THE ROUTLEDGE COM
PHILOSOPHY AND

The Routledge Companion to Philosophy and Music is an outstanding guide and reference source to the key topics, subjects, thinkers and debates in philosophy of music. Over fifty entries by an international team of contributors are organized into six clear sections:

- general issues
- emotion
- history
- figures
- kinds of music
- music, philosophy and related disciplines.

The Routledge Companion to Philosophy and Music is essential reading for anyone interested in philosophy, music, and musicology.

Theodore Gracyk is Department Chair and Professor of Philosophy at Minnesota State University Moorhead, USA. He is the author of *Rhythm and Noise: An Aesthetics of Rock* (1996), *I Wanna Be Me: Rock Music and the Politics of Identity* (2001), *Listening to Popular Music* (2007) and *On Music* (Routledge, 2013).

Andrew Kania is Associate Professor of Philosophy at Trinity University in San Antonio, USA. His principal research is in the philosophy of music, literature, and film. He is the editor of *Memento* (Routledge, 2009).

ROUTLEDGE PHILOSOPHY COMPANIONS

Routledge Philosophy Companions offer thorough, high-quality surveys and assessments of the major topics and periods in philosophy. Covering key problems, themes and thinkers, all entries are specially commissioned for each volume and written by leading scholars in the field. Clear, accessible and carefully edited and organized, *Routledge Philosophy Companions* are indispensable for anyone coming to a major topic or period in philosophy, as well as for the more advanced reader.

The Routledge Companion to Aesthetics, Third Edition
Edited by Berys Gaut and Dominic Lopes

The Routledge Companion to Philosophy of Religion, Second Edition
Edited by Chad Meister and Paul Copan

The Routledge Companion to the Philosophy of Science, Second Edition
Edited by Martin Curd and Stathis Psillos

The Routledge Companion to Twentieth Century Philosophy
Edited by Dermot Moran

The Routledge Companion to Philosophy and Film
Edited by Paisley Livingston and Carl Plantinga

The Routledge Companion to Philosophy of Psychology
Edited by John Symons and Paco Calvo

The Routledge Companion to Metaphysics
Edited by Robin Le Poidevin, Peter Simons, Andrew McGonigal, and Ross Cameron

The Routledge Companion to Nineteenth Century Philosophy
Edited by Dean Moyar

The Routledge Companion to Ethics
Edited by John Skorupski

The Routledge Companion to Epistemology
Edited by Sven Bernecker and Duncan Pritchard

The Routledge Companion to Phenomenology
Edited by Søren Overgaard and Sebastian Luft

The Routledge Companion to Philosophy of Language
Edited by Gillian Russell and Delia Graff Fara

The Routledge Companion to Philosophy of Law
Edited by Andrei Marmor

The Routledge Companion to Social and Political Philosophy
Edited by Gerald Gaus and Fred D'Agostino

Forthcoming:

The Routledge Companion to Seventeenth Century Philosophy
Edited by Dan Kaufman

The Routledge Companion to Eighteenth Century Philosophy
Edited by Aaron Garrett

The Routledge Companion to Theism
Edited by Charles Taliaferro, Victoria Harrison, and Stewart Goetz

The Routledge Companion to Islamic Philosophy
Edited by Richard C. Taylor and Luis Xavier López-Farjeat

The Routledge Companion to Philosophy of Literature
Edited by Noël Carroll and John Gibson

The Routledge Companion to Bioethics
Edited by John Arras, Rebecca Kukla, and Elizabeth Fenton

The Routledge Companion to Ancient Philosophy
Edited by Frisbee Sheffield and James Warren

The Routledge Companion to Medieval Philosophy
Edited by J. T. Paasch and Richard Cross

The Routledge Companion to Hermeneutics
Edited by Jeff Malpas and Hans-Helmuth Gander

PRAISE FOR THE SERIES

The Routledge Companion to Aesthetics

"This is an immensely useful book that belongs in every college library and on the bookshelves of all serious students of aesthetics." – *Journal of Aesthetics and Art Criticism*

"The succinctness and clarity of the essays will make this a source that individuals not familiar with aesthetics will find extremely helpful." – *The Philosophical Quarterly*

"An outstanding resource in aesthetics . . . this text will not only serve as a handy reference source for students and faculty alike, but it could also be used as a text for a course in the philosophy of art." – *Australasian Journal of Philosophy*

"Attests to the richness of modern aesthetics . . . the essays in central topics – many of which are written by well-known figures – succeed in being informative, balanced and intelligent without being too difficult." – *British Journal of Aesthetics*

"This handsome reference volume . . . belongs in every library." – *Choice*

"The *Routledge Companion*s to Philosophy have proved to be a useful series of high quality surveys of major philosophical topics and this volume is worthy enough to sit with the others on a reference library shelf." – *Philosophy and Religion*

The Routledge Companion to Philosophy of Religion

". . . a very valuable resource for libraries and serious scholars." – *Choice*

"The work is sure to be an academic standard for years to come . . . I shall heartily recommend *The Routledge Companion to Philosophy of Religion* to my students and colleagues and hope that libraries around the country add it to their collections." – *Philosophia Christi*

The Routledge Companion to Philosophy of Science

"With a distinguished list of internationally renowned contributors, an excellent choice of topics in the field, and well-written, well-edited essays throughout, this compendium is an excellent resource. Highly recommended." – *Choice*

"Highly recommended for history of science and philosophy collections." – *Library Journal*

"This well conceived companion, which brings together an impressive collection of distinguished authors, will be invaluable to novices and experience readers alike." – *Metascience*

The Routledge Companion to Twentieth Century Philosophy

"To describe this volume as ambitious would be a serious understatement. . . . full of scholarly rigor, including detailed notes and bibliographies of interest to professional philosophers. . . . Summing up: Essential." – *Choice*

The Routledge Companion to Philosophy and Film

"A fascinating, rich volume offering dazzling insights and incisive commentary on every page . . . Every serious student of film will want this book . . . Summing Up: Highly recommended." – *Choice*

The Routledge Companion to Metaphysics

"The *Routledge Philosophy Companions* series has a deserved reputation for impressive scope and scholarly value. This volume is no exception . . . Summing Up: Highly recommended." – *Choice*

The Routledge Companion to Philosophy of Psychology

"This work should serve as the standard reference for those interested in gaining a reliable overview of the burgeoning field of philosophical psychology. Summing Up: Essential." – *Choice*

The Routledge Companion to Nineteenth Century Philosophy

A *Choice* Outstanding Academic Title 2010

"This is a crucial resource for advanced undergraduates and faculty of any discipline who are interested in the 19th-century roots of contemporary philosophical problems. Summing Up: Essential." – *Choice*

The Routledge Companion to Ethics

"This fine collection merits a place in every university, college, and high school library for its invaluable articles covering a very broad range of topics in ethics[.] . . . With its remarkable clarity of writing and its very highly qualified contributors, this volume is must reading for anyone interested in the latest developments in these important areas of thought and practice. Summing Up: Highly recommended." – *Choice*

The Routledge Companion to Philosophy and Music

"Comprehensive and authoritative . . . readers will discover many excellent articles in this well-organized addition to a growing interdisciplinary field. Summing Up: Highly recommended " – *Choice*

". . . succeeds well in catching the wide-ranging strands of musical theorising and thinking, and performance, and an understanding of the various contexts in which all this takes place." – *Reference Review*

The Routledge Companion to Phenomenology

"Sebastian Luft and Søren Overgaard, with the help of over sixty contributors, have captured the excitement of this evolving patchwork named 'phenomenology'. *The Routledge Companion to Phenomenology* will serve as an invaluable reference volume for students, teachers, and scholars of phenomenology, as well as an accessible introduction to phenomenology for philosophers from other specialties or scholars from other disciplines." – *International Journal of Philosophical Studies*

The Routledge Companion to Epistemology

A *CHOICE* Outstanding Academic Title 2011.

"As a series, the *Routledge Philosophy Companions* has met with near universal acclaim. The expansive volume not only continues the trend but quite possibly sets a new standard. . . . Indeed, this is a definitive resource that will continue to prove its value for a long time to come. Summing Up: Essential."– *Choice*

THE ROUTLEDGE COMPANION TO PHILOSOPHY AND MUSIC

Edited by
Theodore Gracyk and Andrew Kania

LONDON AND NEW YORK

First published in paperback 2014
by Routledge
First published 2011 by Routledge
2 Park Square, Milton Park, Abingdon, Oxon OX14 4RN

Simultaneously published in the USA and Canada
by Routledge
711 Third Avenue, New York, NY 10017

Routledge is an imprint of the Taylor & Francis Group, an informa business

Typeset in Sabon by Swales & Willis, Ltd, Exeter, Devon

British Library Cataloguing in Publication Data
A catalogue record for this book is available from the British Library

Library of Congress Cataloging in Publication Data
The Routledge companion to philosophy and music/edited by
Theodore Gracyk and Andrew Kania.
   p. cm. – (Routledge philosophy companions)
Includes bibliographical references and index.
1. Music–Philosophy and aesthetics. 2. Music and philosophy.
I. Gracyk, Theodore. II. Kania, Andrew.
ML3800.R625 2011
781'.1–dc22
2010035122

ISBN: 978–0–415–48603–3 (hbk)
ISBN: 978–0–415–85839–7 (pbk)
ISBN: 978–0–203–83037–6 (ebk)

CONTENTS

CONTENTS

CONTENTS

LIST OF FIGURES

NOTES ON CONTRIBUTORS

Philip Alperson is Professor of Philosophy and Director of the Center for Vietnamese Philosophy, Culture, and Society at Temple University. His interests are in aesthetics, philosophy of the arts, especially music, music education, performance and improvisation in music, creativity, theories of interpretation and criticism, value theory, the philosophy of the visual arts, the theory of culture, and comparative aesthetics including Vietnamese aesthetics. He is the General Editor of the Wiley-Blackwell series *Foundations of the Philosophy of the Arts*. He is also a jazz musician.

Bruce Ellis Benson is Professor of Philosophy at Wheaton College, Illinois. He is the author of *The Improvisation of Musical Dialogue: A Phenomenology of Music*, as well as articles on jazz and the effects of recording on musical identity.

Jeanette Bicknell is the author of *Why Music Moves Us* and essays in *The Journal of Aesthetics and Art Criticism*, *Philosophy and Literature*, and *Philosophy Today*. She lives in Toronto, Canada.

Stephen Blum teaches at the City University of New York Graduate Center. His writings deal with general topics (musical composition, improvisation, analysis) and with music of Iran, Europe, and North America.

Lee B. Brown is Professor of Philosophy Emeritus at The Ohio State University. He has written extensively in many areas of philosophy, including aesthetics. He has specialized recently on philosophical problems concerning popular music, and is currently at work on a book about metaphysical and cultural problems about jazz.

Malcolm Budd is Emeritus Grote Professor of Philosophy of Mind and Logic, University College London, Fellow of the British Academy, and President of the British Society of Aesthetics. His books include *Music and the Emotions*, *Values of Art*, *The Aesthetic Appreciation of Nature*, and *Aesthetic Essays*.

Ben Caplan is an Associate Professor in Philosophy at Ohio State University. He is interested in metaphysics, broadly construed, and has published in the *Journal of Philosophy*, *Mind*, *Philosophical Review*, and *Philosophy and Phenomenological Research*. He grew up in Montreal, once played the violin, and likes collaborating with Carl Matheson.

Noël Carroll is a Distinguished Professor in the Philosophy Program of the City University of New York. His most recent major publication is *On Criticism* (Routledge).

John M. Carvalho is Professor of Philosophy at Villanova University and the author of "Repetition and Self-Realization in Jazz Improvisation," "Creativity in Philosophy and the Arts," "Dance of Dionysus: The Body in Nietzsche's Philosophy of Music" and essays on French and American critical theory and aesthetics.

Eric Clarke has bachelor and masters degrees in music, and a doctorate in psychology for research on rhythm and expression in piano performance. From 1981 he held appointments in the music department at City University in London, was appointed to the J. R. Hoyle Professorship of Music at the University of Sheffield in 1993, and to the Heather Professorship of Music at Oxford in 2007. He has published widely on various issues in the psychology of music, musical meaning, and the analysis of pop music, including *Empirical Musicology* (co-edited with Nicholas Cook), *Ways of Listening*, and *Music and Mind in Everyday Life* (co-authored with Nicola Dibben and Stephanie Pitts). He is an Associate Director for the Research Centre for Musical Performance as Creative Practice. He is an associate editor for the journals *Musicae Scientiae*, *Music Perception*, and *Empirical Musicology Review*, and is on the editorial boards of *Psychology of Music*, and *Radical Musicology*.

James Currie is an Associate Professor in the Department of Music at the University at Buffalo. His work is located at the intersections between music history, philosophy, and politics and has appeared in a wide range of venues, including *The Musical Quarterly*, *The Journal of the American Musicological Association* and *Popular Music*. His book, *Music and the Politics of Negation*, is forthcoming from Indiana University Press and he is also active as a poet and performance artist.

David Davies is Associate Professor of Philosophy at McGill University. He is the author of *Art as Performance* (Blackwell), *Aesthetics and Literature* (Continuum), and *Philosophy of the Performing Arts* (Blackwell, forthcoming). He has also published widely on issues concerning photography, cinema, literature, music, and the visual arts.

Stephen Davies teaches philosophy at the University of Auckland. He is a former President of the American Society of Aesthetics. His books include *Musical*

Works and Performances (Clarendon Press), *Themes in the Philosophy of Music* (Oxford University Press), *Philosophical Perspectives on Art* (Oxford University Press) and *The Philosophy of Art* (Blackwell).

Rafael De Clercq is an Assistant Professor at Lingnan University, Hong Kong, where he is affiliated with the departments of Visual Studies and Philosophy. His research interests lie in aesthetics and metaphysics. He has published several journal articles on aesthetic properties and is currently working on a book on the same topic.

Joseph Dubiel is Professor of Music at Columbia University, teaching composition and theory. His work centers on relationships between music theory and musical experience, and he is writing a book about theory's explanatory claims. A recording of his music is available on Centaur Records.

John Andrew Fisher is Professor of Philosophy at the University of Colorado at Boulder, USA. He is the author of *Reflecting on Art* and articles on various aesthetic themes in the contemporary arts, including the ontology of rock music, mass art as art, the nature of songs, technology and art, and the distinction between high and low art, as well as articles on the aesthetics of nature.

Hannah Ginsborg is Professor of Philosophy at the University of California, Berkeley. Her published work includes articles on Kant and on contemporary issues in theory of knowledge and philosophy of mind. A collection of her articles, *The Normativity of Nature: Essays on Kant's Critique of Judgment*, is due to appear soon with Oxford University Press.

Alan H. Goldman is William R. Kenan Jr. Professor of Humanities and Professor of Philosophy, College of William & Mary. He is the author of seven books, including *Aesthetic Value*, *Practical Rules: When We Need Them and When We Don't*, and *Reasons from Within: Values and Desires*.

Theodore Gracyk is Professor of Philosophy at Minnesota State University Moorhead. He is the author of three philosophical books on music: *Rhythm and Noise: An Aesthetics of Rock* (Duke University Press), *I Wanna Be Me: Rock Music and the Politics of Identity* (Temple University Press), and *Listening to Popular Music* (The University of Michigan Press), as well as many articles on aesthetics and its history.

Thomas Grey is Professor of Music at Stanford University. His original area of research concerned the aesthetic and critical contexts of Richard Wagner's prose writings, especially with reference to theories of musical form and meaning. He is the author of *Wagner's Musical Prose: Texts and Contexts* (Cambridge University Press) and editor of *Richard Wagner: "Der fliegende Holländer"* (Cambridge University Press), *The Cambridge Companion to Wagner*, and *Wagner and his World* (Princeton University Press). Current projects involve the critical history of "absolute music," music and visual culture in the nineteenth century, and music and the Gothic.

Anthony Gritten is Head of the Department of Performing Arts, Middlesex University. He has co-edited two volumes on music and gesture (Ashgate), and is co-editing a volume on music and value judgment (Indiana University Press). He has published essays in the collections *Phrase and Subject: Studies in Literature and Music* (Legenda), *In(ter)discipline: New Languages for Criticism* (Legenda), and *Recorded Music: Philosophical and Critical Reflections* (Middlesex University Press), and in the journals *Musicae Scientiae*, *Dutch Journal of Music Theory*, *British Journal of Aesthetics*, and *Performance Research*, as well as in visual artists' catalogs.

Stephen Halliwell is Professor of Greek at the University of St Andrews, Scotland. His books include *Aristotle's Poetics*, *Plato Republic 10*, *Plato Republic 5*, *The Aesthetics of Mimesis: Ancient Texts and Modern Problems*, and *Greek Laughter: a Study of Cultural Psychology from Homer to Early Christianity*.

Andy Hamilton is Senior Lecturer in Philosophy at Durham University, and Associate Lecturer at University of Western Australia. He has published *Aesthetics and Music* and *Lee Konitz: Conversations on the Improviser's Art*. He contributes to contemporary music magazine *The Wire*.

Anthony Kwame Harrison is an Assistant Professor in the Department of Sociology/Program in Africana Studies at Virginia Polytechnic Institute and State University. He is an Associate Editor for *The Journal of Popular Music Studies*, and author of *Hip Hop Underground: The Integrity and Ethics of Racial Identification* (Temple University Press).

Kathleen Marie Higgins is Professor of Philosophy at the University of Texas at Austin. Her main areas of research are continental philosophy, aesthetics, and the philosophy of emotion. She is author of *The Music of Our Lives* (Temple), and co-editor of *A Companion to Aesthetics* (Blackwell).

Erkki Huovinen is a Finnish musicologist currently working as a visiting professor at the Minnesota University School of Music. After a Ph.D. dissertation concerning experimental music psychology (University of Turku, Finland, 2002), his research has covered issues related to the philosophy of music, methods of music analysis, ancient Greek music theory, and musical improvisation.

Ray Jackendoff is Seth Merrin Professor of Philosophy and Co-Director of the Center for Cognitive Studies at Tufts University. His books include *Semantics and Cognition*, *Foundations of Language*, and with Fred Lerdahl, *A Generative Theory of Tonal Music*.

Jennifer Judkins is an Adjunct Associate Professor at the UCLA Herb Alpert School of Music. She has worked for many years as a professional percussionist in the Los Angeles area, and is particularly interested in the aesthetics of live performance.

Andrew Kania is Assistant Professor of Philosophy at Trinity University in San Antonio. His principal research is in the philosophy of music, literature, and film. He is the editor of *Memento*, in Routledge's series "Philosophers on Film."

Judy Lochhead, a professor at Stony Brook University, is a theorist and musicologist whose work focuses on the most recent musical practices in North America and Europe. Utilizing concepts and methodologies from post-phenomenological and post-structuralist thought, she develops modes of thinking about recent music that address the uniquely defining features of this repertoire. Her work distinguishes between the conceptions of musical structure and meaning that derive from the differing perspectives of performers, listeners, and composers. Some recent articles include: "Refiguring the Modernist Program for Hearing: Steve Reich and George Rochberg," "Visualizing the Musical Object," "'How Does it Work?': Challenges to Analytic Explanation," and "The Sublime, the Ineffable, and Other Dangerous Aesthetics." With Joseph Auner, Lochhead co-edited *Postmodern Music/Postmodern Thought*. She is currently completing a book on the analysis of recent music entitled *Reconceiving Structure: Recent Music/Music Analysis*.

Justin London is Professor of Music at Carleton College in Northfield, Minnesota, where he teaches courses in music theory, aesthetics, music psychology, and the Delta Blues. He has written on a wide range of subjects, from humor in Haydn to the perception and cognition of complex musical meters. He served as President of The Society for Music Theory (2007–09) and is the guitarist and lead vocalist of the New Moon Trio. His webpage can be found at www.people.carleton.edu/~jlondon.

Peter Manuel has researched and published extensively on musics of India, Spain, the Caribbean, and elsewhere. He teaches ethnomusicology at John Jay College and the Graduate Center of the City University of New York.

Carl Matheson is Professor and Head of the Philosophy Department at the University of Manitoba. He has written mainly on the philosophy of art, metaphysics, and the philosophy of science and is currently collaborating with Ben Caplan on a series of papers on the ontology of music. He has played jazz piano for many years with mixed results.

Thomas J. Mathiesen, Fellow of the American Academy of Arts and Sciences, is Distinguished Professor and David H. Jacobs Chair in the Jacobs School of Music at Indiana University. He is a specialist in ancient and medieval music and music theory.

Derek Matravers lectures in Philosophy at The Open University, and is a Bye-Fellow of Emmanuel College, Cambridge. He is the author of *Art and Emotion* and several articles on aesthetics, ethics, and the philosophy of mind.

Fred Everett Maus teaches music at the University of Virginia. He was a Visiting Fellow in Music and Popular Music, University of Liverpool, 2002. His research interests include music theory and analysis, gender and sexuality, popular music, aesthetics, and dramatic and narrative aspects of classical instrumental music.

Allan F. Moore is Professor of Popular Music at the University of Surrey, England. He is series editor for Ashgate's Library of Essays in Popular Music, and an editor of *Popular Music*. His interests lie principally in questions of meaning in popular song, analytical work which draws particularly on the fields of ecological perception and embodied cognition.

Margaret Moore (University of Leeds) is a research fellow with the AHRC aesthetics project "Methods in aesthetics: the challenge from the sciences." Her work focuses on topics in the intersection of the philosophy of music and the philosophy of mind, especially imagination and music cognition. She is also a flutist and violinist.

Alex Neill is Senior Lecturer in Philosophy at the University of Southampton, England. He writes mainly on issues at the intersection of philosophical aesthetics and the philosophy of mind.

Diana Raffman (Ph.D. Yale) is Professor of Philosophy at the University of Toronto. She is a former professional musician and the author of a philosophical book (*Language, Music, and Mind*) and several articles on music perception. She is currently completing a book on vagueness in natural language.

Jenefer Robinson is Professor of Philosophy at the University of Cincinnati, author of *Deeper than Reason: Emotion and its Role in Literature, Music and Art* (Oxford University Press), editor of *Music and Meaning*, area editor for aesthetics in the *Encyclopedia of Philosophy*, and President of the American Society for Aesthetics (2009–11). Her articles have appeared in numerous books and journals including *The Journal of Philosophy*, *The Philosophical Review*, *Australasian Journal of Philosophy*, *Erkenntnis*, *Philosophy*, *Behavioral and Brain Sciences*, *Emotion Review*, *Journal of Literary Theory*, *British Journal of Aesthetics*, and *The Journal of Aesthetics and Art Criticism*.

Tiger C. Roholt is Assistant Professor of Philosophy at Montclair State University. He earned his Ph.D. in philosophy from Columbia University, and is author of "*Musical* Musical Nuance" in *The Journal of Aesthetics and Art Criticism*. Roholt is also a musician.

Roger Scruton is a writer, philosopher, composer, and public commentator, and has written widely on aesthetics, as well as political and cultural issues. He is the author of *The Aesthetics of Music* (Oxford University Press). He is a visiting scholar at the American Enterprise Institute, a visiting Professor in the Philosophy Department, Oxford University, and a Senior Research Fellow at Blackfriars Hall Oxford.

Julia Simon is Professor of French at the University of California, Davis. A specialist in eighteenth-century French literature, culture, and music, she has just completed a book-length study, *Rousseau Among the Moderns: Music, Aesthetics, Politics*.

Robynn J. Stilwell is Associate Professor of Musicology at Georgetown University. Her research interests are primarily in how music circulates meaning and the ways that music function in our lives; topics include film, television, sports, gender, sexuality, ethnicity, and class.

Paul Thom is a Fellow of the Australian Academy of the Humanities. He is an Honorary Professor in the School of Philosophical and Historical Studies at the University of Sydney.

Saam Trivedi is an Associate Professor of Philosophy at Brooklyn College, City University of New York. He has published articles on such topics in the philosophy of music as musical expressiveness and musical ontology in *Metaphilosophy, The Journal of Aesthetics and Art Criticism, British Journal of Aesthetics, Revue Internationale de Philosophie*, and also in edited anthologies.

James O. Young is Professor and Chairman of the Department of Philosophy at the University of Victoria, Canada. He has published extensively on philosophy of language and philosophy of art. His most recent book is *Cultural Appropriation and the Arts*.

PREFACE

Music has been an object of philosophical enquiry since the beginning of philosophy. Reading Plato's *Republic* for the first time, students are often surprised to find that he devotes so much space to music's influence on personal character and social harmony. For Plato and his contemporaries, an account of music was important to issues in metaphysics and epistemology, and philosophy of music was intertwined with moral and political philosophy, and thus, in turn, with basic issues in psychology. Ancient Greek speculation about music also encouraged two millennia of exploration of its relationship with mathematics and, perhaps surprisingly, cosmology and astronomy. Philosophy of music was an important concern for most of the major philosophers of the "modern" period that extends from the scientific revolution until the early twentieth century. It is no exaggeration to say that philosophy of music was central to aesthetic debates in the nineteenth century.

This volume demonstrates that this area of aesthetics is not a historical relic. In the past few decades, there has been exponential growth in philosophy of music. As Stephen Davies memorably put it in 2003: "If medals were awarded for growth in aesthetics in the last thirty years, the philosophy of music would win the gold." Part of this trend arises from the fact that many of the leading aestheticians, such as Davies himself, Peter Kivy, and Jerrold Levinson, have been primarily interested in music. Another reason is the expanding interests of those writing philosophically about music. In addition to the traditional questions of musical aesthetics, there is a burgeoning interest in under-explored areas, such as "impure" music – song and film music, for instance – and musical traditions other than Western classical music – rock, jazz, Balinese gamelan, and so on.

More recently still, there has been a growing return to the field's historical interdisciplinarity. On the one hand, musicologists have become more engaged with philosophical approaches to music, as evidenced by their discussions of books by philosophers and recent plans to hold a joint meeting of the American Society for Aesthetics and the Society for Music Theory. On the other hand, philosophers of music are increasingly drawing on work in other fields, such as psychology and cognitive science, to illuminate traditional philosophical questions, such as music's emotional expressivity.

The Routledge Companion to Philosophy and Music provides a state-of-the-art summary of this complex field, accessible to anyone with an interest in the philosophical study of music. We have aimed at chapters in a non-technical style that will be accessible to readers at different levels – from undergraduates through graduate students to academics – and across disciplines – from philosophers to musicologists and those in related disciplines, such as cognitive science. We hope that the volume thus not only reflects but will also help nurture the growing connections between the philosophy of music and these related disciplines.

We thus take the "and" in our title quite seriously, due to both the necessity of grounding musical aesthetics in a thorough knowledge of music and the interest of musicologists and other scholars in aesthetic issues. This is evidenced in three ways in the contents of the volume. First, there are several chapters on topics that might be thought to be primarily musicological – the nature of harmony, melody, and rhythm, for instance, or the chapter on Wagner's thought. Second, there are several chapters on the various sub-disciplines of music – theory, analysis, composition, and so on. Third, several chapters have been commissioned from specialists in disciplines other than philosophy. We hope that these essays will make philosophers more aware of work relevant to their interests being done in other fields, and will encourage additional exploration and dialogue across disciplinary boundaries. We recognize that our selection of topics reflects a certain degree of subjectivity and personal preference, but our goal has been to give a sense of both what has been accomplished in the field to this point and where it seems to us to be fruitfully headed.

The volume is divided into six parts. The first two contain essays on general philosophical issues that music raises, from the nature of music itself, and various aspects of it (e.g. melodies, musical works, notations), through musical practice (e.g. authentic performance, appropriation, technology), to our experience of music (e.g. understanding, beauty, value). With the exception of a few "cutting edge" topics, the essays in Part I address the major topics that would normally be expected in any attempt to survey the philosophy of music. The relationship between music and emotion, while a general issue, is of such interest and scope that we felt it deserved a part of its own.

Parts III and IV also form a related pair, surveying the history of philosophical thought about music. Part III provides essays covering five major periods of philosophical thought about music. These essays survey historical movements and schools, outlining the relation of musical aesthetics during these periods to other developments in philosophy, music, and history. Given the size of the task, we have not attempted to survey the entire history of the philosophy of music. Instead, we have highlighted broad periods of particular significance – pre-modern thought in Asia, Europe and the Middle East, and the early modern period in Europe – and two philosophical approaches central to contemporary work – the Continental and Anglo-American (or "analytic") schools. We have chosen to supplement the historical surveys with focused explorations of central figures in the philosophy of music, such as Plato, Nietzsche, and Adorno. A number of the other essays also contain a fair amount of additional history, viewed from a particular perspective (e.g. Musicology, Music Theory and Philosophy).

Part V covers different kinds of music. The traditional target of most philosophy of music has been "absolute" or "pure" music – concert music without an accompanying program or text. But there has been much recent interest in "impure" music, in part motivated by the recognition that this may be the kind of music most commonly experienced. So this part includes essays on song, film music, dance music, and so on, in addition to different musical traditions, such as rock and jazz. Taken together, these essays suggest that different kinds of music highlight distinct philosophical issues, and that philosophy of music thus need not converge on a limited set of philosophical problems. Furthermore, the choice to reflect on music beyond the Western "canon" of art music is increasingly important in non-philosophical thought about music, as evidenced by the essays on sociology and cultural studies and on phenomenology of music.

Finally, Part VI contains essays on the relations between the philosophy of music and many of the other disciplines that inform such philosophy. These include many of the sub-disciplines of music scholarship, such as theory, analysis, and composition, and also other subject areas such as politics, gender, and psychology. Besides extending the scope of the book beyond philosophy, the topics in this part also reflect a goal of creating a broadly inclusive companion that goes beyond the concerns of the Anglo-American school that dominates contemporary philosophy of music.

In sum, *The Routledge Companion to Philosophy and Music* constitutes an up-to-date overview of more than four dozen distinct topics relevant to the philosophy of music. To our knowledge it is the first reference work ever devoted exclusively to the philosophical study of music. Many of the essays are contributed by distinguished scholars who have already advanced the field they summarize here; others are by young researchers with a particular expertise. We hope that these essays will inform and engage students and academic professionals alike. But, most of all, we hope that their combination in a single volume will encourage new thinking about music.

Theodore Gracyk and Andrew Kania

ACKNOWLEDGMENTS

Theodore Gracyk would like to thank Andrew Kania for inviting him to join this project. Andrew Kania would like to thank Julie Post and his colleagues at Trinity University, in both the Department of Philosophy and the Writers' Bloc, for their support throughout the project.

Producing a volume such as this requires the support of many individuals and institutions. We would like to thank Justin London, Fred Everett Maus, Nicholas Cook, Roger Scruton, and four anonymous reviewers, for valuable suggestions on the proposed contents of the volume. Tony Bruce and Adam Johnson at Routledge were helpful throughout its production. Thanks to Yvonne Freckmann for transcribing the musical examples. We would like to thank, more generally, the American Society for Aesthetics and the British Society for Aesthetics, without which the philosophical content of this project would be much impoverished.

We would like to thank the original publishers for permission to publish versions of Ray Jackendoff, "Parallels and Nonparallels between Language and Music" (*Music Perception*, vol. 26, no. 3: 195–204. © 2009, The Regents of the University of California. Used by permission. All rights reserved.), Jenefer Robinson, "Music and Emotions" (*The Journal of Literary Theory*, vol. 1, no. 2: 395–419; by kind permission of De Gruyter Publishing), and an English language version of Fred Everett Maus, "Genders, sexualité et sens musical," originally published in the book edited by Marta Grabocz, *Sens et signification en musique* (Éditions Hermann, 2007) (© Éditions Hermann, 2007, pp. 253–71). Images 24.1–24.6 are from *Apollo's Lyre: Greek Music and Music Theory in Antiquity and the Middle Ages* (© 1999 Thomas J. Mathiesen), and are reproduced by kind permission of Thomas J. Mathiesen. Thanks also to Trinity University for financial assistance in obtaining permission to reprint the contributions of Jenefer Robinson and Ray Jackendoff, and in the production of the musical examples.

Finally, we would like to thank the contributing authors, without whose work this book would, of course, not exist.

Part I
GENERAL ISSUES

1
DEFINITION
Andrew Kania

Much of the time most of us can tell whether, and which of, the sounds we are currently hearing are music. This is so whether or not what we are listening to is a familiar piece, a piece we have not heard before, or even music from a culture or tradition with which we are unfamiliar. In cases where we are unsure, or initially mistaken in our judgment, we will often change our opinion based on further information. This near-universal agreement suggests that the concept of music is one shared by different people, and has boundaries which we are implicitly aware of and which we make use of in judging whether something is music or not. The project of defining the term "music" is the attempt to make explicit the boundaries of this concept.

Philosophical definitions

Traditionally, a philosophical definition takes the form of a set of individually necessary, jointly sufficient conditions. A necessary condition on being X is one something *must* meet in order to be X. For instance, being female is a necessary condition on being a niece. Nothing that fails to meet that condition can possibly be a niece. If you specify a necessary condition on the concept you are interested in, you will capture everything under that concept, but the danger is that you will capture *more* than that. (There are plenty of women who are not nieces.) A sufficient condition on X is something that, once met, *guarantees* being X. *Being a woman with an aunt* is sufficient for being a niece, since if you meet that condition, you are thereby a niece. If you specify a sufficient condition, you will capture *only* things that fall under the concept, but you might not capture *enough*. (There are lots of nieces who do not have any aunts.) Philosophers have usually attempted to specify a list of conditions that are each individually necessary, but when taken together are sufficient for falling under the concept in question. For instance, each of the following conditions is necessary for being a niece: (i) being female, with (ii) at least one parent who has a sibling. Taken together, these conditions are sufficient for being a niece. Thus we have produced a traditional philosophical definition of "niece." "Music" is not so easy.

One reason for the difficulty is that there is not universal agreement about what counts as music. One way to overcome this problem is to try to figure out a definition that covers what everyone agrees on, and then see what it has to say about the contentious cases. This will not necessarily settle the matter, since some people might prefer to revise the definition rather than admit the results of its application, but the hope is that the parties to the debate will ultimately be swayed in the same direction by the same reasons. Another reason for the difficulty is that "music" is probably a *vague* concept, that is, one under which not everything either clearly falls or does not (perhaps because one or more of its necessary conditions is vague). On the one hand, this may helpfully allow us to classify disputed examples as "borderline cases." On the other, there may be just as much dispute over whether a particular example is a borderline case or a clear one.

One potential confusion that can be cleared up at the outset is that we are looking for a *descriptive* rather than (purely) *evaluative* definition of "music." There is a temptation to dismiss an example of bad music as not music at all, but this would be incoherent. There is little disputing that there are some terrible musical performances, recordings, and works. However, there may be an evaluative *component* to the definition of "music." Perhaps every piece of music must be *intended* to be rewarding, for instance.

There are some quite general objections to definitional projects of the sort I will be engaging in here. There is no space to consider these objections here, but some good starting points are Davies 2000, Dean 2003, Meskin 2008, and Margolis and Laurence 2008 (especially §§2 and 5).

The history of philosophy of music

Philosophers have been discussing the nature of music since the beginnings of philosophy in both the East and the West, but their work is not much help to the definitional project. This is for two related reasons. First, the theory of music held by each of these philosophies is usually embedded in a much larger theory – often a systematic philosophy that attempts to answer fundamental questions in metaphysics, epistemology, ethics, and political philosophy. Extracting a definition of "music" from so grand a theory is usually absurd. For instance, it makes no sense to consider Schopenhauer's claim that music is *the direct objectification of the will itself* without first understanding what Schopenhauer means by "the will," how it is objectified in "the world of representation" and the various other arts, and the roots of all of this in Kant's "transcendental idealism." Suppose we do understand Schopenhauer's philosophical system. We may now be able to extract a definition of "music" from it, but we are unlikely to be satisfied with the definition of "music," since we probably do not subscribe to the system upon which it depends.

The second reason the history of philosophy is not much help in defining "music" is that most philosophers have simply not been interested in that project. So why are we? Let me note at the outset that many philosophers, musicians, musicologists, and ordinary music-lovers are *not* interested in the definition of "music." Those philosophers who *are* are part of a tradition known as "analytic philosophy," with historical roots in the work of figures such as Frege, Russell, and Wittgenstein. One idea central to early analytic philosophy was that we could make better philosophical progress if we became clear about the precise definitions of our terms, and used them more carefully – an approach modeled in part on successful empirical science. While there are still methodological connections between the various strands of contemporary analytic philosophy and their forebears, few philosophers of music pursue the definition of "music" hoping it will shed much independent light on other aspects of the philosophy of music. Rather, the primary motivation for defining "music" is simply a curiosity about the nature of an art that is central to many people's lives. Whether or not you are grabbed by the topic might depend on whether you are moved more by Marx's claim that "The philosophers have only *interpreted* the world, in various ways; the point, however, is to *change* it" (Marx 1978: 145), or by Harry Frankfurt's that "There are plenty of people and institutions devoted to changing the world, but philosophers are among the few who are devoted to understanding it" (Leimbach 2008: 21).

Working toward a definition of "music"

When we aim at defining "music," what *kinds* of things do we want our definition to capture? Unsurprisingly, the concept of *sound* is central to most definitions of "music." But you might point to a musical score and say, "That's a great piece of music." Scores make no sounds, however. Does that mean they are not really music? We might similarly ask whether we intend to capture musical works, performances, instruments, recordings, and so on with our definition. The answer to these questions is that there is a central concept of a *musical event*, in terms of which we can define the other concepts. (For instance, a *musical instrument* may be a tool whose function is the production of musical events.)

Intrinsic, subjective, and intentional definitions

Even if you think that sounds are necessary for music, they are certainly not sufficient. Sounds occur throughout the world all the time, and very few of these are music. We might describe certain sounds as *music-like* – the babbling of a brook, for instance – yet still deny, when speaking strictly, that these sounds are really *music*. (It is natural to describe such sounds as "musical," but I will reserve that adjective to describe things that are literally music, rather than merely *like* music in some way.) How can we characterize *musical* sounds so as to distinguish them from non-musical sounds?

One obvious way would be to try to figure out the *intrinsic properties* of musical sounds, as opposed to others. For instance, we might begin by figuring out the frequencies of all the sounds emitted by a standard piano keyboard, and say that any musical sound must have one of those frequencies. This is not very promising, however. For one thing, you still make music if you play on an out-of-tune piano. For another, there are many different musical scales, both within Western music and across the globe. Also, there are sounds whose frequencies are irrelevant to their musicality, such as "untuned" percussion (e.g. a snare drum). We could perhaps extend our list of kinds of musical sounds to encompass all of these, but the problem would then be that our definition included far too much. For all sorts of non-musical sounds have frequencies. (I used to have a printer that emitted two sounds alternately, at the interval of a tritone.)

A second strategy would be to adopt a *subjective* definition, claiming, for instance, that whatever sounds like, or is perceived as, music by a given listener *is* music, regardless of its intrinsic properties. This kind of approach gives rise to unintuitive consequences. For instance, if you leave the radio on when you leave the house, the sounds it emits cease being music, according to the subjectivist, since there is no one around to perceive them in the right sort of way. On the other hand, you can transform the sounds of a train into music merely by hearing them as rhythmic. More troublingly, someone ignorant of a particular culture's musical practices may not hear a given performance as music. At best, the subjectivist may say that this performance is not music for this listener, though it may be for other listeners. This seems wrong. This listener is simply mistaken about what he hears, as much as if he denied that the *Mona Lisa* is a painting.

A more promising approach is to adopt an *intentional* definition. According to such a definition, your radio continues to emit music when you leave the house because the sounds it emits are rooted in the music-making intentions of the people ultimately responsible for those sounds. While you cannot turn the sounds of a train into music just by hearing them a certain way, you could turn them into music by repeating them with musical intent (as, for example, Arthur Honegger did in *Pacific 231*). This strategy also seems to give us the right answer with respect to the culturally ignorant listener. He has no effect on whether what he is listening to is music, which turns instead to the intentions of the people producing the sounds he hears.

Are there any sounds we might want to classify as music, yet which are not intentionally produced? When one *improvises*, one does not know in advance all of the particular sounds one will make. But this does not mean that one makes the sounds unintentionally. Paisley Livingston characterizes intentional action as "the execution and realization of a plan, where the agent effectively follows and is guided by the plan in performing actions which, in manifesting sufficient levels of skill and control, bring about the intended [i.e. planned] outcome" (2005: 14). Given this account, it seems plausible that the improviser intends to produce music, even the *particular* notes she produces, as evidenced by Slam Stewart's singing along to his improvisatory performances, though these intentions may be formed very soon before the production of the notes themselves and may not be fully conscious.

What about "music" produced by machines or non-human animals? It seems unlikely that even "higher" non-human animals have the capacity for the complex intentions necessary for the production of music. The animals we characterize as "singing" (particularly birds and whales) do not have the capacity to improvise or invent new melodies or rhythms (though they can make mistakes). Despite the name, then, bird and whale "song" should no more count as music than the yowling of cats. We call these displays "song," of course, because they sound *like* music to us. But sounds can be music-like without being music.

Machines, such as music-boxes, CD players, and iPods emit music, but this music is rooted in the intentions of the musicians behind the sounds, just as in the example of the radio considered above. The case of a computer programmed to compose is slightly different, but I would argue that the sounds or scores produced by such a program should count as music for the same reason. The program is designed by someone to produce certain kinds of outputs (e.g. pitches and rhythms), though the particular outputs may be unpredictable. It is telling that we would not even ask the question about a word-processing program, though it also emits sounds when it operates.

Basic musical features

So far I have implied that what distinguishes musical sounds from others is that they be *intended to be musical*. Initially, this suggestion looks *circular*. A circular definition is one that relies on the term being defined. For instance, defining "dog" as a "canine animal" is circular. While *true*, the definition is uninformative. We can escape the charge of circularity if we can define "musical" without referring to music. Roger Scruton attempts something like this, claiming that a sound is transformed into music when it is perceived as existing "within a musical 'field of force'" (1997: 17), such as the arrangement of pitches in a scale, or beats in a measure. If we can characterize such "fields" independently of the concept of music, we will have escaped the circle. (Scruton's suggestion is subjectivist, since it relies on a listener's perception, rather than a musician's intention, but we can eliminate the subjectivism by replacing it with an intentional condition, and retaining the account of musical "fields of force.")

One concern some people have about defining music in terms of particular musical features, such as pitch or rhythm, is that these might be features of only *some* music, perhaps music in the European tradition (e.g. Levinson 1990a: 270–1). This would incorrectly exclude the music of other cultures from the definition. As it turns out, however, the division of sounds into both *scales*, consisting of series of discrete pitches that repeat at the octave, and *measures*, consisting of a number of equal beats, seem to be culturally universal features of music (Stevens and Byron 2009: 16–18; Stainsby and Cross 2009: 54–6). This may be because all humans share a capacity to produce and understand music as a result of their common evolutionary history (see Wallin, Merker, and Brown 2000; Cross 2009.) If so, this gives us another reason to exclude animal sounds from music.

It is worth emphasizing that there is a difference between the concept of pitch appealed to here, and the concept of frequency, briefly considered above. Frequency is an intrinsic, objective characteristic of all sounds. Pitch, on the other hand, is already in itself a partly intentional concept. Although we may loosely say that the pitch of A above middle C has a frequency of 440 Hz, no one would deny that the note produced by the relevant key on a baroque organ is also an A, though it may produce a frequency of 470 Hz, nor that you continuously play an A on the violin, though you use vibrato throughout (and thus produce a sound with a continuously changing frequency). In short, whether the sound you produce is an A depends more on the place it occupies (or you intend it to occupy) relative to the other notes you are playing (its place in a musical "field of force") than on its frequency. There are also differences between musical pitch and the "pitches" of tonal languages that should allow us to exclude such languages from a definition of music (Stainsby and Cross 2009: 55–6). Similar points can be made about rhythm. Though ordinary speech may have a certain periodicity that might naturally be called its "rhythm," in a definition of music the term would be restricted to a division into stricter units of time, such as characterized by measures of two or three beats.

Combining all of this into a provisional definition, we might say that:

> Music is (1) sounds, (2) intentionally produced or organized, (3) to have at least one basic musical feature, such as pitch or rhythm.

Temporal organization

Jerrold Levinson has argued that music must be "temporally organized" (1990a: 273), and thus that our provisional definition is too broad – it encompasses some items that it should exclude. The solution would be to add a further necessary condition to our definition. What would such a condition amount to? All sounds occur in time, so Levinson must mean something more than this. He asks us to consider "an art in which the point was to produce colorful instantaneous combinations of sounds – i.e. chords of vanishingly brief duration – which [are] to be savored independently," and claims that we would not consider this a *musical* art, since music is "as essentially an art of time as it is an art of sound" (1990a: 273). Suppose it is true that we would not consider this tradition of sonic art a *musical* tradition. It does not follow that we ought to exclude *individual* instantaneous pieces or performances from the realm of music. We might similarly agree that a culture which only produced blank canvases, never applying paint to them, did not have a tradition of painting. It does not follow that there can be no blank canvases in a tradition of painting. If Levinson were offering a definition of "musical tradition," this criticism might be apt, but he is explicitly seeking the correct conception of "an instance or occasion of music" (1990a: 269). (That said, I am not so sure that a tradition of exquisite instantaneous chords should not count as a musical tradition.)

Moreover, there seems to be an actual example of a musical work that violates Levinson's temporal-organization condition. La Monte Young's *Composition 1960 #7* consists of a single open fifth (B and F#), marked "to be held for a long time". This piece is not instantaneous, but it is difficult to see what kind of temporal structure it has that would not be shared by a variant marked "to be held for a short time" or "to be held instantaneously."

Music without basic musical features

A more serious objection to our provisional definition is that it is too narrow, that is, it does not encompass enough. Some music seems intentionally designed *not* to be pitched or rhythmic; for instance, John Cage's *Williams Mix* (1952) – a tape composition painstakingly spliced together out of a variety of sound sources, without regard to their basic musical features – or Yoko Ono's *Toilet Piece/Unknown* (1971) – an unedited recording of a flushing toilet. You might, of course, simply deny that such works are music, though that would require a revisionist view of much of twentieth-century music history. However, it would be wise to investigate why people have been inclined to call such works music before dismissing them.

Precisely in response to the wide variety of sounds employed not only in twentieth-century avant-garde music but also in musical cultures around the globe, Jerrold Levinson defends what might be called an *aesthetic* definition of "music," since it appeals not to features of the intentionally produced sounds but to a certain kind of experience they are intended to elicit. According to Levinson, music is "[i] sounds [ii] temporally organized [iii] by a person [iv] for the purpose of enriching or intensifying experience through active engagement (e.g., listening, dancing, performing) [v] with the sounds regarded primarily, or in significant measure, as sounds" (1990a: 273).

We have already discussed the first three of Levinson's conditions. (We can take "person" to refer to the kind of being capable of complex intentions.) What remains is an aesthetic condition (iv), and a requirement that musical sounds be intended to be heard "primarily . . . as sounds" (v). Levinson introduces the last condition in order to exclude aesthetically pleasing or music-like language, such as poetry and oratory, from his definition. "To hear something *as sounds*," however, must not be a disguised way of saying "to hear something *as music*," on pain of circularity. We might explicate hearing something as sounds in terms of *not* listening to it for its semantic content, or meaning. But many people believe that much music *does* possess meaning of some sort. In fact, it might be argued that even hearing sounds as pitched or rhythmic is to hear them as more than simply sounds, since a dog can hear the sounds coming from your stereo, but not the music (Hamilton 2007: 56–9). Perhaps a better way to exclude artistic language from a definition of "music" is simply to do so explicitly. Levinson almost does this when he introduces this condition, glossing "hearing sounds as sounds" as hearing them "not primarily as symbols of discursive thought" (1990a: 272).

You might think that excluding language will make the definition too narrow, since many musical works include language, notably songs. But if we think of songs as a combination of words and music, then we can understand the definition as capturing the musical element of songs, and ignoring the linguistic element. Roughly, the definition should capture the features of sung words that would be absent if those words were merely spoken.

Let us turn, then, to the central aesthetic condition of Levinson's definition. To my mind, the most troubling counterexamples to this condition are ones of mundane music-making, such as the practicing of scales. Few would deny that such activities produce music, yet it seems questionable at best that such practice is aimed at enriching or intensifying anyone's experience. Indeed, it is not clear that the musician intends these sounds to be attended to at all. (Someone may practice scales simply to keep warm, rather than to work on tone production, or anything else that would require even the musician's own attention to the sounds.)

Levinson presents a thought experiment to defend his aesthetic condition. He asks us to imagine "a sequence of sounds devised by a team of psychological researchers which are such that when subjects are in a semiconscious condition and are exposed to these sounds, the subjects enter psychedelic states of marked pleasurability" (1990a: 273). The idea is that such sounds should not count as music, since they are not intended to be attended to. I am not convinced by the counterexample, since we can use music for all sorts of purposes without its thereby ceasing to be music. I may sneak into a friend's bedroom and play the opening of the first-violin part of Strauss's *Don Juan* to startle him awake, with no intention that either of us attend to or engage with these sounds at all, let alone for the purpose of enriching or intensifying our experiences. In such a case, it seems to me, I have woken my friend up with some loud *music*, not just music-like sounds. Thus, I would want to hear more about the experimenters' intentions regarding the sounds themselves – in particular, whether they are intended to be pitched or rhythmic. A final example we might consider is Muzak. Levinson rejects the idea that Muzak is music for the same reason he rejects the psychological experimenters' sounds – Muzak is not intended to be listened to, but to have a psychological effect on those who hear it (such as being more willing to spend money). But it seems undeniable that Muzak is music, albeit bad music put toward a mercenary end (see also Hamilton 2007: 52–5).

A disjunctive strategy

One advantage of an aesthetic definition is that it can explain why we might consider *Williams Mix* or *Toilet Piece* to be music, despite their lack of basic musical features, namely, by pointing out that these pieces seem to be intended to be listened to in the way in which we listen to other musical works. We can apply this same insight to the basic-musical-features approach to defining music however, thus avoiding the problematic consequences of an aesthetic definition. The idea would be that if you think that *Toilet Piece*, but not the sound of any toilet flushing, is music, you must implicitly believe that we ought to listen to the sounds on the recording against a background expectation of encountering pitches and rhythms. This would be something like *listening for* such features, even if they are absent. Why should we listen for these features in the Ono piece, but not every time we flush a toilet ourselves? Because, presumably, that is what Ono intended us to do by placing it on an album (*Fly* (1971)), that is, a recording consisting mostly of uncontentious examples of music, and which was released (i.e. presented to the public) in the same way as much other music. (This argument resembles one Levinson gives for his definition of "art," which differs markedly from his definition of "music" (1989: 41–2).) Intending people to attend to something for features it does not possess smacks of paradox, but it is common enough. Think of a detective story that does not resolve. You are intended to read it with an eye to discovering who the criminal is, even if you know from the outset that the story will offer insufficient evidence of whodunit.

We now have a tension between two kinds of cases. On the one hand, there is sound with undeniably musical features, but produced without the intention that those features be attended to, such as Muzak or the *Don Juan* wake-up call. On the other, there is sound that lacks any basic musical features, but counts as music because it is intended to be attended to for such features, such as *Toilet Piece/Unknown*. It may be that here, as with several recent definitions of "art," we need to use a disjunctive strategy. Consider the following proposal:

> Music is (1) sounds, (2) intentionally produced or organized (3) *either* (a) to have some basic musical feature, such as pitch or rhythm, *or* (b) to be listened to for such features.

Condition 3a should capture most music across history and the globe, while 3b should capture the remaining modernist and postmodern musical experiments, such as Ono's work and Cage's *Williams Mix*.

Musical silence

We began our discussion of the concept of music with the idea that it is, at least, *sound*. But many pieces of music contain significant periods of *silence*, that is, the absence of sound. In fact, the use of silence is a very common way of structuring sound. In particular, rests make a major contribution to the *rhythmic* organization of music. So when we talk of intentionally produced or organized sounds, we must include silences. The air of paradox here can be dispersed if we replace "sound" in our definition with "anything intended to be heard":

> Music is (1) any event intentionally produced or organized (2) to be heard, and (3) *either* (a) to have some basic musical feature, such as pitch or rhythm, *or* (b) to be listened to for such features.

The rests in an ordinary piece of music would thus count as part of the music. A new question arises of whether there could be musical works that consist of *nothing but* silence. I have argued that there are in fact such pieces (Kania 2010), but I must pass over that topic here.

Conclusion

I have suggested an intentional definition of music that relies heavily on the nature of basic musical features but that also allows for avant-garde music which deliberately flouts such features. To be truly satisfying, this definition would require an account of the features appealed to, such as pitch and rhythm, and arguments for the completeness of the list. There is no space to take on that task here, but see Scruton (1997: 19–79), Davies (2001: 45–58), Hamilton (2007: chs 2 and 5), and, in this volume, "Rhythm, melody, and harmony" (Chapter 3).

One might adopt the general approach taken here, but more conservatively stop short of the disjunctive condition I have suggested, excluding works without basic musical features from the realm of music. But it should be noted that the definition I have suggested is not totally liberal. For there are works of sonic art that will not count as music according to my definition. These are works such as *Toilet Piece/Unknown* that lack basic musical features but (unlike *Toilet Piece/ Unknown*) are not intended to be listened to for such features. (It could be argued that *Williams Mix* is in fact such a piece.) This is an advantage of the definition I have suggested, since there does seem to be just such a division in contemporary art practice between music and sound art (Hamilton 2007: ch. 2).

See also Improvisation (Chapter 6), Psychology of music (Chapter 55), Rhythm, melody, and harmony (Chapter 3), and Silence, sound, noise, and music (Chapter 2).

References

Cross, I. (2009) "The Nature of Music and its Evolution," in Hallam, Cross, and Thaut, pp. 3–13.

Davies, S. (2000) "Non-Western Art and Art's Definition," in N. Carroll (ed.) *Theories of Art Today*, Madison: University of Wisconsin Press, pp. 199–216.

—— (2001) *Musical Works and Performances: A Philosophical Exploration*, Oxford: Clarendon Press.

Dean, J. (2003) "The Nature of Concepts and the Definition of Art," *Journal of Aesthetics and Art Criticism* 61: 29–35.

Hallam, S., Cross, I., and Thaut, M. (eds) (2009) *The Oxford Handbook of Music Psychology*, Oxford: Oxford University Press.

Hamilton, A. (2007) *Aesthetics and Music*, New York: Continuum.

Kania, A. (2010) "Silent Music," *Journal of Aesthetics and Art Criticism* 68: 343–53.

Leimbach, D. (2008) "Interview with Harry Frankfurt," *Aporia: Dartmouth Undergraduate Journal of Philosophy* 26/1: 20–1.

Levinson, J. (1989) "Refining Art Historically," reprinted in Levinson (1990b), pp. 37–59.

—— (1990a) "The Concept of Music," in Levinson (1990b), pp. 267–78.

—— (1990b) *Music, Art, and Metaphysics*, Ithaca: Cornell University Press.

Livingston, P. (2005) *Art and Intention: A Philosophical Study*, Oxford: Oxford University Press.

Margolis, E. and Laurence, S. (2008) "Concepts," in E.N. Zalta (ed.) *The Stanford Encyclopedia of Philosophy*, Fall 2008 edn, available at http://plato.stanford.edu/archives/fall2008/entries/concepts/.

Marx, K. (1978 [1845]) "Theses on Feuerbach," in *The Marx–Engels Reader*, 2nd edn, ed. R.C. Tucker, New York: Norton, pp. 143–5.

Meskin, A. (2008) "From Defining Art to Defining the Individual Arts: The Role of Theory in the Philosophies of Arts," in K. Stock and K. Thomson-Jones (eds) *New Waves in Aesthetics*, New York: Palgrave Macmillan, pp. 125–49.

Scruton, R. (1997) *The Aesthetics of Music*, Oxford: Oxford University Press.

Stainsby, T. and Cross, I. (2009) "The Perception of Pitch," in Hallam, Cross, and Thaut, pp. 47–58.

Stevens, C. and Byron, T. (2009) "Universals in Music Processing," in Hallam, Cross, and Thaut, pp. 14–23.

Wallin, N.L., Merker, B., and Brown, S. (eds) (2000) *The Origins of Music*, Cambridge: MIT Press.

2
SILENCE, SOUND, NOISE, AND MUSIC

Jennifer Judkins

Music has often been simply described as organized sounds framed by silence. Recorded music has always suggested this definition, with increasingly pristine (and now digitized) silences before and after musical works, and between movements. Any extraneous "noises" prior to or within the performance itself, such as instrument squeaks, valve sounds, and even breaths, are often "cleaned up" in post-production. Even the "noisiest" genres, such as heavy metal and other rock music, where fuzz and distortion are used as expressive effects, are often presented on recordings with clean silent frames between the tracks.

Any definition of a musical work relies on assumptions about noise and silence. For instance, we have certain conventions in Western music that enable us to tell when a musical work begins and ends, and what sounds are most likely musical sounds that are part of the work (the sound of the trumpets), and what sounds are probably not part of the work (the cough of the woman in front of you). At classical music concerts, audience members and performers enact a "silence" before a piece begins, and another one when it ends, to frame the work. There may be silences within the piece itself (a grand pause, for instance), and we understand that the work is still ongoing, and that that period of time is meant to be understood as a silence (even as the woman in front of you noisily unwraps her cough drops).

Yet, in addition to the background audience noise of any live performance, there is always some "musical noise" surrounding the means of tone production itself, even in the finest performances. Musical sounds are generated through rhythmic physical motions or air pressure applied to an instrument, and instruments (and humans) are noisy things. We might hear Andrés Segovia's fingers squeak on the guitar strings, or János Starker's bow scrape the cello strings – are these really "noises" that should be removed from a recording or minimized in performance? Glenn Gould was perhaps the most infamously noisy performer, with his grunts and moans riding atop his brilliant performances of Bach. In a New York Philharmonic performance, the noises might be more incidental, but if you were on stage with the orchestra, you might hear air escaping around a clarinetist's embouchure, the clunking of the tuba valves, or the breathing of the trombone section. These noises, though, are closely tied to the nature of the instruments themselves and the process of playing them, much as breathing and the resonance of the human head are attached to the quality of the voice. Most of this noise is quite subtle, and often inaudible to the audience in larger venues, yet it may be quite evident at a chamber music concert. It is usually only in recordings that its presence becomes an artistic question.

Musical sound and musical noise

It can be difficult to draw lines between musical noise (noise resulting from the process of music-making) and regular noise, or less-musical noise and more-musical noise, or even between body and instrument. For example, with the guitar, the fingertip applies force to the string on the fret, and the string vibrates not only on either side but also underneath the fingertip. Thus the "squeaking" noise of the fingers moving along the strings from note to note, or chord to chord, seems more closely connected with sound production than, say, the noise of the keys on a bassoon. The latter seems to be a more discrete relation, as opposed to the more continuous relation of the fingers to strings. Yet bassoonists, or even pianists, who are at some distance from the actual striking of hammer on string, certainly do not feel as though they are working through an intermediary device when they perform. Violinists, for example, do not believe that their right hand (holding their bow) is less connected with sound production than their left hand (on the fingerboard).

We have continued to "improve" upon Western instruments, and yet in many respects most of our orchestral instruments are still quaintly old-fashioned. Many older traditions of instrument-making have survived because the product is successful – Stradivarius did indeed have it right. However, the eccentricities inherent in manufacturing an instrument to play a tempered scale have always made for peculiar idiomatic tendencies, and for the occasional awkwardness. Unidiomatic passages go against the workings of the instrument's acoustics or mechanics, such as fingerings that "just don't lie well." Much of what we hear as musical noise develops from these unidiomatic passages, since usually the player must exert more effort in order to execute them. One would expect more valve noise from a tubist struggling with fast fingerings, and one would expect more pedal noise from a harpist dealing with a very chromatic piece. (Some instruments are also just mechanically noisier than others. It can be difficult to tell the notes from the mechanical noises on a virginal, and its champions would not have it any other way.) Although we may not play the instrument in question, may not have held or even seen one before, we understand how it feels to take deep breaths and to exhale quickly, we understand what it is to pound and strike, and, above all, we understand tools and the joy of action.

In the professional musician, a window of facility outlines the limitations of the body and the instrument. As the edges of the window are approached, there is more noise: the trumpet player squeaking out higher and higher notes, a tenor reaching for a high B-flat, or the sound of János Starker's bow hairs rapidly scraping across the strings in a Bach allemande. For the general audience, these instances in which the instrumentalists have approached the impossible may be the only times they notice musical noise. Virtuosity requires great talent and strength as well as great dexterity, and we forgive the sometimes excessive noise of virtuosic attempts much as we forgive "mistakes" in the improvising jazz player, knowing them to be the residue of risk. As Stan Godlovitch has written: "Talent without skill is like power without authority – unsteady, capricious, unreliable" (Godlovitch 1998: 20).

Certain gray areas exist in the arena of noise in music. For example, instances can be offered which blur any line between "successful performance" and "instrument malfunction." Clarinet squeaks, unlike guitar string squeaks, are unintended accidents that take the place of the intended sound. As such, we might characterize them as malfunctions, and eliminate them from consideration as musical noise. However, gurgles from a horn getting full of water may accompany a successful performance. And what do we say about the "noises" of a Glenn Gould, muttering and singing along to his performances of Bach? When is there "too much" noise? What should be removed from a recording so as to provide the best instance of the work? Is the sound of wind players breathing a noise that should be "fixed in the mix"?

Certainly mistakes are noises – in musicians' lingo, the "clams" or "fraks" that occur in wind instrument playing when notes do not speak, or when the clarinet squeaks in place of a tone. Yet, is a wrong note always noise? As Robert Walser points out, the jazz trumpeter Miles Davis was infamous for missed notes, yet he remains one of the more important musicians in the history of jazz (Walser 1993: 343). Davis played "closer to the edge than anyone else and simply accepted the inevitable missteps" (Walser 1993: 356). There are also, of course, a myriad of extra-musical noises on the part of the performers or the audience which are *un*attached to performance means, such as feet shuffling, rustling, even talking.

Musical noise reminds us of the means of performance and the close relationship of musician to instrument. The intimacy of the singer with her own voice is traditionally appreciated in Western music. (Interestingly, in popular songs, it seems that audiences will accept certain tunes from some singers but not from others, particularly if there is too great an incongruity between that singer's public persona and what is conveyed in the song (Bicknell 2005: 266).) Less well appreciated is the close relationship of instrumentalists to their instruments. The Kpelle of Africa even consider instruments as surrogate participants that cause the human performer's fingers to move. Stephen Davies has written eloquently about musicians and instruments, and he states that in general we treat instruments "with care and respect, even reverence, more so than we accord to many of the other artifacts that are part of our lives" (Davies 2003a: 109). We are upset when they are mistreated or destroyed. Musicians have an immense degree of attachment to and identification with their instruments – a complex interaction unfortunately smoothed over when we speak of "making music." The attachment to the instrument is built not only out of years of practice and devotion, but also from the artistic and physical resonance the instrument brings to the player. Imagine B. B. King without his guitar "Lucille," or Yo-Yo Ma without his Stradivarius cello.

Musical noise and recordings

The issue of musical noise becomes prickly in the recording studio. Today, musicians and engineers must make decisions regarding which sounds are and which sounds are not aesthetically good aspects of the performance. Contemporary digital recording techniques allow us to pick up a very wide band of sounds, and we can manipulate these sounds at an almost microscopic level. Essentially, any layer of sound, no matter how thin or momentary, can be removed or enhanced. In classical recordings, sounds deemed as "noises" are almost always removed or lessened. (Exceptions are in those recordings marketed as "live" – both as an enticement to the public and as a warning of a "noisier" product.)

Tom Leddy has discussed the privileging of the concepts of "neat" and "clean" in a manner that is helpful in discussing recordings: "To say that something can be neatened or cleaned *implies* that there is something underlying that is worthy of neatening/cleaning" (Leddy 1995: 260). He discusses the attractive tension between surface messiness and underlying neatness, as, for example, in an abstract expressionist painting (Leddy 1995: 260). The violent, thick palette strokes of color overlay a "cleaner" structure beneath. Possibly musical noise is an everyday surface quality of live musical performance, a "proto-aesthetic" quality. Like the palette strokes, perhaps we should view the sound of the guitar string squeak or of the air escaping around a clarinetist's mouthpiece as inelim- inable parts of the aesthetic content of the performance, rather than as things to be "cleaned up" in the final mix.

There has been some backlash against the digitization of recordings, especially when it first began in the mid-1980s. Some audiophiles valorized older vinyl recordings as being more "authentic" or true to the performance. Vinyl record- ings (LPs) are analog recordings, that is, the record itself has a groove carved into it that mirrors the original sound's waveform. The record player than transforms this groove to an analog sound signal which can be fed into an amplifier. A CD is digital, that is, the audio information from the recording session is digitized – like many, many snapshots taken in a row, which are then converted to digital information bits. The early public perception was that this digital process left out some of the information, resulting in a more sterile sound, and this indeed may be apparent in some early CDs. These days, however, the sound quality of a digital recording is so much improved (the detail of sound captured and encoded is staggering) that this argument has diminished greatly. Today the most distinguishing feature of an LP is the noise of the needle, a noise that is an artifact of the reproductive technology, and not tied to the musicians' actions.

Musical noise and rock music

In live rock and pop music, sheer volume itself (which exposes even more noise) is an important expressive feature. One of the differences in vocal quality between Frederica von Stade and Sheryl Crow (or any opera singer versus a rock singer) is the "clean," "pure" sound of a classically trained voice, versus the "graininess" and noise of the rock singer. Yet both aspects, the purity and the graininess, add crucial expressive elements to those performances in those genres – possibly because both purity and graininess require effort and artistic manipulation of the "normal" singing voice. This effort is recognized as expressive.

Interestingly, it is only with the advent of rock music and the electric guitar that noise itself becomes such a predominant expressive factor in music. Imagine Jimi Hendrix without distortion in his rendition of the national anthem. Imagine Janis Joplin with a clear, pure sound. It is difficult today to remember how radical it was in the 1960s to push musical noise to the forefront of a performance. Did the increased volume of the new electronic amplification suddenly suggest that what were once small musical noises might be now be showcased as a musical event?

However, as Susan McClary indicates, it is interesting to see what counts as noise, what as order, and who gets to marginalize whom (McClary 1985). Current Western classical music practice has stifled and made tame the concert hall, the recording, and the performance itself, in search of a polished package (McClary 1985: 152), absolutely in contrast to a rock concert. The quiet, controlled, disciplined classical audiences of today are actually an anomaly in music's long history. Before the late nineteenth century, operas were often social events where one ate, chatted to one's neighbors, and heckled those on stage. Lovers escaped to the darkness of the upper balconies. After the late nineteenth century, the invention of the electric light allowed house lights to be lowered – a powerful audience inhibitor – and chairs began to be bolted to the floor facing the conductor (Haynes 2007). Audience attention began to be regimented and restricted, and noise of any kind was proscribed, to the point that today even a candy wrapper can cause immediate silent censure.

Noise in the other arts

Issues of noise surface in other arts as well. We understand the patter of the ballet slippers, and the rustling of costumes on stage to be "noise" attached to those artistic events. In painting, brushstrokes are often visible on the surface of the artwork, left as an artifact of the physical gesture of applying paint to canvas. Consider van Gogh and the expressive nature of his brushstrokes, the rhythm of them running with and against the representation. Sometimes by "muting" the surface noise a different sort of expression is put forward, as we see in the "clarity" of a Vermeer portrait. Think of the chisel marks left evident (or not) on sculpture. And, just for argument, what about "sweetened" background sounds in film: the foot-chase scene where the sounds of clicking heels and doors unlocking are added or enhanced? Or body mics in a live Shakespearean drama? Few in the audience, I would venture, object to sound/noise enhancement on the dramatic stage, and yet many might find hearing more musical noise (as they would if they were actually on stage during a performance), disconcerting. Perhaps it is because most people are more familiar with speaking, walking, and the other noisy mechanics of acting than they are with the mechanics of producing music.

Musical silence

Artworks require frames to help us first to understand them *as* artworks, and second to perceive where they begin and end. These frames may be as structured as a gilded frame around a painting, or as nebulous as the museum space surrounding what would otherwise appear to be a Brillo box. In the performing arts, such as dance, theater, and music, the artwork is not inert: it progresses through time. Without some kind of framing device, the audience might be confused as to when the play started, or when the music began.

In Western classical music, we use silence to frame the artwork, and also as a means of articulating phrasing, form, sections, and movements. Musical silence is an especially dynamic and important component of live musical performance (Judkins 1997). Silences are often the "thread" binding phrases, sections, movements, and even entire works together. They allow us to reflect on form and continuity. Silence is often used as a moment of reflection, anticipation, or summation in music. Musicians indicate musical silences not only by not producing sounds but also by remaining perfectly still.

In live performance, the acoustics and "feeling" of the space create an intimacy between the performers and the building or area in which they perform, greatly influencing the performer's interpretation of silence – especially those silences within the piece. When musicians warm up on stage prior to a concert, they are also testing the quality of silence in that hall. The resonance that a building or a room provides has proven an irresistible attraction to performers throughout music history, and points to a crucial distinction between live and recorded music, as room ambience and other acoustic effects are often artificially enhanced later in the studio.

Kinds of musical silences

There are two general kinds of musical silence. Most internal silences are *measured* – that is, they are short, notated, pulsed moments felt as part of the ongoing musical line. Brief measured silences often become the "breath marks" or punctuation at the end of musical phrases or sentences, not allowing time for reflection or anticipation; they are a part of the fabric weave, not a seam. Measured silences are specified and remain the same from performance to performance, and from performance to recording.

More interesting philosophically are longer, *unmeasured* silences, which are given meaning by the tonal and rhythmic material near them (their musical context) (Clifton 1976). Longer unmeasured silences include framing silences (before and after the work, and between movements), grand pauses, and other long internal silences (fermatas, caesuras). These silences are typically improvised in live performance – never rehearsed – even in a large orchestra. For the musician, long silences present considerable technical problems because of the exposed attacks and releases – the finesse that the arts require in any kind of "edge-shaping." Most longer unmeasured silences vary greatly in length and character in different live performances.

For example, we would think it quite bizarre to have a conductor say "We will take 25 seconds of silence between the first and second movement." The shaping of unmeasured silences is a large part of what is the edge (literally) and excitement of a live performance, playing an important role in stylistic interpretation. Silences can distill the potential energy of the penultimate grand pause, or the inertia of the end of a phrase. Most framing silences typically go unrehearsed, in the knowledge that the sense of "the moment" will determine the appropriate timing between movements, the silence after a fermata, or the length of the final silence after the music ends. What *is* rehearsed is the actual mechanics of stopping and starting the group, or, in the case of the solo musician, the releases and attacks. It is as if musicians have an unspoken understanding that longer, indefinite length silences are one of several musical elements that can only be given their final shape in a specific performance in a specific place.

In jazz performance, nearly all silences are pulsed. In a jazz ensemble situation, the opening "frame" is not silent but rather counted off by the leader. The nature of timekeeping with a drum set necessitates a continuous pulse either articulated in sound or constantly felt beneath any silence. The concluding "frame" at the end of a tune is characteristically blurred with various expressive ventures – the pianist outlines the chordal structure, adding a "color" note at the ninth, the drummer explores the cymbals while slowing the pulse, the bass player adds a glissando down to a final tonic, and lets it ring. This is not to say that silence is not used aesthetically in jazz; it is just usually found in a brief, pulsed context – ironically, silence is often "freer" in classical music. A jazz saxophonist may have many moments of "silence" or gaps in his improvisation, but it is heard over the background rhythm section, and not as silenced time on stage.

Musical silence in recordings

On recordings, musical works are presented much as paintings are on a museum's walls, with engineered silences and clean edges. In live performance, however, musical convention and physical gesture are required to help the audience identify and frame the musical event. We understand that the orchestra is just tuning, not playing a piece, because we know that today conventions require physical stillness on the part of the players, and an effort at producing silence before the work is commenced. One says "today," because, as noted above, this was not always the case. Western classical music has become increasingly silence-framed and formal, some feel to its detriment. (It was not until well into the twentieth century that audiences finally stopped applauding between movements of symphonies.)

Major orchestras, opera companies, and vocal ensembles record in large concert halls, often set up out in the center of the hall (over some of the seats), in an attempt to capture its acoustics. These sessions will invariably also include a recording of the musicians just sitting silently. The resultant recorded "silence" is not, of course, absolutely silent. It captures the "silence" in that hall with all of those individuals in it, and it is used in the recording to enhance the silences framing the piece so that they will not sound too "sterile." Exposed silences in live performance are much less pure, simply because an audience has a certain ambient noise level that comes from simply being alive, not to mention coughing, rustling, or sneezing. In live performance, some of the audience may seize the moment for applause "too soon" after the last note, inadequately framing the ending. Similarly, a final silence can also be stretched to an awkward length by incomplete gestures on the part of the conductor.

Musical silence and contemporary music

In contemporary music, silence is often used as a deliberate, obvious compositional device. Such "playing with time" and pairing of opposites (sound and silence) is an artistic trend perhaps reflective of the many disparities in our times. Today we are presented with many quite discontinuous and seemingly blurred experiences of time and space, from airplanes to particle physics. These incongruities of modern life often find expression in contemporary visual arts and in music, sometimes with materials or formats "incongruous" to that art form and its canon: in music, this is often the use of void or silence. It can make for challenging listening. Of course, just as we see in the visual arts, many musical works are not so much musical events as they are statements about *the nature of* musical events. For example, in John Cage's *4′33″* (1952), the performer simply sits silently for three tacit movements. (It should be noted that Cage indicates in the score that "the work may be performed by any instrumentalist or combination of instrumentalists and last any length of time".) Most writers agree that the musical content of a performance of this work is the ambient sounds that become apparent to the audience within the boundaries of that performance (Davies 1997). However, as Stephen Davies argues, if Cage's point was to draw our attention to the potential of ordinary sounds he failed: "He failed because he intended to create an artwork and succeeded in doing so, thereby transforming the qualities of the sounds to which that work directs our attention" (Davies 1997: 17).

The lessening of internal, formal relationships, whether in the arts or ordinary experience, is extremely disconcerting. When settings and events become increasingly non-related, we have to work hard to find cause-and-effect connections. Unfortunately for the listener, music can become complex more quickly than any other art, since it relies on the perceived coherence of its internal formal relations through time, usually greatly assisted by repetition. Thus both the "spinning out" of a Baroque melody in a Bach partita, and the fluid, seamless vocal writing of Josquin produce continuous musical anchors for the listener – as does the more formal punctuation of Haydn and Mozart. These "anchors" were compromised in the late twentieth century by the shakedown of traditional harmony, and the evolution of tonal systems that offer little redundancy. An overly generous use of musical silence can lessen the perception of internal musical relationships, by actually distancing bits of information further across time. On the other hand, "minimalist" and "New Age" music that employs very little or no musical silence might be viewed as a reaction of sorts to the largesse of silence in the "classical" musics of Varèse, Schoenberg, Boulez, and Ligeti.

In conclusion, during musical silences, rather than being in the "other-worldness" of, for example, film, we become even more intensely aware of our physical surroundings, through the interaction of sound and architecture, actually enlarging our sense of time and our own existence. Sometimes a lack of sensory information actually enhances our awareness of the passage or directedness of time, and even without sensory change or variation we still experience its passage (a phenomenon certainly crucial to appreciation of the repetitive, minimalist works of Steve Reich and Philip Glass). Music may be one of the only ways in which we truly engage the present, especially when musical time is crystallized in musical silence. The characterization of silence in live performance is more than just the articulation of form – it is a large part of helping the audience to know "where they are" in the piece. Consider the quality of the silences between verses of a carol or madrigal, or after the magnificent opening of the Bach D-minor organ toccata. These silences are musical silences, not ordinary silences, whose character is determined by the musical materials around them, their edges.

See also Aesthetic properties (Chapter 14), Classical aesthetic traditions of India, China, and the Middle East (Chapter 23), Definition (Chapter 1), Instrumental technology (Chapter 18), and Performances and recordings (Chapter 8).

References

Attali, J. (1985) *Noise: The Political Economy of Music*, Minneapolis: University of Minnesota Press.

Bicknell, J. (2005) "Just a Song? Exploring the Aesthetics of Popular Song Performance," *Journal of Aesthetics and Art Criticism* 63: 261–70.

Clifton, T. (1976) "The Poetics of Musical Silence," *The Musical Quarterly* 62: 163–81.

Davies, S. (1997) "John Cage's 4'33": Is it Music?" reprinted in Davies (2003b), pp. 11–29.

—— (2003a) "What is the Sound of One Piano Plummeting?" in Davies (2003b), pp. 108–18.

—— (2003b) *Themes in the Philosophy of Music*, New York: Oxford University Press.

Godlovitch, S. (1998) *Musical Performance: A Philosophical Study*, London: Routledge.

Haynes, B. (2007) *The End of Early Music: A Period Performer's History of Music*, Oxford: Oxford University Press.

Judkins, J. (1997) "The Aesthetics of Musical Silence in Live Performance," *Journal of Aesthetic Education* 31: 39–53.

Leddy, T. (1995) "Everyday Surface Aesthetic Qualities: 'Neat,' 'Messy,' 'Clean,' 'Dirty'," *Journal of Aesthetics and Art Criticism* 53: 259–68.

McClary, S. (1985) "The Politics of Silence and Sound," afterword to Attali, pp. 149–58.

Walser, R. (1993) "Out of Notes: Signification, Interpretation, and the Problem of Miles Davis," *Musical Quarterly* 77: 343–65.

Further reading

Kania, A. (2010) "Silent Music," Journal of Aesthetics and Art Criticism 68: 343-53. (A investigation of both the role of silence in music and the possibility of wholly silent pieces of music.)

3
RHYTHM, MELODY, AND HARMONY

Roger Scruton

Music in the Western tradition is spread out in three dimensions: rhythm, melody and harmony. One or other dimension might be lacking, but the possibility of all three, and of music that develops simultaneously along each of the axes that they define, is both distinctive of Western art music and responsible for its many aesthetic triumphs. Other traditions use only one or two of the three dimensions. African drum music, for example, is purely rhythmical, and much of the world's folk music is homophonic or heterophonic, eschewing many-voiced harmony as a distraction from the melodic line. The ancient Greeks, who first inquired into the rules of harmony, distinguished harmonious from cacophonous intervals, and explored the mathematical relations which seemed to them to explain the difference. But *harmonia* meant, for the Greeks, a pleasing melodic line, rather than two or more voices singing simultaneous but consonant melodies. In what follows it will not be possible to review all the many ways in which music has ignored one or more of the dimensions, and I shall focus on the Western tradition as the clearest example we have of music that both uses the three dimensions and consciously distinguishes them.

Rhythm

I begin with rhythm since it seems to be a species-wide phenomenon, and one that has an obvious social function in coordinating the movements of people, when they are working together, worshipping together, or relaxing together in a dance. As that sentence suggests, we are not going to understand rhythm if we ignore its ability to generate a sense of community. Through rhythm people find their activities governed by a *shared force*, and in both the dance hall and the concert hall they submit to that force collectively, in conscious awareness that they do so as a group.

We should not think of rhythm simply as a beat, such as might be produced by regularly striking a drum. Beat is neither necessary nor sufficient to generate rhythm. It is not necessary for the reason that there are rhythms contained in melodic lines which cannot be divided into the relevant sections – such as the extended melisma of Gregorian chant. It is not sufficient, since regular pulse can be heard in things which have no rhythm, such as the pulses of a machine. Of course we can hear such pulses *as* rhythmical, importing in imagination an organization that they do not contain in reality – as when Gershwin began to hear the rhythm of *Rhapsody in Blue* in the clicking wheels of the train in which he was traveling. But that only emphasizes the fact that rhythm is distinct from beat, and must be brought to the beat by the one who listens or moves to it.

The issue here is obscured by the Western habit of *measuring* in bar lines. Rhythm is not measure, though if you are familiar with Western music and understand the ways of measuring it out in bars, you will quickly latch on to the rhythm of any new piece. A bar contains a certain number of beats, which can themselves be divided by two, three, or more to produce smaller beats. Notes can be tied across the beat and also across bar lines, to produce effects of syncopation, as in Figure 3.1. These effects are felt and understood because the ties are forcing the listener to group the notes in a way that conflicts with the underlying movement. Some scholars (e.g. Schuller 1968) argue that the use of syncopation in jazz reflects the origins of jazz rhythms in African drum-music, which is polyrhythmical, that is, it contains conflicting rhythms that serve to shift the accent relative to each other.

The emphasis on measure, and the division of the bar-line, leads to the illusion that rhythm and measure are the same thing. Two important observations count against that. First, there is the example of unmeasured rhythm, as in Gregorian chant. The work of Dom André Mocquereau of the Abbey of Solesmes, subsequently taken up by Olivier Messiaen, has familiarized us with the fact that Gregorian chant is profoundly rhythmical in its organization, even though it is not, and in many instances cannot be, measured out (Messiaen 1996–). In his striking polyphonic and serial tribute to the Benedictine tradition, the *Lamentatio Jeremiae prophetae*, Ernst Křenek produces entirely unmeasured sequences which generate a strong rhythmic pulse through phrasing and grouping alone.

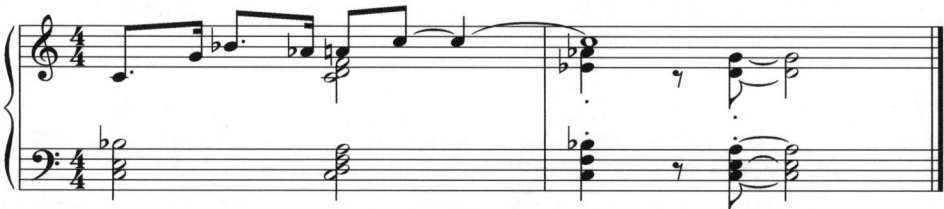

Figure 3.1 Dave Brubeck, "Everybody's Jumpin'"

Second, there is rhythm formed by addition rather than division within the bar-line – a practice again taken up by Messiaen. A leading example is that of the Indian *mâtra*, as set out in the system of *deçi-tâlas* by the thirteenth-century theorist Sharngadeva. Many composers – Boulez and Stockhausen among them – have followed Messiaen in constructing rhythms which resist division into beats, and which are derived by lengthening individual notes as one might lengthen a syllable for emphasis. (That is, indeed, how emphasis was effected in the Sanskrit language, and this feature of the language has carried over into its musical setting.)

Additive measure does not, however, determine rhythmic organization. Some of the measures introduced by Sharngadeva are just too long to be grasped as single units, and the use of the *tabla* and other percussion devices introduces beats and divisions into classical ragas that are not unlike the beats and divisions heard in Western music. This point further emphasizes that measure and rhythm are two different things. In Eastern European folk music, especially Bulgarian and Hungarian, beats are often lengthened, without destroying their number in the bar, as in the Bulgarian Christmas carol in Figure 3.2. This has four beats in the bar, but no bar is the length of four eighth-notes, since in every bar beats occur which have been lengthened by a sixteenth-note. Despite the irregular measure, this is an intensely rhythmical piece, which exerts a strong grip on the listener.

Such examples remind us that measured bar lines may or may not succeed in capturing the real rhythm of a piece. The "Danse sacrale" from the *Rite of Spring* is measured out with irregular bar lines – but measured out differently in the orchestral and the four-hand-piano scores. The *real* rhythm of the opening bars is captured by neither measure, since it arises from an experience of grouping and stress which itself depends on the "slicing" of the silence by the razor-sharp chords.

Such examples point to the importance of grouping. We group notes – whether pitched or percussive – in blocks or sections, and hear a beginning and an end to each block. If these blocks are repeated, even if they are of unequal length, we may hear a kind of pulse, and can "move with" that pulse either bodily or in imagination. Grouping of this kind belongs with those imaginative powers that remain within the province of the will: it is a well-known fact that we can choose to group notes in contrasting ways, and so enjoy the experience of rhythmic ambiguity, stressing now one note, now another, in a regularly repeated sequence, as in the excerpt from Brahms in Figure 3.3.

Figure 3.2 Bulgarian Christmas carol

Figure 3.3 Brahms, "An die Nachtigall": two ways of hearing

The simplest way to explain rhythm is therefore phenomenologically: it is that temporal organization which we hear in the sequence of musical sounds and with which we move, when we move with the music. It is not reducible to beat or measure, does not require regularity, but is sensitive to grouping and stress. This suggests a deep distinction, in conclusion, between two kinds of rhythmic organization – the external and the internal. External rhythmic organization comes from draping the music over bar lines that are defined from outside the melodic line, as by the drum-kit in a pop group, or by an ostinato rhythm in a classical orchestral piece, such as we find in the last movement of Sibelius's Violin Concerto or, more subtly, in the first movement of Walton's First Symphony. Internal rhythmic organization, by contrast, is "precipitated out" from the melodic movement: it arises from stresses and groupings that take shape within the melodic line, and has no independent reality. A prime example is the rhythmic order that we sense in Gregorian chant, and which explains the otherwise surprising fact that Messiaen, in his lectures, constantly reverts to chant as the paradigm of rhythmic organization. While you can tap or beat along with an external rhythm without destroying it, you cannot do this so easily to an internal rhythm, and certainly you cannot do it to a Gregorian chant. Between the two extremes of the drum-kit in pop and the melisma of Gregorian chant there are many intermediate rhythmic experiences, in which internal rhythm is given a measure of external support; for instance, by the use of timpani in a Haydn symphony.

Melody

Melody is as hard to define as rhythm, and – as the last paragraph implies – is often inseparable from rhythm. The shapes, lengths and intervals of melodies vary wildly from culture to culture, and it is difficult to give a general account that distinguishes genuine melody from a mere sequence of pitches. As with rhythm, however, it is safe to assume that melody is something that we hear *in* a sequence of pitched sounds, and which is not a material property of the sound sequence itself. We can therefore hear melody in bird-song, even though this melody is something that birds, which lack imagination and the grouping experiences that derive from it, cannot hear (Scruton 1974: pt. 1).

In the Western classical tradition, it is helpful to distinguish melisma – the melodic organization that extends "horizontally" through a sequence of pitches – from melodies, which are bounded individuals, with a beginning, a middle and (usually) an end. The Gregorian chant is a continuous melisma, which only rarely can be broken down into individual melodies. The same is true of the guitar solos in heavy metal, and certain kinds of jazz improvisation (for example, Charlie Parker and John Coltrane). In the classical tradition, however, melodies play the role of musical individuals, to be transported whole around the pitch spectrum, and to be diminished, augmented, varied and inverted, while remaining in some deep (but purely phenomenological) sense the same. Renaissance polyphony and the ensuing "baroque" show yet another kind of melodic organization, with few clear boundaries, but only half-closures, as the melodic line pauses at places where it can renew its ongoing energy (Szabolsci 1965). A clear example is the last movement of Bach's Third Brandenburg Concerto.

The language with which we refer to melodies indicates some of the differences between them. Not all melodies are tunes: some are too open-ended and elaborate to deserve such a label. (Consider, for example, the long melody that occurs immediately after the opening declamation of Act II of *Tristan und Isolde*.) We distinguish songs and song-like melodies from thematic and theme-like melodies, the first being complete musical individuals that can stand alone, the second being, and sounding like, musical *material*, which will reveal its character only in the course of elaboration and development. Folk songs and hymns have melodies of the first kind, and a strophic form suitable to their use. The instrumental masterpieces of the Western classical tradition often deploy themes that are very unsong-like, however attractive – such as the "thesis" melodies of Bach's keyboard works, or the famous four-note theme that opens Beethoven's Fifth Symphony. Such themes call out for development, and acquire their character only in the course of it. The distinction here is not hard and fast, but depends on context and treatment. Schubert was able to present one and the same melody now as a song, now as a theme in a fully instrumental elaboration – consider "Der Tod und das Mädchen," "Sei mir gegrüsst" and "Getrockene Blumen."

Melodies are also distinguished by the impulses that drive them. Some are driven by word setting, and bear the marks of the words that they set – these we might call logogenic, and they include most hymns in the Anglican Hymnal, and most of the modal folk songs collected by Cecil Sharp in the pubs and marketplaces of Edwardian England. Other melodies are essentially dance tunes. These (the orchegenic) are often not very singable, however compelling in outline: consider the melodies of Dvořák's scherzos, or that of Ravel's *Bolero*, which is both orchegenic and melismatic. Finally there are the harmonegenic melodies, which are driven by harmonic relations among their successive notes and reflect underlying harmonic relations and key relations which may be only implicit, or else filled in by the accompanying voices. Familiar examples are the themes of sonata-form movements in the classical tradition. The first two melodic kinds preserve the memory of social uses: love-song and hymn, dance and choir. Only in the course of time, and as a result of the listening culture that grew in church, in court and finally in concert hall, did melodies begin to take the thematic form which we find in the Western symphonic tradition.

Two features serve to characterize melody in all its forms. First, there is the internal constraint exerted by every note on every other. A melody is a sequence in which no note can be altered without changing the character of the whole. This feature was pointed out by Edmund Gurney: the "wrong note" phenomenon causes us to cry out in protest at every departure from the known musical line (Gurney 1880: 92–4). A non-melodic sequence of tones can be chopped and changed without eliciting protests. But all changes in a melody are noticed, and most condemned as wrong. If a composer is able to change a melody and take it in a new direction – for example, so as to end in another key – this is regarded as an achievement, such as that of Berg in incorporating the whole-tone melody of Bach's *Es ist genug* into the last movement of the Violin Concerto.

The second feature that characterizes melody is that of the boundary. Melodies have a beginning and an end, and often half-endings along the way – though, as I noted above, the ending may be postponed until the close of a section or a movement, as in much Baroque music. Hearing a melody begin is one of the fundamental musical experiences, and it is very difficult to describe what exactly it is that you hear when this happens. Some melodies begin with an up-beat – a passage that leads into them, and which is understood as preparatory, as in Figure 3.4. Sometimes a phrase might sound like an up-beat but turn out to be an indispensable part of the melodic structure, such as the three-note phrase that begins the "Londonderry Air" (Figure 3.5), which is in fact the first of eight such three-note entrance figures, and a key to the character of the melody as a whole.

The word "closure" is often used to describe the ending of a melody, on the analogy with syntactical closure in language. By invoking this analogy we emphasize that, in the classical tradition, the musical movement unfolds along all three dimensions simultaneously, and that the "sense of an ending" in the melodic line may be reinforced at the rhythmical and harmonic level too. A simple example is the "syntactically correct" nursery rhyme, "Baa Baa, Black Sheep" (Figure 3.6), a four-square sixteen-bar tune which moves toward the tonic for a "half closure," goes back to the dominant and then moves step-wise down to the tonic again. It seems illuminating to say that this harmonegenic melody moves toward rhythmic, melodic, and harmonic closure simultaneously, although it is necessary to guard against taking the analogy with linguistic syntax too literally.

Figure 3.4 English folk song, "Daughter in the Dungeon"

Figure 3.5 "Londonderry Air"

Figure 3.6 "Baa Baa, Black Sheep"

The boundary experience and the "wrong note" experience are familiar at the phenomenological level, but they do not correspond to any fixed features of the sound sequence. A melody can pass through any note on the diatonic scale, tonic included, without generating the sense of an ending; and it can also end on any note, even a note that does not belong to the scale, as in Figure 3.7 from Debussy's *Prélude à l'après-midi d'un faune*. There are also recognizable melodies that are not tonal at all, such as that which opens the Schoenberg Violin Concerto, and melodies which appropriate tonality only to ignore its melodic constraints, such as the melody which opens the Violin Concerto of William Walton. The experience of hearing a melody begin and end is, in other words, *sui generis*, and not reducible to the recognition of any definable pattern in a sound sequence. A melody is a purely *intentional* object of musical perception, something we hear in a sequence when we respond to its musical potential.

Figure 3.7 Debussy, *Prélude à l'après-midi d'un faune*

During the course of the nineteenth century, and under the influence of Wagner, melodic boundaries began to weaken: a new kind of melisma emerged, in which tune-like episodes emerge from a continuous musical line, as in the first act of Wagner's *Die Meistersinger von Nürnberg*. A good example of this is the slow movement of Elgar's Violin Sonata, which is melodious without a melody. The melodies that are begun in this piece usually break off, or are overlaid by new beginnings. Many Romantic movements are similar, consisting only of melodic beginnings without endings, as in the tone poem *Don Juan* by Strauss. In describing such works, it is more appropriate to speak of *melodic thinking* than of melodies. Nevertheless, they exhibit the same horizontal order that we hear in a tune by Mozart.

Harmony

The study of harmony in ancient Greece began from the natural intervals – fourth, fifth, and octave – which correspond to elementary arithmetical relations witnessed in the lengths of the strings or pipes used to produce them. However, harmony as we now know it is an intentional object like melody. It is what we hear in two simultaneous pitches when we hear them as a single object. In this sense, harmony, in our tradition, takes two distinct forms: chordal harmony, in which separate pitches sound together as a single chord; and counterpoint, in which separate voices move interdependently, creating an interwoven texture. In both cases, harmony is to be distinguished from *simultaneity*. In certain works of atonal music, such as Schoenberg's *Pierrot Lunaire*, we hear instruments sounding together at different pitches. But we do not (or do not as a rule) hear chords. What exactly is the difference here? One difference seems to be that when two or more pitches are heard as a chord, the phenomenal space between those pitches is *occupied* by the chord. The space between two pitches that form a "simultaneity" remains vacant.

In saying that, I am assuming that the metaphor of musical space is not just a *façon de parler*, but a description of something that we hear. We speak of tones as moving up and down the pitch spectrum, of melodies as occurring now at one place, now at another, and of the music itself as moving forward, and these are all metaphors, which correspond to no actual space in the world of pitches. Nevertheless, we hear music as spatially organized, and if we did not do so we would be unable to understand the art of music as we know it (Scruton 1997). Our experience of harmony belongs to this experience. A chord *occupies* music space. Chords can be heard as excluding melodies from the spaces they occupy, such as the chord that opens the second episode (the "Dance of the Adolescents") in Stravinsky's *Rite of Spring*. Chords can "leak into" each other (as Janáček puts it (1974: 164)) – as the open fifth on A at the beginning of Beethoven's Ninth Symphony leaks into and pollutes the fifth on D that replaces it; they can be transparent, such as the opening chords of *Lohengrin*, or opaque, such as the Stravinsky chord just mentioned.

31

Chords may be harmonically disconnected from their neighbours and still be chords, rather than simultaneities; for example, the whole-tone chords in the chordal melody that opens Debussy's *Pelléas et Mélisande*. More often, however, we hear chords as belonging to sequences, in which each chord places constraints on its successor, compelling us to hear it either as part of the harmonic argument or as an intrusion. Hence there has arisen in the Western tradition an idea of "harmonic progression," according to which sequences of chords are understood as progressing toward or away from a boundary, with the equivalent of the "wrong note" phenomenon in the form of the "wrong chord" (as in the crazy cadence that ends Strauss's *Don Quixote* – and which sounds right in retrospect, when the tonic chord is finally reached).

Understanding harmony in this way, we are led to the view that the distinction between consonance and dissonance is a distinction *within* harmony. The distinction is purely phenomenological and impossible to align with any material property of the sounds in which it is heard. Helmholtz (1954) believed that he could explain dissonance in terms of the beats caused by the clashing overtones of competing fundamentals. However, harmonies cluttered by beats may be heard as entirely consonant – close harmony in the bass, for example, as in late Beethoven sonatas – while uncluttered harmonies can sound highly dissonant, as when open fifths and fourths emerge in polytonal structures (e.g. in Ligeti's Horn Trio). Such examples suggest that consonance and dissonance are heard relative to the stylistic context, so that a chord that is dissonant in Haydn will sound consonant in Berg. Furthermore both are a matter of degree, and are understood as such – such as the dissonances that interrupt the "Ode to Joy" in Beethoven's Ninth Symphony. Hence dissonance can gradually increase and decrease within the musical line.

In the classical tradition these phenomenological features are put to important use in two ways: resolution and suspension. Composers discovered ways of "resolving" the tensions heard in a dissonance through the consonance that follows it. So effective is this device that the syntax of tonal harmony has been almost entirely built upon it. And one way of building on it is through the practice of suspension, in which a note from a consonant harmony is held while the other notes change, so creating a dissonance, which then resolves to consonance as the "suspended" note is allowed to slide home to its proper place. Whole sequences of suspensions occur in the music of Gesualdo and Victoria, often put to exquisite use, and Romantic harmony frequently resolves a suspended note while at the same time changing the rest of the chord, so as to land on another dissonance – the prelude to *Tristan und Isolde* being a vivid instance, in which harmonic closure is deliberately avoided throughout.

In one familiar form of suspension, the tonic is sounded over the chord of the dominant and then resolved on to the leading note (Figure 3.8). Jazz musicians got to like the sound of the first of those chords, with its accumulation of fourths, and, in deference to its classical function, called it the "sus" chord. However, sus

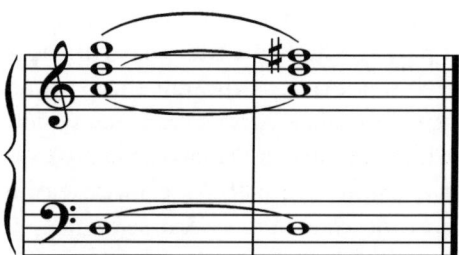

Figure 3.8 Suspension

chords are used in jazz as complete and closed harmonies, and as a rule no listener feels the need to resolve them – a clear illustration of the context-dependence of dissonance in all its forms. The convention arose of turning the upper fourth of the stack into a triad, so that the sus chord on a given root is now understood to include the triad on the note one whole-tone below the root (Figure 3.9). (Herbie Hancock's "Maiden Voyage" consists entirely of such chords.)

The Baroque harmonic idiom, which J. S. Bach shared with Couperin and Handel, deploys recognized "chord progressions," in which each harmony arises naturally from the predecessor, while moving in a goal-directed way toward closure. The Classical style of J. C. Bach, Haydn and Mozart also deploys such chord progressions – though they are rather different. And Romantic composers delighted in exploring novel progressions, which might lead to closure, as in Schumann and Brahms, or might equally seem to "lose their way," as in Wagner (see, for example, the Tarnhelm and Forgetting motifs in the *Ring* cycle). In jazz, however, there is a fertile abundance of progressions, some standard, some not so standard, even though there is as a rule no felt need for a "goal-directed" syntax. The consonance–dissonance distinction is much fainter in jazz than in the classical tradition, on account of the seventh and ninth being treated as natural additions to any triad, the seventh in addition being a melodic note, and not a passing note as it is in most classical music. Indeed, you might conclude from this and other examples that the "goal-directed" character of Western art music is very much a culture-bound phenomenon, and not something that has any special connection with any of the three dimensions of musical syntax.

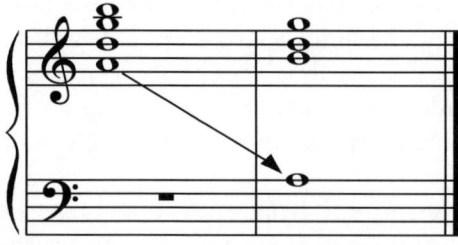

Figure 3.9 Sus chord

Earlier I remarked that the distinction between a simultaneity and a chord could be understood in part through the fact that chords are heard as "filling" the space between their boundaries. Although this is true, it is not the whole truth, and there is a great difference between chords which are heard *simply* as musical units, and chords which are heard as *composed* from the several voices that flow into them. Suspension is in fact a special case of a general principle of Classical harmony, according to which chord sequences arise from the movement of individual voices. In the Classical style, and equally in its Romantic offshoots, voices are required to move naturally, as though singing from one position to the next: disobedience to this rule causes the musical surface to lose its organic integrity, and to acquire a jerky quality which makes it difficult or impossible to hear goal-directed progressions. Jazz too obeys the voicing principle, and insists that each chord be properly spaced, so that no inner parts are heard to leap across unmelodic intervals.

The cadence

An interesting feature of both melodic and harmonic order in our tradition is the "cadence." This word, from Latin *cadere* ("to fall"), indicates a specific kind of boundary – not necessarily a closure, but an effect of "settling," however temporary, in which melodic or harmonic tension is released, and a particular note or harmony emerges as a place of rest. Melodic cadences are very important in Gregorian chant, and in melismatic compositions generally, since they represent pauses in the musical movement that facilitate grouping. Without them both listening and performing would lack an essential aid to the grasp of structure.

Harmonic cadences are similar, and have achieved standard forms in most Western idioms. The V–I cadence is familiar as a concluding moment in the Classical style, as are the II–V–I and the IV–V–I cadences, all known, in this use, as "perfect cadences." The IV–I cadence, known as the "plagal" (oblique) cadence, or "amen" cadence because of its use in the Protestant "amen," also has a concluding function, as in Scriabin's *Poème de l'extase*. Cadences include imperfect cadences, half cadences, interrupted and deceptive cadences – all instantly recognizable to anyone familiar with the Classical style and its Romantic derivations. There is also a distinction between masculine and feminine cadences, the first moving to a metrically strong position, the second to a position which is metrically weak. Needless to say, feminists have objected to this use of language; but the distinction, however described, is very easily heard. (Listen to the beautiful sequence of feminine cadences with which Jenůfa reminds the selfish Števa of her plight, in Act 1 of Janáček's opera, and you will see that the language records something real.)

Cadences that form conclusions in one idiom might have quite a different effect in another. Thus the II–V–I progression which provides the perfect cadence in much classical sonata-style music has another use altogether in jazz. If the chords are voiced without the root and with added seventh and ninth, the progression loses its finality, and becomes an opening gambit, rather than a concluding move – as in "Tune Up" by Miles Davis, which presents a succession of such cadences in different tonal areas.

Whether there is the equivalent of the cadence in rhythmic organization is a moot point. Rhythmic order can certainly work toward and away from boundaries, and it is possible that it can induce the same effect of pause and recuperation that we know from melodic and harmonic cadences. Nevertheless, rhythm is seldom if ever described in this way. As the distinction between "masculine" and "feminine" cadences makes clear, however, melodic and harmonic cadences are affected by rhythmic organization, and heard differently according to the strength of the beat or the rhythmic accent.

Tonality

Central to the Western musical tradition have been the ideas of scale and key, and, arising from these, the notion of the chords of the key, and modulation between keys. Tonality is not a static system, but one that is constantly developing; scales can be modal as well as diatonic; they include chromatic and whole-tone scales, which have no key. Nevertheless, the idea of a tonal centre, with its privileged chords and intervals, has been fundamental to music in the Western classical tradition right up to the present day. It is thanks to tonality that we can hear melodic and harmonic closure as achieved together, and also that we can hear chord sequences as making sense in themselves, as well as being appropriate "accompaniments" to recognized melodies – such as the melodies that we know from the Great American Songbook.

The presence of a tonal centre is vital to a certain kind of long-range symphonic thinking. While a simple song may progress from tonic to dominant and back again in a few bars, large-scale movements in the classical tradition may prolong such transitions over many minutes. This does not mean that a symphonic movement will stay on one chord for all that time. The classical idiom enables the listener to hear, enduring beneath a short-term progression, a single tonal centre, to which the musical movement returns both melodically and harmonically, and from which it departs in ways that do not disrupt the sense of that tonal centre as "home." Tonality creates "regions" of tonal space, in which a single chord prevails, so that other chords are heard as "prolongations." These prolonging harmonies do not, in themselves, turn the music in a new direction, but simply move around the harmony that defines the region in which they occur. This striking phenomenon has been provided with an interesting analysis by Heinrich Schenker, who presents a kind of generative grammar of tonal music, with subsidiary harmonies emerging as "middle ground" structures from background tonal relations (Schenker 1979). However, Schenker's theory has proved controversial and at best of only narrow application. Once again, we seem to be confronted with a striking phenomenological feature of music which cannot be pinned down by a single theory.

Such discussions suggest that the three musical dimensions, although separable in principle, are not easily separated in fact. The emergence of tonal "regions" in musical space is profoundly influenced by rhythmic organization: rhythmic patterns govern the segmentation of what we hear, and can force alien harmonies to relate to each other. Melodies have harmonic as well as rhythmic implications, and can change character entirely when differently harmonized. The slow movement of Schubert's last piano sonata contains a melody first harmonized in C-sharp minor, and then harmonized in E major. And what we hear is two melodies, even though hardly a note has been changed. That which is being played out "horizontally" in the melodic line is heard as expounding, in its own way, the "verticals" on which it rests, just as the ornaments in a classical frieze expound the same Order as the columns beneath them.

What happens to melody and harmony when tonality is abandoned? This is a question that troubled Schoenberg, who believed that he could derive new melodies from his serial technique, and who advocated what he called "the emancipation of the dissonance" (1975: 91), which would remove entirely the feeling of tension and release, the distinction between consonance and dissonance, and the need for dissonances to resolve. The result remains controversial to this day. In particular it remains controversial whether genuine closure can be heard in music that eschews all privileged pitches, and whether real harmonies, as opposed to simultaneities, can be heard in chord sequences that follow no pattern of tension and release.

This controversy lies beyond the scope of the present chapter, but it points to the real need, in the philosophy of music, for clarity concerning the nature of the musical dimensions. Can there be melody without boundaries? Can there be harmonic progression without the dissonance–consonance distinction? Can there be closure without rhythm? Those and many other questions all depend upon our view of the three musical dimensions, and how they connect. So too do questions concerning the place of music in a culture.

For example, we make a distinction between short-term and long-term musical attention. The Western classical tradition is a tradition of long-range musical thought, in which themes and ideas are explored in all their implications, and closures achieved only after extended ventures across musical space. The contrast here with the short-term listening encouraged by pop is both important and difficult to conceptualize. Adorno (1987) wrote in this connection of "the regression of listening," meaning the kind of short-circuiting of musical attention, what we might call the "addictive" aspect of listening, that he discerned in the popular music of his day. Adorno connected his argument – which he took to be a profound objection to jazz and its off-shoots – with a theory of mass culture and its socio-economic origins. This theory is, to say the least, controversial. But many of Adorno's readers have felt that he is getting at a profound truth about music, concerning a real distinction between different kinds of listening, and between the different roles that music might play in the lives of its adherents. However, there is no likelihood that Adorno's criticisms will ever be properly stated, let alone assessed, if they are not connected to a theory of what is going on when a listener follows a rhythmic, melodic, or harmonic argument.

See also Analysis (Chapter 48), Music and imagination (Chapter 11), Music and language (Chapter 10), Music, philosophy, and cognitive science (Chapter 54), Phenomenology and music (Chapter 53), Psychology of music (Chapter 55), Music theory and philosophy (Chapter 46), and Understanding music (Chapter 12).

References

Adorno, T.W. (1987 [1938]) "On the Fetish Character in Music and the Regression of Listening," in A. Arato and E. Gebhardt (eds) *The Essential Frankfurt School Reader*, New York: Continuum, pp. 270–99.

Gurney, E. (1880) *The Power of Sound*, London: Smith, Elder, & Co.

Helmholtz, H. (1954 [1885]) *On the Sensations of Tone as a Physiological Basis for the Theory of Music*, trans. A.J. Ellis, New York: Dover.

Janáček, L. (1974 [1911–20]) *Hudebně teoretické dílo*, vol. 2: *Úplná nauka o harmonii*, ed. Z. Blazek, Prague: Supraphon.

Messiaen, O. (1996–) *Traité de rhythme, de couleur et d'ornithologie*, 8 vols, Paris: A. Leduc.

Schenker, H. (1979) *Free Composition*, trans. E. Oster, New York: Longman.

Schoenberg, A. (1975 [1948]) "A Self Analysis," in *Style and Idea: Selected Writings of Arnold Schoenberg*, trans. L. Black, ed. L. Stein, London: St. Martin's Press, 76–91.

Schuller, G. (1968) *Early Jazz: Its Roots and Musical Development*, New York: Oxford University Press.

Scruton, R. (1974) *Art and Imagination: A Study in the Philosophy of Mind*, London: Methuen.

—— (1997) *The Aesthetics of Music*, Oxford: Oxford University Press.

Szabolsci, B. (1965) *A History of Melody*, trans. C. Jolly and S. Karig, London: St. Martin's Press.

4

ONTOLOGY

Carl Matheson and Ben Caplan

Ontology

Ontologists of music have been interested in a number of questions, including the following ones. Are there musical works? If there are musical works, what are they like? If there are musical works, what relation do they stand in to their performances? In this chapter, we will be focusing primarily on the second of these questions, the question of what musical works are like. In addressing this question, ontologists of music have asked a number of further questions, including the following ones. What ontological category or categories do musical works belong to? Where are musical works located in time? How are musical works individuated?

Let us assume for now that there are musical works. (We will come back briefly to this assumption later.) In particular, let us assume that Beethoven's Piano Sonata No. 29 in B-flat major, Op. 106 – the *Hammerklavier* – exists. First, there are questions about its ontological category. For example, is the *Hammerklavier* a type? Or an event? Or something else? Second, there are questions about its temporal location. For example, did the *Hammerklavier* come into existence when Beethoven composed it, in 1817–18, or did it always exist? And, third, there are questions about its individuation. For example, is the *Hammerklavier* distinguished from other musical works entirely by how it sounds? Or is it distinguished from other musical works in part by the historical context in which it was composed, or by the instrument that Beethoven specified that it should be performed on?

Ontological category

The dominant view in the ontology of music is the *type theory*, according to which the *Hammerklavier* is a type (Wollheim 1980: §§35–7; Levinson 1980: 78–82, 1990a: 216; Currie 1989: 66–71; S. Davies 2001: 37–43; Dodd 2007: chs 1–5, 2008; Kivy 1983: 35–6, 1987: 59–60, 1988: 75; Wolterstorff 1980: pt. 2). A natural starting point for type theorists is the view that the *Hammerklavier* is a type whose tokens are sound events that sound exactly like note-perfect performances of the *Hammerklavier*. This view can then be modified or extended in various ways, for example, by excluding sound events that are not performances of any musical work because they are natural occurrences (such as the wind whistling through the trees), or by including sound events that deviate to some extent from note-perfect performances of the *Hammerklavier*.

But not everyone is a type theorist. Some who reject the type theory think that the *Hammerklavier* is a set, either of correct performances (Goodman 1976: 210) or of possible and exemplary performances (Effingham ms.). The main difference between sets and types is that only the former are *extensional*: necessarily, two sets are identical if and only if they have the same members; but it is possible for two distinct types to have the same tokens. For example, if everyone who is Canadian happens to be a hockey player, and vice versa, then the set of Canucks is identical to the set of hockey players, but the types *Canuck* and *hockey player* might still be distinct, because, for example, being able to skate is one of the requirements on being a hockey player, but it is not one of the requirements on being Canadian (even if all Canadians happen to know how to skate).

Others who reject the type theory think that the *Hammerklavier* is an event, something that occurs in space and time, namely, Beethoven's compositional activity (D. Davies 2004). Still others think that it is a mereological sum of performances: something that each of those performances is a part of and every part of which has a part in common with one of those performances (Alward 2004). And still others think that it is a *sui generis* non-physical object, which is distinct from but nonetheless intimately connected to performances and recordings, copies of the score, and mental representations (Rohrbaugh 2003, ms.), or to a type whose tokens are sound events (Evnine 2009).

Some defend their view on the grounds that it identifies the *Hammerklavier* with something ontologically respectable that is already in their ontology, for example, a set (Effingham ms.). And some defend their view on the grounds that it best explains some feature or features of the *Hammerklavier*. For example, type theorists might say that their view best explains its *repeatability*, how it can have multiple performances: each of the *Hammerklavier*'s performances is a token of it (Dodd 2007: 9–19, 2008). And those who think that the *Hammerklavier* is a *sui generis* non-physical object might say that their view best explains its *temporality* (how it can come into and go out of existence), its *modal flexibility* (how it could have been different than it actually is), and its *temporal flexibility* (how it can change over time). Types might be temporal (see below), but type theorists generally deny that they are modally or temporally flexible (Dodd 2007: ch. 2), whereas *sui generis* non-physical objects might well be temporal, modally flexible, and temporally flexible (Rohrbaugh 2003, ms.).

In response to the claim that their view does not best explain the temporality, modal flexibility, or temporal flexibility of the *Hammerklavier*, some type theorists deny that the *Hammerklavier* has those features and offer an explanation of why it *seems* to have those features, even though it really does not (Dodd 2007: chs 4–5, 2008). Perhaps the *Hammerklavier* is not temporal after all (see below), and even some who reject the type theory admit that it might not be temporally flexible (Rohrbaugh ms.). But the *Hammerklavier* does seem to be modally flexible: it does seem that in composing the *Hammerklavier* Beethoven could have called for a different note here or there, in which case the range of the *Hammerklavier*'s correct performances would have been slightly different. Those who think that the *Hammerklavier* is a modally inflexible type might say that, although the range of the *Hammerklavier*'s correct performances could not have been even slightly different, Beethoven could have composed a different work, the *Near-Hammerklavier*, with a slightly different range of correct performances (Dodd 2007: 90–1, 2008: 1127).

Temporal location

The *Hammerklavier* was composed in 1817–18. Did it come into existence at that time? Opinion is pretty evenly divided. Some say *yes* (Levinson 1980: 65, 1990a: 217; Rohrbaugh 2003, ms.); others say *no*, either because the *Hammerklavier* is not located in time or because it is located at all times (Dodd 2007: 99). (Not being located in time and being located at all times are not often distinguished in the literature.) The conjunction of the type theory and the claim that the *Hammerklavier* and other musical works do not come into existence is known as *musical Platonism* (Dodd 2007: 99). One reason for asserting that the *Hammerklavier* came into existence in 1817–18 is that, in composing it, Beethoven created it; and, in creating it, he brought it into existence (Levinson 1980: 65–8, 1990a: 217–21, 227–31). Of those who deny that the *Hammerklavier* came into existence in 1817–18, some say that Beethoven created it without bringing it into existence (Deutsch 1991), whereas others say that he composed it without creating it and, instead, creatively discovered or selected it (Kivy 1983: 38–47, 1987: 66–73; Dodd 2007: ch. 5). One reason for denying that the *Hammerklavier* came into existence in 1817–18 is that it might be hard to square its coming into existence with the type theory, since types are often thought to exist at all times or outside of time (Dodd 2007: ch. 3). Of those who assert that the *Hammerklavier* came into existence in 1817–18, some say that types can come into existence (Levinson 1980: 79–80, 81–2, 1990a: 259–61), whereas others say that the *Hammerklavier* is not a type (Rohrbaugh 2003, ms.).

Eventually, perhaps millions of years from now, all traces – including all performances, recordings, and memories – of the *Hammerklavier* will have disappeared. Will it go out of existence at that time? Those who deny that the *Hammerklavier* came into existence in 1817–18 deny that it will go out of existence in the distant future (Dodd 2007: 99). Of those who assert that the *Hammerklavier* came into existence in 1817–18, some are ambivalent about whether it will go out of existence in the distant future (Levinson 1990a: 261–63), whereas others assert that it will (Rohrbaugh 2003, ms.). The question of whether the *Hammerklavier* will go out of existence in the distant future has received less attention in the literature than has the question of whether it came into existence in 1817–18 (but see Trivedi 2008), presumably because only the latter question is connected to questions about composition and creativity.

Individuation

Beethoven composed the *Hammerklavier* in 1817–18 and specified that it should be performed on a piano (a "hammer-keyboard" or "*Hammerklavier*"). As it happens, no one else composed a sound-alike musical work – a musical work that sounds exactly like the *Hammerklavier* – 175 years later, nor did anyone else compose a sound-alike musical work and specify that it should be performed on a Perfect Timbral Synthesizer (PTS), an electronic device that can duplicate the timbre of any actual instrument. But those are historical accidents. Suppose that Beethoven composed the *Hammerklavier* in 1817–18; someone else composed a sound-alike musical work, the *1993 Hammerklavier*, 175 years later; and someone else composed another sound-alike musical work, the *PTS Klavier*, and specified that it should be performed on a PTS. According to *sonicism*, the *Hammerklavier*, the *1993 Hammerklavier*, and the *PTS Klavier* are in fact the same musical work, since the *Hammerklavier* is distinguished from other musical works solely by how it sounds (Kivy 1987: 60–6, 1988; Dodd 2007: chs. 8–9). But, according to *contextualism*, the *Hammerklavier* and the *1993 Hammerklavier* are distinct musical works, since the *Hammerklavier* is distinguished from other musical works not just by how it sounds but also by the historical context in which it was composed (Levinson 1980: 68–73, 1990a: 221–7; Currie 1989: 34–40; S. Davies 2001: 72–5). And, according to *instrumentalism*, the *Hammerklavier* and the *PTS Klavier* are also distinct musical works, since the *Hammerklavier* is distinguished from other musical works not just by how it sounds but also by the instrument that its composer specified it should be performed on (Levinson 1980: 73–8, 1990a: 231–47; S. Davies 2001: 60–71).

Contextualists argue that the *Hammerklavier* and the *1993 Hammerklavier* differ in their aesthetic and artistic properties. For example, the *Hammerklavier* is exciting and original in ways in which the *1993 Hammerklavier* is not. So, by Leibniz's Law, they must be distinct (Levinson 1980: 68–9, 1990a: 221–4; Currie 1989: 34–40). Sonicists reply that the *Hammerklavier* and the *1993 Hammerklavier* do *not* differ in their aesthetic and artistic properties. There are various ways for sonicists to say that. For example, sonicists might say that the *Hammerklavier* is exciting in exactly the ways that the *1993 Hammerklavier* is and that, although Beethoven and his compositional actions might be more original than the twentieth-century composer and her compositional actions, neither the *Hammerklavier* nor the *1993 Hammerklavier* is itself original (Dodd 2007: ch. 9).

Instrumentalists can offer a parallel argument: the *Hammerklavier* and the *PTS Klavier* differ in their aesthetic properties. For example, the *Hammerklavier* is thundering in ways in which the *PTS Klavier* is not. So, by Leibniz's Law, they must be distinct (D. Davies 2009: 168–70). Sonicists can offer a parallel reply: the *Hammerklavier* and the *PTS Klavier* have the same aesthetic properties. For example, the *Hammerklavier* is thundering in exactly the ways that the *PTS Klavier* is. But this reply is not available to all sonicists. For example, some sonicists (e.g. Dodd 2007: ch. 8) say that the *Hammerklavier* is thundering in exactly the ways it is only because its performances are correctly heard as performed on a piano (even if they are not in fact performed on a piano). But it might come to be that performances of the *PTS Klavier* are correctly heard, not as performed on a piano, but rather as performed on a PTS. And, in that case, the *PTS Klavier* would not be thundering in exactly the ways that the *Hammerklavier* is (D. Davies 2009: 168). (One might be tempted to draw a different conclusion, one that goes beyond instrumentalism, namely, that a musical work is individuated not just by how it sounds, or by the instrument that its composer specified that it should be performed on, but also by the instrument that its performances are correctly heard as being performed on, even if that instrument is not the instrument that its composer specified that it should be performed on.)

Meta-ontology

Suppose that the goal of a given ontology of music is to handle those intuitions of ours that are relevant. For instance, in considering whether musical works can be created, one might appeal to the commonly held belief that musical works are created and conclude that musical Platonism must be rejected in favor of a theory according to which musical works are the sorts of things that can be created (cf. Levinson 1980: 65–8, 1990a: 216–21). In this case, an ontological issue is settled solely by a direct appeal to our intuitions concerning ontological matters. That is, for the purposes of this little exercise, the only relevant intuitions are ontological intuitions concerning whether musical works can be created.

However, this basic approach faces a few problems. Even if it can be used sometimes – for instance, with respect to creatability – most people do not have enough ontological intuitions to generate a fully fleshed-out ontology of music. Furthermore, those that they do have are rarely the product of careful consideration and often are not very strongly held. At this point, although there might be several candidate theories, we simply do not have enough data to pick a winner. We can augment our list of data by bringing into consideration issues that can be plausibly considered to be relevant and about which non-metaphysicians have strongly held opinions. In other words, we can hold that the goal of an ontology of music is to handle a much broader range of intuitions concerning musical (or critical) practice, that is, what musicians, music audiences, music critics, and music theorists say and do (D. Davies 2004, 2009; Rohrbaugh 2005; Stecker

2009). For instance, consider the claim that the aesthetic or artistic properties that we attribute to the *Hammerklavier* differ from those we would attribute to the *1993 Hammerklavier*. If this claim is true, then, since sound-alike musical works can differ in their properties, sonicism must be false and contextualism true. In this case, our non-ontological intuitions can be used to adjudicate between rival ontologies of musical works.

Appealing to musical practice raises some further questions. Musical practice could have been different in many ways. How would the ontology of music have been different if musical practice had been different? And must the actual ontology of music, now, already be ready to accommodate all of these different possible practices or, at least, all possible extensions of our current actual practice?

But, even putting these large-scale questions aside, appealing to musical practice does not by itself settle the issue between sonicism and contextualism. Sonicists can deny that the differences between the *Hammerklavier* and the *1993 Hammerklavier* should be construed as requiring two works that have different properties. One way to do this would be to regard the case as an example of one work that bears different relations to different audiences – in this case, an audience from 1818, which hears the work as revolutionary, versus an audience from 1993, which hears it as old-fashioned (cf. Kivy 1987: 64–5). Similarly, although a musical Platonist would have to agree that, strictly speaking, musical works fail to be creatable, she would add that acts of composition occur in time and have a beginning. According to the musical Platonist, when we say "Musical works are created," the truth in the vicinity might be that a given work is indicated or conceived for the first time on a certain date (cf. Kivy 1983: 38–47, 1987: 66–73; Dodd 2007: ch. 5).

Each of these strategies relies on a technique known as *paraphrase*. For instance, a philosopher might believe that, strictly speaking, only sensory ideas exist. Nevertheless, she wishes to preserve certain claims such as "My piano is in the corner of the room" by capturing the sentence in the language of ideas. According to her theory, although we are wrong at a fundamental level, we still utter true sentences under her construal or paraphrase of them. Furthermore, our basic error might not require us to change our everyday speech or behavior. However, if paraphrase is permissible and available, then ontological issues might not be decidable. If the sonicist and the musical Platonist can provide friendly paraphrases of what seem to be truths that are problematic for their views, then we do not seem to have a way of adjudicating between those views and their rivals.

If we are to proceed further, we need to bring in this constraint: if our practice implies the attribution of an aesthetic or artistic property to a musical work, then the best ontology of music is one according to which the musical work in question really possesses the property in question (Levinson 1980: 84 n. 29, 1990a: 224; D. Davies 2004: 16–24). Musical Platonism loses on the creatability question under this constraint if it paraphrases claims about a work's being created as claims about the occurrence of an action of composition; sonicism loses the *1993 Hammerklavier* case if it paraphrases claims about the aesthetic or artistic difference between two works as claims about different relations that hold between a single work and different audiences. Another methodological wrinkle stems from the fact that, if one's theory seems not to fit the data supplied by musical practice, one can modify one's data set for ostensibly independently motivated reasons. For instance, if a writer supports some sort of musical empiricism, according to which all of a work's aesthetic properties are in some sense readily hearable, then that writer can simply reject the claim that the *Hammerklavier* and the *1993 Hammerklavier* could differ in their aesthetic properties, since they are sound-alikes (Dodd 2007: chs 8–9). Of course, in the absence of persuasive arguments for musical empiricism, opponents can maintain that a theory's inability to handle our apparent aesthetic judgments about this case should count as a flaw.

The possibility remains that no ontology of music can save all of our current intuitions concerning musical practice, no matter how much creative paraphrasing we employ. Or, perhaps, all of our intuitions can be saved only by an extremely cumbersome and unwieldy theory. In these circumstances it might be best to consider ontological theories that sacrifice a few of our intuitions for the sake of preserving the rest of them in a theoretically virtuous way. Our final theory and the particular claims concerning music it generates might conflict with the views that we started with in important ways, both about basic ontology and about our understanding of musical practice. This methodology is akin to reflective equilibrium in philosophical ethics. Suppose that the ethical theories we start with are in conflict with our intuitions about particular cases. We resolve the conflict by revising our theory and revising our beliefs about particular cases (to the smallest extent possible) so that we eventually arrive at a coherent and powerful ethical theory. However, at the outset, everything is up for grabs, at least in principle. Some writers identify works with things that have long been in our general ontologies. For instance, David Davies (2004) asserts that musical works, and indeed all artworks, are actions that artists perform. As such they form a species of event tokens. Others, such as Jerrold Levinson (1980, 1990a) and Guy Rohrbaugh (2003, ms.), devise new things – types that come into existence or *sui generis* non-physical objects – that are tailor-made to play the role we accord to musical works. Each of these theorists identifies musical works with new or unexpected things, because the old, familiar candidates for being a musical work cannot do the job of preserving all or even most of the things we want to say about musical works.

But not everyone sees the need for reflective equilibrium. Some take musical practice to be sacrosanct because the term "musical work," if it refers at all, must refer to something that conforms completely to what actual musical practice requires (Thomasson 2005, 2006). But, on this view, there is no guarantee that our term "musical work" will refer to anything at all, unless we start with an ontology so plenitudinous that we are guaranteed to refer to something no matter how it is characterized. Others see no need to take into account general theoretical or metaphysical claims beyond those implicit in musical practice, since they see ontology of music as solely being in the business of describing how we think about musical works (Kania 2008b). But ontology of music is not solely in the business of describing how we think about musical works; it is also in the business of describing how musical works are. Others think that preserving what is implicit in musical practice is so easy that no reflective equilibrium is required, since they see ontology of music as solely being in the business of preserving the truth of certain sentences and they think that those sentences can be made true even if there are, strictly speaking, no musical works (Cameron 2008). But, even if our musical practice is coherent and there is a way of simultaneously making true all of the sentences that correspond to it (and at this point there's no guarantee that that is possible), there is more to preserving what is implicit in musical practice than preserving the truth of some sentences: musical practice includes what musicians and audiences do, and one might think that playing and listening to musical works requires the existence of musical works and not just the truth of some sentences about them. In any case, insofar as we care about the truth of sentences about musical works, we think that those sentences are made true by the existence of musical works (Stecker 2009).

Some doubt the usefulness of the ontology of music altogether, because to be useful an ontological theory about the *Hammerklavier*, for example, would have to tell us ahead of time what would count as a performance of that musical work, and there is no way of knowing what would count as a performance of the *Hammerklavier* before hearing all possible performances of it (Ridley 2003). These anti-ontological concerns can be side-stepped, because the usefulness of the ontology of music does not depend on its telling us ahead of time what would count as a performance of what (Kania 2008a). But they can be profitably viewed as a starting point for an examination of the issue of "grounding," which in the ontology of music largely concerns the relation between claims about musical works and claims about their performances. Is the *Hammerklavier* thundering in virtue of the thundering nature of its performances, or are the performances thundering in virtue of the thundering nature of the work? In other words, are the aesthetic or artistic properties of the musical work grounded in the properties of its performances, are the aesthetic or artistic properties of its performances grounded in the properties of the musical work, or neither? This is a metaphysical question; as such, it should be distinguished from a pragmatic or epistemological question, which is also of interest: How should we go about finding out which aesthetic or artistic properties the *Hammerklavier* has? For instance, should we ascertain that the *Hammerklavier* is thundering via a close examination of the score or by an imaginative engagement with possible performances? Although there is renewed interest in grounding among metaphysicians (e.g. Schaffer 2009), philosophers of music have not begun to address the issue.

Critics and musicians frequently distinguish the properties of performances from the properties of musical works. If ontologists of music were to consider grounding, they would be able to address issues of greater importance to musical practice than that of pigeon-holing musical works in some ontological category or other. Until now, ontologists of music have been very active at the theoretical level, but they have tended to simply accept what is said by other participants in the musical community. Perhaps this is due to assumptions they might have made about the limited role of, and possibilities inherent in, the philosophy of art. However, the issue of grounding might sometimes make it possible for ontologists of music to play a part in guiding practice, which would be a very good thing for those philosophers who want to do more than record and regiment what the "real" practitioners are doing.

See also Authentic performance practice (Chapter 9), Jazz (Chapter 39), Medium (Chapter 5), Performances and recordings (Chapter 8), Rock (Chapter 38), and Song (Chapter 40).

References

Alward, P. (2004) "The Spoken Work," *Journal of Aesthetics and Art Criticism* 62: 331–7.

Cameron, R. (2008) "There are No Things that are Musical Works," *British Journal of Aesthetics* 48: 295–314.

Currie, G. (1989) *An Ontology of Art*, London: Macmillan.

Davies, D. (2004) *Art as Performance*, Oxford: Blackwell.

—— (2009) "The Primacy of Practice in the Ontology of Art," *Journal of Aesthetics and Art Criticism* 67: 159–71.

Davies, S. (2001) *Musical Works and Performances: A Philosophical Exploration*, Oxford: Clarendon.

Deutsch, H. (1991) "The Creation Problem," *Topoi* 10: 209–25.

Dodd, J. (2007) *Works of Music: An Essay in Ontology*, Oxford: Oxford University Press.

—— (2008) "Musical Works: Ontology and Meta-Ontology," *Philosophy Compass* 3: 1113–34.

Effingham, N. (ms.) "The Metaphysics of Musical Works," available at http://www.nikkeffingham.com/resources/MusicalWorks.pdf.

Evnine, S.J. (2009) "Constitution and Qua Objects in the Ontology of Music," *British Journal of Aesthetics* 49: 203–17.

Goodman, N. (1976) *Languages of Art: An Approach to a Theory of Symbols*, 2nd edn, Indianapolis: Hackett.

Kania, A. (2008a) "Piece for the End of Time: In Defence of Musical Ontology," *British Journal of Aesthetics* 48: 65–79.

—— (2008b) "The Methodology of Musical Ontology: Descriptivism and its Implications," *British Journal of Aesthetics* 48: 426–44.

Kivy, P. (1983) "Platonism in Music: A Kind of Defense," reprinted in Kivy (1993), pp. 35–58.

—— (1987) "Platonism in Music: Another Kind of Defense," reprinted in Kivy (1993), pp. 59–74.

—— (1988) "Orchestrating Platonism," reprinted in Kivy (1993), pp. 75–94.

—— (1993) *The Fine Art of Repetition: Essays in the Philosophy of Music*, Cambridge: Cambridge University Press.

Levinson, J. (1980) "What a Musical Work Is," reprinted in Levinson (1990b), pp. 63–88.

—— (1990a) "What a Musical Work Is, Again," in Levinson (1990b), pp. 215–63.

—— (1990b) *Music, Art, and Metaphysics: Essays in Philosophical Aesthetics*, Ithaca: Cornell University Press.

Ridley, A. (2003) "Against Musical Ontology," *Journal of Philosophy* 100: 203–20.

Rohrbaugh, G. (2003) "Artworks as Historical Individuals," *European Journal of Philosophy* 11: 177–205.

—— (2005) "The Ontology of Art," in B. Gaut and D. M. Lopes (eds) *The Routledge Companion to Aesthetics*, 2nd edn, London: Routledge, pp. 241–53.

—— (ms.) "Platonism, Particularism, and Puzzles of Repeatability."

Schaffer, J. (2009) "On What Grounds What," in D. J. Chalmers, D. Manley, and R. Wasserman (eds) *Metametaphysics: New Essays on the Foundations of Ontology*, Oxford: Clarendon, 347–83.

Stecker, R. (2009) "Methodological Questions about the Ontology of Music," *Journal of Aesthetics and Art Criticism* 67: 375–86.

Thomasson, A.L. (2005) "The Ontology of Art and Knowledge in Aesthetics," *Journal of Aesthetics and Art Criticism* 63: 221–9.

—— (2006) "Debates about the Ontology of Art: What are We Doing Here?" *Philosophy Compass* 1: 245–55.

Trivedi, S. (2008) "Music and Metaphysics," *Metaphilosophy* 39: 124–43.

Wollheim, R. (1980) *Art and Its Objects: With Six Supplementary Essays*, rev. edn, Cambridge: Cambridge University Press.

Wolterstorff, N. (1980) *Works and Worlds of Art*, Oxford: Clarendon.

5

MEDIUM

David Davies

On the general notion of an artistic medium

We speak of a medium in a variety of contexts where we want to describe something that serves as a means, or instrument, whereby some content is transmitted from a source to a receiver. A spiritual medium purports to mediate between loved ones and the departed, the news media transmit tidings of the latest scandals and disasters, and air and water are media that transmit sounds to our ears. In the arts, one might think, a medium will be the means whereby an *artistic* content is communicated by an artist to receivers. Indeed, one way in which we differentiate art forms from one another is by reference to their media. For example, painting differs from other visual arts in articulating its artistic content through the manipulation of pigment on a surface, and oil painting differs from watercolor in the kind of pigment employed by the artist.

This intuitive view conceals a couple of assumptions. First, it is assumed that there is a way to cash out talk about an artwork's "artistic content." But it does not seem difficult to make good on this commitment. The content of a painting, for example, is just what it represents, or expresses, or manifests in its formal structure. And even though some (e.g. Bell 1914) have questioned whether the representational or even the expressive properties of a painting are properly viewed as part of its content *as an artwork*, this does not affect our ability to identify the medium of a painting in the foregoing sense, since the same "stuff" will be used whether or not we take representational or expressive properties to be part of the artistic content.

But this brings us to a second assumption. The medium of a painting, or of an artwork more generally, was identified with the "stuff" that the artist manipulates in order to produce a manifold that communicates a particular content. There is good reason, however, to resist such a simple identification of media in art with the kinds of stuff manipulated by artists, given our general instrumental conception of a medium. For if we make such an identification, we require a further mediating force to explain how manipulations of this stuff achieve the end of articulating an artistic content. For example, applying pigment to a canvas produces a pigment-covered canvas, yet we take the painter to have represented a certain subject, or expressed certain qualities, in the painting. The need for something that mediates between what the artist does in the purely manipulative sense and what the artist does in the artistic sense is even clearer if we consider how almost identically pigmented canvases can articulate very different artistic contents. This is illustrated by Arthur Danto (1981: 1–2) in a thought experiment involving perceptually identical red rectangles that are very different artworks, and by Kendall Walton (1970) in his thought experiment concerning a "guernica" – an artwork of a novel kind – that differs dramatically as an artwork from a perceptually identical painting.

All this has led philosophers to distinguish between two notions of medium applicable to works of art. First, our interest in a work's medium is indeed sometimes an interest in the kind of stuff employed in the making of the thing that conveys an artistic content – term this thing the "artistic vehicle" and the stuff the "vehicular medium." While this is sometimes called a work's "physical medium" – oil paint and canvas, in the case of a painting, for example – we need a term that can apply even when, as in the case of a musical work such as Sibelius's Second Symphony or a literary work such as *War and Peace*, it is not obvious that it makes sense to think of its vehicle as being something physical.

Second, philosophers have used the term "*artistic* medium" to characterize what bridges the gap between the two ways of describing what the artist does – manipulate a vehicular medium, on the one hand, and articulate an artistic content, on the other (see, for example, Margolis 1980; Beardsley 1982; Levinson 1984: §1; D. Davies 2004: ch. 3). There are two closely related ways of thinking about the artistic medium. First, it can be thought of as a way of characterizing the outcome of the artist's manipulations of the vehicular medium in terms that refer to his or her intentional activity in performing those manipulations. What are, considered in terms of the vehicular medium, mere marks on the canvas are, considered in terms of the artistic medium, "brushstrokes," "impasto," and "firm design," for example. In dance, the mere bodily movements of the dancers' bodies, as the elements making up a dance work's vehicular medium, are, in the language of the artistic medium, "movings" and "posings." This establishes the required bridge between the artist's manipulation of the vehicular medium and the artistic contents ascribable to the artwork. It is, for example, in terms of the brushstrokes, impasto, and firm design of a particular painting that we identify and explain its expressive or representational qualities. A second, closely related, way of thinking about a work's artistic medium is in terms of shared understandings upon which the artist draws as to the specific implications of particular manipulations of the vehicular medium for a work's artistic content. Timothy Binkley (1977), for example, describes an artistic medium as a set of conventions whereby performing certain manipulations on a kind of physical stuff counts as articulating a particular artistic content.

Medium in music

Philosophical attention to the notion of medium in art has concentrated on such questions as the limitations of different vehicular media for the articulation of particular kinds of artistic content (e.g. Lessing 1957), or the problems that arise when different vehicular or artistic media are combined in a single artistic enterprise, as is the case with theatre, sound cinema, and opera (e.g. Arnheim 1964; Levinson 1984). Surprisingly, perhaps, given the instrumental nature of a medium, another contested question is whether artists have an obligation to "respect" the vehicular medium they use in their art. The doctrine of "medium purity" requires that the artist dedicate herself to realizing the distinctive aesthetic potential of the medium she employs (e.g. Greenberg 1961). Medium in *music*, however, has received little explicit philosophical attention. For example, in a discussion of medium purity as it relates to the different arts, Morris Weitz (1950: ch. 7) does not dedicate a separate section to music, recognizing only, in passing, that purist sensibilities have been offended by "program music," which uses musical means for representational purposes. In spite of this, however, views about the nature of the medium in musical art are implicit in some of the central debates in recent philosophy of music, as we shall see. In line with the general considerations about medium in art outlined in the previous section, I shall distinguish between questions that pertain to the vehicular medium of musical works and questions that pertain to their artistic medium.

Vehicular medium in music

If painters work with pigment in creating arrangements of colored marks on a surface, and sculptors work with bronze or marble, and writers work with words, what is the vehicular medium of music? The simplest answer is to say that musical artists work with sound (e.g. Kivy 1995: 229–30). But talk of "musical artists" conceals a nest of difficulties. For, unlike painting and sculpture, but like literature and film, music is usually taken to be a "multiple art" where works (e.g. a film) admit many different instances (e.g. screenings of a film) in which the properties that bear on their appreciation are realized for receivers. (On multiple artworks, see S. Davies 2003.) Unlike literature and film, however, instances of musical works are usually taken to be *performances*. Such performances, which involve interpretation by performers of what the composer has prescribed, may make manifest different appreciable properties of the work. Sibelius's Second Symphony, for example, has been performed by many different orchestras under many different conductors, and these performances can differ quite strikingly while remaining genuine instances of the work. Works for performance of this kind require a more nuanced formulation of the view that the vehicular medium of musical works is sound. For we have taken the vehicular medium to be something that an artist manipulates in order to articulate an artistic content. But the composer does not, in a direct sense, manipulate *sounds*. Rather, she produces prescriptions that she intends others to follow in producing sounds. The artistic content of a musical work for performance is articulated through performances that are guided by these prescriptions.

In the case of musical works for performance, then, the vehicle is the range of particular sound sequences that comply with what is prescribed, or perhaps the type of sound sequence of which those particular sound sequences are tokens. In the case of a performance of a musical work, or a free improvisation, the vehicle is the sound sequence realized on a particular occasion of performance. Is the artistic vehicle of a musical work always a type of sound sequence, or a range of sound sequences, whose realization in performance articulates the work's artistic content? In at least some cases, this is clearly not so. In classical "electronic" music, for example, the vehicle is a sound sequence encoded electronically in some way and made available to receivers through playback. According to Theodore Gracyk (1996), this also applies to rock music. The vehicle is the recording, the electronically encoded result of technological operations that is then played back rather than performed. Andrew Kania (2006) defends a similar view, holding that rock works are "tracks." Stephen Davies (2001: ch. 1), on the other hand, argues that in most cases rock works are works for "studio performance," where the work of technicians and sound engineers necessarily complements the performance of the musicians.

If the vehicular medium of musical works is sound, realized either in single or multiple performances or in the playback of recordings, are there any limitations on the kinds of sounds that can serve as the vehicle for a musical work? Given our general conception of medium in art, the only constraint is that the sounds in question be the vehicle whereby a composer or musician aims to communicate an artistic content of some kind to receivers. This presumably excludes sounds that are inaudible to the human ear. If an artist were to prescribe, for our delectation, the generation of a sequence of sounds audible only to bats, for example, this is best viewed not as a musical work but as a work of conceptual art. There is no principled reason to place further limits on the sounds that can serve as the vehicle for a musical work, however, even if the sounds in question are to be produced by the use of implements not normally thought of as musical instruments. It may indeed have been assumed in pre-modernist musical circles that only certain kinds of sounds were an appropriate vehicle for music. But figures such as Russolo, whose theory and practice advocated seeking out "noise" to use as a musical medium, not to mention rock music in general, give one reason to think otherwise (see Gracyk 1996: 114–18).

Artistic medium in music

What, then, makes a sequence of sounds the vehicle for a musical work, if not intrinsic features of those sounds? The answer, as we have seen, is that the sounds must be used to convey an artistic content. And this, as we have also seen, requires that they are to be apprehended in terms of an artistic medium which both represents those sounds as the product of an agent who is using them to articulate an artistic content and determines what the artistic content is, given the sounds. As mentioned earlier, one way of thinking about an artistic medium is in terms of a distinctive vocabulary by which we describe the artistic vehicle as embodying the intentional activity of its creator. To get a sense of the kinds of terms that enter into this vocabulary in the musical case, it will be helpful to analyze a passage that makes use of some of these terms in relation to the prescribed sound sequence of a particular musical work.

Timothy Day (1991) comments on Sibelius's Second Symphony as follows:

> From his modest orchestral forces, Sibelius is able to conjure up astonishingly varied sonorities, eloquent and powerful in the Finale where he exploits the full range of the brass instruments, or harsh and forlorn, as in the slow movement, with thin textures and the dark colour of the lower registers of the orchestra. Sibelius is rarely serene: the pastoral quality of the opening *Allegretto* is tinged with melancholy and there is a solemnity in the triumph of the work's conclusion.
>
> The first movement is a sonata-form structure. Its themes give the impression of evolving from each other rather than presenting sharp contrasts, and indeed, in the recapitulation, material from the first and second groups of the exposition is contained without strain or distortion. This coherence adds great strength and inevitability to the movement's predominantly sunny and relaxed mood. The second movement is a more rhapsodic structure with a succession of beautiful themes. It begins, slightly menacingly, with a single melodic line played pizzicato by cellos and double basses, joined later by two bassoons in octaves intoning a modal lament, marked *lugubre*. A series of impassioned climaxes ensue and the movement ends in a solemn mood.
>
> The third movement is a scurrying *Scherzo* which erupts in fiery outbursts. Its lyrical trio, *lento e suave*, in which an oboe sings remote, plainsong-like phrases, is reintroduced before the movement surges into the Finale. The slower sections of the last movement recapture the pastoral quality of the first, but the dominant mood of the Finale is heroic, and its big tune undeniably stirring.

Day is describing, here, not a particular performance of Sibelius's work but qualities to be found in any performance that does justice to what the work prescribes. The first thing to note is that the language he uses to characterize the sounds of such performances represents them as organized to serve some purpose. Particular sounds are to be comprehended in terms of their place in a larger structure whereby they contribute to the artistic content of the work, and in terms of the ways in which, as elements in this structure, they develop out of and refer to one another. He talks here of "sonata-form structure," "rhapsodic structure," "coherence," themes "evolving" out of one another, "exposition," and "recapitulation." Sounds that are properly classified as music are to be heard as organized under structural categories of these sorts. But this can encompass the deliberate avoidance of such structural features as "development" – this itself becomes a feature of the ordering of elements in a sound sequence, as perhaps with a rock track such as the Velvet Underground's "Sister Ray."

A second significant feature in Day's commentary is his concern not just with the structure of sounds in a "thin" sense – the pitches of the notes, their duration, harmonies, etc. – but also with the instrumentation prescribed for their execution – brass, cello, and bassoon, for example – and the consequent "color" of the sounds produced, their timbral properties. Described in one way – as, for example, the sound of a given sequence of notes played on a bassoon – this might be part of the vehicular medium of the work. But Day relates these timbral qualities to the ordering activity of the composer in his talk of the "varied sonorities" that Sibelius conjures up, and of Sibelius's "exploiting" the full range of the brass instruments and the "dark colour of the lower registers of the orchestra." His commentary suggests that the timbral properties of the sound sequence are crucial to the artistic content of the work.

This impression is reinforced by the third, and most prominent, kind of observation in Day's commentary. Here he relates the structural and timbral properties of the sound sequence prescribed by Sibelius to the broadly *expressive* content of the musical work. He speaks of passages in the work as "eloquent," "powerful," "harsh," "forlorn," "melancholy," "sunny," and "menacing," for example. He also anchors these expressive properties in prescriptions by the composer, referring to the markings of *lugubre* and *lento e suave* in the score.

The nature of the vehicular medium in music: sonicism and instrumentalism

An artist who seeks to articulate a particular artistic content in a work performs, or prescribes that others perform, certain manipulations of the vehicular medium, thereby generating an artistic vehicle with certain manifest properties. The intended receiver is someone who can apprehend the vehicle in terms of the artistic medium employed by the artist, and thus understand its manifest features in terms of the intentional activity of the artist. Such a receiver will be in a position to grasp the artistic content articulated in the work. In accomplishing this feat, the receiver must first identify the artistic vehicle itself – for example, she must distinguish between the painted canvas and the frame that surrounds it. She must then understand manifest properties of the artistic vehicle in terms of the relevant artistic medium.

In the musical case, the artistic vehicle is a sequence of sounds generated on a given occasion either in a live performance or in a studio. Or, in the case of works for performance, it is a type of sound sequence, or those particular sequences of sounds that occur or can occur in performances that realize in different ways the prescriptions of the work. This we may take in the present context to be uncontroversial. Where we find disagreement is over which features of a performed or played-back sequence of sounds are to be apprehended in terms of the artistic medium in determining a work's artistic content. This is best viewed as a disagreement over which aspects of such a sound-sequence make up the artistic vehicle of the work. It thereby differs from disagreement over whether the representational properties of program music bear upon its appreciation as music. In the latter case, the issue concerns how different aspects of the artistic vehicle are "taken up" into the work by being apprehended in terms of the artistic medium. For example, given that I can hear the song of a nightingale in the timbral qualities of the sound-sequence produced in a performance of a given work, and given that these qualities are partly constitutive of the work's artistic vehicle, is the representation of a nightingale's song part of the work's artistic content? In the former case, the issue is to determine just what the artistic vehicle is. For example, are the timbral qualities of the sound-sequence produced in a performance indeed partly constitutive of the work's artistic vehicle?

Debates about the nature of the artistic vehicle in music have not usually been couched in such terms. Rather, philosophers have debated the nature of the musical work for performance, insofar as it prescribes certain things for its instances. This leads to a focus on the *kinds* of things that a work prescribes. But, as may be clear, to focus on this is just to focus on the features of a work's performances that play a role in articulating its artistic content. And these features, as we have seen, are the ones that are constitutive of the artistic vehicle, the ones that must be apprehended in terms of an artistic medium if the artistic content of the work is to be determined.

There are three ways in which philosophers have delimited those properties of a performance event or played-back recording that are constitutive of the artistic vehicle through which the artistic content of the work performed or the recording is articulated. First, there are two variants on the general strategy that Julian Dodd (2007) terms "sonicism." The sonicist maintains that the artistic vehicle is a certain sequence of sounds at least partly identifiable, in the case of performances of works, by reference to the score from which the performers are playing. The score prescribes (at least) that notes of specified pitches and durations be produced, either simultaneously or consecutively, in a given order, according to a given rhythm and with a particular kind of accentuation. *Pure* sonicists hold that only these kinds of features are constitutive of the artistic vehicle (e.g. Kivy 1983). For the pure sonicist, it is irrelevant whether the pure sonic sequence specified by the composer is performed on, or sounds as if it were performed on, any particular instruments. Others, however, maintain that the *timbre* of the notes produced, which will vary according to the instrumentation used in generating those notes, is an essential part of what the composer prescribes for performances of the work (Dodd 2007: 212–17). The *timbral* sonicist includes such timbral properties among those which are constitutive of the artistic vehicle. As we saw in Day's remarks about Sibelius's Second Symphony, Day treats timbral qualities of the sound sequence produced by the orchestra as elements in the artistic vehicle through which expressive qualities of the work are realized in performance. He includes timbral qualities, and not just pure sonic qualities, in the vehicular medium of such musical works.

The sound sequence generated in a given performance event or playback of a recording has other properties, however. It not only sounds the way a piano would sound, for example, but was also, let us suppose, produced by someone playing a piano. This is a relational property of the sound sequence. Is it also a part of the artistic vehicle of which we must take account in apprehending the sound sequence under an artistic medium? *Instrumentalists* maintain that at least some of the artistic content of a musical work depends not merely upon timbral qualities but also upon the instruments used in producing those qualities. Jerrold Levinson, for example, argues that the specification of "performance means" has been integral to the performed work of classical music since the mid-eighteenth century. The aesthetic attributes of such works "always depend . . . in part on the performing forces understood to belong to them" (1990: 77). He cites, as a particularly dramatic example, Beethoven's *Hammerklavier Sonata* whose "sublime, craggy, and barn-storming" qualities "depend in part on the strain that its sound structure imposes on the sonic capabilities of the piano" (1990: 76–7). Such qualities would be lacking in a performance on a perfect timbral synthesizer that duplicates the timbral sonic properties of the piece, Levinson claims.

If Levinson is right, then, if such expressive properties are rightly included in the artistic content of performances, or of performed works as realized in those performances, we must include in the artistic vehicle these relational properties of the sound sequences generated in performances. The same will apply for musical works that are recordings. In both cases, it is the producing of a given sequence of sounds, in the fullness of their timbral properties, on given instrumentation or by specific means, that is the artistic vehicle that must be apprehended in terms of the appropriate artistic medium if we are to determine the work's artistic content. One response open to the anti-instrumentalist is to argue that the artistic content of a work as realized in a musical performance or recording depends upon *our hearing* the sound sequence *as if* played on particular instruments or generated by specified means, but not upon its actually *being* played on those instruments or produced by those means (Dodd 2007: 230ff). Whether this response succeeds is open to debate, however (D. Davies 2009).

Contextualism and the artistic medium in music

Another relational property of the sequence of sounds prescribed or produced on a given occasion, whether in performance or in the playback of a recording, is the *musico-historical context* in which the prescription or production of that sequence is situated. *Contextualists* hold that at least some aspects of the artistic content of a musical work, performance, or recording depend not merely upon the sound sequence generated and the kinds of instruments used to generate that sound-sequence. They also depend upon contextual features such as the body of existing artworks upon which an artist draws, the intellectual resources available in the culture in which she works, and her own developing oeuvre taken as manifesting more general artistic projects. It is in virtue of these contextual variables that the artistic product serves as the articulation of certain specific artistic contents.

If this is correct, how does it bear on our account of the nature of the medium in musical art? Clearly, the context in which a composer composes or a musician performs cannot be part of the vehicular medium of a work, performance, or recording. For the vehicular medium is what the artist manipulates in order to articulate an artistic content, and (save perhaps in the case of certain conceptual pieces) artists do not manipulate the art-historical contexts in which they find themselves. Rather, the artist produces the artistic vehicle by performing various manipulations *within* a given art-historical context, and, so the contextualist maintains, the context plays a part in determining the artistic content thereby articulated. It thus constitutes part of the *artistic* medium of the work. If the contextualist is right, we need to take account of various aspects of the art-historical context in which an artist is working if we are to characterize correctly the artistic vehicle in terms of "what has been done" artistically.

The most common kind of argument for contextualism asks us to consider situations where artistic products indistinguishable in terms of their manifest properties are generated in sharply different art-historical contexts. Since we generally lack such situations in real life, contextualists offer thought experiments in which we are asked to imagine a situation in which there are such doppelgängers. Levinson (1990) offers five such thought experiments where we have doppelgängers for actual musical works, and argues that, in each case, there are differences in aesthetic or artistic properties bearing on the appreciation of the works that derive from differences in the musico-historical context of composition. To cite one example, Levinson ask us to imagine a work by Beethoven sonically and instrumentally identical to Brahms's Second Piano Sonata. In listening to Brahms's piece, we rightly note the ways in which it reflects the influence of Liszt, but this would be anachronistic if applied to the hypothetical piece by Beethoven. Similarly, we would rightly ascribe a visionary quality to the Beethoven piece but not to the piece by Brahms.

Opponents of contextualism argue that artistic qualities such as originality or influence pertain not to the proper evaluation of musical artworks as aesthetic objects, but to our assessment of their place in art-history (e.g. Dodd 2007: ch. 9). If so, these characteristics are not part of a work's artistic content. Contextualists may respond that to properly evaluate something as an artwork is in part to evaluate its place in art history and not merely to assess it as an aesthetic object. A further anti-contextualist proposal (Wolterstorff 1991) is that contextually based properties of musical works are *relativized* properties of the form: being-x-as-produced-in-art-historical-context-y. A work can quite consistently possess both this property and the property not-being-x-as-produced-in-art-historical-context-z. In that case, nothing privileges one musico-historical context over others in determining the artistic content of a musical work, and thus features of the musico-historical context in which the work or performance originated are not partly constitutive of the artistic medium. Contextualists may respond, however, that this misrepresents the way we talk about works of musical art. A work is taken to be Liszt-influenced *simpliciter*. Resolving this kind of dispute is likely to require more general inquiry into the metaphysics and epistemology of art, and, indeed, into the proper methodology for investigating such matters.

See also Aesthetic properties (Chapter 14), Authentic performance practice (Chapter 9), Ontology (Chapter 4), and Performances and recordings (Chapter 8).

References

Arnheim, R. (1964 [1938]) "A New Laocoön: Artistic Composites and the Talking Film," in *Film as Art*, Berkeley: University of California Press, pp. 199–230.

Beardsley, M. (1982) "What is Going on in a Dance?" *Dance Research Journal* 15: 31–7.

Bell, C. (1914) *Art*, London: Chatto and Windus.

Binkley, T. (1977) "Piece: Contra Aesthetics," *Journal of Aesthetics and Art Criticism* 35: 265–77.

Danto, A. (1981) *The Transfiguration of the Commonplace*, Cambridge, MA: Harvard University Press.

Davies, D. (2004) *Art as Performance*, Oxford: Blackwell.

—— (2009) "The Primacy of Practice in the Ontology of Art," *Journal of Aesthetics and Art Criticism* 67: 159–71.

Davies, S. (2001) *Musical Works and Performances*, Oxford: Oxford University Press.

—— (2003) "Ontology of Art," in J. Levinson (ed.) *Oxford Handbook of Aesthetics*, Oxford: Oxford University Press, pp. 155–80.

Day, T. (1991) "Jean Sibelius: The Symphonies," notes accompanying a recording of Sibelius's symphonies by the Vienna Philharmonic Orchestra conducted by L. Maazel, London Records 430 778–2.

Dodd, J. (2007) *Works of Music*, Oxford: Oxford University Press.

Gracyk, T. (1996) *Rhythm and Noise: An Aesthetics of Rock*, Durham: Duke University Press.

Greenberg, C. (1961) "On Modernist Painting," *Arts Yearbook* 4: 101–8.

Kania, A. (2006) "Making Tracks: The Ontology of Rock Music," *Journal of Aesthetics and Art Criticism* 64: 402–14.

Kivy, P. (1983) "Platonism in Music: A Kind of Defense," *Grazer Philosophische Studien* 19: 109–29.

—— (1995) *Authenticities*, Ithaca: Cornell University Press.

Lessing, G.E. (1957 [1766]) *Laocoön: An Essay on the Limits of Painting and Poetry*, trans. E. Frothingham, New York: Noonday Press.

Levinson, J. (1984) "Hybrid Artforms," *Journal of Aesthetic Education* 18: 5–13.

—— (1990) "What a Musical Work Is," in *Music, Art, and Metaphysics*, Ithaca: Cornell University Press, pp. 63–88.

Margolis, J. (1980) *Art and Philosophy*, Atlantic Heights: Humanities Press.

Walton, K. (1970) "Categories of Art," *Philosophical Review* 79: 334–67.

Weitz, M. (1950) *Philosophy of the Arts*, Cambridge, MA: Harvard University Press.

Wolterstorff, N. (1991) "Review of Gregory Currie, *An Ontology of Art*," *Journal of Aesthetics and Art Criticism* 49: 79–81.

6

IMPROVISATION

Lee B. Brown

The historical data

While it might be thought that musical improvisation is the specialty of American jazz, it has long been a common – indeed, perhaps basic – feature of music throughout the world. Arab, Indian, Iranian, and African musicians have all long been familiar with it. From the Middle Ages through the Renaissance in European music, it was standard practice to improvise a line in counterpoint over a *cantus firmus*. In the classical era, keyboardists often competed with each other in improvisational contests – Mozart, for instance, against Clementi, or Beethoven against rivals such as Hummel. Performances extempore are still standards features of organ recitals.

Improvisation in concert music declined in the nineteenth and twentieth centuries. However, by the late twentieth century, composers and performers began to revive improvisational practice. It has attracted the attention of musicians such as Lucas Foss, Pierre Boulez, and Terry Riley, for example, and groups such as the multi-faceted New York organization "Bang on a Can." Currently, soloists in classical concerti exhibit a trend toward replacing stock cadenzas with novel impromptu efforts of their own.

For many listeners, the paradigm example of improvisation is jazz. In mainstream jazz, a "head" – usually based on a 32-bar jazz "standard," such as "Body and Soul," or 12-bar blues pattern – is played over once, or perhaps twice, framing improvised solos. The improvised melodies are played on the harmonic and rhythmic foundation provided by the head. Alternative chords are often allowed, depending on style. After a sequence of solos, the performance will normally end with a reprise of the head. There are many variations to the basic pattern. Several musicians may trade off with each other. Or, as in classic New Orleans jazz, many musicians can improvise collectively. The basic pattern was challenged by the rise of so-called "modal" jazz in which, instead of improvising on melodies that fit a set of chords, soloists would create wide-ranging variations within a single scale.

Two ideologies of improvisation

Neither of two extreme points of view about improvisation can be sustained. One of these might be termed the *romantic perspective*, according to which improvisation is utterly rule-free music-making – music created "without previous preparation," as one work on piano instruction puts it (Palmer 1992: 109). Too often, though, the *ex nihilo* view is based on an equation of the improvised with the primitive or unschooled. Such a view, as applied to jazz, was popular in the mid-twentieth century among certain French journalists – for example, Robert Goffin, who often extolled the most untrained, most "frenzied," versions of jazz as the most authentic (Goffin 1944: 124).

This sentimental perspective reflects naïveté about the basic resources that improvisational performances inevitably presume. Experts on Iranian instrumental music, for instance, explain that improvisers in that tradition must learn several hundred elements that make up the repertoires of what is called the *radif* (Nettl 1992). Analogous considerations apply to jazz improvisation, as demonstrated by one massive study of the topic (Berliner 1994). Jazz musicians also internalize a cache of musical forms – for example, meters, bar lengths, chord progressions, and even phrase patterns – as frameworks and as material for improvised solos. Whatever Coleman Hawkins was creating in his famous 1939 recording of "Body and Soul," it was not the harmonic motion instanced by that song. He simply accepted it as a pattern for his solo. Even Keith Jarrett's famously "free" piano improvisations were typically built upon a vamp of familiar chords.

The freedom of the improviser is also limited by what she must *not* do. In Ghanaian drum music, for instance, only certain instruments are allowed to improvise and they can do so only within prescribed limits (Chernoff 1982). Unwitting musicians who beat out novel pulses without regard to customary practice could easily confuse the dancers and other musicians. In jazz, too, the most daring soloist realizes that there are any number of things she is not supposed to do. Even in a "free jazz" context, a keyboardist is not normally allowed to interpolate Chopin's Ballade in G minor or to beat the piano with a baseball bat. Further, there are contextual stylistic constraints. It might seem that while playing with Charlie Mingus, Eric Dolphy had as much freedom as could be imagined. In fact, Mingus encouraged those qualities in Dolphy's playing that fit the conception of the music he wanted to realize.

Part of the explanation for the mystificationist perspective on improvisation is that most of us nowadays are mere auditors of the activity rather than participants. A partial antidote is the useful analogy some have suggested between musical improvisation and linguistic activity, in which we all participate. For instance, the highly interactive playing of jazz musicians has been framed as a musical *conversation* (Hagberg 1998: 480–1; Kraut 2007: 57–65, 177–82).

Equally extreme, of course, is the view that, once the materials that go into the process are understood, improvisation can, in effect, be explained away. According to this perspective, what we call "improvising" – unless it be mere noodling – always follows a preconceived plan. However, even if a performance were to consist of a dreary pastiche of learned material, there is no reason not to regard it as genuinely improvisational – unless the sequencing itself had been worked out in advance.

Improvisation and artistic quality

Judgments about improvisation quality have been made from both an extra- and an intramural point of view. Winthrop Sargeant, whose study of the musical elements of jazz betrays a peculiar love–hate relationship with its subject, lodges the complaint that in American jazz in general, "a sturdy repetition" of the music's basic harmonic elements always underlies "the apparent freedom of improvised" jazz (Sargeant 1976: 247). Elaborating the thought, he gives jazz a generally lower place in a scale of musical values, when compared with that of opera and concert music (Sargeant 1976: 253–78). Sargeant's provocative and detailed discussion of the matter merits more attention than we can give here. But he could be faulted for his tacit assumption that forms of music that privilege harmonic variety, at the expense of other values, are superior.

Nevertheless, even when viewed from a properly intramural perspective, issues of improvisational excellence are still complex. Generally, good improvisers will exhibit technical facility and display a resourceful and imaginative reach. But beyond these platitudes it is hard to generalize. Gambits appropriate to one musical genre or style would be inept or meaningless in another. However, the phenomenology of the knowledgeable listener's experience does suggest one additional but fairly constant norm of artistic quality in improvised music.

With any kind of unfamiliar music, one can be interested in how it will go. Where a work is familiar, a listener can take an interest in the interpretive choices of the performer. However, with improvised music a knowledgeable listener's focus of interest is complex from the outset. One will be interested in how the musical line itself unfolds and whether it hangs together. At the same time one will be interested in aspects of the *activity itself* (Alperson 1984: 23; Brown 2000: 121). And this is where a peculiarly salient norm surfaces. Even when a performance is going well, a knowledgeable listener will be alert to the musician's willingness to take *risks*, at the peril of the quality of the musical line. If a performer's choices get her bogged down, or if she runs out of ideas, one worries about how she will deal with the problem. If she pulls the fat out of the fire, we will applaud. This is not only true of jazz. In Iranian instrumental music, again, experts tell us that the unpredicted phrases are most prized (Nettl 1992: 191–2).

However, even here, we find a spectrum of degrees such that knowledgeable judgments will be highly contextualized. Given the style of music he played, we do not mind that Louis Armstrong worked out aspects of his performances in advance. By contrast, listeners have different expectations for music played by Charlie Parker. As alternative takes of his recording of "Embraceable You" for Dial records show, Parker would go in strikingly different directions with a given song, from one performance to an immediately successive one. Further, even more local circumstances make a difference. For instance, a solo in an Ellington concert would be expected to follow a prescribed melody more closely than a jazz jam using the same song – "Take the A Train," for instance.

What is improvisation?

Improvisation and intentionality

Consider the worry of the jazz journalist who complained about hearing pianist Ray Bryant play "After Hours" in what sounded like a note-for-note copy of his famous recording of it on Verve Records (Gioia 1992: 52–3). In a commentary on the example, Andy Hamilton is perplexed to explain a relevant difference between the two, given that the subsequent performance was, like the original, "fine blues piano" (Hamilton 2000: 177–8). In fact, Hamilton has stumbled onto a perfect illustration of the fact that we tacitly appeal to a musician's *intentions* in order to mark an improvisation as such. Hamilton goes on to grant that there is an "improvised feel" in improvised music. But the observation fails to do any work. (What if Bryant's original performance had not, in spite of its "improvisational feel," actually been improvised – that it had been written out, for instance, or was a copy of a previous improvisation?) We may not be able to say with certainty what Bryant was doing on either occasion – but whatever it was depends partly upon his intentions at the time.

Improvisation and composition

It is striking that a principled analysis of the concept of the improvisational has been so elusive. Some have approached the concept by relating it to another supposedly less daunting one – composition, for instance. Here, two opposite strategies open up. One is to illuminate improvisation by *contrasting* it with composition. The other is to try to demonstrate *affinities* between improvisation and composition.

Improvisation versus composition

Borrowing words from the jazz pianist Bill Evans, Ted Gioia states that improvisational jazz differs from many other artistic practices, including musical composition, by its dependence upon a "retrospective" rather than a "blueprint," or "prospective," model. In the prospective model, artists make decisions about what is to come next in light of an overall conception. With the retrospective model, "the artist can start his work with an almost random maneuver – a brush stroke on canvas, an opening line, a musical motif – and then adapt his later moves to this gambit." The jazz improviser may proceed from his opening move in any number of directions (Gioia 1992: 60). However, there is no reason a composer, too, might not begin with a random maneuver and adapt later moves to the initial one. Furthermore, there is no reason why an improvising musician needs to play in the absence of an overall conception of what she is doing.

A novel way of contrasting improvisation and composition was articulated by the composer Ferruccio Busoni. Taking a stand against the common modern platitude voiced by Arnold Schoenberg and others that the performer of a composed work is only the servant of it, Busoni claimed that improvisation is historically, and perhaps logically, more *fundamental* than composition. Compositional notation, he states, "is to improvisation as the portrait is to the living model." It is only "an ingenious expedient for catching an inspiration, with the purpose of exploiting it later." An interpreter of a notated work thus has the obligation to do his best to "restore" what "the composer's inspiration necessarily loses through notation" (Busoni 1962: 84).

Of course, it is difficult to sustain the thesis. First, Busoni appears to assume mistakenly that all musical works for performance are tied to scores. Second, as Stephen Davies has explained, works for performance in general have some degree of *thinness* – that is, some degree to which the work's instructions, whether through a score or otherwise, leave some performance decisions to be determined by the performer (Davies 2001: 3, 20). To add that these decisions should be guided by some more fundamental model lying, so to say, behind the scored work is hardly helpful. (What would the criterion possibly be of a successful restoration?) Third, even if the concept of a musical work has only developed in relatively recent music history, it does not follow that fully fledged musical works are awkward attempts at catching something more original.

Improvisation as composition

An opposed approach is to stress affinities between improvisation and composition. Gunther Schuller, in one of his exhaustive historical studies of jazz, recommends that we should see a jazz soloist's recorded performance as a "work in progress" (Schuller 1968: x). If the similarity of Charlie Parker's recorded solos to compositions seems less than obvious, consider that when he recorded his music, the final product issued to the public would typically be picked as the best of several recording "takes." (And Parker's case is not unique.) So, there may be some correspondence between this practice and the kind of trial-and-error methods of composers.

An example not limited to the territory of recorded music comes from the life of J. S. Bach. While at Potsdam, it is said, Bach improvised a three-part ricercare for Frederick the Great, and wrote the music down only later when he returned to Leipzig. According to Peter Kivy, "the composing was already done" when Bach improvised the piece (Kivy 1983: 124–5). Can we generalize from this kind of case?

In what might have been the first extended philosophical treatment of improvisation in English, Philip Alperson attempts to make the connection between improvisation and composition by means of a rather complex argument. He first establishes a reciprocal relationship between composition and work-performance (Alperson 1984: 19–20). In narrower senses of these concepts, it is customary to distinguish the two. However, in a broad sense, Alperson urges, composing always involves performance – for example, running over music in one's mind if not actually playing it aloud. In a broad sense, too, the converse holds, given that, as already noted, there is always some degree to which the instructions for a work leave some decisions to the performer.

Now, when Alperson turns to improvisation, he says that we have an activity in which the improviser "practices simultaneously the interdependent functions of composition and performance in both the broad and narrow senses of the term" (Alperson 1984: 20). By these moves, the gap between improvisation and composition is gradually closed so as to yield the wanted analysis: improvisation is the composition of a musical work as it is being performed (Alperson 1984: 20).

Alperson was challenged on the grounds that he makes his case only by using the concepts of both *composition* and *performance* too loosely (Spade 1991). When arguing for the necessity of (improvisational) performance to composition, he sticks pretty closely to our standard concept of composition. However, when he turns to the converse point, Alperson is using "composition" in a much looser sense, where it now means something like "determining the sonic properties of a performance." Analogously, part of the time Alperson uses "performance" in a standard sense – roughly, the tokening of a pre-existing work-type. However, when arguing that composition requires performance, he shifts to a loose sense of "performance," where the mere generation of some musical sounds qualifies. The grain of truth in Alperson's view might simply be that both improvisation and composition are creative activities.

If we compare improvisation and composition as *practices*, we can discern general reasons why the one cannot be assimilated to the other (Brown 2000: 114). Let us profile them.

The French existentialists were fascinated by the idea of *forced choice*, according to which every moment in life is latent with an anxiety-charged choice among alternatives. This may be an exaggerated picture of human life in general, but the thought might have some application to improvisation. By contrast with the improviser, the composer can take time out in her project – indeed, set it aside for years. The improviser must plunge ahead and do something. Stretches of silence can be musically functional in all music, whether composed or not. However, a pause in the process of composing a work does not become a potentially unfortunate feature of the work. With improvisation, time-outs resulting from fatigue or a lack of inspiration carry costs.

Indeed Alperson, whose overall theory seems to neglect it, notes such a difference between improvisation and composition (Alperson 1984: 23). At any point, the composer can alter what has so far been laid down. Not only can compositional projects be revised up to the point of publication but they can also perhaps be revised beyond that point, as examples by Stravinsky and others show. A subsequent effort by an improviser might be superior to a previous one, but it cannot count as a revision of an earlier one.

Finally, the improviser's choices ramify, in the sense that she must produce on-the-spot responses to something already laid down. An extended improvisation is a continuous feedback loop, such that later phrases are responses to previous ones.

Now, none of the foregoing rules out that Bach, on the occasion cited earlier, was composing *as* he improvised. However, to generalize from that case to composition as a general practice is implausible. It is part of the *practice* of composing that composers do avail themselves of the conventions that allow the sorts of revisions and time-outs that are not allowed in genuine improvisation. (Imagine the riskiness of composition were it otherwise.)

Improvisation and work-performance

Another way to explicate improvisation is as part of the very concept of *work-performance*. Perhaps, as some have maintained, improvisation is not a curiously separate and distinctive form of performance, but an inevitable dimension of any music-making whatsoever (Gould and Keaton 2000; Benson 2003).

For instance, Carol S. Gould and Kenneth Keaton argue that "all musical performance, no matter how meticulously interpreted and no matter how specific the inscribed score, requires improvisation" (2000: 143). Basic to the argument is the now familiar view – which the theory shares with Alperson's – that musical works underdetermine their performances. The authors go on to claim that such work-performances count as improvisation, for improvisation is "a relation between the score and the performance event" (Gould and Keaton 2000: 145). (Throughout, it should be noted, the authors, like Busoni, assume what might be challenged – that all works are *scored*.)

In order to support this broadening of the concept of improvisation, the authors must interpret *improvisation* in such a way that an improvisation need not be spontaneous (Gould and Keaton 2000: 144–5). So, a specific thickening of the instructions for Beethoven's Op. 135 that the Guarneri String Quartet might work out in advance would, in this theory, qualify as improvisatory. However, this would surely be stretching the concept of improvisation to the breaking point. At the very least, a necessary condition of an improvisation is that it involves spontaneity.

Improvisation and spontaneous creation

In a later essay, Alperson wrote, to "improvise is to do or produce something on the spur of the moment" (Alperson 1998: 478). There must be something to the idea. But can the matter be that simple?

To improvise, let us say, is to make decisions about the music one is playing as one plays. Note that we must of course avoid equating "music" here with "a musical composition." But the formula faces other more serious difficulties of clarification. First, what should we make of the implicit temporal marker in the phrase, "as one plays"? Surely an improviser's decision to go one way rather than another must have been made at least a nanosecond before following through. In fact, though, we may not know enough about the mechanics of mental activity to decide the issue one way or another, so let us leave the matter open: an improvisational move is one made at the time of or slightly before the move itself – where we shall assume that either formulation would make the addition of "spontaneity" in the formulation unnecessary (Kania forthcoming). However, we cannot avoid fuzzy cases here. If Sonny Rollins lays out a second chorus while playing the first, should we regard the second as improvised?

Further, what is it to make "decisions about the music"? Given what we saw about the inevitable resources that are drawn upon in improvisational performance, it is not clear what this concept means, or how it applies. As already suggested, even very free improvisations have some structural guidance. The genuine keyboard improviser, for instance, is not simply noodling.

At one point, I tacitly answered the foregoing question when I wrote, "an improviser makes substantive decisions" about what to play "while playing it" (Brown 1996: 354). But what kinds of decisions are substantive? Elsewhere it has been suggested that, in jazz, "an improvised performance is one in which the structural properties of a performance are not completely determined by decisions made prior to the time of performance," where "structural properties" include melody, harmony, and length as opposed to "expressive properties" such as "tempo, the use of vibrato, dynamic, and so on" (Young and Matheson 2000: 127). But, first, the concept of a structural property remains unclear. (By what criterion would we distinguish between structural properties and others?) More generally, it is difficult to see why the musical properties that can be improvised should be restricted at all – except to those over which the improviser has control.

A matter of degree or of kind?

Let us grant then that an element of spontaneity is involved in any performance we term "improvisational." With that qualification, can we then say that improvisation and work-performance "differ more in degree than in kind" (Gould and Keaton 2000: 143)? One might try to illustrate the view with a thought experiment: imagine a stretch of music consisting of, say, a hundred notes, such that some are specified by a score, with the others to be filled in spontaneously by the performer. Now, imagine many such sets in a spectrum, such that in some of them very few notes are to be filled in, while in others a great many are. The array might be thought to illustrate how the supposed difference between the two kinds of performance is only a matter of degree.

However, the thought-experiment at best illustrates the banality that in such a situation we have potential vagueness, since we cannot indicate a precise point at which a performance is no longer a work-performance but an improvisation. To conclude from that fact that there is no difference between the two kinds would involve a version of the so-called "slippery slope" fallacy. Further, the thought experiment has left out of consideration what the performer *intends* – that is, what she thinks of herself as doing. Does she think of herself as spontaneously fleshing out a work while remaining faithful to its composer's style? Or does she think of herself as exploiting a given musical structure as a point of departure for music of her own?

The difference – *in kind* – between the case where a performer thickens a relatively thin work while performing and the case where she improvises ought surely to go something like this: in the former kind of case, the performer fleshes out a pre-existing structure rather than using it as a springboard for what Stephen Davies terms a "gravity defying" departure from such a structure (Davies 2001: 17).

But there are two grains of truth in the Gould–Keaton view. First, we can envision cases on the boundary between the two types of performance. In jazz pianist Uri Caine's recently recorded performance of Mozart's Sonata in C major, the "wrong" notes throughout can be assumed to have improvisational intention. But the performance does on the whole follow the general structure of the written music. Second, even within the class of uncontentiously improvisational performances, some may be more so than others. A typical solo by Louis Armstrong is less improvisational, for instance, than one by Charlie Parker. However, comparisons across musical genres will be difficult – if possible at all – for it is not clear how to enumerate the available options in one context by a measure that would apply in the other. How could we determine whether a bop solo by Charlie Parker is more or less improvisational than a classical Iranian performance on the *ʿūd*?

The ontology of improvisation

The inclusion of stretches of improvisation in a performance does not rule out that such a performance may still count, ontologically, as being *of* a work. (Consider a piano concerto containing an improvised cadenza.) So should we simply borrow our ontology for improvisational performances from the best available view about musical *works*? Such a view would be hard to generalize because it would leave certain cases homeless – certain free jazz performances, for instance, which are not of any antecedent work. Is it possible that the concept of *work-hood* simply does not apply to such cases? Upon what does the question turn?

First, let us assume that by "art work" we mean something that can be re-identified – revisited, as it were, on multiple occasions. Obviously, a Keith Jarrett improvisation cannot be revisited in the way that we can revisit the *Las Meninas* of Velasquez, which can be found on a wall in the Prado, where we can go see it anytime we can afford to do so. But how could we possibly revisit an improvisation that is, so to say, entirely in-the-moment? As it happens, Jarrett's Cologne improvisations were transcribed and published. However, a performance of one of them from the sheet music, or indeed, a copy of it by any means, whether by Jarrett or by anyone else, would surely lack an essential feature of the original, namely that – with the necessary qualifications – the music was created *as* Jarrett performed it. Given its once-only character, must we conclude that a Jarrett improvisation is not an art work? But now consider a visual work of performance art – such as those organized by Alan Kaprow, which, given their presumed spontaneity, could not be copied without loss of authenticity. In spite of this, such once-only events in visual art are documented and discussed just like art works in general.

Perhaps a musical improvisation is not an art work because an art work is something worked on over time (Kania 2008: 6–7). True, we can cite examples of art works that were *in fact* not worked on over time – Coleridge's poem, *Kubla Khan*, for instance, if we accept the poet's story about its spontaneous genesis. The reply, however, is that Coleridge *could have* worked on it over time.

Another reasonable criterion of workhood is that an art work is the focus of critical attention. By this criterion, Jarrett's performances presumably would be works in their own right – if we are untroubled by the thought that it seems conceptually impossible for these musical works to have more than a single instance.

So with different criteria of workhood we get various problematic results. And sooner or later, we will find ourselves asking whether it is relevant that ECM recorded Jarrett's performances for us to listen to as often as we wish. And would this be relevant because recordings *do* magically allow us to revisit an ephemeral event even though it has slipped into the past? Or is it because the Jarrett recording itself takes on the status of an art work? An ontology for improvised performances remains unfinished business.

See also Jazz (Chapter 39), Ontology (Chapter 4), and Performances and recordings (Chapter 8).

References

Alperson, P. (1984) "On Musical Improvisation," *Journal of Aesthetics and Art Criticism* 43: 17–29.
—— (1998) "Improvisation – An Overview," in M. Kelly (ed.) *Encyclopedia of Aesthetics*, vol. 2, New York: Oxford University Press, pp. 478–9.

Benson, B. (2003) *The Improvisation of Musical Dialogue: A Phenomenology of Music*, Cambridge: Cambridge University Press.

Berliner, P. (1994) *Thinking in Jazz*, Chicago: University of Chicago Press.

Brown, L.B. (1996) "Musical Works, Improvisation, and the Principle of Continuity," *Journal of Aesthetics and Art Criticism*, 54: 353–69.

—— (2000) "'Feeling My Way': Jazz Improvisation and its Vicissitudes – A Plea for Imperfection," *Journal of Aesthetics and Art Criticism* 58: 112–23.

Busoni, F. (1962) "Sketch of a New Aesthetic of Music," in *Three Classics in the Aesthetics of Music*, New York: Dover.

Chernoff, J. (1982) *African Music*, Chicago: University of Chicago Press.

Davies, S. (2001) *Musical Works and Performances: A Philosophical Exploration*, Oxford: Clarendon Press.

Gioia, T. (1992) *The Imperfect Art*, Oxford: Oxford University Press.

Goffin, R. (1944) *Jazz from the Congo to the Metropolitan*, New York: Doubleday.

Gould, C. and Keaton, K. (2000) "The Essential Role of Improvisation in Musical Performance," *Journal of Aesthetics and Art Criticism* 58: 143–8.

Hagberg, G. (1998) "Improvisation: Jazz Improvisation," in M. Kelly (ed.) *Encyclopedia of Aesthetics*, vol. 2, New York: Oxford University Press, pp. 479–82.

Hamilton, A. (2000) "The Art of Improvisation and the Aesthetics of Imperfection," *British Journal of Aesthetics* 40: 168–85.

Kania, A. (2008) "Works, Recordings, Performances: Classical, Rock, Jazz," in M.D. Dack (ed.) *Recorded Music: Philosophical and Critical Reflections*, Middlesex: Middlesex University Press, pp. 3–21.

—— (forthcoming) "All Play and No Work: The Ontology of Jazz," *Journal of Aesthetics and Art Criticism*.

Kivy, P. (1983) "Platonism in Music: A Kind of Defense," *Grazer Philosophische Studien* 19: 109–29.

Kraut, R. (2007) *Artworld Metaphysics*, Oxford: Oxford University Press.

Nettl, B. (1992) *The Radif of Persian Music: Studies of Structure and Cultural Context*, rev. edn, Champaign: University of Illinois Press.

Palmer, K. (1992) *The Piano*, Chicago: NTC Publishing Group.

Sargeant, W. (1976) *Jazz, Hot and Hybrid*, rev. edn, New York: Da Capo Press.

Schuller, G. (1968) *Early Jazz: Its Roots and Musical Development*, New York: Oxford University Press.

Spade, P. (1991) "Do Composers Have To Be Performers Too?" *Journal of Aesthetics and Art Criticism* 49: 365–9.

Young, J. and Matheson, C. (2000) "The Metaphysics of Jazz," *Journal of Aesthetics and Art Criticism* 58: 125–34.

7

NOTATIONS

Stephen Davies

The oldest musical instruments date to about 30,000 years ago (BP), but musical notations did not arrive until much later. The first notations date from 4500–3000 BP in Sumeria and 2400 BP in China, but those with which Westerners are most familiar emerged in Europe around 1200 BP. The earliest European notations assisted singers to recall plainsong melodies by showing the direction and approximate interval size of melodic movement. In other words, these notations belong to the type below called "mnemonic"; they underspecified the melodies they indicated, but showed enough to bring the melody to the mind of someone who was already familiar with it. Subsequent changes to the notation over several centuries (stave lines, indications of relative duration, etc.) permitted a more precise specification of the musical notes and how they are to be sung or played.

It is not necessary to have notation in order to develop a large corpus of works (as the liturgical tradition shows) or to produce long and extremely complex works (as is apparent in Javanese and Balinese music – notations of such music are primarily archival in function and are not usually consulted by practicing musicians). Nevertheless, it probably helps. Singers and musicians in Europe from the fourteenth century or earlier played from notations and were expected to be literate. Works were often issued as part books – that is, as showing the part for each instrument or singer separately – rather than as scores showing all the parts in vertical alignment. Some part books were arranged such that the parts could be read by musicians facing each other, with the book between them. As musical works became more complex and were specified in more detail, scores became more prominent, as did the orchestra's director, who was usually one of its members but later, from the nineteenth century, a conductor.

Generic and instrument-specific notations

One distinction that is sometimes drawn is between generic and instrument-specific notations. The former show the result to be achieved but not the manner of doing so, whereas the latter indicate the manner of eliciting the desired result from the given instrument. Notations of vocal music are generic: they present what is to be sung and not how to arrange one's larynx so that the desired sound issues from it. The best examples – indeed, perhaps the only plausible ones – of instrument-specific notations are tablatures for stringed instruments, such as the guitar and lute. (Some of the oldest are for the Chinese *quin*.) Tablatures show the position of the fingers on the instrument's strings (or, if it has them, frets) and assume or specify a particular tuning of the strings.

The generic notation of pitch might take several forms. It could be that (more or less) absolute pitch is shown, usually involving reference to some standard and presuming certain tonal or modal systems. Modern Western notation is of this kind. Alternatively, a pitch is indicated as relative to an unspecified tonic in a tonal or modal system. Modern solfeggio – the naming of the notes of the scale, as in "do-re-mi-fa-so-la-ti-do" – takes this form. In this system, the "do" is movable but always counts as the tonic. Or relative position in a series of intervals or a scale could be specified. This is the case with Balinese solfeggio. The notes are named "deng, ding" etc. and the intervals are fixed, but any note in the scale could function as the tonic. (The same applies if "do[C]-re[D]- " is used to notate the church modes, since in these the degree of the scale that serves as the tonic varies with the mode.) The notation of music for the Chinese *shamisen* shows intervals (*ma*) rather than pitches when the instrument accompanies a vocalist, because the singer chooses the song's pitch according to his range. Early Indian and Arabic notations employed forms of solfeggio. Cipher notation, in which notes are assigned numbers, is similar to solfeggio and was widely adopted in China, India, and Indonesia 150–100 years ago.

Rather than pitches, the notation might show the harmonic sequence according to its chord type. The notation might be absolute (C, a, F, G^7, C) or relative to a tonal (or modal) system (I, vi, IV, V^7, I), possibly leaving the pitch of the tonic unspecified. A more complex system could imply the bass line by showing the chords' position/inversion (I, vi_b, IV_c, V^7_b, I) or the bass line could be explicitly written with numbers indicating the scale degrees above the bass line of the harmonic middle voices, as in the Baroque "figured bass." Yet more detail would be added by combining pitch and harmonic notation to show a melody and its harmonic accompaniment.

The generic notation of rhythm, rather than showing measures of absolute duration, usually employs a notation for sounded beats (and rests) and their simple multiples and subdivisions (2, 4, 8, 16, 32 or 3, 6, 12, 24). Where groups of beats are organized according to a meter, this might be specified and indicated by bar lines. (If the meter is regular, it is usually indicated only at the outset.) Alternatively, bar lines could be used as a navigational convenience to check for coordination but without implying a meter or stress. The pace of the underlying pulse can be specified, either with somewhat vague verbal terms (*andante*, walking pace) or by metronome markings, but even where there is no explicit indication, usually a tempo (fast, slow, etc.) is implied.

One might have supposed that instrument-specific notations preceded generic ones and that a move from one to the other went with a move toward the standardization of instruments and their combination into various ensembles. There is no evidence for this hypothesis, however, and it is unlikely to be true. The first notations came well after moves to regularize instruments and their combination. In any case, if much of the music first indicated notationally was vocal, as seems likely, we can anticipate that generic notations would be to the fore from the outset.

Generic notations have some obvious advantages. If many instruments play together, generic notation makes it simpler for the composer (or conductor) to grasp how their parts fit together. Such notations are more transparent. And they also facilitate the circulation of pieces from one kind of instrument to another, which is certainly valuable if the composer cannot be sure what resources will be available for the presentation of his work. These advantages can be inappropriately exaggerated, however. As I now discuss, predominantly generic notations quite commonly do not show what is to be done in a literal or translucent fashion.

The fact is, notations are neither purely generic nor purely instrument-specific. If tablatures show rhythmic values, as those for lute usually do, these are indicated in a manner that is not lute-specific. The notation of the relative duration of notes and of rests was standardized from the earliest times. Meanwhile, generic notations constantly employ instrument-specific directions if the desired instrumentation is indicated. Sometimes special notational symbols are used, such as that for a down-bow. In other cases, a written instruction is given, such as *pizz.* (for *pizzicato*) or *sul ponticello* (which means play with the bow close to the bridge). There are literally dozens of terms and symbols dealing with the manner of using the bow, for instance. Obviously, these instructions are addressed to string players; wind instrumentalist do not use a bow and have no strings to bow or pluck. In a similar vein, organ music includes instructions for preferred couplings (resulting in doubling at the octave, for instance) and stops (that reproduce the timbral effects of specific instruments or the voice). Piano music may include specifications about the use of the pedal; harps have seven pedals each of which has three positions and idiomatic harp writing usually indicates how they are to be used.

Sometimes a notational element that appears to be generic because it is addressed to very different kinds of instruments in fact requires modes of execution that are instrument specific. A good example of this is the instruction *con sord* (which means play with a mute). The mute on a stringed instrument is a clamp that attaches to the bridge and dampens the instrument's resonance. By contrast, mutes for brass instruments are cones or hats placed in or over the instrument's bell. Some wind instruments can be muted, though this is not common, by the insertion of a cloth in the instrument's bell. These instrument-specific means of quieting the instrument result in distinctive modifications to the instrument's timbre, and it is these effects, rather than quietness alone, that are often sought by the composer. Another example is the instruction *tr.* (for "trill"). Addressed to an untuned percussion instrument, a roll is called for, whereas a violin rapidly alternates notes at the interval of a semitone or tone, depending on the context.

Another implicitly instrument-specific aspect of standard notations is in the use of clefs. The piano made the use of a G (treble) clef and F (bass) clef standard, with the two sharing middle C one ledger line below the treble clef's five stave lines and one above the bass clef's five stave lines. The parts for most instruments nowadays use one or other of these clefs (sometimes with a transposition up or down an octave, as with the piccolo and double bass). In the past, C clefs, placed variously in relation to the stave's lines, were more common. (This practice apparently did not inhibit the readability of the various parts in vertical relation, from the composer's point of view.) Their use survives for a few instruments. In particular, the viola alone uses the C alto clef (with middle C as the stave's middle line). In their upper ranges, the bassoon and trombone (and less often the 'cello) use the C tenor clef (with middle C on the fourth line of the stave). Presumably, these usages hark back to earlier periods in which certain kinds of instruments were viewed as forming families with ranges overlapping at the fourth and octave.

It was formerly common to produce a kind of instrument as a family or choir, with each individual within the family tuned a fifth or fourth from its nearest siblings. Viols, for example, were arranged as a consort. (The only member of the viol family surviving to the modern orchestra is the double bass.) Recorders were tuned as follows (high to low): garklein (C), sopranino (F), soprano (C), alto (F), tenor (C), bass (F), great bass (C), contrabass (F). In this case, the tuning indicates the instrument's lowest note, with the tenor's being middle C. It is not common for modern instruments to retain the full choir – for instance the flute (C) is usually accompanied only by the piccolo (an octave higher but lacking the lowest C) and the alto flute (a fourth lower, to G) and the oboe is paired only with the cor anglais (a fifth lower at F) – but the saxophone is an exception with sopranino (E-flat), soprano (B-flat), alto (E-flat), tenor (B-flat a major ninth with below middle C), baritone (E-flat), bass (B-flat), contrabass (E-flat).

It is useful for the musician to be able to swap from one instrument to its siblings. To facilitate this, the note designations of the fingerings were kept the same. For example, if the second oboist took up the cor anglais, she would finger a notated C as she would on the oboe, but the note sounded would be the F below this. Or in other words, the notation of the part was transposed up a fifth, so that she could treat the two differently pitched instruments as using a consistent fingering. This flexibility and convenience compromises the clarity of the notation, however. It results in notations showing pitches and keys other than those literally sounded. Moreover, where this occurs the pattern is not systematic because many instruments employing different transpositions may be in simultaneous use. Though the notation has the appearance of being generic and is certainly not instrument-specific, it is significantly affected by the practice of playing that goes with different kinds of instruments.

Transposing instruments as they are called – that is, instruments whose parts are notated at a pitch other than the one sounded – do not always divide up the pitch range so neatly as the recorder or the saxophone. Soprano and sopranino clarinets come in many pitches. Meanwhile, the player of the main clarinet part has two instruments – one transposing to B-flat and the other to A. In other words, a B-flat clarinet sounds a B-flat when the musician fingers what is notated as C, and the A clarinet sounds an A when the musician uses the same fingering, also notated as a C. The B-flat clarinet is better suited to flat keys (it cancels two of the flats in the key signature) and the A clarinet to sharp keys (it cancels three of the sharps in the key signature). No doubt historical contingency played a major role in bringing about this musical anomaly, but one reason for it might have been to avoid forked or half-hole fingerings, with their uneven tone and timbre, which would have been unavoidable for sharpened and flattened notes prior to the introduction of the modern Boehm system for woodwinds, which addresses the problem by adding supplementary holes activated by metal keys.

Prior to valves and slides, brass instruments could play only the fundamental and the natural harmonic series above it (and, for horns, a few other pitches half-stopped with the fist), where the pitch of the fundamental was determined by the tube's length. To get around the limitations this caused on the number of keys in which the instrument could play, it was common to insert "crooks," extra lengths of tubing that altered the instrument's fundamental. Again, pitch was notated as if no crook was in use, and the part was transposed to take account of the crook's effect. The modern introduction of valves did not remove the need for transposition: most brass instruments transpose to B-flat or E-flat. Indeed, the modern French horn in effect conjoins two horns tuned to F and B-flat, and the notational conventions for the instrument are unique, with the part notated a fifth higher than it sounds in the treble clef but a fourth lower in the bass clef.

One final use of instruments that leads to the transposition of the notation of the instrument's part is scordatura, in which there is some departure for a stringed instrument from the standard interval or pitch tuning of the strings. Because the musician is trained to finger the instrument in the normal fashion in producing what is notated, to keep a scordatura part in tune with other instruments the part must be notationally transposed or altered to take account of the unusual tuning.

In a normal orchestral score, the parts of a number of the instruments will be transposed, so that the pitches that are written are not the ones that are sounded (Figure 7.1). This undermines one of the advantages of a generic notation, namely, transparency across the parts of the score, and shows how the practi-

Figure 7.1 Notations of various instruments playing middle C

cal business of dealing with the instruments shapes the notation, even where the notation is not entirely instrument specific in design. Of course, one obvious response to this would be to show all parts in a score at their sounded pitch; the score's indication of the cor anglais's music, say, need not duplicate the part from which the relevant musician plays. This has yet to become the general practice, though, perhaps because it could make communication between the orchestra's director and the musicians difficult or ambiguous.

Because notations are not always to be read literally, their proper interpretation relies on knowledge of both the conventions of the notation system and the background of musical practice it takes for granted.

Functions of notations

We might prefer to classify notations not in terms of their appearance but of their function. A first type was mentioned earlier: mnemonic notations. These are sketchy or gappy notations that serve either to remind the musician of something she knows or to provide something from which she can derive her part. Examples of the latter, perhaps, are Indonesian notations that indicate the melodic spine of the piece, since other instruments improvise around that spine or can derive their parts from it, or, in jazz, a notation of a chord sequence or melody that is the basis for an improvisation. Mnemonic notations do not always go with free or improvisatory pieces. Long and complex pieces can be committed to memory and recalled with great accuracy once the necessary notational (or other) cues are presented, as is apparent in traditions of liturgical chant or in Balinese music.

In the West, a primary function of notations has become that of specifying works. Such notations have a prescriptive force: if you would play my work, make this so! The interpretation of work-specifying notations requires some care: as well as knowing the general conventions of the notation and the practice it assumes, one needs to be aware of others specific to the kind of work notated. For instance, it may be that not everything that is required in delivering the work is indicated in the notation – perhaps melodies must be decorated when repeated. And it may be that not everything that is notated is prescribed, as against recommended – perhaps marked repeats, phrasings, and fingerings are optional.

Such scores can include comments or programs that are not addressed to the performer as such. These, if not solely for the composer's benefit, are usually addressed to the work's listener. Also, the notation might be written so as to have, in addition to its musical import, a pictorial significance. For instance, the notes might be so disposed in the score of a passion to look like three crosses. (Some fifteenth-century composers created "eye-music" in which visual aspects of the score were relevant to the music's subject. A famous example of *c.*1400 is a love song by Baude Cordier in the Codex Chantilly, which is notated in the shape of a heart.) Whereas the visual aspects of concrete poetry surely are to be counted as among the work's elements, the same does not apply here: the score is not the musical work as such and the pictures in the score rarely generate equivalent "aural pictures" when the music is played. Such notational tricks have their interest, of course, but they belong with many other techniques and devices – such as the creation of long-distance derivations and relations between bits of the work – that structure the composer's efforts without being audibly discriminable in how the work sounds.

The use of pictorial elements in scores is not always incidental, however. In the early days of electronic music, pictorial impressions of the music's sound were issued as "scores." From the composer's point of view, this was no idle matter because the law at the time allowed works to be copyrighted only via their notational specifications. And in the 1950s, some composers addressed performers not with standard notational instructions but with pictorial impressions of the sounds they desired the performers to realize. An example is Earle Brown's *Folio* of 1952–53. In such cases, the performer may have considerable freedom not only in the manner of her interpretation of the work but also in her interpretation of the notation that specifies it.

A further principal function of notations is to document musical events. Such notations, known as transcriptions, are descriptive, not prescriptive; they are usually based on a single performance and record what was done. A performance can present more than one musical object: a work (if there is one), a repeatable interpretation of a work (if there is one), and a singular musical event of playing. A documentary notation can target any of these. Musical works can be more or less thick or thin with constitutive detail – one requiring sections of improvisation is thinner than one that indicates each and every note that is to be played – but even in the case of the thickest works for live performance, their renditions always contain sonic detail that is attributable to the performer's interpretation rather than to the work itself. That is, even the most complex notational specifications of the thickest musical works leave many choices to the performer's discretion, as regards both microscopic features, such as phrasing nuance, and macroscopic elements, such as shaping, contrasting, balancing, and emphasizing. Accordingly, a notation intended to capture only the work recovers less detail than one intended to display the performer's interpretation of the work. And whereas both of these may involve the notational correction of what were performance errors, a notation attempting to record the microscopic detail that marks the single performance as an unrepeatable individual act of playing does not. Transcriptions of this third kind are rare, however, because standard musical notations, even when supplemented with specially defined symbols, are not fine-grained enough to capture the shadings of pitch, timbre, attack, rhythmic inflection, etc. that are crucial to the individuality of a single live musical rendition.

Functions apart from these three are served by some musical notations. Notations can be used for pedagogical purposes: for teaching the use of the notation, the playing of musical instruments, orchestration, and so on. As well, musical analysts and historians of music use them to illustrate their accounts. Composers sketch their ideas, doodle, and write drafts of works. These further uses are obviously secondary and derivative.

Nelson Goodman on musical notations

Nelson Goodman is among the few philosophers to have discussed musical notations. He focuses on the work-identifying function of scores and holds that they must uniquely and unequivocally describe the work they specify. To do this the notational system must meet two syntactic requirements – disjointness and finite differentiation – and three semantic ones – unambiguity, disjointness, and finite differentiation (1968: 130–52). The syntactic conditions are met when each notational mark belongs to one and only one "character" (that is, each symbol denotes only one musical element or event). The semantic conditions are met if the notation is unambiguous, all work-relevant musical elements are notationally specifiable, and no two distinct scores could have any accurate copies or performances in common. According to Goodman, a performance must comply exactly with the score to instance the work it specifies and the score must be derivable from a genuine instance of the work.

At first glance, it looks as if Goodman will have to regard as notationally satisfactory only those scores that spell out each and every work-identifying detail that is to be played in instancing the work. A score that invites the performer to decorate melodies when they are repeated, for instance, will lead to non-identical renditions from which a single score is apparently not derivable. Goodman avoids this difficulty by distinguishing different systems of notation, with any given work relativized to only one of these. Provided the instances of a given work form a class that is distinct from the classes of genuine instances of all other works specifiable under the same notational system, it does not matter that the instances comprising the class of the given work vary in respects allowed for within that notational system. For example, though a trio sonata with a figured bass tolerates more than one realization of its middle parts, we could derive a score of the work from any accurate performance provided that we were aware that the work belonged to a notational subsystem allowing this mode of improvisation. Such a work would be distinguishable from different trio sonatas that also use a figured bass. Moreover, though works relativized to a different notational subsystem (for instance, to one that spells out the middle parts and does not permit improvisation) might happen to have compliants intersecting with those of the trio sonata (and hence violating the condition for disjointness), this appearance is illusory given that work identity is a function of the notational subsystem under which the work-identifying inscription falls.

Goodman is not always so accommodating, however. For instance, he regards verbal tempo indications, such as *largo*, as non-notational because they are ambiguous and not finitely differentiated. In dismissing such markings as non-notational, he removes tempo as a work-identifying feature. A genuine performance for such a work might have any tempo, including one so slow as to make the piece unrecognizable. Similarly, the mark *tr.* (trill) is non-notational because it does not specify how many notes should be played, so a performance of Giuseppe Tartini's *Devil's Trill Sonata* would be accurate, according to Goodman, if it contained no trills.

Goodman's is offered as an idealized, revisionary account, but to be acceptable it should at least capture many of our central intuitions regarding notationally specified works. If it is to come close to doing so, it will be necessary to assume there are a great many exclusive musical notational subsystems and that we are (or could be) clear on how they differ. Neither assumption is convincing. A more plausible approach is the one advocated earlier. Instead of leaving the notational system to do all the work, so to speak, which means that many distinct systems will have to be recognized, we should acknowledge that general notations are employed according to a spread of historically grounded conventions concerning how they are to be read, established traditions of performance practice, and characteristics of differing work genres or types.

See also Authentic performance practice (Chapter 9).

References

Goodman, N. (1968) *Languages of Art*, Indianapolis: Bobbs-Merrill.

Further reading

Apel, W. (1953) *The Notation of Polyphonic Music: 900–1500*, rev. 5th edn, Cambridge, MA: Medieval Academy of America. (The classic treatment of Western early music notation.)

Davies, S. (2001) *Musical Works and Performances: A Philosophical Exploration*, Oxford: Clarendon Press. (Chapter 3 is devoted to a discussion of notations.)

Gerou, T. and Lusk, L. (1996) *Essential Dictionary of Music Notation: The Most Practical and Concise Source for Music Notation*, Indianapolis: Alfred Publishing. (A practical guide to Western musical notation.)

Kaufman, W. (2003) *Musical Notations of the Orient: Notational Systems of Continental East, South, and Central Asia*, Bloomington: Indiana University Press. (A description of some classical non-Western notational systems.)

8
PERFORMANCES AND RECORDINGS
Andrew Kania and Theodore Gracyk

The most common musical experience today, across most of the globe, is that of listening to a recording. For many centuries, however, music was only experienced live, since recording technology did not exist. As a result, much of the philosophy of music is rooted in the idea that music is a performance art, and recordings have been met with some skepticism (when they have been discussed at all). In this chapter, we investigate the nature of musical performances and recordings, and compare views about their respective values.

Performances

General features of musical performances

Not just any musical event is a musical performance. Consider a CD playing in an empty house. While there is music going on in the house, there is no performance within its walls. For there to be a performance going on, there must be people performing. Performance is thus a kind of action – something only people (not machines, such as CD players) can do. But not every musical action is a musical performance. We standardly distinguish between just messing around on an instrument, practicing, rehearsing, and performing. What distinguishes performance from the other musical activities in this list seems to have something to do with the presence of an audience. When you mess around, practice, or, rehearse, you play your instrument or sing, but you do not do so *for an audience*.

Is the requirement that a performance be for an audience merely intentional, or is it a success condition, in the sense that if there is no audience, there cannot be a performance? Both Stan Godlovitch (1998: 41–9) and Paul Thom (1993: 190–3) argue for the stronger claim: an actual audience is a necessary condition on there being a performance. They do so on the grounds that performance is essentially *communicative*, and thus requires two parties – performer and audience. Godlovitch describes two situations which, he suggests, we would only describe as "performances" in some secondary or derivative sense. In the first, a performer decides to go ahead with the evening's performance even though no one has turned up to hear him. In the second, the performer plays a politically incendiary work in defiance of the government officials who have locked the audience out of the hall (Godlovitch 1998: 43). These thought experiments do not quite show what they are intended to, however. For in both these cases there is neither an actual audience nor an intended audience in the relevant sense. Of course these performers "intended" to perform for people, but the past tense of the verb is telling. Performances are intentionally for an audience in the sense that one's actions (playing, singing, etc.) are guided by the belief that one is playing for people who are capable of listening to the sounds one is making. The performers in Godlovitch's cases do not have this belief, since they know there is no one else present. One can have the relevant belief mistakenly, though. Imagine a case where the performer comes onstage and plays for the audience in the hall, only realizing after the performance, when the blinding stage lights are dimmed and house lights come up, that there is no such audience. Such a performer has the relevant intention despite the absence of an audience, and thus might be said to have performed. This view does not undermine the analogy with ordinary communication. If one is convinced there is a burglar in the house, one might utter a warning, such as "Who goes there?" Such a speech act is intentionally directed at whoever is in the house, even if it turns out that one is mistaken, and there is no such person. (This kind of thing may happen in cultures where musical works are performed for the gods. If there are two such cultures, with beliefs in incompatible deities, then if Godlovitch and Thom are right, at most one is actually engaged in musical performance. This seems wrong.)

Paul Thom gives a different argument for the necessity of an actual audience, arguing that the address of a performer to an audience is different in kind from that of non-performance artists, such as painters or novelists. The latter make a "hypothetical" address, according to Thom, "to whoever happens to be the addressee," while as a performer, "I make a categorical address to the audience, whom I assume to exist. In performing I believe myself to be referring to present persons, to whom I am in effect saying, 'You, attend to me.'" (1993: 192). To the extent that Thom refers here only to a *belief* or *assumption* that the audience exists, it does not establish the need for an *actual* as opposed to an *intended* audience. What remains is the idea that the audience for a performance must be (at least believed to be) present. But this condition is also too strong. For musicians can perform a live broadcast for "the folks at home" without any audience present where they play. It seems, then, that the attitudes of performing artists are not at base so different from those of other artists. They present their efforts to whomever is in a position to appreciate them. This argument could also be extended to the production of some musical recordings.

In sum, a performance requires the intention to play music for an audience, but there need be no actual audience. You might think this point is usually moot, since the performers themselves may count as the audience, in the absence of any other listeners. But it is not clear that musicians are in the right position to be the audience for their own music-making (Godlovitch 1998: 42–3; Gracyk 1997: 149 n. 6; cf. Thom 1993: 172).

Kinds of musical performances

Many musical performances are performances of independent musical works, that is, works that would exist whether or not these particular, or indeed any, performances of them existed. Philosophers have disputed what is required for a performance to be of a given work. One appealing first pass at an answer is that one must play all the right notes. But most work-performances include wrong notes, and we do not discount them as performances for that reason. On the other hand, it seems clear that if you play *none* of the right notes, you have failed to perform the work in question. The kicker is that it seems an impossible task to decide how many, or what proportion of notes must be correct for a performance to count as of a given work. All this suggests that some other connection between performance and work is at least necessary. One popular suggestion is that the performers must *intend* to play the work in question; others have suggested that there must be a particular kind of causal chain running from the work (or its composition) to each performance. (For an excellent overview of the literature on these questions, and a consideration of how to spell out these proposals, see Davies 2001: 152–84).

Another important part of this debate has been the discussion of "authentic performance practice," which is usually centered around the question of whether a (proper) performance of a musical work ought to involve the use of the kinds of instruments contemporary with the work. The literature on this question dwarfs that on any of the others considered in this chapter; it is thus treated separately in this volume. (See Chapter 9, "Authentic performance practice.")

Many performances, on the other hand, are not performances of works. The most obvious examples are free improvisations. Such performances need not emerge *ex nihilo*; rather, they are cases where any materials they are based on are treated as jumping-off points for the performer's creative activity, instead of something the performer centrally intends to present to the audience through performing it. (See Chapter 6, "Improvisation," this volume.) Are such performances musical works in their own right? The answer turns, unsurprisingly, on the nature of the concept of a musical work. On the one hand, such performances are the primary focus of appreciation in traditions such as jazz, suggesting that if there are works of art in jazz they include such performances. On the other hand, work-performances are a primary focus of appreciation in classical music, yet we do not typically think of these as works. We could, of course, simply stipulate that performances that are of works cannot be works in their own right. It may be, though, that central to our (or one of our) concept(s) of a work of art is the idea that they are enduring entities. If that is right, then we might deny that there are works of art in jazz (and other similar traditions). This may sound like an insult to the tradition, but it should not if the sense of 'work of art' being employed here is not an evaluative one.

Evaluating performances

Some evaluative criteria seem applicable to any kind of performance. The ability to play one's instrument or sing well is valued in any performance, for instance, and it may be exalted in virtuosic performances (Mark 1980). We also evaluate the musical properties of the performance, for example, its melodies or harmonies, and how they are developed over the course of the performance. The way in which such features are evaluated depends upon the kind of performance we are listening to. The virtuosity and musical features of a work-performance will be attributed to the work or its composer, while those of an improvisation might be attributed to the performer. (It is worth remembering that in attending to a work performance we attend to at least two things – the work and its performance.)

Other evaluative criteria depend on the kind of performance evaluated. In evaluating an improvisation, we value the spontaneous risks the performer takes in attempting to fashion a worthwhile musical event in the moment. In evaluating a work-performance, on the other hand, we value a faithful adherence to the work. There are other things we value in work-performances, such as a performer's ability to *interpret* the work, and thereby show us something new and interesting about it. Moreover, as Jerrold Levinson (1990a) has argued, there are many legitimate yet irreconcilable perspectives from which to evaluate a work-performance. A good performance for a first-time listener, for instance, may emphasize broad structural and expressive elements of the piece, while a good performance for a seasoned listener may emphasize the role of a particular motif that should not be foregrounded for a first-time listener. There are, of course, illegitimate perspectives, such as that of the monomaniacal percussionist who values the loudness of the cymbals over all else. And there may be some difficult cases. Levinson judges the perspective of a jaded listener, who values idiosyncratic performances, legitimate (1990a: 380). But there will doubtless be cases that fall in a hazy border between the legitimate and illegitimate. The variety of legitimate perspectives arises precisely because the kinds of musical works we have been considering are intended for multiple performances. This suggests that it is pointless to ask what the *ideal* performance of a given work would be like.

Live non-performance music-making

Musical performances are "art" in the loose sense that they are produced for an audience that is supposed to appreciate the performance in some way. But there is much live music-making that does not fit this description. Two broad types are, or have been, common. The first is communal music-making, such as the singing of hymns in church or folk songs around a campfire. In these cases there is something like a performance of a work – the singers attempt to get the notes, words, chords, etc., right – yet they are not singing for an audience (not even for each other) – in the sense in which the concert performer does. Rather, they are singing *with* each other. The two types of music-making may occur simultaneously, as when the audience joins the band in singing along with a hit song at a concert. The band is performing, in the sense of the term we have been using; the audience is not.

Live music-making can also be *functional*. Examples here include work songs and lullabies. The musicians in these cases produce music primarily for some purpose other than the appreciation of an audience, whether it is to coordinate their actions, make the time pass quickly, lull a baby to sleep, or express one's love. (See Chapter 40, "Song," this volume.)

Musical recordings

"These modern gramophones are a remarkable invention," remarks Sherlock Holmes in "The Adventure of the Mazarin Stone" (Doyle 1921: 296). Holmes has just used a phonograph recording of a solo violin performance of Offenbach's barcarolle from *The Tales of Hoffman* to fool jewel thieves into thinking that he was playing his violin in a neighboring room. Heard through a wall, it is plausible that they might confuse the playing of a primitive recording with a very different thing, a performance. In any case, the phenomenon of recorded music was sufficiently familiar to the general public in 1921 to serve as a plot device in a popular detective story. Fifteen years later, Walter Benjamin and Theodor Adorno staked out opposite positions on the effects and desirability of this "mechanical reproduction" on listeners (Benjamin 1968; Adorno 2002) – after which there is a long silence on this topic in the philosophical literature. As late as 1990, philosophers simply took it for granted that listening to recorded music constitutes listening to music, without pausing to discuss whether audience response differs when listening to recordings (e.g. Levinson 1990b: 306). However, in the ensuing decades a number of philosophers took up the topic of recorded music and its role in musical experience (e.g. Gracyk 1996, 1997; Fisher 1998; Brown 2000; Kania 2009). Two general topics have emerged concerning musical recordings. First, what is the nature of recorded sound and what is its relationship to the music it records? Second, should we be concerned that so much of our musical culture now takes the form of listening to recordings? It is best to take up the two questions in that order, for it is doubtful that we can achieve an evaluative consensus when we do not yet agree on the nature of the phenomenon being evaluated (Kania 2008: 69–73).

Kinds of recordings

Consider the simple case of Sherlock Holmes "playing" Offenbach's barcarolle on his gramophone. In 1921, it would have been a mechanical recording of an uninterrupted performance of that piece. While Offenbach's barcarolle allows for multiple instances through multiple performances, each performance is a singular event. Yet the multiple playbacks of a single gramophone recording (and the multiple playings of multiple copies of the recording) present us with the ontological peculiarity that a single musical performance can be heard by a temporally and spatially dispersed audience. Because one cannot listen to a musical performance years after the performance ends, it seems relatively obvious that audiences for musical recordings do not actually hear the performance. They hear an imitation or representation of the sonic dimension of that performance. (However, see the following discussion of transparency.)

This intuition about representation poses three problems. First, does this relationship hold for all recorded music? As will become apparent, this is unlikely. Second, where it does hold, does the recording provide an instance of the music? Third, where it does hold, can the recording faithfully capture the sonic dimension of the performance?

With the advent of electronic music (both synthesized and musique concrète), it became apparent that some musical works depend essentially on recording technology and playback. Subverting the ontological priority presupposed by Holmes's use of the gramophone recording of the Offenbach barcarolle, these recordings directly instantiate music that cannot otherwise exist. There are no performances of such works, for their only instances are playbacks (e.g. Pierre Schaeffer's *Étude Pathétique* and Milton Babbitt's *Composition for Synthesizer*). Stephen Davies calls these works "for playback, not for performance" (Davies 2001: 7–8). Following Aron Edidin's alternative terminology, these "recording artifacts" should be distinguished from two other kinds of recordings: recordings of performances and recordings of compositions (Edidin 1999). Whereas recordings of performances provide access to musical works by documenting performances of some work (e.g. Holmes's recording of the barcarolle), recordings of compositions employ studio editing and manipulation to construct sonic manifestations of musical works that can also be instantiated in real-time performance. The intended aesthetic appeal of such recordings is not confined to their documentary function of capturing the sonic dimensions of musical performance. Thus, two different recordings of Glenn Gould's interpretation of Bach's *Goldberg Variations* possess distinct functional relationships to Bach's music and thus have different ontological status: Gould's 1981 studio sessions and his 1959 Salzburg live performance furnished a recording of a composition and recording of a performance, respectively. Mere listening does not necessarily reveal the appropriate category. The functional relationship to performance practice, rather than the kind of musical work that is presented, determines which kind of recording presents the music.

Discussing studio recordings of works such as the *Goldberg Variations* (i.e. Edidin's category of recordings of compositions), Davies observes that they normally aim at a simulated performance that emphasizes accuracy, consistency, and finish (Davies 2001: 313–17). However, many such recordings are not limited to the function of simulating a performance. Since the 1960s it has been common for popular music recordings to employ studio techniques that create sonic events with electronic effects that cannot be reproduced in real-time performances. Such effects include movement within the stereophonic soundscape, singers who sing multiple harmonies with themselves and drum kits with cavernous echo that sounds distinctively different from the echo effect on the vocal performances on the same recording. Here, the studio manipulations furnish musical effects that can exist only in playback and which are intended to be appreciated as such. Furthermore, the recording process often serves as a non-documentary compositional tool, allowing new compositions to emerge through trial and error as additions are recorded at different times and by multiple contributing musicians (Gracyk 1996: 46–50).

Like Davies's works for playback and Edidin's recording artifacts, these composite, studio-enhanced "tracks" are distinct musical works, intended to be appreciated for composed musical effects that go beyond real-time performance effects (Gracyk 1996; Zak 2001). We might consider, for example, Pink Floyd's *Dark Side of the Moon*, which employs sound manipulation and montage techniques to create musical patterns from "found" sounds. Such manipulation is particularly conspicuous at the beginning of "Money." Because it is also possible to perform the song live, in real time, Davies contends that the recording is a simulated performance of a musical work of a special type: a work for studio performance (Davies 2001: 34–35). Davies further contends that this composition is the only musical work to be appreciated when listening to the fifth track of *Dark Side of the Moon*. Gracyk (1996) and Kania (2006) contend that non-documentary studio tracks engage listeners with two distinct kinds of musical works. There is a representational display of the basic properties of an ordinary musical composition and there is also the studio-constructed track for playback (i.e. Edidin's categories of recordings of compositions and recording artifacts, respectively).

Against Davies, there is no reason to fabricate a special type of composition for the songs on *Dark Side of the Moon*, nor two types of performance – live and studio. If works for playback by Schaeffer and Babbitt are independent musical works, then so is *Dark Side of the Moon*. We do not require a special ontological category of musical composition for such music. We need only distinguish between three distinct modes of providing access to performable compositions: (1) real-time performance instantiations, (2) recordings of such performances, and (3) studio-constructed representations. Thus Pink Floyd's song cycle can be heard – and differently appreciated – in its performances, in documentary recordings of its real-time performances, and in the recording of the composition that is *Dark Side of the Moon*.

Repeatability and transparency

Christy Mag Uidhir (2007) notes that sound recordings do not necessarily provide repeatable playbacks, for they might play back from a source that can only be used once. However, the recording technologies that interest us here were developed in such a way that complex sound sequences can be preserved and then repeated. Sound recordings are templates for generating multiple aural instances, and they can function as representations of other sound events, just as photography developed multiple-instance representations (Davies 2001: 318–19).

In grounding categories of musical recordings in distinct representational relationships to musical compositions and their performances, we have suggested that the mere activity of listening can be insufficient for determining which sort of recording one is hearing. Listening to Glenn Gould or Pink Floyd, a listener might confuse a recording of a composition with a recording of a performance, and so might admire Gould's precision and Pink Floyd's ensemble interaction on false grounds, the way that a naïve film viewer might attribute the feats of the stunt double to the leading man. Therefore recordings of compositions are sometimes viewed with suspicion as detrimental to musical culture (Gracyk 1997). Lee B. Brown (1996) and Davies (2001) worry that a musical culture centered on recordings will desensitize listeners to music's interactive and performative aspects. Recordings undermine the social practice of performing music, because their repeatability counterbalances their documentary function: "the music stands in an adverse relationship with the calcifying medium with which we document it" (Brown 2000: 122). Furthermore, Brown worries that the technology has a destructive effect on improvisational music, particularly jazz, because it encourages audiences to treat non-repeatable performances as repeatable, re-identifiable compositions (Brown 1996).

The underlying issues involve the evaluative appreciation of music. There is concern that an audience for recordings will form improper expectations for performances, and so will improperly evaluate both performances and undoctored recordings of performances. (These worries are distinct from concerns about auditory degradation, which will be taken up in relation to the issue of transparency.) Such concerns are partially mitigated by noting that audiences bear some burden of responsibility for understanding that different recordings "promote different values" depending on the functional intentions behind their production (Davies 2001: 317). Furthermore, even if recordings do mislead some listeners, they provide many compensatory advantages, such as ease of access to multiple interpretations of the same composition (Gracyk 1997).

While there are important gains in being able to compare Gould's 1955, 1959, and 1981 recordings of the *Goldberg Variations*, and to compare these in turn to Murray Perahia's more recent interpretation, we may remain concerned that all sound recordings lack documentary transparency. Recordings are sonically inadequate to provide the timbral musical nuances that can be heard in a good performance venue. Furthermore, recordings are never stylistically neutral; all recordings of performances introduce some degree of sonic departure from the sound of the documented performances (Gracyk 1997; Hamilton 2003). Against this view, Joshua Glasgow argues that "transparent" recordings are possible. At least some parts of some recordings are qualitatively identical with their sources (Glasgow 2007). While such transparency is not always desirable, Glasgow defends its possibility.

Glasgow's emphasis on sonic accuracy appears to miss the point, developed by Gracyk (1996) and Kania (2009), that transparency is fundamentally an ontological issue. Even allowing for the possibility of recordings that sound just like their sonic sources, does a documentary recording actually permit someone to hear the music? Albrecht Dürer's self-portrait of 1500 may look very much like him, yet one does not literally see Dürer by looking at it. Paintings are not transparent. Glass windows, in contrast, are transparent. In 1500, someone could look through a window and see Dürer on the other side, and the viewer would see him even if the glass was uneven and thus produced distortions in how he looked. Kendall Walton (1984) has argued that photographs are similarly transparent, for they allow us to see (albeit indirectly, and with certain distortions) the actual things that are photographed. Can recordings of performances do the same with music? Do we literally see and hear Judy Garland sing "Over the Rainbow" when we watch *The Wizard of Oz* (1939)?

If sound recordings are transparent in this sense, then recordings of compositions are worrisome entities. Listening to Gould's 1981 Goldberg recording, we cannot hear how many recording "takes" were needed, how many partial performances were spliced together, and how many days of performing were involved to produce the thirty-two musical segments. Therefore it is not possible to evaluate Gould's playing, for we cannot determine his capacity to produce those sounds in the manner Bach intended, that is, by playing them consecutively at one sitting. The "distortion" here is not a matter of sonic fidelity. The distortion comes in a listener's inability to keep track of what performance activity is transparently heard as the music moves forward, instant to instant. Combined with the fact that sonic fidelity is more an ideal than a practice, the merits of transparency are frequently at odds with the effects of studio manipulation and sonic infidelity (though see Kania (2009: 32) for an attempt at resolving this tension).

Conclusion

Musical performances and recordings are all alike in being essentially aimed at providing listeners with musical experiences. But this broad commonality masks a host of differences both between and within each category. Musical performances differ in their nature and aims. Some musical recordings are aimed at replicating the experience of one or another kind of performance. But other recordings are works of art in their own right, to which, in fact, some performances may bear a derivative relation. Philosophers and other theorists of music, particularly those interested in the listener's musical experience, ought not to ignore such matters.

See also Authentic performance practice (Chapter 9), Improvisation (Chapter 6), Jazz (Chapter 39), Ontology (Chapter 4), Popular music (Chapter 37), Rock (Chapter 38), and Song (Chapter 40).

References

Adorno, T. (2002 [1938]) "On the Fetish-Character in Music and the Regression of Listening," in *Essays on Music*, ed. R. Leppert, Berkeley: University of California Press, pp. 288–317.

Benjamin, W. (1968 [1936]) "The Work of Art in the Age of Mechanical Reproduction," in *Illuminations: Essays and Reflections*, ed. H. Arendt, trans. H. Zohn, New York: Harcourt, Brace and World, pp. 219–53.

Brown, L.B. (1996) "Phonography," in D. Goldblatt and L.B. Brown (eds) *Aesthetics: A Reader in Philosophy of the Arts*, Upper Saddle River: Prentice Hall, pp. 252–7.

—— (2000) "'Feeling My Way': Jazz Improvisation and its Vicissitudes – A Plea for Imperfection," *Journal of Aesthetics and Art Criticism* 58: 113–23.

Davies, S. (2001) *Musical Works and Performances: A Philosophical Exploration*, Oxford: Clarendon Press.

Doyle, A.C. (1921) "The Adventure of the Mazarin Stone," *Strand Magazine* 62 (October): 288–98.

Edidin, A. (1999) "Three Kinds of Recording and the Metaphysics of Music," *British Journal of Aesthetics* 39: 24–39.

Fisher, J.A. (1998) "Rock 'n' Recording: The Ontological Complexity of Rock Music," in P. Alperson (ed.) *Musical Worlds: New Directions in the Philosophy of Music*, University Park: The Pennsylvania State University Press, pp. 109–23.

Glasgow, J. (2007) "Hi-Fi Aesthetics," *Journal of Aesthetics and Art Criticism* 65: 163–74.

Godlovitch, S. (1998) *Musical Performance: A Philosophical Study*, New York: Routledge.

Gracyk, T. (1996) *Rhythm and Noise: An Aesthetics of Rock*, Durham: Duke University Press.

—— (1997) "Listening to Music: Performances and Recordings," *Journal of Aesthetics and Art Criticism* 55: 139–50.

Hamilton, A. (2003) "The Art of Recording and the Aesthetics of Perfection," *British Journal of Aesthetics* 43: 345–62.

Kania, A. (2006) "Making Tracks: The Ontology of Rock Music," *Journal of Aesthetics and Art Criticism* 64: 401–14.

—— (2008) "Piece for the End of Time: In Defense of Musical Ontology," *British Journal of Aesthetics* 48: 65–79.

—— (2009) "Musical Recordings," *Philosophy Compass* 4: 22–38.

Levinson, J. (1990a) "Evaluating Musical Performance," in *Music, Art, and Metaphysics*, Ithaca: Cornell University Press, pp. 376–92.

—— (1990b) "Music and Negative Emotion," in *Music, Art, and Metaphysics*, Ithaca: Cornell University Press, pp. 306–35.

Mag Uidhir, C. (2007) "Recordings as Performances," *British Journal of Aesthetics* 47: 298–314.

Mark, T.C. (1980) "On Works of Virtuosity," *Journal of Philosophy* 77: 28–45.

Thom, P. (1993) *For an Audience: A Philosophy of the Performing Arts*, Philadelphia: Temple University Press.

Walton, K.L. (1984) "Transparent Pictures: On the Nature of Photographic Realism," *Critical Inquiry* 11: 246–77.

Zak, A. (2001) *The Poetics of Rock: Cutting Tracks, Making Records*, Berkeley: University of California Press.

Further reading

Davies, D. (forthcoming) *The Performing Arts*, Malden: Blackwell. (An excellent introduction to a range of philosophical issues raised by the performing arts.)

Day, T. (2000) *A Century of Recorded Music: Listening to Musical History*, New Haven: Yale University Press. (An extended exploration of the impact of recording technology on performance practices, particularly in classical music.)

Doğantan-Dack, M. (ed.) (2008) *Recorded Music: Philosophical and Critical Reflections*, London: Middlesex University Press. (A strong collection of essays on recorded music.)

Eisenberg, E. (1987) *The Recording Angel: Explorations in Phonography*, New York: McGraw-Hill. (Essays on recorded music, whose themes were taken up by Lee B. Brown and Theodore Gracyk, among others.)

Katz, M. (2004) *Capturing Sound: How Technology Has Changed Music*, Berkeley: University of California Press. (Trained in both philosophy and musicology, Katz covers some of the same material as Day but extends the discussion by speculating on the impact of digital technology.)

Philip, R. (2004) *Performing Music in the Age of Recording*, New Haven: Yale University Press. (Focusing on classical music, includes an interesting essay on "authenticity" and the Early Music Movement of the twentieth century.)

9

AUTHENTIC PERFORMANCE PRACTICE

Paul Thom

Performance practice, as an academic discipline, is the evidence-based study of the performance of music and other arts at particular historical periods. Types of evidence include actual performance spaces and artifacts, designs and depictions of them, along with theoretical or practical treatises and critical writings. The relationships studied include the conventions for understanding written notations and the context of practices within which instructions for performance were used (Brown et al. 2001).

If the authentic may be defined as that which truly is what it purports to be, then the question of authenticity can be raised in relation to anything that purports to be anything. The term "authentic performance practice" commonly refers to a particular practical approach that is found in the performing arts, one that purports to apply results derived from the academic discipline of performance practice. The question of what practices are authentic arises in all the performing arts (Young 2005: 501); but this chapter will focus on music.

The 1960s saw the rise of certain practices in the performance of Western classical music that claimed the status of authentic performance practice. These practices were generally known under the title of the Early Music Movement – and initially they did have something of the character of a protest movement (Haynes 2007: 41). The movement arose as a reaction against the ways in which music of the seventeenth and early eighteenth centuries had been played in the first half of the twentieth century, when it was given in concert performance on modern instruments, often in arrangements adapted to the sonority of those instruments or in creative transcriptions. These ways of playing music from earlier times left some practitioners feeling aesthetically dissatisfied, and they began looking for alternative ways of playing the music (Young 2005: 501). They quickly found that the music sounded very different when played on the kind of instruments for which it had originally been conceived. Inspired by initial successes, enthusiasts extended this general approach to the music of the Classical and Romantic periods.

Present-day advocates of authentic performance practice are reluctant to use the term "authentic" and the label "Early Music Movement," preferring the banner "Historically informed/inspired performance, or HIP" (Haynes 2007). James O. Young conjectures that this reluctance is the product of two considerations. On the one hand, practitioners in pursuit of authenticity may have become concerned that the goal was unachievable (though Young himself thinks that such a concern would be misplaced). On the other hand, the practitioners may have become increasingly aware that what they were doing was actually falling short of the ideal authenticity that they espoused (Young 2005: 510).

Thanks to the movement's commercial success, support for the pursuit of authenticity has grown in some quarters, as has hostility in others. Arguably, the practices against which the Early Music Movement reacted occurred, and achieved success with audiences, only because the original instrumental specifications for this music had been forgotten, or (where they were known) performers and audiences felt free to disregard them. In other words, the original prescriptions for the performance of this music had to some extent lost their authority: they no longer commanded respect. Thus authentic performance practice can be seen through a political lens as a restoration of lost authority – which may explain why it excites both partisanship and hostility.

There are two main areas of philosophical interest concerning authentic performance practice. First, there are philosophical analyses of various concepts that have been claimed to play a guiding role in these practices. Second, there are questions of ideology and value: to what extent have various concepts of authenticity actually played a role in performance practice, and what has been the value that authentic performance practice has contributed to contemporary culture?

Conceptual analysis

One can distinguish two broad classes of meaning that the word "authenticity" carries in relation to performance. In the first class of meanings, authenticity is judged in relation to a musical work, its sounds, or the intentions behind it. In the other class of meanings, authenticity is judged in relation to a person or culture.

Works

For Stephen Davies, authenticity concerns fidelity to works. "Authenticity is a matter of ontology rather than interpretation. An ideally authentic instance of a musical work is one that faithfully reproduces the work's constitutive properties," that is, one in which the performers successfully follow the work-determinative instructions of the composer (Davies 2001: 212–13, 227). He understands these instructions to go beyond what is explicitly notated in scores of the work, but to include only what is relevant to the work itself and not merely social conventions. In order to find out what a work's constitutive properties are, therefore, we may need to make use of the academic discipline of performance practice.

When Davies says that ideal authenticity is not a matter of interpretation, he does not mean to deny that in preparing a performance aiming at authenticity one has to interpret various things. In applying the discipline of performance practice to a particular planned performance, performers inevitably have to interpret the evidence on which they rely, just as they inevitably have to interpret the scores they use. Nor does he mean to deny that someone may choose to perform a work with less than ideal authenticity; for example, by making cuts or other alterations or additions by way of interpreting what is contained in the work. He is saying that to deliver an ideally authentic performance of the work (i.e. a performance that at least reproduces all of the work's constitutive properties), as such, is not to make a performative interpretation of the work: it is simply to perform the work in the prescribed way.

Doing what is required by the work's determinative prescriptions does not mean doing nothing else. In particular, it does not exclude the practice of performative interpretation whereby performers bring to their realization of the work their own individual ways of executing what the work prescribes, or their own ways of supplementing what the work prescribes, without coming into conflict with the work's requirements. So, authenticity in Davies's sense is not incompatible with performative interpretation (Davies and Sadie 2001). But Davies expressly claims that what is authentic about a performance and what is interpretive about it are disjoint classes (Davies 2001: 209). Against this, some philosophers argue that authenticity itself is an interpretive choice – one among many. Both sides are right, relative to different objects of interpretation. A *score* admits of authentic or non-authentic interpretations; a *work* does not, according to Davies.

It follows from Davies's analysis that authenticity is a relative concept. For example, a performance might be authentic relative to the work's explicit prescriptions but not authentic relative to what is merely implicit. It also follows that authenticity is a matter of degree: performances may be better or worse approximations to what the work prescribes (Young 2005: 503).

Davies's account rests on an analysis of works for performance as prescriptions for performance. If works for performance were simply abstract sound-structures, an authentic performance would be nothing more than one that produces the right sounds. Davies's account also assumes a distinction among the prescriptions constituting a work between those that are determinative and those that are merely recommendatory. Such a distinction is actually drawn by editors and practitioners in relation to musical scores (Davies 2001: 94). Sometimes the score explicitly warrants such a distinction; for example, a passage is marked *ossia*, or the critical apparatus shows a traditional cut or addition as an alternative to the main text. But sometimes the score itself gives no such explicit indication. The score may contain fingerings, dynamics or phrasings without any explicit indication that they are merely recommendatory, and in some cases a critical edition of a score may show that these markings derive from the composer. Davies takes markings in these classes to be merely recommendatory even if they are sanctioned by the composer. He gives the imaginary example of a score in which the composer instructs that the work be performed only once; he observes that such an instruction would not be regarded as legitimate and thus could only be considered as a recommendation. The basis for the distinction, he says, lies in the conventions governing the score and the performance practices contemporaneous with the score (Davies 2001: 106, 141, 147). But, we do not always know exactly where to draw the boundary between a score's determinative and merely advisory prescriptions.

Davies is perfectly consistent in denying any overlap between interpretation and authentic performance. But in order to arrive at a view of a work's identity, much interpretation will be needed. Moreover, in the absence of decisive evidence from the discipline of performance practice, we may never be able to form a soundly based view of the work's identity.

Intentions or sounds

Some philosophers explicate the issue of authenticity in terms of fidelity to the intentions of the composer, or to the sounds of performances at the time of composition (Young 2005: 503).

To define authentic performance practice as compliance with the composer's intentions is too broad, since composers have intentions that are not relevant to performance practice, as in the example just mentioned. Arguably, however, the composer's *relevant* intentions comprise the determinative prescriptions that are enshrined in the work, plus whatever else the composer can be assumed to intend because it was an accepted convention or assumed practice at the time. But with this revision, the definition in terms of intentions takes us back to a Davies-style definition in terms of the work.

The Early Music Movement achieved widespread uptake in the recording industry, and this has led some critics to assume that authentic performance practice is simply an attempt to recreate sounds from the past. Charles Rosen regards the Early Music Movement's concentration on the sound the composer would have heard as a mark of great progress because to concentrate on the notation would be to miss the point that the notation points to real performances. At the same time, he regards the concentration on the sound the composer actually heard as a regression because "many composers write partly with the hope of an ideal performance which transcends the pitiable means and degenerate practice they have to compromise with" (Rosen 2000: 206–13).

To define authenticity in terms of the re-creation of sounds that occurred at the time of the work's early performances could be understood either in terms of the types of sound waves or in terms of the types of auditory experience that are presumed to have occurred at the time of those early performances. We may thus distinguish "sonic" from "sensible" authenticity (Kivy 1995: 48–50). Sensible authenticity may not be attainable given that our experience of music is shaped by experiences that earlier audiences could not have had (Young 2005: 505). Sensible authenticity may be undesirable for similar reasons as sonic authenticity: the experience of early audiences of, say, Beethoven may not be worth reliving if those audiences did not understand the music (Young 2005: 505). In either sense this definition seems too broad, since the work's early performances may not have been any good. It seems better, with Davies, to talk about the original *kind* of sound under optimal conditions. But arguably, the optimal sound will be what is given in the work's determinative prescriptions understood as including background conventions and practices; so we are back with Davies's definition in terms of the work.

Personal and cultural authenticity

In his book *Authenticities* (1995), Peter Kivy devotes some analytical attention to the notion of personal authenticity, raising the question whether authenticity in this sense has anything to do with artistic performance. He argues against analyzing personal performative authenticity in terms of sincerity. Sincerity, according to him, is a feature either of emotional expression or of statements; but, he says, it is not a virtue in a performance to be an emotional expression, and performances do not make statements. Generally speaking, what he says here is true of the performance of classical instrumental music.

On the other hand, Jeanette Bicknell raises the question whether it is true of the performance of popular songs, asking "Would we not be disappointed if we learned that Paul Robeson regarded 'Go Down, Moses' as just a song?" (Bicknell 2005: 261). To deliver a performance that is authentic, in the sense that the feelings it expresses are sincerely felt by the performer, does not in itself amount to authentic performance practice. There may be no determinative prescription explicit or implicit in a work that mandates genuine feeling in the performer. Still, in certain cases there may be such a determinative prescription. Arguably, this is so in the case Bicknell cites, to the extent that the song "Go Down, Moses" is widely understood to implicitly prescribe a genuinely heartfelt performance.

Some writers on popular culture claim to see personal *inauthenticity* as playing a defining role for some performers. Hugh Barker and Yuval Taylor characterize Elvis Presley's voice as an "inimitable combination of playfulness, arrogance, and desire" (2007: 148). This highly crafted mixture, they argue, actually precluded personal authenticity: "In order to make arrogance and desire palatable to American listeners, they could not be genuine; moreover, it's difficult to be simultaneously earnest and playful" (148). In general, they argue, "rock'n'roll was at its core self-consciously inauthentic music" because it "spoke of self-invention" (149). They draw a more general conclusion:

> Music can be great to listen to exactly because it is heartfelt, emotional, honest, personally or culturally revealing, and so on. It's just that when we aggregate all these into an ideal of authenticity we can lose sight of the fact that some of the things that make us judge music as inauthentic – such as theatricality, glamour, absurdity, pointlessness, and cultural cross-pollination – can also enrich our musical experience considerably.
>
> (Barker and Taylor 2007: 336)

Or, as Theodore Gracyk puts it, "it is also important to celebrate artists whose musical performances are unlikely to be taken as authentic expressions of the singer: we need both the Bruce Springsteen model of utter sincerity and the David Bowie model of ironic play-acting" (Gracyk 2001: 216). But the quality that Bicknell expects in Robeson is not the same as the quality Barker and Taylor find in Presley. Whereas the issue there concerned Robeson's personal beliefs and desires, it is not Elvis's personal beliefs and desires that are in question but those of his performing persona. In other words, the question concerns what feelings and beliefs are consistently represented in his performances.

Here, one can ask whether this kind of inauthenticity in the performer's persona amounts to authentic performance practice on the part of the performer! The suggestion is not that this is so as a general rule: in general there is no reason to assume that a work prescribes the projection of inauthenticity in the sense described. But in certain cases there may be such a determinative prescription. Arguably, this is so in the case of certain songs that Presley sings.

Kivy prefers to conceive of personal authenticity neither in terms of the performer's genuine feelings nor in terms of the projected feelings of the performer's persona but in terms of the achievement of a personal style and originality in performance (1995: 100–23). He argues that personal authenticity in this sense is quite compatible with authenticity regarding the composer's intentions. (We may add that it is compatible with work-authenticity, though it does not entail it.) But Kivy believes that personal authenticity in his sense (i.e. the development of a personal performing style) is incompatible with sonic authenticity (1995: 138–41).

This seems wrong: there is no good reason to believe that the pursuit of an authentic sound cannot be combined with the development of a performing style that is distinctive in comparison with the style of other performers who also pursue authenticity of sound. There seems to be plenty of evidence that some musicians pursuing sonic authenticity simultaneously aim at (and sometimes achieve) an original personal style. Think of the highly individual lute-styles of Hopkinson Smith and Paul O'Dette, both of whom pursue sonic authenticity. Any aim at all can take an all-consuming form and thus its actualization may become incompatible with the actualization of other aims. This is true even of personal authenticity in Kivy's sense. In some of Glenn Gould's more extreme performances, personal style is pursued to the exclusion of respecting the composer's intentions. There is no necessary incompatibility between work authenticity and an individual personal performing style (Young 2005: 503).

The question of cultural authenticity in performance practice concerns the extent to which a performance practice truly reflects cultural values that it purports to reflect (Davies 2001: 202). Here, as with personal authenticity, one can distinguish the values a culture represents itself as having from those that it actually has; and correspondingly there will be two types of cultural authenticity in performance.

Ideology

Do any of these philosophical concepts of authentic performance practice accurately match the expressed or implicit aims of practitioners?

Bruce Haynes has been a distinguished practitioner, and as such is able to give an insider's view of the Early Music Movement. In recounting its history, Haynes shows that in the 1960s practitioners had an ideology of replication: makers of authentic instruments wanted to replicate the original instruments they were copying, and the performers wanted to replicate early performances (Haynes 2007: 140–1). An ideology of replication leaves no room for interpretation; and yet interpretation is a necessity, in instrument-building as much as in performance. Richard Taruskin had already pointed to the influence of Modernist style on "period" performances from the 1960s (Taruskin 1995: 136, 168). He had talked about the "straight" style, and he had decried the Early Music Movement as "a branch office of modernism" (Taruskin 1995: 13). Haynes acknowledges these criticisms.

But as time passed, musicians proposed "the performance of a piece in the *style* of its original time" (Haynes 2007: 75), thus acknowledging the necessity for interpretation in playing old music. Haynes contrasts both Romantic and Modern styles with what he calls Rhetorical style. Haynes gives rich descriptions of Romantic, Modern, and Rhetorical styles. The Modern style is characterized by its continuous vibrato, general uniformity of tempo, and its avoidance of individual expression; it is calculated to provide the listener with clear access to the work being performed. Characteristic of the Romantic style is the use of portamento, rubato, sentimentality, and uniform solemnity; here, it is harder for the listener to detach the work performed from its performative interpretation. The Rhetorical style invokes rhetorical techniques and concepts in an attempt to make the music "speak" with the accents of human utterances (Haynes 2007: 165–84). The use of the Rhetorical style provided performers with ways of introducing expression into their performances, thus escaping from the grip of the Modern style in which many of them had been educated, without relapsing into the excesses of Romantic style (Haynes 2007: 48–64).

Haynes quotes Nikolaus Harnoncourt's sleeve-notes to his 1967 recording of Bach's *St John Passion*, which portray Harnoncourt's pioneering efforts as initiating "a process at the end of which stands a performance corresponding to the circumstances at the time of composition in every respect." This can be read as an overblown description of an actual performance located at some distant time in the future; but it is probably better to read it (with Haynes) as an expression of 1960s idealism (Haynes 2007: 45).

By and large, the ideologies propounded by practitioners of authentic performance do not withstand philosophical scrutiny. An ideology of replication all too readily invites the criticism that authenticists are foreswearing any ambition to develop a personal style. And Harnoncourt's vision of a future performance that resembles bygone performances in every respect raises the question of why anyone would want to repeat past fiascos. And yet, it would be churlish to hold against Monteverdi that in his *Orfeo* he failed to achieve the revival of the Greek theatre. Equally one should not complain against the cultural achievements of those pursuing the reinvigoration of historical performing styles that they have sometimes wildly overstated their case. It is not in their attempt to articulate their aims, but in their actual achievements that HIP's contributions to culture reside.

One could even agree with Charles Rosen's judgment when he finds, on the one hand, that the ideologies (he calls them philosophies) propounded by Early Music practitioners are indefensible while, on the other, he lauds their artistic successes. Rosen goes on to claim, paradoxically, that these successes have been achieved because of the flawed philosophy: "it has been by taking the indefensible ideal of authenticity seriously that our knowledge has been increased and our musical life enriched" (Rosen 2000: 221). The paradox can be resolved by remembering that it is not the function of ideologies to be good philosophy; their function is to inspire action.

Value

What, then, has been the value that authentic performance practice has contributed to contemporary culture?

First of all, performance is a practical matter. The pursuit of authenticity in performance has turned out to be of practical value to performing artists. Early sources sometimes contain useful information not only about what effects are to be achieved but also about how to achieve them. As an example, Philip Gossett cites the case of nineteenth-century Italian operas, many of which are still performed today. Before the twentieth century, most operatic sets were based on painted backdrops placed at various "depths" in the stage. These could be quickly raised or lowered, facilitating the almost instantaneous scene-changes that many "period" operas demand. Gossett reports on a revival of Verdi's *Ernani* in Modena in 1984 where set and costume designs contemporaneous with the opera's first productions turned out to be a very practical way of making the scene changes more effective (Gossett 2006: 466–76).

But performance is an aesthetic matter, too. Seeing that the original motivation for the Early Music Movement was an *aesthetic* one, the movement's success or failure ought to be judged, as Rosen implies, on aesthetic grounds. The painted backdrops that Gossett talks about could be things of great beauty, and it is in its contribution to the aesthetic experience of the contemporary world that the pursuit of authenticity has had its biggest impact. Authentic performances, at their best, have distinctive aesthetic qualities (though this is not to say that non-authentic performances of the same works do not also have their own distinctive aesthetic qualities). These qualities derive from a number of sources. First, there is the artistry of a small group of performers – true virtuosi of the Baroque violin, cello, natural trumpet, and many other "early" instruments. Then there is the singular sonority of these instruments. Finally, there are the unique aesthetic qualities of the works performed, revealed afresh. Indeed, the widespread success of authentic performance practice, in performance and through recordings, is indicative of the fact that a new musical aesthetic now stands alongside traditional performance practice. And while some audiences find one of these aesthetics musically rewarding to the exclusion of the other (some preferring their Beethoven on modern instruments, while others prefer period instruments), many listeners have found that their aesthetic experience has been enriched by the appreciation of both.

See also Appropriation and hybridity (Chapter 17), Improvisation (Chapter 6), Instrumental technology (Chapter 18), Notations (Chapter 7), Ontology (Chapter 4), Opera (Chapter 41), Performances and recordings (Chapter 8), and Style (Chapter 13).

References

Barker, H. and Taylor, Y. (2007) *Faking it: The Quest for Authenticity in Popular Music*, New York: Norton.

Bicknell, J. (2005) "Just a Song? Exploring the Aesthetics of Popular Song Performance," *Journal of Aesthetics and Art Criticism* 63: 261–70.

Brown, H.M. et al. (2001) "Performing Practice," in S. Sadie (ed.) *The New Grove Dictionary of Music and Musicians*, 2nd edn, vol. 19, London: Macmillan, pp. 349–88.

Davies, S. (2001) *Musical Works and Performances: A Philosophical Exploration*, Oxford: Clarendon Press.

Davies, S. and Sadie, S. (2001) "Interpretation," in S. Sadie (ed.) *The New Grove Dictionary of Music and Musicians*, 2nd edn, vol. 12, London: Macmillan, pp. 497–9.

Gossett, P. (2006) *Divas and Scholars: Performing Italian Opera*, Chicago: University of Chicago Press.

Gracyk, T. (2001) *I Wanna Be Me: Rock Music and the Politics of Identity*, Philadelphia: Temple University Press.

Haynes, B. (2007) *The End of Early Music: A Period Performer's History of Music for the Twenty-first Century*, New York: Oxford University Press.

Kivy, P. (1995) *Authenticities: Philosophical Reflections on Musical Performance*, Ithaca: Cornell University Press.

Rosen, C. (2000) *Critical Entertainments: Music Old and New*, Cambridge: Harvard University Press.

Taruskin, R. (1995) *Text and Act: Essays on Music and Performance*, Oxford: Oxford University Press.

Young, J.O. (2005) "Authenticity in Performance," in B. Gaut and D. Lopes (eds) *The Routledge Companion to Aesthetics*, 2nd edn, London: Routledge, pp. 501–12.

10

MUSIC AND LANGUAGE

Ray Jackendoff

Formulating the issues

A fundamental question that has animated a great deal of thought and research over the years is: What does music share with language that makes them distinct from other human activities?

This question emphasizes similarities between language and music (see, for example, Patel 2008), sometimes leading to a belief that they are (almost) the same thing. For instance, the prospectus for a 2008 conference in Dijon entitled "Musique Langage Cerveau" ("Music Language Brain") states: "The similarities between these two activities are therefore not superficial: music and language could be two expressions of the same competence for human communication" (my translation). However, the divergences between music and language are also quite striking. So we should also ask:

- How are language and music different?
- Insofar as language and music are the same, are they distinct from other human activities?

The emphasis of this chapter will be on these latter two questions.

These questions are sharpened by the "Chomskyan turn" in linguistics, which focuses on how language is instantiated in speakers' minds, such that they can produce and understand utterances in unlimited profusion, and on how speakers acquire this ability. Lerdahl and Jackendoff's *A Generative Theory of Tonal Music* (GTTM, 1983) advocates a similar approach to music: its central issue is what constitutes musical understanding, such that individuals can understand an unlimited number of pieces of music in a style with which they are experienced, and how individuals acquire fluency in a musical style through experience.

Through this lens, music and language can be compared in the following terms:

- Every normal individual has knowledge of language and music.
- Everyone learns the local variant(s) of both language and music. Normal adults achieve full linguistic competence, but are more variable in musical ability, depending on exposure and talent.

Then the important question becomes: What cognitive capacities are involved in acquiring and using a language, and what capacities are involved in acquiring and using a musical idiom? The question is the same for both capacities, but this does not mean the *answer* is the same.

The issue of particular interest here is: What cognitive capacities are shared by language and music, but not by other cognitive domains?

Similar issues arise with other human capacities; for example, the capacity for social and cultural interaction (Jackendoff 2007). Like languages and musical idioms, cultures differ widely, and an individual's ability to function in a culture requires considerable learning and the use of multiple cognitive capacities. Moreover, the use of language and music is embedded in social and cultural interaction, but that does not entail that the capacity for either language or music is simply a subset of the social/cultural capacity.

A major dispute in the theory of language, of course, is how much of the language acquisition capacity is special-purpose. Many people (e.g. Christiansen and Chater 2008; Tomasello 2003) think that language is acquired through general-purpose learning plus abilities for social interaction. This view is explicitly in opposition to the claims made by generative grammarians up to the late 1990s to the effect that there must be a rich innate language-specific Universal Grammar (Chomsky 1965, 1981). In between these two extremes are all manner of intermediate views (Hauser, Chomsky, and Fitch 2002; Jackendoff 2002; Pinker and Jackendoff 2005).

The parallel issue in music cognition and acquisition arouses less vehement dispute, partly because claims for an innate music capacity have been less highly politicized – and partly because claims that music is an adaptation favored by natural selection are considerably weaker than those for language. At one extreme we find Pinker's hypothesis that music is "auditory cheesecake," constructed adventitiously from parts of other capacities (1997: 534); at the other might be the fairly rich claims of GTTM. In between is, for example, Patel's view that music is a social construction, but that the capacity for pitch discrimination and formation of tonally oriented scales is nevertheless specific to music (2008).

General capacities shared by language and music

Some similarities between language and music are easily enumerated.

- Although many animals have communication systems, no non-humans have language or music in the human sense, and there are no obvious evolutionary precursors for either in non-human primates.

- Language and music both involve sound production (although notice that language also exists in the signed modality and music does not).
- Every culture has a local variant of language, and every culture has a local variant of music. The differences among local variants are, moreover, quite striking; this contrasts with other species, whose communication systems show very limited variation at best.
- In every culture (I believe), language and music can be combined in song.

Looking more cognitively, the acquisition and processing of both language and music call for certain capacities that are shared with other cognitive domains. Here are seven.

First, both language and music require substantial memory capacity for storing representations – words in language (tens of thousands) and recognizable melodies in music (number unknown; my informal estimate easily runs into the thousands). But this is not specific to music and language. Massive storage is also necessary for encoding the appearance of familiar objects, the detailed geography of one's environment, the actions appropriate to thousands of kinds of artifacts (Jackendoff 2007: ch. 4), and one's interactions with thousands of people – not just what they look like but also their personalities and their roles in one's social milieu (Jackendoff 2007: ch. 5).

Second, in order for novel stimuli to be perceived and comprehended, both language and music require the ability to integrate stored representations combinatorially in working memory by means of a system of rules or structural schemata. Again, this characteristic is not specific to language and music. Understanding a complex visual environment requires a capacity to integrate multiple objects into a structured scene; and creating a plan for complex action requires hierarchical integration of more elementary action schemata, in many cases bringing in complex social information as well. (See Jackendoff and Pinker 2005, who argue against Hauser, Chomsky, and Fitch's (2002) hypothesis that the use of recursion is what makes language unique. All cognitive capacities of any complexity have recursion.)

Third (as stressed by Patel (2008)), the processing of both language and music involves creating expectations of what is to come. But visual perception involves expectation, too: if we see a car heading for a tree, we expect a crash.

Fourth, producing both language and music requires fine-scale voluntary control of vocal production. No other faculties place similar demands on vocal production per se. However, voluntary control of vocal production is plausibly a cognitive extension of our species' enhanced voluntary control of the hands, crucial for tool-making and tool use (Calvin 1990; Wilkins 2005), not to mention for signed language and playing musical instruments.

Fifth, learning to produce both language and music relies on an ability – and desire – to imitate others' vocal production. In the case of music, one may imitate other sound-producing actions as well (e.g. drumming, birdsong). This ability to incorporate others' inventions enables both language and music to build a culturally shared repertoire of words and songs. However, this is not specific to language and music either: the richness of human culture is a consequence of the ability to imitate and integrate others' actions (not just others' words) into one's own repertoire.

Sixth, there must be some individuals who can invent new items – words or tunes – that others can imitate. This too extends to cultural practices, be they tools, food, types of clothing, or praxis (customs, trade, games, rituals, etc.).

Seventh, individuals must be able to engage in jointly intended actions – actions understood not just as me doing *this* and you doing *that*, but as us two doing something *together*, each with a particular role (Bratman 1999; Gilbert 1989; Searle 1995). This ability lies behind the human ability for widespread cooperation (Boyd and Richerson 2005; Tomasello et al. 2005), and it is necessary in language use for holding conversations (Clark 1996) and in music for any sort of group singing, playing, dancing, or performing for an audience.

The only capacity on this list not shared with other domains is fine-scale voluntary vocal production, which of course is not necessary for either signed languages or instrumental music. Other primates arguably possess the first three – large-scale memory, combinatoriality, and expectation – though not in their communication systems. The last three – imitation, innovation, and joint action – are not shared with other primates, but are generally necessary for all sorts of cultural cognition and culturally guided action. The point is that these general abilities alone do not specifically determine the form of either language or music.

Differences in ecological function

One fundamental difference between language and music concerns their ecological functions in human life. In brief, language conveys propositional thought, and music enhances affect. (I prefer the broader term *affect* to the more usual *emotion*; see Jackendoff and Lerdahl 2006.) Although this point is hardly new, it is worth expanding in order to make clear the extent of the difference.

Language is essentially a mapping between sound and "propositional" or "conceptual" thought. The messages it conveys can be about people, objects, places, actions, or any manner of abstraction. Language can convey information about the past and the future, visible and invisible things, and what is *not* the case. Linguistic utterances can be used to offer information, make requests for action, ask questions, give instructions and orders, negotiate, undertake obligations (including promises), assert authority, and construct arguments about the differences between language and music. Linguistic messages distinguish information taken to be new to the hearer ("focus") from information taken to be shared with the hearer ("common ground"), and they can incorporate social distinctions between speaker and hearer (as in French *tu* versus *vous* or Japanese honorifics). The gist of a linguistic utterance can be translated from any language into any other, given appropriate vocabulary.

Music can satisfy none of these functions. In particular, linguistic utterances cannot be translated into music. (Even if various drumming and whistling languages use media more commonly deployed for musical purposes, they are codes for language and are not forms of music.)

Consider now the functions of music. Probably furthest from its evolutionary roots are the uses in which people sit and passively listen to a performance. Many different uses of music in traditional cultures have been proposed as the original adaptive function of music (see, for example, the essays in Wallin, Merker, and Brown 2000), but actual evidence is scanty. What the different uses of music have in common is the enhancement of affect associated with an activity. If this is considered "musical meaning" (e.g. Raffman 1993), it still bears no relation to "propositional" linguistic meaning.

In some sorts of music, one person directs music at another: lullabies convey a sense of soothing intimacy; love songs convey affection and passion; ballads convey the emotional impact of a story. Other sorts of music are meant to be sung or played together. Work songs convey the coordinated rhythm of work and the affect of coordinated action. Marches convey the coordinated action of walking, often militaristically or ceremonially. Religious music conveys transcendence and spirituality, with affect anywhere from meditative to frenzied. Dance tunes stimulate affective or expressive body movement. Songs for collective situations such as campfires and bars seem to instill a sense of fellowship. Another genre is children's songs, including nursery tunes; it is not clear to me what their function is. Still other sorts of music, such as muzak and café music, are meant to be perceived subliminally. Their function is evidently to enhance mood. This genre also includes film music, whose effects can be quite powerful. There is no comparable subliminal use of language.

Of course, language *can* be put to affective use. For instance, utterances such as "You are an idiot" and "I love you" convey affect, though in a different way from music. Language also borrows a wide range of rhetorical devices from music. Poetry (especially "folk" poetry) makes use of isochrony or strict rhythm, which brings linguistic utterances closer to the metrical character of music. Poetic rhyme parallels the rhythmic patterns of harmonic/melodic expectation in music (Lerdahl 2003). Poetry's appeal – even to children – partly comes from the affect of such rhythmic patterning. Similarly, call and response patterns (as in certain styles of preaching) evoke strong affect, paralleling the experience of choral singing. More generally, combinations of music and language are ubiquitous – in song, where language follows musical rhythms, in chant (e.g. recitative), where melody follows speech rhythms, and in rap, where words without melody follow musical rhythms. Lerdahl (2003) suggests that these are all hybrids: poetry is the result of superimposing musical principles on linguistic utterances. Thus poetic form conveys affect because it invokes principles of *musical* perception that are not normally associated with language.

Interestingly, poetry in signed languages makes use of alliteration (such as deliberate choice of parallel handshapes), rhythmic patterning, and – unlike spoken poetry – counterpoint (overlapping of signs) (Klima and Bellugi 1979: 340–72). Again, arguably musical types of structure are superimposed on language.

Language and music also both convey affect through tone of voice. However, this does not show that the two capacities are the same: they have each incorporated some of the character of mammalian call systems. Mammalian calls *do* convey both affect (like music) and some very limited sort of conceptual information (like language). But it does not follow that language and music evolved as a single capacity that later split (Brown's (2000) "musilanguage" hypothesis). They could equally be independent evolutionary specializations of primate communication. The next section enumerates differences that favor the latter hypothesis.

To sum up this brief survey: aside from the use of tone of voice shared by language and music, and aside from the mixture of language and music in poetry, the specialization of language to conceptual information and music to affect is actually quite extreme.

Similarities and differences in formal structure

Next consider the formal devices out of which language and music are constructed.

Pitch

Unlike other cognitive capacities, both language and music involve a sequence of discrete sounds: speech sounds in language, tones or pitch events in music. This is one reason to believe they are alike. But the resemblance ends there. The repertoire of speech sounds forms a structured space of timbres that is governed by how consonants and vowels are articulated in the vocal tract. Speech sounds can also be distinguished by length (the shortest differing from the longest by a factor of two or so).

By contrast, tones in music form a structured space of *pitches* and differ over a broad range of lengths (shortest to longest differing by a factor of sixteen or more). In all traditional musical genres that use pitch, the organization of sound is built around a *tonal pitch space*, a fixed collection of pitches whose stability is determined in relation to a tonic pitch. It is well established that the structure of tonal systems is explained only in part by psychoacoustics; the rest is culture-specific (see Jackendoff and Lerdahl 2006 and references therein).

The characteristics of tonal pitch spaces are mostly not shared with language. There are a number of possible parallels. For instance, prosodic contours in language tend to go down at the end, and so do melodies. But both probably inherit this from the form of human and mammalian calls (and possibly from physiology – the drop in air pressure as the lungs are emptied). Thus this common character-istic could be the result of independent inheritance from a common ancestor.

Moreover, only melodies have discrete pitches, while prosodic contours usu-ally involve a continuous rise and fall. Of course there are mixtures. On the one hand, many vocal and instrumental traditions incorporate bending of pitches and sliding between them. And intonation (in many languages) is commonly analyzed in terms of high and low pitches anchored on prominent accents and ends of breath-groups (Pierrehumbert 1980). Thus intonation in language might be fundamentally a two-pitch tonal system, modulated by continuous transitions between the anchoring pitches. However, the high and low pitches are not fixed in frequency throughout an utterance, unlike the fixed dominant and tonic in musical pitch space. So the analogy between intonational systems and tonal pitch spaces is strained at best.

Pitch in language is also used for tone in tone languages such as Chinese and many West African languages. In such languages, the tones form a fixed set that might seem analogous to tonal pitch space. However, since the tones used are determined by the words being used, no tone can function as a tonic – the point of maximum stability at which melodies typically come to rest. Moreover, tones are superimposed on an overall intonation contour. As a breath group continues, all tones drift down, and the intervals between them get smaller (Ladd 1996) – an entirely different use of pitch than in musical pitch spaces. Finally, evidence from tone deafness and amusia (Peretz and Coltheart 2003) suggests that linguistic intonation and musical pitch are controlled by distinct brain areas.

Thus language has no convincing analogue to the musical use of pitch space, despite their making use of the same motor capacities in the vocal tract.

Rhythm

GTTM shows that phonology and music are both structured rhythmically by similar metrical systems, based on a hierarchical metrical grid. This is a parallel perhaps shared by only music and language. However, the domains use the grid differently. The minimal metrical unit in phonology is the syllable, a sequence of speech sounds which corresponds to a beat in the metrical grid. The metrical grid in language usually is not performed isochronously (Patel 2008: 97–154). By contrast, a single note in music can subtend multiple beats, and a beat can be sub-divided by multiple notes. And within certain degrees of tolerance (depending on the style), the metrical grid is isochronous, which makes syncopation possible.

The second component of musical rhythm is grouping, which segments the musical stream recursively into motives, phrases, and sections. Musical grouping parallels visual segmentation, which configures multiple objects in space and seg-ments objects into parts. Though grouping structure is recursive, musical groups simply contain a collection of individual notes or smaller groups. There is no distinguished element in a group that functions as "head," parallel to the heads of syntactic constituents in language (see below). If there is a linguistic analogue to musical grouping, it is probably intonational phrasing. But intonational phrasing forms a relatively flat structure, unlike musical grouping, which extends recursively from small motivic units to an entire piece. Moreover, intonational phrases are made up of smaller prosodic constituents such as phonological words and phonological phrases, each with its own specific properties (Selkirk 1984). Music lacks such differentiation of grouping units into distinct types.

In the rhythmic domain, then, the metrical grid may well be a genuine capacity unique to language and music; musical grouping is shared more with vision than with language, and linguistic intonation contours are partly specific to language.

Words

Beyond the sound system, language and music diverge more radically. Linguistic utterances are built up from words and syntax; pieces of music are built up from individual tones, some formulaic patterns, and prolongational structure. Consider the possible parallels here.

Words are conventionalized sound patterns associated in long-term memory with pieces of meaning (or concepts). Sentences are composed of words plus "grammatical glue" such as agreement, grammatical gender, and case. Musical idioms do incorporate some conventionalized sound patterns such as stylistic clichés and standard cadences, plus larger patterns such as 12-bar blues and sonata form. But these patterns are not associated with concepts. Moreover, melodies are usually not made up exclusively of conventionalized patterns in the way in which sentences are made up of words. (There are exceptions, though, such as much Jewish liturgical chant (Binder 1959).)

The function of conventionalized patterns in music more closely resembles the function of linguistic "prefabs" – clichés, idioms, and figures of speech. Like musical formulas, prefabs are frequent, but utterances are not exclusively made of them: there is still plenty of free choice of words. However, if musical formulas are parallel to prefabs, then words have no musical parallel. And of course musical formulas do not carry conceptual meaning in any event.

Syntax

Language can serve as such an expressive mode of communication because of syntactic structure, a hierarchical structure in which each node belongs to a syntactic category such as noun or adjective phrase. Music has no counterpart to these categories. Syntactic structure is headed: one element of most constituents is designated as its head. The category of a phrase is determined by the category of its head: a noun phrase is headed by a noun, a prepositional phrase by a preposition, and so on. This is the fundamental "X-bar" principle of phrase structure (Chomsky 1970; Jackendoff 1977). Each syntactic category has a characteristic configuration. For example, English verb phrases contain a head verb followed by up to two noun phrases, followed by prepositional phrases, adverbs, and subordinate clauses.

Syntax also contains multiple devices for encoding the dependencies among its constituents, such as agreement, case, reflexivity (and other anaphora), ellipsis, and long-distance dependencies (for instance, when *who* functions as direct object of *meet* in *Who does Joe think he will meet at the party?*). Words often are further differentiated into *morphosyntactic* structure: affixal structures that affect meaning and syntactic category. Sometimes this structure is recursive (as in *antidisestablishmentarianism*), and sometimes templatic (for instance, the underlined French object clitics in *Je le lui ai donné*, 'I gave it to him').

None of this structure has a counterpart in music. It all serves to code meaning relations among words in a fashion fit for phonological expression, namely, linear order and affixation. Of course, meaning expression is absent in music as well.

Prolongational structure

The closest musical counterpart to syntax is GTTM's *prolongational structure*, originally inspired by the reductional hierarchy of Schenkerian theory (Schenker 1979). Prolongational structure is a recursive hierarchy, in which each constituent has a head, and other dependents modify or elaborate the head. But in other respects it diverges from syntax. It has no parts of speech: the tonic/dominant distinction, for instance, is not formally analogous to either noun/verb or subject/predicate/object. The category of a constituent is determined by its head, but it does not parallel X-bar structure in language. For instance, a phrase headed by the note G or by a G major chord is not a "G-phrase," but simply an elaborated G. The difference between the two structures is illustrated in Figure 10.1.

Prolongational relations do not express the regimentation of conceptual relations; rather, they encode the relative stability of pitch-events in local and global contexts. Prolongational structure creates patterns of tensing and relaxing as the music moves away from stability and back toward a new point of stability. GTTM and, in much more detail, Lerdahl (2001) argue that these patterns of tensing and relaxation have a great deal to do with affect in music. Language has no counterpart to this function. Thus, on both formal and functional grounds, syntax and prolongational structure have little in common beyond both being headed hierarchies.

Following the general intuition that the components of music ought not to be *sui generis*, one would hope for a stronger analogue of prolongational

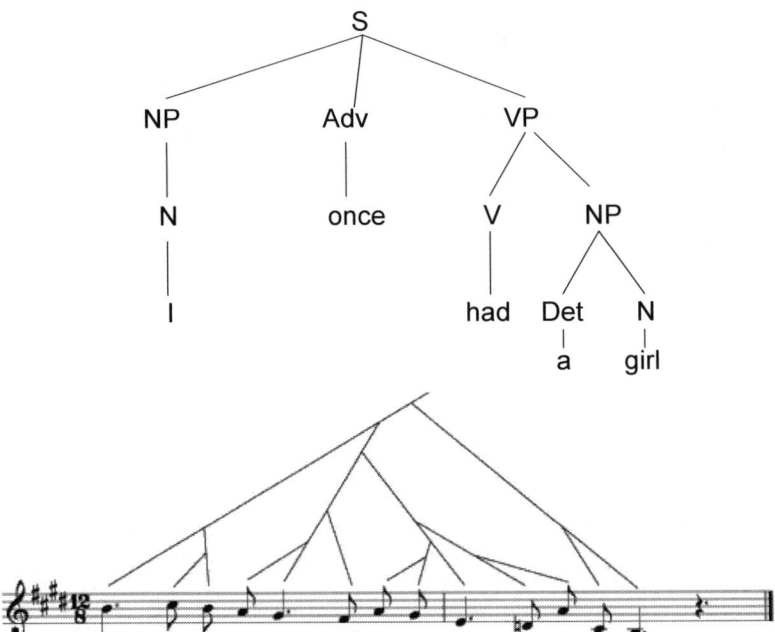

Figure 10.1 Contrast between syntactic and prolongational structure

structure in some other cognitive capacity. However, evaluating the strength of potential parallels with other capacities requires a detailed analysis and comparison of faculties. At the moment, this is impossible: not enough is known about the formal structure of mental representations for any other cognitive capacity.

However, a candidate comparison has recently emerged. Jackendoff (2007: 111–43), drawing in part on work in robotics, suggests that, like syntax and prolongational structure, the formulation and execution of complex actions – actions as ordinary as shaking hands or making coffee – invokes a recursive headed hierarchical structure that integrates and modulates many subactions stored in long-term memory. Patel (2003, 2008) presents experimental evidence that the hierarchical structures of language and music, although formally distinct, are integrated by the same part of the brain, roughly Broca's area. If so, this invites a conjecture that complex action structures are, too. That this area is usually considered premotor would add some plausibility to such speculation. In fact, the integration and execution of complex action might be a strong candidate for a more general, evolutionarily older function that could be appropriated by both language and music, quite possibly independently.

Conclusion

Language and music share a considerable number of general characteristics and one detailed formal one, namely, metrical structure. They also share some brain areas. However, most of what they share does not indicate a particularly close relation that makes them distinct from other cognitive domains. Many of their shared characteristics prove to be domain-general; for instance, recursion, the use of memory, and the need for learning and for a social context. Moreover, the fact that language and music are both conveyed through the auditory–vocal modality, though it places constraints on both of them, does not have much to do with their formal structure. This is pointed up especially by the alternative signed modality for language, which preserves most of the standard formal properties of language. Finally, language and music differ substantially in their use of pitch, in their rhythmic structure, in their "meaning" (propositional versus affective), and in the form and function of their hierarchical structures.

The conclusion, then, is to urge caution in drawing strong connections between language and music, both in the contemporary human brain and in their evolutionary roots. This is not to say we should not attempt to draw such connections. For example, Patel (2008), surveying much the same evidence as this chapter, concludes the glass is half full rather than half (or three-quarters) empty. But if one wishes to draw connections, it is important to do so on the basis of more than speculation. In particular, at the moment we do not have a properly laid out account of even one other capacity against which to compare language and music. It is an interesting question when and how cognitive science will approach such accounts, in order eventually to have a fair basis for comparison.

See also Music, philosophy, and cognitive science (Chapter 54), Psychology of music (Chapter 55), Rhythm, melody, and harmony (Chapter 3), and Understanding music (Chapter 12).

References

Binder, A. W. (1959) *Biblical Chant*, New York: Philosophical Library.

Boyd, R. and Richerson, P.J. (2005) *The Origin and Evolution of Cultures*, Oxford: Oxford University Press.

Bratman, M.E. (1999) *Faces of Intention*, Cambridge: Cambridge University Press.

Brown, S. (2000) "The 'Musilanguage' Model of Music Evolution," in Wallin, Merker, and Brown, pp. 271–300.

Calvin, W. (1990) *The Cerebral Symphony*, New York: Bantam Books.

Chomsky, N. (1965) *Aspects of the Theory of Syntax*, Cambridge: MIT Press.

—— (1970) "Remarks on Nominalizations," in R. Jacobs and P. Rosenbaum (eds) *Readings in English Transformational Grammar*, Waltham: Ginn, pp. 184–221.

—— (1981) *Lectures on Government and Binding*, Dordrecht: Foris.

Christiansen, M. and Chater, N. (2008) "Language as Shaped by the Brain," *Behavioral and Brain Sciences* 31: 537–58.

Clark, H.H. (1996) *Using Language*, Cambridge: Cambridge University Press.

Gilbert, M. (1989) *On Social Facts*, Princeton: Princeton University Press.

Hauser, M.D., Chomsky, N. and Fitch, W.T. (2002) "The Faculty of Language: What is it, Who has it, and How did it Evolve?" *Science* 298: 1569–79.

Jackendoff, R. (1977) *X-bar Syntax*, Cambridge: MIT Press.

—— (2002) *Foundations of Language*, Oxford: Oxford University Press.

—— (2007) *Language, Consciousness, Culture*, Cambridge: MIT Press.

Jackendoff, R. and Lerdahl, F. (2006) "The Capacity for Music: What's Special about it?" *Cognition* 100: 33–72.

Jackendoff, R. and Pinker, S. (2005) "The Nature of the Language Faculty and its Implications for the Evolution of Language (Reply to Fitch, Hauser, and Chomsky)," *Cognition* 97: 211–25.

Klima, E. and Bellugi, U. (1979) *The Signs of Language*, Cambridge: Harvard University Press.

Ladd, R. (1996) *Intonational Phonology*, Cambridge: Cambridge University Press.

Lerdahl, F. (2001) *Tonal Pitch Space*, New York: Oxford University Press.

—— (2003) "The Sounds of Poetry Viewed as Music," in J. Sundberg, L. Nord, and R. Carlson (eds) *Music, Language, Speech and Brain*, London: Macmillan, pp. 34–47.

Lerdahl, F. and Jackendoff, R. (1983) *A Generative Theory of Tonal Music*, Cambridge: MIT Press.

Patel, A. D. (2003) "Language, Music, Syntax, and the Brain," *Nature Neuroscience* 6: 674–81.

—— (2008) *Music, Language, and the Brain*, Oxford: Oxford University Press.

Peretz, I. and Coltheart, M. (2003) "Modularity of Music Processing," *Nature Neuroscience* 6: 688–91.

Pierrehumbert, J. (1980) "The Phonetics and Phonology of English Intonation", Ph.D. diss. Massachusetts Institute of Technology. (Published by Indiana University Linguistics Club, 1987.)

Pinker, S. (1997) *How the Mind Works*, New York: Norton.

Pinker, S. and Jackendoff, R. (2005) "The Faculty of Language: What's Special about it?" *Cognition* 95: 201–36.

Raffman, D. (1993) *Language, Music, and Mind*, Cambridge: MIT Press.

Schenker, H. (1979 [1935]) *Free Composition*, trans. E. Oster, New York: Longman.

Searle, J. (1995) *The Construction of Social Reality*, New York: Free Press.

Selkirk, E.O. (1984) *Phonology and Syntax: The Relation between Sound and Structure*, Cambridge: MIT Press.

Tomasello, M. (2003) *Constructing a Language*, Cambridge: Harvard University Press.

Tomasello, M. et al. (2005) "Understanding and Sharing Intentions: The Origins of Cultural Cognition," *Behavioral and Brain Sciences* 28: 675–91.

Wallin, N.L., Merker, B. and Brown, S. (eds) (2000) *The Origins of Music*, Cambridge: MIT Press.

Wilkins, W.K. (2005) "Anatomy Matters," *The Linguistic Review* 22: 271–88.

11

MUSIC AND IMAGINATION

Saam Trivedi

Imagination

In thinking of imagination in relation to music, it seems clear that the creative imagination is involved in such musical activities as musical composition and improvisation. Perhaps composers, in writing musical works, imagine musical forms, timbres, textures, and the like by creating images of these in their auditory imaginations, and then later often but not always test their hypotheses about these images through actual music-making (Levinson 1992: 84–5). The same might hold true of improvisers in jazz and other oral traditions, such as Indian classical music, which call essentially for improvisation, though the auditory imagination must work much quicker here, since improvisers play or perform what they imagine, or some variant thereof, soon after imagining it, leaving aside what has been imagined prior to the commencement of the improvisatory performance.

Be that as it may, it seems appropriate to begin an inquiry into music and imagination with at least a brief discussion of the nature of imagination. We imagine things in a variety of ways, not all of which are highly conscious or foregrounded (Ryle 1949: ch. 8; Walton 1990; Kieran and Lopes 2003). What follows is a short, non-exhaustive list of different kinds of imaginings.

Imaginings often involve visualizing some thing or event or scene that is not present, as when one tries to picture an ice-cream cone. But imaginings can also involve forming mental images associated with senses besides sight, such as forming an auditory image of the distinctive timbre of a trumpet.

Forming mental images, however, is not the only way of imagining things. Additionally, imaginings can involve fancying or supposing something such as when we are asked to imagine or suppose the denial of a certain proposition at the outset of a *reductio ad absurdum* proof. And imaginings can include pretending to oneself or make-believe, something children often engage in when they play games such as imagining that a tree stump is a bear, or imagining that a block of wood is a truck (Walton 1990: 21–4). Imaginings can also involve entertaining possibilities without actually believing or affirming them, such as when we are asked to imagine Louis XIV is the King of France today, or Lincoln is the US President. Sometimes imaginings can be delusions, such as when a deranged person imagines she is Queen Victoria. Dreaming and daydreaming are also instances of imagining, ones which clearly show we need not always notice that we are engaged in certain kinds of imaginings; we do not always notice that we are daydreaming, but sometimes merely lapse into it, and we rarely if ever realize we are dreaming.

This last fact about dreaming and daydreaming points to something important about the nature of imagination and various kinds of imaginings. Imaginings can be voluntary, that is, under our control, but they can also be spontaneous, non-deliberate, passive rather than intended. They can be constant or they can be intermittent, of a long or a short duration. And one may imagine something without being aware that one is doing so. We can also be engaged in imaginings while caught up with other activities, such as the daydreaming many students do while in class. In what follows, it is important that the reader bears in mind that imagination is not always highly foregrounded and we can engage in certain kinds of imaginings without being aware of doing so.

Imaginative perception and perceptual imagining

As we will see below, the particular notion of imaginative perception (or imaginative hearing in the specific case of music) is applied to the experience of music by some thinkers (such as Roger Scruton). So it seems appropriate to clarify here before proceeding further what imaginative perception is, generally, and how it is different from related phenomena such as perceptual imaginings. To do so, we must briefly look at recent work on imagination in general before turning to music.

A fair bit of recent work on imagination by philosophers and psychologists has focused on engaging with fiction and fictional characters empathetically (Currie 2004: 173–88) or, relatedly, on recreating others' mental states and perspectives (Currie and Ravenscroft 2002), or else on the imaginings of children (Harris 2000). Let us briefly look, as a recent sophisticated example, at the view of imagination provided by Brian O'Shaughnessy (2002: 339–78). O'Shaughnessy identifies several varieties of imagining, but let us restrict ourselves to what he has to say about three sorts of non-propositional, direct-object imaginative experiences: (i) imaginative perceptions, as when we look suitably at and "see three dimensions in" a two-dimensional photograph; (ii) will-susceptible perceptual imaginings, as in the case of common mental imagery; and (iii) will-impervious perceptual imaginings, as in the case of visual hallucinations. Note that while O'Shaughnessy's examples are visual, we will see auditory analogs of these later in this chapter (in the section on musical expressiveness).

In discussing imaginative perceptions, O'Shaughnessy tells us that these are imaginative non-imaginings where the imagination helps generate the internal object of the perceptual experience, that is, what we see. For instance, when seeing a photograph of a landscape, the imagination imposes a second-order interpretation upon our first-order experience of seeing colored expanses on cardboard. We see these in such a way that while remaining expanses of color, they simultaneously bring a landscape into view in a special imaginative sense. There is, O'Shaughnessy claims, one complex phenomenon here with two internal objects – the colored expanses and the landscape – the latter being dependent upon the former; put differently, there is one complex experience here involving two mental representations – one of the colored expanses and one of the landscape. Thus the phenomenon is fundamentally a seeing (an imaginative seeing, that is) rather than an imagining. Moreover, O'Shaughnessy claims it is vital that the colored expanses on the photographic surface share *some* similarity with the landscape (as seen from a point of view), such as their common contours and color-distributions. This combination of some similarity and yet some dissimilarity prompts the imagination to this imaginative seeing, though the imagination need not follow the prompt. O'Shaughnessy claims that a landscape is visible in these marks to those who know the look of landscapes and can also impose second-order imaginative interpretations upon suitable marks on surfaces. The landscape that "appears" to one is not really there; all that is literally there is marks on cardboard, which one sees, even as one also goes beyond them simultaneously in imaginatively seeing a landscape.

Turning to O'Shaughnessy's discussion of perceptual imaginings, which is focused on visual imaginings, we are told that there are three kinds of visual imaginings: mental imagery, visual hallucination, and "dream seeing" (about which O'Shaughnessy does not have much to say). Mental imagery comes in many varieties, of which but one is the common "seeing in the mind's eye." Mental images can be conjured into and out of existence at will, but they often come and go unbidden, such as sexual images, to use an example from Colin McGinn (2004: 14). They are will-susceptible in that even though their arrival may sometimes be unbidden, we bear a limited degree of responsibility for willing their persistence and their course. In contrast, we are usually without choice in the case of both visual hallucinations and "dream-seeing," both of which also involve some measure of weakening of one's sense of reality. Visual hallucinations can be experienced with belief (e.g. Macbeth's hallucination of Banquo), with doubt (e.g. Macbeth's hallucination of a dagger), or with the knowledge that they are illusory (e.g. the first stages of mescaline intoxication). On O'Shaughnessy's view, visual hallucinations and perceptual imaginings generally are imaginings rather than perceptions or seeings. An alcoholic's "seeing" pink elephants, for example, is a visual imagining; it is an apparent visual experience that is the seeing of nothing rather than a real visual experience with a real presence in the visual field (as when we see pink elephants in a picture).

With this overview of imagination in hand, I turn now to various ways in which imagination has been said to play a role in our engagement with music, from our basic perception of music to the construction of musical culture.

Basic musical perception

There is an ongoing debate over whether music perception is (ineliminably) informed by spatial concepts applied metaphorically or imaginatively to sound. Roger Scruton claims that metaphors involve a deliberate transfer of a term or concept from a central context to something known not to exemplify it. In this way metaphors bring dissimilar things together in a highly imaginative fusion (Scruton 1997: 80–96). Metaphors are indispensable, holds Scruton, when how the world seems depends upon our imagination being actively involved with it, and this is the case with musical experience. In describing music, Scruton suggests, metaphors cannot be eliminated, for they define the intentional object of musical experience. For example, sounds do not literally rise and fall, but we often hear music move in this way. Moreover, Scruton claims, musical motion and other musical qualities are aspects or tertiary qualities (which, following Locke, are powers of objects to affect other objects, such as the power of fire to melt wax). These musical qualities, Scruton holds, are only perceived by rational beings via certain exercises of the imagination involving the metaphorical transfer of concepts from other contexts, and so we hear music under indispensable metaphorical descriptions. In hearing sounds, Scruton suggests, we may thus be on the listen-out for imaginative perceptions, hearing sounds and also simultaneously hearing the life and movement in them that is music, situated in an imagined space and organized in terms of such spatial concepts as "up" and "down," "high" and "low," "rising" and "falling," and so on.

Malcolm Budd believes an alternative to Scruton's account of the experience of hearing sounds as music can be offered that does without metaphors and the spatial and other concepts Scruton appeals to (Budd 2003: 211). Budd suggests that one can hear the distinctive timbral character of a note without appealing to a metaphorical description transferred from another domain (Budd 2003: 213–14). Turning next to pitch and melody, Budd rejects as untenable Scruton's claim that without reference to space, tones would no longer be heard as moving away from or toward each other. Continuing to chords, Budd argues that if melody cannot tenably be explained in terms of sounds being heard under spatial concepts, as Scruton thinks, then it seems unwarranted that we hear tones sounding simultaneously (as chords) in terms of tones heard imaginatively as arranged spatially. Finally, as for rhythm, given that Scruton here bases his view on beat as being comparable to the heartbeat, Budd claims that the idea should not be one involving spatial movement but rather of something contracting and dilating, as in the case of the systole and the diastole.

Budd's own positive suggestions on these matters are as follows. Arguing that the literal/metaphorical distinction may obscure things, Budd refrains from claiming (like Stephen Davies (1994: 235–6)) that it is literally true that melodies move up and down. He suggests instead that melodic movement from tone to tone is merely temporal, not spatial, given that relations between tones are due to their positions on the pitch continuum, which is not itself a spatial dimension. "Movement," Budd thinks, does not only mean change in spatial location, but can also mean change along a non-spatial continuum or with reference to a particular variable (Budd 2003: 219–20). As for rhythm, to hear it, Budd claims, may involve imagining the pulsations of life (Budd 2003: 221).

Scruton responds to Budd's criticisms first by trying to clarify what it means for an experience to "involve" a metaphor (Scruton 2004: 185–6). While admitting that we may be up against a sort of bedrock in this dispute, he suggests that seeing a dog, for instance, involves the concept of a dog applied in judgment, whereas seeing a dog in a picture involves the concept of a dog applied in an "unasserted thought" and thus figuratively. It is in a manner similar to the latter, claims Scruton, that we apply the concept of movement to pitches in hearing a melody, since pitches cannot literally move. Scruton also disagrees with Budd's claim that spatial metaphors can be dispensed with in hearing music, and claims in opposition that we must hear music in terms of up and down, toward and away, mirroring, inversion, forward, backward, same direction, and so on, to make sense of it. Finally, Scruton contends that Budd's suggestion that musical movement is temporal rather than spatial is itself metaphorical, and is the same metaphor of movement that Scruton is trying to explicate (Scruton 2004: 187). Scruton grants that merely temporal *Gestalts* may be broken down preconceptually into temporal chunks experienced as unified wholes without appeal to movement, but thinks that this level lies below the experience of music.

In this debate, Budd seems right to object to Scruton with regard to timbres and musical movement. For, *contra* Scruton, the distinctiveness of a timbre might be heard under very different metaphorical descriptions or under none at all; for example, the literally shrill timbre of an oboe holding a high note might be heard as such even by little children incapable of understanding metaphors. And one can hear melodic or musical movement without appealing to Scruton's spatial metaphors. For example, a melody can be heard as moving from the leading note to the tonic in the familiar musicological terms of melodic tension and resolution (or melodic drive or yearning) that we literally hear in the music, or in some such terms that describe the experience without essentially referring to spatial features; musically untrained listeners unfamiliar with notions of musical space might be especially inclined to do so, or else they might hear music as moving from the "unpleasant" to the "pleasant." For example, the supertonic and the leading note have a melodic tendency to go to the tonic, the subdominant to the mediant or dominant, and the submediant to the dominant. There are also notes of emphasis, such as the tonic in tonal music, the *finalis* in modal music, or the *vadi* (or main note) of Indian *ragas*. And there are notes of secondary emphasis such as the dominant in tonal music, the *confinalis* in modal music, or the *samvadi* (often a fifth higher than the *vadi*) of Indian *ragas*. Similarly, there are notes or points of melodic tension and repose. Such features might be especially important in the experience of a lot of essentially monophonic music, such as

Gregorian chant and many non-Western musics, where melody is not just an important element but virtually all there is to the music, barring such things as background drones, pitched rhythmic accompaniment, and the like.

It might also be asked, against Scruton, whether ordinary language metaphors at the very least point to or suggest objective resemblances (or lack thereof in the case of negative metaphors such as "No man is an island," "Life is not a bed of roses," etc.) in certain respects between two or more otherwise very different things, in virtue of which we are prompted to imagine (or not imagine, in the case of negative metaphors) one thing as, or in terms of, another (Trivedi 2008). If such a resemblance-plus-imagination conception of metaphors is right, and metaphors can in principle be paraphrased, then any allegedly metaphorical description of musical motion, expressiveness, and so on, might be explained away via paraphrase in a way that involves resemblance and imagination and, *contra* Scruton, dispenses with the metaphor. It is also possible that musical experience may be organized by concepts that do not apply literally but might only be *imagined* (willy-nilly, readily, and immediately, and in ways that need not be highly foregrounded) to apply to sounds as we hear them, and in a way that need not, *contra* Scruton, invoke or involve metaphors at all.

Imagination and musical expressiveness

To turn now to musical expressiveness, analogs of many of O'Shaughnessy's claims about imagination discussed earlier would seem to apply well to the experience of music, especially to that of hearing musical expressiveness. In hearing absolute or purely instrumental music – music without words or an associated story or program – as sad, happy, anguished, tranquil, and so on, it is clear we are hearing something that is not literally or really true of the music, which after all is without life and consciousness, and so cannot itself have such mental states. It seems plausible, then, that music is not literally sad, happy, etc., but is rather only *imagined* to be so (Levinson 1996; Trivedi 2006). If that is right, then it is possible that music may be imaginatively heard as sad in a variety of ways, given that we imagine things in many ways, as outlined above, and that we may often imagine things without being aware of it. As Stephen Davies puts it, "what goes on in people's heads as they listen attentively to music and . . . its expressive character is very varied" (Davies 2006: 190).

One of the many kinds of imagining involved when we hear music as sad may be our animating the music itself (Trivedi 2001), imaginatively projecting life and life-like qualities, including mental states, onto it and thus imagining that the music *itself* – not something else, such as the composer, performer, or listener, or an imagined persona in the music – is sad. Our animating the music when we hear it as sad involves imaginative perception or imaginative hearing, in something like the manner O'Shaughnessy and Scruton have in mind. We really hear musical sounds in hearing musical expressiveness, and so there is aural perception going on, fundamentally. But at the same time, there is also imagining going on as we imagine readily, immediately, and willy-nilly of these sounds, in ways we are not always conscious of, that they are sad, happy, etc. Furthermore, as in the case O'Shaughnessy deals with, what prompts imaginings in the case of musical expressiveness may be resemblances of various sorts between the music and *something* to do with mental states, either their typical vocal or behavioral expression or their affective feel. In the very midst of hearing musical sounds, there is thus a non-perceptual or non-audible "going beyond" as we imaginatively hear mental states in the music. In accordance with Scruton's claim that the "literal perception and the imaginative perception can cohabit the same experience, since they do not compete" (2004: 184), we literally hear or perceive musical sounds unfolding in time and at the same time also imaginatively hear mental states in them, as part of the same experience.

O'Shaughnessy's discussion of the distinct phenomenon of perceptual imagining might also relate well to a different way of imaginatively hearing musical sadness, etc. One kind of imagining involved in hearing music as sad, say, may be when we imagine an indefinite agent in the music, the music's persona – someone or something, we know not what exactly – expressing its mental states via the music, its gestures, development, and so on (Levinson 1996, 2006; Robinson 2005: pt. 4). Imagining a persona may involve a kind of indeterminate mental imaging, not a visual imaging but an auditory imaging. Along with the kind of visual imaging or "seeing in the mind's eye" that O'Shaughnessy describes, it is also possible, with the help of memory, to form mental images associated with the other senses besides sight so that one might form an auditory image of the distinctive timbre of a trumpet, an olfactory image of the smell of a rose, a gustatory image of the taste of a fine wine, or a tactile image of the prick of a cactus. To be sure, many of these mental images are faint and not very precise or determinate, which also holds for the imagined, indeterminate musical persona. Alternatively, one might view hearing musical expressiveness in terms of a persona as involving a kind of propositional imagining – *that* there is some agent expressing itself musically – though a possible problem here may be that propositional imagining seems to be both more determinate than and not as immediate or direct as hearing musical expressiveness in terms of a persona, which happens readily and immediately and is indeterminate; one *hears* the sadness in the music first – someone or something is crying or wailing in the music – and then forms the belief that the music is an agent's expression. Moreover, as with the visual images O'Shaughnessy discusses, non-visual mental images can be conjured into and out of existence and guided at will, but they often come and go unbidden. In the particular case of imagining an indeterminate musical persona, we may form this kind of auditory image without being aware of doing so, and yet the unbidden image of a musical persona may be terminated at will after we realize we are engaged in imagining it.

Music, imagination, and culture

In an important book, Nicholas Cook has suggested that sonata form, large-scale Schenkerian tonal structures, thematic unity, serial transformations, and other such staples of music theory are not directly audible, but are rather ways of imagining sound as music ("a repertoire of means for imagining music" (1990: 4)) that constitute musical culture – "a tradition of imagining sounds as music" (1990: 223). *Contra* Cook, however, many music theorists would contend that their aim is to understand how music actually works rather than merely create fictive or imaginative accounts of music that do not correspond to listeners' auditory experience (Huron 1995). Indeed, though Cook rejects such claims, it has not infrequently been held that listeners may aurally apprehend sonata forms, serial transformations, and the like not directly but rather indirectly or subconsciously, thus contributing to coherent and unified musical experiences that may consequently please and satisfy (Réti 1961; Schoenberg 1978).

Of particular interest to our topic of music and imagination, leaving Cook's main thesis aside, is his rich discussion of the different aspects of musical imagination. Cook recalls Jean-Paul Sartre's example of imagining a thimble, wherein our image synthesizes within a single awareness the front and back, inside and outside of the thimble, even though in real life we would have to alternate between different viewpoints to see all of the front and back, the inside and outside of the thimble, and could not see them all wholly at the same time (Sartre 1972: 105). Analogously, Cook suggests that both musically trained and untrained listeners can imagine experiences of musical works in ways where all that is heard sequentially is integrated into a single, heightened experience that captures all features of the music, even though there is something illusory about this (Cook 1990: 89). Likewise, Cook follows Sartre's example of imagining the Pantheon where our image is simply "many-columned" rather than one that has a determinate number of columns (Sartre 1972: 100–1), and suggests that we may similarly simply imagine the sound of Dietrich Fischer-Dieskau's voice, say, in at least a partly generic way (imagining the mellowness of his voice, the emphasis of his articulation, etc.), without imagining the specifics of whether he sings loudly or softly, what syllable he sings, whether he sings the beginning of a note or its middle or end, and so on (Cook 1990: 90). Similarly, in trying to recall a familiar musical work, Cook claims we might form generic images of harmonic gracefulness and orchestral luxuriance rather than specific sound-images with these properties (Cook 1990: 92). All these cases, Cook claims, following Sartre, involve "the illusion of immanence," that is, the illusion that is imagined is there before one.

Cook also suggests that a lot of imagery used by musicians in producing or playing music is kinesthetic, or even to some degree visual. For instance, imagining music as fingered a certain way, or writing in a certain fingering as imagined, is one of the ways in which musicians imagine or represent the music they play (Cook 1990: 74–85). Likewise, in trying to recall one musical work while hearing another very different and structurally incompatible musical work being played on the radio, though the work being heard interferes with auditory recall, nevertheless a skilled keyboard player might recall the other work by "playing" it on a silent keyboard, consciously focusing on the movements of her fingers, hands, and arms. Alternatively, a work might be recalled via visual imagery of its score – as when a pianist plays a work from memory and remembers what comes next by "seeing" it halfway down the next page – or visual imagery of the keyboard. The imagery of the voice can also help sometimes in imagining a musical work. For example, reading a score in a library where one cannot sing aloud and is without a piano, one might sense the virtual or even actual tensing of the throat as the vocal line hits a high note or plumbs a low note, and thereby grasp something of the melody's expressive character. *Sotto voce* singing while performed by jazz musicians, the kora players of West Africa, or the great classical pianist Glenn Gould provides a similar sort of security that comes from vocal awareness. There are, then, according to Cook, many sorts of images besides the auditory in terms of which musical works may be represented or imagined – kinesthetic, visual, notational, vocal, etc. – and musicians may first analyze or deconstruct musical works in these different ways before reconstructing them as wholes. Finally, Cook suggests that a composer may conceive or imagine the basic framework of a musical work before starting to write the score. Then the composer elaborates the framework and ties together all sorts of details, just as an experienced public speaker may have the framework (the basic points, etc.) and some specific details (illustrations, jokes, etc.) of her lecture worked out in her head before elaborating the framework and tying the details together in the course of writing her lecture.

See also Analytic philosophy and music (Chapter 27), Composition (Chapter 47), Improvisation (Chapter 6), Music and language (Chapter 10), Music, philosophy, and cognitive science (Chapter 54), Music theory and philosophy (Chapter 46), Psychology of music (Chapter 55), Resemblance theories (Chapter 21), and Rhythm, melody, and harmony (Chapter 3).

References

Budd, M. (2003) "Musical Movement and Aesthetic Metaphors," *British Journal of Aesthetics* 43: 209–23.
Cook, N. (1990) *Music, Imagination, and Culture*, Oxford: Clarendon Press.
Currie, G. (2004) *Arts and Minds*, Oxford: Clarendon Press.
Currie, G. and Ravenscroft, I. (2002) *Recreative Minds*, Oxford: Clarendon Press.
Davies, S. (1994) *Musical Meaning and Expression*, Ithaca: Cornell University Press.
—— (2006) "Artistic Expression and the Hard Case of Pure Music," in M. Kieran (ed.) *Contemporary Debates in Aesthetics and the Philosophy of Art*, Oxford: Blackwell, pp. 179–91.
Harris, P. (2000) *The Work of the Imagination*, Malden: Blackwell.
Huron, D. (1995) Review of Cook 1990, *Music Perception* 12: 473–81.

Kieran, M. and Lopes, D. (eds) (2003) *Imagination, Philosophy, and the Arts*, New York: Routledge.

Levinson, J. (1992) "Composition, Musical," in D. Cooper (ed.) *A Companion to Aesthetics*, Malden: Blackwell, pp. 82–5.

—— (1996) "Musical Expressiveness," in *The Pleasures of Aesthetics*, Ithaca: Cornell University Press, pp. 90–125.

—— (2006) "Musical Expressiveness as Hearability-as-Expression," in M. Kieran (ed.), *Contemporary Debates in Aesthetics and the Philosophy of Art*, Oxford: Blackwell, pp. 192–204.

McGinn, C. (2004) *Mindsight*, Cambridge: Harvard University Press.

O'Shaughnessy, B. (2002) *Consciousness and the World*, Oxford: Oxford University Press.

Réti, R. (1961) *The Thematic Process in Music*, New York: Faber.

Robinson, J. (2005) *Deeper than Reason*, Oxford: Clarendon Press.

Ryle, G. (1949) *The Concept of Mind*, London: Hutchinson.

Sartre, J. (1972) *The Psychology of the Imagination*, London: Routledge.

Schoenberg, A. (1978) *Theory of Harmony*, Berkeley: University of California Press.

Scruton, R. (1997) *The Aesthetics of Music*, New York: Oxford University Press.

—— (2004) "Musical Movement: A Reply to Budd," *British Journal of Aesthetics* 44: 184–7.

Trivedi, S. (2001) "Expressiveness as a Property of the Music Itself," *Journal of Aesthetics and Art Criticism*, 59: 411–20.

—— (2006) "Imagination, Music, and the Emotions," *Revue Internationale de Philosophie* 60: 415–35.

—— (2008) "Metaphors and Musical Expressiveness," in K. Stock and K. Thomson-Jones (eds) *New Waves in Aesthetics*, New York: Palgrave Macmillan, pp. 41–57.

Walton, K. (1990) *Mimesis as Make-Believe*, Cambridge: Harvard University Press.

12

UNDERSTANDING MUSIC

Erkki Huovinen

Music may never be fully understood. An important reason for this is that music, since it is art, often strives for the new, the previously unknown, the unconventional. Some musical thinkers have therefore thought that musical utterances only fulfill their aesthetic goal to the extent that they deviate from what has previously been considered as syntactically normal (e.g. Dempster 1998: 61–2). Considering, say, the twentieth-century musical avant-garde, it may be claimed that an appropriate aesthetic response to these musical phenomena *calls for* a certain bafflement or lack of understanding (Danuser 2004). Following Theodor Adorno (1970: 184), one may even think that *all* true works of art are imbued with a certain enigmatic character that will not let them be fully understood. It is not hard to find something rather persuasive in these thoughts. Perhaps the function of art precludes complete understanding after all. Artworks – including musical works – rarely seem to be made solely for the purpose of, say, communicating a definite content to the public. If no such definite content can be singled out for a musical work, why should one even strive for a once-and-for-all understanding of it? Perhaps a part of the very essence of art is to be in a certain sense indefinite and thus to resist our understanding.

Despite these thoughts, innumerable musicians and musical aficionados remain devoted to the enterprise of understanding music, in one way or another. While perhaps accepting that some aspects of music evade our understanding, they are nonetheless fascinated by the challenge of learning to apprehend it. What is more, there exist many thriving scholarly disciplines, all of which apparently have understanding music as their goal: music historians, psychologists, theorists, and sociologists, ethnomusicologists, and philosophers of music all seem to be driven by the wish to understand music better. This state of affairs suggests a certain relativity of musical understanding: music may, apparently, be understood in many ways that are sometimes even defined in opposition to each other. Furthermore, all of these disciplines – and with them, their respective views of what understanding music consists of – have changed over time, and will probably continue to do so. This alone should motivate the study of musical understanding by philosophers of music, while at the same time cautioning against normative or too universal theories of it. It is far from self-evident that all musical understandings should be commensurable in the sense that their respective "levels" might be evaluated on a single scale (cf. Huovinen 2008). Yet certain broad conceptions of understanding music tend to crop up in the literature, potentially allowing for a comparison between different views. In the following, I will discuss two basic kinds of understanding music that are often referred to, as well as interrelationships between them.

Perceptual and epistemic views of musical understanding

There is an important sense in which one may already speak of musical understanding when a listener perceptually grasps sounds as musically meaningful – for instance, hearing a melody instead of merely registering bursts of noise. In order to understand music in this sense, the listener need not form any explicit beliefs about the heard sounds, or otherwise be conscious of applying concepts to them (cf. DeBellis 1995). Roger Scruton (1983: 78) has called this the intentional aspect of musical hearing, explaining that instead of knowledge concerning the world of material objects, we are here concerned with appearances. Scruton writes that "[u]nderstanding music involves the active creation of an intentional world, in which inert sounds are transfigured into movements, harmonies, rhythms – metaphorical gestures in a metaphorical space" (1983: 100). Whether or not we accept Scruton's metaphorical conception of musical hearing, it is easy to see why he would describe the intentional hearing of musical melodies, harmonies, and rhythms as a necessary (though not a sufficient) condition of musical understanding. Understanding music implies understanding its sounds *as music*. Perhaps this is also how we might read Hans-Georg Gadamer's statement that "[e]ven when we hear, say, absolute music, we have to 'understand' it; and only if we understand it, if it is 'clear' to us, will it be there as an artistic construct" (1965: 87).

Some musical thinkers have concentrated on accounting for this perceptual side of musical understanding from a perspective that is informed by gestalt psychology and cognitive science. Harold Fiske (2008), for instance, equates musical understanding with the listener's ability to mentally construct musical patterns from the sounds received. According to Fiske, as musical listeners we "identify relevant cues, piece the cues together into patterns that can be retained (in echoic memory) long enough for brain mechanisms to examine and create the sense that we can 'look' at music by invoking principles borrowed from vision, and then creating the impression of an auditory 'object'" (2008: 56). Here, the implication is of a "piece" of music that may be "seen" as if it were a fixed object. However, an account of basic cognitive sense-making does not presuppose such a notion. What is material here is that any passage of music is taken to be understood only when it is somehow appropriately represented in the listener's mind (or, as Fiske would have it, brain). I take this to be a perfectly acceptable manner of talking about musical understanding, as long as care is taken to articulate clearly what is at issue. Indeed, cases of so-called amusia can be thought of as cases in which a person is unable to understand sounds as music in this sense. The fact that a comprehensive amusia is a rather rare phenomenon implies that most people show at least some degree of perceptual musical understanding, being able to grasp heard sounds as subjectively meaningful music.

Musicians are often experts in understanding music perceptually: they may have highly developed abilities to grasp even complex sound constructions as musically meaningful. Hence, the early pioneer of computer-aided music research, Otto Laske, framed his theory of musical competence in terms of "actual music understanding systems, *i.e.*, human musicians" (1977: 12). The implication is that musicians' competence represents a central form of musical understanding. Such views have later been called into question by, among others, Benjamin Brinner (1995) who, in his research on Javanese musicians, reports cases which purport to demonstrate that practical musical competence represents neither a sufficient nor a necessary condition for what he prefers to call musical understanding. Despite such empirical studies, there seems to be no consensus about the relationship between musical understanding and practical musical competence among philosophers of music. For instance, Jerrold Levinson has the "intuition" that the ability to musically reproduce (by playing, singing, whistling, etc.) and the ability to continue a given bit of music in an appropriate manner should be taken as "strong evidence of basic musical understanding" (1997: 26–7). Peter Kivy does not accept Levinson's intuition (2001: 200–1). This might of course be taken to show that "Kivy fails to see how reasonable that intuition is" (Levinson 2006: 509), but it might also signal that these two philosophers' conceptions of musical understanding are simply different – that they are talking, in part, of different matters.

Such debates bring out the old and well-known fact that practical musical competence and knowledge concerning music are at least conceptually distinct matters. Even if one should find reason to sympathize with Levinson's view, it is important to remember the traditional tendency in Western culture to value abstract theoretical knowledge concerning music, which is often rather detached from any practical competence. For many theorists, to understand music has been simply to possess knowledge of it. To pick one example, the medieval music theorist Guido d'Arezzo wrote that

> There is a great difference between musicians and singers: the latter vocalize, but the former know what music consists of. For he who makes what he does not understand is defined as a beast.
>
> (d'Arezzo 1963: 25)

According to this epistemic view of musical understanding, real musical understanding requires explicit knowledge concerning music: knowledge articulated in

conscious beliefs and possibly also mediated through language. Practical musicianship, knowing *how* in the world of music, is not sufficient, but perhaps also
not necessary, for such epistemic understanding of music (knowing *that*). From
our present perspective it should be kept in mind, however, that practical musicianship most probably involves the kind of perceptual understanding that was
discussed above. If so, then dismissing practical musicianship as insufficient for
true musical understanding also implies dismissing the perceptual grasping of
music as insufficient for it.

It may be rare nowadays to completely renounce perceptual understanding in
favor of an epistemic view of musical understanding. Instead, there have been
attempts to argue for a substantial bias toward perceptual understanding. One
example of such a theory is Jerrold Levinson's "concatenationism" (1997), which
aims at answering the following questions: "Why do we listen to music, how do
we listen to music, and what is the main source of our satisfaction in listening
to music?" (Levinson 2006: 505). The answer to these questions, according to
Levinson, lies in the way in which music is followed, or attended to, moment by
moment, bit by bit. Levinson's chief objective is to oppose theories which take
the apprehension of large formal structures of music to be an important source
of musical enjoyment and understanding. In the part of his theory pertaining to
understanding, Levinson states that musical understanding "centrally involves
neither aural grasp of a large span of music as a whole, nor intellectual grasp of
large-scale connections between parts; understanding music is centrally a matter
of apprehending individual bits of music and immediate progressions from bit to
bit" (1997: 13). Despite some concessions that Levinson makes to "architectonic
awareness" of music, his main idea is to emphasize the awareness of small-scale
musical features and progressions as central to musical understanding.

Even though his discussion is framed in terms of the distinction between small-
scale bits of music and large-scale "architectonic" features, it is easy to see that
Levinson's view is also a clear statement in favor of what was above called perceptual understanding. One of the intuitions that, according to Levinson, "incline us
in the direction of concatenationism" is that "what we ordinarily count as *knowing* a piece of music, as *grasping* it, or, in a more vernacular vein, as *getting* it" is
a matter of "perceiving it as a developing process" (1997: 22–3). One might nevertheless ask what the philosophical relevance of such a theory should be, beyond
the empirically testable psychological generalizations that it implies. In claiming that musical understanding centrally involves concatenationistic perception,
Levinson might be taken to say that what he *means* by "musical understanding"
is first and foremost bit-by-bit perceptual grasping. Or, he might be interpreted as
suggesting that there are admittedly different types of musical understanding, but
that the most *interesting* or *valuable* ones have to do with perceptually following
the small-scale features of music and their progressions. Either way, it seems that
he just wants to restrict the discussion to one corner of what may have traditionally been seen as instances of musical understanding. Thus, it is not easy to see

the philosophical relevance of the debate between Levinson and those who would like to include more epistemic features in their account of musical understanding (e.g. Kivy 2001). Instead of arguing whether the perceptual or epistemic aspects of musical understanding are "more important," it may be more fruitful to consider their mutual relationships within a more comprehensive account that gives credit to both. Their relative importance may, after all, be a matter of how one *wants* to understand music.

Eggebrecht's comprehensive theory

Discussions of musical understanding are complicated by the lack of consensus on what is meant by the verb "to understand." According to some philosophers, to understand something is merely to have a "sense of comprehension" – a certain "feel" that one has been taught to correlate with the word "understanding" (e.g. Forrest 1991). I assume that many musical listeners are familiar with some difference between having a sense of comprehension when listening to familiar music and lacking such a sense in other cases. It should be clear, though, that one can have a sense of understanding even in cases where some independent evidence would later lead one to realize that one had not really understood the phenomenon in question properly, or even at all. Scientific explanations have notoriously been accepted on the basis of a strong sense of understanding – a sense of "feeling right" that the explanations initially elicited – even though a mere sense of understanding arguably cannot provide any guarantee of the correctness of an explanation (Trout 2002). Such considerations might provide one rationale for reading the verb "to understand" as a success verb that should only be applied to a person who has *correctly* apprehended the phenomenon at issue. In connection with music, too, many informal uses of the verb fall into this category, and it appears to be true that "the distinction between understanding music and misunderstanding it is highly valued in most musical cultures" (Lidov 1992). In sum, there seem to be two conflicting intuitions concerning the meaning of "to understand": a phenomenological intuition emphasizing the subjective sense of understanding, and an epistemological intuition emphasizing the distinction between understanding and misunderstanding.

In order to do justice to both intuitions, one obviously needs a distinction between two different categories of mental states. As an illustrative example, we may consider the account of musical understanding offered by the German musicologist Hans Heinrich Eggebrecht (1999). According to Eggebrecht, musical understanding comes in two stripes which may and should work in tandem. On the one hand, there is the more basic "aesthetic understanding" (*Ästhetisches Verstehen*) that is reminiscent of what I have above spoken of as perceptual understanding. On the other hand, there is another kind of understanding, *Erkennendes Verstehen*, which comes close to what was above called epistemic understanding. In Eggebrecht's view, epistemic understanding is conceptual, mediated by language. As an example of the difference between the two kinds of understanding, Eggebrecht describes how aesthetic understanding allows one to recognize a progression of tones as inherently related, and to recognize reappearances of this close-knit unit; epistemic understanding would then only require the further application of terms such as "motif" or "repetition," which immediately opens the way to conceptual reflection (1999: 118–19).

In Eggebrecht's conception, epistemic understanding is based on and will always refer to prior, non-conceptual, aesthetic understanding. This is because the reality (*Dasein*) of music lies in its aesthetic complexity that "already in its simplest appearance is never fully reached by the knowing, analytically describing understanding" (Eggebrecht 1999: 120). As far as understanding musical *sounds* are concerned, it is hard not to agree: without some connection to the perceptually understood appearances of music, any thoughts concerning heard music would remain empty. However, Eggebrecht follows a Kantian line of thought in emphasizing that neither can the aesthetic understanding be fully realized without concepts. That is, even if a conceptual understanding of music without any perceptually understood content is empty, a mere perceptual understanding without concepts will remain blind (Kant 1966: A51/B75) or incomplete (Eggebrecht 1999: 120). Concepts are thus needed not only for complementing an already fully formed aesthetic understanding with distinct conceptual identifications on a different level, but also the aesthetic understanding itself needs to be informed by concepts.

Let us see how such a two-tiered account of musical understanding helps in accommodating the intuition that music may be misunderstood. Eggebrecht supposes that the more fundamental aesthetic understanding is always directed toward the inherent formal content (*Formsinn*) of a particular musical work, which he identifies with the work's temporally organized pitch structure. Although Eggebrecht notes that the formal content may in some ways be ambiguous or open, he nevertheless claims that aesthetic understanding has an objectivity that is grounded in the correspondence between the formal content of the music and what the listener understands (Eggebrecht 1999: 25–8). Such correspondence implies that musical understanding, on this perceptual level, is not merely subjective but intersubjective (Bandur 2004: 68). Therefore, Eggebrecht also thinks that the musical content of a melody cannot be misunderstood (Eggebrecht 1999: 31). On the other hand, the concept-driven epistemic understanding of music will never be fully objective. Language cannot reach the perceptual complexity of music, and thus the transformation of perceptually grasped, maybe to some extent non-conceptual images into the medium of language may occur in multifarious ways, always involving an element of subjective selection by the understanding subject (Eggebrecht 2004: 19; cf. 1999: 153). Such variability on the conceptual, epistemic level allows for more and less appropriate understandings. If so, Eggebrecht's view seems to be that the distinction between correct understanding and misunderstanding is applicable on the level of epistemic understanding, while the more basic level of aesthetic understanding, in its turn, allows for a listener's subjective sense of understanding.

What seems problematic in Eggebrecht's theory, however, is that it does not seem to leave room for conflicting aesthetic understandings, nor for more or less appropriate ways of *perceptually* understanding music. In fact, musical structures present perceptual ambiguity in so many ways that it may be impossible to draw a strict line between "correct" and "incorrect" perceptual understandings. Even so, there may appear reasons for revising our perceptual understandings in favor of more appropriate ones. Consider, for instance, the question of how Western listeners understand meter in African music: where they locate the "downbeat" and what they consider as the main pulse. Without delving too deeply, suffice it to say that such perceptual, and often largely unconscious decisions do make a difference to the qualitative feel of the perceived rhythms. Now, let us imagine that a Western listener has tended to perceptually make sense of the "standard pattern" of African rhythm (often expressed as a succession of time values 2212221) by counting in three. Then, she meets an expert arguing that a culturally appropriate perceptual understanding of basic African rhythms relies on a metrical framework that only manifests itself in how the dancers move their feet, and, given such evidence, a more appropriate understanding of the standard pattern would be to perceive it by counting in four (cf. Agawu 2006). If the listener values culturally sanctioned understandings or trusts an expert's view more than her own perceptual understanding, she may thus come to see her perceptual understanding as defective and in need of revision. Eggebrecht may be right that, among Western listeners, musical misunderstanding typically becomes manifest on a discursive level where language is involved. However, it is wrong to suppose that perceptual misunderstandings do not occur or that such misunderstandings cannot be manifested non-conceptually. When I was invited to dance at a Bulgarian wedding, at first I indeed committed some perceptual mistakes concerning the rhythms, and also manifested them in my gestures!

States of understanding and states of belief

In order to see what is needed for an account of musical understanding that gives credit both to a perceptual and to an epistemic way of making sense of music, while at the same time allowing for a subjective sense of understanding as well as for the possibility of misunderstanding, we might look for advice in theories of linguistic understanding. David Hunter (1998) has argued that states of linguistic understanding are informational states that belong to the same epistemic category as states of perception or memory. Like states of perception, states of understanding are conscious states that are not normally under voluntary control: in hearing speech or reading texts we simply "take in" linguistic meanings without special effort. Such states of understanding may serve as a basis for belief, but they are not in themselves states of belief or knowledge. This is simply because a person may doubt the reliability or truthfulness of her understanding of a text or speech act and therefore fail to believe what she understands it to mean. A reader may have a certain understanding of the meaning of a written sentence, but upon hearing from her more knowledgeable friend that this is not what the sentence really means, she may doubt the appropriateness of her own understanding. This may be so even if she cannot by herself come to understand the sentence in any other way than she initially did. In Hunter's account, understanding itself is taken to be fallible and revisable, but the major point is that the *sense* of understanding may persist even despite the fact that the subject herself doubts its truthfulness.

Similarly, even though one's perceptual grasp of music is revisable, even culturally incorrect ways of perceptually making sense of music may be accepted as states of musical understanding. A Western listener without theoretical knowledge of, say, Indonesian gamelan music may listen to it and learn to perceptually understand it as music, tapping along with a metrical pulse and finding the melodies comprehensible in relation to it, even if knowledge about the end-accented "colotomic" structures that lie at the bottom of gamelan performance would fundamentally call into question her ways of perceptually interpreting the sounds (see Brinner 2008). The listener may, nevertheless, be able to demonstrate behaviorally a state of understanding induced by the sounds heard, and may even proceed to explicate her understanding verbally, ostensively linking her statements to the sounds. Learning about the theory of this music's end-accented structures will not necessarily affect her old habits of perceptually making sense of the music: although she knows that she should somehow modify her perceptual understanding, she may simply be unable to do so. Listeners may thus entertain perceptual understandings that are discordant with their beliefs about what the appropriate way to understand the music in question would be. Treating states of understanding as distinct from states of belief allows both for a sense of understanding and for the possibility of perceptual misunderstanding of music (with respect to culturally authorized perceptual understandings). Note that this distinction does not rely on any value judgments concerning the relative "importance" of perception and belief.

Construing the understanding of music in terms of perceptual states and accounting for the "epistemic understanding" of music in terms of beliefs casts some light on the common idea of music as a "universal language" – as something that retains a part of its comprehensibility across cultural boundaries. Even without relevant, culturally justified true beliefs, it may often be possible to gain some understanding of the heard sounds as music that may be enjoyed, used, and talked about. This is not always appreciated by music researchers. The popular-music scholar Allan Moore, for instance, suggests that style and genre classifications constitute an organization that is individually and socially imposed on the music, but that "it is also an organization we *must* impose if we are to understand the sounds as music" (2001: 441). To back up his case, Moore gives the example that understanding David Bowie's "Fashion" is "dependent on understanding its irony, which in turn is dependent on understanding the genre conventions of up-tempo dance music" (2001: 441). It is hard to see, however, why entertaining culturally sanctioned beliefs concerning the irony in a piece by Bowie should be necessary for understanding it *as music*. Likewise, a listener may have all that is needed to apprehend the sounds as musically meaningful even if she has no clue of the socially accepted genre classification of the music – be it western swing, neoclassicism, or grunge. Even without such knowledge, the listener may hum along, dance to the sounds, react emotionally to chord changes that seem surprising, or manifest any other activities implying that the sounds have been understood as music.

Some theorists appear to think that all musical understanding should be directed toward true beliefs – say, toward true beliefs concerning compositional intentions (e.g. Gruhn 2004: 189). Given this, one might expect the listener's perceptual understanding to be congruent with such beliefs in order to qualify as understanding. This would be a mistake, however, as it would ignore the possibility of a sense of understanding in cases where some serviceable ways of perceptually grasping a piece of music have little to do with the truth of the beliefs entertained. During my first year as a student, a professor played a recording of Messiaen's *Mode de valeurs et d'intensités* and asked what its rhythmical or metrical construction might be. My immediate and confident response, based on the way that I had subjectively heard the piece, was that it was a waltz. For the rest of the lecture, despite having been taught about the pre-serial construction of the piece, I continued to hear it as a waltz. However I tried, I could not "switch off" my perceptual understanding of the piece, even given my true belief that there was really no basis for it in the composition. The point is that sometimes the only public guidelines for true beliefs about heard music – or for a correct "epistemic understanding" of it, if you will – might not make suitable guidelines for perception. In such cases it may arguably be more helpful to rely on subjective and even idiosyncratic perceptual strategies than on none at all, if one wishes to experience the sounds as subjectively meaningful. A one-sided emphasis on true beliefs as the criterion of appropriate musical understanding thus risks losing the "sense of understanding" which – according to the view adopted here – is relevant for experiencing sounds *as music*.

However, there is no reason to deny that some aspects of the significance of Messiaen's composition as a cultural product may surely be understood – in the distinct epistemic sense of forming appropriate beliefs – by acquiring knowledge concerning its hidden compositional structure, despite the relative unconnectedness of such knowledge to perception. Even in the extreme case in which such beliefs remain "empty" of any perceptual musical significance, they may arguably address important issues about music as a form of cultural activity. If this is so, we might indeed accept a sense of epistemic understanding of music even without the "fusion" of theoretical beliefs and auditory perception – without the "enrichment and extension" (DeBellis 1995: 130) of the perceptual musical experience that we often hope explicit musical knowledge will provide.

Whether our beliefs are taken as a part of understanding music "as music," will depend, then, on our answers to the question of what music is: are we trying to understand music as a human expression, as an artifact, as an experience, as a social activity, or perhaps as a cognitive process? As the multitude of research disciplines dedicated to these phenomena attests, our answers will be different depending on how we conceive of the object of understanding. Even if we follow the curiously persistent tendency of philosophers of music to concentrate solely on the understanding of notated Western musical works, our discussion will depend on our views concerning their ontology. For instance, if musical works are mental entities existing in the minds of the composer and the listener (Collingwood 1958: 139), we will be trying to understand mental entities, but if musical works are, say, conjunctions of sound-structure-and-a-structure-of-performance-means-as-indicated-by-X-at-t (Levinson 1990), the understanding of music accordingly becomes a more multidimensional enterprise.

From a given research perspective, and a concomitant conceptualization of the object of study, it may then seem warranted, say, to insist on the importance of grasping genre classifications for understanding the sounds as music, or to claim that the ultimate goal of musical understanding is knowledge concerning compositional intentions. The only problem is that by generalizing such positions we easily lose sight of other, equally valuable ways of trying to understand the many-faceted phenomenon of music. Common symptoms of such myopia are an exclusive concern for the distinction between correct and incorrect beliefs, and a concomitant neglect of the phenomenological sense of understanding. However one wishes to employ "understanding" as a technical term, there are important issues to be addressed on both the perceptual and the epistemic levels.

See also Analysis (Chapter 48), Music and language (Chapter 10), Phenomenology and music (Chapter 53), Psychology of music (Chapter 55), Rhythm, melody, and harmony (Chapter 3), and Silence, sound, noise, and music (Chapter 2).

References

Adorno, T. (1970) *Ästhetische Theorie*, Frankfurt am Main: Suhrkamp Verlag.

Agawu, K. (2006) "Structural Analysis or Cultural Analysis? Competing Perspectives on the 'Standard Pattern' of West African Rhythm," *Journal of the American Musicological Society* 59: 1–46.

Bandur, M. (2004) "Musikalisches Verstehen – sprachliches Begreifen. 'Begriffslosigkeit' und 'Geschichte' in Hans Heinrich Eggebrechts *Musik verstehen*," in Blumröder and Steinbeck, pp. 65–73.

Blumröder, C.V. and Steinbeck, W. (eds) (2004) *Musik und Verstehen*, Laaber: Laaber-Verlag.

Brinner, B. (1995) *Knowing Music, Making Music: Javanese Gamelan and the Theory of Musical Competence and Interaction*, Chicago: The University of Chicago Press.

—— (2008) *Music in Central Java: Experiencing Music, Expressing Culture*, Oxford: Oxford University Press.

Collingwood, R.G. (1958 [1938]) *The Principles of Art*, New York: Oxford University Press.

Danuser, H. (2004) "Lob der Torheit oder Vom Nicht- und Mißverstehen bei ästhetischer Erfahrung," in Blumröder and Steinbeck, pp. 313–31.

d'Arezzo, Guido (1963 [n.d.]) *Regulae rhythmicae in antiphonarii sui prologum prolatae*, in M. Gerbert (ed.) *Scriptores ecclesiastici de musica sacra potissimum*, vol. 2. (reprint of a 1784 edition), Hildesheim: Olms, accessed at www.chmtl.indiana.edu/tml/9th-11th/GUIRR_TEXT.html.

DeBellis, M. (1995) *Music and Conceptualization*, Cambridge: Cambridge University Press.

Dempster, D. (1998) "Is there even a Grammar of Music?" *Musicae Scientiae* 2: 55–65.

Eggebrecht, H.H. (1999) *Musik verstehen*, 2nd edn, Wilhelmshaven: Florian Noetzel Verlag.

—— (2004) "Verstehen durch Analyse," in Blumröder and Steinbeck, pp. 18–27.

Fiske, H.E. (2008) *Understanding Musical Understanding: The Philosophy, Psychology, and Sociology of the Musical Experience*, Lewiston, Queenston, and Lampeter: The Edwin Mellen Press.

Forrest, P. (1991) "Aesthetic Understanding," *Philosophy and Phenomenological Research* 51: 525–40.

Gadamer, H.-G. (1965) *Wahrheit und Methode: Grundzüge einer philosophischen Hermeneutik*, 2nd edn, Tübingen: J.C.B. Mohr (Paul Siebeck).

Gruhn, W. (2004) *Wahrnehmen und Verstehen: Untersuchungen zum Verstehensbegriff in der Musik*, Wilhelmshaven: Florian Noetzel Verlag.

Hunter, D. (1998) "Understanding and Belief," *Philosophy and Phenomenological Research* 58: 559–80.

Huovinen, E. (2008) "Levels and Kinds of Listeners' Musical Understanding," *British Journal of Aesthetics* 48: 315–37.

Kant, I. (1966 [1781]) *Kritik der reinen Vernunft*, Stuttgart: Reclam.

Kivy, P. (2001) "Music in Memory and *Music in the Moment*," in *New Essays on Musical Understanding*, New York: Oxford University Press, pp. 183–217.

Laske, O.E. (1977) *Music, Memory, and Thought: Explorations in Cognitive Musicology*, Ann Arbor: University Microfilms International.

Levinson, J. (1990) "What a Musical Work Is," in *Music, Art, and Metaphysics: Essays in Philosophical Aesthetics*, Ithaca: Cornell University Press, pp. 63–88.

—— (1997) *Music in the Moment*, Ithaca: Cornell University Press.

—— (2006) "Concatenationism, Architectonicism, and the Appreciation of Music," *Revue internationale de philosophie* 60: 505–14.

Lidov, D. (1992) "Toward a Universal Musicology," *The Semiotic Review of Books* 3: 8–10.

Moore, A.F. (2001) "Categorical Conventions in Music Discourse: Style and Genre," *Music and Letters* 82: 432–42.

Scruton, R. (1983) "Understanding Music" in *The Aesthetic Understanding: Essays in the Philosophy of Art and Culture*, London and New York: Methuen, pp. 77–100.

Trout, J.D. (2002) "Scientific Explanation and the Sense of Understanding," *Philosophy of Science* 69: 212–33.

13
STYLE

Jennifer Judkins

Style is the dress of thoughts.
(Lord Chesterfield, in a letter to his son, November 24, 1749 (Roberts 1992: 176))

The nature of musical style and styles

In music, "style" refers roughly to the manner in which a musical work is executed, its mode of expression. The term "style" might be applied to the music of a particular composer (the musical style of Steve Reich), a particular era (late Baroque style), a particular geographical or social unit (Netherlandish style), a school of composition (minimalist style), a compositional technique (contrapuntal style), a medium (orchestral style), a body of work (the style of Mozart's secular works), or an individual work (the style of Mozart's *Requiem*). Recognizing and being familiar with the style of a musical work is generally thought to be prerequisite to a full and correct understanding and appreciation of it (Goodman 1975; Ross 2003). In fact, style is such a rich and immediate feature of music that only a moment's exposure (a few seconds of listening) is usually enough for us to identify it.

In everyday contexts, "style" is typically a lightweight topic. "Style" as a term is often applied to fashion, or etiquette, or custom in general (especially that of high society), with a corresponding implication of frivolity or lack of substance. It might apply to current versions of dress, décor, or even car design, which, while often aesthetically charged, are not in the end artworks. Or, "stylish" may imply just a certain hip *joie de vivre*, which might be recognized in the carriage and personality of people themselves. "Style" in these ordinary contexts is often viewed as "somewhat trivial, its singleminded pursuit morally questionable, since those cultivating style may be neglecting 'deeper,' more important concerns" (Ross 2003: 228).

Yet in music (and in the arts in general), the term "style" is of great import, and it carries broad implications beyond just formal or surface qualities. Style is the *je ne sais quoi* that holds a musical work together. The world of a work of music is clearly separate from the everyday world, and (ideally) even more internally coherent than those of works of painting or literature. In fact, music is perhaps our only true alternative reality (Sparshott 1987: 71). The coherence of a musical world is articulated in its musical style.

Style, whether in fashion, cars, or the arts, is slippery to define per se. It may be easy to point to certain aspects or characteristics of a particular style, but it is very difficult to discuss style in an overarching way, especially in music. We know it when we hear it. The concept of style in Western music has roots in the rhetorical tradition, stretching back to the distinction the Greeks first made between *what* is said versus the manner *in which* it is said. The use of rhetorical terminology in music theory in regard to style was always more focused on vocal rather than instrumental music however, and was most prominent in writings on early opera in the late sixteenth century. (In early Italian opera, the text was the master of the music, and meant to be an imitation of the clear, expressive text settings believed to be characteristic of Greek epic poetry.) Rhetorical classifications of musical style faded in the eighteenth century, and have not returned.

Leonard Meyer puts forth an oft-heard definition of musical style: "Style is a replication of patterning, whether in human behavior or in the artifacts produced by human behavior, that results from a series of choices made within some set of constraints" (Meyer 1996: 3). According to Meyer, understanding artistic and historical constraints allows us to understand "what might have happened" (and "what could not have happened") at any given point in the musical work, which in turn affects our expectations in appreciation. Style is, in his view, *how* things are stated as opposed to *what* is stated, just as it was for the Ancient Greeks.

Other writers have found this definition of style (choices within constraints) insufficient for capturing all of the nuances that determine musical style. Style is not always dependent upon a composer's conscious choice from among alternatives (Goodman 1978: 23). Much of our knowledge of musical style is deeply imbedded and not easily articulated, which is part of music's delight. Music also does not have a subject that it states things about – music means in ways other than "saying something" (Goodman 1975: 799, 803). Nelson Goodman also notes that only certain aspects of a work (i.e. not all musical choices or constraints) are actually elements of its style: "[a] property counts as stylistic only when it associates a work with one rather than another artist, period, region, school, etc. A style is a complex characteristic that serves somewhat as an individual or group signature" (Goodman 1975: 807). In fact, the more complicated and elusive the style, the more we enjoy its exploration and illumination (Goodman 1975: 811).

Arthur Danto suggests that artistic style, in general, is like a history with its own narrative, in which we can trace not only the style's emergence but also the increasing eloquence with which it becomes perceptible in the work (Danto 1991: 208). (The evolution of Beethoven's symphonic style from his first through ninth symphonies might be an example of this sort of increasing eloquence.) We should be wary, though, of viewing music history (and the history of musical styles) as one continuous narrative, with one development yielding to (or causing) the next development in a linear fashion. However, certainly some features of musical works are made legible only by retroactive study: styles are usually labeled or "discovered" by those looking back on musical works in a larger context.

The constraints on a composer can include everyday practical concerns, in addition to higher-level musical issues. For example, the expectations and requirements of the audience or other patrons can greatly condition musical style; in fact, it was traditional in Western music for composers to be in service to courts, churches, and aristocrats, with all of their concomitant restrictions and requests. Performance resources can also affect style – instruments may be limited (no pedal-tuning kettledrums available), or unique (Haydn writing for Prince Esterházy's peculiar instrument, the baryton). Early Classical composers capitalized on the increased sustaining power of Cristofori's newly invented fortepianos by writing treble-dominated "melody and accompaniment." Some stylistic changes in music are in specific reaction to socio-political or ecclesiastical strictures. For example, Shostakovich and Prokofiev were forced to write in a very constrained style, to remain in accordance with the dictates of government-sanctioned "Soviet Realism."

Yet rebellion against established styles themselves has always triggered the most robust changes in musical style. For example, note the tremendous movement around 1600 away from the Flemish counterpoint tradition (and its obscured text) to accompanied solo songs with clearer settings – a shift that ultimately allowed the birth of opera and the Baroque period itself. Or, witness the early twentieth-century expansion of compositional approaches from (solely) tonal music to serial and other non-diatonic techniques, or the birth of rock and roll (an event so epic as to be always termed a "birth").

Musical genres themselves are not styles – "concerto" is not a style – but a genre is often typified by the use of a particular style (and vice versa), and it can be difficult to tease them apart. The definition of musical genre is almost as difficult as that of musical style. Overall, in music, genre refers to the "what," and style to the "how." Musical genres are best articulated with reference to their historical period. For example, one must specify the historical era in order to know what was meant exactly by, say, the terms "motet," "sonata," or "opera" when speaking of them as genres. We should instead speak of a Flemish motet, a nineteenth-century sonata, or a Baroque opera. Genres, unlike styles, also usually imply specific compositional structures or forms – the bones of the piece – that are then fleshed out by the style. Stylistic features are often defined more functionally and less historically than genres – and they must be recurrent features in order to express meaning (Genova 1979: 324).

Style and the Western musical tradition

Style is never a static concept in music. A style can be a synthesis of other styles ("folk rock," "Latin jazz"), or it can just name a wide range of musical possibilities ("Baroque," "Romantic," "serialism," "minimalism," "rococo," "ragtime," "early Italian monody"). There is a vast number of identified musical styles in Western music today, compared to music in many other cultures, and to previous historical eras. A brief list of just some of the best-known current styles illustrates this amazing range: "zydeco," "new age," "soft rock," "reggaeton," "rhythm and blues," "hip hop," "gospel," "honky-tonk," "Nashville Sound," "avant-garde," "Christian rock," "country," "aleatoric," "gangsta rap," "New Orleans jazz," "heavy metal," "salsa," "Afro-Cuban," and "Europop," to name but a handful. It is well beyond the scope of this chapter to document the incredible explosion of musical styles in today's rock and pop music. Any exploration will reveal dozens of subdivisions within any single category, and any comprehensive list would be immediately dated.

Why have so many very different styles continued to appear over the course of Western musical history? There is some speculation that the growth (beginning around the ninth century) of an increasingly specific musical notation in the West may have been a factor in the blossoming of so many musical styles. More specific notation tends to codify musical pieces, making stylistic features more transparent, allowing pieces to be shared more widely, and then, of course, rebelled against, with seams pushed open so that new styles can emerge. Today, many musical traditions, such as rock, pop, and especially jazz, do not employ notation per se as a codifying agent. Instead, the recording itself has become the locus of the work. Still, the desire for definitive versions either written or recorded in Western music – even if only then to generate variations upon them – has allowed easy and wide transmission of stylistic knowledge, which other musicians then imitate and push against. The exponential increase in the accessibility of recordings due to the rise of the internet has only increased the abundance of musical styles around the world. (It would also be difficult to discount the West's recent political and economic domination from any discussion of why we adopt so many of the world's musical styles today, and why many other cultures have embraced Western musical styles.)

Also, in the West, novelty is typically privileged over tradition in the arts. This is not the case in parts of the rest of the world, where tradition does not have a pejorative connotation, but is instead valued as a stabilizing factor (Nketia 1982: 83). (This is not to say that different musical traditions in certain African societies, for example, do not each have a vast array of musical or dance styles – it is just that these styles often evolve more slowly than Western musical styles.) Japanese aesthetics are also quite conservative and traditional, in an interesting contrast to their First-World, often trend-setting status as a nation.

The myriad of musical styles in Western music may also be related to the relative importance of *personal* style in our artistic tradition, at least in the last 500 years. In classical Western music, musicians sit down deliberately to compose a musical work, writing it down in explicit notation. Even in jazz, there are "charts" or scores that, while not as notationally dense as classical scores, are still quite specific as to structure and melodic or harmonic content. In a metal rock band, a musician makes a conscious decision to "write a song," even though this might mean composing on the guitar, demonstrating it to the group, and never committing anything to paper or computer. The song is "notated" by then being recorded. Western musical works have authors, and they have scores or recordings that act as "recipes" or "blueprints." In comparison, for the Blackfoot nation of Native Americans, songs arrived in dreams, from guardian spirits (Nettl 1996: 174). There is no notation, and no known author or even first intermediary. A Cherokee story tells of how all of their songs were originated by a cannibal monster, named Stonecoat, who was finally captured and burned. As he was burning in the fire, he sang and produced all of the songs the Cherokee will ever need for dances, magic, and curing (Heth, Levine, and Gooding 2005: 149).

The elements of musical style

In Western music, traditionally, the major stylistic elements are form, texture, rhythm, harmony, and melody. (I will focus on form and texture in particular here, since rhythm, harmony, and melody are discussed in Chapter 3.) These five elements are present in most musical works to some extent. Note the caveats here: "*most* musical works to *some* extent." Any one of these stylistic elements may be brought to the foreground (or pushed to the background), or given more (or less) importance in expression and meaning in any given style. In the paintings of Monet, for example, pastel shades play a fundamental stylistic role in his attempt to depict different kinds of light falling on different kinds of surface: "No description of Monet's style could omit a reference to his pastel palette" (Robinson 1981: 9). For another painter – say, Vermeer – blurred pastels do not play a major stylistic role. Yet color, which encompasses both Monet's pastels and Vermeer's black and white floor tiles, will always be a large stylistic element of painting, even if it is its absence or muting that is notable.

In somewhat the same way, in music we have form, texture, rhythm, harmony, and melody as large stylistic elements. In general, the relative success of any musical feature depends upon how that feature contributes to the work's general aesthetic significance. Interestingly, the degree of complexity, variability, or predominance of any stylistic feature may or may not precisely reflect its contribution to the musical style. (And again, in avant-garde works, it may be their absence that is notable.) Harmonic change is simplistic in rock and roll music, and complex in a Wagnerian opera. Yet we would hesitate to say that harmonic change is more "important" in one than in the other – it just plays a larger role in the characterization of Wagner's style. The lack of melodic development in hip-hop music is certainly part of the essence of that style, even though it is not as evolving or variable as the rhythmic interest.

Often, in music, it is only one or two stylistic features that predominate, playing the largest roles. (We would have difficulty aurally understanding works in which all stylistic elements were immensely variable.) Wagner's complex harmony is presented in a rather straightforward rhythmic style, and this helps us follow the intricate harmonic development. On occasion, the strong presence of one stylistic element necessarily mutes another: in a minuet and trio, the strict form precludes any extensive harmonic development.

Thus the major stylistic elements in music, like those in the visual arts, can not only be identified, but also weighed – not for their "importance," but rather for their role in the work. For example, repetitive rhythms play a central role in minimalist style, while there may be no melody at all, or only melodic fragments. This is not the case in Debussy's *Prélude à l'après-midi d'un faune*, where a multi-layered ethereal texture is more prominent than any rhythmic interest. Identifiable rhythm almost evaporates in Gregorian chant, yet loud, regular, even hypnotic rhythmic patterns typify rock music, with its strong drum-set "time." Even within a single work from a specific musical period (e.g. Handel's *Messiah*), there can be drastically different roles for rhythm in each movement– yet all fall within the boundaries of Baroque rhythmic style. Rhythms might be thicker and steadily subdivided (as in the "Hallelujah Chorus"), or they might be rather sparse and improvisational (as in the recitative "Comfort Ye, My People").

"Musical form" is usually taken to mean the form of the musical work in a basic structural sense – something it might share with other works, rather than its unique structural profile. Musical forms often feature a great deal of repetition, as the nature of music itself is that it flows past the listener through time. The audience requires repetition in the musical work (more than in any of the other arts), in order that structural features of the form can be recalled and made intelligible. Contemporary music does not often feature the large repeated sections more typical of earlier music (for example, a Mozart *da capo* aria), and contemporary works are sometimes quite fragmented, or, conversely, quite repetitive on a very small level. Still, the musical form in successful works, however tenuous, must have an organicism – the musical structure must seem to grow from its musical materials and the style overall – and provide some sort of aural signposts for the listener.

Very straightforward musical forms are typical of music through the Classical era, and of many genres and styles even now. Basic musical forms can be quite easy to summarize. A piece might have a binary form (aabb), a ternary form (aba), a rounded binary form (aababa), or a pop-song (32-bar) form (aaba). "The Star Spangled Banner," for example, has a simple aabc form. Historically, music has also often reflected particular dance forms. Some musical forms are very specific to an era or genre, and some are not. The *virelai* (AbbaA), for example, is peculiar to medieval France and fixed forever in that moment in music history. "Sonata-allegro" or "first-movement" form, on the other hand, has taken on a life of its own, perhaps since it is a more flexible framework for musical events. It begins to appear in the Classical era in fairly simple presentation, then is elaborated and greatly expanded in the Romanticism of the nineteenth century, and is even seen in skeletal incarnations in the twentieth century. It can be found in the compositions of Mozart, Haydn, Beethoven, Mahler, Strauss, Stravinsky, and Schoenberg, helping to support and being at the same time the clothing for all of their different musical styles.

Musical forms, like so many elements of musical style, are generally soft concepts that are stretched and manipulated, so that we have to consider each of even the strictest forms (like the *virelai* above) as only a basic outline for a composer. Adding to the difficulty, it is not unusual in popular usage to have musical forms not only conflated with musical styles and genres but also with compositional procedures. The first movement of Beethoven's Fifth Symphony is in sonata form, but the genre of the work is "symphony." We speak of a fugue oftentimes as if it were a form, when it is actually, more strictly speaking, a genre that requires a specific stylistic process.

Although form represents the basic construction or outline of a musical work, we probably recognize musical styles more quickly based on their texture than on any other musical element. In music, much as in ordinary life, "texture" refers to both surface and thickness. The texture of a piece is somewhat like an MRI of that work – a vertical cross-section. Texture is the most open concept in musical style, and comprises many of our instinctive initial impressions. The adjectives "thick," "thin," "light," "dark," and "heavy" are often used, just as when speaking of non-artistic texture. Much more so than forms, certain musical textures are often immediately characteristic of particular musical styles; for example, we need to hear only a few seconds of electronic bass pounding out of the trunk of the car next to us, or a moment or two or a Dixieland band in order to identify their styles.

It might seem initially that certain musical instruments or characteristics would naturally produce denser or darker textures, and certain ones would produce lighter textures. However, "texture" in music refers solely to the resultant soundscape, and not necessarily to the instrumentation or compositional technique. Aaron Copland's "Appalachian Spring" was rescored for full symphony orchestra, yet the resulting texture is often quite light, since, in general, the tessitura (pitch range) is rather high, the pitch intervals are very open, and there are many rests in many parts. A Bach Brandenburg Concerto is written for a very small ensemble, yet the texture can be rather dense. In these concertos, oftentimes, everyone is playing – in that Baroque way of constantly "spinning out" – and the instruments are closely scored in pitch, creating a considerable density within a small chamber work.

There are some traditional terms for the various compositional techniques that produce different textures. In simple terms, music may be contrapuntal (also called "polyphonic"), or it may be homophonic. Contrapuntal music is more horizontally directed, with lines of music each having nearly equal integrity and nearly equal roles in the texture. In a Palestrina mass, for example, each sung part has its own rhythmic integrity, but all parts are equal in weight. Note that music can be contrapuntal without being fugal, which is an imitative process with very strict rules about time and pitch intervals. Homophonic musical texture, in contrast, is more vertically directed, with some lines clearly subservient in importance and in overall texture. Homophonic music customarily features a top melody over an accompaniment, such as we hear in an operatic aria, or a U2 song. A trumpet concerto (or any solo concerto) may also illustrate homophonic texture, with a soloist playing a melody over an orchestral accompaniment. Homophonic music might also adopt a chordal style, as heard in a church hymn: a prominent melody (generally in the highest voice) is supported by multiple other lines, each of which simply emphasizes chord tones in the same basic rhythm as the melodic line (without the independent melodic interest that would be found in contrapuntal music).

Composers, like other artists, thrive when they can play against rules and prescriptions, and this has been as true for texture as for any other musical element. Some of the most dense, almost mathematical organ fugues of Bach are preceded by the lightest and freest of preludes, which seem almost without specific rhythm, as if improvised on the spot. We can speak of tendencies in different eras toward contrapuntal or homophonic textures, but exceptions litter the landscape.

Understanding musical style

In music, it has been noted that style is not as easily isolated from substance as it can be, for example, in literature. The elements of musical style – form, texture, rhythm, harmony, and melody – are not clearly distinct from the substance of the work itself. Musical styles may share elements, and yet each element may have a very different significance in each context. Dotted rhythms characterize the seventeenth-century French overture style, but they are also a feature of Irish jigs and swing music. Stepwise melodic lines characterize both Gregorian chant and twentieth-century minimalist music. Both the monody of Monteverdi (seventeenth century) and the pointillism of Webern (twentieth century) employ thin textures. Thus how each element contributes to the aesthetic significance of the piece is what matters more to the musical style, not the mere fact that a given element is employed (Robinson 1981: 9).

A listener's recognition and appreciation of musical style comes from an understanding of the theories and histories of music, and those theories and histories in turn provide an important framework for the composer's creativity (Carroll 1995: 251). The history of music offers periods of relative stylistic stability (the High Renaissance, the Classical era in general), often alternating with periods of instability and change (the fourteenth-century Ars Nova, the early Baroque after 1600, twentieth-century experimentalism). During these periods of "stylistic flux," the "jostling among conventions, expressive devices, and 'purely musical' procedures is very apparent" (McClary 2000:

4). (McClary uses quotation marks here, as she believes that the term "purely musical" is often inaccurately applied, arguing that we cannot divorce music from culture, gender, and politics.)

Knowledge of stylistic conventions plays a huge role in musical understanding – many scholars point to expectations based on these conventions (which may be fulfilled or defeated) as crucial to appreciation. As conventions are ultimately overused and run-through, new solutions take their place. In painting, the Impressionist movement ran its course, and one can no longer term oneself an "Impressionist painter." So too with music. Time has run out on being a Baroque composer (although one may deliberately compose in a Baroque style). Also, just as in painting, the rise and fall of styles in music are not always as clearly defined as the table of contents in a history textbook would have us believe. What Danto notes of the visual arts is also true for music: "we have cases of movements stopping but not ending, ending but not stopping, ending and stopping, though there is nothing that appears to be neither ending nor stopping. The important consideration is that art is killed by art, and the interesting consideration is why this is so" (Danto 1991: 209).

See also Notations (Chapter 7), and Rhythm, melody, and harmony (Chapter 3).

References

Carroll, N. (1995) "Danto, Style, and Intention," *Journal of Aesthetics and Art Criticism* 53: 251–7.

Danto, A. (1991) "Narrative and Style," *Journal of Aesthetics and Art Criticism* 49: 201–9.

Genova, J. (1979) "The Significance of Style," *Journal of Aesthetics and Art Criticism* 37: 315–24.

Goodman, N. (1975) "The Status of Style," *Critical Inquiry* 1: 799–811.

—— (1978) *Ways of Worldmaking*, Indianapolis: Hackett.

Heth, C., Levine, V., and Gooding, E. (2005) "American Indian Musical Cultures," in E. Kosko (ed.) *Music Cultures in the United States*, New York: Routledge, pp. 139–60.

McClary, S. (2000) *Conventional Wisdom: The Content of Musical Form*, Berkeley: University of California Press.

Meyer, L. (1996) *Style and Music: Theory, History, and Ideology*, Chicago: University of Chicago Press.

Nettl, B. (1996) "Ideas about Music and Musical Thought: Ethnomusicological Perspectives," *Journal of Aesthetic Education* 30: 173–87.

Nketia, J.K. (1982) "Developing Contemporary Idioms out of Traditional Music," *Studia Musicologica Academiae Scientarum Hungaricae* 24, Supplementum: Report of the Musicological Congress of the International Music Council, pp. 81–97.

Roberts, D. (ed.) (1992) *Lord Chesterfield's Letters*, Oxford: Oxford University Press.

Robinson, J. (1981) "Style and Significance in Art History," *Journal of Aesthetics and Art Criticism* 40: 5–14.

Ross, S. (2003) "Style in Art," in J. Levinson (ed.) *Oxford Handbook of Aesthetics*, Oxford: Oxford University Press, pp. 228–44.

Sparshott, F. (1987) "Aesthetics of Music: Limits and Grounds," in P. Alperson (ed.) *What is Music? An Introduction to the Philosophy of Music*, University Park: Pennsylvania State University Press, pp. 33–98.

Further reading

Van Eck, C., McAllister, J., and van de Vall, R. (eds) (1995) *The Question of Style in Philosophy and the Arts*, Cambridge: Cambridge University Press. (A collection of essays that extends the discussion of style to architecture, science, and even philosophy itself.)

14

AESTHETIC PROPERTIES

Rafael De Clercq

The aesthetic appreciation of music, like the aesthetic appreciation of art in general, consists at least in part in the attribution of aesthetic properties of various kinds. Prototypical aesthetic properties include beauty, elegance, gracefulness, balance, harmony, delicacy, loveliness, and unity, and their negative counterparts, for example, ugliness, clumsiness, and disunity. Less prototypical, perhaps, are powerfulness, vividness, and boldness, as well as properties referring to human moods and emotions, for example, being mournful, sad, angry, melancholic, brooding, passionate, and anguished. Similarly, properties connected with a work's position in the history of art such as being original, derivative, influential, impressionist, and expressionist, are less prototypical, although some authors regard them as aesthetic properties. (For a survey of what are considered to be aesthetic properties, see De Clercq 2008.) Perhaps such properties are more appropriately labeled *artistic*. Whether this label carries any definite content, however, remains to be seen. The term "artistic property" has been used to designate a wide variety of properties, including, in addition to the aforementioned historical and stylistic properties, various kinds of representational and semantic properties such as being realistic, being about a certain person or event, and symbolizing the "cycle of death and creation" (Davies 2006: 56). None of these seems to stand out as paradigmatic among the artistic properties. Moreover, it is not clear whether they have anything significant in common except for being occasionally exemplified by works of art – a property they share with an even more gerrymandered set of properties. In comparison, the notion of an aesthetic property seems to be better understood and more likely to correspond to a real distinction.

Obviously, an aesthetic property can be ascribed to a musical work as a whole, to a more or less distinct part of it (for example, a passage, movement, or theme), or to a performance of the work. In the philosophical literature, many questions have been raised regarding the nature, reality, and attribution of aesthetic properties. To mention but a few: What distinguishes aesthetic properties from other kinds of properties? Do such properties exist? Are there objective grounds for attributing them to a work? In what follows, however, the focus will be on questions that concern specifically the aesthetic properties *of music*. In particular: What determines whether a musical piece has a certain aesthetic property? Is music capable of having emotional properties such as sadness? Are there aesthetic properties that music is incapable of having? These questions will be taken in turn in the following three sections.

Formalism

Formalism is a view in the philosophy of art that has been around for some time. Rightly or wrongly, it is associated with such historical figures as Leon Battista Alberti (1404–72), Immanuel Kant (1724–1804), Robert Zimmerman (1824–98), Eduard Hanslick (1825–1904), Roger Fry (1866–1934), and Clive Bell (1881–1964). Although it is difficult to state precisely what formalism consists of in general, formalists share the idea that the class of aesthetically relevant properties of a work of art is smaller and more homogeneous than the class of properties one might be inclined to consider. More specifically, formalists believe that only *immediately perceivable* qualities are relevant. In the case of music, such qualities include pitch, timbre, loudness, duration, and properties directly determined by these such as melody, harmony, rhythm, and dynamics. Excluded, in any case, are properties that relate to the origin of the work: artistic intentions, the cultural circumstances in which the work was created, and so on.

This kind of formalism is implausible as a general thesis about music because it cannot account for the role lyrics, musical allusions, performance means, and extra-musical references play in music appreciation. For example, how the words in a song are to be understood cannot be derived from the way they sound; not even that they *are* words can be so derived. Similarly, the references to non-musical events or states of affairs that are part and parcel of program music cannot be picked up merely on the basis of how a piece of music sounds. Yet in both cases – word meaning and extra-musical reference – we seem to be dealing with something of aesthetic or artistic importance.

A defensible formalism would thus have to involve a restriction, and the restriction can take at least two (logically independent) forms:

1. *Some* musical works are such that *all* their aesthetic properties are entirely determined by the way they sound.
2. *All* musical works are such that *some* of their aesthetic properties are entirely determined by the way they sound.

Here "the way they sound" is to be understood as meaning what sounds – characterized in terms of pitch, timbre, loudness, and duration – occur in what order. And an aesthetic property of a work is considered to be "entirely determined by" the way the work sounds just in case any same-sounding work is guaranteed to have the same aesthetic property. (Although theses 1 and 2 are, strictly speaking, logically independent, thesis 1 implies thesis 2 given an extra assumption that some may be willing to accept: the assumption that the complement of an aesthetic property – for example, *not*-being-beautiful – is itself an aesthetic property.)

The idea behind thesis 1 is to restrict formalism to so-called "absolute" or "pure instrumental" music, as in Zangwill (2001). Thus, Schubert's piano sonatas would have all their aesthetic properties determined by the way they sound, but not necessarily his songs. The idea behind thesis 2, on the other hand, is to restrict formalism to particular aesthetic properties such as *musical beauty*, as (perhaps) in Hanslick (1986). Thus, Schubert's piano sonatas and his songs may both have musical beauty merely in virtue of how they sound, but they could still differ in other aesthetic respects from works that sound the same. If this idea sounds strange, think of musical beauty as a "specifically musical kind of beauty . . . that is self-contained and in no need of content from outside itself, that consists simply and solely of tones and their artistic combination" (Hanslick 1986: 28). If such a distinct kind of beauty exists, and there is also a kind of beauty which is *not* specifically musical (a beauty that can be shared by works in different art forms), then the idea behind thesis 2 should start to make sense. For musical works that sound the same could then differ in respect of this more general kind of beauty without differing in respect of the specifically musical kind.

How plausible are these restricted versions of formalism? They are not much more plausible than the unrestricted version considered earlier. Consider, for example, that the idea behind thesis 1 is that the aesthetic properties of a piece of purely instrumental music are entirely determined by the way the work sounds. This is to rule out that such a piece might derive some of its aesthetic character from musical allusions, as a musical parody does, or from the way it is supposed to be performed. (See, for example, Walton 1970: 349–50 for more on the aesthetic relevance of performance means.) But the two theses also face a more fundamental problem. For suppose that the unrestricted version of formalism is false, in other words, that it is not the case that:

3. *All* musical works are such that *all* their aesthetic properties are entirely determined by the way they sound.

The two restrictions – thesis 1 and thesis 2 – can then be seen as offering different explanations of why thesis 3 is false. According to the first restriction, thesis 3 is false because it makes a claim about all *musical works*. If this explanation is correct, then some musical works have aesthetic properties that are not entirely determined by the way they sound. So, assuming that thesis 1 is true, there would be two kinds of aesthetic property: aesthetic properties that are, and ones that are not, wholly determined by the way a work sounds. (Note that it would go against the idea of determination, as explained earlier, to say that a property is wholly determined by a certain factor in one work but not wholly determined by that factor in another work. That a property of a work is determined by a factor X means that *every* work with X must be indiscernible with respect to the property.)

According to the second restriction, thesis 3 is false because it makes a claim about all *aesthetic properties*. If this explanation is correct, then some of a work's aesthetic properties are not wholly determined by the way it sounds. Again, but now assuming that thesis 2 is true, there would be two kinds of aesthetic property: aesthetic properties that are, and ones that are not, wholly determined by the way a work sounds. But now the important question, touching the motivation behind *both* restrictions, is: what reason do we have to suppose that the aesthetic properties of music fall into these two separate categories?

In response, moderate formalists are likely to point to the different dimensions of music appreciation: musical pieces can be appreciated for the way they sound, and nothing more, but they can also be appreciated for the way they (help to) convey some extra-musical content, for example, how they bring out the emotional quality of a movie scene or induce a particular feeling. In the first, "formal" case, all the features of a work that are not directly audible are ignored, in the second case they are not. If the two modes of appreciation are seen as supplementary, as they often are (see, for example, Levinson 1998), then they should not contradict one another. And how else can they fail to contradict one another than by ascribing aesthetic properties of different kinds? In other words, if the second, more comprehensive mode of music appreciation is not in tension with the first, then there should be aesthetic properties that depend on sound properties (pitch, timbre, loudness, and duration) alone. And that is exactly what the moderate formalist believes.

The desired conclusion, however, does not follow. After all, there is more than one way in which the compatibility of different modes of appreciation of a work can be secured. Let me offer just a couple of suggestions. One: the different modes may be only superficially concerned with the same object. On closer inspection, different objects may turn out to be involved, say, an abstract sound pattern and a musical work – the sound pattern being the object of the formal mode of music appreciation, the musical work being the object of the more comprehensive mode of music appreciation. (See Chapter 4, 'Ontology,' in this volume for more on the possible difference between a sound pattern and a musical work.) Two: it may be that one of the appreciative modes is based on imagining the work in question to be a different kind of work. For example, the formal mode of music appreciation may be based on imagining the work in question to be a piece of absolute music rather than a piece of program music. Because the work may *in fact* be a piece of program music, the aesthetic judgment issued in the formal mode should not be categorical but hypothetical. In other words, a positive judgment made in that mode should take the form "*if* the work's sound structure were the sound structure of a piece of absolute music, *then*, all else being equal, that (absolute) work would be great." The hypothetical form of such a judgment allows it to co-exist with potential negative evaluations of the work made in the more comprehensive mode.

In light of the foregoing, it seems that there is no good reason to suppose that the aesthetic properties of music fall into two kinds: ones that depend on sound properties alone, and ones that do not. The existence of different modes of music appreciation can be explained at least equally well by the assumption that such appreciation is not always directed at the same object or based on the same mental act. Consequently, there is no good reason to suppose that thesis 1 or 2 defines a kind of formalism that is more plausible than the one defined by thesis 3.

For the sake of completeness, let me signal that the term "formalism" has also been used in a slightly different way in recent years, namely, as a name for the thesis that absolute music lacks representational or semantic content. In other words, such music is not supposed to be "of or about" something (Kivy 2002: 67–8). Given plausible assumptions, this thesis may be implied by thesis 3, but it neither implies thesis 3 nor any of the other formalist theses considered so far. The main problem with this thesis is that it is either wrong or trivial. It is trivial if absolute music is conceived as music that is not "of or about" something. It is wrong if absolute music is conceived as music that is not connected to a text – for example, a title or lyrics. After all, a musical parody may lack such a connection and yet be a parody *of* a musical work, genre or style. (The sense in which parodies are "of" other works seems to involve a relation of reference that is plausibly considered "semantic.")

Realism

In aesthetics, realism is the view that at least some things (objects, events) have aesthetic properties; antirealism is the denial of this claim. A striking consequence of antirealism is that none of our aesthetic judgments are, strictly speaking, true. Antirealists are divided with respect to the question of whether that makes all aesthetic judgments false. Some will answer this question in the positive, others will respond that aesthetic judgments simply do not have or express truth-apt contents (propositions). On this second view, what *appear* to be aesthetic descriptions are in point of fact expressions of attitudes such as approval or disapproval. The norm such expressive acts aim to satisfy is not truth but quasi-truth at best. (See Blackburn 1993 for more on quasi-truth, and Hopkins 2001 for a sketch of what a quasi-realist position in aesthetics might look like.)

One can be an antirealist with respect to aesthetic properties for the same reasons that one can be an antirealist with respect to moral properties or values in general: because there is profound disagreement about what has these properties, because the properties are "queer" compared to other properties (for example, physical properties), because they do not figure in important explanations, or because their dependence on so-called natural properties is mysterious. And there are no doubt reasons not mentioned in this list. However, in aesthetics, Roger Scruton (1997) has devised a special argument to show that music does not have the emotional properties we tend to ascribe to it: sadness, joy, melancholy, etc. The argument does not obviously generalize to other aesthetic properties of music, but if it were sound, it would legitimate an antirealist view of a major part of aesthetic discourse. It is worth quoting the argument in full, because an unsophisticated rendering is likely to diminish whatever force attaches to it:

> If we say that the Countess's aria "Dove sono" from *Le nozze di Figaro* actually possesses the sadness that we hear in it, we face the question whether this sadness is the same property as that possessed by a sad person or another property. It surely cannot be the *same* property; the sadness of person is a property that only conscious organisms can possess. But it cannot be *another* property, since it is precisely this word – "sad" – with its normal meaning, that we apply to the music, and that is the whole point of the description. To say that the word ascribes, in this use, another property is to say that it has another sense – in other words that it is not used metaphorically but ambiguously. If that were so, we could equally have used some other word to make the point, and someone could be an expert at noticing the property we describe as musical sadness, even though he vehemently denies that the music can be sad. . . . But that is surely absurd: if he refuses to describe the music as sad, then he has not noticed the sadness. It follows that the word "sad" attributes to the music neither the property that is possessed by sad people, nor any other property. It therefore attributes no property at all.
>
> (Scruton 1997: 154)

As Gary Iseminger (1999) and Malcolm Budd (2005: 114–19) have pointed out, the argument places all cases of ambiguity on a par, and is not sensitive to the connection that may exist between the various properties attributed by means of an ambiguously used word. In the case of metaphor, there is of course always *some* connection, but the connection may vary in strength. For example, when a professor is called a white elephant because he is exceptional and yet of dubious value, the connection is only a contingent, *a posteriori* one. If white elephants had been more common, the connection would have been different and the metaphor an inappropriate characterization of the professor. However, when music is called "sad," the connection between the attributed property and the literal or more common meaning of "sad" may be much tighter. It may be, for instance, that music is sad because it makes one feel sad or because it resembles ordinary sadness in crucial respects. (See the chapters in Part II of this volume.) If an account of musical sadness along such lines is correct, then the connection between the sadness attributed to music and the sadness attributed to living, sentient beings is neither contingent nor *a posteriori*, but rather conceptual or analytic. If this is so, knowing that a piece of music is sad would not be possible without somehow grasping its relation to ordinary, felt sadness. And such a connection is precisely what Scruton seems to be looking for in the passage quoted above.

Of course, Scruton might reply that there is as yet no agreed-upon analysis of what musical sadness is. (By an "analysis" of a property is meant here an explicit definition or a statement in non-circular terms of the necessary and sufficient conditions for the exemplification of the property.) But the idea that there is a conceptual or analytic *connection* between musical sadness and ordinary sadness does not imply that there is an *analysis* of musical sadness in terms of ordinary sadness, let alone that such an analysis has already been formulated in the literature. Compare: the fact that there is a conceptual or analytic connection between knowledge and truth does not imply that knowledge can be analyzed in terms of truth. Moreover, if there is one thing on which the analyses proposed in the literature seem to agree, it is that there is a close conceptual connection between musical sadness on the one hand and ordinary sadness on the other. In sum, Scruton's argument for antirealism is flawed because there is a realist explanation of why ascriptions of emotional properties to music are informed by an understanding of what it means for a conscious being to be sad. (For an alternative explanation, see Zangwill 2001: ch. 10, and for criticism of this alternative explanation, Budd 2005: 115–18.)

Sublimity and profundity

Are there aesthetic properties that music cannot exemplify? When "sublime" is not used as a mere term of praise, roughly equivalent to "excellent," it is often used to designate an aesthetic property that objects exemplify in virtue of being immense, mighty, and even terrifying (see, for example, Burke 1990 and Kant 1998). Accordingly, one's natural attitude toward sublime objects is generally taken to be one of awe, reverence, and even fear. Thunderstorms, mountains, and skyscrapers can easily qualify as sublime in this sense, but what about musical works? Of course, a musical work can be extremely long or loud, and be immense or terrifying as a result, but then it is more likely to inspire irritation than respect. However, it seems that the characteristics in virtue of which objects qualify as sublime need not be *literally* present. For example, a musical work such as Beethoven's Fifth Symphony can be considered sublime even if listening to it acquaints us with something which is only metaphorically "colossal," "immeasurable," and "ever-rising" (Hoffmann 1975: 84). (See Bicknell 2009: ch. 2 for a more comprehensive treatment of the musical sublime.)

Although music may not literally possess the features in virtue of which other objects are called "sublime," there has been more philosophical debate about whether it can be called "profound." For example, Peter Kivy (1990: ch. 10,

1997: ch. 6, 2003) has argued that absolute music cannot be profound. A profound work of art, in Kivy's view, must "(1) have a profound subject matter and (2) treat this profound subject matter in a way adequate to its profundity – which is to say, (a) say profound things about this subject matter and (b) do it at a very high level of artistic and aesthetic excellence" (Kivy 1997: 145). Kivy is flexible about the way in which a work of art can be said to say something about its subject matter. He explicitly states that it need not be "in a direct manner" (1997: 145), as in a journalistic piece or a philosophical work. In his view, it can also happen through "suggestion" or "implication" (2003: 404). Of course, this should come as no surprise. In ordinary conversational contexts, too, what is said often does not coincide with what is literally meant or expressed (Soames 2009). But although we can say something that differs from what our words literally mean, we cannot (literally) say something without using words. To be sure, a thought can be communicated in a variety of ways – by winking, laughing, gesturing – but only its linguistic communication is a way of *saying* something. It is easy to see, then, why Kivy believes that absolute music cannot be profound. Because absolute music does not involve song or an accompanying text it is incapable of literally saying something, which means that condition (2a) cannot be satisfied.

The obvious response to this line of reasoning is to replace "saying" with "communicating" in the formulation of condition (2a). After all, it may be asked, if music can *communicate* profound thoughts, why bother about whether it can literally *say* things? But the problem with this kind of response is that a profound thought need not be communicated by profound means. In fact, it is only in special circumstances that the means of conveying a profound thought are themselves considered profound. For instance, when a profound thought is communicated by linguistic means such as a written text or an utterance, then the profundity is (usually) transferred to these. But when a profound thought is communicated by non-linguistic means such as a wink or a blush, the profundity is not transferred to them. In other words, it is odd to call a wink or a blush profound, but it is not odd to call a text or an utterance profound. What explains the difference is that linguistic items such as utterances can *share* their content with thoughts (one can say what one is thinking); and thoughts are profound in virtue of the content they have. Non-linguistic items such as winks and blushes, by contrast, cannot have the kind of content thoughts have, although they can serve to communicate such thoughts.

So it would not much help a defender of musical profundity to appeal to the capacity of absolute music to communicate or convey thoughts. Non-linguistic items such as winks and blushes also have such a capacity, but they never seem to inherit the profundity of the thoughts they help to convey.

A more radical response to Kivy's line of reasoning is to say that profundity does not have to be understood in a "propositional" manner. On this view, there may be other kinds of profundity in art, not requiring that anything truth-apt be asserted or conveyed. For example, according to Jerrold Levinson, the "*sine qua non*" of a musical work's profundity is its capacity to elicit "an impression of knowledge," a sense of "having seen" (1992: 59–60). Whether the sense or impression is of having acquired propositional knowledge, Levinson leaves open. The problem with this view is that it makes it hard to understand why profundity should be regarded as an aesthetic merit. Why should it be considered more valuable from an aesthetic point of view than a work's capacity to elicit, say, *déjà vu*, or any other curious psychological state? Having an impression of knowledge does not seem to be valuable in itself, and may even be of disvalue where no knowledge is actually acquired. Kivy's account, by contrast, has no problem explaining the aesthetic value of profundity because of its condition (2b).

Stephen Davies has also taken the non-propositional line in defense of musical profundity. According to him, a musical work can be profound in virtue of illustrating "to a jaw-dropping degree the inexhaustible fecundity, flexibility, insight, vitality, subtlety, complexity, and analytic far-reachingness of which the mind is capable" (2002: 351). This kind of profundity, as Davies himself points out, can also be found in chess games, and no doubt also in certain technological and scientific advances, political strategies, and criminal behavior. The obvious problem facing this account is that it seems too coarse or general. Profundity seems to be a matter merely of being able to serve as proof of someone's ingenuity. Stated in this manner, it seems that a musical work could be profound on Davies's account even when the composer's ingenuity has served, say, commercial rather than artistic purposes. This problem is alleviated only a little bit if the composer's ingenuity is explicitly required to serve artistic purposes, for clearly there can be ingenuity in the service of such purposes that does not amount to profundity. Consider, for example, the ingenuity that goes into animation film and various sorts of computer-generated art.

Without doubt there are more ways in which profundity in art can be understood. For example, taking inspiration from Walton's account of style (Walton 1979), one might suggest that a work is profound if it appears to have been made by a profound person (i.e. if it appears that way to a sensitive subject perceiving the work in the right category and so on). In other words, if the choices apparently made in the creation of the work reveal a character or personality that is mindful of valuable things forgotten, ignored, or overlooked, it may qualify as profound. Probably, some absolute music can qualify as profound in this sense. But the problem underlying the whole debate, as should have become clear by now, is that neither common sense nor art-critical practice seem to offer enough guidance to decide the issue of how profundity in art is to be understood. How else could philosophers have ended up with such widely divergent accounts of profundity, not even agreeing about whether it is propositional or not? In any case, the important point for this chapter is that none of the above accounts implies that profundity is a paradigmatic aesthetic property. True, Kivy's account makes explicit reference to "artistic and aesthetic excellence," but that does not necessarily make profundity itself aesthetic. A property defined by reference to aesthetic properties need not itself be an aesthetic property (any more than a person recognized by his shirt need himself be a piece of clothing). As a consequence, Kivy's claim that absolute music cannot be profound *need not* be understood as the claim that absolute music cannot exemplify certain aesthetic properties.

See also Arousal theories (Chapter 20), Hanslick (Chapter 33), Music's arousal of emotions (Chapter 22), Ontology (Chapter 4), Resemblance theories (Chapter 21), and Rhythm, melody, and harmony (Chapter 3).

References

Bicknell, J. (2009) *Why Music Moves Us*, New York: Palgrave Macmillan.

Blackburn, S. (1993) *Essays in Quasi-Realism*, Oxford: Oxford University Press.

Budd, M. (2005) "Aesthetic Realism and Emotional Qualities of Music," *British Journal of Aesthetics* 45: 111–25.

Burke, E. (1990 [1759]) *A Philosophical Enquiry into the Origin of our Ideas of the Sublime and Beautiful*, ed. A. Phillips, Oxford: Oxford University Press.

Davies, S. (2002) "Profundity in Instrumental Music," *British Journal of Aesthetics* 42: 343–56.

—— (2006) *The Philosophy of Art*, Oxford: Blackwell.

De Clercq, R. (2008) "The Structure of Aesthetic Properties," *Philosophy Compass* 3: 894–909.

Hanslick, E. (1986 [1891]) *On the Musically Beautiful: A Contribution towards the Revision of the Aesthetics of Music*, trans. G. Payzant, Indianapolis: Hackett.

Hoffmann, E.T.A. (1975 [1813]) "Beethoven's Instrumental Music," in *E.T.A. Hoffman and Music*, ed. and trans. R.M. Shafer, Toronto: University of Toronto Press, pp. 83–9.

Hopkins, R. (2001) "Kant, Quasi-Realism, and the Autonomy of Aesthetic Judgement," *European Journal of Philosophy* 9: 166–89.

Iseminger, G. (1999) Review of Scruton 1997, *Journal of Aesthetics and Art Criticism* 57: 374–5.

Kant, I. (1998 [1781]) *Critique of Pure Reason*, trans. P. Guyer and A.W. Wood, Cambridge: Cambridge University Press.

Kivy, P. (1990) *Music Alone: Philosophical Reflections on the Purely Musical Experience*, Ithaca: Cornell University Press.

—— (1997) *Philosophies of Arts: An Essay in Differences*, Cambridge: Cambridge University Press.

—— (2002) *Introduction to a Philosophy of Music*, Oxford: Oxford University Press.

—— (2003) "Another Go at Musical Profundity: Stephen Davies and the Game of Chess," *British Journal of Aesthetics* 43: 401–11.

Levinson, J. (1992) "Musical Profundity Misplaced," *Journal of Aesthetics and Art Criticism* 50: 58–60.

—— (1998) "Evaluating Music," in P. Alperson (ed.) *Musical Worlds: New Directions in the Philosophy of Music*, University Park: Pennsylvania State University Press, pp. 93–108.

Scruton, R. (1997) *The Aesthetics of Music*, Oxford: Oxford University Press.

Soames, S. (2009) "The Gap between Meaning and Assertion: Why What We Literally Say Often Differs from What Our Words Literally Mean," in *Philosophical Essays*, vol. 1: *Natural Language: What it Means and How We Use it*, Princeton: Princeton University Press, pp. 278–97.

Walton, K. (1970) "Categories of Art," *Philosophical Review* 79: 334–67.

—— (1979) "Style and the Processes and Products of Art," in B. Lang (ed.) *The Concept of Style*, Philadelphia: University of Pennsylvania Press, pp. 45–66.

Zangwill, N. (2001) *The Metaphysics of Beauty*, Ithaca: Cornell University Press.

15
VALUE
Alan H. Goldman

A mystery

When one truly describes music as sequences of sounds or tones, it immediately seems mysterious how it could have the value for us that it does. Pure instrumental music does not (or need not) represent anything or inform us about anything. It does not teach us about ordinary life or the objects that occupy us within it. Unlike painting and literature, it is an essentially abstract art, lacking referential content and any direct relation to the world of ordinary objects. From literature we can learn how to react to real people by reacting to fictional characters, and we can learn to visually perceive the world in fresh ways by viewing paintings. But we learn nothing of ordinary sounds by listening to music; they only sound worse in comparison. Ordinary sounds can inform us of the nature and location of the objects that produce them, but we do not ordinarily listen to musical tones in order to gain such information. In listening we gain information neither about ourselves nor about the world, despite claims of some theorists to the contrary. And even if they are right and I am wrong about this, we certainly do not typically listen in order to gain such information. Instead, we are interested in organized tones for their own sake, at least when we are aesthetically interested. But why should we be?

Not only do we have this interest, but it also seems to be universal in the human race across times and cultures. Music itself seems nearly ubiquitous. It accompanies our work, eating, shopping, and driving. In these contexts it may be a mere soothing effect we seek, and musical tones certainly are usually more soothing than ordinary sounds. But serious listening seeks a greater value, and yet it is more mysterious what greater value it seeks. Few philosophers of music have addressed this question directly, most concerning themselves with such topics as music's expressiveness, its meaning, or its formal structures. Those who have addressed the question of value have for the most part simply noted a failure to solve the mystery. Peter Kivy, perhaps the most distinguished philosopher of music, cannot answer the question why listeners, including himself, value music they describe as profound so highly (Kivy 1990: 216–17). Malcolm Budd holds that music's expression of emotions contributes only a minor part of its value, and while he notes the formal qualities that we value in musical pieces, he has no theory to explain why we find these qualities valuable, why we respond with such great interest (Budd 1995: 155, 158).

Our first clue to this value is pure music's very lack of relation to the world of ordinary affairs, as well as the related felt ineffability of musical experience – our very difficulty in expressing in words the value that music has for us. Our second clue lies in the other instrumental values (other than soothing us) that music can serve. These instrumental values prominently include both therapeutic and communal uses. Therapeutically, movement disorders can disappear when treated with music, and music can be used to treat memory disorders and autism as well (Sacks 2008: 252, 257, 319). Musical memory survives longer than other forms of memory in those with dementia. Visual and verbal memory fade more quickly with time than musical memory of melodies; and musical accompaniment can facilitate other forms of learning and remembering, which is why musical jingles are used in advertising and rote learning, for example, of the alphabet. The latter uses may be more common than the therapeutic ones, but again do not enter into the reasons why we typically listen to music. Indeed, the same feature of music that confers these benefits can turn negative, as when musical imagery running through the mind becomes so insistent as to be pathological. The feature in question is the way in which music becomes so deeply engrained in our minds or brains, probably because of the way in which it stimulates different areas of the brain – those controlling emotion, movement, and cognition – simultaneously.

The same feature, our second clue to music's value, explains the many related social uses of music. It is used in many diverse social contexts with one principal aim: to bind people together emotionally – to prepare them for battle or confrontation, to celebrate joyous occasions, or to mourn or comfort in sorrowful ones. In these contexts, music's rhythms can infectiously prompt movements and its melodies can alter moods, effects on individuals that can be put to social uses. Once more we see simultaneous effects on the body and on emotional as well as cognitive faculties of mind. Music helps to bind social groups together and can even spur them to action. Such bonding explains much of the attraction of singing in choruses (Storr 1992: ch. 1). Music's emotional effect is obvious also in its use to enhance the dramatic effects of texts and pictures, as in the background of movies and in opera. This enhancement once more testifies to the emotional effect of music itself. Nevertheless, emotional bonding is once more not the reason we listen to music in the privacy of our homes.

Some suggest that emotional arousal in itself accounts for all the instrumental as well as intrinsic value of music. In regard to instrumental value beyond social bonding, it is claimed that we learn about our emotions or learn to master them better by listening to music, or that musical works provide a map of how emotions change through time (Langer 1951: ch. 8). But such claims are implausible. There is no evidence that music lovers master their emotions better than others. (Opera divas provide notorious counter-evidence.) And since expressive qualities in music change so much more rapidly and unpredictably than do emotions in real life, any map that music could provide would be highly inaccurate. Other philosophers – for example, Jerrold Levinson – point to other instrumental values they claim for music: the insights it provides into life experiences and points of view, the reinforcement of moral character, its giving us "a paradigm or practicum of how to move or be" (Levinson 1998: 95–6). But again, I must admit to remaining skeptical of such vague and sweeping suggestions that to my knowledge lack any evidential support.

Our topic here, then, will be the aesthetic value of music. That value is intrinsic, not instrumental. We can define the aesthetic value of music as the value of the way in which music sounds when experienced with understanding. This is the value of the aural experience of music in itself, not that of any external effects such experience might have. In regard to such intrinsic value, it is on initial reflection equally mysterious why we value as we do experiencing the expressive and formal qualities of music. Why, for example, do we want to have our emotions aroused, especially when the emotions often aroused by serious music of greatest value are negative, sorrowful, or anxious, if not tragic? Normally we seek to avoid such emotions instead of relishing them. To say simply that we relish them in the context of art or music is not to explain anything, but rather to pose a question that needs answering. We do not typically listen to music in order to feel the emotions it causes in us (unless we are preparing for battle). We do not listen to the second movement of Beethoven's Seventh Symphony or the fourth movement of Mahler's Fifth in order to expand our capacity for or our experience of grief. The expressive qualities we experience in those movements are instead valued as a part of our access to the music itself and to the unity of these marvelous movements.

The mystery extends from the value of arousing emotions to another claimed source of intrinsic value for the music listener: the recognition of form, often complex and intricate, in musical pieces. We can recognize such forms more easily from reading scores than from listening to the music they represent, yet no one thinks that great intrinsic value lies in reading scores and identifying the complex forms of pieces in that way. The intrinsic value of music must lie instead in actually experiencing works aurally. But why should grasp of form in that way, more difficult and often less accurate, provide such great value to listeners, any more than does emotional arousal? Again, to say that we simply do greatly enjoy or value such recognition of form in experience is to pose a question, not to answer it. Keeping our previous clues in mind, we may turn to a different tack in seeking the answer.

Appreciation

We appreciate the aesthetic or intrinsic value of a musical work only in experiencing it. Since aesthetic value is what we appreciate in such experience, we can perhaps learn of its nature by reflecting on the nature of musical appreciation. The answer to the question what it is to appreciate a piece of music is more readily at hand. We appreciate the value of a piece when we understand it as we experience it and when we evaluate it however positively it deserves. Thus, by describing what it is to understand a piece of music and the criteria according to which we evaluate pieces or judge some better than others, we should discover the nature of the value that at first seems mysterious.

The relevant kind of understanding is once more not to be gained from reading scores (absent accurate imagination of the sequences of sounds). Such understanding consists instead in hearing the music in a certain way. Reading scores can tell us how pieces were constructed or put together, but not why they are as good as they are. We must hear them to understand that. And once more our hearing or listening is not directed toward the satisfaction of any practical interests or development of any of our capacities: it is directed only toward the works themselves. Musical works have their own inner goals, but we have no external goals in listening to them, which is why our interest in them is not exhausted after several hearings (when such goals would be achieved). Grasping these inner goals, like grasping form and experiencing expressive qualities in a piece, are all part of understanding it, and so we must describe in more detail what these types of experience amount to.

What is minimally necessary for understanding or appreciating a piece is not controversial, although there is disagreement about what, if anything, further is necessary for complete understanding. Understanding a piece of pure music is not grasping any reference or representational content, since there is none to grasp. Listeners understand works when they are able to follow them, when they relate what they hear at any given time to what has come before and anticipate what is to come, when they are able to perceptually organize progressions of melodic, harmonic, and rhythmic elements into groupings or gestalts. They then experience the ongoing developments in the pieces as intelligible sequences. When melodic phrases and themes are related to their previous appearances, they are heard as repetitions, elaborations, variations, contrasts, or transitions. Harmonic modulations are heard as such and as pointing ahead to further developments or resolutions. This is not to say that any of this must be verbally formulated as such, but instead that it is perceptually recognized. Musical understanding consists not in applying verbal concepts to stable objects, but in perceptually structuring the aural experience as it proceeds, following themes through their embellishments and variations and harmonies through their modulations. Such hearing is not passive but active listening that projects backward and forward.

When we understand or appreciate the inner logic of a piece in this way, we can hum along with it or reproduce sections in memory. If our listening is interrupted at any point short of the conclusion of the piece, it sounds unfinished. The final cadence itself is heard as the ultimate resolution of what came before and pointed ahead, and previous incomplete cadences are heard as partial resolutions. To hear a melody as such is already to follow a continuous logical sequence up to its final cadence as a unity or gestalt (Scruton 1997: 40). This ability may be innate for most people, or at least nearly universal. We naturally discriminate tones in terms of pitch, duration, intensity, and timbre, and we can as easily relate sequences of them into melodies. It is almost impossible not to hear melodies moving higher and lower through their individual tones. Likewise, we hear chords as consonant or dissonant and as open or dense. Following harmonic modulations is less basic and natural but is also part of musical understanding for the competent listener. As noted, musical competence or understanding requires recognition of repetitions and variations when they occur, but whether grasp of the longer overall forms of movements is required is a matter of dispute (Levinson 1997). For our purposes, we need note only what is involved in the understanding required to appreciate the musical value of a piece, and following relations of what is heard to prior elements and to those to come suffices for that.

Corroborating this account, when one fails to understand a piece of music, when one is at sea at a performance of an atonal piece, for instance, it is because one cannot follow and anticipate its course. One has no sense of being directed toward musical goals, of synthesizing sections into intelligible sequences in the process of hearing. If lack of understanding manifests itself in feeling this inability to follow, remember, and anticipate, then understanding consists in being able to do so. Further corroboration lies in the fact that appreciation of a piece grows instead of diminishing with familiarity. This is because one is able to follow the piece better and anticipate more accurately when one is familiar with it. Certainly one can anticipate better when one knows roughly what is to come, and appreciation lies partly in such anticipation. Reaching the goals of a composition does not end one's listening endeavor once and for all, but instead enables one to return to the piece for greater appreciation.

Understanding music, as a form of understanding more generally, is grasping meanings. Here the meanings are not referential, but internal. Elements of music, whether melodic, harmonic, or rhythmic, point to or imply others, and therein lies their musical meaning. Harmonically, in tonal music, modulation to the dominant, subdominant, or relative minor keys points to a return to the tonic. Rhythmically, unaccented tones point to accented ones. Melodically, gaps point ahead to fills, regular rising patterns to eventual descent, and antecedent phrases, sounding like questions, point to consequents (Meyer 1973). Variations of themes and contrasting themes point ahead to repetitions of the originals. Once more, grasping these meanings or musical implications involves hearing and feeling tensions and resolutions, prolongations, embellishments, developments, variations, and repetitions. Familiarity with a style, if not with a piece itself, facilitates this ability. In short, a competent listener who fully appreciates a piece hears, grasps, and feels the functions of the phrases and chords as they occur, and does so perceptually, not necessarily verbally.

In this act of appreciation, all mental capacities operate together. The cognitive apprehension of form is achieved perceptually through felt tensions and resolutions, and it is expressed through imagined or anticipated musical goals in which our wills seem to be involved as well. Thus, cognition, affect, imagination, and will merge indissolubly in musical appreciation. At the same time, the listener appreciates the sensuous beauty of the tones and the emotional qualities in the music expressed by its imitation of a voice or of the movement of a person in the grip of those emotions (for example, low and slow tones for sadness). Just as humans are naturally sensitive to the musical qualities of the voice as revealing emotional states of speakers, so voice-like properties of music are immediately interpreted as expressive of emotion. This is another level of affect in listening to music, along with the felt tensions emphasized above, just as the appreciation of sensuous beauty in tone is another level of perception, along with cognitive grasp of form. Affect here functions cognitively; form is grasped affectively and perceptually. Feelings are involved not just in detecting expressive or emotional qualities, but also in discriminating and relating elements, especially harmonic progressions, in listening to works. Cognition and affect, like form and content, are inextricable parts of a unified experience.

Such understanding relates directly to evaluation in appreciating musical works. Just as we understand works when we grasp in experience the implications forward and backward among their elements, and when we feel their expressive qualities and sensuous beauty, so we evaluate works more positively the tighter these implications are, and the more expressive and beautiful the works are experienced to be. I do not mean to say that works are always better for being more predictable. Simple and shallow works and more popular forms are far more predictable than complex more serious works. Instead, the best sequences in music follow the pattern that Aristotle ascribed to great drama: subsequent sections should surprise when they occur but feel absolutely necessitated after the fact. Something similar is true of our evaluation of expressive qualities. We do not most value obvious melodramatic outbursts in music any more than in people. We react most deeply to more subtle and sincere expressions of emotion appropriate to their contexts. Perception of both form and expressive qualities is more satisfying after being challenged, and such understanding after challenge leads directly to positive evaluation and hence maximal appreciation. We evaluate pieces according to the ingenuity of their design, the cogency or fluidity of their progressions, and by the depth of their expressive qualities, as these inform our experience of them.

Just as sensory perception, cognition, affect, imagination, and will merge in musical appreciation, and none suffices in itself for appreciating music, so grasp of form and arousal of emotion are not isolated ends in themselves, but are valuable only as parts of this all-encompassing experience. Even the sensuous pleasure of hearing beautiful tone, not to be underestimated when, for example, one hears the tone of Leontyne Price's voice or Jascha Heifetz's violin, is not the end of musical appreciation, but again one contributor to the value of the overall experience. On the objective side, when each musical element is tightly related to preceding and subsequent elements, when music is rich in internal connections not easily predicted in advance, each temporal part is intensely meaningful when heard. On the subjective side, the experience of such musical progressions is itself vivid and rich, as the present is imbued with the past and future. We hear the whole in the parts of such pieces. And, as already emphasized, all our mental capacities are engaged and unified in fully attending to the music.

Just as what it feels like to lack musical understanding provides insight into the nature of such understanding, so negative evaluation of musical works indicates the criteria for positive evaluation. Aesthetic failure in a piece is failure to engage listeners in the way described above. The experience of such a piece is not intense and rich, but narrow, impoverished, or banal. The musical progressions are either completely predictable and therefore uninteresting, or loose and seemingly unconnected, lacking in musical logic. Emotional expression is either lacking or overdone. Perception, cognition, and affect are then either unchallenged or lost and wandering off course. Experience is most satisfying in music, as elsewhere, when our capacities are challenged but ultimately exercised successfully, and when, as Dewey described, the experience builds cumulatively to a unifying conclusion (1958: Ch. 8). Great tonal music provides such experience to those who understand it as they listen. The complex interplay between melody, harmony, rhythm, volume, and timbre challenges as it satisfies. All perception and cognition seek order in complex data, and success in actively finding it is pleasurable.

We can now see why the therapeutic and the social uses of music alluded to earlier are clues to music's aesthetic value. People with memory disorders can nevertheless follow melodic and harmonic progressions and remember them in part because of the tight implications between different temporal parts of those sequences, and this is one criterion for the evaluation of music as well. Furthermore, music is so deeply engrained in the brain because it stimulates different regions simultaneously, and it does so because the engagement of all our mental capacities is required for appreciating the music. The clue with which we began, the complete detachment of music from the world of our practical concerns, remains to be explained and utilized.

The world of music

I have suggested that experience of the type described in which we are fully engaged is its own reward. In this experience lies the value of music. But our question is not yet completely answered. Pure music, as indicated earlier, is the most abstract and yet most immediately expressive of all the arts, and the experience and appreciation of musical works is distinct from the experience and appreciation of painting and literature. This suggests that music has value for us distinct from the values that the other arts afford. Yet we have not yet completely isolated this distinctive value. All the arts engage our cognitive, perceptual, affective, and imaginative capacities (Goldman 1995), and so, while we may have described the nature of aesthetic value in general by using music as our example, we have not yet distinguished the peculiar value of music. To do that, we need to see how the means by which music engages us in this way differs from those of the other arts, such as painting and literature. We began to do this in the first section, when we noted the other-worldly nature of the tones of musical instruments in comparison to the media of the other art forms.

When we are completely engaged in the appreciation of a work of art, we seem to enter another world, divorced from the world of our practical affairs. Many aestheticians historically have pointed to this contrast between the appreciation of art and practical interests. The apt metaphor of another world to capture this contrast is perhaps most natural in reference to fictional literature, especially novels. Great novels seem to project us into full fictional worlds. But these are worlds in which ordinary propositions are fictionally true or false. Literature utilizes language, the primary instrument of our practical affairs, and it typically refers to objects and persons in a world that could be real even when it is not. Painting also often depicts real objects and events, and even when it is abstract, it presents visual forms and colors like those we might see elsewhere. Literature and painting use words and pigments to create worlds that overlap with the real world at many points, in their settings, scenes, events, characters, and broader suggested environments.

Our complete engagement in listening to music and resultant detachment from our ordinary pursuits, the complete loss of our practically oriented selves, justifies the description of seeming to enter another world in this case as well. But the world of a musical work is completely different from both the real world and the fictional worlds of the other arts. This results first from the medium itself. Musical tones are twice removed from the world of ordinary objects. Sounds are first of all more detachable, and experienced as more detached from the objects that produce them, than are visual sensations; we often hear sounds as such and not as objects located in physical space. And second, musical tones are not natural sounds, so that they are easily heard as occurring in an ideal rather than real space. Electronic reproduction enhances this illusion, and attention to the musical qualities of the tones and the musical contexts in which they are embedded accentuates the effect even more.

Structures of musical tones are unlike anything in the world of ordinary objects. A musical work is therefore a self-contained world that provides a more thorough escape from the everyday world in which to exercise our human capacities than the other arts provide. The way in which this world is totally different connects with the felt ineffability of musical experience, the difficulty we have in expressing its value in words. We are focused here on pure instrumental music, as we have been throughout. Songs, for example, in which the human voice is the principal instrument, appear less other-worldly, since the voice in song resembles the voice in speech. But both the mystery of music's value and its solution derive from the highly abstract nature of instrumental music, which is therefore our proper focus. And while the recognition of expressive or emotional qualities such as sadness or anger depends on the resemblance of musical progressions to the voice and movement of people in the grip of those emotions, this resemblance holds only between the formal relations in very different media. The emotional dimension makes the musical world recognizably human, but it remains completely ideal or other-worldly.

The world of music is an ideal world in another sense as well, completely created by composers and tailored to their audiences. In this sense it is a totally human world in which there are no extraneous noises or threats, even when it is tinged with pathos or other negative emotions throughout. Our cognitive and affective capacities, ordinarily exercised in resistant physical and social environments that at best only sometimes or only partially satisfy them, here find complete gratification after effort and full occupation. Here we can truly rely on intelligent design to fashion a benign environment through which we make our way, instead of relying, as we must, on the satisficing mechanisms of natural selection to attune us to the real world. Here we are in a world of sensuous beauty, unthreatening emotion, and perfect coordination of aspects and moments. It is then no longer mysterious why being fully absorbed in this way is highly rewarding.

But there is a final part to our answer only hinted at so far in describing the emotional bonding that takes place immediately in the presence of powerful music. I said earlier that we do not typically, and certainly do not always, listen to music in order to bond with others, since we listen in private more often than in public settings. (I speak here of "we" at the present time; when music could be heard only at live performances, its social effects could have been a more prominent part of its value.) It can be admitted also that we do not intentionally listen in order to escape our everyday worlds or completely exercise our mental capacities. We typically attend to music for its own sake, because of our interest in structures of tones themselves (Davies 2003; Budd 1995). But this does not mean that the rewards I have been describing do not explain the value of pursuing this interest. This explanation of music's value must appeal also to the bonding that occurs not only or mainly between different listeners, but also between a listener and composer, the connection that listening to music affords to the creative human mind. Once more this connection is more immediate in the case of music than in the other arts because of the nature of the medium.

The musical medium is not only other-worldly, but is also immanent, evanescent, ephemeral, transparent. We hear musical tones as wholly present to us, but only for the fleeting moments in which they occur. The feeling of transparency, the fact that our contact with this art appears to be unmediated by physical objects, indicates the purest meeting of minds possible within the confines of the physical world. Indeed, as already noted, the meeting appears to take place in a wholly different, ideal world. The musical object is constantly disappearing as it appears, leaving the creative force behind it more fully exposed. Music then represents the purest kind of Hegelian overcoming of matter by mind, the purest expression of the creative human spirit. Its peculiar value lies not only in its providing us models of perfect order that we seem to cooperate in creating while listening to them, but also in the purity of its revelation of the creative mind itself.

See also Evaluating music (Chapter 16), Music's arousal of emotions (Chapter 22), Psychology of music (Chapter 55), Rythm, melody and harmony (Chapter 3), and Understanding music (Chapter 12).

References

Budd, M. (1995) *Values of Art: Pictures, Poetry, and Music*, London: Penguin.

Davies, S. (2003) "The Evaluation of Music," in *Themes in the Philosophy of Music*, Oxford: Oxford University Press, pp. 195–212.

Dewey, J. (1958 [1934]) *Art as Experience*, New York: Capricorn.

Goldman, A. (1995) *Aesthetic Value*, Boulder: Westview.

Kivy, P. (1990) *Music Alone*, Ithaca: Cornell University Press.

Langer, S. (1951) *Philosophy in a New Key*, New York: Mentor.

Levinson, J. (1997) *Music in the Moment*, Ithaca: Cornell University Press.

—— (1998) "Evaluating Music," in P. Alperson (ed.) *Musical Worlds: New Directions in the Philosophy of Music*, University Park: Pennsylvania State University Press, pp. 93–108.

Meyer, L. (1973) *Explaining Music*, Berkeley: University of California Press.

Sacks, O. (2008) *Musicophilia*, New York: Vintage.

Scruton, R. (1997) *The Aesthetics of Music*, Oxford: Clarendon.

Storr, A. (1992) *Music and the Mind*, New York: Free Press.

16

EVALUATING MUSIC

Theodore Gracyk

What do we evaluate when we evaluate music, and for what purpose? Philosophers generally agree that, apart from other value music has, music is composed and performed for the purpose of providing listeners with a valuable experience, most often a pleasurable one. (It seems wrong to describe the tragic shock that one feels at the end of a good performance of Puccini's *Madame Butterfly* as a feeling of pleasure. Nonetheless, it is rewarding.) For those with sufficient leisure and training to partake of such experiences, the experiences themselves are an independently valuable end that can only be obtained from music. This value is often identified as music's intrinsic value. Strictly speaking, however, only the experience possesses intrinsic value, whereas the music is instrumentally valuable for providing that experience. This approach is normally called the *aesthetic* evaluation of music (Davies 2003; Walton 1993). A piece of music can be evaluated from other points of view, each of which may assign a different level of merit. Evaluated aesthetically, John Lennon and Paul McCartney's "Love Me Do" is a weak song. Nonetheless, it is of some historical interest as their public debut and its copyright has considerable financial value. In contrast, evaluating it aesthetically involves calculating its capacity to provide pleasurable or otherwise rewarding experiences to appropriately knowledgeable listeners who attend to its musical individuality. Although there is considerable debate about why other factors ought to be excluded, I will begin by focusing on the aesthetic evaluation of music.

Two modes of evaluating

Suppose that an inquisitive adolescent music lover decides to consult a range of music criticism in order to identify the greatest individual piece of music ever composed. She intends to fill her life with musical experiences of the highest quality by listening to no other music. Furthermore, she will attempt to listen to it as often as possible. A few days of internet research leads her to conclude that Beethoven's Ninth Symphony is the work she seeks. Recorded performances allow her to sample this work as played by many orchestras and conductors. She occasionally attends a live performance. Listening during all waking hours, her first 100,000 hearings lead her to conclude that Wilhelm Furtwängler's 1951 performance at Bayreuth is definitive. Over the course of her life she listens to it 330,000 more times. To maintain her objectivity, she occasionally listens to other performances, live and recorded, repeatedly confirming that this one remains the best.

This behavior seems bizarre, if not deranged, for it appears to frustrate the purposes of listening to music. Evaluating music is not like evaluating sports contenders; it does not aim at identifying a winner (Davies 2003: 196). As such, the scenario invites us to question a standard assumption about music evaluation. Put simply, it is that evaluation prioritizes. Evaluation is a comparative activity leading to a prescriptive ranking; evaluation ranks music in order to direct listeners toward better music and away from inferior music. (For brevity's sake, this chapter focuses on listeners. With modification, it can be understood to embrace musicians as "listeners" who evaluate their own music-making, as well as composers who "listen" to their own works in progress.) On the standard model, evaluating music is fundamentally aligned with the activity of criticism, a public activity with a prescriptive dimension.

This idea of evaluation as prescriptive criticism is honored by our fictitious music lover. Since it leads our listener astray, we must examine its components. For instance, does the listener's error stem from a lack of warrant for the evaluation? Yet if a weak warrant is the problem, a better justified evaluation need not recommend different behavior. A stronger justification for the same ranking fails to address the fundamental problem, which is the narrowness of this listener's musical life.

Looking beyond the problem of justification, the deeper issue is the question of how we profit from listening. In asking this question, we seek an instrumentalist account of value, in which music is evaluated in terms of its capacity as a means to some identifiable valuable end. We have assumed that that end is aesthetic reward (see Chapter 15, "Value," in this volume).

Let us suppose, for the moment, that justified rankings attain a level of objectivity that makes it plausible to regard them as properly prescriptive. Nonetheless, the criticism model is open to the charge that it puts too much emphasis on publicly articulated evaluations, those with prescriptive force. The process of ranking music and then using the ranking to locate better music might be better understood as secondary activities, offshoots from a more basic evaluative activity. That activity is the operation of musical taste, in which evaluating is an essential element of listening, without which there is minimal reward or pleasure. So it is wrong to regard evaluation as external to – consulted before, or formulated after – listening. If evaluating is internal to listening, then everyone who appreciates music regularly evaluates it. There are relatively fewer occasions that demand construction of an objective ranking of music.

"Taste theories," for example, emphasize that evaluative activity is internal to appreciative listening. Taste theorists argue that musical rewards derive primarily from the active exploration of a musical work's individuality, which includes evaluating it continuously while listening. A listener experiences perceptual features of the work and, more importantly, various features in interaction with one another; the aesthetic reward arises less from the immediate experience than from the exploratory activity of evaluating that experience while having it. Returning to our overly focused listener, what more is there to evaluate in the same recording after several thousand hearings? Taste theories explain why someone is unlikely to reap aesthetic rewards by limiting the experience of music to a small amount of very good music. After a certain point, there is simply nothing left to evaluate – there is no exercise of taste – and the aesthetic effect becomes that of boredom.

One argument for this position observes that much of our aesthetic terminology is intrinsically evaluative without being particularly descriptive. Were it more descriptive, it would lack the wide range of application that we wish it to have. Consequently, one cannot determine whether a particular musical transition is clumsy without hearing the music and deciding whether it sounds clumsy (see Sibley 2001c). However, this decision involves evaluative assessment. Both localized and overall aesthetic properties of any piece of music are only apparent to those who continuously evaluate it while listening, deciding where it is rewarding and where it is not. A very different argument for the same result begins by noting a difference between receiving pleasure, as when soothed by music, and receiving pleasure in admiring how the music is constructed to have that effect. The latter case, appreciating, requires a second-order response that evaluates the relationship between the musical design and one's initial felt response. By itself, a mere liking is not evidence of aesthetic merit (Walton 1993). Requiring a second-order response neatly differentiates appreciating music from merely liking it – one can *like* the sound of Earl Scruggs on banjo without understanding his accomplishment, but one can only *appreciate* it by recognizing how the pleasure is merited. Furthermore, it makes sense of appreciating music that elicits negative emotions, including sadness, allowing us to find value in what is otherwise unpleasant.

Taste theory and the criticism model are not mutually exclusive. The project of objectively ranking music complements the exercise of musical taste in two distinct ways. Rankings can, as is typically thought, direct listeners toward worthwhile music. But objective rankings have a second function. They are epistemically invaluable for codifying convergences of evaluative judgment and thus providing an external measure of the objectivity of a listener's musical taste. However, a listener who does not learn how to evaluate musical works independently will not experience the intrinsic rewards that make good music good.

Finally, both the criticism and the taste accounts become more complex upon recognizing that a listener evaluates different musical objects by shifting the range of musical activity to which the music is compared. Even the same piece of music will be evaluated differently, depending on the evaluator's focus and emphasis. A performance of Beethoven's Ninth can be evaluated as a musical *work*, which we may presume is the sequence of sound-types specified by Beethoven as essential to its various performances. Furtwängler's distinctive contribution should not influence this evaluation, nor should the quality of any of the solo vocalists, for we are only evaluating Beethoven's accomplishment. However, how can anyone evaluate Beethoven's Ninth without evaluating different performances of it (Davies 2001: 13–14)? Composers frequently revise works after hearing them performed, so it appears that even composers' evaluations require perceptual experiences from which emerge the aesthetically valuable features. The problem then arises of determining which properties are due to the work and which are due to the contingencies of its particular realization. Were we in the audience at Bayreuth in 1951, we could evaluate "Furtwängler's Ninth" (Beethoven's work as interpreted by a particular conductor). To be warranted, this evaluation must compare his available performances with those of other conductors. Even here, different members of the audience might evaluate it differently – as a particular Furtwängler performance (where the comparison class is other Furtwängler performances, of Beethoven or otherwise), as a Furtwängler Ninth (a much smaller comparison class), or simply as a performance of Beethoven's Ninth (the comparison class of interest to our overly focused music lover). For twenty-first-century listeners, the experience of that performance is necessarily mediated by its recording, and unless someone regularly listens to older recordings, she is likely to be disappointed that the 1951 recording lacks the sonic range of more recent recordings.

Evaluative principles

How does an evaluation become warranted? In this section I outline several theories that justify particular evaluations by reference to general principles. In the next section I present objections to these approaches.

In a tradition that stretches back to nineteenth-century music critic and aesthetician Eduard Hanslick, an objective evaluation of a work must be defended by reasons, which in turn requires reference to what can be heard in a performance of that work. Attribution of beauty to a particular Chopin nocturne can be dismissed as subjective unless the listener understands how that beauty emerges from the particularity of the musical work (Hanslick 1986: 58–9). In the twentieth century, several philosophers developed this insight by articulating evaluative principles that use general criteria to support overall evaluations (e.g. "This music is very good"). In one of the most influential theories of this sort, aesthetic success is reduced to the interplay of three features that are always desirable in an aesthetic experience: unity, diversity, and intensity (Beardsley 1981: 454–89). However, these reasons reflect overall impressions that tell us nothing about a work's particularity. If two Chopin nocturnes are beautiful, then each will have unity, diversity, and intensity, and so these very general criteria bring us no closer to knowing why the nocturnes are musically good than when we merely attribute beauty to both of them. Consequently, overly general criteria are inadequate as explanatory reasons. We need more specificity in the aesthetic attributions that warrant the overall evaluation of the music, describing how the music impresses knowledgeable listeners who attend to its sonic elements unfolding in time. Locating such criteria, we arrive at myriad principles for aesthetic evaluation (Dickie 1988; Sibley 2001a).

On this model, evaluation takes notice of the music's lowest-order perceptual properties – in the case of a musical work, its lowest-order perceptual property-types, and in the case of performance, of the actual sounds of the performance – in order to attend to aesthetic properties arising from them, such as the foreboding quality of the opening of Beethoven's Ninth and the irreverence of Varèse's *Ionisation* (Levinson 2001). In other words, evaluation is directed at the perceptual appearances that arise from the arrangement of the music's lowest-order properties, together with the affective responses that are typically reported by qualified listeners. Evaluative principles codify perceptual and affective features that regularly reward an intrinsic concern for music. Given a sufficient store of such principles, we can determine which listeners offer cogent reasons for their overall evaluations of particular works.

There is considerable disagreement about whether appropriate aesthetic attributions must be evaluatively neutral descriptions. Some attributions, such as "beautiful" and "maudlin," are irreducibly evaluative. However, irreducibly evaluative attributions are generally rejected as an inadequate basis for an overall evaluation. Such "reasons" cannot be used to justify an evaluation, Jerrold Levinson argues, unless their descriptive content can be separated from their evaluative aspect (Levinson 2001). To function as reasons that can be accepted by others, evaluative labels must be replaced with evaluatively neutralized descriptions of the underlying aesthetic properties. Where their descriptive content cannot be separated out, the criteria beg the question by failing to specify just what a knowledgeable listener ought to be able to hear in the music in order to find it rewarding.

On this approach, evaluation proceeds by assembling an evaluatively neutral description of the music, to which we apply many principles of the following sort:

> Music rewards intrinsic concern in so far as it is P.
> Music frustrates intrinsic concern in so far as it is Q.

P and Q are placeholders for evaluatively neutral aesthetic attributions, and these are either affective or perceptually emergent characteristics (e.g. "cheerful" and "balanced," respectively). An example would be the claim that Varèse's *Ionisation* rewards intrinsic concern in so far as it is irreverent. Because music is good when it rewards intrinsic concern, the music's irreverence counts in favor of its being good.

However, even if such principles serve as limited indicators of value, there remains the concern that they are insufficient to tell us which music is good. Overall evaluations do not arise from isolated elements, but from taking everything into account. For example, suppose that a composer compiles a list of principles indicating merit and a list of those indicating deficiency. A work could be created that possesses multiple properties that are merit-qualities and avoids all properties that are deficit-qualities. One moment might express foreboding and, in so far as it expresses foreboding, it has merit. The next moment is irreverent, and, in so far as it is, it has merit. The next moment is intensely joyous, and so on. Every moment has merit in so far as it has the property it has in that moment. Nonetheless, the piece might be a hodgepodge of merit-qualities that lack internal connection to one another. (Such music might be composed by appropriating snippets from a range of familiar compositions, or by juxtaposing fragmentary pastiches, as in They Might Be Giants' track "Fingertips.") As Levinson observes, one might say "I like how it sounds" at any given moment, but the music will not reward an aesthetic interest in it unless we also like "how it goes," that is, how it progresses from moment to moment and passage to passage while presenting its various merit-qualities (Levinson 2006: 197–8).

Consequently, Levinson argues that these lower-level principles must be supplemented by an interest in the overall construction of the music *as music*. Minimally, he thinks that an overall evaluation must proceed from consideration of two dimensions of the music's designed progression: as configurational form and as expressive gesture. In turn, these two aspects must be evaluated for their "specific fusion of human content and audible form" (Levinson 2006: 201). A musical work is good in so far as it is rewarding to follow its tonal process, it is good in so far as it is rewarding to respond to what it conveys, and it is good in so far as it is rewarding to experience how what it conveys is embodied in its particular tonal process (Levinson 2006: 203). This strategy of identifying universally valuable dimensions of music is reminiscent of Beardsley's postulation of unity, diversity, and intensity as the general criteria of aesthetic value. Both grant, for instance, that a high degree of reward in one dimension will generally reduce attention to one or both of the other two. However, Levinson argues that his model is more informative than Beardsley's, for Beardsley sought criteria that apply to every art form, whereas Levinson offers principles that are specific to music.

Criticisms of evaluative principles

It will be useful to address two common but misguided objections to evaluative principles before proceeding to more serious problems with their claim to securing evaluative objectivity. First, it is sometimes claimed that aesthetic properties are not objective properties of objects. Because aesthetic attributions describe phenomenal characteristics, they do not refer to objective properties, at least not in the way that the year of the debut of Beethoven's Ninth is a matter of historical fact. Lacking objectivity, these principles confer no prescriptive force. This common objection has been frequently answered. The classic reply is that the same emergent characteristics are recognized by most, if not all, listeners who have considerable experience with that kind of music. The convergence of agreement about these properties is no less than holds when recognizing color distinctions, the presence of a visual pattern, or the sweetness of honey. Therefore aesthetic attributions should be regarded as furnishing appropriately objective descriptions of what is heard by knowledgeable listeners (Sibley 2001b; Levinson 2001). In turn, the fact of convergence can itself be employed to test the objectivity of a critic, and so a music lover who cannot hear that "the opening of Beethoven's Ninth Symphony is dark and foreboding" is not competent to say what is present in music of this kind (Levinson 2001: 80).

A second baseless criticism holds that aesthetic evaluation reflects the interests of an elite population and that it is based on principles that privilege fine art. Consequently, it improperly undervalues popular, folk, and non-Western music, which are of value for rather different reasons. In response, at least some "low" music succeeds admirably when evaluated in terms of standard aesthetic values (Shusterman 1991). More importantly, it is clear that non-elite and non-Western cultures employ recognizably aesthetic standards for their cultural productions (Dutton 2000), including music (Davies 2001: 268–73). The fact that evaluative criticism is frequently derailed by cultural biases is no evidence that aesthetic evaluation is essentially elitist, or that beauty is an elitist value.

More serious difficulties arise with low-level principles involving particular aesthetic attributes. One problem is that they operate in terms of isolated features, none of which are necessary for a positive overall evaluation. The principle that witty music is good, to the extent that it is witty, does nothing to help evaluate music that lacks wit. Thus, it tells us that Gilbert and Sullivan's "patter" songs are to some degree good, but tells us nothing about the Adagietto movement of Mahler's Fifth Symphony. For Mahler's Adagietto we need another principle, but it will not always be evident which is the most appropriate. And because they are indefinitely many in number, our inventory will never be complete (Beardsley 1981: 509). At best, our present stock of such principles provides a reminder of the wide range of different norms that apply in various cases. Even in the best cases, we cannot be confident that we possess the principles that justify a positive or negative evaluation; the skeptic says we can never be confident.

Another difficulty with low-level principles is that they treat evaluation as an additive process. Guided by principles, we can articulate how many distinct ways a work is good. However, there are no principles for evaluating interactions among the relevant artistic and aesthetic properties. A piece of music might be good for its expressive melancholy (e.g. the country music standard "He Stopped Loving Her Today"). Another might be good because it features frequent inversions of standard musical syntax. Each of these features is normally rewarding and an intrinsic good. Nonetheless, either can lead to an extrinsic deficit, as happens when one intrinsic good interferes with our appreciation of another (Gaut 2007: 62–3). For example, expressive melancholy and disruptions of standard musical syntax tend to interfere with one another when combined in the same piece. Thus, when Haydn writes a melancholy song, such as "She Never Told Her Love," he eschews the musical playfulness he displays at the close of "The Joke" String Quartet (Op. 33 No. 2). So it appears that evaluative principles will frequently mislead us unless they receive a host of additional qualifications about their extrinsic entanglements. To remain useful, they must take this form:

Music rewards intrinsic concern in so far as it is P, unless it is also Q.

But the list of entanglements is so open-ended that we can never be confident that we have the full list. Because we can only evaluate these interactions by observing them, case by case, our principles do not guide overall evaluations of any music. We gain nothing by incorporating qualifiers about negative interactions with other aesthetic properties. In the end, principles never license an evaluative conclusion stronger than "the music has some aesthetic merit in so far as it is P" (Gaut 2007: 65; see also Dickie 1988: 159–60).

As a result, principles themselves do not seem to warrant the rankings that we need on a criticism model of evaluation. The rankings are not straightforward products of the principles.

George Dickie offers a partial solution (Dickie 1988). Suppose two works have a common set of aesthetic features, so that both are subject to exactly the same principles, and one is superior with respect to all of these properties. That one is the better of the two. (Imagine that the two works are two variants of the same folk ballad.) A third work that shares the same properties can then be compared with those two, then a fourth with those three, and so. We can thus plot a matrix of better and worse works. Faced with a work that has a property not yet in our matrix, the work can be ranked against otherwise similar works by imagining an additional work possessing all of these properties, and then ranking all of them in relation to that possibility. By gradually comparing actual and imagined works, we can roughly rank most works into the categories of excellent, good, and poor.

While a system of this type may be our only method for comprehensive ranking, it does not get us far. First, comparisons are made to imagined works, which overlooks the way in which composers can be surprised by their own works when they are realized in performance. Second, it retains the problem that the interaction of two independently valuable properties cannot be calculated by appeal to a principle. One (or both) might be of lesser value due to the presence of the other, and the resulting level of reward in the context of the interaction can only be determined by appeal to the consensus of qualified listeners. Hence, even the best scenario for constructing objective rankings is subject to the complaint that the rankings are really a consensus of taste. As such, the principles are ultimately dispensable.

This problem of interaction is marginally addressed by Levinson's more general principle about the interaction between tonal process and whatever is conveyed by a work. Unfortunately, as Levinson acknowledges, he has simply reintroduced a variant of the problem, for his interaction principle does not rule out the possibility that "works of a markedly representational character" might be of a sort that "harmfully competes with attention to the configurational" (Levinson 2006: 204). He offers no examples, but racist and misogynistic songs illustrate the problem. However well written, the repugnance of the musical persona might negate any rewards to be had from the way that the musical processes support the hateful message. We are thrown back, each time, to an evaluative decision that receives insufficient warrant from our principles.

A third serious difficulty is that principles only emphasize what is typical, for they are generalizations from a range of examples. As such, it is not clear that they are even correct when restricted to saying that music rewards intrinsic concern in so far as it is *P*. Considered in isolation from its interaction with other properties, a "universally" desirable property might sometimes make a work unrewarding. For example, consider Beardsley's proposal that a work is always good in so far as it has intensity. Yet we can imagine cases of intense works that are unrewarding (Sibley 2001a: 113). A variant objection is that the phrase "too *P*" implies fault, and the modifier can be applied to any property to which our principles assign value. Unless mitigated by its interaction with other features, the intensity of a piece might be too great in its overall effect – an intensely sad work, for instance, might be *too* sad. Given that it is difficult to test our generalization by locating a work that possesses only a single, isolated property (and, even if we could, one that does not induce boredom), the "too *P*" problem is difficult to defuse. Hence, principles are merely rough heuristics for evaluating partial aspects of works, and they may fail us altogether when the property in question is an overall characteristic of the work in question. The problem arises equally for low- and high-level principles.

Non-aesthetic evaluation

There remains an obvious, frequently raised objection to the philosophical focus on evaluating music aesthetically. Most music, in most of human history, was created as a means to some other purpose. Music created to reward an intrinsic concern for its musical individuality is the exception and not the rule – most music accompanies and supports some other activity, and so on. A few of these purposes include encoding and transmitting histories, myths, and so on, in preliterate cultures, coordinating the movements of groups of people (including, but not limited to, dancing and military maneuvers), frightening enemies, facilitating healing, and indicating and reinforcing social differences. Aesthetic evaluation imposes a distorting perspective on such music, which is not designed to reward an interest in it for itself alone (Merriam 1964: 260–3). Therefore each piece of music should be evaluated functionally, as a means to its culturally intended purpose. If there is no justification for evaluating most music aesthetically, then different ends will separate music according to multiple, incommensurable ranking systems.

Some philosophers counter that there is at least one other common purpose, one to which art traditionally subordinates aesthetic purpose. Art and music express and transmit the values of their originating culture (Scruton 1997: 457–508; Kaufman 2002). Hence, there is an independent basis for commensurate comparison of different musics. Religious or secular, "art" or not, we can ask how well a particular piece of music embodies the values of the culture in which it functions, and we do not have to *endorse* those values in making this determination. Unfortunately, this position faces the standard criticisms aimed at ethical relativism, including the problem that it does not give positive value to alterity, the music of "otherness," nor to any music that subverts the dominant culture (see also Gracyk 2007: 167–75).

Furthermore, valuing music for its capacity for cultural integration and solidarity provides no reason for members of one culture or subculture to value the music of another group. In the same way in which one can grasp the value of golf for avid golfers without thereby receiving any reason to golf, one can recognize that opera lovers have reasons to value European opera without therefore receiving a reason to value it. In fact, this strategy provides a reason *not* to value European opera if it is not part of one's cultural inheritance, for it will be at the expense of investment in one's own culture. In short, objective evaluations of cultural products have no prescriptive force unless they are relevant to the life projects of concrete individuals. Far from being a universal language, music appears to be a divisive force.

Happily, this argument overstates the problem. While it is false that music is a universal language, music-making is a universal human activity. Aesthetic rewards are part of the explanation for music's prominence in diverse cultural activities. Combining music with a cultural activity attaches aesthetic value to that activity, which furnishes an independent incentive to cooperate socially, namely, in order to have access to aesthetically enjoyable music. However, it cannot function as an incentive unless it supplies its *own* value to a practice or activity. In effect, most "functional" music has very little value unless it also has the potential to become a common bond among individuals who have no other reason to interact. (For example, consider how Haydn's reputation in England led him to travel there.) Thus, it is not an error to evaluate music for rewarding an aesthetic interest in it. Aesthetic evaluation can be legitimately directed at all music (Gracyk 2007: 41–72).

See also Aesthetic properties (Chapter 14), Authentic performance practice (Chapter 9), and Value (Chapter 15).

References

Beardsley, M.C. (1981) *Aesthetics: Problems in the Philosophy of Criticism*, 2nd edn, Indianapolis: Hackett.

Davies, S. (2001) *Musical Works and Performances: A Philosophical Exploration*, New York: Oxford University Press.

—— (2003) "The Evaluation of Music," in *Themes in the Philosophy of Music*, New York: Oxford University Press, pp. 195–212.

Dickie, G. (1988) *Evaluating Art*, Philadelphia: Temple University Press.

Dutton, D. (2000) "'But They Don't Have Our Concept of Art'," in N. Carroll (ed.) *Theories of Art Today*, Madison: University of Wisconsin Press, pp. 217–38.

Gaut, B. (2007) *Art, Emotion, and Ethics*, New York: Oxford University Press.

Gracyk, T. (2007) *Listening to Popular Music: Or, How I Learned to Stop Worrying and Love Led Zeppelin*, Ann Arbor: University of Michigan Press.

Hanslick, E. (1986 [1891]) *On the Musically Beautiful*, trans. G. Payzant, Indianapolis: Hackett.

Kaufman, D. (2002) "Normative Criticism and the Objective Value of Artworks," *Journal of Aesthetics and Art Criticism* 60: 151–66.

Levinson, J. (2001) "Aesthetic Properties, Evaluative Force, and Differences in Sensibility," in E. Brady and J. Levinson (eds) *Aesthetic Concepts: Essays after Sibley*, New York: Oxford University Press, pp. 61–80.

—— (2006) "Evaluating Music," in *Contemplating Art*, New York: Oxford University Press, pp. 184–207.

Merriam, A.P. (1964) *The Anthropology of Music*, Evanston: Northwestern University Press.

Scruton, R. (1997) *The Aesthetics of Music*, New York: Oxford University Press.

Shusterman, R. (1991) "Form and Funk: The Aesthetic Challenge of Popular Art," *British Journal of Aesthetics* 31: 203–13.

Sibley, F. (2001a) "General Criteria and Reasons in Aesthetics," in *Approach to Aesthetics: Collected Papers on Philosophical Aesthetics*, ed. J. Benson, H.B. Hildred, and J.R. Cox, New York: Oxford University Press, pp. 104–18.

—— (2001b) "Objectivity and Aesthetics," in *Approach to Aesthetics: Collected Papers on Philosophical Aesthetics*, ed. J. Benson, H.B. Hildred, and J.R. Cox, New York: Oxford University Press, pp. 71–87.

—— (2001c) "Particularity, Art, and Evaluation," in *Approach to Aesthetics: Collected Papers on Philosophical Aesthetics*, ed. J. Benson, H.B. Hildred, and J.R. Cox, New York: Oxford University Press, pp. 88–103.

Walton, K. (1993) "How Marvelous! Toward a Theory of Aesthetic Value," *Journal of Aesthetics and Art Criticism* 51: 499–510.

17

APPROPRIATION AND HYBRIDITY

James O. Young

Conceptual clarifications

Musicians have always appropriated ideas from other musicians. In recent years appropriation of musical ideas has been subjected to scrutiny, particularly when musicians borrow ideas that originate in cultures other than their own. Borrowing from indigenous and minority cultures has been particularly controversial. Other forms of appropriation, particularly that known as sampling, have also been widely discussed. Reflection on appropriation, especially cultural appropriation, and the hybridity that can result from appropriation, gives rise to both aesthetic and ethical questions. This chapter will introduce readers to the range of such questions.

The concepts of appropriation and hybridity are in need of clarification. Begin with the concept of appropriation. To appropriate is simply to take something for one's own use. The appropriation with which this chapter is concerned is the taking of something produced by musicians. Usually, other musicians do the taking and they are engaged in the production of new musical works and performances. Appropriation takes two basic forms: appropriation by means of recordings and appropriation of musical content. Here 'musical content' refers to compositions, themes, styles, motifs, and other musical structures.

Let us begin by considering appropriation of musical content. Appropriation of content can involve taking over a complete composition. This occurs when a band "covers" a song originally produced by another group. Charles Avison's arrangement of Domenico Scarlatti's harpsichord sonatas as concerti grossi is a related example of this sort of appropriation. Elements of a composition can also be appropriated. For example, composers will often appropriate a theme from another composer. Examples include Brahms's *Variations on a Theme by Handel*, Op. 24 and Beethoven's *Diabelli Variations*, Op. 120. Appropriation of a theme is commonplace in jazz performance. Styles can also be appropriated. The use of jazz or blues styles by non-African Americans is a case of such appropriation. When such appropriation occurs, a new composition in an old style is produced. Sometimes something less than a complete style is appropriated. Stravinsky (*Ragtime*) and Darius Milhaud (the jazz fugue in the second section of *La Création du Monde*) appropriated elements of jazz styles without producing jazz compositions.

Appropriation can also be done by means of recordings. In the contemporary world, sampling (the re-use of a portion of a recording in a new recording) is a common sort of appropriation. Sampling was employed as early as the 1960s, and became commonplace on rap recordings in the 1980s. Sampling has also been widely used by experimental bands such as Negativland. A quite different sort of appropriation results from recordings made by ethnomusicologists. Ethnomusicologists have recorded music by indigenous people from Africa, Australasia, and the Americas. The use of recordings made by ethnomusicologists has been the source of concerns about the proprietary rights of individual musicians and cultures.

Cultural appropriation of music is appropriation which occurs across cultural lines. That is, individuals from one culture appropriate something that has been produced by musicians who belong to another culture. (For a discussion of cultural appropriation in the arts see Young 2008.) One widely discussed example of cultural appropriation has already been mentioned: appropriation of African American musical styles. (For discussions see Rudinow 1994; Taylor 1995; Gracyk 2001.) Appropriation of jazz styles has been going on since at least Bix Beiderbecke in the 1920s. Appropriation of blues styles continues in the music of Marcia Ball, Eric Clapton, John Hammond, Stevie Ray Vaughan and other non-African Americans. African Americans have also engaged in cultural appropriation. Herbie Hancock, on his album *Headhunters* (1973), appropriated the *hindewhu* style of the pygmies of central Africa. This appropriation was mediated via another act of appropriation: *The Music of the Ba-Benzélé Pygmies* (1966), a recording made by two French ethnomusicologists, Simha Arom and Geneviève Taurelle (Feld 1996). (The cycle of appropriation continued when Madonna used a short sample from *Headhunters* in the song "Sanctuary" on her 1994 CD, *Bedtime Stories*.) Paul Simon, who appropriated the music of South Africa's townships, and Steve Reich, whose studies with a drummer of the Ewe people of Ghana have influenced his minimalist compositions, are two more examples of musicians who have engaged in cultural appropriation.

Not all appropriation across cultural lines counts as cultural appropriation. Something counts, for present purposes, as cultural appropriation only if something is taken in which an entire culture has a stake. Suppose that someone in China (that is, someone culturally distinct from me) brings out a pirate edition of my original compositions. The fact that the pirate belongs to another culture is not an interesting feature of the appropriation. If someone from my own culture pirated my compositions, the act would be wrong for the same reason. It is just garden-variety theft of intellectual property. For this reason, the appropriation of Solomon Linda's composition "Mbube" ("The Lion Sleeps Tonight") by The Weavers (1952), The Tokens (1961), and subsequently by the Disney Corporation does not count as cultural appropriation for present purposes. This is appropriation across cultural lines (Linda was a Zulu), but it does not count as cultural appropriation since something was appropriated from an individual. (This is not to say that Linda was fairly treated. He and his heirs likely received only a fraction of the royalties they were owed. A lawsuit with Disney was settled out of court.) If the entire Zulu culture were adversely affected by the appropriation of the song, or if the Zulus had a collective claim on the composition, then the appropriation would be cultural appropriation.

Turn now to an analysis of the concept of hybridity. A work of music can be hybrid in many senses, but usually to call a work hybrid is to say that it displays the influence of more than one style. Both compositions and performances can be hybrid in this sense, but this chapter will focus on compositions. The compositions Stravinsky produced during his neo-classical period are a good example of stylistically hybrid works. They are a composite of the composer's earlier expressivism and elements of Classical and Baroque music. The most controversial sort of hybridity results from cultural appropriation. Many Western composers have appropriated musical content from non-Western cultures, including Native American, Balinese, African, and Middle Eastern cultures.

While appropriation and hybridity are both discussed in this chapter, the two are not necessarily connected. A musician could appropriate from another musician without the work being hybrid in any interesting sense; for example, if a musician working in a given style appropriated musical content from another musician working in the same style. When Handel appropriated from Bononcini, the resulting works were not stylistically hybrid: they both composed in the Italian Baroque style. Conversely, a musical work could be hybrid without its production involving cultural appropriation. This would be the case when a composer employs two styles both of which are native to his culture. Nevertheless, when appropriation is involved in the production of a work, it will often be stylistically hybrid. This is true, for example, of Stravinsky's *Ragtime* and many compositions by Western composers that appropriate from non-Western cultures.

Can appropriation be aesthetically successful?

The musician who engages in appropriation might be thought to produce something aesthetically flawed. The appropriator's work will, one could argue, be derivative and inauthentic. Music that is hybrid may seem to have other aesthetic flaws since unity of style may seem to be a precondition for aesthetic success. While completely derivative work will have little aesthetic value, a general aesthetic case against appropriation in music is harder to mount. Similarly, it is difficult to argue that all hybrid music is aesthetically flawed.

Examples of successful appropriation are easy to find. Johann Sebastian Bach borrowed freely from Vivaldi, Albinoni, and other composers with great success. Handel was an inveterate appropriator of musical content from other composers, yet the musical results were excellent. Uvedale Price remarked that, "If ever there was a truly great and original genius in any art, Handel was that genius in music; and yet, what may seem no slight paradox, there never was a greater plagiary. He seized [that is, appropriated], without scruple or concealment, whatever suited his purpose" (Price 1842: 573). These are, however, not clear examples of cultural appropriation. Even if appropriation can produce good works of music, one might still think that cultural appropriation will lead to disappointing music.

This claim is often made about the appropriation of African American music. Amiri Baraka (formerly LeRoi Jones) has maintained that in order to perform the blues a musician requires "the peculiar social, cultural, economic, and emotional experience of a black man in America. . . . The materials of the blues were not available to the white American" (Jones 1963: 148). A similar claim could be made about any style of music: in order to employ a style successfully one must have a particular cultural background. We may call this the cultural experience argument.

The cultural experience argument cannot show that all appropriation will be aesthetically unsuccessful. At best it shows that musicians cannot completely adopt the style of another culture. In many cases, however, musicians do not attempt to mimic the styles of other cultures. Rather, they take from another style and form a new, hybrid style. Steve Reich has written that, "Instead of imitation, the influence of non-Western music structures on the thinking of a Western composer is likely to produce something new" (Reich 1974: 40). Nothing in the cultural experience argument shows that innovative appropriation of the sort Reich has in mind will be aesthetically unsuccessful. Even Baraka admits as much. He has stated that Beiderbecke "played 'white jazz' . . . music that is the product of attitudes expressive of a peculiar culture." Still, Baraka grants that Beiderbecke was "a serious white musician" and the hybrid music he produced was a successful creative re-use of the appropriated materials (Jones 1963: 154).

It is not even clear that the cultural experience argument is able to show that non-innovative appropriation of musical styles will be aesthetically unsuccessful. Sometimes appropriation of a musical style is unsuccessful, but no necessary correlation can be identified between cultural background and success in a particular musical style. One sometimes hears that only Italians can successfully sing Italian music, but the empirical evidence suggests otherwise. By most accounts, Kathleen Battle (African American) and Kiri Te Kanawa (Maori) have mastered bel canto singing as well as Cecilia Bartoli. Similarly, many authorities believe that non-African Americans have created aesthetically successful jazz and blues performances. Eric Clapton, Stevie Ray Vaughan and other non-African Americans are widely regarded as leading blues musicians. Ray Eldridge, the African

American jazz trumpeter, was an advocate of the cultural experience argument. Despite his standing as the greatest trumpet soloist of his time, in a blind listening situation, he misidentified the cultural background of performers more than half of the time (Feather 1959: 47).

The examples just given may indicate that appropriation can give rise to good music. Examples of good hybrid music are just as easy to find. In addition to the example of Beiderbecke's "white jazz" given above, much German Baroque music (including that of Bach) was a composite, or hybrid, of the Italian and French styles. Mozart's *Rondo alla Turca* (from the Piano Sonata in A, K. 311) is only the best known of many great compositions that are hybrids of Turkish and European music. George Gershwin and Irving Berlin produced masterpieces of hybrid music by appropriating from African American culture. In the past forty years, aesthetically valuable hybrid compositions have become too common to enumerate. While it must be admitted that not all hybrid compositions are worth hearing, arguably hybridity is the most important source of new and aesthetically valuable ideas in contemporary music.

Proprietary questions

Appropriation gives rise to debates about the ownership of musical content. These debates see considerations about artistic creativity and freedom pitted against concerns about the proprietary rights of individual musicians and (in many cases of cultural appropriation) entire cultures. Resolving these debates can be quite complex. They often have a legal dimension. Legal questions can be complicated by the fact that different cultures and nations have different legal regimes. At the root of the debates are moral questions about what ought to be regarded as property.

Sometimes the answers to moral questions about the ownership of musical content are readily apparent and many legal systems track these answers quite reliably. Unauthorized duplication of entire copyrighted recordings and scores for commercial gain is clearly wrong. On the other hand, as long as appropriation of musical content results in a work that is not substantially similar to another work, the appropriation is permissible. This seems to be the correct position since appropriation that results in substantially new works does not adversely affect the economic opportunities of an original creator. A good balance is struck between encouraging musical innovation by permitting creative re-use and encouraging innovation by ensuring that creators are fairly rewarded.

Appropriation by means of recording gives rise to some difficult questions. In particular, the use of sampling has been widely debated. In the USA, the UK, and other jurisdictions, the courts have ruled that the use of any element of a sound recording without permission, no matter how small it may be, is actionable. For example, a US court has ruled that even the use of three notes constitutes a violation of copyright (*Bridgeport Music Inc. v. Dimension Films*, 410 F.3d 792

(6th Cir. 2005)). Now the use of samples is routinely cleared with copyright holders.

While the legal status of samples has been settled (at least for the time being), the moral question remains open. From a moral point of view, one can hold that artistic innovation has been wrongly sacrificed in favor of property rights, usually the property rights of corporations. The band Negativland holds this position, writing that

> Artists who routinely appropriate . . . are not attempting to profit from the marketability of their subjects at all. They are using elements, fragments, or pieces of someone else's created artifact in the creation of a new one for artistic reasons.
>
> (Negativland n.d.)

The use of sampling does not normally cut into the market for the sampled recording. So normally no economic harm is done to the owner of the original copyright. Consequently, a situation in which sampling is used is arguably a Pareto improvement relative to a situation in which it is not employed. (An action is Pareto efficient, or a Pareto improvement, if it improves the well-being of some people without making anyone worse off.) One could conclude from this that sampling is not wrong.

Perhaps, however, economic considerations are not the only relevant ones. It has been argued that the use of sampling can devalue sampled works. Samples of some composition could be used, for example, in a parody of the composition. Still, it is not obvious that sampling devalues the sampled work, even if it is used in a parody. No one thinks any the worse of the *Mona Lisa* just because Duchamp parodied it in his *L.H.O.O.Q* (1919), a postcard reproduction of Leonardo's painting, on which Duchamp drew a moustache and goatee. By parity of reasoning, the use of sampling should not hurt the reputation of a work or an artist. On the other hand, restrictions on sampling are certainly limiting musical innovation. Clearance fees are often very high and even when artists pay these fees, they sometimes still face legal challenges to their appropriation.

Sometimes music is regarded as the property, not of an individual composer but of an entire culture. This is a claim often made about the traditional music of indigenous cultures. In Western law, no one in the cultures in which the music originated has any proprietary rights to the music since it has no identifiable creator. Such music is regarded in Western law as "traditional" or "folk music" and anyone may freely appropriate it. Indigenous cultures, however, often regard this music as the property of an entire culture or of some clan within the culture. Sometimes cultures are said to own more than just particular compositions. Amiri Baraka has described blues as "the basic national voice of the African American people." Its use by non-African Americans he describes as the "Great Music Robbery" (Baraka and Baraka 1987: 226, 328). Baraka and others believe that

African Americans own not just particular compositions but collectively own an entire style of composition. Similar claims are sometimes made about the music of indigenous cultures.

It is easy to be sympathetic to indigenous and minority cultures from whom music is appropriated. They are often economically disadvantaged and it seems unfair that they should not benefit from something created by their culture. (It seems even more unfair when anthropologists who have recorded the music may receive compensation if their recordings are sampled.) Nevertheless, questions about whether cultures have proprietary rights to music are difficult to resolve.

Begin by considering the question of whether musical styles can be owned. The case that they can is difficult to make. The first reason is that styles can be difficult to individuate. Quite similar styles can come into existence at different times and in different cultural contexts. Consequently, assigning to a single culture proprietary rights over a style is likely to be unfair to other cultures that have just as good a claim on the style as another culture. (One could argue that two styles are distinct simply in virtue of having originated in different cultural contexts. Suppose this point is granted. Determining the style to which some new work belongs may still be difficult or impossible. A composer may have appropriated from some culture without it being possible to determine which.) A second, related reason for doubting that styles can be owned is that cultures have been interacting for a long time. As a result, a culture can seldom, if ever, claim sole credit for the development of a musical style. Without sole credit for developing a style, there is little basis for a claim to exclusive ownership. Finally, one can argue that the general interest is best served by allowing unfettered access of musicians to musical styles. Everyone's interests are served when cross-fertilization of musical styles is permitted and even encouraged. Moreover, allowing members of one culture to use the styles of another does not deny opportunities to anyone. The members of the original culture can still employ their own styles. That is, the free exchange of musical content is likely Pareto efficient.

This leaves to be considered questions about proprietary rights to individual traditional compositions and recordings of such compositions. It is hard to see how the traditional compositions of certain cultures could be owned while those of other cultures are in the public domain. Certainly indigenous people ought to have unhindered access to any recordings already made of their music, particularly when these recordings may have a legal function. (The recordings could have a bearing on the resolution of land claims by indigenous people, for instance.) If the use of the recordings generates royalties, the performers ought to be compensated. If the performers belong to a culture that has not been integrated into the market economy, they will have no use for money. In such a case, royalties can be used to establish a fund that benefits the performers' culture. Such a fund could, for example, be used to purchase land that would protect an indigenous people against unwanted intrusions.

Concerns about appropriation of music are sometimes linked to concerns about the appropriation of an audience. That is, there is a fear that when outsiders appropriate a musical style they may monopolize the market for performances in that style. This sort of concern has been raised both with regard to appropriation from African American musicians and from non-Western cultures. Paul Simon's *Graceland* has often been regarded as an example of the latter. This fear may seem particularly well grounded when outsiders have better access to recording contracts and performance opportunities. Arguably this was the case when non-African Americans first appropriated jazz and blues styles.

The available evidence suggests that fear of the appropriation of audiences may be exaggerated. The argument is based on the assumption that musicians are playing a zero-sum game: any gain for one musician comes at the expense of another. In fact, the demand for music in a given style is elastic. There is no more a fixed market for music in a given style than there is a fixed market for books about wizards or murder mystery novels. Arguably Simon's appropriation of South African music opened up opportunities for South Africans rather than closing them down. In the wake of Simon's appropriation, the Zulu choir Ladysmith Black Mambazo rose to international prominence. A similar point could be made about appropriation from African American musicians, particularly in the 1950s and earlier. White American musicians took advantage of opportunities that were not available to their African American counterparts. Even here, however, one can argue that White musicians made audiences aware of the music of African Americans and, in this way, helped open up opportunities for minority musicians.

Other forms of harm

Many moral questions, besides proprietary questions, have been raised about appropriation of music from minority cultures. This section will address two of these additional issues. The first is the suggestion that appropriation can lead to the harmful misrepresentation of a culture. The second is the charge that appropriation can lead to the assimilation and distortion of minority cultures.

Begin by considering the first of these charges. Musicians from mainstream Western cultures are often held to have misrepresented non-Western cultures, indigenous cultures, and African American culture. This misrepresentation is thought to involve stereotypes that create or perpetuate cultural prejudices. Both Mozart, in *Abduction from the Seraglio* and Borodin, in *Prince Igor*, appropriate elements of non-Western music. Both have been suspected of Orientalism (the presentation of misleading stereotypes of Eastern cultures). Gershwin's *Porgy and Bess* appropriates elements of African American music and this has led to charges of caricaturing African Americans: "black characters are commonly represented as 'simple,' either by folky pentatonics or the banjo tunes of 'I Got Plenty o' Nuttin''" (Born and Hesmondhalgh 2000: 23). Tommie Shelby raises the possibility that the appropriation of musical styles from African American culture leads to another danger. Suppose that non-African Americans were to produce bad jazz and blues performances. "The uninformed or naïve will mistake the fake stuff for the real thing, coming away with a distorted view of the value of the original" (Shelby 2005: 191; Shelby does not endorse this argument.)

These sorts of observation are most often made by musicologists. Not being philosophers, they are not always explicit in drawing moral conclusions from these and similar observations about appropriation. Presumably, however, the implication is that the misrepresentation of other cultures is morally wrong, particularly when it creates or perpetuates harmful stereotypes. This point ought to be conceded. The creation of a Hollywood Western that misrepresents Native Americans as dim-witted or duplicitous is clearly morally wrong. If a work of music similarly misrepresents the members of a culture, its creation is also wrong. Some philosophers believe that when artworks express flawed moral perspectives, they are also aesthetically flawed (Gaut 1998). If they are right, then musical works that harmfully misrepresent cultures are also aesthetically flawed. Such works need not, however, be completely without aesthetic value. Few would deny that *Abduction from the Seraglio* is a masterpiece, even if Mozart is guilty of Orientalism.

While harmful misrepresentation in music is wrong, we have little reason to believe that all cultural appropriation of music involves misrepresentation, harmful or otherwise. As we have seen, Baraka is no admirer of cultural appropriation, but he grants that some appropriation can be helpful. He wrote that Beiderbecke's appropriation of jazz "served to place the Negro's culture and Negro society in a position of intelligent regard it had never enjoyed before" (Jones 1963: 151). If appropriation from African American culture is not harmful, appropriation from other cultures could also be benign or even beneficial. That a composition has been produced by cultural appropriation or is hybrid does not, by itself, demonstrate that the work is morally objectionable or aesthetically flawed.

Turn now to the second of the issues to be addressed in this section. Some writers have objected to cultural appropriation of music on the ground that it can contribute to the distortion or assimilation of minority cultures. It is easy to imagine how appropriation could lead to the distortion of a culture. Suppose that outsiders appropriate musical content from an indigenous culture. When these musicians engage in appropriation, they alter, perhaps subtly, the music that they appropriate. That is, the music becomes hybrid. Now one can easily imagine that musicians from the indigenous culture hear performances by the outsiders. The outsiders are likely to have greater access to recording contracts and performance opportunities than do musicians from the indigenous culture. The indigenous musicians may begin to adapt their music so that it sounds more like the music produced by outsiders. In time, the music of the indigenous people may be distorted. Since, in many cultures, music is an essential part of spiritual and ritual practices, distortion of a culture's music can have far-reaching cultural implications. It may even contribute to the assimilation of cultures.

This argument correctly identifies the single biggest threat facing minority cultures and, in particular, indigenous cultures: assimilation. It is not clear, however, that it shows that musicians always act wrongly when they appropriate from minority and indigenous cultures. In an increasingly cosmopolitan world, it is difficult, if not impossible, to prevent cultures from influencing each other. Likely minority musical traditions are influenced as much (or more) by completely different musical traditions as they are by musicians who have appropriated elements of the minority cultures. Consequently, it seems that whatever musicians from majority cultures do, they may have an impact on minority culture. So, if the mere act of creating music that influences another culture can be regarded as wrong, musicians are damned if they appropriate and damned if they do not. Some responsibility for maintaining the integrity of minority musical traditions has to lie with the members of these cultures. If they wish their traditions to remain intact, then they need to take care to ensure that traditional training is preserved. For their part, musicians from outside a culture ought to ensure that they do not misrepresent their works, which will often be hybrid in style, as authentic expressions of the culture from which they borrow.

Offensive appropriation

A final objection to the cultural appropriation of music remains to be addressed. Music can have more than aesthetic significance in many cultures. In certain cultures, particularly indigenous cultures, music can often have important spiritual or legal importance. For example, among the Kwakwaka'wakw people of the Pacific Northwest, the Blackfeet of Montana, and the Yolngu of Australia, songs can be seals of authority and indications of legal rights (Coleman et al. 2009: 186–7). Particularly when music has an important ceremonial or spiritual significance within a culture, its appropriation may be regarded as offensive or sacrilegious. This could be because its appropriation is regarded as a desecration of something sacred. In some cultures, for example, certain songs are to be sung only by persons properly initiated in certain rituals or secrets. A violation of this norm can be deeply offensive.

Musicians need to be aware of this possible consequence of their appropriation. This is not to say that the creation of an offensive work of art is always wrong. Carlos Serrano's *Piss Christ* (a photograph of a crucifix immersed in the artist's urine) is offensive, and offensive because it involves desecration. Still, it is not obvious that Serrano acted wrongly in creating this work. Few would want to say that he acted wrongly if he was engaged in an act of self-expression. (If he was simply trying to be gratuitously offensive, his actions would be assessed differently.) By parity of reasoning, musicians could engage in offensive cultural appropriation without acting wrongly. Nevertheless, gratuitous offensiveness is wrong. Consequently, when appropriation will cause deep offense in some culture, musicians ought to have compelling artistic or other reasons for their appropriation. Musicians may also be morally required to observe time and place restrictions on appropriation. If, for example, large numbers of Australian Aboriginals are profoundly offended by the appropriation of their music, then outsiders likely ought not to perform on the didgeridoo at a festival of aboriginal arts.

See also Authentic performance practice (Chapter 9), Music and dance (Chapter 43), Opera (Chapter 41), Song (Chapter 40), and Style (Chapter 13).

References

Baraka, A. [L. Jones] and Baraka, A. (1987) *The Music: Reflections on Jazz and Blues*, New York: William Morrow.

Born, G. and Hesmondhalgh, D. (2000) "Introduction," in *Western Music and its Others: Difference, Representation, and Appropriation in Music*, Berkeley: University of California Press, pp. 280–304.

Coleman, E. and Coombe, R. with MacArailt, F. (2009) "A Broken Record: Subjecting 'Music' to Cultural Rights," in J. Young and C. Brunk (eds) *The Ethics of Cultural Appropriation*, Malden: Wiley-Blackwell, pp. 173–210.

Feather, L. (1959) *The Book of Jazz*, New York: Meridian.

Feld, S. (1996) "Pygmy POP: A Genealogy of Schizophonic Mimesis," *Yearbook for Traditional Music* 28: 1–35.

Gaut, B. (1998) "The Ethical Criticism of Art," in J. Levinson (ed.) *Aesthetics and Ethics: Essays at the Intersection*, Cambridge: Cambridge University Press, pp. 182–203.

Gracyk, T. (2001) *I Wanna Be Me: Rock Music and the Politics of Identity*, Philadelphia: Temple University Press.

Jones, L. [Baraka, A.] (1963) *Blues People*, New York: William Morrow.

Negativland (n.d.) "Changing Copyright," available at www.negativland.com/news/?page_id=22.

Price, U. (1842) *On the Picturesque: With an Essay on the Origin of Taste*, Edinburgh: Caldwell, Lloyd and Co.

Reich, S. (1974) *Writings about Music*, Halifax: Nova Scotia College of Art and Design.

Rudinow, J. (1994) "Race, Ethnicity, Expressive Authenticity: Can White People Sing the Blues?" *Journal of Aesthetics and Art Criticism* 52: 127–37.

Shelby, T. (2005) *We Who Are Dark: The Philosophical Foundations of Black Solidarity*, Cambridge: The Belknap Press of Harvard University Press.

Taylor, P. (1995) ". . . So Black and Blue: Response to Rudinow," *Journal of Aesthetics and Art Criticism* 53: 313–16.

Young, J. (2008) *Cultural Appropriation and the Arts*, Malden: Blackwell.

18

INSTRUMENTAL TECHNOLOGY

Anthony Gritten

Our writing instruments contribute to our thoughts.
(Nietzsche, quoted in Kittler 1990: 195)

This chapter considers the significance of instrumental technology. The primary focus is on the conventional acoustic instruments used in the Western classical tradition, the repertoire that developed alongside them, and the strategies that performers develop to deal with both.

Human technology

Technology, often defined as the practical application of knowledge, has affected biology, environment, society, economy, culture, and community in numerous ways, and has raised ethical and social questions in the process. It has helped First World economies to advance and to raise living standards. The term "technology" refers to material objects such as industrial machines and kitchen forks, and also to computer software as well as organizational techniques and protocols. It has even become a barometer of demographic shifts, with "the digital divide" replacing "the class divide" as the pre-eminent measure of social progress and cohesion. Technology also affords social practices, providing both the time (indirectly) and the means (directly) for the leisure classes to indulge their desires in artistic practices such as performing music.

The discovery and manipulation of fire was a turning point in the technological evolution of humankind, perhaps the greatest after the evolution of opposable thumbs. Archaeological data suggests that humans domesticated fire by 1,000,000 BCE, and controlled it sometime between 500,000 BCE and 400,000 BCE. Clothing and shelter were similarly momentous technological advances, and the adoption of both was central to the survival, and subsequent domination, of humankind.

Turning to more conceivable history, technology and "techne" (craft) have a long and respectable genealogy. Plato (2006), considering techne as a potential threat to civic balance, treated the understanding of it as the proper foundation for governing the polis. Aristotle (1999) described it as one of the five virtues of thought. Marx (1990) contributed to the critique of technology in his work on labor, noting that machines objectify human knowledge and extend the reach of the human brain, and arguing that technical evolution requires its own theory independent of Darwin's theory of biological evolution. Freud (2002) emphasized that tools perfect humanity's organs, expand their limits, and remove their constraints, though he had misgivings about the role of technology. In the twentieth century, Heidegger (1993b) provided what has since become the classic articulation of the subject in "The Question Concerning Technology." McLuhan (1962, 1964) explored the impact of mass communication technologies, while Baudrillard, Haraway, Deleuze, and Stiegler, among others, turned to technology, techne, and "technics" in order to articulate humanity's position in the world and its future potentialities.

This brushstroke genealogy highlights the immense ambition of humanity with regard to technology. Only recently, with the rise in public awareness of climate change, has the speed and importance of high investment technological progress – the First World ideology of "Research and Development" – been seriously questioned.

Musical instruments

Performing much music requires various forms of technology, of which the most obvious is the musical instrument. (Whether the voice is an exception deserves consideration elsewhere.) Musical instruments have existed as long as the cultures which they partly constitute. Generally speaking, a tool is an object mediating between two domains and affording productive action, that is, a means of passing energy between domains in order to achieve some desired end, as with the transformation of potential into kinetic energy when bowing a violin string. A musical instrument is a tool designed to make musical sound; most have been acoustic, and put to the use for which they were designed. In principle, anything that produces sound can serve as a musical instrument, whether bone, ebony, or silicon, and every musical tradition maintains acoustical, symbolic, ergonomic, and aesthetic systems by which instruments are calibrated, used, and valued – by which musical tools are used to fulfill the desires and intentions of their performers.

> Musical instruments are formed, structured, and carved out of personal and social experience as much as they are built up from a great variety of natural and synthetic materials. They exist at an intersection of material, social, and cultural worlds where they are as much constructed and

fashioned by the force of minds, cultures, societies, and histories as axes, saws, drills, chisels, machines, and the ecology of wood.

(Dawe 2003: 275)

Indeed, instruments tend to be valued anthropomorphically (Lane 2000: 31–2), as if they were human, as Gerard Hoffnung's cartoons suggest. Famous violins are thought to have sonic "personalities" that their performers exploit to great effect, just as orchestras have "the Philadelphia sound" and there is a French school of flute playing descended from Claude-Paul Taffanel. In other words, we often recognize particular instruments by their trademark timbre. Instruments also have an aesthetic value: "at once physical and metaphorical, social constructions and material objects" (Dawe 2003: 276), they are pleasing to look at and can be expensive pieces of property, as with gilded harpsichords and cathedral organs. All these are reasons why we sometimes feel a vicarious pain when they are damaged or misused, whether by removal men or as part of an aesthetic event (Davies 2003b) – or when just carelessly played.

Noting the categorization of instruments in terms of strings, membranes, and resonators, or idiophones, aerophones, chordophones, and membranophones, this chapter is concerned with what instruments have in common, which is their use as tools and machines. Instruments are broadly ergonomic systems, designed with the local ecology of the parent musical practice in mind: ergonomic in that they are task-focused in their construction, operation, and maintenance, and reward a particular kind of trained manipulation; ecologically grounded in that their history both as individual instruments and as a genus can be traced alongside the very practices in which they are designed to be used. (They can also be used for "extended" practices, as with Cage's music for prepared piano.) From an ergonomic perspective, the central component of a musical instrument is the "interface" with which the performer engages in order to produce musical sound. This interface, whether keys, holes, fingerboard, or double reed, consists of various devices by which the performer measures and manipulates one or more variables or processes that contribute to the production of musical sound. From the perspective of the instrument-makers and technicians that support the performer, the interface is also the "instrumentation," so to speak, of the instrument: those parts of its engineering with which technicians work in order to improve the instrument's stability, optimization, safety, reliability, and above all productivity – to prepare for and facilitate the performer's musical task. In this sense, a musical instrument provides the performer with two things: first, a tool through which she can exercise and embody her intentions with respect to her performance and, second, a prosthetic extension of her body. Even conventional acoustic instruments are thus, in principle at least, distantly related to virtual reality, second life, and other emerging technologies that claim to generate and improve upon life (rather than merely mimic it). Indeed, it is curious that Baudrillard did not consider music in detail, for its practices would have made an interesting focus for his interest in simulation and simulacra (Baudrillard 1983).

Technical thinking

In the Western classical tradition, the musical instrument is tied into the logic governing the performer's primary task, namely, to perform the musical work, with all the nuances that are associated with "perform" in this context: compliance, representation, authenticity, expression, spontaneity, singularity, and so on. Thus the role of the instrument is to facilitate the execution of the performer's intentions unobtrusively, the paradigmatic use of the instrument being congruent with the following belief: "The outstanding performance of a fine musical work is, I suggest, an invitation to transcendental listening, in that, paradigmatically, it avoids drawing attention to itself *as* a performance (whether for positive or negative reasons)" (Johnson 1999: 85). Using the instrument should be effortless for the performer and transparent to the music. If the performer is a postman carrying and transmitting the musical package for and to the listener, then the instrument is the postman's van, designed to run smoothly and well oiled by the discourse of musical appreciation on the one hand and the exercise of the performer's skill on the other, but not primarily appreciated for its own qualities. Underlying the ergonomically couched advice about music "strategies" in empirical writings on performing (e.g. Parncutt and McPherson 2002; Williamon 2004) is the assumption that using the instrument should be effortless, the instrument functioning entirely within the performer's reach and being entirely focused on the task at hand, namely, to communicate the musical work with clarity and commitment.

It should be noted that there are at least two senses of "technical" at issue in the performer's engagement with her instrument: one ontological, one ergonomic. First, all performing is technical because it involves physical training and implementing bodily and instrumental movements in strategic ways that respond to the demands of the musical work as specified and implied in the score. Second, only certain styles of performing are technical, that is, embody what can be called "technical thinking": those that, as a result of direct intervention, use the body in ways that have been specifically selected because they expend less energy than other ways of acting. Indeed, according to this second sense of technical, in the game of performing "a technical 'move' is 'good' when it does better and/or expends less energy than another" (Lyotard 1984: 44), when it helps the performer to reach goals quicker and to operate the game's controls and tools – her instrument – in a more productive and efficient manner.

The question, then, concerning the technology of the instrument and the technical status of the performer's actions concerns "functionality" (Lane 2000: 32–5). Performing must make something with the instrument and show evidence of craftsmanship in its execution. The discourse of Western classical music has almost universally assimilated this idea into its ideology, concluding that performing is therefore governed by technical thinking, and by a mentality of "problem solving."

Tools and machines

Technology and aesthetic judgment have always been intertwined, and have developed alongside each other. How they interrelate has not always been straightforward, especially in the modern era. To use Heidegger's analogy (1993b: 321), where once humanity harnessed nature harmoniously in the windmill, now it challenges nature with the hydroelectric power-plant, and technology – technical thinking – is the means through which it implements this challenge. In recent decades, the rise of technical thinking and the digital turn have colluded to set in motion a paradigm shift. We have drifted from a situation in which instruments are mimetic and geared toward the prior desires and intentions of performers, toward a situation embracing instruments as the autonomous generators of new and unexpected expressions. This chapter is more concerned with the first of these situations and the first type of instrument. Nevertheless, while the implications of meta-instruments, software hacking, electroacoustic music, and other forms of digital activity for the question concerning technology deserve treatment elsewhere, an excursus on the digital instrument frames the particular qualities that the acoustic instrument brings to the performance of Western classical music.

Thanks to Marx's work on labor (1990) and Heidegger's on *techne* (1993b), we can distinguish between tools and machines. The tool does not completely displace the performer from its operation. The machine, increasingly though not necessarily digitally driven, is set in motion by its user but operates semi-autonomously and contains within itself the means for further self-generation and self-development; as Stiegler notes, it enables "the pursuit of life by means other than life" (1998: 17–18). A tool extends its user's reach; a machine displaces it (Bajorek 2003: 49–51; Marx 1990: 548).

Machines are premised upon the gathering, institution, organization, and production of clearly defined and repeatable data. Their focus is thus not on the unique, the unrepeatable, the messy, or the loose, but on what can be measured, abstracted, ordered, and represented in a symbolic system. This means that machines are entirely driven by the question of form, rather than content, ordering life but not creating it. Indeed, it is precisely this factor that affords machines their greatest strength, namely, that they facilitate a certain kind of labor. This machinic labor, however, short-circuits human labor with a quicker and more efficient means of getting the job done, with the implication that humans now have to develop skills to match those of today's machines, or risk becoming obsolete like yesterday's machines. For whereas humanity once bore tools (and now makes machines), machines themselves have gradually become the predominant tool bearers, and humanity has thus become less technological in the strict sense of the term; technology, not humanity, now seems to direct nature (Stiegler 1998: 23–4).

Returning to music, the musical instrument often embodies the qualities of both tools and machines. As tool, it extends the performer's reaching for personal musical expression and affords her the productive illusion that she is "saving time" or "acquiring knowledge" by using the instrument in this precise manner rather than any other (Reybrouck 2006). As machine, it also generates unexpected forms of temporal articulation. The boundary between tool and machine is not always rigid, as illustrated by Music-Minus-One recordings, which inhabit a realm somewhere between tool and machine (Davies 2003a); they are not merely tools, because they maintain a certain autonomy of their own, but they are not fully machines, because they still require the performer to play along and complete the illusion of performing in ensemble. The underlying point is that instruments present the performer with two simultaneous sets of opportunities, and it is her responsibility to decide what ratio of instrument-as-tool to instrument-as-machine to create as she performs. Improvisers, for example, make particular use of the machinic potential of their instruments, one of their tasks being to challenge conceptions of what is ergonomic and practical for the instrument (such is also the effect of virtuosity). Many classical instrumentalists emphasize the prosthetic qualities of their instrument-as-tool and its ability to facilitate a musical sound or style that mimics, or at least is analogous to, vocal production, as with the way pianists often perform ascending anacrustic gestures at phrase beginnings. Interestingly, the analysis and performance literature (e.g. Rink 1995, 2002) tends to take a functionalist approach to the issue, configuring music's technological apparatus more as a machine than as a tool; the question of whether this approach is thus able to consider fully the role of aesthetic value judgment in performing (a frequent anecdotal criticism performers make) deserves consideration elsewhere.

The rise of the machines

If technology now leads the way, then the paradox of the performer's relationship to her musical instrument is that, *qua* technology, "[t]o be commanded, technology must first be obeyed" (Winner 1977: 262; cf. Bajorek 2003: 56). Indeed, it is not pushing the point too much to claim that technology produces performing to a significant degree, that performing is necessarily technological. Configuring performing in terms of technical thought, in terms of the instrument and its technical values, has consequences.

Our social practices evolve alongside our use of new tools and the refinements we make to existing tools, in the sense that "if a new technology extends one or more of our senses outside us into the social world, then new ratios among all of our senses will occur in that particular culture. It is comparable to what happens when a new note is added to a melody" (McLuhan 1962: 41). Stiegler

(1998) argues that it is not the case simply that humanity is the subject of its own history and technology its object, the means by which humanity implements its projects; their interrelationship (both genetic and causal) is more complex. This is the issue of what Katz (2004) terms "technology effects":

> People no longer know or control what they have made. Their tools, far from being neutral and amenable to different purposes, have become a "second nature" with its own self-determining ends. . . . Human beings objectify their energy into the technological world which then becomes "animate," while they become inanimate, passive and lifeless.
>
> (Herf 1977: 183)

Now, it may be the case, in what looks superficially like the tail wagging the dog, that technology has allowed instruments to lead the development of performing styles and musical repertoires, from the invention of the saxophone to Vanessa-Mae's turn to the electric violin; from Josef Hofmann's personal Steinway, made with thinner keys to fit his tiny hands, to the mechanical and timbral advances of Cavaillé-Coll organs in nineteenth-century France; from the gradual adoption of vibrato on the violin to Hendrix's inverted guitar technique. It may be the case that, metaphorically speaking, tools and machines are infantile in that they behave how they want much of the time, with little loyalty to the performer, and it can sometimes feel as if "no matter which aims or purposes one decides to put in, a particular kind of product inevitably comes out" (Winner 1977: 278). It may be the case that technology exists in its own world and holds an alienating mirror up to the performer, reflecting back at her all her technical and aesthetic inadequacies while absorbing all her gifts and abilities without a note of thanks (the horn player's necessary spittle release brings the instrumental technology down to earth). It may simply be the case that, as potential tool and machine, the instrument provides a degree of alienation and resistance (Evens 2005: 160–73). But the performer must find a way not to reject but to live with this alienation and resistance. She must turn it to her advantage as she searches for her voice, for "[w]hile McLuhan was right to stress technology's shaping role in modern life, the human side of the equation cannot be ignored" (Katz 2004: 191).

The dark side of technology

Before exploring some of the ways in which the performer can turn the potential alienation and resistance of instrumental technology to her advantage, a note on what a failure to do so might entail, a scenario often envisaged by pessimists (*in extremis*, Luddites).

Optimists and pessimists alike note that technology, in the form of ever more competent, autonomous, and intelligent machines, is making numerous decisions for us, that instruments are controlling an increasing number of the parameters of our interaction with the world, and that tools are taking over more and more dirty manual work (in the First World, at least); indeed, the very term "interaction" is gradually being replaced by the rhetoric of "interface." Technology is assuming its own momentum and pace of innovation, and we are witnessing a divorce between the rhythms of technical and cultural development, the former evolving much quicker than the latter; predictions that technology will one day survive without humankind are no longer just a classic science fiction fantasy.

In many situations this is a relief, since it affords the use of time for other activities (such as performing music). Whether, however, technology is appropriately focused toward performing music (and aesthetic activity in general) needs debate. Aden Evens, for example, writes that "extraction, distribution, and refinement are the most efficient path to a given end; they are modern technology's techniques, through which it institutes its *order*" (2005: 64). Read literally (as intended), this statement describes how digital computers deal with the data on CDs. Read metaphorically, it describes, *inter alia*, a business plan for capturing natural petroleum resources. What is interesting is the relative balance of these two readings, the metaphorical being much more than a literary conceit, since it is clear that technology and its rhetoric have deeply infiltrated world, thought, and praxis.

Assumptions that technological development has generally beneficial effects sometimes lead to predictions that humanity will control the world using technology or that humanity will *become* technology (as opposed to being technological, which it has always been). Such views are epitomized by Paul Virilo's work on speed (1995). Debates about musical technology, and in particular the future of musical instruments, include similar assumptions and predictions, from advocates of distributed performance networks (Harris 2006) to Stelarc (Caygill 1997). While it is perhaps unnecessary to overdo "the threat of a whole-scale absorption into the digital" and the "nightmare of a world where creativity is left to the computer" (Evens 2005: 131), it is important to retain some skepticism about ideologies of techno-utopianism and caution regarding the notion of human betterment which they tend to assume. Some, such as Heidegger (1993b), hold reservations about technology but maintain the importance of the issue. Others, such as Marcuse (1964), argue more forcefully that societies become more technological at the cost of their moral freedom and psychological health. Others still, such as Bakhtin, are highly critical of the abnegation of human responsibility that excessive reliance on technology seems to imply:

> Thus instruments are perfected according to their own inner law, and, as a result, they develop from what was initially a means of rational defense into a terrifying, deadly, and destructive force. All that which is technological, when divorced from the once-occurrent unity of life and surrendered to the will of the law immanent to its development, is

frightening; it may from time to time irrupt into this once-occurrent unity as an irresponsibly destructive and terrifying force.

(Bakhtin 1993: 7)

Adorno has broadly the same attitude as Bakhtin, though is more caustic:

Not least to blame for the withering of experience is the fact that things, under the law of pure functionality, assume a form that limits contact with them to mere operation, and tolerates no surplus, either in freedom of conduct or in autonomy of things, which would survive as the core of experience, because it is not consumed by the moment of action.

(Adorno 1978: §19; cf. §§76, 77, 81, and 125)

Even taking their respective historical–political contexts into account, though, both thinkers overstate the case. Despite that fact that "schemes [for considering musical instruments] are culture-specific in one way or another and are tied to hegemonic systems of one sort or another" (Dawe 2003: 275), human responsibility nevertheless remains central to the performer's task in the wake of any technological change to society's – and hence the performer's – musical instruments. What is required is less the "either-or" rhetoric of Bakhtin and Adorno (technology or humanity) and more the "both-and" of responsible aesthetic judgment as practiced by the performer: How can the instrument be both her tool and her machine? Should she use general registration pistons in the performance of Buxtehude's organ works, even although such playing aids were unknown to the composer?

I'll be back, or, the return of the performer

Despite these claims for the autonomous power and ambition of technology as embodied in musical instruments, and the continuing rise of machines to unprecedented levels of performance and capability, it remains the case that, against the odds, human intervention is needed for performing acoustic Western classical music. Indeed, while this year's cutting-edge technological innovations will become next year's landfill, the technological antiquity of the acoustic instrument does not present an insurmountable problem for the performer, since antiquity does not imply obsolescence; like wine, some instruments get better with age. If instrumental antiquity were a problem, then Stan Godlovitch's admirable stand against the development of synthesizers and other artificial performing devices, arguing that technological "challenges [to the traditional model of performing] fail to damage the model's internal coherence or show it to be inconsistent" (Godlovitch 1998: 4), would have been indispensable.

While instrument manufacturing has become quicker and cheaper, benefitting countless households, there have been fewer labor-saving benefits for the performer. It may be that there are certain situations in which live human presence is less necessary than it used to be, as with bomb disposal or the computing power needed to profile national demographic shifts, or even with aspects of the manufacture of musical instruments themselves. But performing acoustic Western classical music is not one of these situations, even though technology provides a range of tools and machines, including musical instruments, and deepens the performer's awareness of what constitutes a tool and what can be used vicariously as one.

Performing is not only a technical activity. Indeed, the problem of technical thinking is that, as Heidegger argues, it tends to reduce thinking to a process "in the service of doing and making," while actually "[i]t is as revealing, and not as manufacturing, that techne is a bringing-forth . . . where *aletheia*, truth, happens" (Heidegger 1993a: 218–19). It is for practical reasons, then, that performers sometimes have an ambivalent relationship to music's technologies, often only listening unwillingly to recordings (Katz 2004: 198–9 n. 61). Beyond a threshold concern for the technician's assurance that the instrument is prepared and the keypads are no longer sticking, and notwithstanding the varying obsessions with, for example, scraping new reeds or experimenting with new rosins, the performer has other imperatives to fulfill and values to create, champion, and critique. Her task is to overcome the potential alienation of her technological situation, of the simultaneous tool and machinic qualities of her instrument, and turn it to her aesthetic advantage.

In general, rather than becoming "transfixed in the will to master" the instrument's technology, the performer must turn her attention elsewhere (Heidegger 1993b: 337) and focus on passing the threshold between green room and stage. What music psychologists call "expert performing" (because they see it as an example of technical thinking), amateurs "professional playing" (because they are not "in the know" technically), and listeners "beautiful, sublime, wonderful, tasteful," and so on (because technique is not their primary concern), happens when the performer acts as if she is not using technology, as if using the instrument is effortless and it is neither tool nor machine.

For the duration of this valuable illusion, which is the duration of performing, questions of the profitability of technical thinking and the efficiency of technology are distracting. They tempt the performer away from the more important questions around the aesthetic judgments that, for the duration of performing, remain a vital input *and* output of the performer's activity. Given that such judgments are effectively para-technological, this makes performing a slow, prosaic, loose, reflective, and messy activity.

Conclusion

This chapter has followed technology through its role in human life and in music performance, noting its extraordinary influence on thinking, its recent division into tools and machines, and its current development beyond the reach of the human mind. Some of its many advantages have been mentioned, along with a few disadvantages. Returning to the human pre-history mentioned at the start, it is worth recalling the Prometheus myth and its association with techne (Meagher 1988): fire is domesticated from a state of wildness, and always threatens to flare up and become wild once again, to expose our essential mortal powerlessness. This is the predicament we live through alongside "our" musical instruments. Will they do what we want? For this reason, as Heidegger (1993b) and Davies (2003b) both argue, they deserve our respect.

See also Adorno (Chapter 36), Authentic performance practice (Chapter 9), Medium (Chapter 5), and Performances and recordings (Chapter 8).

References

Adorno, T. (1978 [1951]) *Minima Moralia: Reflections from Damaged Life*, trans E.F.N. Jephcott, London: Verso.

Aristotle (1999) *Nicomachean Ethics*, trans. T. Irwin, Indianapolis: Hackett.

Bajorek, J. (2003) "Animadversions: Tekne after Capital/Life after Work," *Diacritics* 33: 42–59.

Bakhtin, M. (1993 [1919–21]) *Toward a Philosophy of the Act*, trans. V. Liapunov, Austin: University of Texas Press.

Baudrillard, J. (1983) *Simulations*, trans. P. Foss, P. Patton, and P. Beitchman, New York: Semiotext(e).

Caygill, H. (1997) "Stelarc and the Chimera: Kant's Critique of Prosthetic Judgement," *Art Journal* 56: 46–51.

Davies, S. (2003a) "So, You Want to Sing with the Beatles? Too Late!" in *Themes in the Philosophy of Music*, Oxford: Oxford University Press, pp. 94–107.

—— (2003b) "What is the Sound of One Piano Plummeting?" in *Themes in the Philosophy of Music*, Oxford: Oxford University Press, pp. 108–18.

Dawe, K. (2003) "The Cultural Study of Musical Instruments," in M. Clayton, T. Herbert, and R. Middleton (eds) *The Cultural Study of Music: A Critical Introduction*, New York: Routledge, pp. 274–83.

Evens, A. (2005) *Sound Ideas: Music, Machines, and Experience*, Minneapolis: University of Minnesota Press.

Freud, S. (2002 [1930]) *Civilization and its Discontents*, London: Penguin.

Godlovitch, S. (1998) *Musical Performance: A Philosophical Study*, New York: Routledge.

Harris, Y. (2006) "Inside-out Instrument," *Contemporary Music Review* 25: 151–62.

Heidegger, M. (1993a [1946]) "Letter on Humanism," trans. D.F. Krell, in *Basic Writings*, San Francisco: Harper Collins, pp. 189–242.

—— (1993b [1949]) "The Question Concerning Technology," trans. D.F. Krell, in *Basic Writings*, San Francisco: Harper Collins, pp. 283–317.

Herf, J. (1977) "Technology, Reification, and Romanticism," *New German Critique* 12: 175–91.

Johnson, P. (1999) "Performance and the Listening Experience: Bach's 'Erbarme dich'," in N. Cook, P. Johnson, and H. Zender (eds) *Theory into Practice*, Leuven: Leuven University Press, pp. 55–101.

Katz, M. (2004) *Capturing Sound: How Technology has Changed Music*, Berkeley: University of California Press.

Kittler, F. (1990) "The Mechanized Philosopher," in L. Rickels (ed.) *Looking After Nietzsche*, Albany: State University of New York Press, pp. 195–207.

Lane, R. (2000) *Jean Baudrillard*, London: Routledge.

Lyotard, J.-F. (1984 [1979]) *The Postmodern Condition: A Report on Knowledge*, trans. G. Bennington and B. Massumi, Minneapolis: University of Minnesota Press.

Marcuse, H. (1964) *One-Dimensional Man*, Boston: Beacon.

Marx, K. (1990 [1867]) *Capital*, Volume 1: *A Critique of Political Economy*, trans. B. Fowkes, London: Penguin.

McLuhan, M. (1962) *The Gutenberg Galaxy*, Toronto: University of Toronto Press.

—— (1964) *Understanding Media*, New York: McGraw Hill.

Meagher, R. (1988) "Technê," *Perspecta* 24: 159–64.

Parncutt, R. and McPherson, G. (eds) (2002) *The Science and Psychology of Music Performance: Creative Strategies for Teaching and Learning*, Oxford: Oxford University Press.

Plato (2006) *The Republic*, trans. R.E. Allen, New Haven: Yale University Press.

Reybrouck, M. (2006) "Music Cognition and the Bodily Approach: Musical Instruments as Tools for Musical Semantics," *Contemporary Music Review* 25: 59–68.

Rink, J. (ed.) (1995) *The Practice of Performance: Studies in Musical Interpretation*, Cambridge: Cambridge University Press.

—— (ed.) (2002) *Musical Performance: A Guide to Understanding*, Cambridge: Cambridge University Press.

Stiegler, B. (1998) *Technics and Time*, vol. 1: *The Fault of Epimetheus*, trans. R. Beardsworth and G. Collins, Stanford: Stanford University Press.

Virilo, P. (1995) *The Art of the Motor*, trans. J. Rowe, Minneapolis: University of Minnesota Press.

Williamon, A. (ed.) (2004) *Musical Excellence: Strategies and Techniques to Enhance Performance*, Oxford: Oxford University Press.

Winner, L. (1977) *Autonomous Technology: Technics-out-of-Control as a Theme in Political Thought*, Cambridge: MIT Press.

Part II
EMOTION

19
EXPRESSION THEORIES
Jenefer Robinson

Many theorists claim that to say music is expressive of emotion is simply to attribute to the music "expressive qualities." Others claim that music can be an expression of emotion in a more full-blooded way. In this chapter I will be defending the idea that at least some music can be a genuine expression of emotion in the sense that it can be a manifestation of emotion that someone (although perhaps a fictional someone) actually feels. I will not be talking directly about the emotions music *arouses* in listeners, although what the music arouses and what it expresses, if anything, are clearly connected. And I will not be arguing that *all* music expresses emotions. The mature compositions of Milton Babbitt, for example, exhibit little interest in emotion. My discussion will be focused on Western art music that is clearly emotionally expressive, most notably, music in the Romantic and post-Romantic style.

Animating music: musical expressiveness as "hearing-as"

For many people, to say that a piece of music "expresses sadness" simply means that the music has a certain quality that is named by an emotion word: the music "is sad." (See, for example, John Hospers 1955; Tormey 1971.) Expression in this view is simply a matter of possessing expressive qualities, and expressive qualities are simply "aesthetic qualities" like any others, such as dynamism or freshness. But music can be sad by virtue of *conventions* (it is in the minor key) or cultural *associations* (it is used at funerals) without expressing much, if any, emotion. Like the upside-down smiley-face, music can be sad without being very expressive.

The doggy theory: appearance expressionism

According to Stephen Davies, the expressiveness of music consists in its "presenting emotion characteristics in its appearance" (1994: 228). Just as the face of a basset hound is called "sad" because that is the way sad people typically look when they are expressing their sadness, so music is called "sad" because it sounds or moves like a person who is sad. Music is *expressive* of sadness without being an *expression* of anyone's sadness, that is, without revealing anything about anyone's actual state of mind. Similarly, in *The Corded Shell* (1980), Peter Kivy argues that music is expressive of emotion by virtue of sharing the "contours" of vocal or behavioral expressive gestures made by human beings when in the throes of emotion. Like Davies, Kivy compares musical expressiveness to the expressiveness of a dog's face, in his case the St. Bernard. (Both Kivy and Davies also recognize the role of conventions in musical expressiveness. See also Kivy 2002, which partially repudiates his earlier view.)

This "doggy" theory of musical expressiveness emphasizes how a musical line can be heard as expressive of grief by virtue of its resemblance to the "contour" or intonation pattern of a grief-stricken voice, as in the famous "weeping figure" at the beginning of Monteverdi's *Arianna's Lament*, or by virtue of how musical movement mimics expressive behavior, especially "the gait, attitude, air, carriage, posture, and comportment of the human body" (Davies 2006: 182). For Davies, "the resemblance that counts most for musical expressiveness ... is that between music's temporally unfolding dynamic structure and configurations of human behavior associated with emotion" (2006: 181). We experience movement in music not only in terms of "progress from high to low or fast to slow," but also in "the multistranded waxing and waning of tensions generated variously within the harmony, the mode of articulation and phrasing, subtle nuances of timing, the delay or defeat of expected continuations, and so on" (2006: 181–2). Davies thinks that "this movement is like human behavior in that it seems purposeful and goal-directed" (2006: 182).

To those who object that there is no greater "objective" resemblance between musical movement and emotions than between musical movement and various natural phenomena – the weather, the moods of the sea – Davies responds that the degree of resemblance is beside the point: listeners simply do experience a resemblance between the music and "the realm of human emotion." Listeners make the connection between music and emotion by an "*experience* of similarity" (2006: 182), not a mere *recognition that* there is a similarity. And our interests shape how we experience the world. As he says, we are more likely to see a weeping willow as a downcast person than as a frozen waterfall, even if the similarity between the willow and the waterfall is no less than that between the willow and the droopy person. We hear music as expressive of emotions because in listening to music, we *anthropomorphize* or "animate" it so that we *hear* it *as* expressive of emotion.

One limitation of the doggy theory is that it allows for music to express only those emotional states that exhibit characteristic vocal intonations or expressive behaviors. This has three important consequences. First, it is hard to see how music can express patterns of feeling, such as the way in which despair is with difficulty overcome and transforms gradually into resignation. Second, and relatedly, it seems to follow that cognitively complex emotions cannot be expressed by music: there are no distinguishing vocal or behavioral marks of resignation, for example. Third, the theory does not explain why listeners are so powerfully moved by emotional expression in music. We are not particularly moved (except perhaps to laughter) by the sad doggy faces of the St. Bernard and the basset hound. Why, then, should we be moved by the sad appearance of music?

Davies has responded to all three objections. First, he has argued that a pattern of feeling can be expressed by an appropriate sequence of musical gestures. Thus, "just as music might present the characteristic of an emotion in its aural appearance, so too it might present the appearance of a pattern of feelings through the order of its expressive development" (Davies 1994: 263). But if what we are listening to is a sequence of expressive "contours" without any underlying psychological reality, there is no organic connection between one expressive "appearance" and the next: they are simply concatenated. It is like watching a series of expressions moving across someone's face. If there is a pattern, it is only because of the thoughts, desires, intentions and so on that underlie the sequence. If it is just a series of facial contortions, why call this a *pattern* of expressions?

Second, Davies has defended the idea that music can express cognitively complex emotions, arguing that a piece of music can express hope, for example, if the "emotion characteristics in appearance" of a longish piece or passage of music are judiciously ordered (1994: 262–4). But again, a mere sequence of expressive gestures is not enough to distinguish a cognitively complex emotion such as hope, whatever the order in which these gestures occur. If all you have to work with are expressive gestures, then the best you can do to express hope in music is to have a cheerful passage followed by a sad one or a passage in which cheerfulness and sadness somehow intermingle or something of this sort. But the expression of hope requires the expression of desires and thoughts. A hopeful person is one who *wishes* for something to happen that he *construes* as good. Hope cannot be expressed merely by a succession of bodily gestures and vocal intonations. (See Karl and Robinson 1995 for a detailed discussion of this point.)

More recently, Davies has conceded that only a few emotional types "can be individuated solely on the basis of observed bodily comportment" (2006: 183). His candidates for expressible emotions include sadness and happiness, timidity, anger, "swaggering arrogance, the mechanical rigidity that goes with repression and alienation from the physicality of existence, ethereal dreaminess, and sassy sexuality" (2006: 183). Notice, however, that apart from sadness, happiness and anger, the rest of these examples are not strictly speaking emotions at all, but rather *behaviors* that could but need not be indicative of some emotion. As for more complex emotions, Davies is cautious: "where deep sadness gives way gradually to joy and abandonment, it may be reasonable to regard the transition as consistent with acceptance and resolution" (2006: 185). But notice here that "acceptance" and "resolution" are inner states, requiring beliefs, desires, and intentions. It is implausible that the transformation of a deeply sad appearance (such as a grieving facial expression) into a joyful appearance (such as a smile) is capable of expressing a complex shift in one's inner states, involving *thoughts* of acceptance, an *intention* to be courageous, a *wish* that things had been different conquered by a *desire* for the capacity to deal with things as they are, and so on. In general, if all musical expression could be explained according to the doggy theory, then music would be able to express very little about our inner life.

The final problem concerns why expressive music should be moving, if the doggy theory is correct. Here Davies relies on the idea that expressive music is "contagious" (1994: 279–307, forthcoming). There is indeed evidence that music can affect the motor system and to some degree change people's behavior and mood (see Robinson 2005: ch. 13). But we are not typically moved by an expression of emotion in a musical "appearance" in the way in which we are moved by an expression of genuine emotion. Even if I am affected physiologically and motorically by a piece of expressive music, this does not explain the power of our emotional responses to expressive music. After all, I am powerfully moved not because my friend has a sad-looking face, but only because that sad-looking face is a sign that she really is sad. In Bill Viola's slow-motion video installation, *The Quintet of Remembrance*, five actors perform different emotions (sadness, anger, and so on) via gradually changing facial expressions and gestures. The people in the group do not appear to interact, and there is no hint as to why they are expressing these emotions. The result is that the piece is both lifeless and melodramatic. Yet this installation is supposed to get its expressiveness in just the same way as the doggy theory claims music does.

The persona theory

Jerrold Levinson propounds a variation of the "animation theory," which, unlike the doggy theory, accepts that what we experience as musical expressiveness is an experience as of someone genuinely expressing his or her emotions. In Levinson's formulation, "a passage of music P is expressive of an emotion E if and only if P, in context, is readily heard, by a listener experienced in the genre in question, as an expression of E" (Levinson 2006: 193; see also Levinson 1996). It is crucial to Levinson's view that expression "requires an expresser" (Levinson 2006: 193). He believes that when we hear music as expressive of emotion, we hear or imagine an agent or persona in the music, the "owner" of the states expressed. Now, when we listen to a lyric song such as "Gute Nacht" from Schubert's *Winterreise*, we naturally hear it as emanating from a person or character in the music who is expressing his gloomy state of mind. In Levinson's view, however, we also hear all purely instrumental music ("absolute music") that is expressive of emotion in the very same way, namely, as emanating from a persona in the music, which may be a "character," or the composer himself, or a persona of the composer.

There is much to be said in favor of Levinson's view. It allows for musical expressiveness to be treated as the genuine expression of emotion. It permits us to hear extended passages of music as expressing unfolding psychological states, rather than as mere sequences of expressive "appearances." And once we hear the music as genuinely expressing a sequence of emotions, it is possible to find "patterns of feeling" in the music as well as the expression of cognitively complex emotions such as hope. If we hear a persona in the music, we can hear him as *seeking* or *striving toward* certain goals (as fragments of a theme struggle to transform into another theme with a different character), as *desiring* certain things and rejecting others (as a sequence of harmonies yearns toward resolution but is turned aside into an alien key which it then struggles to resist), or as *remembering* past events with nostalgia or bitterness (as when an early sunny theme is recalled later in a piece with reassuring or troubling effect). Emotion characteristics in appearances do not strive or seek or desire or remember, but people do. Through positing a persona in the music, Levinson allows us to hear the music as expressing the inner states of this persona. Finally, because it allows us to hear the music as a genuine expression, it makes sense that we would be moved by music's expressiveness. (See Karl and Robinson (1995) for a case study of Shostakovich's Tenth Symphony. For a recent study that emphasizes how the listener not only *hears* what the music expresses but also *enacts* virtual expressive behaviors afforded by the music, see Nussbaum 2007.)

Despite its many virtues, however, there are problems with Levinson's theory: in some respects it goes too far and in other respects it does not go far enough. First, Levinson means his theory to be a general account of expressiveness in music. But there are many pieces which in common parlance are said to "express melancholy" even though we have no inclination to posit a melancholy persona in the music. As we have seen, a piece can be "sad" or "cheerful" for diverse reasons: associations or conventions may play the major role. Other pieces can be explained simply by reference to the doggy theory: we hear a piece as sad because of its sad "contours." Perhaps we should stipulate that the term "musical expression" should be confined to those pieces that fit Levinson's theory, but then we need to know how to determine which those are.

This brings me to my second objection to Levinson's theory: in some respects it does not go far enough. For Levinson, like Kivy and Davies, expression in music is primarily something determined by the experience of listeners or audiences, not primarily something achieved by artists. Now, it is true that emotional expression in ordinary life is a means of communication – looking at your gait and posture tells me how you are feeling – but it is also true that the reason why expression is such a good means of communication is that, when it is sincere, it accurately reveals genuine inner states. In other words, expression is primarily something achieved by expressers, not something noticed or experienced by spectators or audiences.

In conclusion, there is much expressiveness that does not need Levinson's persona, and there is some expressiveness that does require the persona but as a genuine (dramatic) protagonist genuinely expressing his or her emotions, not merely as something imagined or postulated by listeners. (For further discussion of Levinson on expression and expressiveness see Robinson 2007b.)

Music as the expression of emotion: a Romantic theory

The Romantic movement at the end of the eighteenth and beginning of the nineteenth centuries spawned the idea that one of the main goals of the arts is to express the emotions of artists. One of the most carefully worked out versions of the expression theory comes from the philosopher R. G. Collingwood (1963). Collingwood claims that *all* "art proper" is expression. But I will treat his view as a theory of expression in art, not a theory of art in general. According to Collingwood, in both the expression of emotion in ordinary life and the expression of emotion in artworks someone who is in an emotional state communicates that state to other people. But artistic expression also differs from what we call expression in ordinary contexts in at least three ways.

First, to "express" an emotion in real life means that you manifest or show this emotion by means of facial or vocal expressions, by the visible concomitants of autonomic arousal (trembling, weeping, blushing), or through "action tendencies" (fist-clenching, hiding, caressing). But Collingwood says that expression in music (and the other arts) is quite distinct from displaying *symptoms* of emotion (as he calls blushing and fist-clenching and so on). A flood of tears *betrays* an emotion willy-nilly; a symphony that expresses emotion is an object *intentionally constructed* so as to express that emotion.

Second, an artistic expression is distinguished from merely *describing* or *labeling* an emotion: when I say "I love you," that would seem to be a paradigm expression of love in ordinary life, but it is not an expression at all in Collingwood's sense, because describing my emotion as "love" *generalizes* it; my words do not capture the specificity of my love for you and distinguish it from all other loves. Artistic expression, on the other hand, *individualizes* an emotion. If the funeral march of Beethoven's "Eroica" Symphony expresses sorrow, this is a quite distinct sorrow from that expressed by the funeral march in Chopin's B-flat minor Piano Sonata. (See Ridley 1995 for one way of explaining the difference.)

Third, Collingwood notes that expression in art cannot be identified with the *arousal* of emotion in audiences: an artist "proper" should not be aiming to arouse emotions in audiences, because that would be manipulating other people's emotions rather than sincerely expressing his own. However, if a composer genuinely succeeds in expressing an emotion in a piece of music, then the audience should, as a kind of by-product, be able to experience it for themselves.

What really makes the difference between ordinary expression and the expression of emotion in music and the other arts for Collingwood is that artistic expression is essentially a *cognitive* process, a matter of articulating an emotion in such a way that the nature of the emotion is clarified for the understanding. Here we see indirectly the influence of Hegel, who thought of the arts as a mode of *understanding* distinct from both religion and philosophy. Collingwood's main examples are literary: the poet who wants to express his emotions in a poem but does not know exactly what emotions he is feeling, yet who, *in writing the poem*, reflects upon and thereby comes to *understand* that emotion. An emotion that was unclear in the poet's mind is clarified once it has been articulated in a structure of words, imagery, rhythm, and other poetic devices. As for the reader, Collingwood claims that in order to understand what a poem expresses, the reader should experience it for herself and come to grasp what is expressed by recreating in herself the emotions of the artist that are expressed in the poem. So the poet is not *aiming* to arouse our emotions, but if he does a good job, he will have created a poem that will in fact enable us to recreate his emotions and feel them for ourselves. Thus Keats's "Ode to a Nightingale" *expresses* the poet's longing for an unchangeable world of art and beauty far away from "the weariness, the fever, and the fret" of our mundane world, and as we read the poem, we imagine the poet's situation and come to experience the emotions with which he responds to it.

It is important to remember that the concept of art as a personal expression of emotion originated in Romanticism. Keats's Ode is a paradigm of expression because in it the poet – or his persona – is expressing some complex emotional state that he is actually experiencing and there is development in this emotional state from the beginning to the end of the poem. This is what expression is in its fullest sense: an achievement by an artist, not a mode of experiencing by a reader or listener.

But how can music express in this full-blooded way? The doggy theory rightly suggests that we can experience music as resembling the vocal expressions and the motor activity – including expressive bodily gestures and action tendencies – that characterize particular emotions. But music can also to some extent express the appraisals in emotion: we can hear in the music when things are going along in a regular, pleasant way, and when they take a turn for the worse. There are also ways in which music can express desire, aspiration, or striving: a theme may struggle to achieve resolution, fail, try again, and finally achieve closure; or one theme may gradually and with apparent difficulty transform into a theme with a different character. There are many different strands in our emotional life, as different emotions ambiguously intertwine, morph from one to another, or blend to make a new emotional state. It would seem, then, that music, which is also woven of many strands, is peculiarly well suited to mirror our emotional life.

In a Romantic *lied*, such as "Gute Nacht" words and music collaborate to express the protagonist's unhappiness at having been rejected by his beloved and his sense of defeat and abandonment. The *Winterreise* is of course both an actual and a psychological journey, but even this one song is a mini-drama in itself: the wanderer's emotions shift and change from the beginning to the end. From the first bars, the funereal D minor harmonies, the descending notes of the piano accompaniment, and the harsh dissonance on the penultimate harmony of the cadence tell us that we are in a dark, cold world both physically and psychologically. We hear the wanderer trudging along in the repeated chords of the piano accompaniment, which continue throughout the piece. The repetitive character of the accompaniment seems to mirror his obsessive thinking about what he has left behind. But in the fourth and final verse, D minor changes to D major with the words "*Will dich im Traum nicht stören, wär Schad' um deine Ruh.*" Suddenly a hopeful vista seems to open that had been closed off before. The wanderer nostalgically remembers his beloved and in his imagination tenderly tells her that he will not awaken her but will instead inscribe "*Gute Nacht*" on the gate as he departs, so that she will know that he was thinking of her. But as he repeats "*An dich hab' ich gedacht*" a second time, the piece sinks back into the darkness and despair of the tonic D minor.

The words and music of "Gute Nacht" *articulate* the development of the protagonist's emotions in just the same way as in Keats's Ode. The *lied* illustrates how music can convey the way things seem to be going from good to bad or from bad to good, a sense that desires have been gratified or disappointed, and a sense that memories have engulfed a person or been swept away. What is even more interesting, however, is that some "pure" or "absolute" music can express the emotions of a protagonist in a very similar way.

Every piece of music, says Edward T. Cone, has an "expressive potential" (1974: 171) able to be realized in different ways in different contexts, but with broad limits on what it can express. Thus the expressive potential of a piece can include a movement from grief to joy, from being oppressed by difficulties to overcoming them, or from dreading a direful fate to resignation. The possibilities are extensive, but they do not include just anything. In particular they do not permit joy turning into grief, or a sunny life that turns sour.

Why should we interpret music as "mirroring" emotional processes rather than processes in inanimate nature: clouds followed by the sun or a stormy sea gradually calming down? In the case of "Gute Nacht," it is clear from the words that the song is about the protagonist's emotions. But what about "pure" instrumental music? The answer is that in the nineteenth-century Romantic tradition, it was thought normal and reasonable for music without words to express the emotions of characters or composers. Indeed, new forms or adaptations of old ones – nocturnes, impromptus, tone poems, and program music of all sorts – were created partly in order to increase the possibilities of emotional expressiveness. When Schumann wrote music expressing the conflict between his two personae, Florestan and Eusebius, when Shostakovich imprinted his signature motif on symphonies and string quartets, when Mahler composed symphonies that morphed into mini-operas or oratorios, they were following a Romantic tradition of expressing the self (and its various personae) in their music.

Not all expressive music is populated with personae who are expressing their emotions, however. If we are listening to an Impressionist work of program music (e.g. *La Mer*), we know we should not be looking for a persona in the music (although one could interpret this piece as somebody's *impression* of the sea, rather than a straightforward pictorial characterization of the sea). If we know we are listening to a Baroque character piece, such as Couperin's "La Superbe," then it is reasonable to hear a particular type of person in the music, but not reasonable to think we are experiencing an outpouring of emotion by that person. Sometimes, we will know we are entitled to find a persona in a work of instrumental music because the composer has given us an evocative title, such as Schubert's *Wanderer Fantasy*. But even where there is no special hint, it is reasonable to interpret certain kinds of Romantic instrumental music as expressions of emotion in a persona, because that was how composers of the time thought of (some of) their compositions. (For further discussion and defense of this view, see Robinson 2007a. For excellent examples of this type of criticism see Newcomb 1984 and 1997. For a recent full-bore attack on this approach see Kivy 2009.)

The *Wanderer Fantasy* is not the only late work of Schubert's in which we find the theme of the "wanderer," who is an outcast from the world just like the protagonist of *Winterreise*. Cone has argued that the A-flat *Moment Musical*, Op. 94 No. 6, "dramatizes the injection of a strange, unsettling element into an otherwise peaceful situation" (Cone 1986: 26). This idea has great "metaphorical resonance" in Anthony Newcomb's phrase, suggesting the idea of the stranger or outsider, the "Fremdling" of Georg Philipp Schmidt von Lübeck's poem "Der Wanderer," which Schubert set to music as a song that later he used as the theme for the Adagio of the *Fantasy*. Newcomb has christened these kinds of story structures in music "plot archetypes" (Newcomb 1984).

Charles Fisk (2001) has made a particular study of the trope of the wanderer or outcast in Schubert's late music. For example, in the first movement of the Piano Sonata D960 in B-flat there is a harmonic "outsider," embodied in the strange trill on G-flat which interrupts the cheerful ambulatory music that opens the piece. Fisk describes how the music seems to dramatize a search for reintegration of this "alien" element, as the music wanders into far distant keys, and he tells a psychologically convincing tale in which the wanderings are those of a persona, whom he identifies for various reasons with the composer himself, who is seeking to be integrated into the "normal" group. Fisk's underlying premise is that there are suggestions in Schubert's cyclic forms and tonal structures of larger dramatic structures, in which there are agents or personae expressing complex emotions and desires.

Once we hear the structure of a piece of music as a psychological as well as a musical structure, then we are able to hear in it not just specific emotions but patterns of emotion. Moreover we can hear in it not only the effects noticed by the doggy theorists but also more complex emotions such as yearning, nostalgia, and resignation, all prime examples of Romantic emotions. And it is no surprise that we are moved by such expressions, because they are not just emotional appearances but have psychological reality, although the psychology in question may be that of a fictional persona.

See also Arousal theories (Chapter 20), Music's arousal of emotions (Chapter 22), and Resemblance theories (Chapter 21).

References

Collingwood, R.G. (1963) *The Principles of Art*, Oxford: Clarendon Press.

Cone, E.T. (1974) *The Composer's Voice*, Berkeley: University of California Press.

—— (1986) "Schubert's Promissory Note: An Exercise in Musical Hermeneutics," in W. Frisch (ed.) *Schubert: Critical and Analytical Studies*, Lincoln: University of Nebraska Press, pp. 13–30.

Davies, S. (1994) *Musical Meaning and Expression*, Ithaca: Cornell University Press.

—— (2006) "Artistic Expression and the Hard Case of Pure Music," in M. Kieran (ed.) *Contemporary Debates in Aesthetics and the Philosophy of Art*, Oxford: Blackwell, pp. 179–91.

—— (forthcoming) "Infectious Music: Music-listener Emotional Contagion," in A. Coplan and P. Goldie (eds) *Empathy: Philosophical and Psychological Perspectives*, New York: Oxford University Press.

Fisk, C. (2001) *Returning Cycles: Contexts for the Interpretation of Schubert's Impromptus and Last Sonatas*, Berkeley: University of California Press.

Hospers, J. (1955) "The Concept of Artistic Expression," *Proceedings of the Aristotelian Society* 55: 313–44.

Karl, G. and Robinson, J. (1995) "Shostakovich's Tenth Symphony and the Musical Expression of Cognitively Complex Emotions," reprinted in Robinson 1997: 154–78.

Kivy, P. (1980) *The Corded Shell: Reflections on Musical Expression*, Princeton: Princeton University Press.

—— (2002) *Introduction to a Philosophy of Music*, New York: Clarendon.

—— (2009) *Antithetical Arts: On the Ancient Quarrel between Literature and Music*, Oxford: Oxford University Press.

Levinson, J. (1996) "Musical Expressiveness," in *The Pleasures of Aesthetics*, Ithaca: Cornell University Press, pp. 90–125.

—— (2006) "Musical Expressiveness as Hearability-as-expression," in M. Kieran (ed.) *Contemporary Debates in Aesthetics and the Philosophy of Art*, Oxford: Blackwell, pp. 192–204.

Newcomb, A. (1984) "Once More 'Between Absolute and Program Music': Schumann's Second Symphony," *19th Century Music* 7: 233–50.

—— (1997) "Action and Agency in Mahler's Ninth Symphony, Second Movement," in Robinson (1997), pp. 131–53.

Nussbaum, C. (2007) *The Musical Representation: Meaning, Ontology, and Emotion*, Cambridge: MIT Press.

Ridley, A. (1995) *Music, Value and the Passions*, Ithaca: Cornell University Press.

Robinson, J. (ed.) (1997) *Music and Meaning*, Ithaca: Cornell University Press.

—— (2005) *Deeper than Reason: Emotion and its Role in Literature, Music, and Art*, Oxford: Clarendon Press.

—— (2007a) "Can Music Function as a Metaphor of Emotional Life?" in K. Stock (ed.)

Philosophers on Music: Experience, Meaning, and Work, Oxford: Oxford University Press, pp. 149–77.

—— (2007b) "Expression and Expressiveness in Art," *Postgraduate Journal of Aesthetics* 4: 19–41, available at www.british-aesthetics.org/uploads/Expression%20and%20Expressiveness%20in%20Art.pdf.

Tormey, A. (1971) *The Concept of Expression: A Study in Philosophical Psychology and Aesthetics*, Princeton: Princeton University Press.

Further reading

Budd, M. (1985) *Music and the Emotions*, London: Routledge and Kegan Paul. (An examination of several of the classic accounts such as those by Schopenhauer and Langer.)

Goodman, N. (1968) *Languages of Art*, Indianapolis: Bobbs-Merrill. (Chapter 2 contains an important account of musical expression as metaphorical exemplification. For Goodman more than just emotional properties can be expressed in works of art and music.)

Langer, S. (1957) *Philosophy in a New Key*, 3rd edn, Cambridge: Harvard University Press. (A classic theory of musical expression as a kind of symbolism.)

20
AROUSAL THEORIES
Derek Matravers

An arousal theory of expression is one that analyses the expressive qualities of a piece of music in terms of the feelings aroused in listening to the music. The theory flows from three springs. First, it accounts for expression using only elements that are present in the listeners' experience: the music and aroused feeling. Second, and relatedly, it has a pleasing simplicity: it posits nothing metaphysically dubious (such as hypothetical personae in expressive music) and there is no need (at least at first) for risky philosophical moves. Finally, it answers to a common intuition: that hearing the emotion in the music has *something* to do with how it makes us feel. The theory surfaces often in discussions by the philosophically unsophisticated, and is occasionally defended by the more philosophically sophisticated. The arousal of emotions by music is of increasing interest to psychologists, but the theory has never gained wide acceptance in philosophy; indeed, it is no exaggeration to say that it is usually regarded as crude and naive. Nonetheless, discussion of the theory, or variants on the theory, emerged in philosophy in the 1980s and 1990s (Mew 1985; Speck 1988; Ridley 1995; Matravers 1998) and more recently (Robinson 2005; Nussbaum 2007). As is usual in discussions of expression, I will confine my discussion to (so-called) Western art music, that is, instrumental music of the period from around 1430 CE to the present day.

It is difficult to describe the phenomenon of expression in music without either advantaging or disadvantaging putative accounts of it, but I will make the following three assumptions. First, "expression" is an audible feature of the music; we hear the music *as* sad (or whatever). Second, the judgment that a piece of music is expressive is intersubjective, that is, expression is a feature available to all competent listeners to the music. Third, an account of expression should at least not rule out an explanation of how expression contributes to the value of a piece.

We can divide the ways in which music can arouse feelings or emotions into three broad kinds. I shall call the first "associative," where the connection between the music and the emotions is merely contingent and external. One example is the "our song" phenomenon, where an association between a piece of music and some event in the listener's past provokes an emotional reaction. Another example might be an emotional reaction to the way in which the piece is played (if, say, the musicians are drunk or obviously indifferent). A third example might be where the music sets the listener off on a train of thought, and the content of that train of thought provokes an emotional reaction. The second kind of emotional reaction to music might be called "affective." These reactions differ from the first kind in that they are explicitly caused by attention to the properties of the music considered as music. Examples include being bored by the music, being irritated by the music, or being excited by the music. It is characteristic of this second kind that there is a single emotion that the music provokes (for example, boredom) which does not then change as the music changes. This distinguishes the second from the third kind, where one's feelings or emotions seem to change with the music. For example, a listener might feel something akin to anxiety which becomes relief as the tension in the music resolves. I shall call these "music-specific" emotional reactions. I do not claim this is the only or even the most perspicuous way in which the arousal of emotions by music could be categorized. It is, however, the most useful for the purposes of this chapter.

Having distinguished the ways in which music can arouse the feelings and emotions, I will now distinguish two ways of approaching the topic. The first is to consider what it is about the music that arouses the feelings or emotions, that is, to identify the mechanisms underlying our response. The second is to use those aroused feelings to provide a constitutive account of expression. The first inquiry is properly the domain of psychology; the second is properly the domain of philosophy. (I shall consider two philosophers who reject the distinction between these two inquiries below.)

I shall say little about the first, psychological, inquiry as this is an empirical matter. Clearly there are many different mechanisms by which music can arouse the emotions. The psychological work on this is less helpful in thinking about expression than it might be, as it tends to consider all mechanisms by which music arouses feelings and emotions as being on a par. That is, it does not distinguish between the three ways in which music arouses emotions described above. Thus, it does not distinguish between mechanisms that are not specific to music (associative and affective arousal) from those that are (music-specific arousal) and does not distinguish between mechanisms that are (arguably) irrelevant to expression (associative and affective arousal) from those that are relevant (music-specific arousal) (for example, Juslin and Vastfjall 2008). The standard way of construing the second, philosophical, inquiry is as the task of providing a constitutive analysis of expression; of saying what expression actually is. As indicated above, expression is something heard in the music, hence the task is to throw light on the nature of that experience.

The problem of negative emotions

Any theory that claims that music arouses the feelings or emotions needs to explain why listeners are motivated to listen to music that arouses negative feelings or emotions. That is, the theory appears to be committed to the following inconsistent triad:

1. People avoid negative feelings or emotions.
2. Some pieces of music arouse negative feelings or emotions.
3. People do not avoid such pieces of music.

All sides agree on the truth of (3). The fact that arousal theories are premised on accepting (2) rules out some of the standard solutions to the problem; for example, that music arouses a *sui generis* "musical" emotion (Kivy 1989: ch. 12) or that the aroused feeling is transformed so as to lose its negative hedonic tone (Hume 1993). Some philosophers have argued for the truth of (1) and hence the falsity of (2), thus using the argument to reject the arousal theory (see, for example, Kivy 1989: 23). Any theory that incorporates arousal thus has to argue that (1) should, at least, be modified. There are a number of attempts to do this, notably those by Jerrold Levinson (1982) and Stephen Davies (1994) – neither of whom is an arousal theorist of musical expression, but both of whom agree that music's arousal of emotions is real and significant (see also Ridley 1995: ch. 7). Furthermore, any acceptable solution should propose an internal connection between (2) and (3); any general solution that licenses the thought that people are motivated to listen to a piece of music *despite* it arousing the negative emotions is, for that reason, unacceptable.

It is common ground between Levinson and Davies that, as the aroused feeling or emotion is not about anything actual, it has no "life implications." Hence, we can read (1) weakly: it is not that we have to explain why people willingly embrace events in their lives for which negative feelings or emotions are appropriate; we need only explain why they willingly embrace those negative feelings or emotions. It is intrinsic to those feelings or emotions, nonetheless, that they be identified as negative. Levinson co-opts some aspects of earlier solutions into his account: that emotional response "facilitates our grasp, assessment, and description of the expression in a musical work" (1982: 323, a view associated with Nelson Goodman 1976: 248–51), and that the experience can be cathartic. To this he adds six further explanations of his own, to do with the value accrued from taking reflective attitude to the feeling or emotion aroused (1982: 324–9). Davies's solution is that we are motivated to understand significant works of art, and that negative feelings and emotions are "integral" to such understanding (1994: 318). It is an open question whether bona fide arousal theories would be able to incorporate these solutions, as the bare feelings postulated by such theories may not be significant enough to play the roles on which the solutions depend.

Arousal in non-arousalist theories

An unambitious way of using aroused feelings and emotions to explain something about musical expression (so unambitious, in fact, that it would not count as an arousal theory) is to allow that they might have a role in causing the experience of expression (Levinson 1996). That is, the music arouses various feelings in us, and these (in part) cause us to experience the music as expressive, where that experience can be characterized independently of those feelings. A slightly more ambitious account takes aroused feelings to have an epistemological role, that is, the aroused feelings are the way in which we detect the expressive structure of the piece. This has been put forward by Aaron Ridley (1995) and Jenefer Robinson (2005). I will discuss the latter theory as it is the more developed.

Robinson provides ample psychological evidence that music arouses emotions. Her view is that these emotions "alert listeners to what is *expressed* in the music" (2005: 366). Obviously, this can only be so if Robinson has an independent account of expression. This she provides:

If an *artwork* is an expression of emotion, then

1. the work is evidence that a persona (which could but need not be the artist) is experiencing/has experienced this emotion;
2. the persona's emotion is perceptible in the character of the work;
3. the work articulates and individuates the persona's emotion; and
4. through the articulation and elucidation of the emotion in the work, the audience can get clear about it and bring it to consciousness.

(2005: 271)

What, then, is the relation between the expressed emotions and the aroused emotions? Robinson's general view is that "*expressive qualities* are *qualities that can be grasped through the emotions that they arouse*" (2005: 291–2). Clearly, much depends on the nature of this "grasping" relation. In the examples Robinson gives, she takes it to be the usual case that the emotion aroused is the same as the emotion expressed: we are calmed by calm music, made nervous or anxious by the nervous or anxious qualities of a piece, and so on. However, she is clear that the feelings or emotions induced by a piece are not necessarily the emotions expressed by a piece: one can be surprised by a harmony modulating from major to minor while that passage expresses not surprise, but rather radiant harmony (2005: 367). Hence, it is clearly not her view that we detect an expressed emotion in the music simply by the music arousing that very emotion. Her view appears to be that, in the usual case, these emotions are aroused *directly* by the music without the music arousing, for example, the thought that the music resembles a person expressing an emotion or the listener imagining, of the music, that it is the expression of emotion by a person. Listeners then reflect upon their reactions and, through this process, grasp the expression in the music.

Questions might be raised about the scope of Robinson's account. Whilst there are occasions in which our aroused emotions can perform an epistemic function – the fact that a person is making us anxious might alert us to their being anxious

– there are other occasions in which they do not – the bare patch on my lawn might make me anxious without that telling me anything about the bare patch on my lawn. In as much as emotions aroused by music are assimilated to the second sort of case, as Robinson allows, it is unclear they can perform an epistemic function even if they are "*appropriate* to" the music (2005: 375). Clearly, music might arouse boredom or irritation in me without that resulting in my judgment that the music *expresses* boredom or irritation. Such reactions are unlikely to tell us much about the expressive structure of the piece other than, perhaps, that it is not very good. In terms of the distinction between ways in which music arouses emotions given above, her claim seems to cover both affective and music-specific arousals of emotion. Indeed, looking at her examples, being "calmed down" or "cheered up" by a piece of music is more likely to be an affective reaction to the music than anything to do with its expressive structure.

Arousal theories

A more ambitious way of using aroused feelings and emotions is to argue that they have more than an epistemological role: they are, in fact, a constitutive part of expression. I shall state the theory in its strongest, simplest, and least plausible version as that will allow me to illustrate the problems that need to be overcome.

The simple theory

A piece of music expresses E if and only if that piece of music aroused E in the listener.

Three putative problems can be dealt with immediately. First, the theory need not claim that an expressive piece of music arouses a feeling or emotion in every listener on every occasion: like other theories of expression (or theories of secondary properties generally) it can invoke the appropriately skilled listener in the right perceptual circumstances. I shall assume this qualification in what follows. Second, it might be held that in the relevant circumstances we react to the music with an emotion *because the music expresses an emotion*: I react to sad music with sadness, and joyful music with joy. Hence, the theory presupposes, rather than provides, an account of expression. That is to misunderstand the nature of the theory. The claim is that the music has certain properties, whatever they might be, that cause certain feelings, and the resultant experience (that of the music and these feelings) is constitutive of expression. The theory seems no worse off than other theories which analyze expression in terms of some experience the music causes in the listener, such as imagining of the music that it is thus-and-so (Levinson 1996). In reply, we can strengthen the objection: it is not that the reaction of the listener presupposes that the music expresses an emotion, but that the experience the listener has is not of reacting to purely musical features, but *of reacting to the expression of emotion* (Kingsbury 2002). Once again, an account of expression is presupposed. It is difficult to adjudicate on this question. It is related to others in the dark heart of metaphysics: is our reaction to a fire engine *caused by* or *constitutive of* its redness? To an extent this issue resurfaces in a grave objection to the theory considered below, namely, where, on the arousal theory, expression is actually located. Finally (taking again our placeholder judgment that the music is sad), it cannot be sadness that the music arouses in the listener, as sadness is an emotion and emotions include in them some propositional component: in the case of sadness, some thought that a bad thing has happened to something I care about. This requires some amendment to the theory: what is aroused is not an affective state with a propositional component but rather some feeling state identifiable as E, or appropriately related to E. (For doubts about this move, see MacKinnon 1996.)

One might feel some skepticism about these replies, particularly the second and third, which will return in a different form later. Let us press on to seemingly more serious problems: doubts about the necessity and the sufficiency of the account. First, is arousal necessary for expression? It seems clearly possible that a listener could experience a piece of music as expressive whilst denying that they are feeling whatever it is that the account claims that they are feeling (the "dry-eyed listener" (Bouwsma 1954)). The arousal theorist might attempt to reply by claiming that the dry-eyed listener is recognizing the piece as the sort of music that, in different circumstances, would arouse the requisite feeling. Apart from the worrying commitment to general aesthetic principles, this reply does not meet the challenge; the claim is not that the dry-eyed listener can correctly judge the music to express E, but that they actually experience the music as expressing E. A better response would be for the arousal theorist to claim that the dry-eyed listener, while correct to deny that he or she is experiencing a feeling in some full-blooded sense, has enough of a feeling to do the work that the theory requires of it. Of course, such a reply is vulnerable to the dry-eyed listener simply denying that they are experiencing any feeling at all.

The claim that the theory is not sufficient gets to the heart of its most serious problem. The arousal of feelings by an object seems independent of considerations of expression. A tree root on which I stub my toe, and which arouses irritation in me, does not thereby express irritation (Ridley 1986: 69). The first move an arousal theorist can make in reply is to point to the different ways in which music can arouse emotions described above: the associative, the affective, and the music-specific. The first two ways (the associative and the affective) are, the arousal theorist can agree, irrelevant to expression; the claim is only that music-specific emotions are so relevant. In short, the theory needs to specify some role for music-specific feelings in expression that cannot be played by either associative or affective feelings. There is a clear candidate for such a role: the feelings must be co-instantiated in the listener's consciousness with the music and change as the music changes (that is, the feeling is experienced as "tracking" the music). This is not true for either associative or affective emotions. A counter-example to the sufficiency of the theory would have to be a music-specific emotion that was irrelevant to expression. Provided the tracking relation is specified tightly enough (without, of course, begging the question) there is reason to think a counter-example will be difficult to find. Clearly, examples such as irritation caused by stubbing one's toe need not trouble the theory as they are clearly affective rather than expressive (Matravers 1998: 165–87).

This reply, however, does not take the theory all the way to meeting the objection. Even if it is granted that the arousal theory can pick out expressive emotions in a non-circular manner, the question remains as to the relation between an aroused emotion – even an emotion that tracks the music – and expression. We can see this if we try to fit the arousalist model to the three features of expression I gave at the start. Allowing an "aptly backgrounded listener" enables the theory to at least make a start on explaining the intersubjectivity of expressive judgment. However, the first and the third features are unexplained. How can an aroused emotion – even one that is experienced as tracking the music – be heard as an audible feature of the music? There are in fact two problems here. First, according to the theory, expression involves two experiences rather than one: those of the music and the aroused feeling. That seems wrong: hearing music as sad is not equivalent to hearing music and feeling sad. Second, putting the point crudely, the feeling ends up in the wrong place: not in the music, but in the head of the listener. Expression is a matter of hearing the feeling *in* the music; the theory gives us only having the feeling *and* hearing the music.

The third feature – the relation with value – is also unexplained. It might be thought that an answer could be constructed out of the two thoughts that feeling an emotion is valuable, and hence that music that arouses such feelings would be valuable. However, that would be to attribute to music's expressivity merely instrumental value (a value it no doubt possesses). That is not sufficient; whatever the instrumental value, it is also the case that the value of music *as music* is the non-instrumental value of the experience to which the music gives rise (Budd 1995: ch. 1; see also Davies 1987).

Can the arousal theory respond to these two problems? The first problem, in particular, seems impossible to solve. It is definitive of the theory that it analyses the experience of expression in terms of the music arousing a feeling or emotion, so it is difficult to see how it can avoid the accusation of involving two experiences. An account of the connection with value does not look forthcoming either.

Two sophisticated arousal theories

Something of the view can be salvaged, however, by limiting its scope. (The following was suggested to me by Malcolm Budd.) In a careful and considered paper, Kendall Walton has argued that the phenomenon of musical tension is, in part, a matter of the feeling the music arouses in us. I cannot here do justice to the subtle arguments Walton advances for this position. Walton claims that it sometimes happens that – in the simplest case – we experience a person as feeling like *this*, where the "this" refers to some feeling that person has aroused in us. For example, the belief that Nellie is nervous may be caused by Nellie's arousing nervousness in us, and then our experiencing Nellie as feeling as we do (1999: 425). Walton's hypothesis is that the same mechanism is at work for attributions of musical tension. The music arouses a certain feeling together with an experience of "there being something or someone or other, or several such, that/who is/are in this state – the state I am in. *Musical tension* is the property of being apt to elicit an experience of this kind" (1999: 433). Walton claims that musical tension and relaxation "have a lot to do with music's expression of emotions" (1999: 436) although he does not pursue this. What is distinctive about Walton's view is that although there are two experiences – the feeling and the music – the feeling goes along with the experience of there being something in the environment (quite what is left indeterminate) that feels that same way. Hence, this can be used to reply to the principal problem for the arousal theory outlined above. Our experience is directed outwards, that is, we experience the music as being infected with the feeling that we have. The extension to expression is obvious. Some music is such as to give rise to a feeling of sadness (say) together with the experience of there being one or more things or persons or groups of persons "in the music" (1999: 432) which or who, is or are, sad. For a piece of music to be expressive of sadness is for it to have the property of being apt to elicit an experience of this kind. It should be conceded immediately that this will not be an account of expression generally, or even expression as I have characterized it above. However, as Malcolm Budd has been impressing on us for some time, the notion of expression encompasses a variety of different experiences of the relation between music and the emotions (1995: 138–42). This account might capture the way in which some music wears the aura of emotion – for example, Satie's *Gymnopédies* – as opposed to music which expresses (in the sense of communicates) an emotion – such as the great Romantic symphonies.

An arousal theory (or at least "a version of the arousal theory") has recently been put forward by Charles O. Nussbaum (2007: 189–258). Nussbaum's theory is remarkably ambitious; it draws on resources provided by the author's extensive knowledge of music, as well as biology, psychology, and philosophy, and it resists easy summary. His view is that music is a complicated mode of representation and that to listen to music is to engage with this representation. One element of the representation is a form of mental model, in particular, a model that embodies analogues of Gibsonian "affordances." An affordance is an environmental invariant that presents itself to perceiving organisms as affording possibilities of action, that is, it stimulates a range of possible relevant motor responses (2007: 33). So, for example, we see a chair as something upon which we can sit. Music presents a "virtual scenario" in which musical patterns ("including symmetry, parallelism, contrast, and large scale formal structure" (2007: 82)) are analogues of environmental invariants. In recovering this representation from the musical surface we "specify motor hierarchies and action plans, which, in turn, put the listener's body into off-line motor states that specify virtual movements through a virtual terrain or a scenario possessing certain features" (2007: 47, emphasis removed). Put another way, "music puts the listener's body into states that would fit with or be appropriate to interacting with and simulating scenarios and terrains with certain features and with varying emotional valence" (2007: 82).

The arousal of emotions (or related affective states) by music plays a complicated role in Nussbaum's conception of the experience of music. First, any successful musical performance arouses in the listener a basic emotion of a positive hedonic tone (2007: 209–11). Nussbaum calls this "joy," although he warns us not to take this too narrowly; it is more the experience of a touch that is "overwhelmingly benignant and . . . promis[es] more of the same" (2007: 211). That is, there is a "real touch effect" of music prior to any judgments being made or descriptions being applied, which endows it with its "curiously immediate emotionally gripping quality" (2007: 211). However, this is merely the reaction to "well-produced musical sound" (2007: 214). To understand the work means engaging with the cognitive content of the work itself, that is, with the represented mental model described above. Nussbaum takes from Nico Frijda the claim that emotions are "action tendencies (or changes in action readiness) as well as evaluative perceptions or appraisals of environmental affordances" (2007: 189–201, 256). Music arouses the emotions because of the "ongoing attempt to negotiate a musical virtual terrain, to act in accordance with its musical affordances, dealing with surprises, impediments, failures, and successes along the way, and requiring the constant reevaluation of strategy to which emotional response is keyed" (2007: 214). What of the problem for traditional arousal theories, namely, that there are two experiences – of the music and the feeling – and the first arouses the second? Nussbaum claims that "the arousal depends on acting off-line on a particular musical plan and interacting with a particular musical virtual environment, and could be produced in no other way" (2007: 246). That engaging with the music is the only way to produce the emotion is insufficient to rebut the charge that it will involve two experiences rather than one. Indeed, one might wonder in general whether Nussbaum is limited to only two experiences: it is difficult to see exactly what the relations are between the experience of music, the imagined exploration of the virtual terrain, and the aroused emotion.

Whether Nussbaum's account is ultimately defensible rests on empirical as well as purely philosophical matters. It has several strengths including that it attempts answers to both the psychological and the philosophical questions described above. That is, it provides a convincing psychological background to substantiate a philosophical account of the experience of expression. It claims to overcome the objection that arousal involves two separable experiences (about which I have expressed some doubt). It can make a claim for intersubjectivity, since it depends on nothing idiosyncratic about particular listeners. This leaves only an account of the link between the arousal of emotion and value. Looked at one way, there is nothing distinctive about Nussbaum's account of musical value; he self-consciously borrows from both Kant and Nietzsche (and echoes can also be found of more recent writers, especially Robinson (2005: 405–12)). His view is that "an important direct proper function of musical representations remains . . . group unification and the evocation in performers and listeners of the emotionally charged twilight state. Both afford a temporary assuagement of the horror of the contingent, the original religious and didactic significance of such group experiences now having atrophied and fallen away" (2007: 293). What Nussbaum brings to these time-honored views is a wealth of empirical evidence, from both anthropology and psychology, of the sort needed to make the account convincing.

In summary, the prospects for arousal theories of expression are mixed. The early revived arousal theories encountered grave conceptual difficulties, although perhaps such theories can account for some forms of expression. There is an increasing interest within psychology in the arousal of emotions by music, although the primary focus of that interest is not accounting for musical expression. However, psychologically informed theories in which the arousal of emotions plays an important role have once again made philosophically respectable the beguiling thought that the arousal of emotions must have *something* to do with expression.

See also Expression theories (Chapter 19), Music, philosophy, and cognitive science (Chapter 54), Music's arousal of emotions (Chapter 22), Resemblance theories (Chapter 21), and Value (Chapter 15).

References

Bouwsma, O.K. (1954) "The Expression Theory of Art," in W. Elton (ed.) *Aesthetics and Language*, Oxford: Blackwell, pp. 73–99.

Budd, M. (1995) *Values of Art: Pictures, Poetry and Music*, Harmondsworth: Penguin.

Davies, S. (1987) "The Evaluation of Music," in P. Alperson (ed.) *What is Music? An Introduction to the Philosophy of Music*, Pennsylvania: Haven, pp. 303–26.

—— (1994) *Musical Meaning and Expression*, Ithaca: Cornell University Press.

Goodman, N. (1976) *Languages of Art*, 2nd edn, Indianapolis: Hackett.

Hume, D. (1993 [1757]) "Of Tragedy," in *Selected Essays*, eds. S. Copley and A. Edgar, Oxford: Oxford University Press, pp. 126–33.

Juslin, P.N. and Vastfjall, D. (2008) "Emotional Responses to Music: The Need to Consider Underlying Mechanisms," *Behavioural and Brain Sciences* 31: 559–621.

Kingsbury, J. (2002) "Matravers on Musical Expressiveness," *British Journal of Aesthetics* 42: 13–19.

Kivy, P. (1989) *Sound Sentiment: An Essay on the Musical Emotions*, Philadelphia: Temple University Press.

Levinson, J. (1982) "Music and the Negative Emotions," in *Music, Art, and Metaphysics: Essays in Philosophical Aesthetics*, Ithaca: Cornell University Press, pp. 306–35.

—— (1996) "Musical Expressiveness," in *The Pleasures of Aesthetics*, Ithaca: Cornell University Press, pp. 90–125.

MacKinnon, J.E. (1996) "Artistic Expression and the Claims of the Arousal Theory," *British Journal of Aesthetics* 36: 278–89.

Matravers, D. (1998) *Art and Emotion*, Oxford: Oxford University Press.

Mew, P. (1985) "The Expression of Emotion in Music," *The British Journal of Aesthetics* 35: 33–42.

Nussbaum, C.O. (2007) *The Musical Representation: Meaning, Ontology and Emotion*, Cambridge: MIT Press.

Ridley, A. (1986) "Mr. Mew on Music," *British Journal of Aesthetics* 26: 69–70.

—— (1995) *Music, Value and the Passions*, Ithaca: Cornell University Press.

Robinson, J. (2005) *Deeper than Reason: Emotion and its Role in Literature, Music and Art*, Oxford: Clarendon Press.

Speck, S. (1988) "'Arousal Theory' Reconsidered," *The British Journal of Aesthetics* 28: 40–7.

Walton, K. (1999) "Projectivism, Empathy, and Musical Tension," *Philosophical Topics* 26: 407–40.

Further reading

Budd, M. (1985) *Music and the Emotions*, London: Routledge. (A classic of the modern literature on expression that was critical of all existing theories at the time, including arousal theories.)

21
RESEMBLANCE THEORIES
Saam Trivedi

Introduction

Purely instrumental musical passages and works without words or an associated program or story are often experienced, by many laypersons and musicians, as being sad, happy, calm, angry, and so on. However, as something that has neither life nor consciousness, music cannot itself possess such mental states. And this leads to the philosophical problem of musical expressiveness, the problem of how something *inanimate* and *insentient* such as music can be, and be heard as, sad, happy, and the like; other formulations of the problem ask how music can be described as sad (Kivy 1989: 6–10), or how it can possess or have sadness "inhering" in it (Kivy 2002: 31–2), or how emotions could be expressed in it (Davies 1994: x, 2001: 169, 173), but let us focus on many people's ready and immediate *experience* of music as sad rather than descriptions of this experience, though the positive view advanced in this chapter can also answer these other formulations of the problem, as we will see later.

To begin, let us address a couple of clarifications before proceeding further. First, at least since Alan Tormey (1971), philosophers have distinguished between expression and expressiveness. To express a mental state is to display outwardly an actual occurrent state in one's psychology, whereas being expressive of a mental state involves merely displaying outwardly features typically associated with that state, without necessarily having or feeling that state; the performance of actors, for example, is usually expressive of mental states that actors do not actually feel while acting. Second, one might ask about the truth of claims about musical expressiveness: why is it true, or what makes it true, that Samuel Barber's *Adagio for Strings*, for example, is sad or mournful (or something in that ballpark)? One might give an error-theory in answer, claiming that such truth-judgments involve an error for music cannot be literally sad. Or one might say they are metaphorically true (Scruton 1997), though it is unclear what the alleged metaphor ultimately amounts to (Davies 1994: 150–62; Levinson 1996: 105–6). Alternatively, it might be claimed that such truth-judgments are literally true but in a secondary sense (Davies 1994: 162–6), though here one might doubt if the literal/metaphorical distinction ultimately illuminates much (Budd 2003: 220), and also whether appeals to it are too influenced by the linguistic turn in analytic philosophy some decades back. Other possible answers may involve the suggestion that such judgments are only imagined to be true, or that they are true in virtue of resemblance between music and something to do with mental states, or that the truth-maker here is the consensus of competent (but fallible) listeners, or some combination of these. One might also step back from the entire question of truth, and claim as above that the *experience* of music in terms of mental states has primacy over linguistic descriptions of the experience and the truth of these, and so we should focus on that experience instead.

Peter Kivy and Stephen Davies, amongst others, have tried to solve the problem of musical expressiveness by appealing to various perceived or experienced resemblances between music and the vocal, bodily, and behavioral expression of various mental states (Kivy 1989, 2002; Davies 1980, 1994, 2001, 2006), though Kivy has recently distanced himself from the resemblance theory, and now claims it is unknown how music possesses the emotions we hear in it (Kivy 2002: 47–8). In this chapter I will first briefly summarize these resemblance theories, and then I discuss criticisms of these views, and some possible replies to these criticisms. I will conclude by sketching a resemblance-plus-imagination, or imaginationist, view of musical expressiveness, which *builds* on the many insights of resemblance theories, instead of throwing away the baby with the bath water. Progress in intellectual inquiry of many sorts, including philosophy, usually involves building on the achievements of one's predecessors; Newton, for example, famously claimed that if he had seen further than others, it was only by standing on the shoulders of giants, referring thereby to such physicists before him as Kepler and Galileo.

Resemblance theories

My summary of resemblance theories of musical expressiveness begins with Peter Kivy's theory, which he sometimes calls the contour-convention view (Kivy 1989: 71–83). Kivy claims that expressive properties are "objective" qualities that are recognized or perceived in the music just as we recognize sadness in a St. Bernard dog's face, rather than being something the music only has in virtue of arousing or evoking mental states in listeners. Musical expressiveness is a complex, emergent quality. We hear musical sounds as expressive of sadness because we hear them as human utterances, as structurally similar to our voices when we express sadness vocally. Additionally, Kivy says musical contour or shape can also resemble our expressive behavior – movement, gesture, posture, and the like. We hear sadness in music because we hear it resembling the gestures and bearing of sad people. Likewise, happy music is heard as such because it resembles the motion and gestures of happy people in being expansive, vigorous, "leaping," and so on.

Kivy also claims that we tend to animate all kinds of sights and sounds, and cannot but perceive expressiveness in them, in ways that are not always conscious or noticed (1989: 57–9, 2002: 41–3). A piece of cloth tied around a wooden spoon will be taken by children to be a doll; a circle with three short lines in it (two on top, adjacent to each other, and one below and parallel to them) is seen as a face. Likewise, claims Kivy, we see figures in clouds, and hear gesture and utterance in music, even though we are not conscious of our animation of it that allows us to hear it as expressive. We may, he suggests, be evolutionarily hard-wired to animate things, as this is conducive to our survival; for example, seeing a stick as a snake puts us on our guard, whereas doing the reverse would be disastrous. Similarly, we may animate sounds subliminally.

The final element in Kivy's resemblance theory is his appeal to musical conventions (1989: 80–3). He claims it is only due to the customs or conventions of the Western musical tradition that the major scale, triad, and third are heard as upbeat, while minor keys, chords, and the minor third are heard as expressive of grief, sorrow, etc. Likewise, musical conventions account for why chromaticism is heard as expressive of sorrow, pain, and the like. Thus, claims Kivy, contour, or resemblance, and convention together explain musical expressiveness, sometimes separately and sometimes jointly.

Stephen Davies's resemblance theory is quite similar to Kivy's (Davies 1994: 221–67). Davies claims that inanimate and insentient things such as weeping willows, cars, and St. Bernards may display features that resemble what he terms "emotion characteristics" of human sadness in their overall bearing, posture, or appearance, and are thus seen as expressive. Similarly, argues Davies, music presents emotion characteristics associated with human expression of emotions in its aural appearance or sounds, and thus is expressive of emotions it does not itself possess. Musical expressiveness, claims Davies, is a public, objective property of the music, one that it possesses literally, and which mainly depends on perceived or experienced resemblances between the dynamic character of music and the demeanor of the human body – its movement, gait, bearing, carriage, and so on. In sum, in Davies's view, music is expressive in virtue of presenting the outward features associated with sadness or happiness in general. Music is expressive in resembling the bodily stance, gait, bearing, carriage, and gestures typically expressive of particular emotional states. Just as sad people often walk slowly, hang their heads low, droop in their bodily stance, and are generally subdued, similarly sad music is often slow, has a downward tendency, is quiet, and so on. Likewise, just as happy people tend to skip and leap quickly and lightly and make expansive gestures, happy-sounding music is often similarly lively and exuberant.

A different kind of resemblance theory that there is not enough space here to discuss at length but should be mentioned at least briefly has been offered by Malcolm Budd (1995: 133–57) who claims, following the American psychologist Carroll Pratt (1931), that music sounds the way emotions feel: there are cross-categorial similarities between music and the emotions, as music mirrors our inner lives in having tension and resolution, in having intermediate and final goals that it strives toward, and so on. Budd's view has been criticized elsewhere (Trivedi 2001) on grounds very similar to those offered below against Kivy and Davies. Another view that should be mentioned here briefly in passing is that of Suzanne Langer (1942), who claimed that music is an iconic symbol of the emotions on account of isomorphisms between music and the emotive life in general. Langer's view has been criticized at length by Stephen Davies (1994: 123–34).

Criticisms

Let us now consider four criticisms of resemblance theories, as well as possible replies to some of these criticisms. To begin with, one might doubt if music really resembles the emotions, or something to do with them such as emotional behavior (Madell 2003). It should not be too hard for resemblance theorists to reply to this concern, appealing to two moves. As a first move, they can point to various resemblances between music and *something* to do with mental states, either their vocal or bodily or behavioral expression or their affective tones. A lot of music seems to sound like human vocal expression: think of rapid runs and glissandi on clarinets, saxophones, and electric guitars which often sound like someone crying or wailing, the opening clarinet glissando of Gershwin's *Rhapsody in Blue* being one example of this. In addition, a lot of music is readily and immediately experienced by many as resembling the way sad people often walk slowly: the music is slow in tempo, low in pitch, and soft in volume, just as sad people hang their heads low, droop in their physical stance and gait, and talk softly. The opening passages of the second movement of Beethoven's "Eroica" Symphony provide a well-known example of this. Also, along the lines of Budd's suggestions briefly mentioned above, musical passages are often heard right away, both by musicians and by laypersons, as having tension, which may or may not be resolved later, and as having points of repose as well as final resting-points or goals (such as the tonic chord or key) which may be arrived at after intermediate goals (such as the dominant chord or key) have been reached, mirroring the way our lives often have tense moments, which may or may not be resolved, and the way we strive for and arrive at our intermediate and final goals.

Additionally, there is a second move resemblance theorists can make in reply, borrowing a leaf from those who criticize appeals to resemblance (especially when it comes to pictorial depiction). It is sometimes said that resemblance is a very broad (and vague) notion, so broad that just about anything can resemble anything else in some respect; for example, unicorns and Alpha Centauri might be said to resemble each other in that they are both mentioned in this sentence. Even if their critics are right about this point, resemblance theorists can go on to claim that it should not surprise us then that music resembles mental states in *some* way, such as the ways briefly discussed above.

Here is a second criticism, this time specifically against Kivy's version of the resemblance theory. It might be doubted if we really animate sounds (Kivy 2002: 46–7). In reply, the resemblance theorist can offer the following two scenarios as examples of our animating sounds (Trivedi 2006). Very often, while walking down quiet, empty city streets late at night, one might hear a noise. Immediately, one is on guard, thinking that the sound might be coming from another person (perhaps a potential mugger) or some creature (such as a vicious dog on the loose). It turns out, however, that the sound is only that of a leaf rustling in the wind. Similar things happen when one hears a sound while going round the bend on a quiet, lonely mountain trail. Once again, one is on guard immediately, fearing the sound might be coming from a creature (such as a bear) or another person (perhaps someone dangerous). It turns out, however, that the sound is only that of a branch breaking off a tree. Both these cases provide clear sonic analogs of Kivy's example of animating the stick in the forest as a snake, as this helps our survival. Now it certainly seems to be the case, as Kivy has suggested before, that as a species we depend more on sight than on hearing for survival; and it is also true that our noise-filled modern lives are rarely filled with silence for very long. Add to this the fact that the animation of sounds may be very dim or subliminal, and you begin to get some sense of why it is hard to detect the animation of sounds, making some skeptical of this.

A third criticism of the resemblance theory seems more pressing. Besides the fact that resemblance and expressiveness are philosophically and logically quite distinct as concepts, perceived resemblances by themselves are not sufficient for expressiveness, nor for hearing it, though resemblance may be causally necessary for expressiveness. All kinds of things may resemble how we vocally or physically or behaviorally express various mental states or the affective tones of these mental states, but they are not thereby expressive of these mental states, even if we perceive these resemblances. For example, turtles move slowly, with their heads hung low, and their bodies very close to the ground, resembling the way sad people often walk. But such resemblances and perceptions of them do not by themselves necessarily lead to our seeing turtles as sad, or as expressive of sadness. To see turtles as sad, we need to add to the account something more than merely these resemblances that we perceive.

Now, Kivy and Davies are aware of the concern that resemblance is not a sufficient condition for expressiveness. Kivy characterizes the sufficiency objection to resemblance theories as follows: according to resemblance theories, music should be expressive of *everything* it resembles, such as ocean waves, the rise and fall of the stock market, and so on, which is clearly not the case (Kivy 1989: 61–2). In reply, Kivy claims that it makes no sense to say that music is expressive of ocean waves or the stock market. Expressiveness must be *of mental states*, thus the objection flouts a "logical" condition of expressiveness. It is important to see here, however, that Kivy has not stated or addressed our objection above that perceived resemblances are not sufficient for expressiveness, even if he may have stated and answered a related objection. Our objection is *not* that music should be expressive of everything it resembles, such as ocean waves and the stock market. Rather, our objection is that all kinds of things, such as turtles, may resemble our vocal or bodily or behavioral expressiveness, or the affective feel of mental states such as emotions, moods, and feelings, and we may perceive these resemblances, but that alone does not make them expressive. The same holds for music.

Davies also tries to answer the concern that perceived resemblances are not sufficient for expressiveness (2001: 184). As he states this worry, it is that resemblance alone cannot ground musical expressiveness or explain why we experience music as expressive, for resemblances can be found between music and many things in addition to the resemblances between music and expressive appearances. Davies replies that we can simply say that "this is how we hear" the music (as expressive), without being committed to explaining what mechanisms underlie and trigger this response. Many insentient things, such as pictures of the human face, crude masks of tragedy and comedy, and Edvard Munch's "scream" face, are likewise experienced as being expressive. The resemblance theory is no worse on this count, asserts Davies, than other theories, which he claims are in no better position to go beyond perceived resemblances in explaining expressiveness. Once again, it is worth noting here that, like Kivy, Davies has not quite addressed our concern. Our worry is not about things resembling *music* in their expressivity, as Davies puts it. Instead, it is about things such as turtles resembling our vocal or bodily or behavioral expression or the affective feels of mental states, which are *not* thereby expressive, even though we may perceive these resemblances consciously or otherwise. The concern, then, is why the case of musical expressiveness should be any different, why perceived resemblances alone should suffice to make music expressive. To be sure, Davies claims that this is just how we are *psychologically*, "this is how we hear" the music (as expressive), thus making the question not one for philosophers to answer. But *contra* Davies, it is not clear that we have here a brute fact not amenable to further philosophical explanation, and one might instead be able to dig deeper and say more, building on the notion of perceived resemblances and adding something more to the picture, as is attempted in the next section of this chapter.

I turn now to a fourth, and arguably the most formidable criticism of resemblance theories of musical expressiveness in general. The resemblance theories of Kivy, Davies, and Budd, even when combined, give us the causal grounds or mechanisms underlying musical expressiveness. They may tell us what causes or allows music to be, and to be heard as, expressive, to wit, perceived resemblances between music and something to do with mental states such as emotions, moods, and feelings. Put differently, these views tell us *why* we hear music as expressive: we hear music as sad, happy, etc., *because* or *in virtue of* various resemblances we consciously or otherwise hear between the music and something to do with such mental states. However, merely giving us this causal story underlying musical expressiveness does not tell us how something *inanimate* and *insentient* such as music can be, and be heard as, sad, happy, and the like, which is the basic problem of musical expressiveness. How can music, a sequence or set of sounds *without* life, consciousness, or mental states be sad or somehow have sadness "in" it, and be experienced to be so? This question is not adequately answered by resemblance theories. There must thus be doubt about whether resemblance theories even address let alone solve the basic problem of musical expressiveness, instead of giving us a mere causal story about what makes music expressive (Levinson 1996: 106; Scruton 1997: 147).

Resemblance-plus-imagination

I will now sketch a resemblance-plus-imagination, or imaginationist, view of musical expressiveness, taking the resemblance theory as the causal foundation of the imaginationist view, and adding an imaginative component that shields it from the objections discussed above.

The imaginationist grants three claims made by resemblance theorists: (1) that there exist various sorts of resemblances between music and something to do with mental states such as emotions, moods, and feelings; (2) that listeners may hear these resemblances in not always highly foregrounded or conscious ways; and (3) that these resemblances may provide the causal basis or ground of why we hear music as expressive.

Here is a very brief, rough statement of the resemblance-plus-imagination view of musical expressiveness, also argued for at length elsewhere (Trivedi 2001, 2003, 2006): music is willy-nilly, readily, and immediately *imagined* by listeners in various, not always highly conscious, ways to be sad, happy, and so on, *because* it is consciously or otherwise perceived to resemble something to do with mental states such as emotions, moods, and feelings, such as their vocal or bodily or behavioral expression, or their affective feel or tones. Note in passing that this view can also answer the other formulations of the problem of musical expressiveness that we saw at the very start of this chapter: music is not literally or really sad but is rather only *imagined* to be so; it is only imagined that sadness "inheres" in it; it is only imagined to express sadness, which it cannot really do.

What follows is a non-exhaustive list of various, not always highly conscious, ways in which we imagine the music is sad, happy etc. because we consciously or otherwise perceive it to resemble something to do with mental states. One kind of imagining involves our animating the music, imaginatively projecting life and life-like qualities, including mental states, onto it willy-nilly, readily, and immediately. This kind of imagining may happen especially when we listen to very intense music, such as passages in Beethoven's late string quartets. In such cases, we may hear *the music itself* – not something besides it, such as the composer or performer or the musically aroused listener or an indeterminate, imagined persona in the music, or something else – as the very thing that is emotionally expressive. Animating the music is very similar to the kind of animation that we as a species engage in when we imaginatively see faces in clouds or rocks, as our pagan ancestors did in seeing life and gods in the sun, thunder, the ocean, and so on. And animating the music is similar to what we do when we see comic strips and imagine within the world of the comic strip that the talking and expressive cars, trains, trees, or sun we see in them are *themselves* sad, happy, etc. Animation films provide an even better example, for they consist of changing images, just as musical passages are dynamic processes. Animating music involves a very similar, if not the same kind, of imagining, except that it is harder to detect musical animation due to both the abstract nature of music as an art and the fact that we engage in various imaginings without always noticing at the time that we are doing so (Trivedi 2001). Note incidentally that this notion of animation is "thicker" than the one which Kivy appeals to, for it involves not just Kivy's idea that we hear gesture and utterance in the music but also requires in addition that we imaginatively project life and mental states onto the music. Note also that our animating the music in this manner provides the simplest and most natural solution to the problem of musical expressiveness: we hear something *inanimate* and *insentient*, such as music, as sad for we imaginatively project life and mental states onto the music, imagining that it is alive and possesses the mental states we hear in it.

Alternatively, we may sometimes imagine of the music that it is the expression of a mental state by an indeterminate, imagined persona in the music, as claimed by Jerrold Levinson and Jenefer Robinson, amongst others (Levinson 1996, 2006; Robinson 2005). In such cases, we may form an auditory image and imagine that someone or something, we know not exactly who or what, is crying or laughing or dancing or expressing themselves somehow in the music. Note that imagining a musical persona is different from the animation of music described above (Trivedi 2001: 416): The persona is someone or something "in" the music and is thus philosophically *distinct* (even if not detached) from the music rather than being the music itself; and in imagining a musical persona, the persona is imagined to have the mental states heard in the music, whereas in animating the music, *the music itself* is imagined to have the mental states heard. Note also that to imagine the music itself is experiencing mental states need not involve imagining the music is an indeterminate persona or a product thereof, though of course the music itself is imagined as something capable of having mental states.

Third, we may sometimes imagine in ways not highly foregrounded that it is the musical instrument(s) that are sad, happy, and the like. Witness, in this vein, talk of wailing violins, weeping guitars, etc. Likewise, one might also sometimes imagine that the composer(s) or performer(s) are expressing their emotions musically.

A fourth kind of imagining involves imaginative identification, and this can happen in various ways. Sometimes we may imagine of our auditory experience of hearing the music that it is an experience of our feeling the mental state we hear the music as expressive of (Walton 1988, 1994). In such cases we imaginatively identify one experience with another experience, imagining our having the feeling that we hear the music as expressive of. On other occasions, we may imaginatively identify with the music, imagining that it is expressive of our own emotion; in doing so, we may feel as if we *are* the music (Budd 1995: 168). Alternatively, one might imaginatively identify with the performer(s), or with the musical persona, or with some (fictional) persona of the composer, and so on.

There may be ways of imagining musical expressiveness besides those adumbrated above. This should not surprise us, given the many ways in which we imagine things, and the fact that we may often imagine things without being aware at the time that we are engaged in certain imaginings that are not very highly foregrounded.

Conclusion

Resemblance theories of musical expressiveness appear to get a lot of things right. It seems there are resemblances of various sorts between music and something to do with mental states; that we perceive these resemblances consciously or otherwise; and that resemblances account for the causal story underlying what allows music to be heard as expressive. However, resemblance theories have some drawbacks, two of which seem especially troublesome. First, besides resemblance and expressiveness being distinct concepts, mere resemblance does not seem sufficient for expressiveness. This is partly what motivates adding imagination to resemblance to complete the picture. Second, while resemblance may give us the causal story behind expressiveness, it does not explain by itself how something *inanimate* and *insentient* such as music can be and be heard as sad, unless one also claims, as the positive view advanced above does, that we *imagine* the music is sad, often animating it, imagining that the music itself is alive and possesses the mental states we hear in it.

See also Analytic philosophy and music (Chapter 27), Arousalist theories (Chapter 20), Expression theories (Chapter 19), Hanslick (Chapter 33), Music and imagination (Chapter 11), and Music's arousal of emotions (Chapter 22).

References

Budd, M. (1995) *Values of Art*, London: Penguin.

—— (2003) "Musical Movement and Aesthetic Metaphors," *British Journal of Aesthetics* 43: 209–23.

Davies, S. (1980) "The Expression of Emotion in Music," reprinted in Davies (2003), pp. 134–51.

—— (1994) *Musical Meaning and Expression*, Ithaca: Cornell University Press.

—— (2001) "Philosophical Perspectives on Music's Expressiveness," reprinted in Davies (2003), pp. 169–91.

—— (2003) *Themes in the Philosophy of Music*, Oxford: Oxford University Press.

—— (2006) "Artistic Expression and the Hard Case of Pure Music," in M. Kieran (ed.) *Contemporary Debates in Aesthetics and the Philosophy of Art*, Oxford: Blackwell, pp. 179–91.

Kivy, P. (1989) *Sound Sentiment*, Philadelphia: Temple University Press.

—— (2002) *Introduction to a Philosophy of Music*, Oxford: Clarendon Press.

Langer, S. (1942) *Philosophy in a New Key*, Cambridge: Harvard University Press.

Levinson, J. (1996) "Musical Expressiveness," in *The Pleasures of Aesthetics*, Ithaca: Cornell University Press, pp. 90–125.

—— (2006) "Musical Expressiveness as Hearability-as-Expression," in M. Kieran (ed.) *Contemporary Debates in Aesthetics and the Philosophy of Art*, Oxford: Blackwell, pp. 192–204.

Madell, G. (2003) *Philosophy, Music and Emotion*, Edinburgh: Edinburgh University Press.

Pratt, C. (1931) *The Meaning of Music*, New York: McGraw-Hill.

Robinson, J. (2005) *Deeper than Reason*, Oxford: Clarendon Press.

Scruton, R. (1997) *The Aesthetics of Music*, Oxford: Oxford University Press.

Tormey, A. (1971) *The Concept of Expression*, Princeton: Princeton University Press.

Trivedi, S. (2001) "Expressiveness as a Property of the Music Itself," *Journal of Aesthetics and Art Criticism* 59: 411–20.

—— (2003) "The Funerary Sadness of Mahler's Music," in M. Kieran and D. Lopes (eds) *Imagination, Philosophy, and the Arts*, New York: Routledge, pp. 259–71.

—— (2006) "Imagination, Music, and the Emotions," *Revue Internationale de Philosophie* 60: 415–35.

Walton, K. (1988) "What is Abstract about the Art of Music?" *Journal of Aesthetics and Art Criticism* 46: 351–64.

—— (1994) "Listening with Imagination: Is Music Representational?" *Journal of Aesthetics and Art Criticism* 52: 47–61.

Further reading

Budd, M. (1985) *Music and the Emotions*, London: Routledge. (The classic treatment of several earlier theories about music and the emotions.)

Davies, S. (1999) "Response to Robert Stecker," *British Journal of Aesthetics* 39: 282–87. (Defends Davies's resemblance theory against Stecker 1999, below.)

Hjort, M. and Laver, S. (eds) (1997) *Emotion and the Arts*, New York: Oxford University Press. (Useful anthology of fifteen essays.)

Matravers, D. (1998) *Art and Emotion*, Oxford: Clarendon Press. (Criticizes resemblance theories and other theories of musical expressiveness, and advances a moderate arousalism.)

Ridley, A. (1995) *Music, Value, and the Passions*, Ithaca: Cornell University Press. (Criticizes resemblance theories, and advocates a moderate arousalism that mediates between resemblance theories and strong arousalism.)

Robinson, J. (ed.) (1997) *Music and Meaning*, Ithaca: Cornell University Press. (Ten interdisciplinary essays on musical meaning, language, metaphor, imagination, emotion, and drama.)

Stecker, R. (1999) "Davies on the Musical Expression of Emotion," *British Journal of Aesthetics* 39: 273–81. (Criticizes Davies 1994, above.)

22
MUSIC'S AROUSAL OF EMOTIONS

Malcolm Budd

Emotion and musical appreciation

By music's arousal of emotions I shall understand the arousal of emotions by music in the very act of listening to it (not in performing it, or dancing to it, for example). And by music I shall understand pure instrumental music – instrumental music that lacks a text, a dramatic context, a program that it seeks to illustrate, or anything else that might enable it to have a representational content that it would otherwise lack. Pure instrumental music undoubtedly has the power to arouse emotions in listeners. If ways that are irrelevant to appreciation of the music are not excluded, music can arouse emotions of every kind, including fear, anger, jealousy, hatred, despair, remorse, envy, patriotism, and embarrassment, for instance, rather than the relatively few emotions, such as joy, sadness, and excitement, that music is most commonly thought of as evoking. In fact, given any emotion and any piece of music whatsoever, no matter how poor it may be, that emotion might be elicited in someone by an appropriate relationship in which the listener stands to the music. This might be by means of a purely personal association or by some more general kind of association, a cultural one, perhaps, as with Elgar's "once in a lifetime" tune (the Trio of *Pomp and Circumstance March No.1*) now tarnished by its regrettable association with hearty, feel-good English patriotism. But the musical arousal of emotions by associations that are not integral to the appreciation of the music is philosophically uninteresting. What I shall be concerned with is an aesthetic matter, the arousal of emotion in the appreciation of music as music, by the character of the music itself, not by the music's being associated in the mind of the listener with something not in the music and irrelevant to its appeal as music, without which association the music would lack its power to excite the emotion. (This allows that associations of various kinds might well be exploited by composers – as often they are – and so be relevant to the appreciation of the musical works in question.) The crucial issue is what role, if any, the arousal of emotions plays in the understanding, appreciation, and value of (pure instrumental) music, and, in particular, what contribution, if any, it makes to the musical value of a piece. The important questions are these: Which emotions, if any, can music arouse in an aesthetically relevant manner? Why these and only these? In what way or ways does music manage to arouse them? What is the aesthetic significance of their arousal?

There is no consensus about the crucial issue. At one extreme is the view that the cupboard of emotions that can be experienced outside a musical context ("extramusical" emotions), and that music can arouse in an aesthetically relevant manner, is bare: there are no such emotions (Hanslick 1986). The opposite extreme is, I believe, unoccupied: nobody holds that music can relevantly arouse emotions of every kind (self-contempt, for example). The middle ground is occupied by the great majority. These thinkers believe that the cupboard is not bare, but neither is it full. Some of them claim that it contains relatively few emotions (Davies 1994). But within the middle camp there is disagreement both about the number and identity of the emotions music can arouse and about the way or ways in which music arouses them.

The nature of emotions

A very great deal depends on the correct conception of the emotions (considered as occurrent experiential states). A common view is the so-called cognitive theory of the emotions, which is adhered to by the principal philosophical skeptic about music's ability to arouse emotions of the "garden variety" (Kivy 2001a, b). The cognitive theory exists in many forms, which differ in both the number and the nature of the elements of which emotions are said to be composed. The crucial cognitive element of emotion has sometimes been thought to be a belief, but that is not essential to a cognitive theory and it is certainly too strong, ruling out emotions based not on belief, but imagining. What is definitive of the theory is that it represents each type of emotion as being defined by a particular kind of proposition or thought plus some combination of bodily sensations, "feelings," hedonic tones, or whatever, so that when the emotion is experienced, prompted by something perceived, imagined, or thought about, it will have a real or imaginary object upon which it is directed, the emotion being about this intentional object. So, for example, the propositional element of fear is (something like) the thought of danger to oneself or someone or something one cares about, and the perception, realization, or imagination of such a danger engenders whatever else constitutes the emotion of fear (increased heart rate, etc.), the intentional object of the emotion being the represented dangerous thing.

Skepticism about pure instrumental music's ability to stimulate extra-musical emotions in a listener in an artistically relevant manner arises at once from the fact that music is a non-representational form of art, presenting no scenes or actions that the listener might respond to emotionally as the viewer of a film or the reader of a novel might. There are two sides to this skepticism. The first is that there is no relevant intentional object for the emotion, that is, the lack of any real or imagined object for an emotion to be directed upon: there is no counterpart to the scene in Tolstoy's *Anna Karenin* as Anna walks along the railway lines to her death, or the scene in Kurosawa's *Ikiru* as the final minutes of Kanji Watanabe's life unfold as he sits on a swing in the playground he had fought so hard to get built. From this follows, second, the unavailability of the mechanisms of empathy and sympathy (or antipathy) active in appreciation of the representational arts. Now even if this skeptical line of thought has some plausibility, there are obvious exceptions. Admiration, repulsion, excitement, and amusement, for instance, are all emotions and, if aroused by the character of the music in listening to it, as they may well be, will have the music as their object. These and all other emotions whose intentional object is the music are unproblematic for a cognitive theory (or, indeed, for whatever is the correct theory of the emotions).

But a cognitive theory of the emotions is open to doubt. Two somewhat similar, but significantly different, non-cognitive theories deserve attention here, according to which, first, emotions are not in themselves cognitive states and, second, emotions do not in general need to be caused by cognitive states. Each theory is based on the idea of an emotion as a non-cognitive "appraisal" combined with physiological changes; both theories are contentious.

Jenefer Robinson represents emotion as a process in which a very fast, automatic, rough and ready "affective appraisal" concerning things that matter to the organism occurs without any conscious deliberation or awareness or any complex information processing, this appraisal inducing characteristic physiological and behavioral changes, which are likely to be followed by cognitive monitoring, which may change the experience (Robinson 2005, forthcoming a). So, seeing a stick beside me that resembles a snake, an affective appraisal concerning danger might be triggered, which induces bodily changes relevant to being endangered, only for me to realize that it is just a stick, which cognition calms me down, although perhaps my heart is still left racing somewhat. Robinson leaves the precise character of an affective appraisal uncertain (although "That's offensive" or "Loss!" or "I like this" might, she thinks, be reasonable conceptualizations of such things). There is also a significant gap in her theory, for no account is offered of what makes an emotion process an experience of a specific emotion (jealousy, pity, nostalgia, amusement, grief, embarrassment, hatred, self-contempt, etc.). This leaves open the possibility that for at least some commonly recognized emotions an element of cognition (of a specific kind) is essential to them: only when this cognition enters the emotion process does it become an experience of that specific emotion. However, given her view that an emotional response is a response set off by a non-cognitive affective appraisal, it follows immediately that whenever pure instrumental music does not (in the aesthetically relevant manner) cause an affective appraisal, music does not arouse any emotions. Robinson herself accepts that in general music does not cause an affective appraisal, but nevertheless attempts to avoid the conclusion that music does not in general engender emotions – as I shall explain later.

For Jesse Prinz, emotions have two aspects: they are both "valent" and "embodied appraisals" (Prinz 2004). Embodied appraisals are embodied mental representations of a certain kind. They represent what they do by monitoring changes in one's body, and what they represent is not a particular object or event but a relational property in which various objects might stand to oneself. More specifically, emotions are perceptions of (or as if of) changes in one's body in virtue of which they represent something that has some bearing on one's concerns or well-being, the emotions being differentiated by, on the one hand, the different contents of the representations, that is, by which concern is implicated, and, on the other, by their so-called valence. (Note that whereas Robinson's affective appraisals cause physiological changes, Prinz's embodied appraisals are perceptions of physiological changes already taking place.) Valence, which may be intrinsically positive, negative, or mixed, or which may be variable, is a matter of one's attitude to the emotion: whether one wants to sustain or be rid of it. So, for example, sadness represents the loss of something valued by one, having a negative affect, whereas pride represents merit for a valuable object or achievement with which one identifies, this time with a positive affect. Each emotional experience consists of feeling (or apparently feeling) certain changes in one's body, the changes (in general) varying from emotion to emotion (and also, sometimes, within the same emotion), the perception of the changes possessing the relevant positive or negative quality. Although generally emotions do not need to be caused by cognitive mental states, there are exceptions. These are the so-called higher cognitive emotions, the identities of which are, in part, determined by relevant judgments, beliefs, or thoughts of the subject and which can be experienced only by those who possess the appropriate concepts. These emotions, like all other emotions, are not in themselves cognitive states, but, unlike other emotions, derive their identities from being caused by a relevant cognitive state. For example, an emotion is self-contempt only if it has been caused by the thought of being worthless.

This account of the emotions has two significant implications for the musical arousal of emotions: it removes what might seem an insuperable barrier and allows us to circumscribe those emotions that music might relevantly arouse. In the first place, if it should be wondered how purely instrumental music can arouse any emotion the identity of which is determined by what it represents, the difficulty is mitigated by the realization that a perceived or imagined object does not need to present such a state of affairs in order to induce in the subject the experience of sadness, for example: all music needs to do is to bring about any bodily changes that mediate what sadness represents (the loss of something valued by one), thereby engendering the feeling intrinsic to sadness of the loss of something valuable (which does not need an intentional object). And – leaving aside a certain possibility – how music manages to do this is a scientific, not philosophical, matter. The second implication is that, given that pure instrumental music does not cause, in an aesthetic response, any of the cognitive states that determine the identity of the "higher cognitive emotions," there is – leaving a related possibility aside – no question of its arousing any of those emotions in an aesthetically relevant manner. It might seem, therefore, that the issue of the arousal of emotions in listeners reduces to, on the one hand, the question of which of the emotions that lack the need for a cognitive stimulus can be aroused by music (in the relevant manner) and, on the other hand, a scientific explanation of this power that identifies both the brain mechanisms that mediate the musical arousal of emotion and, for each emotion, the properties of a musical work that arouse that emotion through the operation of these mechanisms – which concatenation of properties produces emotion E1, which emotion E2, and so on. But, as I have indicated, both of the above implications need to be qualified. For a significant feature of musical appreciation is awareness of music's expressive qualities, and in particular its emotional qualities or the emotions it is expressive of; and a principal way in which music has been thought to elicit emotion is in response to the qualities of emotion that are heard in it. If this is right, it would allow a different explanation from the scientific (although one complementary to it); and if awareness of these emotional qualities consists in cognitive states, this might endow music with the power to arouse certain emotions of the higher cognitive kind.

The musical expression of emotion and the emotional qualities of music

A distinction is sometimes drawn between music that possesses an emotional quality and music that is expressive of that emotion. And it is indeed the case that if M is a musical passage and F a property, it is not always true that if M possesses F, then M is expressive of F: empty music is not necessarily expressive of emptiness, nor is jolly music always expressive of jollity (Scruton 1997: 155). But another distinction is needed also: the distinction between a piece of music that possesses an emotional quality and a piece of music that, in virtue of its possession of emotional qualities and various of its other features, can properly be said to be a musical expression of emotion. By a musical work's being an expression of emotion I shall mean that it should be interpreted as displaying the experience of emotion in a persona (or number of characters): the listener is right to imagine, in accordance with the nature and development of the music, a persona (who need not be the composer) undergoing an emotion or series of emotions, or a number of characters doing so. I shall consider, first, the idea that the emotional qualities of music are such that they are liable to induce an emotional response in the listener. Note that this liability need not be thought of as a disposition of the emotional quality of a piece of music to arouse a corresponding emotion in listeners who perceive the quality. For that would be to focus on the emotional quality in itself, neglecting how it is realized in the music, and the liability need cover, for listeners who appreciate the character of the music, no more than impressive music with an emotional quality, not mediocre or poor music with that quality. In other words, the idea can be limited just to music that (for the listener) both possesses an emotional quality and is expressive of that kind of emotion – a restriction from which the idea would certainly benefit, since if one is listening to music that one finds unimpressive, one is unlikely to respond positively to its emotional quality, and may even resist responding to it. The second idea I shall consider is that listening to a musical work that is an expression of emotion is liable to induce an emotional response in the listener – or, more strongly, must do so if the listener is properly to appreciate the work.

Responding to the emotional qualities of music

The plausibility of the idea that the emotional qualities of music are liable to induce an emotional response in the listener depends on the correct account of what it is for music to possess an emotional quality (and to be expressive of that kind of emotion). Although there is agreement about the aesthetic relevance of these emotional qualities, there is no consensus as to how they should be understood. If an arousalist theory, which construes the possession of emotional qualities as a disposition to arouse the emotion in qualified listeners, were correct, the aesthetic relevance of the emotions aroused by music in virtue of its emotional qualities would be secured immediately; but the unacceptability of arousalist theories would still leave open the possibility that the emotional qualities of music play a crucial role in music's arousal of emotions. Opposed to arousalist theories are perceptual property theories (the principal resemblance theory falling under this head) and imagination theories (of which expression theories are one kind). Perceptual property theories construe the emotional quality of a piece of music as a pure perceptual property of the music. If they do not elucidate the connection between the emotional quality of a piece of music and that emotion itself, they are thereby unable to offer any plausible account of how the perception of such a quality might arouse emotion in a listener. But explanations are open to perceptual property theories that specify the relation in question.

A perceptual property theory of the resemblance kind maintains that to hear an emotion in music is to experience the music as resembling a vocal or non-vocal expression or betrayal of the emotion. The outstanding advocate of such a theory is Stephen Davies, who construes the resemblance as obtaining between the music and non-vocal expressions of the emotion – the dynamic character of music is heard as being like actions that express or display the emotion – and who has offered an explanation of how the perception of music that possesses an emotional quality might well arouse that emotion in a listener. The explanation is, crudely, by contagion: the perception of the emotional quality is liable to induce a mirroring emotional response (Davies 1994, forthcoming a).

Of course, there is a significant difference between the musical and a real-life case in which we are infected with another's (apparent) emotion: in the one we perceive a person apparently in a certain emotional state, in the other we hear a piece of music the character of which is heard as resembling the character of the behavior of someone displaying that emotion. So the explanation, more precisely, is that as in ordinary life a mirroring emotion can be aroused by the perception of expressed emotion, so a mirroring emotion can be aroused by musical passages that are heard as being similar to expressions of emotion.

Robinson opposes to Davies's explanation her own, based on what she calls the Jazzercise effect (Robinson 2005: 391–410). Her idea consists of two parts. The first is that music that presents an emotional quality of happiness, sadness, restlessness, or calm induces corresponding states of arousal that can be called "moods," in which physiological changes, motor activity, and action tendencies take place, bringing in their wake an inclination to view the world in a way characteristic of the emotion. The second is that the musical arousal of such a state puzzles the listener, who then engages in cognitive monitoring, labeling the state in one way or another, ascribing to herself a certain emotion, which activity is likely to bring about corresponding affective appraisals, thus making it true that she is undergoing the named emotion. But this explanation is not a serious competitor to Davies's. For, even if cognitive monitoring of a "mood" (state of arousal) is liable to trigger an affective appraisal (which seems unlikely but is required by Robinson), (i) on Robinson's account it is not the (emotional quality of the) music as such that arouses an emotion of a certain kind but the listener's puzzled reflection on her state of arousal, and (ii) if cognitive monitoring is essential to turn a process begun by music's triggering changes in the body into one in which the emotion of nostalgia, triumph, or whatever, is experienced, then, in general, such emotions are not aroused by music, since we do not engage in such monitoring while listening (cf. Kivy 2006: 308–10).

Responding to the musical expression of emotion

I have said that for a musical work to be an expression of emotion is for it to be correctly heard as presenting the experience of emotion of a persona (or number of characters). If the work is of any length, it will constitute a series of psychological episodes, a drama of the inner life, one emotion following another. If a musical work is heard as presenting the emotional experience of a persona or characters, then, as with fiction or drama or film or real life, a listener's emotional response to the musical presentation of the persona's experience, which could be empathic, sympathetic, or antipathetic, is unproblematic for a cognitive theory of the emotions, since it has an intentional object (the persona). It is unproblematic also for Robinson's theory if she is right to claim that affective appraisals are triggered equally by imagination and reality. But are any works of pure instrumental music expressions of emotion in the sense at issue? There are three possible views that might be held about music that is expressive of emotion: a persona is correctly heard in (i) all (Cone 1974; Levinson 1996, 2006), (ii) only some (Robinson 2005, forthcoming b; Ridley 2007), or (iii) none (Davies 1997; Kivy 2006).

If a work that is expressive of emotion can be heard as a musical expression of emotion and in composing it the composer intended it to be so heard, then it is right to hear it in that way. But what exactly is a listener to imagine in listening to such a work? One indisputable point is that there is a marked disanalogy between the musical expression of emotion and the representational arts, which calls into question, if not the viability, at least the significance of the musical expression of emotion and its effectiveness in engendering emotion in listeners. For the "narrative" or "dramatic" content of a musical work that supposedly presents the emotional experience of a persona will inevitably be both indefinite and minimal, the work being incapable of presenting the sex, identity, thoughts, age, or moral character of the persona, the circumstances in which emotion is experienced, the number of characters involved, or any other of the multifarious facts available to fiction, drama, and film, all of which features serve to determine the nature and power of the emotional responses of the reader or viewer (cf. Kivy 2006: 298–304; Davies forthcoming b). And there is a further problem for any work that supposedly has a single persona, which concerns the continuity of the "soliloquy," "monologue," narration, or drama and so the continuity of the listener's imagining of the persona's experience. For it is doubtful whether there is any musical work, except a miniature, for which a listener imagines, continuously throughout the work, a persona undergoing a series of emotional states.

Given the inevitable thinness of the content, the emotional power of a work that is a musical expression of emotion would have to depend entirely on the mode of presentation – in the first place, the very fact that the presentation is by music, and, more importantly, the quality of the musical presentation. But what character might a musical work possess to compensate for the poverty of the story line, empowering it to move us deeply, not just in virtue of the emotional qualities it possesses and all the other qualities that can figure in the experience of a listener who does not imagine a persona in the music, but also because of the emotional history of a persona that it unfolds? Jenefer Robinson has claimed that music can mirror not only the appearance of emotions, but also cognitive or evaluative aspects of them, and, most importantly, the streams of emotional experience, the ways in which emotions change, blend, conflict, or become or remain ambiguous (Robinson 2005: 311–12, 325). However, this by itself is insufficient to overcome the marked difference in detail with the representational arts, for the features of the emotional life she indicates can be conveyed equally by works of fiction, for example.

But although this account fails to close the wide gap between the content of a work that is a musical expression of emotion and the content available to works of fiction, perhaps it explains the emotional power of a musical expression of emotion. For hearing a persona's experience in music not only enables the listener to imagine that experience but, it is claimed, to undergo it: the music, imagined as a presentation of the emotional experience of a persona, induces physiological changes characteristic of that experience. However, granting the additional aspects of emotional processes that music can "mirror," and accommodating the further point that the music presents the pure feelings of emotions uncluttered by thoughts, from the point of view of explaining the emotional power of music the introduction of a persona into a musical work would appear to be an unnecessary shuffle. For if the emotional qualities of music – in Davies's terms, "emotion characteristics in appearances" – are fit to arouse the corresponding emotions in the listener, so are the other aspects of emotional processes that Robinson specifies: in each case the music does no more than resemble, perhaps strikingly, the aspect of emotion it "mirrors," and if resemblance in one case is sufficient to generate emotion, so it is in the other. If the listener's mirroring emotional response tracks the progress of the musical features, the resulting emotional experience will mirror that of the suppositious persona without any imagining of such a persona, who therefore can be discarded. If music is the most emotionally moving of the arts because it affects us more powerfully than any other in a direct physiological manner (Robinson 2005: 376), it has no need of a persona to explain its emotional power.

The aesthetic significance of music's arousal of emotions

What is the aesthetic significance of the musical arousal of emotions by the emotional qualities of music? Admittedly, this may constitute evidence that a listener has perceived the music's emotional qualities (Davies 1994: 314–15), but that does not endow them with aesthetic significance in themselves. A rather different idea is that the arousal of an emotion may help a listener to understand, and so to appreciate, the musical work, alerting the listener to what the music is expressing (Robinson 2005: 348–78, forthcoming b). But, granted that this is a possibility, a crucial question remains: is the arousal of emotions that mirror the emotional qualities of the music essential to understanding the music? Or can those who insist that the perception of the emotional qualities of music does not arouse corresponding emotions in them nevertheless understand the music just as well? Moreover, these kinds of question apply equally to the grasp of characteristics of music other than emotional qualities – to structural aspects, for example, or expressive qualities other than emotional ones. Is the arousal of emotion necessary for the grasp of these features of a musical work? Suppose that none of these aspects of music require the arousal of emotion. This would not mean that the musical arousal of emotions would be of no aesthetic importance. However, its importance would be rather slight. That importance would be increased if the arousal of emotions were to enhance the appreciation of the music in the sense that it makes the experience of the music more valuable to the listener – but that claim would be hard to defend.

See also Arousal theories (Chapter 20), Expression theories (Chapter 19), Music and imagination (Chapter 11), and Resemblance theories (Chapter 21).

References

Cone, E. (1974) *The Composer's Voice*, Berkeley: University of California Press.

Davies, S. (1994) *Musical Meaning and Expression*, Ithaca: Cornell University Press.

—— (1997) "Contra the Hypothetical Persona in Music," in M. Hjort and S. Laver (eds) *Emotion and the Arts*, New York: Oxford University Press, pp. 95–109.

—— (forthcoming a) "Infectious Music: Music-Listener Emotional Contagion," in A. Coplan and P. Goldie (eds) *Empathy: Philosophical and Psychological Perspectives*, Oxford: Oxford University Press.

—— (forthcoming b) "A Philosophical Perspective," in P.N. Juslin and J. Sloboda (eds) *Handbook of Music and Emotion: Theory, Research, Applications*, Oxford: Oxford University Press.

Hanslick, E. (1986 [1891]) *On the Musically Beautiful*, trans. G. Payzant, Indianapolis: Hackett.

Kivy, P. (2001a) "Auditor's Emotions: Contention, Concession, Compromise," in *New Essays on Musical Understanding*, Oxford: Clarendon Press, pp. 71–91.

—— (2001b) "Experiencing the Musical Emotions," in *New Essays on Musical Understanding*, Oxford: Clarendon Press, pp. 92–118.

—— (2006) "Critical Study: Deeper than Emotion," *The British Journal of Aesthetics* 46: 287–311.

Levinson, J. (1996) "The Concept of Musical Expressiveness," in *The Pleasures of Aesthetics*, Ithaca: Cornell University Press, pp. 90–125.

—— (2006) "Musical Expressiveness as Hearability-as-Expression," in *Contemplating Art*, Oxford: Clarendon Press, pp. 91–108.

Prinz, J. (2004) *Gut Reactions*, New York: Oxford University Press.

Ridley, A. (2007) "Persona Sometimes Grata: On the Appreciation of Expressive Music," in K. Stock (ed.) *Philosophers on Music: Experience, Meaning, and Work*, New York: Oxford University Press, pp. 130–46.

Robinson, J. (2005) *Deeper than Reason*, Oxford: Clarendon Press.

—— (forthcoming a) "Emotion," in J. Prinz (ed.) *The Oxford Handbook of Philosophy of Psychology*, Oxford: Oxford University Press.

—— (forthcoming b) "Emotional Responses to Music: What Are They? How Do They Work? And Are They Relevant to Aesthetic Appreciation?" in P. Goldie (ed.) *The Oxford Handbook of Philosophy of Emotion*, Oxford: Oxford University Press.

Scruton, R. (1997) *The Aesthetics of Music*, Oxford: Clarendon Press.

Further reading

Levinson, J. (1990) "Music and Negative Emotion," in *Music, Art, and Metaphysics*, Ithaca: Cornell University Press, pp. 306–35. (Explores what reasons there might be for valuing music that arouses negative emotions.)

—— (2006) "Musical Chills," in *Contemplating Art*, Oxford: Clarendon Press, pp. 220–36. (An exploration of the nature of musical episodes that arouse tingles along the spine.)

Part III
HISTORY

23
CLASSICAL AESTHETIC TRADITIONS OF INDIA, CHINA, AND THE MIDDLE EAST

Peter Manuel (India) and Stephen Blum (China, the Middle East)

In India, China, and the Arab Middle East, pre-modern philosophers and writers on music generated substantial sets of treatises – primarily in Sanskrit, Mandarin, and Arabic, respectively – dealing with what could broadly be termed the philosophy of music. Despite marked differences in approach and content, within each culture writers established intellectual traditions animated by a sense of historicity, a combination of mystical and empirical approaches, and earnest attempts to hypothesize the relation of music to society and the cosmos in an era pre-dating modern science.

India

Indian music aesthetics, if broadly conceived as explicitly articulated "thinking about music," constitutes a vast semantic field, including but not limited to a substantial corpus of Sanskrit treatises. As in most discussions of the topic, primary emphasis here will be on art music, although it should be remembered that the popularity of the classical fine arts has always been limited to the relatively elite minority; similarly, customary casual generalizations about, for example, "the Indian way of thinking" do not do justice to the prodigious social diversity of South Asia, whether in the present or in prior millennia.

Classical cosmologies and music

If music aesthetics is understood in the most expansive sense as comprising conceptions about music's relation to epistemologies or conceptions of reality, then a voluminous body of classical Sanskritic philosophical and music theory must be considered in a thorough apprehension of Indian music ideology. The relevant body of literature consists primarily of a set of Sanskrit texts (or *shâstras*) dating roughly from the latter part of the first millennium BCE to the sixteenth century CE. The literature is diverse in several ways: texts focus variously on religion, philosophy, music theory, poetry, or phonetics; they are penned by scholars separated by centuries, thousands of miles, and in some cases contrasting schools of thought. At the same time, they are linked by a common language (Sanskrit) and literary style, by familiarity with and references to a revered body of texts, and – differences notwithstanding – by a shared philosophical basis and sense of historicity. Some of the landmarks in this literary tradition are: the *Nâtyâshâstra* (henceforth "*NS*," second century BCE to second century CE?), on dramaturgy and its music; the *Nâradishikshâ* (*c*.500 CE), a phonetic manual regarding Vedic chant and music mythology; the *Brhaddeshi* ("*BD*," *c*.800), on music; the *Abhinâvabharati* ("*AB*," *c*.1000), a recension of and commentary on the *Nâtyashâstra*; and the *Sangîtratnâkara* ("*SR*," 1240) on music theory. Despite being handwritten on perishable palm leaves, texts such as the *NS* and *SR* were fairly widely disseminated among Hindu literati throughout the subcontinent; several treatises, although themselves lost, are quoted and discussed in other surviving manuscripts. Taken collectively, the series of texts represents, whether explicitly or implicitly, a relatively coherent and consistent body of cosmological discourse relating directly or indirectly to music – especially ritual music and what may be retrospectively understood as art music, that is, that sustained by elite patronage and grounded in theory explicitly articulated in the *shâstras*. What is less clear, as suggested below, is the impact of these esoteric notions on musical form and the layperson's apprehension of it.

A recurrent notion in texts such as the *BD* and *SR* is that musical sound is quintessentially vocal rather than instrumental (in contrast to Greek acoustic conceptions), and proceeds along a spiritual pathway from an unmanifested ideal form, through the navel, heart, throat, and finally the mouth. Vocal music, generated by vital breath and thus linked to cosmic energy, was conceived as a sublime manifestation of *nâda-brahma*, a sort of primordial and divinely animating substratum of cosmic sound. In this esoteric view influenced by Tantric and Yogic notions, musical utterance at once worships the gods Brahma, Vishnu, and Shiva, recapitulates the act of cosmological creation, and acquires value less as an instance of human innovation or mundane expression than as the audible revelation of a deeper stratum of sublime, imperceptible reality. Such a cosmology cohered with a general social and philosophical conservatism which revered Sanskritic tradition and, in the realm of music and aesthetic theory, perpetually sought to reconcile contemporary practice with the supposedly timeless truths presented in ancient texts, especially the *NS*. (In contrast to Chinese and Japanese aesthetics, little literary interest was taken in hypothesizing relations between music and ethics, numerology, acoustics, or natural beauty.)

Much discourse in the *shâstras* regarding music and its broader associations took the standard Sanskritic form of elaborate – and some would say, obsessive – taxonomies and enumerations. Some of these, such as the classifications of phonetics and musical instruments, were rigorously empirical and logical; others would strike the modern (and especially Western) reader as fanciful and gratuitous rhetorical exercises bearing little relation to any form of reality outside the texts themselves. For example, the *Nâradishikshâ* related each of the seven notes of the scale to a color, social caste, animal sound, deity, and so on. Such extra-musical associations could be regarded as aspects of music aesthetics in the sense of representing a music ideology relating formal features (in this case, notes) to other natural phenomena and belief systems (see, for example, Rowell 1992: 330). A contrasting point of view would hold that considerations of *nâda-brahma*, ritual roots of chironomy, and Tantric speculations constitute arcane esoterica cultivated in an essentially autonomous Sanskritic literary tradition which had little bearing on the meaning art music had for either its performers or listeners (most of whom, in North India from the twelfth century, were likely in any case to be Muslims unfamiliar with Sanskrit and its literature). Hence, for example, North Indian classical music has long been greatly enjoyed by diverse listeners, both Indian and non-Indian, Hindu and non-Hindu, who have been unfamiliar with and uninterested in Hindu cosmology (see, for example, Clayton 2000: 18).

Similarly contrasting perspectives could be obtained regarding the sixteenth- and seventeenth-century tradition of *râga-mâla* painting, in which a given *râga* or melodic mode is portrayed as personified by a standardized set of icons (see Ebeling 1973; Powers 1980). Such paintings might also be accompanied by short, evocative *râga-dhyâna* (*râga*-contemplation) verses, which were also included alongside the more technical *râga* descriptions in some music treatises. Thus, for example, *Todi râga* is generally portrayed as a damsel playing a *vîna* zither, attended by one or more enchanted deer, with an inscribed *dhyâna* depicting her charming appearance and the dulcet tones of *Todi* that she plays. One could argue (as does Gangoly 1989) that such paintings and poems constitute parts of a coherent musical synaesthetic, and they are indeed reflective of the way in which the individual *râgas* have distinct characters and lend themselves to extra-musical associations. Alternatively, such paintings and verses could be regarded as thoroughly autonomous visual-art and literary traditions, having very little to do with music or even "thought about music."

Classical aesthetic theory

More explicitly relevant to music is the tradition of Sanskritic aesthetic theory, especially that concerned with *rasa* (colloquially pronounced *ras*, rhyming with "bus"). The first surviving exposition of *rasa* theory is in the *Nâtyashâstra*, the dramaturgical treatise attributed to the sage Bharata, though evidently a compilation of earlier works. As schematically presented in the *NS* and elaborated in subsequent works, *rasa* (literally "flavor," "juice," "essence") can denote both the sentiment expressed by an art and the viewer's experience of that emotion. A companion term is *bhâva*, which, depending on context and interpretation, denotes either real-life emotions or the manner of expressing them in art. The *NS*'s sixth chapter succinctly enumerates the eight *rasas*, namely, *sringâra* (the erotic), *hasya* (the humorous), *karuna* (the sorrowful), *raudra* (the angry), *vira* (the heroic), *bhayânaka* (the frightful), *vibhatsa* (the odious), and *adbhuta* (the wonderous). These are to be regarded as aesthetic counterparts to eight basic real-life emotions (*sthâyi-bhâvas*). Chapter 29 specifies associations of the particular *rasas* with melodic modes (*jâtis*, the precursors to *râgas*) and, less plausibly, with individual notes of the scale.

The Sanskrit drama discussed in the *NS*, like such still-extant genres as Keralan *kathakali* and *kuttiyâtam* dance-drama, employed highly stylized rather than naturalistic portrayals of characters. *Dramatis personae* consisted of stock stereotypes (*nâyikâs*, e.g. *vipralabdha nâyikâ*, the woman berating but secretly desiring her wayward lover), whose portrayal relied on standardized *bhâvas* encompassing gait, garb, facial expression, and the like, and who were accompanied by music expected to cohere with and enhance the appropriate *rasa*. While the *NS*'s enumerations of *rasas* might strike a modern reader as artificial, they may have been quite apt as descriptive and prescriptive references to such a stylized theater tradition. As Sanskrit drama eventually died out, the art music discussed in texts became autonomous, and documented interest in *rasa* theory surfaced only irregularly until Abhinavagupta's impressive *Abhinâvabharati*. The *AB* elaborates *rasa* aesthetics, stressing the importance of a disinterested attitude on the part of the viewer, and contrasting aesthetic experience with everyday emotions. Although aspects of *rasa* theory are seen by this time as better applied to drama, poetry, visual arts, and dance than to art music, music treatises such as the thirteenth-century *SR* reflect the *AB*'s influence and reiterate associations of *rasas* with songs and *râgas*.

As Katz (1996: 416) and others have pointed out, the ultimate merit of *rasa* theory may lie less in its taxonomies and enumerations of emotion-types than in its presentation (however contested and ambiguous at times) of a theory of artistic poetics and reception. As an empirical attempt to rationally explain artistic (including musical) enjoyment and evaluation, *rasa* theory bears striking compatibilities with the orientation of modern Western aesthetic scholarship (as well as corresponding contrasts with, for example, Japanese and Chinese aesthetics). Indeed, further parallels could be noted, including the emphasis on disinterested perception, the distinction (still debated in the West) between aesthetic and real-life experienced emotions, and the idea that however nuanced and diverse expressive forms may be, the goal of artistic contemplation is a generalized aesthetic pleasure (thereby resolving, for its purposes, the ongoing "negative emotion" debate in Western music aesthetics).

From the Muslim period to the present

From around the thirteenth century, most of North India – and at times, much of the South as well – was ruled by Muslim dynasts. With a few exceptions, from the early fifteenth century Muslim rulers and nobles were ardent patrons of the classical music system they inherited, and in the North, Muslim musicians (including many low-caste Hindu converts and their descendants) dominated the performance scene. A few Muslim rulers took an eclectic interest in Sanskritic learning and commissioned translations of treatises (including texts on music) into Persian. However, beyond a superficial familiarity with the basics of *rasa* theory, it may be said that Muslim patrons and performers had little engagement with Sanskritic aesthetic theory. Meanwhile, although Arab theorists such as the tenth-century al-Fārābī had written on music aesthetics, it cannot be said that the Indo-Muslim rulers introduced a dramatically distinctive or explicitly elaborated theory of music aesthetics. Between the socio-religious extremes of fundamentalists who scorned music and Chishti Sufis who embraced it as a form of devotion and a route to mystical ecstasy, most Muslim patrons apprehended it as one of the fine arts (*funûn-e-latifah*), made all the more worldly by its lack of institutional Islamic support (unlike music in Hindu culture).

The primary effect of Muslim rule on North Indian classical music was to intensify its secular character at the expense of its associations with Hindu cosmology. In the twentieth century, many Hindu writers on music denounced the Muslim patrons for depriving music of its (Hindu) spiritual associations and grounding it not in the temple but in the hedonistic world of the court and courtesan's salon. Yet it could be counter-argued that in secularizing Hindustani music, Muslim patrons helped make it compatible with modernity and confrontation with the West, thereby contributing to what must be regarded as its formidable vitality at present. For its part, South Indian music enjoys its own prodigious dynamism and bourgeois popular support, while retaining a more overt devotional Hindu dimension (which the listener, however, is free to ignore).

Meanwhile, if classical Sanskritic philosophy has long since ceded prominence to cosmopolitan Western-influenced scholarship, *rasa* theory retains a certain attenuated presence in musical thought. At the very least, aesthetic terms dating back to the *NS* provide a familiar colloquial descriptive vocabulary, e.g. "*Râg Khamâj* is well suited to *sringâr ras*," "Abdul Karim Khan's voice drips with *karun ras*," or, among cognoscenti, "This song portrays a *vipralabdha nâyikâ*." While a mechanistic identification of *rasas* with *râgas* is no longer seen as plausible, such past conventions, along with *râgamâla* paintings, are recognized as expressions of the ways in which *râgas* possess distinctive individual expressive characters.

Despite the past cosmological dimensions of Indian art music and whatever lingering presence they may have, both North and South Indian classical musics have become essentially secular fine arts. Performed in concert halls, reviewed in newspapers, and increasingly learned in conservatories, Indian art musics are enjoyed in much the same way as Western concert music, evaluated with many of the same criteria, and amenable to being discussed in the terms of Western academic writing on music aesthetics.

China

Music and ritual

As an indispensable component of rituals and ceremonies deemed essential to the very survival of the state, music has long been an object of philosophical reflection in China. The philosophy of music outlined by two Confucian philosophers active in the third century BCE, Hsün Tzu and his student Han Fei Tzu, formed the basis of such later works as the *Record of Music* (one section of the *Record of Rites*) and the chapter on music in Ssuma Ch'ien's *Records of the Historian*.

In the classic formulation of the *Record of Music*, "to unite the emotions and to polish external appearances – these are the affairs of Ritual and Music. . . . Music comes out from within; Ritual comes into being from without" (Cook 1995: 42–3). Through a reciprocal process joining inner feeling to outward manifestation, ceremonial performance of properly regulated music upholds the social order and fulfills a vital obligation to ancestors. When music transgresses its proper limits, the Confucian ideal of harmonious relations within the family and the state is seen as seriously threatened. Hence the state must ensure that a correct standard of pitch is maintained as bronze bells or stone chimes are constructed for use in imperial rites.

The rationales offered by ruling elites in support of state ceremonies are inevitably subjected to critique. Mo Tzu, writing perhaps toward the end of the fifth century BCE, argued that "making music is wrong!" inasmuch as the high cost of manufacturing musical instruments and ceremonial costumes induces rulers and ministers to exploit the general population (Mo Tzu 1963). Complaints that Confucian ritual music was boring, like that attributed to Duke Wen of Wei in the *Record of Music*, may have been more common than critiques of exploitation. Of the many varieties of ritual music cultivated in China up to the present, only a select few have been constrained by Confucian standards.

Silence, sound, and music

A conception of sound as "a manifestation of Nature in equilibrium and disequilibrium" (Needham 1962: 131) is compatible both with the Confucian assumption that poorly regulated music is symptomatic of social disorder and with a

Daoist interest in experiencing "reverberations (*yün*) of the vitalizing force in nature (*ch'i*)" (Chou 1991: 184) by contemplating sounds as they emerge from and fade into silence. As the *ch'in*, a zither with seven silk strings, became the instrument of Confucian scholars, introspective cultivation of inner feeling while alone or with a few friends might be valued more highly than ceremonial action within a large group, at least by philosophers and other scholars. Music for introspection and music for group solidarity could be experienced as complementary, with each considered appropriate to certain moments in one's life.

Chinese musicians have long cultivated a keen interest in the different timbres or qualities of sound, such as those of the metal bells and stone chimes used in ceremony and those of the *ch'in*'s silk strings. A typology of eight material sources of sound was correlated with directions and seasons (see Needham 1962: 153–5). According to the *Tso Commentary on the Spring and Autumn Annals*, "dancing is that by which one regulates the eight sources of sound, and thereby conducts the right winds" (Needham 1962: 145). One could channel the energies of winds through instruments of the appropriate material, such as bamboo flutes and pipes in spring. Hsün Tzu's attempt to spell out "the symbolism of music" connects instruments to spiritual states and feelings associated with seasonal changes: "the drum represents a vast pervasiveness [winter]; the bells represent fullness [autumn]; the sounding stones represent restrained order [autumn–winter]; the mouth organs represent austere harmony [spring–summer]; the flutes represent a spirited outburst [spring]" and so on (Hsün Tsu 1963: 117).

Aesthetic terminology

A statement in the *Book of Documents* outlines a sequence of phases advancing from a silent thought or emotion to a harmonious configuration of tones: "Poetry expresses the mind, the song is a (drawing out =) chanting of (its) words, the notes depend upon (the mode of) the chanting, the pitch-pipes harmonize the notes" (Karlgren 1950: 7). This linear progression became the subject of commentary in the *Record of Music*, the "Great Preface" to the Mao edition of the *Book of Songs* (25 CE), and K'ung Ying-ta's seventh-century commentary on the Great Preface (Saussy 1993: 77–88). According to the *Record of Music*, sound (*sheng*) arises in the heart in response to an external stimulus, music (*yin*) is produced as sounds of contrasting pitches and timbres respond to one another, and a more elaborate music (*yüeh*) is achieved with the addition of ceremonial implements (Cook 1995: 24–5; Chou 1991: 180). The progression from thought through poem, chanting, notes, and harmonization culminates in government, and for that reason "Music is investigated to know administration" (Cook 1995: 33–4).

A state that holds music to be symptomatic of sentiments can sponsor projects of collection and revision aimed at replacing features suggestive of undesirable sentiments with others that might instill sentiments the state desires, and nowhere has this model of state policy toward music been more highly developed than in China (Trebinjac 2000). All the same, a critique of the belief that musical sound is an index of feeling was voiced by Hsi Kang (223–262 CE) in a "Discourse on the Nonemotional Nature of Sound" (DeWoskin 1982: 104). Hsi Kang recognized that two listeners may respond differently to the same music, and a single listener may respond differently when the same music is performed on a later occasion.

A sophisticated aesthetic terminology in Chinese was first developed for music, then transferred to literature and painting (DeWoskin 1983: 198–205). Among the fundamental terms are *tao* (way) and *ch'i* (vitalizing force or configured energy). This common terminology has fostered "a close-knit relationship among the poetic, graphic and sonic arts across much of Asia" (Chou 1991: 181). One key text is the *Rhymeprose on Literature* of Lu Chi (261–303 CE), which explores the interdependence of five aesthetic qualities: *ying* (response, resonance), *ho* (harmony), *pei* (gravity of feeling), *ya* (restraint in expression), and *yen* (richness of texture). Each quality serves as a control on the others: "The advances of one meet the retreats of another; the assertions of one control the excesses of another" (DeWoskin 1983: 205). The resulting balance may approach the ideal of "blandness," in which no single quality stands out. Likewise, the way of life appropriate to a sage is often described as requiring a disciplined avoidance of any inclination to favor one tendency over others, so that the sage can experience the world in its wholeness (Jullien 1991: 41–7). Music and the other arts enable us to achieve and sustain a sense of poised equilibrium.

Arabic and Persian writings in the early centuries of Islam

Philosophical treatment of music in the early centuries of Islam began with the assimilation and extension of Greek musical thought, enriched through close attention to the existing musical practices of Arabs, Persians, and their neighbors. Two of the greatest Muslim philosophers, al-Fārābī (d. 950) and Avicenna (980–1037), wrote extensively on the discipline known in Arabic as *mūsīqī* (from Greek *mousiké*), which was treated as a branch of mathematics and contrasted in various respects with traditional arts of singing (Arabic *ghinā'*).

Music and other sciences

The adaptation of Ancient Greek and Byzantine music theory by Muslim scholars extended from the late eighth century through much of the tenth. The first major philosopher involved in this effort was al-Kindī (d. *c*.866), whose surviving works include four brief treatises on music. One of these deals with "the instrument of philosophers," namely the lute (*'ūd*). Another is a systematic presentation of the knowledge needed for composition of melodies: knowledge of tones, intervals, species of tetrachord, combinations of tetrachords, modulation, and the workings of melodies on the soul (Greek *ēthos*, Arabic *ta'thīr*). From the ninth century onward, music theorists writing in Arabic described intervals between pitches with reference to the locations of frets on the neck of a lute, or to the points where the single string of a monochord could be stopped.

Aristotle's *Rhetoric* and *Poetics* are placed among his logical works in the pedagogical ordering of scientific disciplines developed by the Aristotelians of Alexandria, which was transmitted to Muslim scholars by Syrian Christians. Avicenna's masterful *Kitāb al-shifā'* (*Book of Healing*) proceeds in a conventional order through the branches of logic (including poetics), physics, mathematics (including music), and metaphysics. Fārābī and Averroës (1126–98) also wrote commentaries on the *Poetics* that touch on key issues in the philosophy of music, such as listeners' responses to the "imaginative representation" (*takhyīl*) or "imitation" (*muhākāh*) of human actions.

From the late tenth century onward, some Muslim authors (such as al-Khwārizmī in his *Mafātīh al-'ulūm* (*Keys to the Sciences*), *c*.985) classified the disciplines that had been developed on the basis of Greek precedents as "foreign sciences," in contrast to such "Arab sciences" as linguistics, jurisprudence, and theology. This dichotomy was retained as "new" (Muslim) versus "ancient" by al-Amolī (d. 1352) in the Persian encyclopedia *Nafā'es al-fonun* (*Treasures of the Sciences*), and as "traditional" versus "intellectual" in the great *Muqaddima* (*Introduction [to History]*) of Ibn Khaldūn (d. 1406). Arab and foreign, old and new, traditional and intellectual could be understood as complementary, or as incompatible in some or even all respects. Debate over this set of issues became ever more intense as Muslim thinkers were confronted with the challenges of European scientific advances and imperial projects.

The composition and reception of music

The Platonic and Aristotelian conception of music as composed of tone-relationships (*harmonía*), structured movement (*rhythmos*), and words (*lógos*) was as pertinent to the arts of *ghīnā'* as to the discipline of *mūsīqī*. The great singer Ishāq al-Mausilī (d. 850) named four "domains" of knowledge as indispensable to the musician's art: *nagham* (tones), *ta'līf* (their "harmonious arrangement"), *qisma* (the "apportionment" of tones to song lyrics), and *'īqā'āt* (metric cycles). Ishāq's contemporary, al-Kindī, distinguished three types of melody with which poetry may be "clothed" by the size and arrangement of intervals: "the contracting" (*al-qabdī*), evocative of melancholy; "the temperate" (*al-mu'tadil*), appropriate to praise and the experience of the sublime; and "the expansive" (*al-bastī*), associated with delight. Kindī added that a composer's choice of a slow, moderate, or quick metric cycle must match his choice of melodic framework if the composition is to bring about the desired movement of the soul. Like the Greek conception of *ēthos* on which it was modeled, this typology posits a neutral point from which movement in either of two opposite directions raises or lowers the level of activity or effort.

Fārābī defined melody (*lahn*) as an ordered succession of tones that is or is not combined with voweled and unvoweled consonants; melody in the fullest sense of the term includes verse. Like Kindī, Fārābī classified melodic frameworks as relatively strong, temperate, or soft. Strong frameworks allow for representation of enmity, cruelty, anger, and boldness; soft frameworks are appropriate to fear, compassion, anxiety, and cowardice. Fārābī and Avicenna were interested in the experience of listening, such as ways in which listeners' expectations may or may not be fulfilled.

An argument that listeners are capable of directing their experience of music in ways that are ethically appropriate rather than reprehensible is central to the influential defense of music offered by the theologian Abu Hamīd al-Ghazalī (1058–1111). Members of many Sufi orders have shared this understanding of the potential spiritual value of music, which extends to purely instrumental melody and the movements it may inspire in performers and listeners. The fourteenth-century Persian poet Hāfez often speaks of "messages" conveyed by instruments: "Sounding in a high register, rebec and harp say, 'Listen closely to the message of those who are intimate with the secret'." Another of his lines depicts the coordination of voice and instrument with structured movement in ceremonial performance: "Now that you have a good instrument in hand, minstrel, sing a good song / that all of us may throw up our hands, dance, and shake our heads as we perform a ghazal."

See also Aesthetic properties (Chapter 14), Antiquity and the Middle Ages (Chapter 24), Composition (Chapter 47), Ethnomusicology (Chapter 49), Rhythm, melody, and harmony (Chapter 3), Silence, sound, noise, and music (Chapter 2), Sociology and cultural studies (Chapter 51), and Value (Chapter 15).

References

Chou, W.-C. (1991) "Asian Esthetics and World Music," in H. Ryker (ed.) *New Music in the Orient: Essays on Composition in Asia since World War II*, Buren: Frits Knuf, pp. 177–88.

Clayton, M. (2000) *Time in Indian Music: Rhythm, Metre, and Form in North Indian Rāg Performance*, Oxford: Oxford University Press.

Cook, S. (1995) "*Yue Ji . . . Record of Music*: Introduction, Translation, Notes, and Commentary," *Asian Music* 26: 1–96.

DeWoskin, K. (1982) *A Song for One or Two: Music and the Concept of Art in Early China*, Ann Arbor: Center for Chinese Studies, University of Michigan.

—— (1983) "Early Chinese Music and the Origins of Aesthetic Terminology," in S. Bush and C. Murck (eds) *Theories of the Arts in China*, Princeton: Princeton University Press, pp. 187–214.

Ebeling, K. (1973) *Râgamâla Painting*, New York: Ravi Kumar.

Gangoly, O.C. (1989) *Râgas and Râginîs: A Pictorial and Iconographic Study of Indian Musical Modes Based on Original Sources*, Delhi: Munshi Manoharlal.

Hsün Tsu (1963) "A Discussion of Music," in *Hsün Tsu: Basic Writings*, trans. B. Watson, New York: Columbia University Press, pp. 112–20.

Jullien, F. (1991) *Eloge de la fadeur: à partir de la pensée et de l'esthétique de la Chine*, Arles: Actes Sud.

Karlgren, B. (1950) *The Book of Documents: The Shu King*, Göteborg: Elanders Boktryckeri Aktiebolag.

Katz, J. (1996) "Music and Aesthetics: An Early Indian Perspective," *Early Music* 24: 407–20.

Mo Tzu (1963) "Against Music," in *Mo Tsu: Basic Writings*, trans. B. Watson, New York: Columbia University Press, pp. 110–16.

Needham, J., with Wang Ling and Robinson, K.G., (1962) *Science and Civilisation in China*, vol. 4, pt. 1: *Physics*, Cambridge: Cambridge University Press.

Powers, H. (1980) "Illustrated Inventories of Indian Râgamâlâ Painting," *Journal of the American Oriental Society* 100: 473–93.

Rowell, L. (1992) *Music and Musical Thought in Early India*, Chicago: University of Chicago Press.

Saussy, H. (1993) *The Problem of a Chinese Aesthetic*, Stanford: Stanford University Press.

Trebinjac, S. (2000) *Le pouvoir en chantant*, vol. 1: *L'art de fabriquer une musique chinoise*, Nanterre: Société d'Ethnologie.

Further reading

India

Pandey, K.C. (1959) *Comparative Aesthetics*, vol. 1: *Indian Aesthetics*, Varanasi: Chowkhamba Sanskrit Series. (The first volume of an extended study by a respected Sanskritic scholar.)

Rangacharya, A. (1996) *The Nâtyasâstra: English Translation with Critical Notes*, Delhi: Munshi Manoharlal. (Currently the most accessible translation of the Nâtyâshâstra.)

Sharma, P.L. (1970) "Rasa Theory and Indian Music," *Sangeet Natak Akademi Bulletin* 16: 57–64. (A representative commentary by a modern Indian musicologist relating traditional Sanskritic theory to modern North Indian practice.)

Singh, T.J. (1970) "Aesthetics of Hindustani Musical Forms," *Sangeet Natak Akademi Bulletin* 16: 23–33. (Another representative commentary by a modern Indian musicologist relating traditional Sanskritic theory to modern North Indian practice.)

China

Fei, F.C. (1999) *Chinese Theories of Theater and Performance from Confucius to the Present*, Ann Arbor: University of Michigan Press. (Extracts from writings on the performing arts, with emphasis on responses of spectators and listeners.)

Gulik, R.H.v. (1940) *The Lore of the Chinese Lute*, Tokyo: Sophia University. (A classic work on the ideology of the ch'in, a zither long regarded as the instrument of Confucian scholars.)

Kaufmann, W. (1976) *Musical References in the Chinese Classics*, Detroit: Information Coordinators. (Chinese texts of passages on music with English translations and commentaries.)

Liang, M.-Y. (1985) *Music of the Billion: An Introduction to Chinese Musical Culture*, New York: Heinrichshofen. (Combines a survey of Chinese music history with essays on major topics.)

So, J. (ed.) (2000) *Music in the Age of Confucius*, Washington: Freer Gallery of Art and Arthur M. Sackler Gallery, Smithsonian Institution. (Essays on string, wind, and percussion instruments based on archaeological findings.)

The Middle East

Blum, S. (forthcoming) "Foundations of Musical Knowledge in the Muslim World," in P. Bohlman (ed.) *The Cambridge History of World Music*, Cambridge: Cambridge University Press. (Summarizes a few of the leading ideas about music articulated in Arabic and Persian writings between the eighth and fourteenth centuries of the "Common Era.")

Erlanger, R.d' (1930–59) *La musique arabe*, 6 vols, Paris: Paul Geuthner. (French translations of several important Arabic treatises followed by two volumes on theory and practice in the first half of the twentieth century.)

Haas, M. (2006) "Griechische Musiktheorie in arabischen, hebräischen und syrischen Zeugnissen," in T. Ertelt, H. v. Loesch and F. Zaminer (eds) *Geschichte der Musiktheorie*, vol. 2: *Vom Mythos zur Fachdisziplin: Antike und Byzanz*, Darmstadt: Wissenschaftliche Buchgesellschaft, pp. 635–716. (A survey of adaptations and extensions of Greek music theory made by authors writing in Arabic, Hebrew, and Syriac.)

Kemal, S. (1991) *The Poetics of Alfarabi and Avicenna*, Leiden: Brill. (A comparative analysis of the aesthetic theories developed by Fārābī and Avicenna in their commentaries on the *Poetics* of Aristotle.)

Neubauer, E. (1998) *Arabische Musiktheorie von den Anfängen bis zum 6./12. Jahrhundert: Studien, Übersetzungen und Texte in Faksimile*, Frankfurt: Institute for the History of Arabic-Islamic Science. (A reprint of important essays and translations by the author, to which facsimiles of the pertinent Arabic texts have been added.)

Shehadi, F.A. (1995) *Philosophies of Music in Medieval Islam*, Leiden: Brill. (An introductory survey.)

Shiloah, A. (1993) *The Dimension of Music in Islamic and Jewish Culture*, Aldershot: Variorum. (A collection of previously published essays.)

—— (1995) *Music in the World of Islam*, Detroit: Wayne State University Press. (A survey that combines deep knowledge of Arabic writings with extensive experience of contemporary cultures.)

—— (2007) *Music and its Virtues in Islamic and Jewish Writings*, Aldershot: Ashgate. (A second collection of previously published essays.)

24
ANTIQUITY AND THE MIDDLE AGES

Thomas J. Mathiesen

A full treatment of the philosophy of music in antiquity, let alone the Middle Ages, would need to take into account not only the familiar "ancient" classical cultures of Greece and Rome but also those of eastern Asia, India, Mesopotamia, and Egypt. Inasmuch as even a cursory overview of all these cultures would be impossible in a short chapter, the Pythagorean tradition will be a useful place to start: first, because Pythagoras himself has been credited with coining the terms "philosophy" and "philosopher"; and, second, because the tradition absorbed important elements of many ancient cultures, as well as unquestionably exerting an enormous influence on the musical philosophy of classical antiquity and the Middle Ages.

Pythagoras and the Pythagoreans

The historical Pythagoras is an elusive character. Born perhaps on Samos, he is presumed to have lived between 570 and 480 BCE. According to his biographers, he was educated by Hermodamas of Samos, Thales, and Anaximander of Miletus, as well as by the learned figures he encountered in his travels in the Near East and Egypt (and possibly even in India). After some years of teaching on Samos following his return to the island, he emigrated to Croton in southern Italy where he attracted a large community of followers. Unrest eventually arose, and Pythagoras emigrated to Metapontum and remained there until his death, the precise date and circumstances of which have been matters of dispute, even among the early Pythagoreans.

According to Heraclides Ponticus (*fl.* fourth century BCE), Pythagoras was the first to use the term "philosophy" (*philosophia*) and to call himself a "philosopher" (*philosophos*) because "no one except god is wise [*sophos*]" (Diogenes Laertius Proem. 12). In other words, Pythagoras "called 'fond of wisdom' – that is, 'philosophos' – those who, regarding all else as nothing, ardently contemplated the nature of things" (Cicero *Tusculanae disputationes* 5.3.8).

Pythagoras taught his students privately (and secretly) rather than developing his ideas systematically in a series of treatises, but many of his teachings were preserved in the writings of his followers, who split into two groups (probably in the fifth century BCE) – the acousmatics and the mathematicians. The acousmatics were particularly interested in Pythagoras's teachings in the area of ritual life (e.g. eschatology, diet, sacrifice, purification, burial, reincarnation, and so on) while the mathematicians were interested in the four primary Pythagorean scientific disciplines (geometry, astronomy, arithmetic, and music), which Pythagoras is supposed to have developed from his studies with the Egyptians and Chaldeans. The mathematicians regarded it as their particular task to disseminate and develop these disciplines (Archytas fr. 1; Aristotle *Metaphysics* 1.5).

The Pythagoreans (and presumably Pythagoras himself) regarded number as central to all knowledge: "everything that can be known has a Number; for it is impossible to grasp anything with the mind or to recognize it without this" (Philolaus fr. 4). In particular, the series of the first four numbers, the *tetraktys* of the decad, held significance because it embodies all the musical consonances (the octave, 2:1; the fifth, 3:2; the fourth, 4:3; the twelfth, 3:1; and the fifteenth, 4:1) and all the geometric elements (point, 1; line, 2; plane, 3; and solid, 4); moreover, the sum of the first four numbers returns to the perfection of 1, now in the base 10 ($1 + 2 + 3 + 4 = 10$).

According to legend, Pythagoras discovered the numerical basis of the musical consonances when walking by a blacksmith's shop: he heard the consonant sounds of the octave, fifth, and fourth; noticed that the various pitches producing the consonances corresponded to the weights of the hammers (12, 9, 8, and 6); replicated these sounds by suspending the weights from strings; and noted the ratios between the weights. He is then supposed to have observed these same ratios in the lengths of strings, pipes, and so on. As it happens, unison strings under these proportional tensions (whether produced by weights or any other means) do not sound these intervals, which actually result from the proportional resonance of unison strings. Nevertheless, the basic consonant ratios embodied in the first four numbers remained inviolable, with a very few notable exceptions, throughout antiquity and the Middle Ages.

The Pythagoreans viewed these musical consonances and their ratios as broadly paradigmatic: "they took the elements of numbers to be the elements of everything and the whole heaven to be *harmonia* and number" (Aristotle *Metaphysics* 1.5). From this, the notion of the cosmos as a musical harmony emerged (including the harmony of the spheres in Plato *Republic* 10.616c–17c) and concomitantly the conception of music (*mousikê*) as a science that reveals the secrets of nature and exerts a powerful force on the character (ethos) of individuals and society as a whole, as is conveyed in the widely repeated story of Pythagoras calming an inebriated (or lustful) youth by changing the *harmonia* (on this term, see below and Mathiesen 2001a) of the music he was hearing and in Socrates' argument against musical innovation as a threat to the fundamental structure of the state (Plato *Republic* 4.424b–c). In a real sense, music and philosophy are inexorably linked in the Pythagorean tradition.

Plato and Aristotle

The influence of the Pythagorean tradition is strong in the work of Plato (*c*.429–347 BCE), especially in *Timaeus* but also in *Republic* and *Laws*. The *Timaeus* (34b–37c; see Plato 1998b), for example, makes frequent use of the term *harmonia* and its related forms in describing the parts of the universal soul in terms of Pythagorean musical ratios, while in *Republic*, *harmonia* is used both in the characterization of various ethnic musical types – Dorian, Phrygian, Lydian, and so on (3.398c–403c; see Plato 1998a) – and in reference to the proper state of the individual soul, as when Socrates says: "he who best blends gymnastics with music (*mousikê*) and applies them in the most measured way to the soul is the one we should most rightly consider to be the most perfectly musical and harmonious" (Plato *Republic* 3.412a). *Republic* also includes the famous Myth of Er, in which a Siren on each orbit in the cosmos (seven planetary and an outer orbit of fixed stars) produces a single pitch, the eight of them together forming "a single *harmonia*" (10.616d–17d). (For a fuller discussion, see Chapter 28, in "Plato," in this volume.)

Aristotle (384–322 BCE) and the Aristotelian *Problemata* have much to say about music, but the material is more often historical or technical rather than philosophical. Aristotle's *On the Heavens*, however, is devoted to a refutation of the Pythagorean "harmony of the spheres" (*De caelo* 2.9), while *Metaphysics* 14.6 debunks the notion of number as reality. In Book VIII of *Politics*, Aristotle turns his attention to the power of music to amuse and relax, instill ethical virtue, and stimulate the intellect (see Aristotle 1998). He acknowledges the powerful influence of music, but his view of music is less dogmatic than Plato's: for Aristotle, the propriety of music (and education in music) is a relative matter, depending on time, place, purpose, age, and station.

Aristoxenus

Aristoxenus of Tarentum (*c*.350–310 BCE), Aristotle's student, seems to have been the first to develop a comprehensive phenomenology of music, leading one recent scholar to call him "the founder of musicology" (Gibson 2005: 2). Unfortunately, his treatises on harmonics (the phenomena of musical sound) and rhythmics do not survive intact, and some parts of his phenomenology can only be conjectured from treatments (often critical) written in later antiquity.

Aristoxenus clearly identifies his study of harmonics as in accord with Aristotle's third type of science, the theoretical, which transcends the limitations of sensory experience in the exercise of pure reason (*Topics* 6.6, *Metaphysics* 1.1, and *Nicomachean Ethics* 10.7). Recalling Aristotle's method in *Physics*, Aristoxenus begins by defining the constituent parts of musical reality: motion, pitch, compass, notes, intervals, genera, scales, musical line (*melos*), synthesis (i.e. the way in which notes and intervals, like letters and words, are placed in natural order), and position or placement of the voice. Later on, these constituent parts are recast as a set of seven categories (notes, intervals, genera, scales, *tonoi*, modulation, and melic composition [*melopoiïa*]), framed by hearing and intellect on the one hand and comprehension on the other. The phenomena, he says, cannot be properly grasped without a sharp sense of hearing, and their function cannot be understood without intellect. Beyond this, because music passes through time, it is both a Becoming and a Having Become. Thus, in order to have musical comprehension, it is necessary to have a sense of the Becoming and a memory of the Having Become.

In his definition of the three basic genera of melodic lines (enharmonic, chromatic, and diatonic), Aristoxenus abandons traditional Pythagorean ratios in favor of a geometric idealization in which two fixed notes – hypate and mese – defining the interval of a fourth (not, however, specified as a Pythagorean interval in the ratio 4:3) surround two other notes – parhypate and lichanos – that define six specific shades by moving within a spatially defined area, measured in parts of a tone (see Figure 24.1).

This extraordinarily bold conception was routinely attacked and derided by theorists throughout antiquity and the Middle Ages as empirically faulty and mathematically impossible, but Aristoxenus was well aware that musical phenomena had not been and could not be adequately explained by the limited

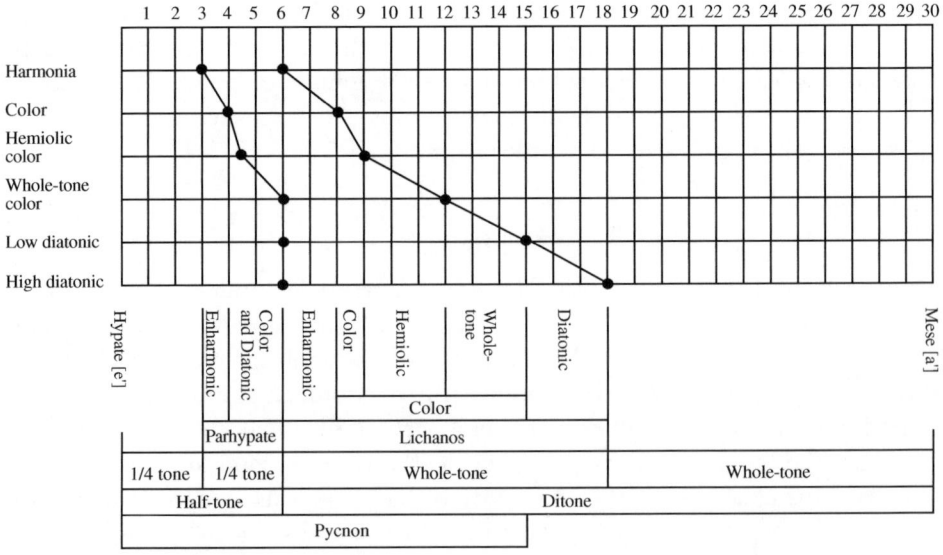

Figure 24. 1 The Aristoxenian shades (Mathiesen 1999: 313)

means of Pythagorean mathematics. By applying a geometric model, Aristoxenus recognized the possibility of transcending these limits. His larger philosophical view seems to have escaped even his followers, who tended to reduce his system to a series of simple descriptive categories, but his application and development of Aristotelian principles and categories established a philosophical alternative to the Pythagorean (and Platonic) view of music. (For a fuller treatment of Aristoxenus, see Mathiesen 1999: 294–344.)

Epicureans and Skeptics

Epicurean and Skeptic philosophers generally rejected the idea that music represented anything beyond itself or held any special power to affect human character (*ethos*). In Book IV of his fragmentary treatise *De musica*, the Epicurean Philodemus (*c*.110–*c*.40 BCE) summarizes and systematically refutes each argument of the Stoic Diogenes the Babylonian (*c*.240–152 BCE), who represents a synthesis of Pythagorean, Platonic, and Aristotelian viewpoints. For Philodemus, music is irrational and, at best, a simple pleasure, invented by man. It has no metaphysical significance and manifests no ethical effects. A similar type of treatment is provided by the Skeptic Sextus Empiricus (*fl.* second century CE), who reviews and debunks the various traditional claims for music, after which he demonstrates that music cannot even be an object of study because it is predicated on elements that cannot be demonstrated to exist (see Sextus Empiricus 1998).

Early Latin writers: Cicero and Varro

Although there are many musical references in Latin literature from the second century BCE through the imperial period, the majority of these are allegorical, metaphoric, technical, or historical; with the exception of Cicero (106–43 BCE) and Varro (116–27 BCE), musical philosophy as such seems to have been left to writers in Greek. Cicero's view of music generally accorded with Philodemus, but he also developed his own treatment of the harmony of the spheres in *Somnium Scipionis* (*Republic* 6.9–29; cf. *De natura deorum* 3.27), which would be highly influential as transmitted throughout the Middle Ages together with an extensive commentary by Macrobius. Further echoes of Plato appear in Cicero's *Laws* 2.15.38–39, which offers brief comments on musical *ethos*. Varro's encyclopedic treatment of the seven liberal arts (in the order grammar, dialectic, rhetoric, geometry, arithmetic, astronomy, and music, as later followed by Martianus Capella) plus medicine and architecture has not been preserved, but references to him appear in the writings of Pliny, Quintilian, Censorinus, Augustine, Cassiodorus, Isidore of Seville, and others. The famous definition "music is the science of effectively modulating the voice," found in Censorinus's *De die natali* 10 and repeated in various forms in many other places, is commonly but insecurely attributed to Varro.

Philo Judaeus

In the first century CE, Philo Judaeus (*c*.20 BCE–*c*.50 CE) attempted a synthesis of pagan and Jewish philosophy in his allegorical method of expounding scripture – a method in which music and number played a significant role. In his view, the beautiful things of the world were based on prefigurations that were part of God's creation (*De opificio mundi* 3–6). Because everything in the cosmos is numerically related, the arts should lead to philosophy and ultimately to God. Thus, musical *harmonia*, as an imitation of cosmic harmony, enables a recognition of this higher harmony that can in turn lead to a transcendent state (*De somniis* 1.35–37; *De opificio mundi* 53–54, 69–71). In a similar manner, the lyre serves as a metaphor for the harmonious soul, which is a "concord of virtues and the beauties in nature" (*Quod deus sit immutabilis* 24.4–5). Philo's allegorical method (emerging from a long tradition of allegorical interpretations of Homer and Hesiod) influenced Origen and Sts Ambrose, Jerome, Augustine, and Gregory, eventually becoming a standard for Biblical exegesis as well as for the interpretation of Greek and Roman secular literature. One of the important philosophical streams from antiquity to the Middle Ages, it nevertheless remains somewhat peripheral to the mainstream of musical philosophy because it is so closely linked with theology and the aesthetic dimension of religious experience.

Greek writers of later antiquity

All the traditions of musical philosophy retained separate identities in later antiquity, but the Pythagorean/Platonic and Aristotelian/Aristoxenian traditions merged to some extent in treatises such as *De musica* attributed to Plutarch of Chaeronea (*c*.50–*c*.120), the *Manuale harmonices* of Nicomachus of Gerasa (*fl.* late first–early second century), and the *Harmonica introductio* of Gaudentius (*fl.* late third or early fourth century; see Gaudentius 1998), all of which provided treatments of Pythagorean mathematics and music combined with historical and technical details of considerable interest to historians of music theory. Other writers of the same period, such as Cleonides and Theon of Smyrna, generally disregard philosophical aspects in providing primarily technical treatments, respectively, of the Aristoxenian and Platonic traditions. None of these shorter treatises, however, can compare with the two capstones of later Greek musical philosophy: the *Harmonica* by the Alexandrian scientist Claudius Ptolemy (*c*.90–161), who attempted a critique and developmental reconciliation of Pythagorean and Aristoxenian music theory, together with a consideration of the musical features of the cosmos; and the *De musica* of the neo-Platonist Aristides Quintilianus (*fl.* late third–early fourth century), perhaps the most "intricate and elaborately unified philosophical discourse in which music provides a paradigm for the order of the soul and the universe" (Mathiesen 1999: 525; for a fuller treatment of all these figures, see Mathiesen 1999: chs. 4–6).

Plutarch

Musical references abound in the *Moralia* of Plutarch, but two of the treatises are especially important in the present context: the unquestionably authentic *De animae procreatione in Timaeo*, essentially a commentary on Plato's *Timaeus*; and the pseudonymous *De musica*, written in the form of a dialogue among a practitioner, a "theorist," and a precentor. *De animae procreatione* 27–33 provides a detailed and useful exegesis of the musical ratios and mathematical means that appear in Plato's psychogony, leading to the conclusion that the ratios and numbers used by the Demiurge represent "the musicality and *harmonia* of the soul herself with herself, by which she, engendered with myriad goods, has filled the heaven" (1030c). Likewise, in *De musica*, the practical and historical discussion of Lysias is extended by the theorist Soterichus into the realm of Pythagorean mathematics and music as he describes the ways in which the Platonic ratios of *Timaeus* 35b–36b should be assigned to specific musical notes in the famous interlocking Pythagorean *harmonia* (Figure 24.2)

Following further consideration of the natures of the Unlimited, the Limited, and the Even-Odd (cf. Philolaus fr. 1–3), Soterichus observes that music is elevating, instructive, and useful. In summarizing the disciplines of harmonics and rhythmics, he moves from his predominantly Pythagorean position to draw on Aristoxenus in his recognition that the mind relies on a sharp sense of hearing in order to understand the continuity of effects and form critical judgments about the nature and *ethos* of music. The precentor Onesicrates caps the dialogue by returning the discussion to the Pythagorean realm, concluding that neither the universe nor the motion of the stars could have been established without music because God has arranged everything in accord with *harmonia*.

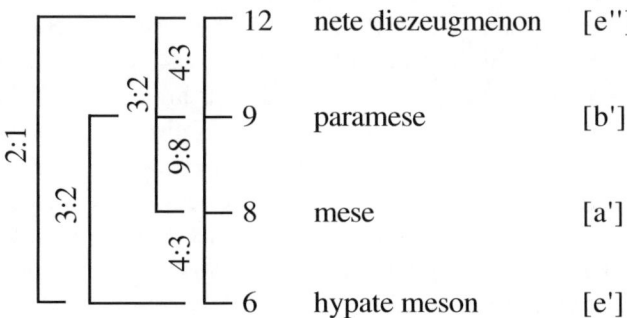

The mese (8) provides the harmonic mean between
the nete diezeugmenon (12) and the hypate meson
(6); the paramese (9) provides the arithmetic mean.

Figure 24.2 The description in *De musica* 22 (1138e–1139b) (Mathiesen 1999: 313)

Nicomachus of Gerasa

The writings of Nicomachus of Gerasa are among the most important sources for the tradition of Pythagorean mathematics and musical philosophy, especially his *Introductio arithmetica*, which survives in Greek and in a Latin translation by A. M. S. Boethius; his *Introductio musica*, which though lost in Greek is generally thought to be the source for the first four books of Boethius's *De institutione musica* (see below), the most influential work on music in Latin from at least the Carolingian period until well into the Renaissance; and his little *Manuale harmonices* and a few additional fragments. The *Manuale harmonices*, written in the form of a letter to a noble lady, is essentially a series of unrelated summaries that nonetheless preserve important Pythagorean source material. The third "chapter," for example, presents the planetary harmony as a prototype for the earliest scale of earthly music, which was originally a heptachord in imitation of the higher harmony. In the following chapters, Nicomachus explains how sound and number are related, how the planetary heptachord was expanded into an octave by Pythagoras, how Pythagoras discovered the basic harmonic ratios, how the mathematical means of the *Timaeus* can be understood, how the Pythagorean Philolaus constructed the *harmonia* of the octave (Philolaus fr. 6), and how the notes and tetrachords of the Greek musical system evolved from the old heptachord into their current arrangement.

Claudius Ptolemy

The *Harmonica* of Claudius Ptolemy, like *De musica* of Aristides Quintilianus, is arranged in three books, but the second and third books were either left incomplete at his death (as one of the scholia states) or partially lost at an early date. As it survives today in three somewhat different versions, Books I and II of the *Harmonica* explore both the Pythagorean and Aristoxenian traditions, which are then reformulated by Ptolemy himself to propose a more coherent and consistent system; the third book, which represents the work of Ptolemy's later redactors, relates the technical details of music to the order of the universe, addressing such topics as the harmoniousness of all things; relationships among consonant musical intervals, the parts of the soul, the primary virtues, and the aspects of the zodiac; and affinities among the sequence of notes and tetrachords in the Greek scale, the various genera, the *tonoi* (on this term, see Mathiesen 2001b), and the organization of the planetary spheres in the cosmos. Ptolemy does not provide illustrations of these relationships, but Figures 24.3 and 24.4 can be constructed from his descriptions.

All the parts in Figure 24.3 form a concord: in the soul, this is righteousness, and the entire *harmonia* of the system is the disposition of the philosopher. The arrangement in Figure 24.4 complements the threefold division of the soul and relates the various sciences to the three musical genera. Ptolemy provides only

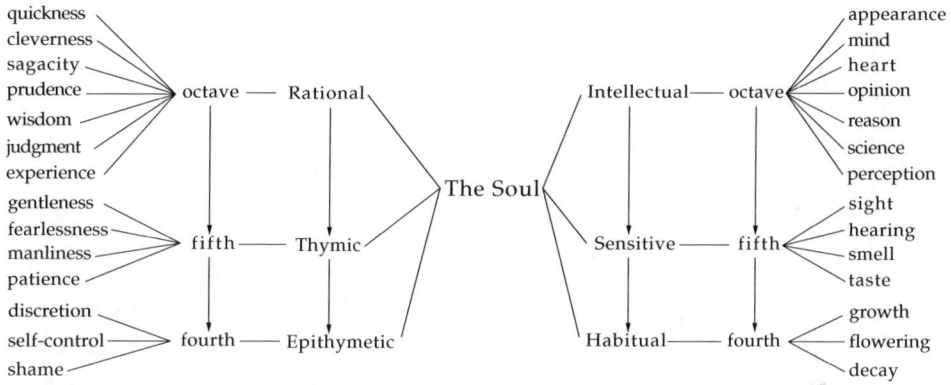

Figure 24.3 Ptolemy's construction of the soul, based on *Harmonica* 3.5 (Mathiesen 1999: 481)

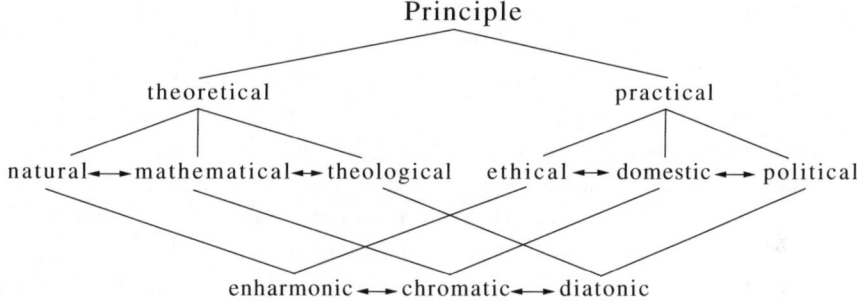

Figure 24.4 Ptolemy's construction of the soul, based on *Harmonica* 3.6 (Mathiesen 1999: 482)

vague reasons for the associations with the enharmonic and diatonic; for the chromatic, he emphasizes the importance of mathematics as a necessary intermediary in understanding the relationship between nature and the god, domestic action as an essential link between ethics and politics. All these interlocking relationships naturally lead to the conclusion that the various *tonoi* can affect the disposition of the soul, and Ptolemy (or his redactors) conclude Book III by showing the relationships among the various *tonoi*, the planetary spheres, and the zodiac.

Aristides Quintilianus

Aristides Quintilianus's *De musica* is a more systematic work: every technical detail of the Aristoxenian categories of harmonics, rhythmics, and metrics laid out in Book I (for the section on harmonics, see Aristides Quintilianus 1998) is related in one way or another in Book II to the effect of music on *ethos* and its role in education, and all of this material is then related to the soul and the order of the universe in Book III. For Aristides Quintilianus, music is an art transcending time and physical nature that reveals the order of the soul and the universe, as he makes clear in his initial definitions of music, the last of which marks out a neo-Platonist epistemology: "Music is a science of melos and of those things contingent to melos. Some define it as follows: 'the theoretical and practical art of perfect and instrumental melos'; and others thus: 'an art of the seemly in sounds and motions.' But we define it more fully and in accordance with our thesis: 'knowledge of the seemly in bodies and motions'" (*De musica* 1.4). These definitions lead to his famous classification of music (Figure 24.5).

Building upon the treatment of the Technical and Application subclasses in Book I, Aristides Quintilianus devotes Book II to the subclass of Expression in three topics, beginning with the soul and the use of music in education (based on Plato's *Phaedrus, Timaeus, Republic*, and *Laws*; Aristotle's *Politics*; and Cicero's *Republic*). He then considers the actualization of music and ways in which music influences behavior through its delivery and the sympathetic resonance of its masculine, feminine, and medial qualities with those of the soul (drawing on Damon of Athens, an elusive figure on whom Plato may have relied for many of his observations about music). This in turn leads to the ways in which musical instruments themselves possess genders and communicate ethical characteristics.

In its treatment of the remaining subclass, the Natural, Book III explains the ultimate goal of music, as anticipated at the very beginning of the treatise (1.1): "it [music] explains both the nature of numbers and the variety of proportions; it gradually reveals the *harmoniai* that are, through these, in all bodies; and . . . it is able to supply the ratios of the soul – the soul of each person separately and, as well, even the soul of the universe." Book III is divided into the two parts of the Natural subclass of music, the Arithmetic part reviewing the elements of Pythagorean musical mathematics, possibly drawn from Plutarch's *De animae*

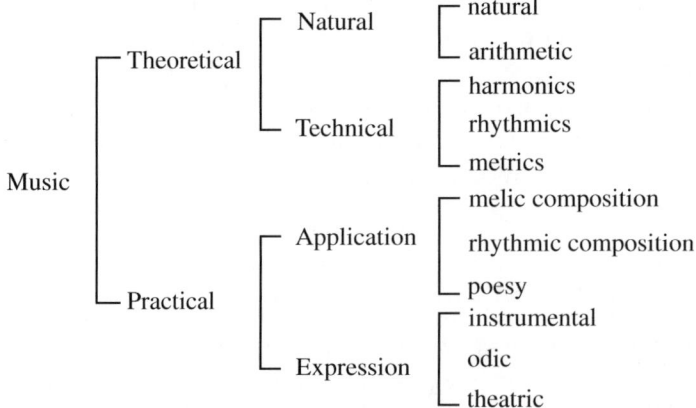

Figure 24.5 Aristides Quintilianus' subclasses of music in *De musica* 1.5 (Mathiesen 1999: 527)

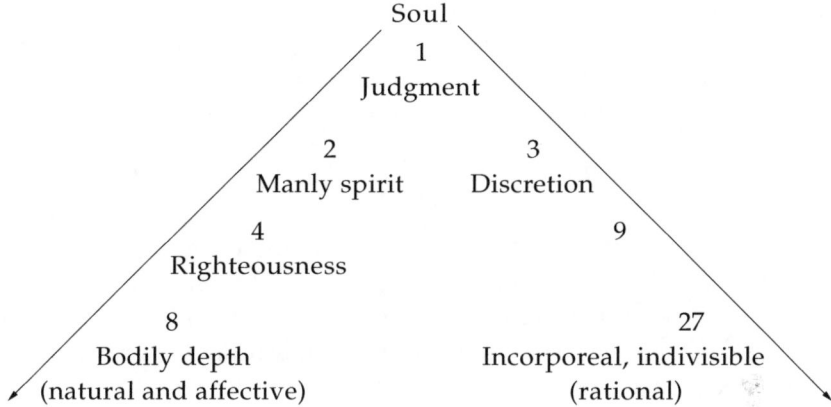

Figure 24.6 Aristides Quintilianus's design of the soul in *De musica* 3.24 (Mathiesen 1999: 575)

procreatione (see above) and Theon of Smyrna, while the Natural part relates "each particular to the universe altogether" (3.9). Every musical element (the genera, individual notes, tetrachords, intervals, scales, *tonoi*, etc.) is associated with some natural element (geometric shapes, five senses, four elements plus the ether, four seasons, the gestation of animals, the four triangles of the zodiac, the astrological actualities, and so on), leading to the relationships among the soul of the universe, the harmonic numbers and means, the virtues, and individual souls, all of which is essentially a gloss on Plato's *Timaeus* 35a–c (Figure 24.6)

Book III further notes that different types of melody may be seen as paralleling the two types of future (recalling Plotinus's *Enneads* II.3 [52], ch. 9, and III.1 [3], ch. 1; Plato's *Laws* 4 and 11 and Cicero's *Republic* 10.14–16): conjunct melody moving in sequential order is likened to the "what-will-be"; disjunct melody to the "what-may-be." Modulation in music, like other types of changes that occur in nature, can thus be further likened to a change of the "what-may-be." With all its paradigmatic qualities, Aristides Quintilianus concludes that music provides an agreeable preliminary study to philosophy as her "greatest consort and attendant." Thus, "we must afford to both philosophy and music their proper worth and honor; and we must unite their conjunction as most fit and legitimate" (*De musica* 3.27).

Latin writers of later antiquity

Latin writers of the first centuries of the Common Era were generally uninterested in musical speculation or a philosophy of music, and as the Latin West began to lose a first-hand knowledge of Greek, authors – insofar as they wished to speak of music at all – increasingly relied on intermediate encyclopedic works such as the *Disciplinae* of Varro, Vitruvius's *De architectura*, and Pliny's *Naturalis historia*, and on Cicero, Seneca, and Quintilian as accessible alternatives to

Plato and Aristotle. In these early centuries, only St. Augustine (354–430) and Anicius Manlius Severinus Boethius (*c*.480–525/26) devoted entire treatises to music, but several more centuries would pass before these treatises would begin to exert a substantial impact on medieval musical thought.

Augustine

The first five books of Augustine's *De musica* (written prior to his conversion) are devoted to a definition of music and a study of rhythm, relying on number and proportion. The sixth book (written after his conversion) is entirely different in style, tone, and content: here, number and proportion are projected from the corporeal to the incorporeal. Music has a sensory (and sensuous) dimension, but it also causes the soul to imitate the harmony of number in proportion, leading it to a love of God. By absorbing the neo-Platonic view of music and adapting it to Christianity, Augustine (in parallel with other Fathers of the Church, East and West) provides a compelling argument for music not only in Christian worship but also as a legitimate field for philosophical and theological study. These roles are pursued in two types of medieval musicography: the so-called *cantus* tradition of early medieval music theory, which evolves into the tradition of *musica practica*, and the tradition of *musica theorica* or *musica speculativa*.

Boethius

Boethius, fearing that knowledge of the Greek intellectual and scientific tradition was being lost in the decline of civilization, intended to undertake paraphrase translations of the major Greek texts in the four Pythagorean scientific disciplines (which he called the *quadrivium*); all of Aristotle's works on logic, ethics, and physics; and all of Plato, as well as showing the inherent harmony of these philosophical schools. He was unable to carry out such an ambitious program but did translate Porphyrius's *Isagoge*, most of Aristotle's *Organon* (with commentaries), and Pythagorean treatises on arithmetic and music by or based on Nicomachus (see above), all of this in addition to numerous theological works and *The Consolation of Philosophy*, his most famous work, written at the close of his life.

Book I of *De institutione musica* introduces the study of music as understood by the Pythagoreans, laying out a threefold division of *musica mundana, humana*, and *instrumentalis* and the distinction between the practitioner of music (*cantor*) and the true *musicus*, "one who exhibits the faculty of forming judgments according to speculation or reason relative and appropriate to music" (Boethius 1989: 51). The first four books are devoted to *musica instrumentalis* (i.e. the elements of harmonics and other principles of Greek music theory). Books II and III draw on Boethius's earlier *De institutione arithmetica* to demonstrate the Pythagorean mathematical tenets of Book I, while Book IV is devoted to a detailed (although somewhat confused) treatment of musical notation, the three genera of melody, and the "modes [*modi*], also called *tropoi* or *tonoi*." Book IV, in particular, had a profound influence on the system of modes (or tones) applied to the medieval system of classifying liturgical chant. Book V, which is incomplete, is based on the first book of Ptolemy's *Harmonica* and thus, as noted earlier, provides a sort of reconciliation of the Platonic and Aristotelian traditions, one of Boethius's aims in his grand intellectual project.

It seems that Boethius intended to include the second and third books of Ptolemy's *Harmonica* as Books VI and VII; had this been done, *De institutione musica* would indeed have ended with treatments of *musica humana* (the blending of the elements of the body and the soul (see Figures 24.3 and 24.4 above)) and *musica mundana* (the music of the cosmos). Nevertheless, even without this material, *De institutione musica* becomes the fundamental text for the study of *musica* within the quadrivium and is inescapable throughout the entire medieval tradition of *musica theorica*, into the Renaissance, while Boethius himself comes to be seen as an archetypal *musicus*.

Other authors

Apart from Augustine and Boethius, the most important Latin authors of the first seven centuries of the Common Era who made more than passing mention of music in their treatises include Censorinus (*De die natali*), Calcidius (*In Timaeum Platonis*), Macrobius (*In somnium Scipionis*), Martianus Capella (*De nuptiis Philologiae et Mercurii*), Cassiodorus (*Institutiones*; see Cassiodorus 1998), and Isidore of Seville (*Etymologiae*; see Isidore 1998). All of them convey some version of Pythagoras's discovery of the harmonic numbers, and some of them also include Pythagorean references to the harmony of the spheres (especially Calcidius and Macrobius, as would be expected) and the ability of music to influence behavior. Pythagorean and Aristoxenian references are frequently found together, sometimes conscientiously contrasted (as in Censorinus), sometimes without comment (as in Martianus Capella). These are highly eclectic works in which the musical content is primarily an intellectual adornment. Nevertheless, all of them were widely read in the Middle Ages and exerted considerable influence on later musical thought. (For a fuller treatment of all these figures, see Mathiesen 1999: ch. 7.)

The Carolingian Renaissance and beyond

The period following the death of Isidore (d. 636) until the establishment of the universities at Bologna, Paris, Oxford, and Cambridge in the eleventh and twelfth centuries was not propitious for further developments in musical philosophy in the East or West. The school of philosophy in Athens was closed in 529, and the university at Constantinople was replaced in the seventh century by the

Ecumenical College (controlled by the Church), which was closed in turn during the Iconoclast controversies in the eighth and ninth centuries. Emperor Justinian (r. 527–65) and his successors were preoccupied with the control (political and ecclesiastical) of the Western territories, the rise of Islam, and the depredations of Iconoclasm, which left little time for an interest in philosophy, literature, and the ancient sciences.

The ninth century, however, was a period of intellectual renewal – in the East under the Macedonian dynasty (867–1056), in the West following the coronation of Charlemagne as Holy Roman Emperor in 800, and in the Islamic empire with the establishment of the *House of Wisdom* (832) by the caliph al-Ma'mūn. Unfortunately, a short chapter such as this must limit itself to the barest outline of developments in the West, leaving it to readers to pursue the various figures and subjects, according to their interests (see the respective articles in Sadie 2001 for further information on almost all of the following figures; their names are given as in that reference work).

Invited by Charlemagne in 781 to join the palace school at Aachen, Alcuin of York (*c*.735–804) became Charlemagne's personal tutor and author of his educational program, including the *Admonitio generalis* of 789, which specifies the curriculum for the church schools to be established throughout the kingdom and – later – empire. Alcuin emphasized the study of the seven *artes* as the basis for philosophy and theology, which helped insure their acceptance as legitimate subjects in a Christian context, leading in turn to a renewed interest in the work of Martianus Capella and Boethius. The importance of music, in particular, was stressed by Johannes Scotus Eriugena (or Erigena; *c*.810–*c*.877), who undertook a fully comprehensive philosophy in *De divisione naturae*, as well as translations of the pseudonymous neo-Platonic *De caelesti hierarchia* (in which the orders of angels replace the sirens or muses in a new celestial harmony) and *De divinis nominibus*, both attributed (in 532) to Dionysius the Areopagite. Since, for Johannes, music and the universe are related through *harmonia* (*De divisione naturae* 3), art aids human beings in returning to the beautiful oneness of God (*De divinis nominibus* 4.7).

With music fully established in the Carolingian curriculum as one of the *artes* and as central to establishing and codifying a uniform liturgy throughout the empire, there was a demand for treatments explaining the theoretical principles of music while finding ways to make use of existing principles (frequently glossed with scriptural parallels) to address current practical issues, such as the organization of chant into a series of eight "tones" (four "authentic" and four "plagal"); classification of chants within the tones according to their *differentiae*; relationships of the eight tones to the Greek *tonoi*; definition of pitches and intervals, located through mathematical principles; relationship of the tones one to another by characteristic species of intervallic structure in a defining octave, fifth, or fourth; parsing musical structures into phrases, clauses, and sentences; rhythm and meter; systems of notation to assist in defining and stabilizing individual chants; polyphony (*organum*); and pedagogy. These treatments drew heavily on Boethius, the Latin grammarians, and to a lesser extent Macrobius, Censorinus, Martianus Capella, and Isidore. Thus, they reflected the approaches characteristic of these authors of late antiquity, as described above.

By the eleventh century, many of the practical issues had been addressed, especially those of definition and classification, and in the following centuries (until the mid-fifteenth), musical writings expanded in various different directions, some of which were broadly philosophical (e.g. those involving the classification of knowledge by William of Conches, Hugh of St. Victor, Alan of Lille, Raoul de Longchamp, Dominicus Gundissalinus, etc.; or those influenced – positively or negatively – by the revival of Aristotelianism such as Robert Grosseteste, Robert Kilwardby, Albertus Magnus, Thomas Aquinas, and Roger Bacon); some were practical and pedagogical (e.g. treatises by Guido of Arezzo, Johannes Cotto Afflighemensis, Johannes de Garlandia, Franco of Cologne, Johannes de Muris, Robert de Handlo, Marchetto da Padova, and various anonymous authors), although many of these contain philosophical analogies and observations, exhibit an interest in the identification and classification of musical genres (e.g. Johannes de Grocheio's *De musica*), or are adaptations of earlier works (e.g. Johannes de Muris's *Musica speculativa*, essentially an abridgment of Books I–III of Boethius's *De institutione musica*); and some attempted grand *summae*, perhaps influenced by Vincent de Beauvais or Aquinas (e.g. Hieronymus de Moravia, Walter Odington, Jacobus of Liège, John of Tewkesbury, Ugolino of Orvieto, and others). There was also a growing concern with the relationship between time and music (emerging from earlier treatments of rhythmics and metrics), especially within polyphonic compositions where the various lines might measure different simultaneous times. Thus, proportions and the nature of numbers, which had previously been considered primarily in regard to sound, play an increasing role in explaining the ever more complicated relationships of counterpoint.

Medieval interests in *harmonia*, mode and *tonos*, the influence of music on behavior, the measurement of time, the nature of sound, definitions of consonance and dissonance, the place of music in education and society, the harmony of the spheres, and so on, did not die out by any means with the rise of humanism, but by the mid-fifteenth century, writers concerned with music, whether they were philosophers such as Marsilio Ficino, pedagogues such as Vittorino da Feltre and Giorgio Anselmi, or theorists such as Johannes Gallicus, had found new sources of inspiration and a new approach to philosophy and music.

See also Music theory and philosophy (Chapter 46), Plato (Chapter 28), and Rhythm, melody, and harmony (Chapter 3).

References

Aristides Quintilianus (1998) "From *On Music*," in Strunk, pp. 47–66.

Aristotle (1998) "From the *Politics*," in Strunk, pp. 23–34.

Boethius, A.M.S. (1989) *Fundamentals of Music*, ed. C.V. Palisca, trans. C.M. Bower, New Haven: Yale University Press.

Cassiodorus (1998) "From *Fundamentals of Sacred and Secular Learning*," in Strunk, pp. 143–48.

Gaudentius (1998) "Harmonic Introduction," in Strunk, pp. 66–85.

Gibson, S. (2005) *Aristoxenus of Tarentum and the Birth of Musicology*, New York: Routledge.

Isidore of Seville (1998) "From the *Etymologies*," in Strunk, pp. 149–55.

Mathiesen, T.J. (1999) *Apollo's Lyre: Greek Music and Music Theory in Antiquity and the Middle Ages*, Lincoln: University of Nebraska Press.

—— (2001a) "Harmonia," in Sadie, vol. 10, pp. 851.

—— (2001b) "Tonos," in Sadie, vol. 25, p. 608.

Plato (1998a) "From the *Republic*," in Strunk, pp. 9–19.

—— (1998b) "From the *Timaeus*," in Strunk, pp. 19–23.

Sadie, S. (ed.) (2001) *The New Grove Dictionary of Music and Musicians*, 2nd edn, London: Macmillan.

Sextus Empiricus (1998) "Against the Musicians," in Strunk, pp. 94–109.

Strunk, O. (ed.) (1998) *Source Readings in Music History*, rev. edn L. Treitler, New York: Norton.

Further reading

Dyer, J. (2007) "The Place of *Musica* in Medieval Classifications of Knowledge," *Journal of Musicology* 24: 3–71. (This article and the next together provide an excellent treatment of the further development of *musica* in the Middle Ages.)

—— (2009) "Speculative 'Musica' and the Medieval University of Paris," *Music and Letters* 90: 177–204.

Schueller, H.M. (1988) *The Idea of Music: An Introduction to Musical Aesthetics in Antiquity and the Middle Ages*, Kalamazoo: Medieval Institute Publications, Western Michigan University. (Provides an extended and generally excellent treatment of the field.)

25

THE EARLY MODERN PERIOD

Jeanette Bicknell

The seventeenth and eighteenth centuries were a period of intense intellectual activity and exchange. The ongoing "scientific revolution," with its emphasis on rationality, experimentation, and systematicity, and the new ways of viewing the world that came with it, affected every area of scholarly interest, including music theory. This period marks more generally the birth of aesthetics as a separate philosophical specialty, as several important aesthetic concepts, including representation and expression, begin to take their modern forms. Music loses its status as an object of mainstream scientific study to take its place as one of the newly emerging "fine arts" in the modern system of the arts. The social context of listening changes, moving from church and court toward the concert hall. The Renaissance pre-eminence of vocal music gives way to the growing importance of instrumental music, thus increasingly changing the view of music from that of a rhetorical art to that of a language in its own right, a process that would be accomplished only by the end of the period.

This chapter surveys some of the major trends in early modern philosophy of music, placing them within the context of the philosophy and aesthetics of the time.

Music and rationalism in France

By the end of the sixteenth century, the empirical study of sound and vibration, undertaken both for practical purposes related to tuning and for its intrinsic interest, had upset traditional musical theory. This had been a blend of myth, scholastic dogma, mysticism, and numerology (Palisca 1961). One testimony to music's importance as an object of scientific study can be seen in the interest it held for the young and ambitious René Descartes (1596–1650). His first work was the *Compendium Musicae*, written in 1618 and presented to his friend and fellow scientist Isaac Beeckman. Posthumously published in 1650, an English translation appeared in 1653 and a French translation followed in 1668. Descartes's approach in the *Compendium* is predominately mathematical and mechanical. He discusses a number of themes, including physical acoustics, sensory perception, mathematical proportions and structures in music, and the effect of music on listeners. Although it was published posthumously, the *Compendium* was discussed earlier by other mathematicians and scientists, including Marin Mersenne (1588–1648), with whom Descartes exchanged letters on a number of musical topics (Descartes 1936–63, see in particular the letters of 4 and 18 March 1631, October 1631, April 1634 and 14 August 1634). Mersenne wrote voluminously on music, both in his correspondence with other researchers and in his published works. Although he thought mathematics of key importance in understanding aspects of sound and music, he insisted on rigorous experimentation and empirical testing of hypotheses. His huge and digressive *Harmonie universelle* (1630) brought to the fore the conflict between mean tone tuning and equal temperament for keyboard instruments (Cohen 1984).

Descartes's thought had a large impact on the intellectual currents taking shape over the next couple of centuries, no less in the philosophy of art and music than in other domains. His influence over the philosophy of music went in two different directions. First was his influence on the composer and music theorist Jean-Philippe Rameau (1683–1764). Rameau sought to unify Descartes's deductive and rationalist approach with the growing body of empirical findings on pitch and tone (Katz and HaCohen 2003). With Descartes's *Discourse on the Method* as his guide, Rameau attempted to rationalize and simplify the many rules that guided musical practice and composition and to reduce them to a few clear and evident axioms. Systematic reflection on music in the eighteenth century was dominated by Rameau's work, and his theory of the *corps sonore* ("sonorous body") has been identified as the most important contribution to that era's music theory (Thomas 1995). Drawing on the empirical work of Mersenne and Joseph Sauveur, Rameau claimed (erroneously) that all vibrating bodies, whether plucked strings, keyboard instruments or woodwinds, resonate consonant overtones (Paul 1970). The *corps sonore* provided the fundamental axiom of musical harmony. This had tremendous importance as it allegedly supported Rameau's view that melody is the unfolding of harmony. One practical result of Rameau's influence on eighteenth-century Classicism was the simplification of all musical language, especially harmony (Palisca 1961). Rameau went on to extend this theory beyond music to the other arts and science. In later years he was inspired by the occasionalism of Nicolas Malebranche (1638–1715) to apply the *corps sonore* to religion as well. His last works may be seen as occasionalist interpretations of music (Paul 1970).

Descartes's second important influence on philosophy of music was through his last published work, *The Passions of the Soul* (1649). In it, Descartes departed from tradition by proposing to treat the passions clinically, with the goal of understanding rather than judging them. The effect of the passions is mental but their cause is physical. Passions arise from the movement of "animal spirits" throughout the living body; Descartes offers detailed mechanistic explanations of the arousal of the different passions. Each of the passions is an expression or combination of one or more of the six different "primitive" passions – wonder, love, hatred, desire, joy and sadness. Descartes's conception of the passions influenced thinking about both the visual arts and music, the latter through the doctrine of the *Affektenlehre*. This was the idea that a musical work should represent abstract affections – one affect per work – by utilizing stereotyped musical figures. Descartes's theory of the passions provided a rationalist foundation for the *Affektenlehre* and helped broaden it beyond its origins in the theory of rhetoric (Neubauer 1986). Although the *Affektenlehre* had dominated Baroque composition, its influence gradually declined throughout the eighteenth century (Maniates 1969). It persisted among philosophers, especially those in France and Britain, longer than among composers (Schueller 1948)

Music and the French Enlightenment

On the frontispiece of the *Encyclopédie ou dictionnaire raisonné des sciences, des arts et des métiers* (1751–72) is an allegorical engraving illustrating the order and arrangement of the sciences, arts, and trades; it is revealing of eighteenth-century attitudes to music (Rex 1981). It depicts Music as sitting together with the imitative arts of Painting, Sculpture, and Architecture; yet she is slightly apart and situated behind them, gazing down modestly; her figure is partially obscured by the three other imitative arts. The imitative arts sit below larger figures that symbolize the different forms of poetry, with pride of place given to Epic Poetry. Music, depicted between the imitative arts (which appeal to the senses) and poetry (which appeals to the imagination), presumably appeals to both. However while Music is clearly allied with the imitative arts, she is nonetheless overshadowed by them. Her primary role is as their imitator. Music's status as an imitative and dependent art had been assumed in Abbé du Bos's (1670–1742) widely read "Réflexions critiques sur la poësie et sur la peinture" (1981). Du Bos was one of the first French writers to discuss the relationship between music and emotion (Maniates 1969). Just as painters imitate the forms and colors of nature, so too do musicians imitate the sounds that are natural signs of the passions. Art, whether poetry, painting, or music, will move an audience only if it is imitative.

A recurring theme in eighteenth-century French aesthetics was the hope of establishing an underlying unity for the fine arts (Maniates 1969). Aristotle's principle of imitation was expected to provide such a unity. The first systematic formulation of this hope was the widely read and frequently translated *Les beaux arts reduits à un meme principe* by Charles Batteux (1713–80). All of the arts imitate "beautiful" nature; music portrays the passions. The "natural" sounds associated with emotions are in music regulated, intensified, and polished. Batteux's account of musical imitation is more suggestive than clear or coherent. While some music is said to be similar to landscape painting, other music may express animate sounds which correspond to feelings, and is more like portrait painting. As he writes: "The heart has its intelligence independent of words, and when it is touched it has understood everything" (Batteux 1986: 266). Although Batteux's work was thoroughly criticized and seen to fall short of its target, his central conception of art as imitation became the received opinion (Neubauer 1986).

Several central themes of French Enlightenment thought on music are evident in the work of Jean le Rond d'Alembert (1717–83) who, as chief editor of the *Encyclopédie*, may be seen as a touchstone for the age. First is the centrality of the idea that music imitates the passions, a conviction shared by nearly every contemporary writer on music. In the "Preliminary Discourse" to the *Encyclopédie* (1995), he insists that music is a "kind of discourse" which expresses the passions. Composers may also imitate objects by imitating those passions that the objects typically arouse, although those of "vulgar senses" may not always grasp the imitation. Famously, d'Alembert claims that music which does not portray something is only noise. Second, is the attitude toward instrumental music, which was seen as decidedly inferior to vocal music. D'Alembert found little of distinction in the non-programmatic instrumental music of his day (Rex 1981) and he rejected the very idea of composing a flute sonata, since the flute properly expresses only sadness and tenderness (Oliver 1966). These ideas were echoed by the anonymous author of the article "*Instrumentale*" (possibly d'Alembert himself), who argues that musical instruments are to be classed as good or bad, depending on how closely they resemble the tonal qualities of the human voice (Oliver 1966). Finally, d'Alembert was typical of his age in his grappling with the influence of Rameau. D'Alembert simplified and popularized Rameau's theories in his *Elémens de musique théorique et pratique suivant les principes de M. Rameau*, thereby helping to disseminate Rameau's ideas throughout Europe (Christensen 1989). While Rameau was initially appreciative of the younger man's efforts on his behalf, the relations between him and the Encyclopedists deteriorated with the *Querelle des Bouffons* – the famous controversy that concerned the relative merits of French and Italian opera.

Denis Diderot (1713–84), d'Alembert's co-editor of the *Encyclopédie*, and their collaborator Jean-Jacques Rousseau (1712–78) also contributed to the era's music theory. Although they shared some basic presuppositions about music with d'Alembert and with their contemporaries, each succeeded in being more than an outlet for received views. Diderot did not produce a systematic aesthetic theory, but he tried to resolve some of the tensions in the prevailing neo-Classical views (Verba 1993). In his *Lettre sur les sourds et muets* Diderot assumes that music is imitative; yet he offers the intriguing suggestion that an artist's conception of nature can be a more important source of beauty than natural phenomena (Rex 1981). Although his early *Memoires* is very close to Rameau, in *Le neveau de Rameau* he allies himself with the views of Rousseau, against Rameau. While the 1771 *Leçons* is an explicit rejection of Rameau, especially the latter's Cartesian rationalism, Diderot ultimately re-asserted the values of reason and reflection even in music (Verba 1993). Like the work of Diderot, much of Rousseau's writing on music contends with the thought of Rameau. While Rameau's theory of the *corps sonore* implied that harmony was primary and natural, Rousseau defends the view that melody is primary, and that both harmony and melody are intrinsically linked to custom and convention (Thomas 1995). Rousseau was also typical of his age in accepting that instrumental music was inferior to vocal, and that music imitates the passions and objects that arouse passions. While Rousseau's debates with Rameau can be seen as part of an overall attack on Cartesian rationalism (Katz and HaCohen 2003), it is worth remembering that many of these debates took place within larger areas of agreement (Verba 1993).

By the final decades of the century, the idea that music is imitative was no longer accepted without question. Boyé (dates unknown) and Michel-Paul Guy de Chabanon (1730–92) were two forceful advocates of sensualism in music who rejected both imitation and expression in music. In his 1779 pamphlet "Musical Expression Relegated to the Ranks of Chimeras," Boyé denied that music could express emotion (Boyé 1986). He argued that music was more properly seen as a pleasure of the senses, not of intelligence. His work was known to and influenced the nineteenth-century formalist critic Eduard Hanslick (Maniates 1969), and through him, many later thinkers. Chabanon also denies that music is an imitative art, and seems to be the first to recognize fully the possibility of instrumental, non-programmatic music (Chabanon 1986; see also Neubauer 1986).

Philosophy of music in Britain

A few differences between early modern French and British philosophy of music are important and deserve note. Unlike the French (or the Germans), British writers on aesthetics were preoccupied by the project of finding similarities among the fine arts as a step in the search for a unified theory. A great number of pamphlets, essays, and treatises appeared that compared music with architecture, painting, and poetry. This search for correspondences among the arts contributed to the decrease in importance, in aesthetic theory, of imitation and the resultant increased importance of the concept of expression (Schueller 1953). Fewer of the participants in the debates over music in Britain were musicians or involved in practical problems of tuning and harmony. Most were men of letters interested in academic issues, and they tended to think in literary terms (Schueller 1948, 1950). This may have contributed to the durability of the idea, in Britain, that vocal music was clearly superior to instrumental. Finally, British aestheticians were influenced by the work of empiricist philosophers – specifically the doctrine of the association of ideas in John Locke (1632–1704) and David Hume (1711–76), and in the latter's doctrine of sympathy.

Locke's conception of the mind and its powers clearly influenced Francis Hutcheson (1694–1746), and this is apparent in his *An Inquiry concerning Beauty, Order, Harmony, and Design*. Although the work is concerned primarily with the visual arts, it does contain a discussion of beauty and the sources of pleasure in music. Just as we appreciate visual beauty by means of an internal sense of beauty, we appreciate harmony (the beautiful in music) by means of an internal "good ear." A person may see or hear well enough, yet be deficient with respect to the natural internal sense that allows one to take pleasure in the beautiful. Beauty in music may be "original," that is, it may refer to nothing but itself. The beauty of harmony is an example. Comparative or "relative" beauty in music arises from the musical imitation of the passions, which in turn causes the same passion is listeners, through a sort of sympathy or contagion. Hutcheson's ideas provide a backdrop against which many later writers form their own theories about music.

A Discourse on Music, Poetry, and Painting (1783) by James Harris (1709–80) is typical of its time in its arrangement of the arts in a hierarchy of value (with music occupying the lowest rung), its assumption that music is an imitative art, and its exclusive focus on music accompanying a text. Also typical is the assumption that music arouses affections in listeners. These affections in turn, through the power of association, raise ideas, which may themselves also raise affections. Although poetry is superior to music, poetry accompanied by music is more powerful that either of these arts can be on its own. A musical setting prepares the mind for the poetry that is sung and helps reinforce the affections and thus the ideas raised by poetry.

In Britain as in France, the idea that imitation provided the underlying unity among the fine arts began to be challenged in the latter half of the eighteenth century, and the idea of expression came to replace that of imitation in thinking about music. The doctrine of expression emerged from the doctrine of imitation yet differed from it. It was both a response to considerations of contemporary musical practice and a justification of those practices (Schueller 1948). Composer Charles Avison (1709–70), while generally approving of Harris's *Discourse*, argued in his very influential "An Essay on Musical Expression" (2004) that the concept of expression (by which he meant the arousal of affections) should replace imitation in thinking and writing about music. Avison's discussion continues the trend of discussing music that accompanies a text, rather than instrumental music. Composers should aim to express a poem's "general drift" and music is most powerful in the service of poetry when it does not draw attention to itself. It is worth noting that the "expression" promoted by Avison and his contemporaries was not private or individual; the feelings expressed by music were limited to positive social emotions (Schueller 1948). Indeed, Avison's work provides a foundation for the eighteenth-century evasion of violent and negative passions in music (Lippman 1992).

Daniel Webb (1719–98) similarly rejected the idea that music could express wholly painful emotions. In *Observations on the Correspondence between*

Poetry and Music he assumes (but does not wholly endorse) the Cartesian view of the passions and describes four ways in which music acts as a mechanism to bring about four different kinds of emotional responses in the soul (Webb 1986). When music is combined with words, the general responses become specific passions. Webb gives an important place to motion in music. Sound is not a single impression but a succession of impressions. Music can affect the passions because both have their origin in movement – the latter in the movement of animal spirits. Motion also helps explain the pleasure that we take in music. When we listen to music, pleasure arises from the succession of impressions that is created, and is augmented by the gradual transition from one kind of sound vibration to another. Webb's work was very influential and a German translation was published in 1771 (Lippman 1992).

Webb's interest in the sources of pleasure in music was shared by some of his contemporaries. Writers interested in this topic tended to rely heavily on the association of ideas (Schueller 1950). It was allowed that some of music's appeal is "natural" – coming from the sounds themselves, their succession, and their combination in pleasing concords. Yet much of pleasure we take in music was thought to come from the associations it aroused in the mind. The leading psychologist David Hartley (1705–57), in his *Observations on Man, His Frame, His Duty, and His Expectations* (1749), provides an explanation of pleasure in music within the context of his more pressing interest, the association of ideas. Richard Payne Knight (1750–1824), whose *Analytical Inquiry into the Principles of Taste* was published in 1805, is best discussed in the context of eighteenth-century classicism. He provides a thorough defense of associationism in music, distinguishing between "sentimental" pleasures that arise from habitual associations and could be felt by anyone, and "intellectual" associations available only to the learned. This indicates a departure from associationism proper.

The essay by Adam Smith (1723–90) on imitation and the arts (from his *Essays on Philosophical Subjects*) deserves to be better known, both for its influence and for its intrinsic value. It provides a comprehensive, carefully worked out account of imitation in the different arts. Pleasure arises from the disparity between an imitated object and its imitative medium. With regard to music, the disparity is between musical sound and the sounds of human emotion or of voices engaged in conversation. Music can effect states of mind and arouse the passions through a kind of "correspondence" between it and mental states. In keeping with eighteenth-century taste, Smith denies that music can easily imitate unsocial passions, and finds the imitative powers of instrumental music to be limited. Yet his views on instrumental music are more forward looking than those of most of his contemporaries. A work of instrumental music can "fill up" the mind on its own, without suggesting any imitated object, and its meaning may be complete on its own without requiring any interpretation: "[Instrumental] music seldom means to tell any particular story, or to imitate any particular event, or in general to suggest any particular object, distinct from that combination of sounds of which itself is composed" (Smith 1982: 205).

Thinking about music in Germany

Like their British counterparts, German theorists of music were influenced by the French, both positively and negatively. Descartes's rationalization of the emotions and mechanistic account of their functioning provided support for the *Affektenlehre*. Batteux's *Les beaux arts reduits à un meme principe*, translated into German in 1751 (Lippman 1992), inspired discussions over the role and limitations of imitation in music. As in France, Rameau's work prompted both praise and critical discussion. The earlier part of the period under discussion was marked by a defense of "galant" style – characterized by an emphasis on melody with light accompaniment only. While music and art in galant style appeared throughout Europe, its explicit philosophical defense was a German phenomenon, probably because it there co-existed with and was a contrast to the well-developed tradition of polyphonic music (Lippman 1992). In writing about music later in the eighteenth century, we find the emergence of proto-Romantic tendencies. Early modern German philosophy of music is different from that coming out of France and Britain in two important ways. First, most eighteenth-century German writers did not assume that instrumental music was inferior to vocal music (Katz and HaCohen 2003). Second, a long tradition in Germany, operative well into the nineteenth century, insisted on the ethical and religious significance of music (Lippman 1992).

Johann Mattheson (1681–1765) was an important and influential proponent of the new imported galant style. While his *Der Vollkommene Capellmeister* is firmly grounded in the conception of music as a rhetorical art and assumes the Cartesian psychology of the passions, its central purpose is an aesthetics of melody (Lippman 1992). Mattheson presents his own ideas in contrast to Rameau's "inexplicable contemplations" (Mattheson 1981: 488). He insists, contra Rameau and sounding very much like Rousseau, that pure melody is "the most beautiful and most natural thing in the world" and that harmony emerges from melody, not vice versa (Mattheson 1981: 300–1). The primacy of melody contributes to Mattheson's views on instrumental music. The human voice is natural and inborn, while musical instruments are a form of artifice. The relationship between vocal and instrumental music is like that between a mother and a daughter – the latter must try to emulate the former (Mattheson 1981: 418–19). Furthermore, an instrumental melody attempts to express without words as much as a vocal melody can express with words.

Mattheson is sometimes grouped together with Alexander Baumgarten (1714–62) and Moses Mendelssohn (1729–86) as the German rationalist aestheticians (Neubauer 1986). Baumgarten wrote nothing on music yet his writings on poetry influenced the emerging discussion on instrumental music. Influenced by Hutcheson, Mendelssohn continued the project of bringing the arts under a common principle, but rejected imitation as the comprehensive principle. Rather, he defined art as the sensuous expression of perfection. Mendelssohn contrasts "natural" signs, such as the human bodily movements and sounds that express the passions, with "arbitrary" signs such as words (Mendelssohn 1997: 177). Painting, sculpture, music, and dance employ natural signs; poetry and rhetoric, which appeal to the mind rather than to the senses, employ arbitrary signs. When music and poetry are combined, poetry is dominant. The expression of sentiment in music may be intense and moving, but it is indeterminate and general; the expression is individualized through words (Mendelssohn 1997: 185–7).

The final decades of the eighteenth century witnessed a marked change in the attitude to instrumental music and an interest in experiencing a broader range of expressivity in music. An aesthetics of "sentiment and yearning" with regard to music is found in novels of the period (Lippman 1992: 126). It is also evident in the writings of Wilhelm Heinrich Wackenroder (1773–98). He claims that there are two ways of listening to music: simple absorption in sound, or a kind of spiritual activity that music generates and sustains (Wackenroder 1981). Music, unlike poetry, seems capable of leading a separate existence. Music means "both everything and nothing" and is both finer and subtler than language (Wackenroder 1981: 250). Instrumental music's lack of determinate propositional content is linked with its capacity to prompt spiritual reveries. These themes are taken up and elaborated in the nineteenth century. Wackenroder was influenced by Karl Philipp Moritz (1757–93), another aesthetician who wrote little on music yet whose ideas contributed to the movement from a Rationalist to a Romantic aesthetics of music. Moritz dedicated his article "On the Concept of Self-Contained Perfection" to Mendelssohn. In it he proposes separating an internal, autonomous order of art from objectivist considerations (Neubauer 1986) and in doing so opens the door to the association of music with the ineffable.

See also Arousal theories (Chapter 20), Kant (Chapter 30), Opera (Chapter 41), Resemblance theories (Chapter 21), Rhythm, melody, and harmony (Chapter 3), and Rousseau (Chapter 29).

References

Alembert, J. Le Rond d' (1995 [1751]) *Preliminary Discourse to the Encyclopedia of Diderot*, trans. R.N. Schwab with W.E. Rex, Chicago: University of Chicago Press. Reprinted (2009) [ebook] by The *Encyclopedia of Diderot & d'Alembert Collaborative Translation Project*, available at University of Michigan Library, http://hdl.handle.net/2027/spo.did2222.0001.083.

Avison, C. (2004 [1752]) *Charles Avison's Essay on Musical Expression: With Related Writings by William Hayes and Charles Avison*, ed. P. Dubois, Aldershot: Ashgate Publishing.

Batteux, C. (1986 [1743]) "Les Beaux arts réduits à un meme principe," in Lippman (1986), pp. 259–67.

Boyé (1986 [1779]) "L'Expression musicale, mise au rang des chimères," in Lippman (1986), pp. 285–94.

Chabanon, M.P.G. de (1986 [1779]) "Observations sur la musique," in Lippman (1986), pp. 295–318.

Christensen, T. (1989) "Music Theory as Scientific Propaganda: The Case of D'Alembert's *Elémens de Musique*," *Journal of the History of Ideas* 50: 409–27.

Cohen, H.F. (1984) *Quantifying Music: The Science of Music at the first stage of the Scientific Revolution, 1580–1650*, Dordrecht: Kluwer Academic Publishers.

Descartes, R. (1936–63) *Correspondance*, 8 vols, ed. C. Adam and G. Milhaud, Paris: Presses universitaires de France.

—— (1961 [1650]) *Compendium of Music*, trans. W. Robert, Rome: American Institute of Musicology.

Du Bos, C. (1981 [1719]) "Réflexions critiques sur la poësie et sur la peinture," in le Huray and Day, pp. 17–22.

Harris, J. (1783) *A Discourse on Music, Poetry, and Painting* in *Three Treatises*, 4th edn, London: C. Novrge, pp. 47–103.

Hartley, D. (1749) *Observations on Man, His Frame, His Duty, and His Expectations*, 2 vols, Bath and London: Samuel Richardson.

Hutcheson, F. (2002 [1728]) *An Essay on the Nature and Conduct of the Passions and Affections, with Illustrations on the Moral Sense*, ed. A. Garrett, Indianapolis: Liberty Fund.

Katz, R. and HaCohen, R. (2003) *Tuning the Mind: Connecting Aesthetics to Cognitive Science*, New Brunswick: Transaction Publishers.

Knight, R.P. (1805) *Analytical Inquiry into the Principles of Taste*, London: T. Payne.

le Huray, P. and Day, J. (eds) (1981) *Music and Aesthetics in the Eighteenth and Early-Nineteenth Centuries*, Cambridge: Cambridge University Press.

Lippman, E. (ed.) (1986) *Musical Aesthetics: A Historical Reader: From Antiquity to the Eighteenth Century*, vol. 1, New York: Pendragon Press.

—— (1992) *A History of Western Musical Aesthetics*, Lincoln: University of Nebraska Press.

Maniates, M. (1969) "'*Sonate, Que me veux-tu?*': The Enigma of French Musical Aesthetics in the 18th Century," *Current Musicology* 9: 117–40.

Mattheson, J. (1981 [1739]) *Der Vollkommene Capellmeister: A Revised Translation and Critical Commentary*, trans. E.C. Harriss, Ann Arbor: UMI Research Press.

Mendelssohn, M. (1997 [1757]) "On the main principles of the fine arts and sciences," in *Philosophical Writings*, D.O. Dahlstrom (ed. and trans.), Cambridge: Cambridge University Press, pp. 169–91.

Neubauer, J. (1986) *The Emancipation of Music from Language: Departure from Mimesis in Eighteenth-Century Aesthetics*, New Haven: Yale University Press.

Oliver, A.R. (1966) *The Encyclopedists as Critics of Music*, New York: AMS Press Inc.

Palisca, C. (1961) "Scientific Empiricism in Musical Thought," in *Seventeenth Century Science and the Arts*, H.H. Rhys (ed.), Princeton: Princeton University Press, pp. 91–137.

Paul, C.B. (1970) "Jean-Philippe Rameau (1683–1764), the Musician as Philosophe," *Proceedings of the American Philosophical Society* 114: 140–54.

Rex, W.E. (1981) "A Propos of the Figure of Music in the Frontispiece of the *Encyclopédie*: Theories of Musical Imitation in d'Alembert, Rousseau and Diderot," in *International Musicological Society Report of the Twelfth Congress Berkeley 1977*, D. Heartz and B. Wade (eds), Basel: Bärenreiter Kassel, pp. 214–25.

Schueller, H.M. (1948) "'Imitation' and 'Expression' in British Music Criticism in the 18th Century," *The Musical Quarterly* 34: 544–66.

—— (1950) "The Pleasure of Music: Speculation in British Music Criticism 1750–1800," *Journal of Aesthetics and Art Criticism* 8: 155–71.

—— (1953) "Correspondences between Music and the Sister Arts, According to 18th Century Aesthetic Theory," *Journal of Aesthetics and Art Criticism* 11: 334–59.

Smith, A. (1982 [1795]) "Of the Nature of that Imitation which takes place in what are called the Imitative Arts," in *Essays on Philosophical Subjects*, W.P.D. Wightman and J.C. Bryce (eds), Indianapolis: Liberty Fund, pp. 176–213.

Thomas, D. (1995) *Music and the Origins of Language: Theories from the French Enlightenment*, Cambridge: Cambridge University Press.

Verba, C. (1993) *Music and the French Enlightenment: Reconstruction of a Dialogue 1750–1764*, Oxford: Clarendon Press.

Wackenroder, W.H. (1981 [1799]) "Phantasien über die Kunst," in le Huray and Day, pp. 241–50.

Webb, D. (1986 [1769]) "Observations on the correspondence between Poetry and Music," in Lippman (1986), pp. 201–14.

26

CONTINENTAL PHILOSOPHY AND MUSIC

Tiger C. Roholt

Since the second half of the twentieth century, Anglo-American philosophers have drawn a distinction between analytic and Continental philosophy. The distinction does not delineate two unified and methodologically distinct branches of philosophy; instead, one branch is defined in terms of methodology, the other in terms of place (Williams 2002). Classification by location is, of course, problematic in that some Continental philosophers hail from the United States or Britain, and some analytic philosophers from Europe. Unfortunately, the distinction often results in the impression that Continental philosophers are methodologically unified, whereas they are far from it; there is no unified Continental philosophical tradition (Critchley 1997, 2001).

Analytic and Continental philosophers share the broader philosophical tradition from the Presocratics through Kant; following Kant, the traditions diverge. The subsequent specifically Continental tradition involves a handful of often-disparate movements:

- *Nineteenth-Century German philosophy*; for example, J.G. Fichte (1762–1814), G.W.F. Hegel (1770–1831), F.W.J. Schelling (1775–1854), Arthur Schopenhauer (1788–1860), Friedrich Nietzsche (1844–1900).
- *Phenomenology and existentialism*; for example, Søren Kierkegaard (1813–1855), Edmund Husserl (1859–1938), Martin Heidegger (1889–1976), Jean-Paul Sartre (1905–80), Maurice Merleau-Ponty (1908–61).
- *Marxism and critical theory*; for example, Karl Marx (1818–1883), György Lukács (1885–1971), Walter Benjamin (1892–1940), Theodor W. Adorno (1903–1969).
- *Structuralism*; for example, Ferdinand de Saussure (1857–1913), Claude Lévi-Strauss (1908–2009).
- *Post-structuralism and postmodernism*; for example, Roland Barthes (1915–1980), Michel Foucault (1926–1984), Jacques Derrida (1930–2004).

A more thorough list would include hermeneutics, psychoanalysis, and French feminism.

In spite of the diversity of these movements, there are a few main themes that go some way toward circumscribing Continental philosophy; this chapter is structured around these themes: (1) history, (2) the sociopolitical, and (3) anti-scientism. (For other, related, ways of distinguishing between Continental and analytic philosophy see Cooper 1994 and Levy 2003.) Although a given philosopher may emphasize one or the other of these themes, typically, more than one theme runs through his or her work; nevertheless (in a decidedly un-Continental maneuver), for clarity's sake, I separate the themes; in each section, I focus upon one example of philosophy of music that is illustrative of a theme.

History

One sort of historicism involves the claim that our concepts, values, and institutions are not eternal. If what it means to be good, for example, is different from one historical period to the next, then we cannot make sense of what it means to be good at a given time without considering the concept's relations to various aspects of that historical context. What is more, a concept's elements may be particularly multi-layered, in time, and more or less hidden. In such a case, disambiguating the concept will require examining its historical development. Nietzsche's genealogical method is fit for this task; an illuminating reference to the method comes in his discussion of the "meaning" or purpose of punishment, found in his *On the Genealogy of Morality*: "(Today it is impossible to say for sure why we actually punish: all concepts in which an entire process is semiotically summarized elude definition; only that which has no history is definable.) . . . In an earlier stage, by contrast, the synthesis of 'meanings' still appears more soluble" (Nietzsche 1998: 53). As Maudemarie Clark writes,

> Nietzsche suggests that concepts influenced by history are like ropes held together by the intertwining of strands, rather than by a single strand running through the whole thing. To analyze such concepts is not to find necessary and sufficient conditions for their use but to disentangle the various strands that may have become so tightly woven together by the process of historical development that they seem inseparable.
>
> (1994: 22)

Lydia Goehr's *The Imaginary Museum of Musical Works* offers a genealogical account of the musical work. Goehr refers to her account as "historical" or "historically based ontology" but grants that genealogy is also an apt description (1992: 7, cf. 90 n. 1). Goehr's key methodological move is to shift the project of musical ontology away from the analytic approach of finding "the best description of the kind of *object* a work is" (1992: 4) toward giving an account of the emergence and function of the *concept* of the musical work in musical practice.

Her book is particularly instructive for highlighting core themes in Continental philosophy of music, because it involves examinations of paradigmatically analytic ontologies of musical works, criticisms of which bring out contrasts between the analytic and genealogical methods. According to Goehr, analytic philosophers have not been able to produce an adequate account of the musical work because they prioritize pure ontological concerns over aspects of musical practice: "While the analytic method has given theorists a way to account for the logic of phenomena, this has not been true for their empirical, historical, and, where relevant, their aesthetic character" (1992: 86). The misplaced priorities of analytic philosophers result in claims that clash with pretheoretical intuitions, and which fail to adequately account for the phenomena under consideration. An example is Nelson Goodman's position that even in the case of a brilliant performance of Beethoven's Fifth Symphony, if the performance contains a one-note mistake, it does not count as a performance of that work (see 1992: 40).

One reason Goehr prioritizes musical practice is that it is in the practice that we find data for properly elucidating the work-concept. In Goehr's account, "a methodological priority is given to making ontological claims compatible with the historical and conceptual complexity of the subject-matter with which they are associated" (1992: 89). Through an examination of the changes in the actions and attitudes of composers, audiences and conductors, changes in the ideals of notation and performance, changes in the function of scores, the shifting currents of aesthetics, etc., Goehr concludes that the concept of the musical work fully emerged around the year 1800. After 1800, the concept of the musical work had significant regulative force in the practice; for example, at around 1800, composers began to view their compositions as ends in themselves rather than as music to serve a religious or social function, notation became more specific, and audiences were increasingly reverent. "The ideal of *Werktreue* emerged to capture the new relation between work and performance as well as that between performer and composer. Performances and their performers were respectively subservient to works and their composers" (1992: 231). The ideal of *Werktreue*, in fact, "pervaded every aspect of practice in and after 1800 with full regulative force" (1992: 242). Lying behind these changes in musical practice were the emerging influences of idealist, formalist, and Romantic theories of art. Although music (with words) had previously attained fine art status as a mimetic art, through the influence of ideas such as artistic autonomy, expression, disinterested aesthetic experience, and genius, instrumental music rose in status to become "emancipated from the extra-musical" (1992: 155); the theoretical groundwork for the emergence of the work-concept was set: "Music would have to find an object that could be divorced from everyday contexts, form a part of a collection of works of art, and be contemplated purely aesthetically" (1992: 173–4).

The work-concept is, according to Goehr, a cultural concept, an emergent, open-textured concept. The continuity of open concepts "prompts us to trace the genealogy of the concept or the history of its meaning as it has functioned within the relevant practice as a way to understand both the concept and the associated practice" (1992: 93). The work-concept cannot be treated scientifically or naturalistically – such concepts are neither historically nor ideologically neutral. The work concept is also projective; works have a kind of fictional, "as if" existence as objects. (These details, it should be noted, take Goehr beyond Nietzsche.) Importantly, the work-concept is also regulative: "In their normative function, regulative concepts determine, stabilize, and order the structure of practices. Within classical music practice we compose works, produce performances of works, appreciate, analyse, and evaluate works. To do this successfully we need a particular kind of general understanding. Every time we talk about individual musical works we apply this general understanding to the specific cases. This understanding focuses upon one or more regulative concepts" (1992: 102–3). It is important to emphasize, however, that the work-concept does not regulate all musical practice; this aesthetic is not an ahistorical key to understanding all music; in her final chapter, Goehr notes that failing to keep this in mind "leads to our alienating music from its various socio-cultural contexts" (1992: 249). The warning delivers us to our next theme.

The sociopolitical

The relationship between music and politics is prominent in the Continental tradition. (See Chapter 36, Adorno, in this volume.) I opt here to consider the more specifically sociological view of art and music developed by Pierre Bourdieu (1930–2002). In explaining social phenomena, Bourdieu attempts to forge a middle path between two views he rejects: subjectivism and objectivism. Regarding subjectivism, Bourdieu rejects explanations of social phenomena given only in terms of an individual's free choices; one main target is Sartre's existentialism. Regarding objectivism, Bourdieu rejects the determinism and ahistoricism of some Marxism and structuralism. Structuralists (Claude Lévi-Strauss, for example) seek to explain social phenomena in terms of underlying, unconscious, universal patterns – deep structures, which are taken to be static, and examined synchronically. Although Bourdieu embraces certain aspects of structuralism, his analysis is decidedly historical. Bourdieu's notions of field and *habitus* are at the center of his attempt to avoid the subjectivist and objectivist positions, and at the center of his claims about art. A field ("the political field," "the academic field," "the artistic field") is an objective but not ahistorical social structure of relations between the positions individuals occupy, institutions, and unseen social forces against which individuals struggle. A field is more or less autonomous in the sense that it is "capable of formulating and imposing its own ends against external demands" (Bourdieu 1987: 256). The artistic field includes artists, art institutions such as galleries, academies, art schools, and "specialized agents" such as critics, art historians, and art dealers. The *habitus* is *not* a system of conscious, cognitive attitudes or beliefs, but rather, a system of *dispositions* acquired through one's experience in a social context; it is a system of acquired habits, an orientation or "feel for the game" (Bourdieu 1990b: 9). Maurice Merleau-Ponty's influence is manifest in Bourdieu's characterization of the *habitus* as "techniques of the body" or "embodied schemes" (Bourdieu 1984: 466–7). While the *habitus* is developed through engagement in a social context, it also shapes and sustains that context. The dispositions of the *habitus* are "principles which generate and organize practices and representations that can be objectively adapted to their outcomes without presupposing a conscious aiming at ends or an express mastery of the operations necessary in order to attain them" (Bourdieu 1990a: 53). One's *habitus* is not mechanistically determined by one's social context; it is constrained by it: "As an acquired system of generative schemes, the *habitus* makes possible the free production of all thoughts, perceptions and actions inherent in the particular conditions of its production – and only those. Through the *habitus*, the structure of which it is the product governs practice, not along the paths of mechanical determinism, but within the constraints and limits initially set on its inventions" (Bourdieu 1990a: 55).

Bourdieu takes the predominant view of art to be that artworks are autonomous objects which can only be recognized as such through disinterested perception, emphasizing form over extra-artistic function and over content (this description emerges largely from his interpretation of Kant). The aptitude for understanding and perceiving art in these terms is "the aesthetic disposition," the aesthetic *habitus*; a person with such competency has "taste," the ability to exercise "the pure gaze" (Bourdieu 1987). In his criticism of this tradition, Bourdieu argues that philosophers are mistaken in basing universal, ahistorical claims on a historically contingent attitude; philosophers do not realize that the *data* for these claims consist of their own experience, rather than a "pure" experience: "Kant's analysis of the judgment of taste finds its real basis in a set of aesthetic principles which are the universalization of the dispositions associated with a particular social and economic condition" (Bourdieu 1984: 493). Bourdieu argues that the aesthetic disposition is much more prevalent in individuals with bourgeois origins, and much less prevalent in working-class individuals. (Many of Bourdieu's claims are informed by surveys conducted in France in the 1960s and 1970s; while Bourdieu acknowledges the potential problem of relying upon such surveys in making the same claims about other cultures, he believes that cultural similarities provide traction for doing so (see Bourdieu 1984: xi–xiv).) The bourgeoisie treat the aesthetic disposition as if it were a natural gift possessed by superior individuals; according to Bourdieu, it is a historical invention. The aesthetic disposition is a product of formal education, but even more importantly, of social origin; it is a kind of cultural code which is cultivated through a bourgeois home life, frequenting of museums, a privileged education, etc. Thus, the artistic field fosters the aesthetic disposition in individuals who occupy various roles; artworks are cultural objects constituted within an artistic field by individuals possessing the aesthetic disposition; and the field is sustained by that very disposition.

Working-class individuals tend to be interested in art for reasons of content rather than form, preferring artworks on the basis of the real-world values depicted. According to Bourdieu, this "popular aesthetic" is not a true aesthetic (for a criticism, see Shusterman 2000); rather, it is defined negatively in contrast to the bourgeois aesthetic. Thus, for Bourdieu, one possesses the bourgeois aesthetic disposition or one lacks taste. It is possible to determine which class a person belongs to by determining which kinds of art she prefers; taste is a mark of distinction. Moreover, when one manifests one's taste, those preferences *justify* her class status. Bourdieu claims that the aesthetic disposition is required in order to appreciate the trappings of a bourgeois lifestyle (fine furniture, haute couture, gourmet meals, etc.); therefore, when a person prefers popular music, for example, this preference demonstrates that she does not have taste, which *justifies* her not having access to fine art *and* the finer things in general. It is in this sense that taste functions as a tool of domination; taste not only *marks* those with different preferences as lower in social status, it also *legitimizes* the status.

Instrumental music stands out as an art that *distinguishes* more clearly than other arts. Not possessing the code for understanding art is most obvious in cases where representational elements are not present to allow one lacking the *habitus* leverage for a partial understanding: "nothing more clearly affirms one's 'class', nothing more infallibly classifies, than tastes in music" (Bourdieu 1984: 18). In addition, the opportunities for acquiring the requisite dispositions are more difficult to come by for working-class individuals; for example, attending concerts is rarer than attending museums. Referring to the bracketing of real-world concerns required of disinterested perception, Bourdieu writes, "music represents the most radical and most absolute form of the negation of the world, and especially the social world, which the bourgeois ethos tends to demand of all forms of art" (1984: 19). Thus, even more than challenging arts such as post-impressionist painting (think of Cézanne's perspectival "distortions"), music *marks* class distinctions.

Bourdieu also considers a fine-grained way of distinguishing among those who possess the aesthetic disposition. Consider two *manners* of engaging with art that betray the conditions of acquisition of the *habitus*. There is a subtlety and ease of engagement in the artistic field that a person with working-class origins is unlikely to acquire, even once he acquires the aesthetic disposition through formal education. The bourgeois individual has the benefit of a slow inculcation within the family and social circles, which allows her to internalize the aesthetic disposition prior to formal education; this slow inculcation "confers the self-certainty which accompanies the certainty of possessing cultural legitimacy, and the ease which is the touchstone of excellence; it produces the paradoxical relationship to culture made up of self-confidence amid (relative) ignorance and of casualness amid familiarity, which bourgeois families hand down to their offspring as if it were an heirloom" (Bourdieu 1984: 66).

When the child grows up in a household in which music is not only listened to (on hi-fi or radio nowadays) but also performed (the 'musical mother' of bourgeois autobiography), and a fortiori when the child is introduced at an early age to a 'noble' instrument – especially the piano – the effect is at least to produce a more familiar relationship to music, which differs from the always somewhat distant, contemplative and often verbose relation of those who have come to music through concerts or even only through records.

(Bourdieu 1984: 75)

Anti-scientism

Scientism is the view that the model of the natural sciences should be the model for all philosophy, or, more generally, all knowledge acquisition. Key aspects of this model include the belief in the possibility of objective observation (Thomas Nagel's detached, impartial "view from nowhere" (1989)) and, relatedly, the viability of removing the object under investigation from its context. Anti-scientism involves the claim that there is no "view from nowhere," and that abstraction is not the preferred mode of examining every kind of phenomenon. Anti-scientism resonates throughout much Continental philosophy (see Cooper 1994). If one believes that there are phenomena which cannot be elucidated through scientific investigation, value-laden phenomena such as music are likely to be high on that list. Anti-scientism is implicit in the historical and social themes discussed above: investigating music abstractly illegitimately sets aside its historicity and social context; if the investigator takes herself to be a purely objective observer, she fails to consider the way in which she, herself, is situated in a context that has shaped her perspective.

In this section, I want to focus upon a particular stripe of anti-scientism in phenomenology, centering on Heidegger's distinction between presence-at-hand (*Vorhandenheit*) and readiness-to-hand (*Zuhandenheit*) (Heidegger 1962); I will work up to this distinction by considering *possession*, the centerpiece of the final chapter of Thomas Clifton's (1935–1978) *Music as Heard* (1983). Clifton holds that music cannot be distinguished from mere sounds by examining sound-events alone: "music, whatever else it is, is not factually in the world the way trees and mountains are" (1983: 3); "there is no empirical difference between sound and music, the difference is decided by human acts" (1983: 272). Listeners *constitute* music; listeners bring music into being. (For Clifton, constitution is much more individualistic than it is for the likes of Bourdieu.) Mere sounds do not become music as long as they are experientially *separated* from the listener. A certain kind of perceptual activity closes the experiential gap between sounds and a listener; this gap-closing is possession.

Among the elements of possession are belief, freedom, willing, caring, and consent. Possession involves two different kinds of belief acts, which typically

290

go unnoticed. First, when I experience music, I believe that it is *music* that I am experiencing, and that the experience is *mine*. This is how the music becomes a phenomenon *for me*. Second, in the actual moments of such an aesthetic experience we *neutralize* our beliefs concerning empirical facts about the music: "neutralizing all references to its purely physical qualities" (Clifton 1983: 281). ("Neutralization" is the term Clifton prefers for Husserl's "phenomenological reduction," which is a methodological change in standpoint in which we set aside naturalistic assumptions.) Regarding freedom and will, Clifton points out that hearing mere sounds does not require an act of will; we involuntarily notice sounds, whereas the experience of music requires an act of will that involves consent and care; "we cannot simply will music into existence" (1983: 276), but we can, by an effort of will, engage with sounds presented to us, organizing them. Moreover, we do not have a neutral, give-or-take attitude toward the emerging music, as when we merely notice sounds, which keeps them at a distance, but one of care, which is "a fundamental feeling stemming from an attitude of concern for the object of possession" (1983: 281). Our care or concern for the music motivates us to close the gap between ourselves and music, and while this results in a loss of freedom, our yielding or consenting to the music is voluntary.

The chapter in which Clifton discusses possession is called "The Stratum of Feeling." Possession is the central concept in the chapter because Clifton claims that possession is a primordial feeling which "underlies and prepares [the way] for more recognizable feelings" (1983: 272). (Possession is a kind of gap-closing between the experiencer and another person, an object, or event, which makes feeling or emotion possible.) As a result of possession:

> The self enters the phenomenal world of the music by neutralizing all references to its purely physical qualities . . . The self-sphere extends its perimeter to include music. If I become tender and dignified, it is because the music is tender and dignified . . . In the presence of music, I qualify my own ontology: I *am* tender and dignified.
>
> (Clifton 1983: 281–2)

Clifton is explicit that this is not a mere arousal of emotions but ontology; it "signifies an accord with a world of music" (1983: 284).

Clifton characterizes his account of possession in terms of Heidegger's distinction between presence-at-hand and readiness-to-hand. A few words on the distinction: pieces of *equipment* are items we use in order to accomplish something (a hammer, a writing pen, shoes). We can *make sense of* a hammer in two ways. First, a hammer can be rendered intelligible as a self-sufficient substance with properties (it might have a brown, wooden handle, a shiny metal head, and weigh 5 pounds). This is the "way of being" (mode of intelligibility) called presence-at-hand. Second, according to Heidegger, this is not the way of being of equipment. Rather, equipment is understood holistically in terms of what it is used for, that is, in terms of its function in an equipmental whole; this is the *way of being* (mode of intelligibility) called readiness-to-hand. Thus, a hammer is properly understood as a thing for pounding nails, in connection with wood, carpenters, cabinets, houses, and so on. If we want to understand a piece of equipment properly (in accord with its way of being), we should not rely on detached observation (the latter is how we would discover its properties in present-at-hand terms). In order to understand a piece of equipment we must *use it* (Heidegger 1962; see also Dreyfus 1990). Loosely speaking, one might think of this as a way of drawing a distinction between understanding an object from a *detached* (present-at-hand) perspective, on the one hand, and an *engaged* (ready-to-hand) perspective, on the other.

Returning to music, consider that we can make sense of sounds in either of these two ways. Treating the sounds made by an orchestra performing Beethoven's Fifth Symphony as mere sounds is to remain disengaged, detached; it is to characterize them as present-at-hand. Clifton suggests that possession involves rendering sounds intelligible as equipment; through an engaged perspective, we *use* sounds musically. When sounds are musical, they are ready-to-hand; once we *possess* the sounds, music emerges, the sounds acquire musical meaning and value. "In a sense, the present-at-hand is always there, just as the sounds of a melody are always there, but to the degree that the thing (the melody) has value, we don't notice it as a mere acoustical event" (1983: 291). "In other words, prior to the music's being ready-to-hand, its sounds already occupy a definite position in objective space-time. They lie *there*, up there on the stage, or coming out of a speaker. With the possessive act, this relation is changed . . . the sounds *of* music comprise the equipment which we use to accomplish the task of discovering sense *in* the music" (1983: 292).

In what way does this view constitute a potential criticism of, or challenge to, the scientific investigation of music? If we accept Heidegger's distinction between presence-at-hand and readiness-to-hand, and Clifton's application of it to music, then we will find fault with experiments in which music is treated in present-at-hand terms. For example, we will most likely not accept the relevance to music of a psychology experiment that involves subjects reporting on their perceptions of sine tones presented in no musical context; in such a case, the subjects are reporting on their perceptions of sounds rather than music. What should we say about experiments that involve subjects reporting on perceptions of, for example, a recording of Beethoven's Fifth? Even though the stimulus is a musical recording, that does not guarantee that the subjects are reporting on engaged musical experiences; they may be reporting on detached perceptions of the recording. We will want to know just how the experiment is devised so as to ensure engaged perception. Finally, even if psychologists ensure that their subjects are reporting on engaged experiences of music, in drawing conclusions based on such reports, we will want to ensure that psychologists do not themselves *make sense of* the reports in present-at-hand terms.

Above, we have considered three senses in which Continental philosophers reject the viability of examining music in the abstract.

See also Adorno (Chapter 36); Kant (Chapter 30); Music and gender (Chapter 52); Music and politics (Chapter 50); Nietzsche (Chapter 32); Ontology (Chapter 4); Phenomenology of music (Chapter 53); Psychology of music (Chapter 55); Schopenhauer (Chapter 31); and Sociology and cultural studies (Chapter 51).

References

Bourdieu, P. (1984 [1979]) *Distinction: A Social Critique of the Judgement of Taste*, trans. R. Nice, Cambridge: Harvard University Press.

—— (1987) "The Historical Genesis of a Pure Aesthetic," *The Journal of Aesthetics and Art Criticism* 46: 201–10.

—— (1990a [1980]) *The Logic of Practice*, trans. R. Nice, Palo Alto: Stanford University Press.

—— (1990b) *In Other Words: Essays toward a Reflexive Sociology*, trans. M. Adamson, Palo Alto: Stanford University Press.

Clark, M. (1994) "Nietzsche's Immoralism and the Concept of Morality," in R. Schacht (ed.) *Nietzsche, Genealogy, Morality: Essays on Nietzsche's Genealogy of Morals*, Berkeley: University of California Press, pp. 15–34.

Clifton, T. (1983) *Music as Heard: A Study in Applied Phenomenology*, New Haven: Yale University Press.

Cooper, D.E. (1994) "The Presidential Address: Analytical and Continental Philosophy," *Proceedings of the Aristotelian Society* 94: 1–18.

Critchley, S. (1997) "What Is Continental Philosophy," *International Journal of Philosophical Studies* 5: 347–65.

—— (2001) *Continental Philosophy: A Very Short Introduction*, Oxford: Oxford University Press.

Dreyfus, H. (1990) *Being-in-the-World*, Cambridge: MIT Press.

Goehr, L. (1992) *The Imaginary Museum of Musical Works*, Oxford: Clarendon Press.

Heidegger, M. (1962 [1927]) *Being and Time*, trans. J. Macquarrie and E. Robinson, New York: Harper and Row.

Levy, N. (2003) "Analytic and Continental Philosophy: Explaining the Differences," *Metaphilosophy* 34: 284–304.

Nagel, T. (1989) *The View from Nowhere*, New York: Oxford University Press.

Nietzsche, F. (1998 [1887]) *On the Genealogy of Morality*, trans. M. Clark and A. J. Swensen, Indianapolis: Hackett.

Shusterman, R. (2000) *Performing Live: Aesthetic Alternatives for the Ends of Art*, Ithaca: Cornell University Press.

Williams, B. (2002) "Contemporary Philosophy: A Second Look," in N. Bunnin and E.P. Tsui-James (eds) *The Blackwell Companion to Philosophy*, 2nd edn, Malden: Blackwell, pp. 23–34.

27
ANALYTIC PHILOSOPHY AND MUSIC

Stephen Davies

Reflecting in 2000 on the first forty years of the *British Journal of Aesthetics*, its then editor, Peter Lamarque, notes a remarkable growth in the number of submissions and printed papers on music, to the point where "the need has arisen to turn down papers on music just for the sake of balance in the journal. This growth of interest is noteworthy for it was not predictable twenty years ago" (Lamarque 2000: 15). "Twenty years ago" – that is, 1980 – saw the publication of several works that played an important role in awakening interest in the philosophy of music and in identifying key topics and positions. They were Peter Kivy's *The Corded Shell* and my "The Expression of Emotion in Music," which presented similar analyses of music's expressiveness, according to which, like the face of the basset hound, music displays an expressive appearance rather than an experienced emotion; Jerrold Levinson's "What a Musical Work Is," which focused attention on questions of musical ontology, such as whether musical works are created or discovered; Thomas Carson Mark's "On Works of Virtuosity," which dealt with the nature and purpose of performance, and Malcolm Budd's "The Repudiation of Emotion: Hanslick on Music," which revealed Eduard Hanslick's nineteenth-century formalist arguments as relevant to the contemporary debate. While such writings had predecessors and precedents to which I return below, Lamarque is correct to observe that the number and influence of these would not have led one to predict the expansion of interest in music aesthetics over the past three decades. (To give just one indication of this growth, recent years have seen five book-length introductions to the philosophy of music.)

The term "analytic" philosophy is used to refer to the style, method, and subject matter of much English-language philosophy from the early twentieth century, especially as originally practiced by Bertrand Russell and G. E. Moore. The contrast is with Continental philosophy, an approach that is often subjectively focused and involves the creation of all-encompassing, elaborate metaphysical systems, or alternatively is directed to elucidating and comparing the theories of the "great men" of the tradition. Analytic philosophy supposedly differs in its commitments to objective, clear argument and to an interpersonal, empirically oriented approach, and it eschews grand theories in favor of treating specific philosophical issues and problems in a piecemeal or cumulative fashion.

As we have just seen, the analytic philosophy of music achieved its current prominence only recently. Accordingly, in the final part of this chapter, I focus on the literature since about 1980. But the roots of analytic philosophy generally and of musical aesthetics reach deep into the philosophical past, so I begin with a survey of earlier thought on music, before briefly reviewing what analytic philosophers wrote about music between 1900 and 1980.

Music in the development of aesthetic thought

Greek philosophers were principally interested in two matters regarding music. One was the systematization of the mathematical features underpinning acoustic phenomena. This topic was not of purely theoretic interest; it supposedly provided a route to understanding the inner harmony of the cosmos and the principles of creation (see Chapter 28, "Plato," in this volume), though Aristotle ridiculed the idea of cosmic music (Aristotle 1939: 90b12–291a25). The second concern was the influence of music on feeling, character, and action. As well as discussion of music theory, this involved reflection on the connection between music and ethics, on the proper role of music in education, and on the control of music in the state. Aristotle did treat music as a topic in its own right (Aristotle 1953: 917b19–923a4), but his concerns there were mainly about acoustics and the rules governing the scales of the Greek modes.

As in other matters, Greek models of music dominated into the Renaissance. In *De Musica*, Augustine analyzes music in terms of the mathematical principles it exemplifies, with these connecting to the form of the human soul and a hierarchy of divinity; he also considers what makes for good, which is to say ethically proper, music. The tradition of treating music as a sub-branch of mathematics, persisted – for example, in Aquinas and, later, Leibniz – as did the doctrine that music is correlated with the movement and astrological function of the planets – for example, in Boethius and in Johannes Kepler's *Harmonices mundi libri V* of 1619. To such views, ancient church philosophers added the doctrine that it is the function of music to make sacred texts vivid and beautiful and to exhibit the perfection of creation. The sensuous appeal of music was perceived to be in tension with music's higher purposes, however. The church authorities constantly strove to curb moves to melisma and polyphony, to the extent that these got in the way of the devotional text's clear expression, and frowned on any purely aesthetic enjoyment of music's voluptuousness. Augustine is typical; in his *Confessions* he uses music as an example of the seductiveness of worldly matters. (For discussion, see Schueller 1988.)

With the growing secularization of music as power shifted from the church to the court, a new kind of theory took root, beginning with *Musica reservata* and *Maniera* in the sixteenth century. These movements, as presented by composers and music theorists, saw the function of music as the imitation of nature, especially through the expressive interpretation of the sung text, and led at the beginning of the seventeenth century to the *Camerata* and the earliest operas. In the eighteenth century, these ideas were expressed as the "doctrine of affect," *Affektenlehre*, which held that music could associate tones with feelings by employing the expressive principles of rhetoric and oratory. (For discussion, see Kivy 1999: 108–17.)

Whereas music was traditionally grouped with astronomy and mathematics, the modern classification of the arts that emerged in the eighteenth century linked it with poetry, drama, painting, sculpture, and architecture. The same period saw the emergence of theories of aesthetics. These were sometimes taken up by composers and music theorists. Among philosophers, Hume and Kant affirmed the centrality of aesthetics in philosophical thought, and both are important influences on analytic philosophy, but neither had much to say about music in particular. Hume often mentioned music but did not offer a distinctive aesthetic theory concerning it. Kant was notoriously uninterested in music and ranked it low among the arts – nearer the agreeable than the beautiful – and compared it to wallpaper. (But see Schueller 1955.)

It was Arthur Schopenhauer, in *The World as Will and Representation* of 1818 (with a second volume in 1844), who provided the first major philosophical treatise to make music pre-eminent among the arts. Whereas the other arts are copies of the Ideas, which are in turn copies of the Will, music is an ideal, unmediated expression of the Will itself; it presents not examples of life and things but, directly, their necessary essences. This is because its elements and structure are analogues of the elements and form of the Will. Moreover, whereas life and our experience of the Will are ordinarily painful, the encounter with music is free from pain and therefore uniquely valuable. (For discussion, see Budd 1985; Lippman 1992.)

Schopenhauer's views profoundly influenced both Richard Wagner (Tanner 1996) and the philosopher Friedrich Nietzsche (Higgins 1986), but their impact is not apparent in contemporary analytic music aesthetics. No doubt this is because Schopenhauer's account of music is hostage to his unappealing and obscure metaphysics, as well as to his pessimistic characterization of human existence as necessarily one of frustration and pain. A similar difficulty attends G. W. F. Hegel's theory (lectures on aesthetics 1820, 1823, 1826) according to which each of the arts, including music, functions as a distinct step in a historical process through which the nature of Spirit is progressively revealed. The arts discharged their functions in this process prior to the Christian era. The place of music in this process was to represent feeling, but it is inferior to poetry because of its non-conceptual nature (Bungay 1984).

The Romantic movement of the time took from Kant his views both of genuine creation as unconstrained by rules and of great artists as geniuses, and married these with the importance of expression (rather than imitation or representation), especially self-expression, in art. But Kant's formalism and his account of the cognitive value of art (as arising from free play between the imagination and understanding) was no less influential, and the tension between these models provoked the polemical debates that pitted, for example, the music of Wagner against that of Johannes Brahms. Within analytic aesthetics, the debate continues with Peter Kivy's defense of an enhanced formalism and Jenefer Robinson's defense of a Romantic account of musical expression (Kivy 1980, 1989; Robinson 2005).

A partisan in this exchange, the music critic Eduard Hanslick, authored one of the most enduringly influential works in music aesthetics, *On the Musically Beautiful*, which first appeared in 1854 but was reissued in a series of editions, the eighth and last of which was in 1891. Hanslick, who is regarded as an arch-formalist, argued that music is not capable of expressing emotion, but that its tonally moving forms are a source of a special kind of beauty. (For a much earlier version of a similar view, see Philodemus' *On Music* of the first century BCE.) Hanslick's approach points the way for the analytic philosophy of music not only because his position is closely argued with musical examples and in it he clearly distinguishes properties of the music from the listener's response, but also because he has a "modern" view of the emotions, according to which they are not merely sensational or visceral motions but are directed to objects and involve the cognitive characterization of those objects under emotion-relevant descriptions or conceptions.

Hanslick's formalism echoes the medieval equation of beauty with balance, proportion, and unity, as well as Kantian aesthetic formalism. And he was hardly alone in regarding music's expressiveness as the central topic to be addressed in a philosophy of music. But more than any other, he established the agenda for the debate that was to follow. The key move in Hanslick's challenge to claims for music's expressive power lies in his view that music cannot present the cognitive, intensional elements that are central to cases of genuine emotional experience and expression. One way or another, many late-twentieth century theories focus on how to address this issue, arguing either that music can present sufficient of the cognitive aspects of emotions to express them, or that not all emotions involve such elements. (For discussion, see Budd 1985; Kivy 1990a; Lippman 1992; Davies 1994.)

The psychologist Edmund Gurney attempted to adopt a scientific approach to music aesthetics in his *The Power of Sound* of 1880, a wide-ranging (and verbose) book that covers acoustics, composition, rhythm, melody, the place of music in society, and music criticism. Gurney's theories were largely ignored by philosophers and music theorists, but it is noteworthy that they are critically discussed alongside those of Schopenhauer and Hanslick by Malcolm Budd

(1985) and that they have inspired a distinctive account from Jerrold Levinson (1997) of how musical understanding proceeds. Levinson defends Gurney's view that large-scale form is, at most, of minor relevance to the appreciation and evaluation of music. What is important for musical appreciation and enjoyment, rather, is awareness of the concrete detail of the musical surface and its quality and connectedness from moment to moment. This position presents a challenge, now as much as in Gurney's time, to the account most favored by musicologists, according to which the experience of large-scale form and closure is essential to the fullest appreciation of music.

Others who adopted a scientific music aesthetic – such as the physician and physicist Hermann von Helmholtz in 1862 and the engineer William Pole in 1879 – were inclined to reduce aesthetic phenomena to the principles of acoustics. Their work is an important historical antecedent of the discipline now known as cognitive science of music, which has attracted the attention of a number of analytic philosophers of music (e.g. Raffman 1993; Nussbaum 2007).

Philosophy of music 1900–80

In its early days in the twentieth century, the focus of analytic philosophy was not on aesthetics. Its proponents were more concerned to integrate philosophy with science. The minor philosophers who wrote on aesthetics and the philosophy of music at the time, such as Halbert Britan, tend to be Kantian formalists (Britan 1911). With the rise of psychology as an experimental science, music and the listener's response attract more attention there (for a literature review, see Hevner 1936). The gestalt psychologist Carroll C. Pratt not only presents relevant empirical data in *The Meaning of Music* of 1931 (see also 1952), he critically reviews theories propounded by philosophers and carefully distinguishes between music's arousal and expression of emotion. His conclusion is that music is replete with tertiary qualities that duplicate very closely our experience of our muscles and viscera, with the result that music sounds as though saturated with mood and feeling. His position, expressed as a pithy apothegm, is that music sounds the way emotions feel. (For discussion, see Budd 1985.)

In 1938 Ludwig Wittgenstein lectured on aesthetics, but notes taken at the time were not published until 1966. He is primarily concerned with the nature of aesthetic judgment and reason giving and he reveals a deep distrust of psychologists' causally based explanations of these. He did not develop an account of music as such, or any systematic theory of aesthetics, but here and throughout his later lectures and writings he often uses musical examples to make points within aesthetics and other areas of philosophy. (For discussion, see Scruton 2004; Ahonen 2005.)

Perhaps the first philosophically motivated and argued account of music was Susanne Langer's *Philosophy in a New Key* (1942). This draws on the theory of linguistic meaning presented in Wittgenstein's *Tractatus Logico-*

Philosophicus (1922) in developing an account of music as a non-linguistic form of iconic symbolism that presents an expressive meaning that cannot be discursively communicated. Music pre-eminently (but also, in their own ways, the other arts – Langer 1953) symbolizes the general form of feeling by duplicating that form while transforming it into the temporal medium of sound. (For discussion, see Budd 1985; Davies 1994; Addis 1999.)

Two important works with a far-reaching influence were produced by musicologists in the 1950s. Deryck Cooke's *The Language of Music* (1959) catalogues the association throughout several centuries of Western classical tonal music of certain musical intervals and figures with specific expressive states (and sung texts). Cooke interprets his data as showing that music's expressiveness is natural at heart, though then shaped by convention. (For discussion, see Davies 1994.) Leonard B. Meyer's *Emotion and Meaning in Music* (1956) combines principles of gestalt psychology with information theory in describing how composers set up expectations concerning the music's progress. These are often temporarily defeated, which results in experiences of musical tension and resolution. Meyer's theory made an important contribution to our understanding of the way in which musical pattern and structure is experienced, though the account of musical expressiveness he attempts to build on this is not ultimately convincing. (For discussion, see Budd 1985; Davies 1994.)

Aesthetics took a semiotic turn in the 1950s to 1970s, including further work on music in a Langerian vein by Gordon Epperson (1967) and an anti-Langerian attempt to argue that music is a language-like symbol system by Wilson Coker (1972). (For discussion see Davies 1994.) Other work on expression in art in the same period (Hospers 1955; Beardsley 1958; Wollheim 1964; Elliott 1967; Tormey 1971; Urmson 1973) is more directly illustrative of the analytic paradigm.

The Polish philosopher Roman Ingarden wrote on the ontology of art from the perspective of the Continental phenomenological tradition. Though literature is his focus, he worked on *The Work of Music and the Problem of Its Identity* between 1928 and 1957, but it was not published in English translation until 1986. A number of analytic philosophers became interested in musical ontology prior to that date, however. The first to address the topic is Nelson Goodman in his highly original *Languages of Art* (1968). Goodman distinguishes between *allographic* and *autographic* artworks; the former, which can be notationally specified and are multiply instantiable, include musical works, whereas the latter, which are necessarily singular, include oil paintings. Goodman focuses on the work-specifying function of the musical score and on the relation between the work and its genuine performances. In both cases his position is counterintuitive. For instance, because verbal tempo terms are ambiguous he concludes that they have no work-specifying significance and, hence, that a performance with a tempo that renders the work unrecognizable (one quarter note = ten years, say) is not one jot less authentic on that ground. At the same time, he holds that a performance with a single wrong note completely fails to instance the work it is of, even if that work can be recognized in its performance. As these corollaries make clear, Goodman's agenda is a revisionary one. (For discussion, see Davies 2001.)

Goodman also presents a theory of music's expressiveness, according to which it expresses properties that it metaphorically exemplifies. Exemplification is a matter of referring to a property through possessing it, that is, by serving as a sample. (As a nominalist, Goodman avoids talk of properties and of reference, but I avoid debating that different issue here.) And, since music cannot literally present emotions, the idea is that it possesses its expressive properties only metaphorically. So, music expresses sadness, say, by metaphorically possessing the property of sadness and by referring to sadness via its doing so. This view invites two obvious objections: music is not always about the emotions it expresses and the notion of what it is for a property to be possessed or instanced metaphorically is inexplicably obscure. (For discussion, see Scruton 1974; Davies 1994.)

Another influential book of the period, Roger Scruton's *Art and Imagination* (1974), also includes consideration of music's expressiveness. In this regard, Scruton makes use of Wittgenstein's account of aspect perception, or "seeing as," and of the role of imagination in this mode of perception. His suggestion is that, as a result of entertaining unasserted thoughts about the music and the character of its progress, we hear it under expressive aspects. At much the same time, Kendall Walton (1973) also applied the notion of make-believe to an account of how we engage with art, though he did not detail his theory with respect to the musical case until later (1990, 1994).

Analytic philosophy of music since 1980

In this final section I list the major topics explored by analytic philosophers of music since 1980. Inevitably, the debate on the expression of emotion in music and on the listener's response to this endures. (See Davies 1994, 2007; Kivy 1989; Levinson 1996, 2006; Madell 2002; Matravers 1998; Ridley 1995; Robinson 2005; Scruton 1997; Walton 1994.) Meanwhile, discussion continues on other familiar topics: the experience of music, musical understanding, and the value of music, including the place of musical analysis and what kind of experience and knowledge is presupposed in the competent listener. (See Davies 1994; DeBellis 1995; Kivy 1990b; Levinson 1990, 2006; Nussbaum 2007; Raffman 1993; Robinson 2005; Scruton 1997.) As well, connections between music and ideology, ethics, and identity have been further explored. (See Goehr 1992, 1998; Gracyk 2001; Higgins 1991; Robinson 2005; Sharpe 2000; Young 2007.)

Among the comparatively new topics in the philosophy of music, the ontology of musical works has garnered increasing attention. Issues include whether works are discovered or created, whether their instrumentation features among their identity conditions, whether the work's identity depends on its composer's identity, and the nature of the relation between the work and its instances or performances. (See Davies 2001; Dodd 2007; Fisher 1991; Goehr 1992; Gracyk 1996; Kivy 1995; Levinson 1980, 1990.) The nature and creativity of performance more generally have also been considered. (See Davies 2001; Godlovitch 1998; Kivy 1995; Thom 1993, 2007.)

A recent trend is toward the application to the philosophy of art of ideas developed in other areas of philosophy (such as philosophy of language, of emotion, and so on), as well as consideration of the data and theories of psychologists, neuroscientists, evolution scientists, and so on. This is apparent also in recent writing on the philosophy of music. (See Dodd 2007; Higgins 2006; Nussbaum 2007; Raffman 1993; Robinson 2005.)

To date, the analytic philosophy of music had displayed consistent biases toward the point of view of the listener rather than of the composer, performer, or analyst; toward art music rather than popular and/or functional kinds; toward music of the eighteenth and nineteenth centuries rather than medieval and renaissance music or modernist and avant-garde music; toward instrumental rather than vocal or electronic music; and toward Western rather than non-Western music. (Of course, there are exceptions to these trends; for example, Godlovitch (1998) and Thom (2007) take the side of the performer.) These biases are predictable and understandable, I think. Quite rightly, philosophers write about the music they know best, and those with a historical and technical background are mostly schooled in Western classical music. And issues of music's expressiveness are at their most acute in the case of instrumental music, whereas it can be difficult to disentangle the contributions of words and music in song.

Nevertheless, a more comprehensive and sophisticated philosophical consideration of music will depend on a more catholic approach. Fortunately, a broader range of musics is now being considered, for instance, jazz (Alperson 1991; Brown 2000a; Hagberg 2006; Hamilton 2000) and rock (Gracyk 1996, 2001, 2007). Reflection on recordings in both contexts has brought fresh perspectives to the discussion of musical ontology and performance (see Brown 2000b, 2000c; Davies 2001; Fisher 1998; Gracyk 1996; Kania 2006). Meanwhile, the relevance of comparative musicology and ethnomusicology has begun to interest some philosophers (Alperson et al. 2007; Davies 1994, 2001, 2007; Higgins 2006). The analytic philosophy of music will be enriched if such trends continue.

References

Addis, L. (1999) *Of Mind and Music*, Ithaca: Cornell University Press.
Ahonen, H. (2005) "Wittgenstein and the Conditions of Musical Communication," *Philosophy* 80: 513–29.
Alperson, P. (1991) "When Composers Have To Be Performers," *Journal of Aesthetics and Art Criticism* 49: 369–73.
Alperson, P., Nguyen, C.B. and To, N.T. (2007) "The Sounding of the World: Aesthetic

Reflections on Traditional Gong Music of Vietnam," *Journal of Aesthetics and Art Criticism* 65: 11–20.

Aristotle (1939) *On the Heavens*, trans. W.K.C. Guthrie, London: Heinemann.

—— (1953) *Problems; Books 1–21*, trans.W.S. Hett, Cambridge: Harvard University Press.

Augustine (1948) *De Musica*, trans. R.C. Taliaferro, in L. Schopp (ed.) *The Fathers of the Church: Writings of Saint Augustin*, vol. 2, New York: Cima Publishing, pp. 153–379.

—— (1991) *Confessions*, trans. H. Chadwick, Oxford: Oxford University Press.

Beardsley, M.C. (1958) *Aesthetics: Problems in the Philosophy of Criticism*, New York: Harcourt Brace.

Britan, H. (1911) *The Philosophy of Music*, New York: Longmans, Green & Co.

Brown, L.B. (2000a) "'Feeling My Way': Jazz Improvisation and Its Vicissitude—A Plea for Imperfection," *Journal of Aesthetics and Art Criticism* 58: 112–23.

—— (2000b) "Phonography, Repetition and Spontaneity," *Philosophy and Literature* 24: 111–25.

—— (2000c) "Phonography, Rock Records, and the Ontology of Recorded Music," *Journal of Aesthetics and Art Criticism* 58: 361–72.

Budd, M. (1980) "The Repudiation of Emotion: Hanslick on Music," *British Journal of Aesthetics* 20: 29–43.

—— (1985) *Music and the Emotions: The Philosophical Theories*, London: Routledge & Kegan Paul.

Bungay, S. (1984) *Beauty and Truth: A Study of Hegel's Aesthetics*, New York: Oxford University Press.

Coker, W. (1972) *Music and Meaning: A Theoretical Introduction to Musical Aesthetics*, New York: Free Press.

Cooke, D. (1959) *The Language of Music*, London: Oxford University Press.

Davies, S. (1994) *Musical Meaning and Expression*, Ithaca: Cornell University Press.

—— (2001) *Musical Works and Performances*, Oxford: Clarendon Press.

—— (2007) "Balinese Aesthetics," *Journal of Aesthetics and Art Criticism* 65: 21–9.

DeBellis, M. (1995) *Music and Conceptualization*, Cambridge: Cambridge University Press.

Dodd, J. (2007) *Works of Music: An Essay in Ontology*, Oxford: Oxford University Press.

Elliott, R.K. (1967) "Aesthetic Theory and the Experience of Art," *Proceedings of the Aristotelian Society* 67: 111–26.

Epperson, G. (1967) *The Musical Symbol: A Study of the Philosophic Theory of Music*, Ames: Iowa State University Press.

Fisher, J.A. (1991) "Discovery, Creation, and Musical Works," *Journal of Aesthetics and Art Criticism* 49: 129–36.

—— (1998) "Rock 'n' Recording: The Ontological Complexity of Rock Music," in P. Alperson (ed.) *Musical Worlds: New Directions in the Philosophy of Music*, University Park: The Pennsylvania State University Press, pp. 109–23.

Godlovitch, S. (1998) *Musical Performance: A Philosophical Study*, London: Routledge.

Goehr, L. (1992) *The Imaginary Museum of Musical Works: An Essay in the Philosophy of Music*, Oxford: Clarendon Press.

—— (1998) *The Quest for Voice: On Music, Politics, and the Limits of Philosophy*, Oxford: Clarendon Press.

Goodman, N. (1968). *Languages of Art*, Indianapolis: Bobbs-Merrill.

Gracyk, T. (1996) *Rhythm and Noise: An Aesthetics of Rock Music*, Durham: Duke University Press.

—— (2001) *I Wanna Be Me: Rock Music and the Politics of Identity*, Philadelphia: Temple University Press.

—— (2007) *Listening to Popular Music: Or, How I Learned to Stop Worrying and Love Led Zepplin*, Ann Arbor: University of Michigan Press.

Gurney, E. (1880). *The Power of Sound*, London: Smith, Elder.

Hagberg, G. (2006) "Jazz Improvisation: A Mimetic Art?" *Revue Internationale de Philosophie* 60: 469–85.

Hamilton, A. (2000) "The Art of Improvisation and the Aesthetics of Imperfection," *British Journal of Aesthetics* 40: 168–85.

Hanslick, E. (1891 [1885 7th edn]) *The Beautiful in Music*, trans. G. Cohen, London: Novello & Ewer.

—— (1986 [1891 8th edn]) *On the Musically Beautiful*, trans. G. Payzant, Indianapolis: Hackett.

Hegel, G.W.F. (1975 [1835–8]) *Hegel's Aesthetics: Lectures on Fine Art*. 2 vols, trans. T.M. Knox, Oxford: Oxford University Press.

Helmholtz, H.L.F. (1912 [1862]) *On the Sensations of Tone as a Physiological Basis for the Theory of Music*, trans. A.J. Ellis, 4th edn, New York: Longmans, Green, and Co.

Hevner, K. (1936) "Experimental Studies of the Elements of Expression in Music," *American Journal of Psychology* 48: 246–68.

Higgins, K.M. (1986). "Nietzsche on Music," *Journal of the History of Ideas* 47: 663–72.

—— (1991) *The Music of Our Lives*, Philadelphia: Temple University Press.

—— (2006) "The Cognitive and Appreciative Impact of Musical Universals," *Revue Internationale de Philosophie* 60: 487–503.

Hospers, J. (1955) "The Concept of Artistic Expression," *Proceedings of the Aristotelian Society* 55: 313–44.

Ingarden, R. (1986) *The Work of Music and the Problem of Its Identity*, trans. A. Czerniawski, Berkeley: University of California Press.

Kania, A. (2006) "Making Tracks: The Ontology of Rock Music," *Journal of Aesthetics and Art Criticism* 64: 401–14.

Kivy, P. (1980) *The Corded Shell*, Princeton: Princeton University Press.

—— (1989) *Sound Sentiment*, Philadelphia: Temple University Press.

—— (1990a) "What was Hanslick Denying?" *Journal of Musicology* 8: 3–18.

—— (1990b) *Music Alone: Philosophical Reflection on the Purely Musical Experience*, Ithaca: Cornell University Press.

—— (1995) *Authenticities: Philosophical Reflections on Musical Performance*, Ithaca: Cornell University Press.

—— (1999) *Osmin's Rage: Philosophical Reflections on Opera, Drama, and Text*, 2nd edn, Ithaca: Cornell University Press.

Lamarque, P. (2000) "The British Journal of Aesthetics: Forty Years On," *British Journal of Aesthetics* 40: 1–20.

Langer, S.K. (1957 [1942]). *Philosophy in a New Key*, 3rd edn, Cambridge: Harvard University Press.

—— (1953) *Feeling and Form*, New York: Scribner.

Levinson, J. (1980) "What a Musical Work Is," *Journal of Philosophy* 77: 5–28.

—— (1990) *Music, Art, and Metaphysics*, Ithaca: Cornell University Press.

—— (1996) *The Pleasures of Aesthetics*, Ithaca: Cornell University Press.

—— (1997) *Music in the Moment*, Ithaca: Cornell University Press.

—— (2006) "Musical Expressiveness as Hearability-as-expression," in M. Kieran (ed.) *Contemporary Debates in Aesthetics and the Philosophy of Art*, Oxford: Blackwell, pp. 192–204.

Lippman, E. (1992) *A History of Western Musical Aesthetics*, Lincoln: University of Nebraska Press.

Madell, G. (2002) *Philosophy, Music and Emotion*, Edinburgh: Edinburgh University Press.

Mark, T.C. (1980) "On Works of Virtuosity," *Journal of Philosophy* 77: 28–45.

Matravers, D. (1998) *Art and Emotion*, Oxford: Clarendon Press.

Meyer, L.B. (1956) *Emotion and Meaning in Music*, Chicago: Chicago University Press.

Nussbaum, C.O. (2007) *The Musical Representation: Meaning, Ontology, and Emotion*, Cambridge: MIT Press.

Philodemus (1884) *De Musica*, trans. von Kempke, Leipzig, s.n.

Pole, W. (1879) *The Philosophy of Music*, London: Trübner.

Pratt, C.C. (1931) *The Meaning of Music*, New York: McGraw-Hill.

—— (1952) *Music as the Language of Emotion*, Washington: The Library of Congress.

Raffman, D. (1993) *Language, Music, and Mind*, Cambridge: MIT Press.

Ridley, A. (1995) *Music, Value and the Passions*, Ithaca: Cornell University Press.

Robinson, J. (2005) *Deeper than Reason: Emotion and Its Role in Literature, Music, and Art*, Oxford: Clarendon Press.

Schopenhauer, A. (1969 [1818, 1844]) *The World as Will and Representation*, 2 vols, trans. E.F.J. Payne, New York: Dover.

Schueller, H.M. (1955) "Immanuel Kant and the Aesthetics of Music," *Journal of Aesthetics and Art Criticism* 14: 218–47.

—— (1988) *The Idea of Music: An Introduction to Musical Aesthetics in Antiquity and the Middle Ages*, Kalamazoo: Medieval Institute Publications, Western Michigan University.

Scruton, R. (1974) *Art and Imagination*, London: Methuen.

—— (1997) *The Aesthetics of Music*, Oxford: Clarendon Press.

—— (2004) "Wittgenstein and the Understanding of Music," *British Journal of Aesthetics* 44: 1–9.

Sharpe, R.A. (2000) *Music and Humanism: An Essay in the Aesthetics of Music*, Oxford: Oxford University Press.

Tanner, M. (1996) *Wagner*, London: Harper Collins.

Thom, P. (1993) *For an Audience: A Philosophy of the Performing Arts*, Philadelphia: Temple University Press.

—— (2007) *The Musician as Interpreter*, University Park: Pennsylvania State University Press.

Tormey, A. (1971) *The Concept of Expression*, Princeton: Princeton University Press.

Urmson, J.O. (1973) "Representation in Music," *Royal Institute of Philosophy Lectures* 6: 132–46.

Walton, K.L. (1973) "Pictures and Make-Believe," *Philosophical Review* 82: 283–319.

—— (1990) *Mimesis as Make-Believe: On the Foundations of the Representational Arts*, Cambridge: Harvard University Press.

—— (1994) "Listening with Imagination: Is Music Representational?" *Journal of Aesthetics and Art Criticism* 52: 47–61.

Wittgenstein, L. (1922 [1921]) *Tractatus Logico-Philosophicus*, trans. C.K. Ogden, London: Routledge & Kegan Paul.

—— (1966) *Wittgenstein: Lectures and Conversations on Aesthetics, Psychology and Religious Belief*, ed. C. Barrett, Oxford: Blackwell.

Wollheim, R. (1964) "On Expression and Expressionism," *Revue Internationale de Philosophie* 18: 270–89.

Young, J.O. (2007) *Cultural Appropriation and the Arts*, Oxford: Blackwell.

Part IV
FIGURES

28
PLATO

Stephen Halliwell

Plato (*c.*427–347 BCE) is the first Western thinker in whose work we can trace an extensive critical interest in music. The subject provides material for philosophical analysis in his dialogues on four main levels: first, as a set of practices whose widespread social, religious and educational uses in the Greek world prompt general questions about music's cultural influence; second, as a particularly potent art form (or an element in several art forms) whose effects on the mind raise issues of philosophical psychology; third, as an exemplar of values and qualities (concord, integration, unity) which function as a model for other human activities and experiences, including philosophy itself (called "the greatest music" by Socrates at *Phaedo* 61a); finally, as a system of ordered beauty which may even reflect, and be a guide to, the fundamental nature of the cosmos. Although the hundreds of references to music in Plato's dialogues cover a multitude of details, from the practical to the theoretical, the most prominent concern is with the challenge which the intense, seductive yet obscure pleasures of music pose to any attempt to philosophize the operations of the mind. For the purposes of this account, I draw no distinction between Plato's authorial position and the views put in the mouth of Socrates.

Cultural context

Plato was born and spent most of his life in a cosmopolitan and democratic city, Athens, whose culture (including its social and religious festivities) was saturated with forms of music. Most of this music, as in the Greek world at large, was performed by a solo wind or stringed instrument: principally, the reed-pipe, *aulos* (usually the double-*aulos*, i.e. a pair played by one person) and the lyre, of which there were several varieties. Most music also served as an accompaniment to sung/chanted words (especially in the performance of poetic genres) or to dance, and sometimes to both, as, for example, in the choral odes of tragic and comic drama. Relatively little Greek music was purely instrumental, though in Plato's own lifetime a trend of avant-garde musical experimentation, often called the "New Music" by modern historians (West 1992: 356–72; D'Angour 2006), produced a heightened interest in melodic complexity and ornamentation which sometimes broke free from a song-text: this is clear from the complaint voiced by a Platonic character at *Laws* 7.669e. Although the New Music is referred to more than once in Plato's work (see below), for the most part his dialogues address questions relating to long-established and deeply embedded features of music's pervasive importance in Greek culture.

That importance was crystallized, among other things, in a set of educational practices and values. Learning to sing and to dance, especially in a group (a Greek *choros* was in the first instance a dance-group, secondarily a singing "chorus"), had long been a typical part of the upbringing of young males of the leisured classes; many girls too received such training. More variable, though not uncommon, was the acquisition of some facility in playing a lyre; the *aulos* was always more the preserve of professionals. Ability to participate in and/or to appreciate the beauty of song and dance became entrenched as a central element of Greek musical sensibility; Greeks imagined even their Olympian deities, including the lyre-playing Apollo and the ecstatic figure of Dionysus (for the relationship between these gods, see below), as devotees of music. It is standard for characters in Plato's dialogues to share this perspective on music's life-enhancing status: Protarchus, at *Philebus* 62c, anticipates Friedrich Nietzsche's "without music life would be a mistake" by saying that music is essential "if our life is really to *be* a life of some kind." (See Chapter 32, "Nietzsche," in this volume.) But the idea of music as necessary for a fulfilled existence is both expanded and complicated, by Socrates in the *Republic* and by the Athenian in *Laws*, into a distinctively Platonic conception of music's (dangerously) powerful role in the shaping of both individual and collective psychology.

Greek views of music's potency were reinforced by the fact, already indicated, that most music was an accompaniment to poetic texts. This meant that appraisals of music's value tended to become part, as we shall see, of a larger conception of the value of song. This did not, however, block the appreciation of qualities of musical form (i.e. melodic, rhythmic and, in a broad sense, harmonic features) in their own right. The two sides of this picture can be seen even in a brief passage such as *Protagoras* 326a–b. There the sophist Protagoras explains how one stage in the education of Greek boys involves being taught to sing poetry by a lyre-teacher (a *kithara*-player). Protagoras suggests that the benefits of the experience come partly from the insights contained in the poetic texts. But he also speaks of rhythms and melodic modes, tunings or pitch-patterns (*harmoniai*, plural of *harmonia*) as being assimilated into the children's souls and conduct: "all human life needs beauty of rhythm and melody." This ethical-cum-existential conception of music's significance lies at the root of the extended Platonic passages to be considered below.

One consequence of the cultural landscape sketched above is that the Greek term *mousikê* itself – literally "art/activity of the Muses" – came to be used, in Plato and elsewhere, with a flexible semantics. In its narrower usage, it refers to structures of rhythm and melody/pitches per se. But it can also designate the larger cluster of poetico-musical arts, including dance; and, more broadly still, it comes to denote the whole sensibility and refined cast of mind which sustained appreciation of these arts was believed to inculcate.

That normative sense of "musical" value had in turn been carried further by one particular group of Greeks, the followers of Pythagoras. Although the details are obscure, Pythagorean thought was certainly known to Plato and had some influence on him. Two ideas in particular stand out here. One is the notion of "the harmony of the spheres" or music as a sort of (symbolic) cosmic concord: this is undoubtedly in the background in a passage such as *Republic* 10.617b–c, a mythical and astronomical vision of the ordered beauty of the universe (Halliwell 1987: 181–2). The other is the view of music as a form of soul-changing therapy. Among various testimonies to this view is the claim of Aristotle's student Aristoxenus that Pythagoreans "used medicine to purify the body and music to purify the mind/soul" (West 1992: 31–3); the likelihood that some Pythagoreans espoused a conception of the soul itself as an "attunement," *harmonia*, of the body (see *Phaedo* 85e–6d), may also be pertinent here. While this precise model of psychotherapy is not found in Plato's own writings, it is likely that Pythagorean convictions about the power of music helped to shape the seriousness with which its psychological effects are probed in the dialogues. A connection can be detected, moreover, between the astral and the psychological aspects of Pythagorean influence on Plato. This is clearest in the idea at *Timaeus* 47c–d that music connects the "orbits" in the soul with the orbits of the cosmos: musical order is a link between microcosm and macrocosm. On the other hand, passages such as *Republic* 530e–31c and *Philebus* 56a–c show that Plato was resistant to (Pythagorean) attempts to turn the study of music into a mathematical science.

Music in the *Republic*

The *Republic*'s main discussion of music occurs in Book 3, 398c–403c. Two general features of this discussion bear out points already adumbrated above: first, the treatment of music stands as an adjunct to, and complements, the principles laid down for the content and form of poetic texts at 2.376e–3.398b; second, the whole poetico-musical side of education (the part dealing with the psyche just as gymnastics deals primarily with the body) is called *mousikê* at 2.376e and subsequently. So the analysis of music proper is presented as one facet of the philosophical regulation of an educational, psychological and cultural constellation of activities. Socrates considers rhythmic and melodic structures (the latter taking the form of *harmoniai*: tunings, modes or scales, Barker 1984: 163–8) as elements in compound art forms; they work in liaison with the discursive *logos* of the texts they accompany (398d). But he nonetheless ascribes to those musical structures expressive qualities of their own.

The nature of those qualities is brought under the heading of mimesis, a concept normally rendered as "imitation" by most modern translators and scholars but which often functions in ways that overlap with later ideas of representation and expression (Halliwell 2002). Socrates introduces mimesis at 2.373b as a compendious category of imaginative simulation as practiced in both visual and musico-poetic art. He later employs a narrower definition of the term to cover the dramatic or "enactive" mode of poetic discourse (3.392d) as opposed to poetry in third-person narrative. These uses of the terminology of mimesis cannot be reduced to a conceptually tidy essence. When Socrates starts to speak of melodic/modal mimesis at 3.399a–c, his meaning is not self-evident. But he clearly supposes some kind of expressive correspondence or correlation (a sort of isomorphy of "movement," according to *Politicus* 306c–7c, a later work) between musically organized sounds and the emotional-cum-ethical traits of characters depicted in poetic texts. On this understanding, followed in many respects by Aristotle *Politics* 8.5 (Halliwell 2002: 234–49), music allows processes and impulses of feeling to be captured in the movements of sound and thereby transmitted to and replayed by other minds.

Socrates advances here a fundamentally "narrative" model of musical semantics. He works with a principle on the lines of "prima le parole, poi la musica" (399e–400a, 400d). His prescriptive choices/exclusions of musical modes (un)suitable for the poetry which will be performed by young guardians, that is, future rulers, in the ideal city (Callipolis) are an extension of the judgments which he earlier made on (un)desirable poetic representations of characters and their attitudes. Thus, for instance, his exclusion of modes or tunings expressive of "lamentation" (398d–e) is aligned with his earlier repudiation of poetry which depicts gods as causing, and heroes as afflicted by, circumstances of tragic suffering (387d–8d). Socrates (or Plato) does not purport to be offering a comprehensive account of the possibilities or uses of music. He is testing the logic of a model of musical significance (ultimately, its capacity to find expressive equivalents to the defining qualities of particular paradigms of "life," 399e–400a) as applied to the art forms of an imaginary society in which certain ethical, political and cultural goals are to be pursued with ideological single-mindedness.

Socrates seeks a kind of "purity" or simplicity which will avoid complexity in the melodic and rhythmic constituents of music (399e, cf. 404e) and in the experiences such complexity stimulates in the minds of hearers. Complexity is regarded as threatening the overriding principles of psychic unity and stability; note the pointedly musical comparison for unity of soul at 4.443d–e. There is also a hint at 399e that complexity is Dionysiac rather than Apollonian; the satyr Marsyas, mentioned here, has links with Dionysus (Rocconi 2009: 570; cf. Plato, *Symposium* 215b–c). Apollo and Dionysus are later mentioned together, in connection with religious festivities (and their music), at *Laws* 2.653d: Nietzsche knew both these passages well. In associating styles of music with kinds of character and "life," Socrates professes to be guided by the theories of a contemporary intellectual called Damon (400b–c; West 1992: 246–7). According to 4.424c, Damon claimed that no change in musical styles could take place without (causing? and/or reflecting?) a corresponding change in the general values of a society. This remarkable tenet clearly left its mark on Plato's lifelong interest in music. It is subtly echoed later in the *Republic* by the premonition that even the ideal society will decline when its guardians neglect the standards of music (8.546d, 548b). It is also the earliest known version of a doctrine of music's necessary implication in the dynamics of a culture as a whole – a doctrine whose modern adherents include Adorno.

While the discussion in *Republic* Book 3 stresses the need to make music "fit" and "follow" the content of a verbal text, Socrates does allow for distinctively musical beauty of rhythmic and melodic form (400c ff.). However, the relationship between such beauty of form and its discursively underpinned expressiveness is not transparent. At 400d–e it is suggested that formal beauty may involve correspondence ("likeness") to the verbal content and ethical tenor of the total art form. But the larger aesthetic of beautiful form (in both artifacts and nature) at 401a–d, an aesthetic which treats a culture as a holistic fabric of value (Burnyeat 1999), cannot be exhausted by the kind of meaning which is explicable in wholly discursive terms, since it encompasses objects (such as buildings and plants) which typically lack a narrative content. Socrates seems to allow at any rate that melodic and rhythmic patterns in music can possess an orderliness which is good in its own right, even if he ultimately wants it to be held accountable to an ethical, "life"-defining reckoning. When he calls formal properties "akin to" as well as mimetically expressive of ethical qualities (401a), he perhaps implies that music can itself serve as a model for, and not just a reflection of, the beauty of a unified soul.

This implication is extended at 401d–e. Socrates says there that rhythm and melody "reach into the interior of the soul," take hold of it, and impress on it a good (or bad) form. So if music can embody patterns which somehow correspond to the qualities of a soul figured in the music, the response to musical beauty on the part of the listener equally involves psychic "internalization" and assimilation of the musical order (Schofield 2010). This process is initially a matter of sub-conceptual feeling (i.e. prior to *logos*, 402a), though ethical values are already being shaped at that level (400d–2d). The more experienced listener will develop ways of hearing which are both affective and cognitive. It is a premise of this phase of the argument that a cultivated responsiveness to artistic beauty involves a capacity to "recognize" images, as well as the intrinsic forms, of good and bad states of mind/soul (402a–c). The implications of this premise, for music as for other art forms, are much more sympathetic and positive than the notorious (and rhetorically provocative) treatment of poetry and other mimetic image-making in Book 10 of the *Republic*. Despite the restrictions he had previously placed on the music allowed in Callipolis, Socrates' case builds to the resounding proposition that the goal of all music (here in its wider cultural sense) is "the erotics of beauty" (403c). At least part of the force of this proposition is an acknowledgment of music's power to arouse feelings which carry with them an impetus of intense desire.

Music in the *Laws*

The *Laws* returns to and reconsiders many of the same principles of musical education that Socrates had outlined in the *Republic*. Although the work is sprawling, unfinished, and without the dramatic flair and finesse of the *Republic*, it is nonetheless remarkable for the way in which it persistently circles round the importance for the well-ordered society of *mousikê* in both the narrower ("music") and the wider ("education"/"culture") senses of the term. This material can be examined only selectively here.

The most sustained passage on music per se is in Book 2 (653c–671b). The Athenian, the work's main speaker, thinks of musico-poetic performances, not least those of choruses (who dance as well as sing), as belonging above all to communal festivals which both unite a society and connect it to its gods (including Apollo and Dionysus, 653d: see above). To that extent his conception of music is culturally normative. But it is also biologically rooted. (One might note here, obliquely, the soothing and entrancing power which music is said to exercise even over certain animals at *Politicus* 268b.) The Athenian regards rhythmic and melodic form as reflecting a fundamental human capacity for, and pleasure in, "ordered movements," which can be physically embodied in dance but are equally enacted in the patterns of sound itself (653e, cf. e.g. 664e–5a, 672e–3a). At the same time, these movements synchronize, as it were, body and soul: just as Socrates spoke of music "reaching into the interior of the soul" (see above), so the Athenian speaks of the movements of the (singing) voice as "penetrating as far as the soul" (673a). Accordingly, in *Laws* as in the *Republic* "good" musical forms are deemed to be images of ethically admirable traits (655a–b). All music is counted as a kind of mimetic (representational-cum-expressive) "image-making" (668a–b), though it will be suggested later in the dialogue that when stripped of a discursive (poetic) basis the mimetic meaning of music becomes obscure or uncertain (669b–670a).

All this draws the Athenian into wrestling with the problem of musical pleasure. He is anxious to assert the need to recognize "correct," that is, ethically grounded, standards of (psychological) pleasure and pain, and to deny that pleasure in itself can be the sole criterion of musical value (654c–d, 655c–d, 667e–8a). He suggests that in responses to music an interplay takes place between the hearer's own character and the kinds of qualities expressed in the music itself; but if the latter is enjoyed, then the hearer's soul is inevitably assimilated to the musical patterns (655d–6b). The Athenian knows that *prima facie* music generates its own, pleasure-driven standards of stylistic evolution and cultural success. This makes him all the keener to ward off what he sees as the threat posed by the predilections of "mass" audiences (657e–660c; cf. *Republic* 6.493d), a move which prefigures many modern debates over musical values. In a striking gesture, he holds up a non-Greek society, that of Egypt (interpreted here as unbendingly traditionalist), as the only one to have laid down and maintained appropriately strict norms of musical (and other artistic) form (656c–7b, cf. 7.799a–b).

Despite what is obviously, on one level, the statement of a deeply conservative stance, the Athenian's reflections can also be read as groping for a formulation which will manage to integrate plural criteria of aesthetic merit; Plato signals at least some awareness of the difficulty of doing so (Halliwell 2002: 65–71). The Athenian speaks of pleasure, "correctness" (in part a measure of how far artistic form does justice to its content), and "benefit" (the ultimate effect on the audience's lives) as the three essential criteria in question (667b–c). In attempting to configure the relationship between these, he uses also the vocabulary of "beauty," a vocabulary which in Greek always has the scope to embrace both sensory appearances and ethical excellence. In a very difficult passage, he sums up his view by saying that good music involves "likeness to the representation of what is beautiful/good" (668b). The obscurity of this phrase need not prevent us, given the larger context, from seeing that the Athenian wants to acknowledge a role for both "internal" (formal) and "external" (world-reflecting) factors in all mimetic art, including music. He remains troubled, however, by a possible tension between these: even the creators of musical works may themselves be expert in rhythms and melodies while not knowing whether what they produce is beautiful or good (670e, cf. 7.802b–c).

That last complaint opens the way for the Athenian to undertake a larger critique of musico-poetic history. This critique is an extension, *au fond*, of the *Republic*'s Damon-indebted model (see above) of music's place within the larger dynamics of a culture. In Book 3 of the *Laws* (700a–1b) the Athenian uses music to illustrate the thesis of a supposedly general Greek decline from cultural "lawfulness" to "lawlessness." There once prevailed, he claims (with a convenient disregard for various complicating factors), a musical culture in which established genres of song had their clearly marked rules and could not be mixed; a culture, moreover, in which audiences were obedient, accepting recipients of what was offered to them. But what has now come about, he continues, is an era of constant experimentation, innovation, and genre-crossing in both poetry and music. Composers have laid claim to a freedom which recognizes no standard of "correctness" other than the hearer's pleasure, and audiences have become correspondingly assertive as the collective arbiters of taste: musical "aristocracy" (rule of the best) has been replaced by "theatro-cracy" (rule by mass audiences), 700e–701a. What's more, music has been central to the wider dissemination of the idea that everyone can judge everything: music (of certain kinds), it seems, is a breeding-ground for an ideology of the supremacy of popular opinion and taste.

The Athenian's sweepingly elitist attitudes imply censure of the democratic culture which his own city had developed over the previous century and more. The censure encompasses, among much else, aspects of the theatre of tragedy and comedy, themselves forms of "music drama" (note e.g. the later allusion to tragic music at 7.800d, matching *Republic* 3.398d–e, mentioned above). But his picture of a collusion between composers and general public, bringing about a radical shift from conservative traditionalism to experimental modernism, applies more specifically to the phenomenon of the New Music (see above). This is particularly clear in the description of promiscuous innovation and "rule-breaking" – including daring juxtapositions of register, novel rhythmic figurations, and "heterophonic" instrumental accompaniments – at 669c–e, 700d, and 7.812d–e. The last of those passages, ascribing a penchant for "bacchic frenzy" to modern composers, gives a Dionysian shading to the disapproved styles in question.

But when the Athenian returns to the subject of music in Book 7 (798d–802e), a paradox emerges from the heavily negative slant of his argument. Having originally defined music as intrinsically concerned with "order" (*taxis*) of sound and movement, his case for the re-imposition of supposedly traditional standards and values leads him to distinguish between "ordered" and "disorderly" music (802c–d). Yet he does not actually count the latter as non-music; indeed, he stresses the pleasure popularly derived from it by those immersed in its styles through their upbringing, just as, for that matter, he had earlier acknowledged the natural creative talents of the composers of such music (700d). Although close in places to a parody of ultra-conservative conformism, his position depends on a recognition of the psychic potency of richly intricate musical textures. Like Socrates in the *Republic*, the Athenian is not simply dismissive of new types of music. He even allows himself, at one juncture in Book 2, to admit a need for constant change and variety in order to maintain the city's appetite for and gratification in music (*Laws* 665c). But he is nonetheless fearful of ways in which the impact of novel musical forms can change both the individual soul and the entire sensibility of a society. Between them, the main speakers in Plato's two longest dialogues represent an anxiety about substantial musical innovations which has had many analogues right up to the cultural clashes of modern times.

Epilogue: philosophy as music

Many references to music in Plato are related either to ideas of system and order or to the "soul-changing" power of musical expressiveness. There is always a tacit and sometimes an explicit connection between these two things. The soul itself, *qua* plurality of psychological functions, needs ordered unity above all else. The power of music can either foster that unity by its own patterned movements or threaten it by its transformative capacity to excite complex, shifting states of mind. In the *Republic* and *Laws* the issues raised by what is perceived as this ambivalent power are pursued, as we have seen, on the level of an authoritarian cultural critique, though more subtly and tentatively in the earlier of the two dialogues. But the authoritarianism is always a response, at its roots, to what is taken to be music's potential for deep psychological penetration.

The double upshot of this Platonic perspective is not only an attempt to philosophize the value of music but also to turn philosophy itself into a kind of "music" ("the greatest music," as Socrates, possibly echoing a Pythagorean motif, says at *Phaedo* 61a when interpreting a dream-injunction to "make music" during the final days of his life). At *Republic* 3.412a, for instance, the most truly "musical" person (here, the successfully trained young guardian in the ideal city) is not the technically adept musician but someone whose soul possesses the highest degree of harmonious integration. But since that integration has (hypothetically) been achieved by means, above all, of musico-poetic education and culture themselves, the notion of the philosophically "musical" soul is not purely metaphorical. In the passage which has led up to this, in fact (410d–11e), Socrates very closely associates the virtues and balanced passions of "the philosophical nature" with a life which uses music as such correctly: a life which allows musical sensuousness to soften harsh, aggressive instincts, but which neither succumbs so completely to music's melting effects that the soul is made effete nor shuns music altogether and thereby remains trapped in a beast-like savagery.

The "music" of philosophy, then, in some sense grows from and even models itself on the music that is conveyed in sound. At the same time, Platonic philosophy aspires to arrive at a position of transcendence beyond the material world, including the physical sounds of music. *Republic* 7.522a–b refers back to the music (including poetry) of the education system sketched earlier in the work as incapable of reaching the higher realms of philosophical truth. Real music, Glaucon (Plato's brother) obligingly reminds Socrates, uses resources of rhythm and pitch-structures to educate by "habituation," not by intellectual knowledge. It instills patterns of order and harmony in the soul's impulses and ethical sensitivities, but it does not have a discursively transparent content which the rational faculty of the mind can grasp.

In the eyes of Platonic philosophy, music is both alluring and elusive. Its capacity to captivate and move the soul through the play of sounds makes it a model for a kind of beauty which fuses outer form with inner feeling; but the enigmatic nature of that capacity stands also as a challenge to the commanding authority of philosophical explanation. Even after the influences of Damon and Pythagoreanism have been factored in, therefore, it is legitimate to see Plato as instigating the history of the philosophy of music. The Platonic legacy to that history is no monolithic scheme of ideas but a set of problems as abidingly fascinating as they are resistant to confident solution.

See also Antiquity and the Middle Ages (Chapter 24), Arousal theories (Chapters 20), Music and politics (Chapter 50), Music education (Chapter 56), and Music's arousal of emotions (Chapter 22).

References

Barker, A. (1984) *Greek Musical Writings, Volume I: The Musician and his Art*, Cambridge: Cambridge University Press.

Burnyeat, M.F. (1999) "Culture and Society in Plato's *Republic*," *The Tanner Lectures on Human Values* 20: 217–324.

D'Angour, A. (2006) "The New Music – So What's New?" in S. Goldhill and R. Osborne (eds) *Rethinking Revolutions through Ancient Greece*, Cambridge: Cambridge University Press, pp. 264–83.

Halliwell, S. (1987) *Plato: Republic 10*, Warminster: Aris & Phillips.

—— (2002) *The Aesthetics of Mimesis: Ancient Texts and Modern Problems*, Princeton: Princeton University Press.

Rocconi, E. (2009) "Music," in G. Boys-Stones, B. Graziosi, and P. Vasunia (eds) *Oxford Handbook of Hellenic Studies*, Oxford: Oxford University Press, pp. 569–78.

Schofield, M. (2010) "Music All Pow'rful," in M. McPherran (ed.) *Plato's "Republic": A Critical Guide*, Cambridge: Cambridge University Press.

West, M.L. (1992) *Ancient Greek Music*, Oxford: Clarendon Press.

Further reading

Barker, A. (2005) *Psicomusicologia nella Grecia antica*, Naples: Guida Editore. (An advanced study of the philosophical psychology of music in Plato and other ancient thinkers.)

Cooper, J.M. (ed.) (1997) *Plato Complete Works*, Indianapolis: Hackett Publishing. (The best complete translation of Plato.)

29

ROUSSEAU

Julia Simon

Better known for his critiques of the project of the Enlightenment and for the rhetorical barbs he aimed at the *philosophes*, Jean-Jacques Rousseau (1712–78) is not normally considered to be a defender of civilization or a champion of the arts and sciences. In his *Discourse on the Arts and Sciences* (1750), written in response to the Academy of Dijon's question, "If the reestablishment of the sciences and the arts has contributed to the purification of manners and morals," Rousseau answers with a resounding "no," citing the corrupting effects of the arts and sciences on human nature. According to Rousseau, it is the arts and sciences that have led throughout history to the division of labor, increasing social dependence, the downfall of the ancient democratic republics, and the lack of satisfaction generally in public life. Nonetheless, Rousseau wrote articles and essays on music, copied musical manuscripts, composed an opera, gave music lessons, and worked as a performer and as a tuner. For nearly the entirety of his life, from roughly 1719 until close to his death in 1778, he engaged with music in a variety of forms. How can we to reconcile the contradiction between Rousseau's philosophical positions and his musical corpus? One thing remains consistent throughout Rousseau's thought: an insistence on originality, authenticity, and self-expression uncorrupted by social pressures and constraints, alongside of a championing of greater social and political equality and justice. This insistence on originality, authenticity, and self-expression is evident in works as diverse as his treatise on education, *Emile, or Education* (1762), his novel, *Julie, or the New Heloise* (1761), and his *Confessions* (1781), but also informs his writing on music.

Early work in music

In order to understand the relationship between Rousseau's social and political philosophy and his work on music, it is important to understand not only the main currents of his thought but also the prevailing opinions of his day on musical questions. Born in Geneva to an artisan father, Rousseau studied music in a cathedral school in Annecy, studied with private music teachers, learned to play the flute and violin, performed in small chamber groups in private homes, and was exposed to Italian music while living in Venice. Rousseau was an autodidact who, according to his *Confessions*, studied the great composer and theoretician Jean-Philippe Rameau's *Treatise on Harmony Reduced to its Natural Principles* (1722) to educate himself further in the field of music (Rousseau 1959: vol. I, 184). Like many people in eighteenth-century Europe, in addition to viewing music as a form of entertainment after dinner, Rousseau valued the study of music as an academic discipline that bridged the arts and sciences. According to Enlightenment thought, music is an art because of its mimetic abilities – its ability to imitate nature, in particular – but it is also very close to the sciences because of the mathematical ratios that explain acoustical properties and harmonic relations. Studying music as both an art and a science, and valuing the study of music as an academic enterprise worthy of reflection alongside other philosophical questions, contextualizes Rousseau's engagement with music as typical for his day. When he decided to leave the countryside of Chambéry to seek his fame in Paris, he set out with a work entitled *Project Concerning New Signs for Music*, which he presented to the Academy of Sciences in 1742. Rousseau sought to simplify the musical notation system to make music easier to learn to read and more affordable, by eliminating the staff lines in favor of sequences of numbers separated by commas. The democratic undertones of his later thought are already apparent in the *Project*, which urges wider accessibility through the use of a more transparent and self-evident form of notation. According to Rousseau, students using his system of notation will learn to sing more quickly and easily. Music will become more affordable due to the savings in space and paper, ultimately producing a broadening of the music-reading public (Simon 2005a). The *Academy of Sciences* did not view Rousseau's new notation system favorably, criticizing the difficulty of quickly glimpsing ascending or descending lines without the spatial display of notes on the staff. Undeterred, Rousseau published his *Dissertation on Modern Music* (1743), a direct appeal to the public aimed at building support for a simplified system of musical notation. In this work, he goes to great pains to explain the advantages of his notation as well as aspects of harmonic systems to the non-specialist.

Following on the heels of this entrée onto the Parisian intellectual scene, Rousseau was invited by Denis Diderot and Jean le Rond d'Alembert, editors of the *Encyclopedia, or a Systematic Dictionary of the Sciences, Arts, and Crafts*, to author virtually all of the articles pertaining to music. Over the course of several years, Rousseau penned about 375 articles for the quintessential Enlightenment project. His contributions sparked criticism quickly, from none other than the composer Rameau, who had turned down Diderot and d'Alembert's offer to author the articles himself. In a published pamphlet entitled "Errors on Music in the *Encyclopedia*," Rameau was especially critical of Rousseau's accounts in "accompaniment," "chord," "dissonance," and later in "enharmonic." The criticisms from Rameau already indicate the seeds of what will become a major point of contention between the two: whether one privileges harmony over melody (Rameau) or melody over harmony (Rousseau) in music. While there are technical disputes that demonstrate Rousseau's insight into weaknesses in Rameau's harmonic system – for example, Rousseau's perceptive insight that Rameau cannot derive the minor third from his theory of the fundamental bass (an overtone series) (O'Dea 1995: 17–18) – much of the dispute rehearses what will become full blown in the *Querelle des Bouffons*: a difference in taste between French and Italian style music.

Le Devin du village: a new style of opera

In August 1752, a troupe of Italian musicians came to Paris to perform Giovanni Battista Pergolesi's *La serva padrona*, touching off a dispute among intellectuals that came to be known as the *Querelle des Bouffons* (named after the Italian *buffoni* or comic actors who performed the comic opera). Pergolesi's highly melodic comic intermezzo contrasted sharply with traditional French opera, especially that of Rameau, that offered tragic material often in mythological or historical contexts. Two camps formed, one on the side of "French" opera and the other defending "Italian" opera, at times necessitating the appearance of armed guards to keep the peace at the opera. Rousseau's participation in the quarrel, the *Letter on French Music* (1753), went so far as to conclude that "the French have no music and cannot have any, or if they ever do have any, it will be too bad for them" (1995: vol. V, 328). Solidly on the "Italian" side, Rousseau links the weaknesses of French opera to the French language. He critiques French opera for its bad use of recitatives, its tedious declamation style constrained by French prosody, and an overly academic adherence to harmonic development. He even goes so far as to engage Rameau directly in a counter-reading of an aria from Jean-Baptiste Lully's *Armide* (1686), disagreeing with Rameau's assessment of the perfect expression of sentiment in its chromatic development. Rousseau found the aria dull and flat compared to the expressiveness of Italian opera, insulting not only Rameau, but also the composer who most embodied the glory of French opera in the seventeenth century, Lully. The *Querelle des Bouffons* provoked the major thinkers of the day to enter into a dispute whose implications went far beyond the musical questions at hand to engage major ideological questions pertaining to taste, aesthetics, epistemology, politics, and even religion (Johnson 1986).

Never one to shy away from self-contradiction, Rousseau, in spite of his statements in the *Letter on French Music*, composed his own opera: *Le Devin du village* (*The Village Soothsayer*, 1752). The opera, with a libretto in French also penned by Rousseau, offers the simple story of two peasants, Colin and Colette, who suspect one another of infidelity, only to be reconciled by the village divine. The naïve simplicity of the plot is matched by music that resembles the vaudeville airs, folk songs, and French dance music popular at the time (Heartz 1997).

Rousseau reports in the *Confessions* that even Louis XV could sing Colette's opening air, "J'ai perdu mon Serviteur" ("I lost my servant") (1964: vol. III, 380). The opera was enormously successful throughout the latter half of the eighteenth century, judging by the 350 performances over the next fifty years (Kaufman 1998). Using the pastoral mode and the musical genre of romance, Rousseau revived traditions that were well worn in France at the time, creating a taste for a "new" style of music that emphasized melodic line over the intricacies of harmonic counterpoint and polyphony.

Social and political philosophy

In a text composed in 1761, the *Essay on the Origin of Languages*, Rousseau develops the thesis that music and language share a common source in human beings' need to communicate feeling. Rousseau argues that while our physical needs may be communicated by simple gestures, our feelings and passion must have originally motivated the development of spoken language and music (Rousseau 1995: vol. V, 380). Rousseau imagines a common origin for language and music, with the two forms being slowly differentiated over time. While language, according to Rousseau, progressively loses its ability to communicate feeling and passion (largely due to the influence of writing), music maintains the potential to access emotion, given proper forms of expression. The *Essay* contains an argument concerning the privileging of melody over harmony that dovetails with the positions that were already evident in the *Letter on French Music* and in the compositional choices in Rousseau's opera. Rousseau argues that while harmony produces an agreeable sensation, melody imitates "the inflections of the voice express[ing] complaints, cries of pain and joy, threats, wails" (1995: vol. V, 415–16). In this respect, he argues, melody "speaks and its inarticulate but energetic, lively, ardent, passionate language has one hundred times more energy than speech itself" (1995: vol. V, 416). It is this potential to communicate great emotion that draws Rousseau to emphasize melodic line in music.

The emphasis on the communication of emotion through music may be related to Rousseau's philosophical positions concerning human sociability and political formations in the texts for which he is best known. In the *Discourse on the Origin of Inequality among Men* (1754), Rousseau answered another question posed by the Academy of Dijon: "What is the origin of inequality among men and if it is authorized by natural right?" In a response that did not garner a prize as his earlier *Discourse on the Arts and Sciences* had, Rousseau laid out a philosophical position concerning the development and spread of inequality through the growth and development of human social institutions. In answering the question, Rousseau maintains that it is necessary to posit a hypothetical "state of nature" in order to understand man as he truly is, that is to say, before the changes wrought by civilization. Underlying this philosophical inquiry is the critical and potentially radical position that inequality may be mitigated, minimized, or even eliminated through appropriate social and political reform.

The hypothetical state of nature, as Rousseau conceives it, includes natural inequalities of age, size, sex, physical force, etc. (Rousseau 1964: vol. III, 131). Because natural man lives in isolation from other humans, these inequalities remain largely inconsequential. As Rousseau traces the development of social life out of the state of nature, human beings slowly and progressively lose their more animalistic characteristics to become socially oriented beings. While this development brings about many positive changes – cognitive development, language, friendship, conjugal love, and family – it also sets in motion a number of changes that will institutionalize inequality.

Rousseau is often misunderstood as promoting a "return to the state of nature" or for romanticizing the concept of the "noble savage." In reality, man in the Rousseauian state of nature lives a limited existence bounded by his needs and physical capacities. Rousseau imagines natural man as a being with limited cognitive abilities, no language, no sense of temporality, and only limited self-consciousness, but one who is free and responds empathetically to the suffering of others. Without the development of language or cognitive ability, and without a shared social existence, the isolated natural man sleeps under trees, gathers food to eat, and dwells in the present moment (Rousseau 1964: vol. III, 140, 160). In spite of his social, psychological, and cognitive limitations, natural man does possess what Rousseau calls natural pity. Although not a social being, natural man has the capacity to feel empathy for other suffering beings when he encounters them (Rousseau 1964: vol. III, 154–5). The feeling of pity will enable socialized man to develop moral relations with his fellow humanity, but even in the state of nature, pity provides a mechanism for man's identification with suffering beings.

Contact with other humans will set in motion a series of changes in natural man's mode of living that will bring civilization into being. Human beings first form loose associations to aid each other in hunting and other endeavors necessary for survival, dissolving these temporary forms of society as soon as the goal at hand is met (Rousseau 1964: vol. III, 166–7).

The gradual development of social life entails the appearance of small family groups housed in huts, meeting their basic survival needs with simple tools (Rousseau 1964: vol. III, 168). Rousseau places great emphasis on the expansion of the human heart in this phase of social development, stressing the appearance of language within the family setting. Eventually, the introduction of agriculture and metallurgy will produce a revolution in early social life, necessitating the division of labor and increasing social dependence (Rousseau 1964: vol. III, 171–2). Rousseau's account of the development of complex social relations dialectically argues that each new social innovation, although designed to free man to enjoy life, paradoxically leads to the further enslavement of man both to others and to material objects. Ultimately, the account of the development of social life in the *Discourse on the Origin of Inequality* describes the emergence of an illegitimate social contract that ties the weak to the strong, increasing social and political inequality to the point that the nascent society pulls apart at the seams. Extreme inequality leads back to the beginning: human beings revert to a new "state of nature," this time as a result of extreme corruption and political despotism (Rousseau 1964: vol. III, 191).

The critique of the institutionalization of inequality as illegitimate provides a window onto an alternative social existence in which human beings retain a greater degree of freedom and independence by meeting their basic needs within the confines of small social groups. This idealized portrait of an earlier phase of social existence includes an account of music. Consistent with the dialectical argument that subtends the account of the emergence of social life in the *Second Discourse*, music produces happiness and joy, but also leads to comparisons, and eventually vices, as people begin to compete for public recognition:

> They became accustomed to assembling in front of the huts or around a great tree: song and dance, true children of love and leisure, became the amusement or the occupation of idle men and women gathered together. Each one began to look at the others and wanted to be well-regarded; public esteem had a price. He or she who sang or danced the best, the most beautiful, the strongest, the most adroit or the most eloquent became the most considered, and that was the first step toward inequality.
>
> (Rousseau 1964: vol. III, 169)

While Rousseau emphasizes the advent of inequality in his account of these early scenes of joy and spontaneous celebration, he also asserts that they were among the happiest times in man's entire existence. Communal life in this idealized form entails the sharing of celebrations and feelings through song and dance, a theme echoed in the account of the rise of language in the *Essay on the Origin of Languages* (Rousseau 1995: vol. V, 405–6).

Building on the critique of institutionalized inequality and alienated social relations in the *Second Discourse*, the *Social Contract* (1762) provides a theoretical foundation for a form of political association that will "defend and protect with the whole force of the community the person and goods of each associate, and by which each individual uniting with all the others obeys only himself and remains as free as before" (Rousseau 1964: vol. III, 360). Rousseau imagines a social contract in which the individuals assemble to form a social group governed by the "general will." This general will expresses the common good or general interest of the community (Rousseau 1964: vol. III, 361). In Rousseau's version of the social contract, the people remains sovereign, retaining the right to dissolve the government when it no longer instantiates the general will or, in other words, works in the common interest (Rousseau 1964: vol. III, 362–3, 434–9). Legitimate forms of government entail that each citizen, as a member of the sovereign body, agrees to follow the laws, because as a citizen s/he has made the laws. Moral or political freedom for Rousseau means adherence to the self-prescribed law (Rousseau 1964: vol. III, 365). Although Rousseau does not mention music specifically in the *Social Contract*, he does suggest that civic celebrations will help foster the bond of community in *Considerations on the Government of Poland* (Rousseau 1964: vol. III, 962–3) and encourages the types of public festivals that occurred in Sparta in the *Letter to d'Alembert* (Rousseau 1995: vol. V, 123–4).

Together, the *Social Contract* and *Discourse on the Origin of Inequality* provide a portrait of an idealized form of social and political existence that minimizes social and political inequality by fostering simpler forms of community than existed in eighteenth-century France. Eighteenth-century France was officially divided into three estates – the Church, the nobility, and the Third Estate (everyone else) – each with corresponding privileges and distinctions. The reality was that 98 percent of the population (the Third Estate) was politically and socially disenfranchised and subject to cycles of poverty and famine. Rousseau's alternative vision of social and political life favors small homogeneous communities in which civic celebrations (with song and dance) help citizens bond with one another. Natural pity from the state of nature develops into a moral bond that ties members of the community together. Rather than seek to exploit and destroy one another, Rousseau envisions a community tied together through common interest and genuine feelings of affection for one another. He holds that the legitimate community will work together for the common cause and, in that way, each individual will also help him or herself, all the while retaining and protecting individual freedom and autonomy (Rousseau 1964: vol. III, 373).

Music and community

If Rousseau critiques the social and political inequality of his day, he also feels that humans are responsible for their own present predicament (Berger 2007: 142–58). Following from the arguments laid out in the *Discourse on the Origin of Inequality*, human beings have no one but themselves to blame for their current state of dependence on one another and enslavement to the social hierarchy. Social and political reform may be achieved through a return to values characteristic of simpler modes of existence, specifically, agrarian forms of social organization. In order to achieve the goal of greater social and political equality, it will be necessary to free men from the fetters of highly differentiated social structures that include intricate divisions of labor. It will also be necessary to forego the corrupting forms of power and prestige characteristic of contemporary society in favor of egalitarian self-sufficiency. This will require not only a social and political reorganization, but also a moral reform as well. In the *Social Contract*, as well as in the *Project of Constitution for Corsica* (1765) and the *Considerations on the Government of Poland*, Rousseau recommends eschewing luxury, commerce, wealth, and especially dependence on other nations, in favor of a return to agrarian values and social structures in which everyone knows everyone else. In the *Social Contract*, he recommends keeping a check on manners and morals through public opinion and a censorship tribunal (Rousseau 1964: vol. III, 458). The watchful gaze of fellow citizens keeps the conduct of the members of the community in check, both policing private conduct and limiting the disparities of wealth that would lead to greater social and political inequality.

Rousseau does not mention a role for the arts in achieving these social and political goals. The *Discourse on the Arts and Sciences* blames "advances" in the arts and sciences for corrupting human nature. In the *Letter to d'Alembert on the Theatre* (1758), Rousseau argues that the theatre has a tendency to reinforce the values and often negative attributes of a community and therefore cannot be used as a vehicle for positive change (Rousseau 1995: vol. V, 18). Arguing against Aristotle's theory of catharsis, Rousseau believes that theatre only augments self-interest and stirs the passions, encouraging people to become more adept at hiding their vices from others. Furthermore, the desire to see and be seen turns the theatre into a kind of public spectacle that exacerbates social inequality, privilege, and distinction. Finally, Rousseau believes that audience members experience plays in silent isolation from one another: "We believe that we gather together in the theatre, and it's there that each one is isolated, it's there that one goes to forget one's friends, one's neighbors, one's relatives, to take an interest in fable, to cry over the misfortunes of the dead or to laugh at the expense of the living" (1995: vol. V, 16). Rousseau sees the theatre as a corrupting rather than a corrective or purifying force within a democratic republican community, one that only heightens self-interest to the detriment of the bonds of community.

His assessment of the effects of novel reading on the public is most succinctly summarized in the preface to his own novel, *Julie, or the New Heloise* (1762), in which he proclaimed: "Theatre is necessary in great cities as are novels for corrupt peoples," and "a chaste young woman never read a novel" (1964: vol. II, 5, 6). While his preface emphatically asserts the corrupting effects of novels, the fan mail that he received in response to the novel documents the existence of an eighteenth-century public that fiercely identified with the emotional lives of the characters (Darnton 1985; Paige 2008). The fan mail suggests that readers felt that the sentiments expressed in *Julie* were "true," in the sense that they were authentic, emanating from the novel's author, Jean-Jacques Rousseau (Paige 2008). In this respect, the historical reception of the novel provides a model for aesthetic reception that underscores the importance of emotional response, although in an individualized way, one reader at a time. Thus, novels elicit an emotional and moral response, but individually, and the theatre corrupts an audience by isolating its members and emphasizing self-interest.

Turning to Rousseau's writing about music, the potential to elicit a strong emotional response in a group of listeners at the same time makes musical performance a possible vehicle for promoting the ties of social, moral, and political community. According to Rousseau, music has the ability to tap the emotions of listeners through a kind of mimesis. In both the *Essay on the Origin of Languages* and the entry "imitation" in the *Music Dictionary* (1767–68), he asserts that the power of music to stir emotion lies in imitation:

> [T]he art of the musician consists in substituting for the imperceptible image of the object the movements that its presence excites in the heart of the one who contemplates. Not only will he agitate the sea, animate the flame of fire, make the streams run, the rain fall and the torrents swell; but he will paint the horror of an awful desert, darken the walls of an underground prison, calm the tempest, make the air tranquil and serene and will spread a new freshness over the groves from the orchestra. He will not directly represent these things, but he will excite in the soul the same movements that one feels in seeing them.
>
> (1995: vol. V, 861)

The musician does not directly imitate the sounds of nature, but rather makes the listener feel the same feelings as if s/he were before nature. In other words, the art of the musician lies in moving the passions. Rousseau claims that this is accomplished through a number of features in music, but especially by accent and melody. By accent, Rousseau means "any modification of the speaking voice, in its duration or in the tone of the syllables and the words of which the discourse is composed" asserting that there exists "a very precise relationship between the two uses of *Accents* and the two parts of melody, namely rhythm and intonation" (1995: vol. V, 613). In other words, tonal variation as well as rhythm produce accent in music and language. The most expressive type of music is one in which accent in language aligns with accent in music in such a way as to communicate feeling and emotion to the audience through song.

Melodic line also contributes to the communication of emotion for Rousseau. He argues that "[s]ounds in melody not only act on us as sounds, but also as signs of our affections, of our sentiments; it is in this way that they excite in us the movements that they express" (1995: vol. V, 417). When we are moved by melody, it is not only because the music is pleasing, but also because the movement is communicated to the heart, stressing the moral component of the experience. Like pity in the state of nature, music enables human beings to identify with one another as they communicate emotion.

One last concept from Rousseau's *Music Dictionary* provides insight into how music realizes its potential to stir the emotions in a moral way. Rousseau defines "unity of melody" as "a successive *Unity* that relates to the subject and through which all the well-linked parts form a single whole, of which we perceive the ensemble and all the relations" (1995: vol. V, 1143). He claims that he composed *Le Devin du village* according to this principle, which he first articulated in his *Letter on French Music* (Rousseau 1995: vol. V, 1146; Waeber 2009). Rousseau maintains that unity of melody enables us to hear a piece composed of multiple parts as a whole, rather than be distracted by polyphonic lines or harmonically driven counterpoint. Rousseau imagines an audience of listeners, such as those who first heard his opera, being moved by the music because of the emotions expressed through the accent of passion and the uncluttered melodic lines. This audience – unlike the theatre audience – would feel the emotion together, as a group, and therefore bond in recognition of their common moral feeling.

Such a vision of aesthetic reception overcomes the alienation that Rousseau diagnosed in theatre audiences by using aesthetic form to shape reception. Unity of melody and accent elicit emotions in the listeners without enabling them to become distracted or self-interested. Rather, music penetrates their ears and they feel the emotions communicated by the composer and musicians. Ideally, the strong pull of moral emotion reinforces the bonds of community that exist. Rousseau argues that we are interested in music because it announces the presence of another human being: "Birds whistle, only man sings, and one cannot hear song or a symphony without immediately saying: another sentient being is here" (1995: vol. V, 421). Like the pull of natural pity, the sound of music taps the natural emotions that originally motivated humans to communicate with one another. Through musical expression, Rousseau seems to suggest that the bonds of community might be strengthened. Strengthening the moral bonds of community ultimately works in the service of the social and political reforms that he proposes in his most famous texts on social and political theory. Music, in the service of shared human moral expression, Rousseau intimates, could help to reinforce our most positive qualities, enabling the overcoming of self-interest in favor of justice and equality for all human beings.

While Rousseau's *Social Contract* poses the modern question of political legitimacy and his *Confessions* usher in a representation of the modern self, his emphasis on the redemptive role music might play in countering the alienation and self-interest of modern life prefigures developments in German Romanticism, modernism, and the theorists of the Frankfurt School. His writings on music link concerns of his social and political thought with a possible remedy in artistic expression (Simon 2005b). In a parallel development, his comparative explorations of the musical expression of non-Western peoples introduce European thought to the field of ethnomusicology. Finally, Rousseau's compositional emphasis on melody heralds the decline of counterpoint in favor of the strong melodic lines of Hayden, Beethoven, and Schubert.

See also The early modern period (Chapter 25), Music and language (Chapter 10), Music and politics (Chapter 50), and Rhythm, melody, and harmony (Chapter 3).

References

Berger, K. (2007) *Bach's Cycle, Mozart's Arrow: An Essay on the Origins of Musical Modernity*, Berkeley: University of California Press.

Darnton, R. (1985) *The Great Cat Massacre and Other Episodes in French Cultural History*, New York: Vintage Books.

Heartz, D. (1997) "Italian by Intention, French of Necessity: Rousseau's *Le Devin du village*," in M.-C. Mussat, J. Mongrédien, and J.-M. Nectoux (eds) *Echos de France et d'Italie: liber amicorum Yves Gérard*, Paris: Buchet/Chastel Société française de musicologie, pp. 31–46.

Johnson, J.H. (1986) "The Encyclopedists and the *Querelle des* Bouffons: Reason and the Enlightenment of Sentiment," *Eighteenth-Century Life* 10: 12–27.

Kaufman, C. (1998) "Questions and Answers about Rousseau and *Le Devin du village*: An Interview with Charlotte Kaufman," *Embellishments 5*, available at www.areditions.com/rr/embellish/1998_05/rousseau.html.

O'Dea, M. (1995) *Jean-Jacques Rousseau: Music, Illusion and Desire*, New York: St. Martin's.

Paige, N. (2008) "Rousseau's Readers Revisited: The Aesthetics of *La Nouvelle Héloïse*," *Eighteenth-Century Studies* 42: 131–54.

Rousseau, J.-J. (1959–95) *Oeuvres complètes*, ed. B. Gagnebin, 5 vols, Paris: Gallimard.

Simon, J. (2005a) "Singing Democracy: Music and Politics in Jean-Jacques Rousseau's Thought," *Journal of the History of Ideas* 66: 433–54.

—— (2005b) "Rousseau and Aesthetic Modernity: Music's Power of Redemption," *Eighteenth-Century Music* 2: 41–56.

Waeber, J. (2009) "Jean-Jacques Rousseau's 'unité de mélodie,'" *Journal of the American Musicological Society* 62: 79–144.

Further reading

Scott, J.T. (ed.) (1998) *Jean-Jacques Rousseau: Essay on the Origin of Languages and Writings Related to Music, The Collected Writings of Rousseau, Vol. 7*, Hanover: University Press of New England.

30

KANT

Hannah Ginsborg

Introduction

Immanuel Kant (1724–1804) was one of the most important philosophers of the modern period. He is best known for contributions to metaphysics and epistemology (*Critique of Pure Reason*) and to ethics (*Groundwork of the Metaphysic of Morals, Critique of Practical Reason*), but his work in aesthetics (*Critique of Judgment*, first published in 1790) is equally groundbreaking. In this chapter, I focus on his aesthetics, with emphasis on elements relevant to philosophical thinking about music.

Kant follows eighteenth-century tradition in distinguishing two aesthetic categories, the beautiful and the sublime, and his aesthetic theory includes discussions of both. I focus primarily on the beautiful, both because it is more relevant to the aesthetics of music and because his account of the beautiful represents a more original contribution to philosophy.

Kant on beauty

Judgments of beauty: non-cognitive but universally valid

The core of Kant's discussion of beauty is contained in the "Analytic of the Beautiful," Sections 1–22 of his *Critique of Judgment*. (Throughout, I cite the standard Academy Edition page numbers (Kant 1908), which appear in all recent editions; all further references to Kant are to this work.) Kant's discussion is framed in terms of "judgments of beauty" or, equivalently, "judgments of taste." It is a controversial question exactly what Kant means by a judgment of beauty, and in particular whether it consists only in the explicit claim that an object is beautiful, or whether it can also be the feeling of pleasure in an object's beauty. Here, relying on an interpretation I have defended elsewhere (for references, and details of the controversy, see Ginsborg 2005), I take the view that Kant does not draw a sharp distinction between aesthetic experience and aesthetic judgment, and that a judgment of beauty is best understood as the pleasurable experience that we might call "finding" something beautiful, and which might or not be articulated as the explicit thought or statement that the thing is beautiful.

Kant's theory of beauty can be seen as addressing a dilemma about the objectivity of aesthetic experience and judgment. When we experience a thing as beautiful, are we registering a genuinely objective property that the thing has independently of our response to it? Or are we simply reacting to it subjectively, as when we feel pleasure or displeasure in something we eat or drink? Relatedly, when we say that something is beautiful, are we making a conceptual claim about it, which could in principle either be verified or shown to be false? Or are we merely expressing our liking for it, without any implications about the objective properties of the thing? The dilemma here is manifested historically in two contrasting eighteenth-century approaches to aesthetic judgment. On the "rationalist" approach, influenced by Leibniz, and adopted by Meier and Baumgarten, a feeling of pleasure in the beautiful is a kind of cognitive representation – a "confused" representation, but objective nonetheless – of a genuinely mind-independent feature of an object, namely, its goodness or perfection. On the contrasting "empiricist" approach, associated with Shaftesbury, Burke, and to some extent Hume, there is nothing objective or cognitive about the feeling of pleasure in beauty. While we can make a cognitive judgment which ascribes to the object a disposition to produce that kind of feeling in normal perceivers, the feeling itself does not register an objective property of the thing.

Kant responds to this dilemma by arguing that judgments of beauty are neither objective nor merely subjective. He argues against their objectivity by emphasizing their dependence on the individual's own affective response to an object. Someone can judge that an object is beautiful only if she herself experiences pleasure in the object. She cannot infer its beauty on objective grounds; for example, that it meets certain supposed criteria for beauty or that other people describe it as beautiful. There is thus an ineliminably subjective element in the judgment of beauty, which distinguishes it from all cognitive judgments (including judgments of the good or of perfection, which for Kant are a species of cognitive judgment). But in spite of this dependence on the individual's own affective response, Kant argues, judgments of beauty should not be regarded as merely subjective. For, in contrast to someone who expresses pleasure in food or drink (the paradigm example of what Kant calls "pleasure in the agreeable"), someone who claims that an object is beautiful makes a normative claim on everyone else's agreement: she claims that everyone ought to share her pleasure in the object. Judgments of beauty, unlike judgments of the merely agreeable, are thus not merely expressions of the individual's own liking for the object, but, in Kant's terms "universally valid." Someone who judges an object to be beautiful speaks, as Kant puts it, with a "universal voice" (§8, 216) claiming to represent not just her own attitude, but rather the attitude which everyone who perceives the object *ought* to take to it, whether or not they in fact do so.

Kant's answer to the dilemma can be put in contemporary terms by saying that he is not a realist about beauty, but that he still thinks that aesthetic judgments have a kind of (what would now be called) objectivity, in that they make a legitimate claim to universal agreement. It is a corollary of this point (emphasized in the Antinomy, §§ 56–7), that there can be genuine aesthetic disagreement, as opposed to mere difference in aesthetic reaction, even though such disagreement cannot be conclusively resolved by means of argument. The point that aesthetic judgments cannot be proved by argument (emphasized in §§32–3) might seem to conflict with the possibility of critical discourse about works of art. But there is still room for critical discourse and even argument in Kantian aesthetics, as long as the argument is understood not as aiming to prove that the object is beautiful, but rather as getting one's interlocutor to experience the object in such a way that she herself comes to judge it to be beautiful.

Disinterested pleasure

Kant develops his view of aesthetic judgment in part by contrasting the pleasure we feel in beauty with other kinds of pleasure, in particular pleasure in the agreeable and pleasure in the good. The upshot is the historically influential claim that pleasure in the beautiful is "disinterested," which is roughly to say that it does not depend on the object satisfying a desire for the object. Our experience of an object as beautiful, unlike our appreciation of its goodness, does not require that we take it to fulfill any goal or purpose; nor, unlike pleasure in the agreeable, does it intrinsically involve the arousal and satisfaction of desire for the object. This is not incompatible with the claim that we can in fact take an interest in the preservation and protection of beautiful things, and that we can desire to experience them.

The free play of the faculties

How is it possible for there to be a kind of judging which is not objective, yet involves a claim to universal validity? Kant's answer, introduced at Section 9, is in terms of the notion of the "free harmonious play" of understanding and imagination, which are the two faculties operative in ordinary objective cognition. In ordinary empirical cognition, paradigmatically the perceptual recognition of an object as having certain features (for example that this is a purple flower with oval leaves), imagination and understanding work harmoniously together, but in such a way that imagination is governed by concepts (here "purple," "flower," "oval," etc.) which function as rules, so that imagination is, as Kant puts it, constrained by understanding. In the experience of the beautiful, imagination and understanding harmonize as in ordinary cognition, but the imagination is "free" rather than governed by concepts. Kant sometimes describes the free play as an activity in which the imagination and understanding do what is normally required for the application of concepts to the object, but without any particular concept being applied, so that we have, in effect, conceptualization without determinate concepts. According to Kant (in a "deduction of taste" sketched briefly at §9 and §21, and presented officially at §38), this "free play" manifests a "subjective condition of cognition in general" and thus can make the same claim to universal validity that is made in a cognitive judgment. Many commentators question the success of this argument, on the grounds that if the free play is a genuine condition of cognition, as the argument seems to require, then we would have to judge every cognizable object to be beautiful. The success of the argument seems to depend on providing an interpretation of the free play on which its universal validity follows from the universal validity of cognition, but without its being the case that the free play actually takes place in every act of cognition.

The free play of the faculties is often thought of as a distinctive psychological occurrence which we can be aware of through introspection, and which is manifested paradigmatically by the experience of looking at an abstract painting, where one might try out various ways of perceiving the relations among the elements without settling on any determinate one. One might suppose that the same kind of imaginative play is involved in listening to music in which, again, there is scope for hearing the same arrangement of sounds in a variety of different ways (for example a particular melodic line can be heard either as an accompanying figure or as a melody in its own right, or an F major chord as the subdominant in C or the dominant in B-flat). But there is a great deal of controversy about the proper interpretation of the free play, due partly to difficulties in understanding Kant's "faculty psychology" in general, and partly to the obscurity of the notion of the free play itself. Rather than the free play corresponding to a phenomenologically identifiable element of the experience of a work of art, I take Kant's talk of the free play to be a metaphorical way of describing the non-conceptual claim to universality implicit in the judgment of beauty itself (for more on the controversy, and references, see Ginsborg 2005).

Purposiveness without a purpose

Kant describes the experience of the beautiful in terms of the apparently paradoxical idea of "purposiveness without a purpose" [*Zweckmäßigkeit ohne Zweck*] (sometimes translated with "end" for "*Zweck*" and the neologisim "finality" for "*Zweckmäßigkeit*"). This feature is variously ascribed to the activity of the cognitive faculties in the experience of the beautiful, to the relation between the faculties and the beautiful object, and to the beautiful object itself. The significance of these ascriptions is disputed, but they can be read as very closely related to the point that a judgment of beauty makes a claim to universal validity but does not ascribe an objective property, in particular a property of goodness. In judging a thing to be beautiful, I take there to be a relation of fitness or appropriateness ("purposiveness") between my mental activity and the object, such that everyone else ought to judge the object in the same way. I thus take my activity and its relation to the object to be purposive in the sense of not being arbitrary or random: I am judging the object as it ought to be judged, not just as I happen to judge it. Yet I do not judge the object to have the objective property of satisfying some particular aim or purpose, nor is my mental activity aimed at any purpose (for example, that of getting information about the object), so that the purposiveness can be said to be without a purpose. Kant conveys the same idea by speaking of "formal purposiveness," which has been partly responsible for his reputation as a formalist (see section on Kant's alleged formalism below.)

Impure judgments of beauty

So far our discussion has concerned what Kant calls "pure" judgments of beauty. But there are two different ways in which judgments of beauty can fall short of being pure. They can involve an element of pleasure which does not derive from the cognitive faculties, in particular "charm" (*Reiz*) or "emotion" (*Rührung*). In that case they fall short of being disinterested because they involve an experience of the agreeable, which in turn depends on the arousal and satisfaction of (sensory) desire. Alternatively, they can be contingent on the application of concepts to the object. Here again they fall short of disinterestedness because they involve the recognition of the object as satisfying a purpose, and hence as meeting a (rational) desire. Judgments which fail to be pure in this second sense are referred to by Kant as judgments of "accessory" or "dependent" (*anhängend*), as opposed to free, beauty. Representational art would seem, for him, to fall into the category of dependent beauty, but music – or more specifically music not set to words – is cited by him as an example of "free beauty" (§16, 229).

Kant on sublimity

Kant follows other eighteenth-century thinkers, in particular Burke, in recognizing two distinct kinds of aesthetic experience, that of the beautiful and that of the sublime. He describes the feeling of the sublime as involving displeasure as well as pleasure, at one point comparing it to a "vibration" between repulsion and attraction to the same thing (§27, 258). As in the case of the beautiful, the feeling is explained in terms of the activity of our cognitive faculties, but in the case of the sublime these are imagination and reason rather than understanding. In the "mathematical" sublime, we feel the inadequacy of the imagination to grasp the immensity of an object presented to us, but this awakens the awareness in us of our power of reason, which is capable of grasping the infinite. In the "dynamical" sublime, we are aware through imagination of the power of the object and its potential to be physically dangerous to us, but at the same time we feel ourselves to be, as rational beings, superior to nature rather than dominated by it. Kant thinks that it is primarily nature which offers examples of sublimity, although he does cite examples of artifacts as well (the Pyramids, St. Peter's in Rome). It has been proposed (Parret 1998) that if Kant had been able to listen to Strauss or Mahler, he would have characterized their works as sublime. A possible connection between music and the sublime is suggested by Kant's association of the sublime with emotion (*Rührung*) (§14, 226; see also §23, 245) and his claim that music is particularly suited to the arousal of emotion (§53, 328ff.).

Kant on art

Kant often discusses artistic beauty tangentially in his treatment of judgments of beauty in general, but he addresses the topic of "fine art" or "beautiful art" (*schöne Kunst*) systematically at Sections 43–54. Kant is concerned here with distinguishing fine art from the production of artifacts more generally (for example, craft or handwork) and in particular with the differentiation of fine or beautiful art from art which is "merely agreeable"; for example, the arts of social entertaining.

Genius

An important part of Kant's discussion of art concerns the question of how beautiful art objects are produced. Since there are no rules or criteria for determining the beauty of something, we cannot explain the production of beautiful art, as we can the production of artifacts more generally, by supposing that the artist is guided by rules or prescriptions. The answer is that the artist has a natural faculty of "genius" which enables him to produce beautiful works without being consciously guided by rules. Beautiful objects are thus in a sense products of nature operating through the artist. This has implications for the teaching and transmission of art. The artist can learn from examples, and his own works can be examples for future artists, but the capacity to produce beautiful art cannot be acquired through learning and internalizing rules.

Aesthetic ideas

Kant's discussion of "beautiful art" introduces a new element which does not figure, at least not explicitly, in the Analytic of the Beautiful, namely, that art is the expression of "aesthetic ideas." Kant describes an aesthetic idea as "a representation of the imagination which occasions much thinking, but to which no determinate thought, i.e. concept, can be adequate" (§49, 314). In his initial characterization of aesthetic ideas, he describes them as the "counterpart" of "rational ideas," whose objects, unlike those of empirical concepts such as *dog* or *table*, cannot be represented by the senses or the imagination. Kant gives as examples of these rational ideas the ideas of invisible beings, hell, eternity, and creation, and he also mentions the ideas of death, envy, love, fame and the virtues and vices more generally, which can indeed be realized in experience, but only incompletely. Aesthetic ideas provide an imaginative correlate to rational ideas, in that sense attempting to play the same role with respect to rational ideas as, say, the image of a dog plays for the empirical concept *dog*: they "strive towards something that lies beyond the bounds of experience, and hence try to approach to an exhibition [*Darstellung*] of concepts of reason (intellectual ideas), so that these [the concepts of reason] are given a semblance of objective reality" (§49, 314). Thus the artist, in creating a work which expresses aesthetic ideas, is also attempting to give sensible expression to rational ideas "in a way which goes beyond the limits of experience" (§49, 314).

In a subsequent section, Kant seems to suggest that there can be aesthetic ideas which are not connected with rational ideas, and that this is the case in particular for those expressed by music: "the form of the arrangement of these sensations (harmony and melody) . . . serves only to express, by means of a proportioned attunement of the sensations, the aesthetic idea of a coherent whole of an unutterable [*unnennbar*] wealth of thought" (§53, 329). Similar interpretive difficulties arise here as in the case of the free play of the faculties: how can music express a wealth of thought without expressing any thought in particular? But the suggestion seems to fit something about the phenomenology of musical experiences, which is perhaps captured in Roger Scruton's suggestion that we can think of music as "expressive" in an intransitive sense, prior to thinking of it as expressing anything in particular (158).

Kant's alleged formalism

Kant is often thought of as the originator of formalism in aesthetics, and, largely as a result of his influence on Eduard Hanslick, in the aesthetics of music more specifically. But it is an open question whether Kant himself deserves to be called a formalist. The question is complicated by unclarities in the very notion of formalism, in particular the degree to which it is compatible with expressivism.

Kant's reputation as a formalist derives primarily from the Third Moment of the Analytic of the Beautiful, in which Kant argues that a judgment of beauty is based on the "mere form of purposiveness" in the representation by which an object is given to us (§11, 221). Kant goes on to equate the "form of purposiveness" of an object, or the representation of it, with the "purposiveness of [its] form," saying that beauty should concern only form and not matter (§13, 223). In illustrating the point at Section 14, he seems to identify "form" with the spatial and temporal arrangement of sensory elements (colors and musical tones). Here he argues that colors and tones, which he regards, following Euler, as vibrations of the ether and of the air respectively, could count as beautiful only if the mind could perceive the vibrations by reflection as well as by sense. That is, for the experience of an individual tone or color to be one of beauty as opposed to mere agreeableness, the vibrations would need not merely to affect us in such a way as to give rise to a pleasant sensation, but would also have to be in some way perceived by the cognitive powers, so that we could recognize their spatial and temporal structure. (It is not clear whether Kant thinks that this condition is satisfied, since he seems to take conflicting positions on this point in different editions; he does make clear that he thinks it could be satisfied at most for "pure" colors and tones.) He also claims that, in the visual arts, it is design rather than color that is essential for beauty, and, similarly, in music, that what matters for beauty is not the agreeable tone of an instrument but rather the "composition" of tones, suggesting again that pleasure in the beautiful is derived from the perception of the spatial and temporal arrangement of elements of the beautiful thing.

Another, and perhaps more significant, reason for regarding Kant as a formalist is his denial, made especially clear in the Second and Fourth Moments, that a judgment of beauty is conceptual. This seems to rule out ascribing beauty to a work of art on the basis of its representational or expressive character, since recognizing what is represented or expressed would seem to require the application of concepts. Kant does allow, in the Third Moment, that there can be judgments of beauty which are conditional on the object being brought under concepts (as when one judges that something is a beautiful shoe, or a beautiful horse, but not necessarily beautiful *tout court*). These are the judgments of dependent beauty mentioned above, and they would seem to include judgments about the beauty of representational art. But his characterization of them as "impure" has led many philosophers to assume that he does not regard them as genuine judgments of beauty and that representational art for him has a second-class status. This would again seem to support the formalist reading, in that it suggests that the success of a work, say of music, in representing or expressing a reality external to that work (for example, in the case of music, human emotion) could not be a ground for regarding it as beautiful.

However, a number of considerations can be raised against the formalist reading. First, regarding the Third Moment, it is not obvious that Kant is genuinely committed to the view that beauty concerns only the spatial and temporal relations among the elements of a thing. It is possible to understand "form" in a broader sense which allows the experience of an object's "form" to include everything about its appearance as such, excluding only its immediate sensory effects on us and our grasp of what kind of object it is and the uses to which it can be put. (On the restrictiveness of the notion of form in Kant, see Guyer 1979, ch. 6 and Allison 2001, ch. 6).

Second, regarding the non-conceptual character of the judgment of beauty, it can be argued that "dependent beauty," including the beauty of representational art, does not have second-class status for Kant (see Schaper 1979). As we shall see below, Kant's discussion of art gives a privileged status to art which is connected with moral ideas, in particular poetry and representational painting.

Moreover, as we saw above, Kant sees art as the expression of "aesthetic ideas," and this doctrine appears on the face of it to be incompatible with formalism, at least as it is usually understood.

Kant on music

Kant wrote very little about music as such. Most of what he did write is in Sections 51–4 of the *Critique of Judgment*, in the context of his account of art, but music is also discussed or at least mentioned in Section 14 (on the beauty or otherwise of individual musical tones), in Section 16 (on music as "free beauty"), and in Section 44 (on *Tafelmusik*, that is, music as background to a dinner party).

At Section 51 Kant classifies the fine arts in a tentative scheme corresponding to three elements of linguistic communication: word (oratory and poetry), gesture (visual art, including sculpture, architecture, landscape gardening and painting), and tone, which includes music and "the art of color," both of which he refers to as offering "a play of sensations." One of his concerns in this section is the question, already discussed in Section 14 (see above under "Kant's alleged formalism"), of whether individual musical tones can be beautiful. This is important for determining the status of music, Kant says, because if the tones are beautiful, then "music is wholly beautiful art," but if not, then it is at least in part "only agreeable art" (§51, 325). At this point though it is left open that, even if individual musical tones are merely agreeable, a musical piece can still be beautiful by virtue of its overall composition.

At Sections 53–4, however, Kant gives indications that music overall is merely agreeable rather than beautiful, and also that its aesthetic value is less than that of the other arts. In Section 53 he ranks the various arts, giving poetry the highest place, and then saying that "if our concern is with charm and the movement of the mind," then music should be ranked next, above the visual arts. But he goes on to say that if we assess the value of the fine arts by the "cultivation" which they offer the mind, then "music, since it merely plays with sensations, has the lowest place among the fine arts." He criticizes music for the transitory character of the impressions it produces and also for its lack of "urbanity," in that music imposes itself on others in the vicinity and thus "impairs the freedom of those outside of the musical party" (§54, 330). (This last point is often ridiculed, but it reflects Kant's deep commitment, emphasized elsewhere in his philosophy, to the importance of freedom, specifically in the exercise of one's mental capacities.) At Section 54 he expands on the suggestion that pleasure in music is merely sensory by saying that it consists in a feeling of bodily health brought about by the lively alternation of the various emotions it arouses. And he compares music to the telling of jokes, claiming that both deserve to be considered more as agreeable arts than as beautiful arts.

It is important to note that Kant's account of music, in particular his reductive view of pleasure in music and consequent dismissal of music's claims to be beautiful, does not represent a commitment of the core aesthetic theory presented in the Analytic of the Beautiful. On the contrary, the discussion at Sections 51–4 seems to be based on assumptions which conflict with the Analytic of the Beautiful, in particular that the experience of beauty must include the entertaining of moral ideas "which alone carry with them an independent liking" (§52, 326). Kant seems to assume, in these passages, that the only alternative to a pleasure which is associated with moral ideas is sensory or bodily gratification. But this seems to run counter to a (perhaps *the*) central theme of the Analytic of the Beautiful, which is that pleasure in the beautiful is a distinctive kind of pleasure, associated with the functioning of the cognitive faculties, which is independent both of sensory gratification and of moral feeling. If we privilege the Analytic as the heart of Kant's aesthetic theory, then it would seem that music's lack of association with moral ideas should constitute it as a paradigm of the beautiful in art (as indeed suggested by Kant's characterization of it at Section 16 as "free beauty").

Conclusion: a Kantian philosophy of music?

I have suggested that Kant's aesthetic theory commits him neither to musical formalism nor to his own reductive characterization of musical experience at Sections 53–4. What, then, are its positive implications for philosophical thinking about music? As I understand his account, it leaves open a wide range of views about the appreciation of music, including views which ascribe meaning to music or take it to express emotions. But I take a view of music that is Kantian in spirit to be committed at least to the following claims:

1. The beauty of a piece of music (and by extension, other aesthetic features we might ascribe to it) is not a real or objective feature of it.
2. The pleasure of listening to music does not derive merely from the senses, but from an exercise of the same capacities that are required for cognition, in particular imagination.
3. There can be genuine agreement and disagreement about judgments of the aesthetic value of music; in other words, divergence in such aesthetic judgments is not just a matter of differing likes and dislikes.
4. While there is a genuine point to critical discourse about music, and musical analysis more specifically, claims that are made in critical discourse do not have the status of rational arguments.

Among contemporary philosophical accounts of music, Scruton (1997) seems to me to come closest to a view which is Kantian in the sense suggested here.

See also Aesthetic properties (Chapter 14), Hanslick (Chapter 33), Music and imagination (Chapter 11), and Understanding music (Chapter 12).

References

Allison, H. (2001) *Kant's Theory of Taste*, Cambridge: Cambridge University Press.

Ginsborg, H. (2005) "Kant's Aesthetics and Teleology," in E.N. Zalta (ed.) *The Stanford Encyclopedia of Philosophy*, available at http://plato.stanford.edu/archives/fall2008/entries/kant-aesthetics/.

Guyer, P. (1979) *Kant and the Claims of Taste*, Cambridge: Harvard University Press.

Kant, I. (1908 [1790]) *Kritik der Urteilskraft*, in *Gesammelte Schriften*, vol. 5, ed. Akademie der Wissenschaften, Berlin: Walter de Gruyter.

Parret, H. (1998) "Kant on Music and the Hierarchy of the Arts," *The Journal of Aesthetics and Art Criticism* 56: 251–64.

Schaper, E. (1979) *Studies in Kant's Aesthetics*, Edinburgh: Edinburgh University Press.

Scruton, R. (1997) *The Aesthetics of Music*, Oxford: Clarendon Press.

Further reading

Bicknell, J. (2002) "Can Music Convey Semantic Content? A Kantian Approach," *Journal of Aesthetics and Art Criticism* 60: 253–61. (Applies Kant's views on aesthetic ideas to contemporary questions about the experience of music.)

Kant, I. (1987 [1790]) *Critique of Judgment*, trans. W. Pluhar, Indianapolis: Hackett. (One of two recommended translations; readable and accurate, but less scholarly than the Guyer edition.)

—— (2000 [1790]) *Critique of the Power of Judgment*, ed. P. Guyer, trans. P. Guyer and E. Matthews, Cambridge: Cambridge University Press. (Less readable than the Pluhar translation, but contains much useful editorial material.)

Kivy, P. (1991) "Kant and the Affektenlehre: What He Said, and What I Wish He Had Said," in R. Meerbote (ed.) *Kant's Aesthetics* (Vol 1, NAKS Studies in Philosophy), Atascadero: Ridgeview, pp. 63–73. (Addresses Kant's relation to formalism in music.)

—— (2009) *Antithetical Arts*, Oxford: Oxford University Press. (Ch. 2 contains more recent reflections on Kant and musical formalism.)

Weatherston, M. (1996) "Kant's Assessment of Music in the Critique of Judgment," *British Journal of Aesthetics* 36: 56–65. (Examines Kant's negative characterization of music.)

31

SCHOPENHAUER

Alex Neill

Arthur Schopenhauer (1788–1860) begins his main discussion of music, in Section 52 of *The World as Will and Representation*, by noting that "It stands quite apart" from all the other forms of art (1969: vol. 1, 256). (All further references to Schopenhauer are to this work.) "[M]usic is by no means like the other arts, namely a copy of the Ideas," he writes, but is rather "a *copy of the will itself* . . . For this reason the effect of music is so very much more powerful and penetrating than is that of the other arts, for these others speak only of the shadow, but music of the essence" (vol. 1, 257). This is a claim that composers and musicians have, perhaps unsurprisingly, found extremely seductive: Richard Wagner, for example, held that Schopenhauer captures "the position of music among the fine arts with philosophic clearness," and in doing so "recognises the true nature of music" (Goehr 1996: 201); other admirers included Liszt, Brahms, Rimsky-Korsakov, Mahler, Schoenberg and Prokofiev. But why did Schopenhauer hold that music "stands quite apart" from the other arts? Just what does he mean when he says that it, unlike them, speaks "of the essence" of things? These are the central questions facing anyone wanting to understand Schopenhauer's theory of music, and in what follows I shall sketch (the beginnings, at least) of answers to them.

Schopenhauer's philosphical framework

First, however, a reminder of the metaphysics and philosophy of art that underpins the theory will be useful. As an Idealist, Schopenhauer holds that the true nature of things is quite different from that which is presented to us in sense experience. But his take on the nature of reality is highly distinctive: reality, he argues, is will, a single arational, impersonal force that is constantly "striving" or in flux. Like the Kantian noumena, will "is that of which all representation, all object, is the phenomenon, the visibility . . . It is the innermost essence, the kernel, of every particular thing and also of the whole" (vol. 1, 110). Unlike the Kantian noumena, however, will is, if not directly knowable by human beings, to some extent accessible, for it "manifests" or "objectifies" itself, with varying degrees of clarity, in phenomena: in forces of nature, in organic and inorganic matter, in sentient creatures, and most clearly or perfectly of all in human beings.

Schopenhauer's point is not that will objectifies itself to a greater or less *extent* in different phenomena, in such a way in which, for example, there might be more of it in a plant than there is in a rock; what varies in degree is rather the objectification itself – the will is more "visible," or more clearly objectified, in the plant than it is in the rock, and more clearly in an animal than in a plant. "Indeed," he writes, "the will's passage into visibility, its objectification, has gradations as endless as those between the feeblest twilight and the brightest sunlight, the loudest tone and the softest echo" (vol. 1, 128).

It is at this point that what he calls the Platonic Ideas come into Schopenhauer's picture. As he writes, "These different grades of the will's objectification, expressed in innumerable individuals, exist as the unattained patterns of these, or as the eternal forms of things" (vol. 1, 129). It is to these patterns or what might be called templates that Schopenhauer is referring in his talk of Ideas: modes of objectification of will that are expressed in particular individuals in space and time. With the exception of music, the point of art, in Schopenhauer's scheme, is to facilitate our recognition of these Ideas or templates of objectification of will, and hence, in effect, to give us access to reality. The different forms of art, he argues – again, with the exception of music – are suited to the presentation of different Ideas, and just as the Ideas can be ranked, so to speak, according to the grade of objectification of will of which they are the pattern or prototype, so the various forms of art can be ranked according to the Ideas which it is their particular function to present or express. In short, the higher the grade of objectification of will represented in an Idea, the more valuable, because the more revelatory of the nature of reality, is the art form which presents and expresses that Idea. Poetry (and in particular tragedy), whose subject is the Idea of "man in the connected series of his efforts and actions" (vol. 1, 244), the Idea in which will is manifests itself most clearly, is at the top of the hierarchy; architecture, the artistic purpose of which is to express "some of those Ideas that are the lowest grades of the will's objectivity," such as those of "rigidity" and "hardness" (vol. 1, 214), is at the bottom.

The argument for music's unique status

Why is it, then, that music "stands quite apart" from this hierarchy, as a "copy" not of the Ideas, but of the will itself"? In the opening pages of Section 52 of *The World as Will and Representation*, Schopenhauer offers what amounts to a simple – at least in terms of structure – argument in support of his claim. The first premise is that "In [music] we do not recognise the copy, the repetition, of any Idea" (vol. 1, 256). The second is that music is nonetheless "in some sense . . . related to the world as the depiction to the thing depicted, as the copy to the original" (vol. 1, 256). And his conclusion, as we have seen, is that music is "a copy of the will itself." Understanding Schopenhauer's view of music depends on understanding why he makes and what he means by each of these statements, and in what follows I attempt to elucidate all three.

What then of the first premise, the assertion that "In [music] we do not recognise the copy, the repetition, of any Idea?" Schopenhauer offers no explicit defence of this claim, but the standard assumption by commentators is that his underlying thought is that music does not "copy" any Idea simply by virtue of the fact that music is not representational: Jerrold Levinson, for example, presents Schopenhauer as holding that "being non-representational, [music] presents for contemplation no Ideas, no perceivable objectifications of willing" (Levinson 1998: 249). However, while at first glance this may appear obvious – for if music is not representational then surely it cannot represent Ideas – the suggestion is nonetheless too quick. The non-representational character of music, the fact that it does not depict phenomena or individual things, would be a sufficient reason for thinking that music's function as a form of art has nothing to do with the Ideas only if the depiction of phenomena were the sole way of providing epistemic access to the latter. And that, on Schopenhauer's own theory of art, is not the case.

Section 52 is misleading on this matter. As we have seen, Schopenhauer says there that music "stands quite apart" from all the other arts in not offering us a copy of any Idea, and he says too that the provision of knowledge of the Ideas "by depicting individual things is the aim of all the other arts" (vol. 1, 257). What he suggests, that is, is (a) that music is unique in not offering copies or representations of the Ideas, and (b) that all the forms of art that do trade in Ideas – that is, all the non-musical forms of art – do so by way of "copying" or depiction. But on Schopenhauer's own account of the non-musical arts, neither of these suggestions is accurate. For the first two forms of art that he discusses, namely, architecture and "hydraulic" art – "the artistic arrangement of water" in landscape design (vol. 1, 217) – he also holds to be non-representational. "Architecture is distinguished from the plastic arts and poetry," he writes, "by the fact that it gives us not a copy, but the thing itself. Unlike those other arts, it does not repeat the known Idea" (vol. 1, 216–17). Works of architectural (and indeed hydraulic) art present to us things that works of the other, non-musical, forms of art (to the extent that they were concerned with those things at all) would copy, or *re*present, by depiction. Nonetheless, Schopenhauer suggests, architectural and hydraulic art – despite being non-depictive, non-representational – are continuous with the other non-musical forms of art in being concerned with the Ideas. In architectural art, "the artist simply presents the object to the beholder, and makes the apprehension of the Idea easy for him" (vol. 1, 217), and works of hydraulic art "reveal the Ideas of fluid heavy matter in exactly the same way as the works of architecture unfold the Ideas of rigid matter" (vol. 1, 218).

In short, if architectural and hydraulic art, despite being non-representational, nonetheless function aesthetically in such a way as to facilitate "the apprehension of the Idea," then an appeal to the fact that music is non-representational gives at best an incomplete explanation of why Schopenhauer holds that music "passes over the Ideas" and hence must function to give us access to "the essence" of things in a way fundamentally different from that in which the other arts do so.

A better explanation is this: the Ideas are essentially templates of the will's objectification in phenomena, which is to say in configurations of matter. Some of them are expressed in particular configurations of matter (such as the Ideas of particular species of animal); some of them are expressed in any and every configuration of matter – such as those of "the most universal forces of nature" (vol. 1, 130), which it is the business of architectural and hydraulic art to make clear. To recognise an Idea, then, one has either to see it in an actual configuration of matter (as Schopenhauer holds that one does in successful architectural/hydraulic art), or in the representation of a particular configuration of matter (as he holds that one does in successful artistic paintings, for example). Non-representational music, however, can present us with neither representations of configurations of matter, nor with matter itself. Hence music cannot give us epistemic access to the Ideas.

Music and the phenomenal world

But at this point, a question that has been lurking in the wings becomes unignorable: on what basis is Schopenhauer assuming that music is (at any rate paradigmatically) non-representational? Is it not quite obvious that at least some music just *is* representational? Schopenhauer – as of course he must – accepts that this is so. However, he suggests, such music

> does not express the inner nature of the will itself, but merely imitates its phenomenon inadequately. All really imitative music does this; for example, *The Seasons* by Haydn, also many passages of his *Creation*, where phenomena of the world of perception are directly imitated; also in all battle pieces. All this is to be entirely rejected.
>
> (vol. 1, 263–4)

When he speaks of "The inexpressible depth of all music" (vol. 1, 264), then, or makes statements such as "[M]usic . . . is also quite independent of the phenomenal world" (vol. 1, 257), it is clear that Schopenhauer does not mean *all* music, but *good* or successful music; it is clear that he is using the term in an evaluative sense rather than a strictly classificatory one. (Indeed, this is true of his talk of the arts in general. As Schopenhauer uses the term, "art" refers to works that are, in his terms, aesthetically successful.)

One worry about any such usage, of course, is that it may be in one way or another question-begging or merely stipulative with regard to what is good or aesthetically successful. However, it is hard to level this charge against

Schopenhauer; if he is right that there is music that expresses the very essence of the world, that puts us more closely in touch with the nature of reality than can any other form of art, it is hardly unreasonable to regard this as being music of the very highest value. His objection to representational music requires rather more by way of explanation, however. Representational music is "to be entirely rejected," he says, inasmuch as it "merely imitates" phenomena, and is "imitation brought about with conscious intention by means of concepts," as opposed to an expression of the composer's "immediate knowledge of the inner nature of the world" (vol. 1, 263–4). These remarks reflect Schopenhauer's view that the primary value of good art is a function of its capacity to reveal something of the nature of reality. Given his idealist metaphysics, this means that the creator of successful art must have transcended the everyday phenomenal world, the structure of which is governed by space, time, and causality, and have glimpsed its underlying reality, the world as will. Schopenhauer holds that this process of transcendence is not something that an individual can deliberately bring about. Furthermore, inasmuch as the world as will cannot be conceived in spatial, temporal or causal terms, Schopenhauer holds that concepts are wholly inadequate to grasping or communicating the nature of the latter, and hence are "eternally barren and unproductive in art." It follows, then, that music (or indeed painting or sculpture or poetry) that is initiated by "conscious intention by means of concepts" cannot point beyond the phenomenal world, cannot be genuinely revelatory of the nature of reality, and hence cannot be good art (vol. 2, 235).

But must all representational music be of this sort? What rules out the possibility of music that is genuinely revelatory by means of representation? Why should we think that representational music is necessarily "brought about with conscious intention by means of concepts," so that musical representation may only be of "phenomena of the world of perception" (vol. 1, 264)? The answer, though Schopenhauer never states this explicitly, is that, as we saw earlier, the Ideas are templates of the will's objectification in configurations of matter, and it is simply not possible to represent the template of a configuration of matter in sound. There is no difficulty in seeing how the sound made by a particular (sort of) configuration of matter may be represented in music – a bird call, say, or (in a more complex sense) the sound of a canon being fired. But whether what is represented is an individual sound event (the opening canon shot of a particular battle, say) or (as Schopenhauer would insist, through abstraction) a kind of sound event, it clearly belongs to the phenomenal world.

However, this is not to say that music that reaches beyond the phenomenal world – music that is genuinely revelatory – is necessarily non-representational. Schopenhauer allows that "we are able to set a poem to music as a song, or a perceptive presentation as a pantomime, or both as an opera" (vol. 1, 263) in such a way that the work is genuinely expressive of will. This will only be successful, however, when the representational aspect of the work remains firmly in a "subordinate position": "if music tries to stick too closely to the words, and to mould itself according to the events, it is endeavouring to speak a language not its own" – "a great misconception and an utter absurdity" (vol. 1, 261–2). This is presumably what Schopenhauer thinks is wrong with the Haydn oratorios he refers to in the passage quoted earlier. By contrast, "No one has kept so free from this mistake as Rossini; hence his music speaks its *own* language so distinctly and purely that it requires no words at all, and therefore produces its full effect even when rendered by instruments alone" (vol. 1, 262).

There are at least two points worth remarking on here. First, the coherence of the thought that music that is composed to have a vocal component should, if it is really good music, "produce its full effect" when that component is left out is to say the least questionable. But it may be that this is simply an overstatement of the view that in genuinely revelatory music that is accompanied by words, the relation between the words in question and the music must be very loose. As he writes, the "individual pictures of human life" painted by the words and

> set to the universal language of music, are [in good music] never bound to it or correspond to it with absolute necessity, but stand to it only in the relation of a particular example, chosen at random, to a universal concept. . . . Even other examples, just as arbitrarily chosen, of the universal expressed in a poem could correspond in the same degree to the general significance of the melody assigned to this poem; and so the same composition is suitable to many verses.
>
> (vol. 1, 263)

This thought is certainly more intelligible than the view that in good music with a vocal element the latter is dispensable with altogether. But it is nonetheless a very long way short of being persuasive. Recall Bach's setting of the aria "Mache dich, mein Herze, rein," in the *St. Matthew Passion*, for example, and the way that Bach spreads these words – has *worked* to spread just *these* words – so sinuously over a melodic line that seems unending. The thought that the words here could be replaced by other ("arbitrarily chosen"!) words that express the same thoughts, leaving "the music" (as if the latter could be isolated from the sung words) somehow untouched, is little short of grotesque. Indeed, only the crudest of analysis could see words and music here as related to each other in such a way that notions of subservience/dominance could have any purchase at all. But if all this is right, Schopenhauer's theory directs us to conclude, Bach's setting of the aria must – precisely in virtue of these facts – be deeply flawed. It is hard not to see this as a *reductio*.

Second, and more positively, if there can be genuinely revelatory music that has representational elements in the form of words or "perceptive scenes" or both (as in opera), we might ask why Schopenhauer does not – or at any rate, does not explicitly – allow that there may also be genuinely revelatory music with representational elements that are *musical*. Fortunately, there appear to be no theoretical considerations that rule this possibility out, for unless it *is* a possibility, there would seem to be no way for Schopenhauer to acknowledge as valuable a great deal of music that one might expect him to value (Rossini's *William Tell* overture, for example); and no grounds (other than what are – in Schopenhauerian terms – more or less superficial ones, such as technique, complexity and the amount of pleasure provided by each) for valuing Beethoven's Pastoral Symphony, say, more highly than the music that accompanies Wile E. Coyote's attempts to catch the Road Runner.

To conclude our consideration of what I identified earlier as the first premise of the argument that structures Schopenhauer's main discussion of music, then: the fact that "we do not recognise the copy, the repetition, of any Idea" (vol. 1, 256) in music is due not to the fact that music is non-representational, but rather to the fact that the Ideas are simply not the sort of thing that can be represented in sound. Indeed, although Schopenhauer does not explicitly acknowledge the fact, there is no reason that good music – music that is revelatory of the nature of reality – cannot represent aspects of the phenomenal world. All that his theory demands in this regard is that such music not be *purely* representational in this way – that it should not be, as he characterizes the Haydn oratorios referred to earlier, "*really* imitative" (vol. 1, 263; my emphasis).

The difference between "representational" and "imitative" is suggestive here, however. For while Schopenhauer is clearly committed to the view that good music cannot be more than superficially imitative of the phenomenal world, he is also committed to the thought that good music is in a different sense representational through and through. The fact that music does not represent Ideas, he suggests, does not imply that it is no more than the purely formal arrangement of sounds, something that can be grasped entirely (as the Pythagorean tradition has it) in logical or mathematical terms: as he says, "we certainly have to look for more than that *exercitium arithmeticae occultum nescientis se numerare animi* which Leibniz considered it to be" (vol. 1, 256). This brings us to the second premise that I identified earlier: the claim that music is "in some sense . . . related to the world as the depiction to the thing depicted, as the copy to the original" (vol. 1, 256).

Music's representational character

It has to be said that the argument that Schopenhauer offers in support of the second premise is not impressive, and Eric Payne's translation renders it even less so:

> That in some sense music must be related to the world as the depiction to the thing depicted, as the copy to the original, we can infer from the analogy with the remaining arts, to all of which this character is peculiar; from their effect on us, it can be inferred that that of music is on

the whole of the same nature, only stronger, more rapid, more necessary and infallible.

(vol. 1, 256)

This is confused. The argument that Schopenhauer actually has in mind, I take it, is in essence as follows: (1) the non-musical arts are related to the world "as the copy to the original"; (2) music's effect on us is "on the whole of the same nature" (albeit "stronger, more rapid, more necessary and infallible") as the effect on us of the non-musical arts; therefore (3) music is related to the world "as the copy to the original." However, while this is more coherent than Payne's rendition of the argument, as it stands it is hardly compelling. To strengthen the argument, much more would have to be said about both the extent and the relevance of the analogy cited in (2); in particular, more would have to be said about the effect of music on us. And what Schopenhauer does say about the latter in effect renders the argument by analogy redundant. His thought is that we simply do not *experience* (good) music as merely a formal arrangement of sounds; or, rather, we experience it as something more than this, as something that is somehow getting at – putting us in touch with – something deep, something of profound significance:

> [I]t is such a great and exceedingly fine art, its effect on man's inner nature is so powerful, and it is so completely and profoundly understood by him in his innermost being as an entirely universal language, whose distinctness surpasses even that of the world of perception itself . . . [and in] which we see the deepest recesses of our nature find expression. Therefore . . . we must attribute to music a far more serious and profound significance that refers to the innermost being of the world and of our own self.

(vol. 1, 256)

It is clear – and this is no criticism – that (despite the "therefore") there is no argument in all this; Schopenhauer is simply appealing to our experience of (in his terms, good) music. To a person who has not had (or at least been persuaded that others have had) the sort of experience that he refers to, the appeal will be unsuccessful, of course; but then so will be the argument by analogy, since fleshing out the second premise of the latter in Schopenhauerian terms will in effect involve appeal to just the sort of thing he appeals to in the passage quoted above. But for anyone whose experience of music is consonant with that described by Schopenhauer, the argument by analogy will be simply redundant; anyone in this position will need no further persuasion that music is not merely a formal arrangement of sounds, that it in some sense or other refers or points to something beyond itself.

But refer or point to what? Schopenhauer's argument thus far has been that music cannot represent the Ideas, but that nonetheless we experience (good) music as somehow revelatory of the "innermost being" of things. Music must, therefore, he concludes, be a representation or "copy" of "the will itself" (vol. 1, 257).

As Schopenhauer acknowledges, this conclusion is deeply problematic, for his own metaphysics dictates that the will – noumenal reality – can "never be directly represented." Hence, as he says, "it is essentially impossible to demonstrate" that music represents the will. Nonetheless, he suggests, his conclusion "is quite sufficient for me, . . . and will be just as illuminating also to the man who has followed me thus far, and has agreed with my view of the world" (vol. 1, 256). But this is wholly unconvincing. The fact of the matter is that either Schopenhauer's metaphysics, holding as it does that the will cannot be object of representation, falsifies his conclusion regarding the nature of music, or that conclusion falsifies his metaphysics – and indeed his theory of music, since that is based on his metaphysics.

Music's expressive character

So what has gone wrong? Why does Schopenhauer insist that music is "a copy of the will itself," despite being committed to the position that the will cannot be represented? At least part of the reason is that he is hugely over-impressed by a range of what he calls "analogies" between music and the Ideas, which is to say between music and the phenomenal world. With one exception – of which more in a moment – these range from the fanciful (e.g. "the definite intervals of the scale are parallel to the definite grades of the will's objectification, the definite species in nature" (vol. 1, 258)) to the ludicrous (e.g. "impure discords, giving no definite interval, can be compared to the monstrous abortions between two species of animals, or between man and animal" (vol. 1, 259)). Only someone as immersed in Schopenhauerian metaphysics, as committed to the revelatory power of music, and as determined to show that each explain and confirm the other as Schopenhauer himself could find them compelling. And Schopenhauer clearly does find them compelling. Although he does not explicitly express it in this way, his thought seems to go something like this: "Given that the phenomenal world is the objectification or expression of the will, and that music in so many respects mirrors or parallels aspects of that world, surely music too must be an objectification or expression of the will."

However, his final "analogy" between music and the Ideas suggests an alternative to this conclusion – and an indication that in the argument that he does explicitly offer for it ("music does not represent the Ideas; it is nonetheless revelatory of reality; music must therefore represent the will") Schopenhauer simply commits the fallacy of false dilemma. The analogy in question is this: "Finally, in the *melody* . . . I recognise the highest grade of the will's objectification, the intellectual life and endeavour of man." In particular, he suggests, melody "relates the most secret history of the intellectually enlightened will, portrays every agitation, every effort, every movement of the will, everything which the faculty of reason summarizes under the wide and negative concept of feeling" (vol. 1, 259).

It is important to note that the will referred to in the latter quotation is not the will that we – and Schopenhauer – have been referring to thus far. Here, "will" refers not to noumenal reality, but to the *human* will. And a strong case can be made for the view that Schopenhauer ought to have restricted himself to the thought that music represents some of the most fundamental aspects of the human will, or of human willing, rather than making the much more ambitious claim that "music expresses . . . the inner being, the in-itself, of the world" (vol. 1, 264). For one thing, all that he has to offer by way of justification of the latter claim is the series of analogies referred to above, none of which are remotely compelling. For another, the less ambitious claim has the significant advantage of not rendering his theory incoherent, for there is nothing in his metaphysics that entails that the human will cannot be object of representation. Finally, the idea that melody "relates the most secret history of the intellectually enlightened will" promises to deliver as much as Schopenhauer could reasonably want or is entitled to by way of content for the idea that music can be a source of profound insight. Indeed, in some of his remarks about the cognitive significance of music, this idea seems to be all that he has in mind; for example, the suggestions that "The inexpressible depth of all music . . . is due to the fact that it reproduces all the emotions of our innermost being" (vol. 1, 264), and that the significance of music refers to the "innermost being" of "our own self," that in it "the deepest recesses of our nature find expression" (vol. 1, 256). In the end, then, the most charitable way of understanding Schopenhauer's theory of music is to discard what many have seen as its most distinctive feature – the thought that music is somehow a direct expression of the ultimate foundation of reality – and to regard it instead as a distinctive version of expression theory.

See also Expression theories (Chapter 19), Nietzsche (Chapter 32), and Wagner (Chapter 35).

References

Goehr, L. (1996) "Schopenhauer and the Musicians: An Inquiry into the Sounds of Silence and the Limits of Philosophizing about Music," in D. Jacquette (ed.) *Schopenhauer, Philosophy, and the Arts*, Cambridge: Cambridge University Press, pp. 200–28.

Levinson, J. (1998) "Schopenhauer, Arthur," in M. Kelly (ed.) *Encyclopedia of Aesthetics*, vol. 4, New York: Oxford University Press, pp. 245–50.

Schopenhauer, A. (1969 [1818, 1844]) *The World as Will and Representation*, 2 vols, trans. E.F.J. Payne, New York: Dover.

Further reading

Budd, M. (1985) *Music and the Emotions: The Philosophical Theories*, London: Routledge & Kegan Paul. (Ch. 5 critiques Schopenhauer as an expression theorist.)

Kivy, P. (1997) *Philosophies of Arts: An Essay in Differences*, New York: Cambridge University Press. (Ch. 7 critiques Schopenhauer's philosophy of music in the course of an argument to the effect that absolute music lacks content.)

Magee, B. (1997) *The Philosophy of Schopenhauer*, rev. and enlarged, Oxford: Oxford University Press. (Ch. 8 explores Schopenhauer's philosophy of music within the context of his broader philosophy of art.)

Tanner, M. (1999) *Schopenhauer*, London: Routledge. (Explores Schopenhauer's philosophy of music within the context of his broader philosophy of art.)

Young, J. (2005) *Schopenhauer*, New York: Routledge. (Chs. 5 and 6 explore Schopenhauer's philosophy of music within the context of his broader philosophy of art.)

32

NIETZSCHE

John M. Carvalho

The spirit of music

Music is clearly very important to Friedrich Nietzsche (1844–1900) and his philosophy. Nietzsche's first book was originally titled *The Birth of Tragedy Out of the Spirit of Music* (1872). He commented on classical music and the music of his day throughout his writings. He composed music and was an accomplished interpreter and improviser on the piano (Liébert 2004: 13–29). He wrote to Hermann Levi, "Perhaps there has never been a philosopher who, to such a degree, was at bottom so very much a musician as I am" (Schacht 2003: 131). Yet, Nietzsche nowhere gives us a discreet philosophy of music, never goes so far as to specify what he thinks music is. We will attempt to fill part of that void here by connecting what Nietzsche says about music with what he says about philosophy and by highlighting how Nietzsche uses Dionysus as a figure for both. As we shall see, everything there is to say about philosophy and music in Nietzsche's writings passes through the figure of Dionysus. A careful consideration of the way Nietzsche figures Dionysus in his writings – from the earliest to the last – will clarify what very well may have been Nietzsche's considered views about music, philosophy, and the relations between the two.

Nietzsche introduces Dionysus in *The Birth of Tragedy* as, precisely, the *spirit of music* from out of which tragedy is born. Dionysus is not the same as music on this account. The god rather figures or represents, Nietzsche says, the spirit of a music that stands alongside a fascination with the image rich world of dreams and illusions figured for the ancient Greeks in the divinity of Apollo. For the concept of music, Nietzsche tells us, the Greeks substituted the "intensely clear" figure of Dionysus, an image of a "non-imagistic" art, the representative of a great musical impulse in nature itself (1967: 33). This figure of music is associated for the Greeks with intoxication, ecstasy, dancing and self-forgetfulness. It prepares those who grasp its deep psychological import for a connection with their fellows and a reunion with a natural world that had become hostile, alien and a threat to their humanity. "In song and in dance man expresses himself as a member of a higher community," Nietzsche writes. "He feels himself a god"

(1967: 37). So conceived by Nietzsche, music is a very powerful force in the life of the pre-tragic Greeks.

Yet, Nietzsche goes on to say, this force was not originally powerful enough to challenge the influence of Apollo on these ancient Greeks. The calm restraint and sun-like eye of the soothsaying god, Apollo, held out for the Greeks the seductive illusion of a dream world which, even in its intensity, preserved for them the sensation that it was mere appearance. They believed this world was beautiful despite the fact that they knew it was not real. And, for a long while, the beauty of these appearances and the illusion preserved in them held their own against the wilder emotions and collapse of the *principium individuations* – the principle of individuation – promised in the music of Dionysus. That Apollonian tendency was even forceful enough among the Greeks to hold out against a more virulent Dionysian tendency, "that horrible mixture of sensuality and cruelty" celebrated in the festivals and rites of the so-called "barbarian," that is to say, non-Greek people. Doric art, famously, immortalizes for Nietzsche "this majestically rejecting attitude of Apollo" (1967: 39).

The majesty of this rejection would not hold out forever, though. In art, generally, the passing of Doric for Ionic style reflected the beginning of a reconciliation of the Apollonian tendency to the more barbarous Dionysian impulses that emerged "from the deepest roots of the Hellenic nature" itself. In other words, Nietzsche suggests, something of the "witches brew" of sensuality and cruelty was already contained in the Greek figure of Dionysus but held back and restrained. When it eventually "made a path" for itself, the resulting destruction of the *principium individuationes* was, for the first time, Nietzsche says, "an artistic phenomenon" (1967: 39). And this is an important transformation. As one of two fundamental impulses in nature, music is figured by the Greeks as a god of dancing, drinking, percussive and harmonic musical sounds content to live alongside the impulse to indulge the images in dreams and the shimmering appearances of our wakeful life. When that dancing, drinking impulse finally expressed a force that was latent in it but not yet manifest because held back by that equally powerful impulse to calm restraint, then the music figured for the Greeks in the dancing god, Dionysus, produced something more vibrant, challenging and distinctly artistic. In fact, it became, for Nietzsche, an emblem of art itself.

These more powerful Dionysian energies which, as it turns out, were always already embodied in Greek music, did not produce an effect on the Apollonian impulse to clarity and calm restraint by simply asserting themselves against or offering themselves as a fresh alternative to the ancient Greek fascination with images and appearances. Nor did these competing tendencies reach a dialectical reconciliation of forces that otherwise naturally opposed one another. Rather, Nietzsche leads us to believe, the more primitive Dionysian impulses forced themselves on the Apollonian, shaping and forming the fascination and restraint associated with the images and illusions of dreams and appearances. This shaping of itself and its object is the meaning and effect of the aesthetic phenomenon Nietzsche attributes to the spirit of music figured in Dionysus. The plasticity of the Dionysian tendency is not a separate or new force but a capacity of that impulse to form itself to and, thereby, remake the shape of the forces it affects. Music, as figured in the god Dionysus, is an especially good candidate for such a plastic power.

That is because this music affects us more immediately and more deeply than the other arts. It produces effects in us that, arguably, all the other arts are striving to achieve. This music is felt as much or more than it is perceived. It reverberates in our bodies and our soul, moving us to sway and dance, to tap our fingers and our feet, to leap out of our seats and clap our hands in appreciation, to swoon and lose ourselves in a transport of thoughts and feelings, dreams and expectations. This music is felt as such a force by performers and listeners alike. In the first, it motivates and informs the transformation of scored notes into audible sounds. In the second, and also in the first, since the performers also listen, it shapes and informs the transformation of audible sounds into dance and daring emotions and ideas.

Nietzsche once located the source of this power in a "tonal subsoil," what he described then as the universally comprehended and communicated "expressions of one primal cause unfathomable to us" (1978: 21; see Allison 1996). The Schopenhauerian inflection, here, is unmistakable. Music represents, for Nietzsche throughout the early 1870s, a primal force, a felt immediacy we vainly articulate in the arbitrary gestures of consonants and vowels that make up the so-called natural languages. "As our whole corporeality stands in relation to that original phenomenon, the 'Will,'" Nietzsche writes, "so the word built out of its consonants and vowels stands in relation to its tonal basis" (1978: 22). What is comprehended and communicated in this *Tonbild* are pleasure and pain, biologically based states which are the common, primal cause in all humans and, so, the shared basis for an understanding that overcomes the differences in native languages. Kathleen Higgins connects this common biological existence – "all that is entailed by 'being alive'" – to the figure of Dionysus and, through Dionysus, to a mode of self-awareness and self-understanding she describes as an appropriately Dionysian self-forgetfulness (1986: 665).

Music of the sort associated with Dionysus, then, is capable of making us forget ourselves, the better to share with others like us an awareness and understanding that linguistic expression only ever obscures. It is the basis for a shared communicability that the human voice struggles to preserve in song but loses as soon as it resorts to words. (This is the sense to make of Nietzsche's remark, in the "Attempt at a Self-Criticism," that *The Birth of Tragedy* "should have sung" (1967: 20).) The Dionysian music that preserves this shared sensibility and sensitivity to the feelings of pleasure and pain is modeled, for Nietzsche, on the dithyramb of the ancient choral song. In the dithyramb, generally thought to have been an antistrophic verse in iambic meter, the devotee puts on the god and makes himself as "divine" as the limitations of his singing and dancing allow. Nietzsche wants to capture in this dithyrambic music the physicality of bodily engagement and "the emotional power of the tone" through which "something never before experienced struggles for utterance" (1967: 40). What is struggling to be heard in the dithyramb is music itself, a music we are only ever on the verge of hearing, a truly Dionysian music that must be distinguished from Apollonian music, on the one hand, and the special art of music, in Nietzsche's day and in ours, on the other.

Apollonian music was Doric, Nietzsche tells us: solid, restrained, "architectonics in tones . . . that were merely suggestive, such as those of the cithara" (1967: 40). The notes of the cithara (or lyre) set a tone for the poetry or dramatic scene they accompanied. They were a scaffolding. They did nothing to direct the action or the melodic line, to mobilize the plot or the harmony, to set a rhythm for the narrative or the musical score. In this music, the non-imagistic Dionysian impulses have been subordinated to the image rich symbolism of the lips, the face, and speech. Apollonian music subordinates the emotional power of the tone, the uniform flow of the melody and the incomparable world of harmony to the message it seeks to communicate and the world it seeks to represent (Nietzsche 1967: 40).

It was as rare to find these properly Dionysian qualities – the emotional power of tone, the uniform flow of melody, the incomparable world of harmony – in the music of Nietzsche's day, as it still is in ours. The music of Wolfgang Amadeus Mozart or the Jimi Hendrix Experience may have a privileged access to the essence of Dionysian music by virtue of growing from the tonal subsoil which sustains that essence, but that is no guarantee that all music or even this specific music expresses the spirit of Dionysus (see Nietzsche 1986: 345, 348). There is so much that can and does get in the way: forced ornamentation, staged distractions and, especially, words, which sacrifice music for a message the artist wants to communicate for an audience that demands to understand. If "life without music would be a mistake," as Nietzsche is so often quoted as remarking (2003: 232; see also 1954: 471), then a tragic reading of Nietzsche's philosophy – one following the wisdom of Silenus, say – would have us believe that there has not been music enough in the special art of music to save life from falling into error (Nietzsche 1967: 42–3).

The case of Wagner

At the time he wrote *The Birth of Tragedy*, Nietzsche was under the impression that the music of Richard Wagner could be appropriately salvific:

> Out of the Dionysian root of the German spirit a power has arisen, which, having nothing in common with the primitive conditions of Socratic culture . . . is rather felt by this culture as something terribly

inexplicable and overwhelmingly hostile – *German music* as we must understand it, particularly in its vast solar orbit from Bach to Beethoven, from Beethoven to Wagner.

(1967: 119)

Nietzsche commends Wagner for confirming the "eternal truth" of Schopenhauer's aesthetics (1967: 100) and cites a long passage from Schopenhauer's *The World as Will and Representation* as an exemplification of what Wagner himself believes he has accomplished (1967: 101–3).

"Music," says Schopenhauer there, "if regarded as an expression of the world, is in the highest degree a universal language, which is related indeed to the universality of concepts, much as they are related to the universality of things" (Nietzsche 1967: 101; Schopenhauer 1907: 339). "This relation may be very well expressed in the language of the schoolmen," Nietzsche adds by way of additional quotation, "by saying, the concepts are the *universalia post rem*, but music gives the *universalia ante rem*, and the real world the *universalia in re*" (Nietzsche 1967: 103; Schopenhauer 1907: 340). This account of Wagner's German music is meant to contrast strongly with the *culture of opera* in his day to which Nietzsche attributes a *stillo rappresentativo* and a powerful, non-aesthetic yearning for the "idyllic," for "Alexandrian flatteries" and for "a superficial pleasure in the play of line and proportion" that has become "an empty and merely distracting diversion" (1967: 118). It would not go too far to describe much of the music of our day as such an empty distraction.

Yet, Nietzsche tells us, his regard for Wagner and his music began to wane in the year the first edition of *The Birth of Tragedy* was published, with the groundbreaking for the Festival Theater at Bayreuth in May, 1872 (1997: 195–9). He reveals this to us in "Richard Wagner at Bayreuth," the fourth of the *Untimely Meditations*, published two years before a second, virtually unchanged edition of *The Birth of Tragedy* appeared in 1878. There, Nietzsche contrasts Wagner with Goethe and connects him with a *"poeticizing folk"* (1997: 229). Out of pity for this folk, Nietzsche says, Wagner became a *"social revolutionary."* He saw the folk – not the people of his day but a mythically artistic people – as "the only spectator and listener who might be worthy of and equal to the power of his artwork as he dreamed of it" (1997: 230). Where Goethe is represented as discriminating, one of the "last great followers of the Italian philologist-poets," Wagner is said to "no longer recognize any distinction between the cultivated and the uncultivated" (1997: 249). Through his music, Nietzsche concludes, Wagner sought to resurrect a folk who would confirm his greatness, and he sought this precisely not by speaking to the future but by interpreting and transfiguring the past (1997: 250).

We might say Nietzsche comes to hear an absence of the truly Dionysian impulse in Wagner's music after Bayreuth. Better put, there is an absence of a truly artistic phenomenon, a shaping of the Dionysian tendency to fit and form an equally powerful tendency to calm restraint that is also there in that music. Wagner's "higher self no longer condescends to serve its violent, more earthly brother," Nietzsche writes, "it *loves* it and cannot but serve it" (1997: 228). If Wagner's music still sounds "Dionysian" to some, it can only be as echoes of the primitive "witches brew" and no longer in what Nietzsche recognizes as the art in music. Where does Nietzsche continue to find the truly Dionysian tendency, music as exemplary of art itself, in the period after his falling out with Wagner? Not immediately in any music extant in his time. No, in fact, not in music at all, not even his own music, but rather in his writings. (Walter Kaufmann reports that Nietzsche had virtually stopped composing once he started publishing (Nietzsche 1978: 17).) And among those writings, not in the first stabs at *Human, All Too Human* or its two sequels, *Assorted Opinions and Maxims* and *The Dawn*, or even in *The Gay Science*. He finds it in the narrative and the grand style given to that "Dionysian monster who bears the name of Zarathustra" in the book Nietzsche named after him (1966: 26).

Philosophy and Dionysian music

Beginning in 1886, Nietzsche began revising his earlier writings, and these revisions, including the "Attempt at a Self-Criticism" added to both editions of *The Birth of Tragedy*, are revealing. In these revisions, and in the books published from 1886 to the end of his life, Dionysus is figured as a productive force. Not only singing and dancing but also creating: creating worlds, creating "truths," creating forms of life. In these writings, Dionysus is the creative force in everything that is alive. This creative force is, of course, what Nietzsche will come to call the will to power. Dionysian music, and philosophy, as we shall see, expresses this will to power. And, insofar as everything that lives returns eternally, about which we have more to say below, that force always creates difference. Dionysus is no longer a force alongside nature but nature itself entirely animated by this difference-making Dionysian force. That very same force animates Nietzsche himself to ask, in the "Attempt at a Self-Criticism," "what would a music have to be like that would no longer be of romantic origin, like German music – but *Dionysian?*" (1967: 25).

There was clearly something Nietzsche admired in the figure of Dionysus from his first book. In that book, however, as we have seen, he associated the sylvan god precisely and closely with Wagner's German music. In his writings after 1886, by contrast, we see a distinct shift in the valence of the Dionysian forces and that there are clearly, now, multiple forces. Arguably, the difference in Nietzsche's thinking and writing, generally, and his figuring of Dionysus, in particular, can be attributed to the work completed from 1883 to 1885 in the four parts of *Thus Spoke Zarathustra*. More specifically, it can be attributed to the "fundamental conception of this work, the idea of the eternal recurrence, this highest formula of affirmation that is at all attainable," the thought that came to him in August 1881,

"6000 feet beyond man and time" (2000: 751). The idea of the eternal recurrence or return gets a preview in the penultimate section (§341) of the 1882 edition of *The Gay Science* (Nietzsche 1974: 273–4), and in the final section of that edition, titled "*Incipit tragoedia*," Nietzsche introduces the figure of Zarathustra with a text that rehearses the "Prologue" for part one of his next book.

This is not the place for us to rehearse all the complexities of Nietzsche's most demanding thought. It will be enough if we restrict our remarks to the significance of the eternal return for Nietzsche's thoughts about music. Nietzsche himself suggested that "the whole of *Zarathustra* may be reckoned as music; certainly a rebirth of the art of *hearing* was among its preconditions" (2000: 751). And what we are advised to "*hear* aright" in that text is "a voice bridging centuries," the "halcyon tone" of that voice and the tempo of its speeches, described as a "tender adagio" (2000: 675). It might seem odd that the thought of the eternal return, that (to put it most succinctly) were there a point to life we would have realized it by now, could produce the calm, richness and joy promised in such a halcyon tone. But this is exactly what we find in the "wisdom" that concludes Nietzsche's extended ruminations on the eternal return in Part Three of *Zarathustra*: "Sing! Speak no more! Are not all words made for the grave and heavy? Are not all words lies to those who are light? Sing! Speak no more!" (1966: 231). With this ode to eternity – *For I love you, O eternity!* – Zarathustra embraces the fate promised by the thought that everything that *can* happen *has*, that everything returns eternally.

If the point of the eternal return is that there is no single end toward which everything in its own unique way is tending, there can be no one unfathomable cause or truth that the tone in our voices is struggling to utter. Rather, the richness and wealth of this tone, the source of its joy, is that there are many, many reasons for living, many, many truths struggling to be heard. Words, once thought too arbitrary to express the truth of nature, are now deemed too heavy and grave to negotiate the multiplicity of truths nurtured in the tonal subsoil. Zarathustra sings, and with his songs he begins to correct at least part of what Nietzsche found lacking in *The Birth of Tragedy* – "It should have *sung*, this 'new soul' – and not spoken!" (1967: 20).

> [H]e that has had the hardest, most terrible insight into reality, that has thought the "most abysmal idea," nevertheless does not consider it an objection to existence, not even to its eternal recurrence – but rather one reason more for being himself the eternal Yes to all things.
>
> (Nietzsche 2000: 762)

Zarathustra sings this eternal Yes, and this singing, this affirmation, Nietzsche tells us, "*this is the concept of Dionysus once again*" (2000: 762).

So, in Zarathustra's singing affirmation of the eternal return and of life in the face of the thought that everything in life returns eternally, Dionysus is transfigured. He no longer represents a tendency to unprincipled abandon plasticizing itself to and forming a powerful fascination with images and appearances. He no longer promises the "metaphysical comfort . . . that life is at the bottom of things, despite all the changes in appearances, indestructibly powerful and pleasurable" (1967: 59). Through the songs of Zarathustra, Dionysus has become the dancing, singing god who affirms "the art of *this-worldly* comfort" (1967: 26; see Conway 1992). Through the songs of Zarathustra, Dionysus has learned to laugh, to leap and side-leap, even, in a fitting image of inversion, to stand on his head (1967: 26). Dionysus, transfigured through Zarathustra and the thought of the eternal return, becomes a new model of music for Nietzsche.

To get a fuller appreciation of this new Dionysian figure of music, and to follow the reasoning that has taken us to this point, we must not get so caught up in what Zarathustra sings and affirms that we fail to notice the more important aspect, the tone of those odes and Yes-sayings. We find that tone in Nietzsche's style or, as Alexander Nehamas would have it, Nietzsche's styles (Nehamas 1985: 13–41; see also Kofman 1993). *Zarathustra* deploys a dizzying array of styles and voices, and songs and affirmations make up a large part of that array. With every other style in that text, these songs and affirmations are uniformly joyful, rich, and tempered, free of rage and turpitude. The text as a whole is truly carried away by this tone, but it is not all joyful, playful celebration. The music of *Zarathustra* makes a serious point without arguing for it, and in the course of making that point, and refiguring it musically, Nietzsche refigured Dionysus as the multiple, difference-making force he becomes in the later writings.

To retell our story, Nietzsche borrowed Dionysus from the ancient Greek figure for a fundamental impulse to make non-imagistic music. He attributed that impulse to Wagner's German music. When Wagner's music failed to live up to that Dionysian standard, Nietzsche tried to find it in his own writings. He abandoned the model of his first five books, extended treatments of some one subject, and experimented with paragraphs of varying length, including aphorisms, on a number of related subjects, finally developing a style that became fruitful and multiplied in *Zarathustra*. With the eponymous hero of that book, Nietzsche experimented with the Dionysian impulse and made a monster of that hero. Transfigured through Zarathustra and the thought of the eternal return, Dionysus becomes a multiple, difference-making force and figures for Nietzsche the impulse to create new worlds, new truths and new forms of life. This Dionysian impulse is especially in evidence in the tone of Zarathustra's songs and affirmations and in Nietzsche's styles, more generally. Finally, this Dionysian music, the multiplicity of styles in Nietzsche's writing, is the creative force behind Nietzsche's perspectivist philosophical position.

This tells us that Nietzsche viewed music, Dionysian music, as the fundamental artistic impulse behind all the special arts and philosophy. What is distinctive about this impulse is that it is creative and that it bears this mantle lightly, calmly and with a joyfulness that enriches everything touched by it. This is characteristic of Nietzsche's writings in the last years of his life, up to and including the letters at the end signed "Dionysus." In the special art of music, there is the well-known example of *Carmen*:

> Yesterday I heard – would you believe it? – Bizet's masterpiece, for the twentieth time. . . . How such a work makes one perfect! One becomes a "masterpiece" oneself. . . . To sit five hours: the first stage of holiness!
>
> (Nietzsche 1967: 157)

Especially in the context of the thought of the eternal return, what must have impressed Nietzsche about *Carmen* is how it makes a way for itself without any end given to it from the start, how out of all the songs and tones available and without a strict model for getting from the beginning to the end, Bizet selects those tones and songs that give style to his music:

> This music is evil, subtly fatalistic; at the same time it remains popular – its subtlety belongs to a race, not to an individual. It is rich. It is precise. It builds, organizes, finishes: thus it constitutes the opposite of the polyp in music, the "infinite melody."
>
> (Nietzsche 1967: 157)

Around the story of a woman's unbridled passions, and the passions she inspires, Bizet composed the means for a distinctly Dionysian music to be heard.

In the end, what Nietzsche expects of music and philosophy is not so hard to understand. He expects music, Dionysian music and philosophy to express the multiple possible forms of life available to creative, daring souls ready to act on the knowledge that there is no one reason for living, no one primal truth we are always struggling to utter. He expects this music and philosophy to be soaked through with the urge to dance, to laugh, to throw off the weight of the *stillo rappresentativo*, to make the god, Dionysus, appear, not on a tragic stage but on a stage set to celebrate life conscious of the thought of the eternal return. He expects music and philosophy to give us the palpable sense of being alive. However distracting much of our music (and philosophy) is today, there are still moments when this Dionysian music is heard.

See also Aesthetic properties (Chapter 14), Schopenhauer (Chapter 31), and Wagner (Chapter 35).

References

Allison, D.B. (1996) "Some Remarks on Nietzsche's Draft of 1871, 'On Music and Words'," *New Nietzsche Studies* 1: 15–41.

Conway, D.W. (1992) "Nietzsche and the Art of This-Worldly Comfort: Self-Reference and Strategic Self-Parody," *History of Philosophy Quarterly* 9: 343–57.

Higgins, K.M. (1986) "Nietzsche on Music," *Journal of the History of Ideas* 47: 663–72.

Kofman, S. (1993) *Nietzsche and Metaphor*, trans. D. Large, Palo Alto: Stanford University Press.

Liébert, G. (2004) *Nietzsche and Music*, trans. D. Pellauer and G. Parkes, Chicago: The University of Chicago Press.

Nehamas, A. (1985) *Nietzsche: Life as Literature*, Cambridge: Harvard University Press.

Nietzsche, F.W. (1954 [1889]) *Twilight of the Idols*, in *The Portable Nietzsche*, trans. and ed. W. Kaufmann, New York: Penguin Books.

—— (1966 [1883–85]) *Thus Spoke Zarathustra: A Book for All and No One*, trans. W. Kaufman, New York: Viking Press.

—— (1967 [1872/1888]) *The Birth of Tragedy and The Case of Wagner*, trans. W. Kaufmann, New York: Random House.

—— (1974 [1882/1887]) *The Gay Science: With a Prelude in Rhymes and an Appendix of Songs*, trans. W. Kaufmann, New York: Random House.

—— (1978 [1871]) "On Music and Words," trans. W. Kaufman, *The Denver Quarterly* 13: 16–30.

—— (1986 [1880]) *The Wanderer and His Shadow* in *Human, All Too Human: A Book for Free Spirits*, trans. R.J. Hollingdale, Cambridge: Cambridge University Press, pp. 301–95.

—— (1997 [1876]) "Richard Wagner at Bayreuth," in *Untimely Meditations*, ed. D. Breazeale and trans. R.J. Hollingdale, Cambridge: Cambridge University Press, pp. 195–254.

—— (2000 [1908]) *Ecce Homo*, in *Basic Writings of Nietzsche*, ed. and trans. W. Kaufmann, New York: Random House.

—— (2003) "An Heinrich Köselitz in Venedig," in *Sämtliche briefe: Kritische Studienausgabe in 8 Bänden*, 2nd edn, G. Colli and M. Montinari (eds), vol. 8, Berlin: Walter de Gruyter, pp. 231–3.

Schacht, R. (2003) "Nietzsche, Music, Truth, Value, and Life," *International Studies in Philosophy* 35: 131–46.

Schopenhauer, A. (1907 [1818]) *The World as Will and Idea*, 6th ed., vol. I, trans. R.B. Haldane and J. Kemp, London: Kegan Paul, Trench, Trübner and Company.

Further reading

Babich, B. (1996) "Nietzsche & Music: A Selective Bibliography," *New Nietzsche Studies*, 1: 64–78. (An extensive list of resources for further reading.)

Benson, B.E. (2008) *Pious Nietzsche: Decadence and Dionysian Faith*, Bloomington: Indiana University Press. (Includes an alternative perspective on Nietzsche on music.)

Higgins, K.M. (2003) "Music or the Mistaken Life," *International Studies in Philosophy* 35: 117–30. (Discusses Nietzsche's thesis that music is crucial to human life.)

Klosowski, P. (1997) *Nietzsche and the Vicious Circle*, trans. D.W. Smith, Chicago: The University of Chicago Press. (A book-length study of the difficult concept of eternal recurrence.)

Nietzsche, F.W. (2003) *Writings from the Late Notebooks*, ed. R. Bittner, trans. K. Sturge, Cambridge: Cambridge University Press. (The notebooks provide Nietzsche's final thoughts on music. Selected notes were published as the book *The Will to Power*.)

33

HANSLICK

Thomas Grey

The most influential philosopher of music in the nineteenth century, and probably since, was by trade a music critic and journalist. As a philosopher and as a historian of music, in which latter capacity he was eventually awarded a more-or-less honorary professorship at the University of Vienna, Eduard Hanslick (1825–1904) was a talented autodidact. This mixed profile has much to do with the signal success of his contribution to the philosophy of music. Unlike any professionally trained philosophers of his day or the professional musicians who sometimes thought to emulate them (such as Richard Wagner), Hanslick was able to ground his discussion of aesthetic principles in a solid, empirical understanding of the modern musical canon and to express his views on matters of genuine philosophical significance in terms immediately intelligible to laymen as well as professionals in either field.

Hanslick was born in Prague to German-speaking parents of musical, scholarly, and literary inclinations. His father Joseph Adolph Hanslik (as he spelled the name) was a pianist and singer who gave lessons as well as working in the university library. Above all he was an enthusiastic amateur scholar who taught for a time philosophy and aesthetics, edited a volume of *Vorlesungen über Ästhetik* by one Johann Heinrich Dambeck (Prague, 1822), and followed closely, too, the work of the empiricist philosopher Friedrich Eduard Beneke (1798–1854). Hanslick's mother, Caroline, was the daughter of a successful Jewish merchant, Salomon Abraham Kisch (she converted to Catholicism at the time of her marriage), who passed on to her son an enthusiasm for literature and the theater, as Hanslick recalls in his substantial memoir, *Aus meinem Leben* (1894). As a young man in Prague he was trained in music by the leading native composer of the era, Vaclav Jan Tomásek (or Wenzel Johann Tomascheck, 1774–1850), and became acquainted with such contemporaries as Robert Zimmermann (1824–98) and August Wilhelm Ambros (1816–76), who later became notable figures in philosophy and music historiography, respectively. Like Beneke (the figure admired by Hanslick's father), Zimmermann was a follower of the philosopher and psychological theorist Johann Friedrich Herbart (1776–1841) who, along with Immanuel Kant, is regarded as an important source of "formalist" aesthetics (Hanslick 1986: xv).

In the later 1840s, Hanslick started writing music criticism for various journals and newspapers in Prague and Vienna. In 1846 he published a lengthy, highly appreciative review of Wagner's new opera, *Tannhäuser*, in the *Wiener Allegemeine Musik-Zeitung*, at a time when the composer (Hanslick's notorious nemesis of later years) was as yet little known to the European public. A law degree from the University of Vienna in 1849 opened the way to a career in the Hapsburg bureaucracy, a typical livelihood for amateur scholars of the time, working first for the ministry of finance and later the ministry of education. Following his initial appointment as a part-time lecturer or *Privatdozent* in 1856, Hanslick was promoted to a professorship in "the history and aesthetics of music" at the University of Vienna in 1861. This enabled him to leave the civil service, although he derived his income principally from his work for the *Neue freie Presse* (of which he was a founding editor, in 1864, when it broke off from *Die Presse*). Hanslick continued to cover musical life in Vienna, with frequent journeys to other European capitals, up through the early years of the next century. His single text on matters of musical philosophy, which earned him his initial appointment at the university, was published in 1854, before he had turned thirty: *Vom Musikalisch-Schönen* (*On the Beautiful in Music*, or *On the Musically Beautiful*). It was the product of extensive reading in music history, aesthetics, and criticism conducted in spare time during his early years in Vienna and, before that, as a civil servant in Klagenfurt. Despite the widespread attention his short treatise continued to attract, he published nothing further, either in monograph or article form, devoted expressly to issues of philosophical aesthetics. As a historian Hanslick published only one study, his 1869 *Geschichte des Concertwesens in Wien*, a history of musical life and institutions in Vienna from the time of Haydn and Mozart to the present. His later publications were all collections of reviews and other journalism.) However, Hanslick did continue to revise and further annotate *On the Musically Beautiful* throughout ten subsequent editions that appeared in his lifetime. This concise essay is regarded as the first and most influential theory of absolute music and musical formalism.

The term "absolute music" occurs only once in *On the Musically Beautiful*, in Chapter 2, maintaining the necessity of grounding philosophical claims regarding the expressive capacity of music in the example of "pure instrumental music" ("for it alone is pure, absolute musical art") (Hanslick 1990: vol. 1, 52). Nonetheless, it is fair to say that Hanslick's book is, as much as anything, a theory of absolute music, to which virtually all subsequent arguments about the autonomy of musical form (or more simply, "formalism") and about the expressive and semantic capacities or limitations of European tonal music must make some reference.

The remainder of this chapter offers a brief overview of the contents of *On the Musically Beautiful*, considers Hanslick's role in the emergence of "absolute music" as a term and as a concept, evaluates his reputation as an advocate of formalism (and hence of musical analysis as the correct means of understanding music), and concludes with comments on his role as a critic with strongly historicist, but by no means antiquarian, tendencies.

On the Musically Beautiful

Hanslick subtitled *On the Musically Beautiful* "a contribution toward the revision of the aesthetics of music." The objective of this revision is explained in the brief foreword to the first edition: "it will be enough if I succeed in providing an effective battering ram against the decayed aesthetics of feeling, and at the same time some foundation stones for a new structure to be erected in its place" (Hanslick 1990: vol. 1, 9). For at least a hundred years, as long as there had been a philosophical discourse of aesthetics, the meaning and value of music had been equated with the "feelings" it was thought to express or represent. Eighteenth-century attempts to include music within a theory of the fine arts unified by a principle of imitation (Aristotelian mimesis) generally yielded or adapted to the alternative that music imitated, represented, or expressed not natural objects but subjective emotions (see Chapter 25, "The early modern period," in this volume). Provoked by the ubiquity of this opinion and the endemic lack of rigor with which it was circulated, Hanslick set about to challenge it as the reigning assumption of musical aesthetics.

   The first two chapters of *On the Musically Beautiful* (Hanslick 1986 – all page numbers in this section refer to this edition) are devoted to this so-called "negative thesis," namely, that neither the subjective arousal of "feelings" (*Gefühle*) nor their objective representation constitutes the essential purpose, value, or "content" of music (xxiii). The first chapter, concerned with demonstrating the failings of the conventional "aesthetics of feeling," is above all aimed at redirecting the attentions of aesthetic inquiry from the subjective response of the listener to the objective evidence of the musical composition. Although he acknowledges the origin of aesthetics as a philosophy or science of "sensations" (*Empfindungen*) analyzing the effects of the fine arts on a discriminating audience with reference to categories of taste and perception, Hanslick sees modern aesthetics as becoming re-oriented to models of the natural sciences (via, perhaps, the example of Herbart's empiricist psychology). Progress in aesthetic thought will also depend, he asserts, on increased attention to the specifics of the individual medium, and be less concerned with supposedly common principles uniting all the arts. Imagination, as the faculty of aesthetic perception, is not merely disinterested, as Kant asserted, but also involves an active engagement with the object perceived, as "contemplating with active understanding" (4). Aesthetic understanding and judgments issuing from such active engagement will necessarily be grounded in knowledge of the nature and "rules" of the medium, and will focus more on the fixed constitution of the work than on the variable effects produced in the listening subject. An appendix to the first chapter catalogues representative examples of the doctrine of "music as an art of feelings" from Johann Mattheson through the 1840s (examples from Wagner's writings were added only in the sixth edition, 1881; see 86–91).

The case against "feelings" is articulated more systematically in Chapter 2. The argument is not that feelings or emotions are irrelevant to the experience of music, but that they do not constitute its actual "content," nor can they provide the basis for judging the artistic value or beauty of a musical work. (Up to this point Hanslick accepts the validity of a form-content dichotomy in the arts, as well as Hegel's notion of art as the sensual appearance of the "idea.") Because most of the "garden-variety emotions" (as Peter Kivy calls them; Kivy 1990, 2002) such as love, jealousy, anger, and the like require a defining object unavailable in a purely instrumental musical context, they cannot plausibly constitute a content to be represented by music, Hanslick argues. (He also distinguishes, along the way, between music's ability to arouse feelings and the question of their representation per se.) Music's alleged expressive or representational power is better understood in terms of the dynamic principles it is much more able to articulate: softness and loudness, consonance and dissonance, rising and falling contours, variations of speed, and so on. In this way music may provide a metaphorical exemplification of emotional properties, a system of "tone symbolism," loosely defined (11). By way of confirming these claims, Hanslick comments on various examples of instrumental music (e.g. Beethoven's overture to *The Creatures of Prometheus*) and operatic works as evidence of the generally fluid character of musical expression and its resistance to unequivocal, exclusive forms of signification.

Where Chapters 1 and 2 are concerned with discrediting the "decayed aesthetics of feeling," Chapter 3 turns to the positive thesis, an account of the "beautiful" in music, from whence the book derives its title. As Geoffrey Payzant notes, the Leipzig publisher Rudolph Weigel may have imposed this main title on the book as a whole, which Hanslick had only thought to identify as his contribution "toward a revision of the aesthetics of music" (xii). Chapter 3 does indeed contain the essentials of a theory of "absolute music" for which the author is best remembered, whatever questions remain about his identification with that term as such (see Pederson 2009). Elevating the chapter title "The Beautiful in Music" or "The Musically Beautiful" ("Das Musikalisch-Schöne") to the general title highlights a problem Hanslick faced in trying to construct a "positive thesis," or even to lay the foundation stones of one upon the ruins of the now discredited aesthetics of feeling. Where Peter Kivy, in analyzing the negative thesis of Chapters 1 and 2, posed the heuristic question "What was Hanslick Denying?" (Kivy 1990), the remainder of the book, especially Chapter 3 and the final Chapter 7 ("The Concepts of 'Content' and 'Form' in Music"), might prompt the question, "What was Hanslick Asking?" At first that might seem to be: "What is the true content of music, or the nature of that content, if it is not feelings (neither their arousal nor their representation)?" But once the positive thesis is underway in Chapter 3, the question seems to turn in the direction of: "What is the nature of musical 'beauty'?" and "Wherein resides the value of successful musical works?" The chapter suggests a set of equivalencies, without quite explicitly spelling them out as such: "Content = Beauty = Value." More crucially, and somewhat more explicitly, Hanslick introduces another equivalence: "Content = Form." These equivalences provide the foundation of his theory of absolute music and his aesthetic of musical formalism, as we would identify these today.

Subtending all of these equivalencies is a key phrase, "tönend bewegte Formen," rendered by Geoffrey Payzant as "tonally moving forms" (29), although a more literal, if cumbersome, version might be "forms in sounding (musical) motion." Such forms constitute the actual "content" of music. (The content of music is what you hear.) In the first edition these "sounding forms" are called "the unique content and object of music" (Hanslick 1990: vol. 1, 75). To convey the essentially abstract, formal nature of musical "beauty" or content Hanslick further advances the figure of the "arabesque," translated into sounding form and "coming into being in continuous self-formation before our eyes," or ears. Along the same lines he proposes the image of a kaleidoscope, similarly translated to a "higher sphere of ideality" (29). At pains not to compromise music's status as a fine art, however, Hanslick emphasizes that, despite the abstract and seemingly decorative nature of these figures for musical form, the work of composition remains "a work of mind upon material compatible with the mind" ("ein Arbeiten des Geistes im geistfähigen Material"; 31; Hanslick 1990: vol. 1, 79). The remainder of the third chapter works through the implications of these claims and dismisses some of the critical fallacies engendered by traditional ways of viewing musical content. If content resided in "feelings," for instance, the success of a composition would be proportionate to the accuracy or success with which those feelings were portrayed. Hanslick assumes no one truly believes that to be the case. The modern Romantic trend of looking for the "composer's feelings" or life experiences encoded in the composition (as say, in the works of Beethoven) is also exposed as an untenable corollary of the old views.

Chapter 7 of *On the Musically Beautiful*, "The Concepts of 'Form' and 'Content' in Music," revisits the form-content dichotomy as a kind of unfinished business, suggesting either that Hanslick himself was not entirely satisfied with the attempt to collapse it in Chapter 3, or that he was not confident that his audience was prepared to accept that move. In addition to the basic term "content" (*Inhalt*), he scrutinizes several related categories: object (*Gegenstand*), material (*Stoff*), and substance (*Gehalt*), of which the last comes closest to conveying the kind of medium-specific, form-immanent content described in Chapter 3. In particular, he revisits the question of whether music, without text, is capable of conveying a representational content in the manner of poetry or painting, such as the punishment of Orestes by the Furies or William Tell's rebellious defiance of political authority. Not surprisingly, he answers in the negative: music "reiterates no subject matter already known and given a name; therefore it has no nameable content for our thinking in concepts" (80). The growing popularity of associating just these kinds of content with music in the form of "programmatic" concert overtures or tone poems probably explains why he felt it necessary to revisit this aspect of the "content" question at all. Elsewhere Hanslick provided the tools for constructing an alternative theory, whereby music might represent the underlying mythic or narrative archetypes of these stories in terms of analogous "dynamic principles" and contours; yet he does not consider that alternative in Chapter 7. Instead, he concludes with a provisional theory of "melodic content." In Chapter 3 "rhythm" had been proposed as the basis of a hierarchical theory of temporal *form* (seen as "large-scale rhythm" breaking down into sections, periods, phrases). Now in Chapter 7 melodic themes or motives are proposed as the basis for a purely musical kind of *content*, reminiscent of the figure of "invention" borrowed from rhetoric in earlier eras. Hanslick likens themes to the principal characters in a novel (82), reflecting an awareness and acceptance of narrative paradigms increasingly common in nineteenth-century musical thought. But he reiterates his belief that content, as "spiritual substance," is immanent, autonomous, and not representational.

The intervening Chapters 4 through 6 of *On the Musically Beautiful* analyze aspects of the receptive role of the listener (Chapter 4, "Analysis of the Subjective Impression of Music," Chapter 5, "Musical Perception: Aesthetic vs. Pathological") and the question of how the materials of music, either as a system of tone-relations or as individual composition, relate to materials or prototypes of the natural world (Chapter 6, "The Relation of Music to Nature"). Thus Chapters 4 and 5 continue to work through the whole matter of music and "feelings," further stressing the importance of disinterested, objective contemplation of the aesthetic object as "form," on the model of Kantian aesthetics. Chapter 4, in which Hanslick's grounding in early theories of psychology is most in evidence, locates an alternative agency for the expression of feelings in the role of the performer. Though only briefly developed, the remarks here on the activity of the performer, as mind and body, and on performance as acoustic "presence" (vs. the disembodied state of the work as text) anticipate a variety of critical turns in recent musicological writing (for example Abbate 2004 or LeGuin 2006). Chapter 5 casts a skeptical eye on the classical tradition of musical "ethos" as a primitive if not downright superstitious relic of a culture still unacquainted with notions of composition as musical artwork. In asserting the lack of any plausible prototypes for music in nature (whether for scales and harmonies or for the composition of musical works), Chapter 6 also considers the relation of music to language. Viewed as modes of communication or utterance, neither music nor language has any explicit prototype in nature (70–1). But whereas poetry does, like painting, transform objects given in nature by way of its "content" (the content of communication or utterance), the same does not apply to music. This is yet another reason for the fundamental autonomy of music as an art, regardless of what extra-musical combinations or uses it may be subjected to.

"Absolute music" and the idea of musical formalism

In a recent essay surveying the critical history of the term "absolute music," Sanna Pederson reminds us that Hanslick did not himself employ the phrase in any direct or self-conscious way (Pederson 2009: 250–5). It is also worth adding that in the single instance where he did approximate the phrase, speaking of instrumental music as the "pure, absolute" genre of "musical art" ("reine, absolute Tonkunst"; Hanslick 1990: vol. 1, 52), he was making a clinical or empirical distinction, not a value judgment. Like E.T.A. Hoffmann before him, Hanslick stresses here that any claims about music's capacity to express feelings or represent content must be tested on examples of music without verbal text, for self-evident reasons. "Absolute" here is a synonym and perhaps mild intensifier of the adjective "pure" (granted, not a neutral or value-free term), which is otherwise the standard way of distinguishing instrumental from vocal or programmatic music for Hanslick as for the preceding generation. It also seems clear that Hanslick is not making any conscious reference to Wagner's extensive use of the phrase "absolute music" in the latter's writings from 1849 to 1851, where it is used with negative polemical import, though ultimately synonymous with Hanslick's usage (cf. Pederson 2009: 253). In neither case is the term infused with the idealist, Hegelian sense of the "absolute" as a quality of the infinite or transcendental, even if both Wagner and Hanslick understood music's potential claims to traffic with some such higher realm. (Hanslick's efforts to purge the remnants of Hegelian idealism from later editions of his book are well known; see Dahlhaus 1989: 27–9; Bonds 1997: 43–20; Hanslick 1990: vol. 2, 88–114).

All the same, as I have suggested, *On the Musically Beautiful* can certainly be read as a theory of what we have come to call absolute music, most explicitly in the effort to construct a "positive thesis" about the nature of musical form *as* content in Chapter 3. If Hanslick's use of the adjectives "pure" or "absolute" may be more or less neutrally descriptive but another phrase, "the specifically musical," is used throughout the book with clear polemical intent. This phrase was also notably taken up in the debates over Hanslick's text and the claims of the "New German School" around Wagner and Liszt over the following decades. Reiterating in Chapter 5 earlier claims about the essential identity of form and content, for instance, Hanslick writes:

> Precisely the "specifically musical" part [of a composition] is the creation of the artistic spirit, with which the contemplating spirit unites in complete understanding. The ideal content of the composition is in these concrete tonal structures, not in the vague general impression of an

abstract feeling. The form (as tonal structure), as opposed to the feeling (as would-be content), is precisely the real content of the music, is the music itself, while the feeling produced can be called neither content nor form, but actual effect.

(1986: 60)

Insofar as Hanslick insisted that claims about expressive content, beauty, or aesthetic value in music had to be relatable to the empirical data of the work as sounding form (*tönend bewegte Formen*), it is reasonable to identify him with an aesthetics of musical "formalism." The "revision of the aesthetics of music" to which he contributed can indeed be described as a turn from an older aesthetics of content (*Inhaltsästhetik*, as German scholarship has traditionally labeled it) toward one oriented to form. But while the modern discipline of "formalist" musical analysis can legitimately invoke Hanslick's ideas as a philosophical foundation, it seems unlikely that Hanslick himself had any notion of such an edifice to be built upon those "foundation stones" he thought to be providing, once having cleared away the debris of the "decayed aesthetics of feeling." German music theorists such as A.B. Marx, Gottfried Weber, Siegfried Dehn, Moritz Hauptmann, and Hugo Riemann had provided tools for a discipline of analysis (especially harmonic) during Hanslick's lifetime, but he seems to have paid scant attention either to the theory or to its potential analytical application. Committed as he was to his principal lifelong vocation of journalistic music criticism, and secondarily to lecturing on music history and appreciation, it is highly unlikely that he would have viewed a specialized discourse of musical analysis as a satisfactory means of articulating "the beautiful in music." (See, for example, his remarks on "dry technical definitions" as the unsatisfactory alternative to metaphorical discourse (1986: 30)).

Aesthetics, criticism, and history

In his memoir *Aus meinem Leben*, published in 1894, a year before he retired from full-time service as music editor of the *Neue freie Presse*, Hanslick reflected on his original intention to follow up *On the Musically Beautiful* with a fully fledged treatise on the aesthetics of music, to which the earlier publication would have been merely the prolegomenon. "I was well aware," he admits, "that its polemic, negative aspects far outweighed the positive, systematic aspects in scope and acuity" (Hanslick 1987: 153). But by the time his career change from civil servant to university professor allowed more ample opportunity for such a project, in the early 1860s, he found himself becoming disillusioned about the prospects. In part, his activity as a critic and now as a historian began to persuade him of the impossibility of constructing a single valid aesthetic discourse of "music," in view of the infinite contingencies of history, culture, and taste (see also Karnes 2008: 48–75).

At first blush this gesture of cultural relativism may sound unlikely. The scattered references to folk, popular, and especially non-European musics in *On the Musically Beautiful* seem to echo all the expected biases of a mid-nineteenth-century Viennese music "professional." And throughout his life Hanslick made no secret of his predilection for the Classical and Romantic canon, viewing even Bach and Handel with a certain skepticism, let alone any "ancient music" preceding the high Baroque. Yet his confession is congruent with the positivist, empiricist, and materialist strains of thought evident in much of *On the Musically Beautiful*. While, as Mark Evan Bonds (1997) has argued, Hanslick's arguments about musical autonomy and the immanence of value and "meaning" in form are to a certain extent predicated on the intellectual legacy of German idealism, the more strictly formalist implications of these arguments are incompatible with the idealist tradition. (Not only did he erase the more overtly "idealist" strains from subsequent edition of *On the Musically Beautiful*, but a majority of later insertions concern perspectives offered by different historical repertoires.) Given Hanslick's commitments to empirical psychology and cultural history, he could not claim a single, fixed, quantifiable measure of "beauty" for any configuration of "forms in sounding motion." Rather, that measure must vary according to the constitution of the listener no less than the time, place, and quality of the performance, among any number of factors. If value, meaning, and the perception of beauty – or for that matter, feelings – all had to be referable to the "music itself," for Hanslick, the autonomy of any music was of a limited and highly contingent sort, as his unwritten "supplement" to *On the Musically Beautiful* would, it seems, have gone on to emphasize.

See also Analysis (Chapter 48), Kant (Chapter 30), Music's arousal of emotions (Chapter 22), Nietzsche (Chapter 32), Psychology of music (Chapter 55), and Wagner (Chapter 35).

References

Abbate, C. (2004) "Music, Drastic or Gnostic?" *Critical Inquiry* 30: 505–36.

Bonds, M.E. (1997) "Idealism and the Aesthetics of Instrumental Music at the Turn of the Nineteenth Century," *Journal of the American Musicological Society* 50: 387–420.

Dahlhaus, C. (1989) *The Idea of Absolute Music*, trans. R. Lustig, Chicago and London: University of Chicago Press.

Hanslick, E. (1986 [1891 8th edn]) *On the Musically Beautiful*, trans. G. Payzant, Indianapolis: Hackett Publishing.

—— (1987 [1894]) *Aus meinem Leben*, ed. P. Wapnewski, Kassel: Bärenreiter.

—— (1990 [1854]) *Vom Musikalisch-Schönen*, 2 vols, ed. D. Strauss, Mainz: Schott.

Karnes, K.C. (2008) *Music, Criticism, and the Challenge of History*, Oxford: Oxford University Press.

Kivy, P. (1990) "What was Hanslick Denying?" *Journal of Musicology* 8: 3–18.

—— (2002) *Introduction to a Philosophy of Music*. Oxford: Clarendon Press.

Le Guin, E. (2006) *Boccherini's Body: An Essay in Carnal Musicology*, Berkeley and Los Angeles: University of California Press.

Pederson, S. (2009) "Defining the Term 'Absolute Music' Historically," *Music & Letters* 90: 240–62.

Further reading

Abegg, W. (1974) *Musikästhetik und Musikkritik bei Eduard Hanslick*, Regensburg: Bosse. (The first scholarly evaluation of Hanslick's aesthetic treatise in light of his music criticism.)

Bujic, B. (1988) *Music in European Thought, 1851–1912*, Cambridge: Cambridge University Press. (An anthology of source readings in translation, including an alternative translation by Martin Cooper of chs 1, 3, and 7 of Hanslick's *Vom Musikalisch-Schönen.*)

Burford, M. (2006) "Hanslick's Idealist Materialism," *19th-Century Music* 30: 166–81. (Following Bonds 1997, argues that *On the Musically Beautiful* sought a middle way between older idealist traditions of philosophical aesthetics and a modern "materialism" foregrounding the concrete empirical data of the artwork and the specificity of medium.)

Chua, D.K.L. (1999) *Absolute Music and the Construction of Meaning*, Cambridge: Cambridge University Press. (Broadly deconstructive essays on a range of categories related to the concept of absolute music, including a brief discussion of Hanslick.)

Gay, P. (1978) "For Beckmesser," in *Freud, Jews, and Other Germans: Masters and Victims in Modernist Culture*, New York: Oxford University Press, pp. 257–77. (An appreciative re-assessment of Hanslick's role as a writer on music and a spokesperson for the educated middle class in late Hapsburg Austria.)

Hanslick, E. (1950) *Vienna's Golden Years of Music 1850–1900: Eduard Hanslick*, ed. and trans. H. Pleasants, New York: Simon and Schuster; reprinted as (1988) *Hanslick's Music Criticisms*, New York: Dover. (A lightly annotated collection of Hanslick's music criticism. Still the only such selection available in English translation.)

—— (1993–) *Sämtliche Schriften: Historisch-Kritische Ausgabe*, ed. D. Strauss, Vienna and Weimar: Böhlau-Verlag. (A collected critical edition of Hanslick's music journalism, with notes and scholarly essays; six volumes to date, covering 1844 to 1863.)

Karnes, K.C. (2008) *Music, Criticism, and the Challenge of History*, Oxford: Oxford University Press. (Chapters 1 and 2 explore Hanslick's relationship to the emerging discipline of musicology at the University of Vienna in the latter half of the nineteenth century.)

Kivy, P. (1990) *Music Alone: Reflections on the Purely Musical Experience*, Ithaca and London: Cornell University Press. (As per the subtitle, essays not so much on Hanslick's ideas as such, but on their implications for the experience of listening to and understanding music.)

Landerer, C. (2002) "Nietzsches Vorstudien zur *Geburt der Tragödie* in ihrer Beziehung zur Musikästhetik Eduard Hanslicks," *Nietzsche-Studien* 31: 113–33. (Hanslick's ideas on absolute music and his anti-Wagnerian critical bias are explored as early seeds of Nietzsche's later turn against the composer, already germinating at the time of *The Birth of Tragedy*.)

Maus, F.E. (1992) "Hanslick's Animism," *Journal of Musicology* 10: 273–92. (Points to the prevalence of organic, bodily, and even ambivalently erotic discourse in *On the Musically Beautiful*, encouraging modern critics and aestheticians to pursue such aspects as remained partially latent in Hanslick's thinking.)

McColl, S. (1996) *Music Criticism in Vienna 1896–97: Critically Moving Forms*, New York: Oxford University Press. (Looks at a little over one year in the musical life of the Austrian capital through the lens of musical journalism toward the end of Hanslick's career.)

Payzant, G. (1981) "Hanslick, Sams, Gay, and 'tönend bewegte Formen'," *The Journal of Aesthetics and Art Criticism* 40: 41–8. (Argues for the rendition of this key phrase as translated in Hanslick 1986 as "tonally moving forms," emphasizing, in Payzant's view, Classical–Romantic tonality as the essential context of Hanslick's thought.)

—— (2003) *Hanslick on the Musically Beautiful: Sixteen Lectures on the Musical Aesthetics of Eduard Hanslick*, Christchurch: Cybereditions. (Payzant's lectures explore various aspects of *On the Musically Beautiful*.)

Taruskin, R. (1998) "A Myth of the Twentieth Century: *The Rite of Spring*, the Tradition of the New, and 'the Music Itself'," in *Defining Russia Musically*, Princeton: Princeton University Press, pp. 360–88. (Distinguishes a twentieth-century brand of musical formalism from nineteenth-century ideas of absolute music still beholden to idealist philosophical traditions.)

Yanal, R.J. (2006) "Hanslick's Third Thesis," *British Journal of Aesthetics* 46: 259–66. (A close reading of Hanslick's arguments for distinguishing musical beauty from its expressive properties.)

Zangwill, N. (2004) "Against Emotion: Hanslick Was Right About Music," *British Journal of Aesthetics* 44: 29–43. (Reviews and defends Hanslick's primary arguments for the so-called "negative thesis.")

34
GURNEY
Malcolm Budd

Edmund Gurney (1847–88), a British intellectual, psychologist, and psychical researcher, who was greatly admired by William James, had a profound love of music and deeply regretted his lack of natural facility and early musical training, which condemned him, as he confessed, to expressing himself *about* music, instead of *in* it. His monumental treatise on the philosophy of music, *The Power of Sound* (1880), is the most impressive, thorough and carefully argued work ever written on musical aesthetics, exploring every aspect of the subject, from the nature of sounds and the distinctive character of the perception of them by the ear, to the distinctive nature of music and the way in which it is perceived, the expression by music of feelings, concrete objects and abstract ideas, the relation between words and music in song and opera, and, finally, the scope and limits of musical criticism, with frequent illuminating contrasts and comparisons with the other arts. In this vast book, which is packed with insights and powerful arguments, Gurney attempts to show that the capacity to appreciate music is a unique and isolated faculty, and which has essentially nothing to do with intellectual or moral character: it is not dependent upon the possession of certain desirable intellectual or moral qualities, and listening to music, even the finest works, has no direct effect on a person's moral worth.

The non-representational nature of music

Gurney's most basic thought is that music is first and foremost an art of presentation, not representation. In its essential nature music does not represent any aspects of things found in the world outside music and which are recognized in the representation of them, as a picture represents something of a kind found in the outside world and which can be recognized in the picture by anyone who knows what that kind of thing looks like. A musical work consists, rather, of abstract forms, representative of nothing in the external world that a listener familiar with their appearance should recognize in the music. Accordingly, its appeal to the ear owes nothing to anything that it represents in an attractive fashion. But this appears to make its power to affect us so powerfully mysterious. How can a short piece of music, a melody, say, be so moving, given that it is not about anything? It consists of tones, abstract and insignificant in themselves, bound together by various degrees of resemblance or relationship into something that is still abstract. And there seems to be nothing in this to explain its emotional effect.

An examination of the abstract element in our appreciation of phenomena that are not abstract – concrete objects, both animate and inanimate, and in particular works of architecture, the only other art that Gurney recognizes as presentative, not representative – serves only to emphasize profound differences with the appreciation of musical forms. The most immediately relevant difference is the absence of the mass of association with other features of the world present in the appreciation of the forms of non-abstract objects (the existence, nature and history of which is easily traceable in the case of architecture). When he focuses on the abstract forms of music themselves, Gurney identifies as apparently promising elements of melodic pleasure not just the suggestion by melody of physical movement, and the suggestion of pace and physical force, but a direct impulse to move in response to a melody. But neither the suggestions of physical movement, force and pace, nor the impulse to bodily movement, considered on its own account as having a physically pleasurable character, nor all these combined, are sufficient to account for the emotional effect of melody. Indeed, Gurney declares, "their inadequacy in the way of explanation is almost ludicrous" (1880: 110).

Musical emotion

This inadequacy becomes apparent if we now introduce Gurney's conception of the emotional effect of fine melody, the "extraordinarily deep and passionate emotions of music" (1880: 123 fn1). In brief, his view is that "Music is perpetually felt as strongly emotional while defying all attempts to analyze the experience or to define it even in the most general way in terms of definite emotions" (1880: 316):

> the prime characteristic of Music, the alpha and omega of its essential effect [is] its perpetual production in us of an emotional excitement of a very intense kind, which yet cannot be defined under any known head of emotion . . . it seems like a fusion of strong emotions transfigured into a wholly new experience.
>
> (1880: 120)

We might try to describe this emotional excitement in such terms as "triumph and tenderness, desire and satisfaction, yielding and insistence," but any suggested description will not do justice to the "fused and indescribable emotion" aroused by music. This emotion is "unknown outside the region of musical phenomena" (1880: 317). It is clear that a "high-pitched excitement" (1880: 120) of this kind stands in need of an explanation, and this explanation cannot be provided by appeal to the various suggestions Gurney has already considered.

Music, emotion and Darwin

At this point Gurney makes a vital move. For if the associations he has explored do not do the trick, this does not mean that the search for association is wrong-headed. For this overlooks the possibility of *inherited* association – association with a powerful emotional source that we are not now conscious of. So his view is that if we are to resolve the mystery of music's emotional power, which, he believes, must after all derive from some kind of association, albeit an inherited one, we must delve as far back as possible in the history of musical phenomena and identify its origin. If the ultimate source of musical phenomena turns out to involve emotion of the strongest kind, and if the connection with this emotion has descended, although not being apparent, to us, then the capacity of melodic forms to affect us so powerfully will no longer be mysterious. And, Gurney claims, this is indeed the case. Here he has recourse to Darwin's theory of the origin of vocal, and so of musical phenomena.

According to Darwin, musical notes and rhythm, and even the requisite power of voice or, more generally, of generating sounds through their bodies, were first acquired and then perfected by insects, amphibians, animals, and birds, the progenitors of humanity, in order to call or charm the opposite sex. Darwin draws attention to a number of facts about music, which include these: (i) music excites feelings of "tenderness, love, triumph and ardour for war," which may be mingled together; (ii) similar, but less complex, emotions are probably felt by birds "when the male pours forth his full volume of song, in rivalry with other males, for the sake of captivating the female"; (iii) musical notes are produced and appreciated by human beings of all races, although these abilities are of no direct use in ordinary (extra-musical) life; (iv) these capacities may have been possessed by our half-human progenitors and some rude form of music may have existed in half-human times. Darwin's view is that these facts become intelligible on the assumption that

> musical tones and rhythm were used by the half-human progenitors of man, during the season of courtship, when animals of all kinds are excited by the strongest passions. In this case, from the deeply laid principle of inherited associations, musical tones would be likely to excite in us, in a vague and indefinite manner, the strong emotions of a long-past age.
>
> (1880: 119)

This fits neatly with Gurney's conception of the emotional effect of music as a fused and indescribable emotion of great power. So the suggestion is that in the remote past the musical faculty, linked with the deepest and strongest emotions, existed in an embryonic form, and in its present, greatly developed form, possessed by most of humanity, inheritance has endowed it with the power to arouse the "sublimated quintessence" (1880: 194) of these emotions.

But there is a problem with this explanation, a problem that Gurney recognized at the time he wrote *The Power of Sound* and that later led him to lose confidence in the explanation (1887: 297–8). The difficulty concerns the process by which contact with Darwin's proposed emotional spring is supposed to be made with impressive, but broken with unimpressive, melodic forms. For the idea is not that the melodic forms that move us are the same as or closely resemble those used and responded to by our semi-human progenitors. The idea is, rather, as I have stated, that these ancestors possessed the same faculty that we possess to hear and enjoy a number of successive tones as a unit, a bit of melody, albeit in an embryonic, rather than our much more developed, form. But the generality of this precludes its explaining why some melodic forms are heard as impressive, others not. Hence, as Gurney realized, to adhere to the Darwinian explanation we must hold both that the musical faculty has an independent power of discriminating satisfying from unsatisfying melodic forms and that "the satisfactory result is *not felt* in independence of the emotional flow from the emotional source to which it opens a passage, and to which the satisfactoriness or impressiveness *as we know it* should be mainly due." "This difficulty," Gurney confessed, "seems to me scarcely less than that of leaving Darwin's suggestion on one side" (1887: 298).

Impressive and unimpressive musical forms

The difficulty of using Darwin's theory of the origin of music in the expression and arousal of primitive sexual emotions is intensified by Gurney's principal claim about melodic forms. An obvious set of facts is that nobody, at any stage in their life, finds every melodic form equally impressive, or impressive at all; which melodies impress us change over time; and people often differ over which melodies they find impressive. Gurney argues that neither in general nor in any individual's case is it possible to specify a criterion that identifies all and only those melodic forms that are impressive – a principle that distinguishes the impressive from the unimpressive – by indicating a property (other than their characteristic emotional power) possessed uniquely by impressive melodic forms. Appeal to a melody's suggestion of physical movement or impulse or to its suggestion of the cadences of emotional speech provides no such criterion, and no principle concerning the structure of a melody fares any better. So for every one of us, the impressiveness of melodic forms is anomalous. And if this claim is correct, there is no possibility of explaining the supposed opening and closing of the passage to the Darwinian source of the emotion that might be aroused by a melody by identifying some property distinctive of impressive melodies and then somehow aligning that property with the opening of that passage.

Ideal motion as the distinctive character of abstract musical forms

Gurney claims that the abstract forms that compose any piece of music have a unique character. This character derives, at bottom, from the ultimate constituents of music, tones, and musical sounds of a definite pitch. For:

> among the simple impressions of sense, differences of pitch present the absolutely unique peculiarity, that they are neither differences of *kind*, as between red and blue colours, or between bitter and sweet tastes, or between a violin-note and a clarionet-note; nor differences of *strength* or *degree of intensity*, as between bright and moderate light, or between very sweet and slightly sweet tastes, or between a loud note and a soft note; but they are differences of distance and direction, clearly and indisputably felt as such.
>
> (1880: 139)

But music possesses another dimension, time: a musical work is a temporal series of sounds of definite pitch. However, when we listen to music we do not hear it as simply a series of notes that follow one after another. Rather, we hear the notes as related to one another in various ways. In particular we hear some of them as being grouped together into melodic forms, which are constituted by "the fusion with rhythm of the pitch-element in which tone-relationship is the all-important feature" (1880: 173). Now consider a melody and the experience of hearing the tones (and rests) that constitute it as forming a melody. One of Gurney's principal ideas is that this experience has a distinctive character, present in a rudimentary form even in mere change of pitch from one note to another, which gives "the impression of passage from point to point" (1880: 141). For a melodic form unfolds itself in time and the "form is perceived by continuous advance along it" (1880: 164). And this distinguishes the perception of melodic form from the perception both of visible form and of physical motion:

> It is the *oneness of form and motion* which constitutes the great peculiarity of melody and of the faculty by which we appreciate it. As we derive our primary ideas of sensible form from visible objects, a form which presents the character of *motion* in that it advances or is advanced along, in one order at one pace from end to end, is a novelty; as we derive our primary ideas of motion from physical motion, a *motion* which presents the character of *form*, in that bits of it separated by other bits and by wide distances are yet felt as indispensable parts of one unity, is a novelty. When a melody is familiar to us we realise it by a gradual process of advance along it, while yet the *whole* process is in some real manner present to us at each of the successive instants at which only a minute part of it is actually engaging our ears.
>
> (1880: 164–5)

Our perception of a melodic form, which is "a unity to which all the parts are necessary in their respective places" (1880: 165), is constituted by our proceeding along it from beginning to end, and to this unique musical process or progressive form Gurney gives the name "Ideal Motion."

This conception of Ideal Motion (which Gurney extends from simple melodic forms to polyphonic and harmonic forms) is rendered liable to misunderstanding by the name Gurney has given to it. It is important to realize that Gurney is not likening a melody (or its perception) to any kind of spatial movement (or its perception), such as that of a rubber ball bouncing up and down as it hits the ground after having been thrown in a certain direction. Indeed, he is concerned to expose the inadequacy of an analogy between a melody and something moving through space and he emphasizes that the result of an attempted translation of a piece of Ideal Motion into terms of physical motion would be "the faintest metaphor" (1880: 337). His coinage of the term "Ideal Motion" is intended to highlight two distinctive features of the perception of a melody. In the first place, the perception of a melodic form is unlike the perception of a spatial form in that, necessarily, the parts of the form must be perceived in a specific order and at a specific rate. Second, the perception of a melodic form is unlike the perception of non-musical, temporal series of events in that the series of events is perceived as, in Gurney's sense, "a unity to which all the parts are necessary in their respective places," the parts not being substitutable by different parts.

Impressive and expressive music

Gurney rightly distinguishes between two ideas: music being impressive and music being expressive – expressive in the sense of being an expression of feelings or qualities or external objects and events or abstract ideas, phenomena known to us outside music. Of course, one and the same piece of music can be both impressive and expressive, but its being one of these things is not the same as its being the other. For Gurney, music is an expression of a certain feeling if it "summons it up within us," and it is an expression of a certain quality if it summons up the feeling "corresponding" to the quality, which may be different from the quality attributed to the music:

> The special feeling corresponding to melancholy music is melancholy, but the special feeling corresponding to capricious or humorous music is not capriciousness or humorousness, but surprise or amusement: clearly, however, this mode of feeling is sufficiently identified with the contemplation of the quality.
>
> (1880: 313 n. 1)

Likewise, music is expressive of some external object or event if it arouses in us a concrete image of the object or event, and it is expressive of an abstract idea if it awakens that idea in us. So Gurney considers the musical arousal of three kinds of phenomena: emotional feelings, concrete images of external things, and abstract ideas. In each kind of expressive music Gurney's concern is twofold: to identify the features of music responsible for the arousal of the feeling, image or idea, and to assess the contribution of the expressive aspect of a piece of music to its musical value.

The conclusion of Gurney's investigation of the suggestion by music of external objects and events, that is, the awakening of concrete images of them, is that this takes place either through perceptual resemblances of the sounds (bells, birdsong) or the motions (rides, gondolas), which may be close or remote, real or fanciful, or by the possession of very general qualities shared with what is suggested (summer, moonlight), the suggestions nearly always being very indefinite, allowing a wide latitude of choice, and usually indicated by the title of the music, without which listeners, if they form an image of anything, are likely to diverge widely. And he argues that the musical expression of extra-musical abstract ideas, which is severely limited, is possible only through the expression of feelings, and in particular through there being different feelings expressed in different parts of a work. In both cases, the enhancement of musical value afforded by the expressive aspect is minimal or entirely lacking.

Gurney argues that it is mainly from the two features that it shares with physical motion – pace and rhythm – that music derives what power it has to express feelings (or qualities), although this power is sometimes traceable to other characteristics of Ideal Motion or the process by which we follow it. But he allows this power only a limited value. His main target is the view that music is primarily an art of emotional expression, its power and value deriving from its expression of extra-musical emotional feelings. He makes two principal claims about the musical expression of feelings (the first of which applies to all kinds of musical expression). The first is that expressiveness "is absent or only slightly present in an immense amount of *im*pressive music" (1880: 214). For a quality to be only slightly expressed by a piece of music is for a word for that quality to be a fairly appropriate characterization of the music for a listener, but for that fact to play little or no role in the listener's response to the music. (Here and elsewhere Gurney appears to slip between two understandings of "summoning up" a feeling, which should be distinguished: on the one hand, arousing a feeling, and, on the other, suggesting a feeling, in the sense that an adjective drawn from the category of the emotions would or does strike the listener as being a suitable description of the music.) Second, "no music is really expressive in any valuable way which does not also impress us as having the essential character of musical beauty; an unpleasing tune may be lugubrious but not melancholy" (1880: 314). This second claim appears to have two implications: (i) impressive music that is also expressive can be expressive in a valuable way, and (ii) to be expressive in a valuable way is to be expressive of certain kinds of quality (melancholy, for instance) and to be expressive of qualities in a unvaluable way is to be expressive of qualities of other kinds (lugubriousness, for example). The second implication is obscure, and, since Gurney does not develop it, I shall leave it aside

A substantial part of Gurney's view of the musical expression of feelings follows more or less directly from his conceptions of musical impressiveness and expressiveness, these being different aspects of music, a particular piece possessing one, both or none of these aspects. For a piece of music to be impressive is for the intrinsic nature of its progressive form or Ideal Motion to yield the distinctive emotional pleasure of music, the origin of which Gurney has traced back to primitive sexual arousal. This emotional excitement is unknown outside music and resists all analysis in terms of definite extra-musical emotions (1880: 316–17). For it to be expressive of an emotional feeling is for it to give rise to it. So if a piece of music is both impressive and expressive, this means that it arouses the emotional pleasure distinctive of music and also the feeling of a definable emotion. On the other hand, if it is unimpressive and yet expressive, this means that the only feeling it arouses (except repulsion or boredom) is the feeling of a definable emotion, which emotion will be either negative (as with fear) or positive (as with triumph). Now even if the definable emotion of a piece of expressive music is positive, if the music is unimpressive it will lack the crucial, all-important, high emotional excitement of impressive music, and its expressive aspect will be an inadequate compensation for what it lacks. On the other hand, if a piece of music is both impressive and expressive, Gurney regards this as a kind of plus, the feeling of the emotion expressed (melancholy, say) receiving an extraordinary intensification (1880: 340) from the distinctive emotion of impressive music, which, in itself "a perfectly distinct though unique and undefinable affection" (1880: 316), takes on the coloring of the extra-musical emotion the music is expressive of (1880: 338).

Musical criticism

It is unsurprising that Gurney has little room for musical criticism – criticism of a work of music itself, not a particular performance of it – whether the criticism is in the form of interpretation, description or argument. In the other arts, interpretation of the meaning of a work is the highest function of an art critic, but in music, which consists of abstract, non-representational forms, thus ruling out the possibility of comparisons with other representations of the same subject, there is nothing to be explained, the "meaning" of music residing in the intrinsic nature of these progressive forms themselves, rather than anything else. So as far as interpretation is concerned, the only interpretation of a musical work is the shaping by the performer of the precise nature of the forms that compose the work. On the other hand, descriptions of a work, whether in technical or extra-musical terms, are usually unenlightening, at best merely spelling out what an attentive listener can hear equally well without such attempted aids, at worst distracting or misleading, although Gurney makes an exception of a certain kind of judicious account or analysis of a work, necessarily somewhat technical, which guides the listener's attention to noteworthy points in the piece. As for the evaluation of music, argument is fruitless and proof impossible. For

> the word *bad* may be fairly used (absolutely or relatively) of music – (1) which gives no pleasure, (2) which gives extremely slight and transitory pleasure, (3) which gives pleasure superior in these respects, but shown by experience to be incompatible with more deep and lasting pleasure given by other music.
>
> (1880: 530)

And although musical taste can be educated and developed, there are ultimate differences of taste which just have to be accepted and which (outside the range of the above criterion of value) preclude a demonstration that one piece of music is superior to another.

See also Arousal theories (Chapter 20), Evaluating music (Chapter 16), Music's arousal of emotions (Chapter 22), Psychology of music (Chapter 55), Rhythm, melody, and harmony (Chapter 3), Understanding music (Chapter 12), and Value (Chapter 15).

References

Gurney, E. (1880) *The Power of Sound*, London: Smith, Elder, & Co.
—— (1887) "The Psychology of Music," in *Tertium Quid: Chapters on Various Disputed Questions*, vol. II, London: Kegan Paul, Trench, & Co, pp. 251–302.

Further reading

Budd, M. (1985) *Music and the Emotions: The Philosophical Theories*, London: Routledge & Kegan Paul. (Chapter IV is a greatly more detailed exposition of the principal elements of Gurney's theory of music and a critique of certain aspects of his thought.)
Epperson, G. (1997) *The Mind of Edmund Gurney*, Madison: Fairleigh Dickinson University Press. (Gurney's biography, including further details about his correspondence.)
Levinson, J. (1993) "Edmund Gurney and the Appreciation of Music", *Iyyun, The Jerusalem Philosophical Quarterly* 42: 181–205. (An excellent exposition and outline defense of Gurney's view, which Levinson refers to as concatenationism, that prioritizes the grasp of small-scale musical forms and their cogency of sequence in the appreciation of music.)

35

WAGNER

Thomas Grey

The inclusion of Richard Wagner (1813–83) as the sole composer meriting an individual entry in the *Routledge Companion to Philosophy and Music* (assuming we are to regard Rousseau principally as a philosopher, not as a musician) should come as no surprise. Many musicians have written on issues of musical theory, contributed to aesthetic debates on music and culture, and above all written musical criticism, but none approaches the scope of Wagner's literary output, much of it devoted to central issues of philosophical aesthetics concerning music and language, meaning and signification, the social value of music, and, most famously, theories of a synthetic "total work of art" (*Gesamtkunstwerk*). More than any other composer, Wagner read and responded to important contemporary thinkers such as Hegel, the French social theorist Pierre-Joseph Proudhon, the materialist "Young Hegelian" Ludwig Feuerbach, the anarchist Mikhail Bakunin, and, most fundamentally, Arthur Schopenhauer, whose ideas shaped the later music dramas from *Tristan und Isolde* to *Parsifal* and, arguably, the composition of the *Ring* cycle. Similarly unique is the impact he himself exerted on the figure of Friedrich Nietzsche (or, for that matter, on the modernist aesthetics of the French symbolists). "There is no other example in the whole of our culture," writes Bryan Magee about the case of Nietzsche, "of a creative artist who is not himself a philosopher having a *philosophical* influence of this magnitude on someone who was indeed a great philosopher" (Magee 2000: 81). Beyond the vast corpus of published writings, correspondence, and autobiography, Wagner's contribution to the philosophy of music might also be sought in the musical works, the later so-called "music dramas," which variously exemplify, refine, and even critique the theoretical perspectives of the writings.

Indeed, the status of Wagner's writings in isolation from his creative oeuvre is problematic in assessing his importance as a "philosopher" of music and the arts. His activity as a writer was intermittent, eclectic, undisciplined, and generally self-serving. Not only did he change his views about the nature and purpose of music and opera over time, but also the views themselves are frequently expressed in a style of such unexampled obfuscation that it is often extremely difficult to arrive at any clear reading of their significance. His own intellectual idol, Schopenhauer, offers a diagnosis of the problem when he describes in the preface to the second edition (1844) of *The World as Will and Representation* the ill effects of his intellectual nemesis, Hegel, with regard to the vacuous prolixity of German philosophical writing in the early decades of the nineteenth century. Without having acquired a proper understanding of Kant's legitimately difficult idealism, writers of the post-Hegelian generation "are early accustomed to regard the hollowest verbiage as philosophical thoughts, the most miserable sophisms as sagacity, and silly craziness as dialectic; and by accepting frantic word-combinations in which the mind torments and exhausts itself in vain to conceive something, their heads are disorganized" (Schopenhauer 1969: vol. 2, xxiv). As he moved from the occasional journalism of his earlier years to tackling a large-scale systematic aesthetic critique in the so-called "Zurich" writings produced during the first years of his political exile (1849–52), Wagner found himself enmeshed in just such neo-Hegelian discursive toils. His passionate views about the relation of art and artists to society, of music to poetry and drama, of his own works to Beethoven or Weber (or for that matter, Meyerbeer) are by no means without substance; but they are routinely "tormented" by just the kind of "frantic word-combinations" Schopenhauer had complained of (Schopenhauer 1969: vol. 1, xxiv), leaving the reader more exhausted than enlightened. Wagner himself was well aware of this, and it is one reason there still exists no practical English translation of his major writings. After starting the *Ring* cycle and after his initiation into Schopenhauer, the writings are fewer, shorter, and concern a broader range of subjects. The style itself, however, was never substantially reformed.

The following short analysis of Wagner's relevance to the philosophy of music summarizes some themes, terminology, and relevant cultural networks of the major groups of his published writings: the casual musical journalism up to his time as Kapellmeister in Dresden in the 1840s; the "Zurich" essays written in the aftermath of the 1848–49 political insurgencies across the European continent, outlining a new genre of musical drama; and some isolated essays on musical-aesthetic topics published during the period of his mature works, notably the retrospective on his earlier theories published under the title "*Zukunftsmusik*" ("*Music of the Future,*" 1861 (Wagner 1979)) and the Schopenhauer-influenced essay for the 1870 Beethoven centennial (Wagner 1895–99: vol. 5).

Opera or symphony?

As he gravitated toward a career in music from the late 1820s and into the 1830s, Wagner was torn between a cultural and perhaps philosophical allegiance to the symphonic tradition of Viennese classicism, above all the recently canonized genius of Beethoven, and a temperamental affinity with the conjunction of poetry, music, and theater in opera. By 1833 at the latest (when he composed his first operatic score, *Die Feen*), he had definitively cast his lot with opera, and despite unrealized hopes to write additional symphonies or symphonic poems of some kind in his retirement (that is, after *Parsifal*, 1882), he rarely strayed from his chosen vocation. The allegiance to Beethoven and a "German" symphonic ideal continued to be carefully cultivated as part of his artistic persona, however, as evidenced throughout his writings, his autobiographical texts, and his activity as a conductor.

A dialectic of symphony and opera is fundamental to Wagner's musical aesthetics, despite their shifting contours, throughout his life. The dialectic is fundamental to many issues in the philosophy of music during the whole nineteenth century, and, indeed, across much of the history of Western music, if we use it to frame questions about the relation of music to language, whether in evolutionary terms, in terms of musical expression and signification, or in terms of compositional technique. Wagner continually interrogated the sophisticated symphonic language his generation had inherited from Beethoven, on one hand, and the highly evolved conventions of opera as he learned them from Mozart, Weber, Marschner, and the major Italian and French composers of the early nineteenth century, on the other. Critics since the later Nietzsche have been skeptical about Wagnerian claims for a perfected, higher synthesis of symphony and opera. But as a theorist of operatic "reform" and as a composer for the theater, Wagner was always looking to both traditions in debating questions as to what music can signify or express on its own, how it is inflected by the words it sets, by the gestures and larger structures of drama, and by the images, symbols, or archetypes of myth.

The pattern of Wagner's education and early professional career – a reverent absorption of German/Viennese instrumental classics (plus a little Bach) followed by an apprenticeship in the field of opera – is also reflected in the themes of his earlier writings. Almost from the beginning he understood it as his mission to advance the existing German hegemony in the realm of instrumental music into the wider musical public sphere of opera. This mission is adumbrated already in the very first paragraph of his very first published work, a brief article "On German Opera" in the *Zeitung für die elegante Welt* (10 June 1834). "By all means, we have a field of music which belongs to us by right, – and that is Instrumental-music; – but a German Opera we have not, and for the selfsame reason that we own no national Drama. We are too intellectual and much to learned to create warm human figures" (Wagner 1895–99: vol. 8, 55). Contemporary German opera composers such as Weber and Spohr are seen to lack a proper sense for "song," by which the young Wagner means the art of singing, generally, but also its perfection in the *cantabile* of Italian bel canto opera. "Song, after all, is the organ whereby a man may musically express himself; and so long as it is not fully developed, he is wanting in true speech" (Wagner 1895–99: vol. 8, 55). Channeling the paradigmatically German art (or science, *Wissenschaft*) of music into a new form of "national" drama, animating this with "warm human figures" (what he would later celebrate as "the purely human"), and communicating it through the "true speech" of singing – all this would continue to define the aims of the great Wagnerian project up to the end of his life.

Even at the moment he was completing what was to be his big operatic break-through, *Rienzi* (1838–40), a work one might fairly describe as "absolute opera," Wagner could extol the essentially German virtues of purely instrumental music and the culture of private domestic music-making or *Hausmusik*. An essay "On German Music," published in the Parisian *Revue et gazette musicale* in 1840, paraphrases E. T. A. Hoffmann's paean to the Romantic values of instrumental music, where the listener's imagination "is not restricted to the expression of a single specific passion," and where he can "lose himself in the great realm of indefinite feeling" (Wagner 1973: 41). At the same time he also echoes the ear-lier writer's belief in the potential of a new Romantic genre of German opera, as expressed in Hoffmann's 1813 vignette "The Poet and the Composer." For the young Wagner, however, there are two routes toward this ideal: the application of the German's "universalizing" genius to the advancement of contemporary international (Italian and French) operatic idioms, and a synthesis of operatic and symphonic languages into a new, more potent (German) genre.

The lodestar of this second route was a work Hoffmann never knew, the Ninth Symphony of Beethoven. In another piece from 1840, imagining the "pilgrim-age" of an idealistic young German musician to Beethoven in Vienna in the early 1820s, Wagner turns the aging symphonic composer into a mouthpiece for the "musical-dramatic artwork of the future" he would later go on to theorize at length. "Why shouldn't vocal music be considered as great and serious as instru-mental music?" asks Wagner's Beethoven. The symphony thrives on the expres-sion of infinitely malleable, indefinite feelings, intimations of the sublime and the infinite. "The genius of the voice," this fictive Beethoven opines, "is completely different: this represents the human heart, the separate individual sensibility, lim-ited, but clear and definite. Imagine, now, these two elements brought together and united!" (Wagner 1973: 80). Modern opera had cultivated all the advances of instrumental virtuosity in its orchestral accompaniments, and its vocal writing had emulated these as well. What it lacked, however, was a symphonic ambi-tion of Beethovenian proportions. While Wagner understood that Beethoven's choral-symphonic setting of Schiller's ode "To Joy" in the finale of the Ninth was no more explicitly "dramatic" in genre than the orchestral movements pre-ceding it, the gesture of appending this vocal movement to his last and most audacious symphony was of immense symbolic value. When Wagner conducted the Ninth in April 1846, in Dresden, he published a hermeneutic gloss on the whole symphony drawing on quotations from Goethe's *Faust*. Like many of his contemporaries, he believed that music of this kind possessed an expressive or imaginative "content" that could be poetically intimated, if never semanti-cally fixed. He locates the symbolic crux of the work not so much in the hymn-like setting of Schiller's verses, but in the way in which Beethoven moves from tones to words. With the shattering harmonic dissonances that open the finale and the urgent instrumental recitative that follows, the music "leaves behind the character of pure instrumental music . . . the realm of infinite and indistinct expression," preparing "the entrance of language and the human voice as something both anticipated and necessary"; "nearly transgressing the boundaries of absolute music, this recitative engages the other instruments with its powerfully emotional discourse, pressing for some resolution, and finally issuing in a lyrical theme" (trans. Grey 2009: 376). It was not the musical style but the revolutionary gesture of this passage that would fuel much of the theoretical speculation Wagner was soon to undertake as a prelude to the creation of his magnum opus, the *Ring of the Nibelung* cycle.

Music as means or end?

The overriding message of the three increasingly lengthy essays Wagner wrote during the first three years of his political exile in Zurich – *Art and Revolution* (1849), *The Artwork of the Future* (1849), and *Opera and Drama* (1850–51) – was that the arts, in order to remain culturally relevant in the life of modern peoples and nations, needed to collaborate in a new way. The truly relevant arts, however, were really just drama and music. The imperfect wedding of these in the existing genre of opera is critiqued in first of the three parts of the longest essay, *Opera and Drama*, starting from a manifesto-like statement embedded in the preface to the book: "The error of the genre of opera has consisted in this: that a means of expression (the music) has been made the end, while the end of this expression (the drama) has been made a means" (Wagner 1984: 19). The three large parts of *Opera and Drama* then go about detailing the shortcomings of conventional operatic practice, in which more or less "purely musical" values provide a framework for mere vocal display and theatrical spectacle (part 1); reflecting on the nature and history of spoken drama and the importance of myth (part 2); and outlining in general terms the nature of the musical-dramatic "artwork of the future" that must supplant the failing genre of opera (part 3), including proposals about language (*Stabreim* or alliterative verse), the hierarchical integration of "poetic-musical periods," and a network of associative "melodic moments" or what would later be known as "leitmotifs." Music may be, in the end, the most potent element of this new genre (one Wagner could not bring himself to saddle with a specific generic designation). However, its ultimate cultural significance rests on its presentation of a mythic content in dramatic form, speaking to the entirety of the *Volk* (people) and not just to affluent fans of music and singing.

The revolutionary impulse that gave rise to these "Zurich" essays is more overt in the preceding two, which also concern a revaluation of ends and means, in a broader sense. The title *Art and Revolution* might suggest that Wagner was advocating the use of art as a means toward achieving social or political reforms, in the manner of politically committed artists in the twentieth century. While he does claim that art must be regarded as "the outcome of political life" and as "a social product" (Wagner 1888: vol. 3, 9), he is not thinking here in terms of agitprop. His notion of the "ends" of art is rather more in line with those of the Weimar classicism of Goethe and Schiller, above all the notion that drama has the potential to educate and edify the public in ways that will contribute to a gradual improvement of society and its institutions. Art (drama) *is* to this extent a means to a social-political end, albeit a vague and idealized one, tending toward that of cultural nation-building. As a means, the individual arts must be re-integrated into a collective art such as the Greeks had once possessed in their tragedy.

The Wagnerian coinage *Gesamtkunstwerk* – the total, collective, or communal work of art – is first applied by Wagner to that ancient Greek tragedy (1888: vol. 3, 12). With the decline of ancient tragedy, he explains, art ceased to be "the expression of public consciousness." "The drama was dissolved into its constituent parts: rhetoric, painting, music, and the rest all left one by one, the circle in which they had once moved in concert, so that each alone might pursue its own path and develop independently, but egoistically" (Wagner 1888: vol. 3, 29). Wagner admits (somewhat grudgingly) that the long development of autonomous artistic media in the hands of professional castes had actually performed important work. Now, however, it is essential to avoid an alienating specialization on the part of these professional castes, on one hand, and to avoid the commodification of their production on the part of modern market forces, on the other. The modern or future *Gesamtkunstwerk* would avoid these perils in reconnecting art with the *Volk*; the *Volk* would then come to realize that art in this new sense is for them a genuine "need" and not merely an appetite artificially generated by commercial interests.

Apollonian representation or Dionysian will? (the beautiful or the sublime?)

Other dichotomous rhetorical questions might be posed with the aim of highlighting important questions about Wagner's later theory and practice. For instance, "Culture, National or Universal?" with regard to the messages of *Die Meistersinger* and the agenda of the Bayreuth Festival; or "Drama, Sacred or Profane?" with regard to that agenda again, the diffuse and often questionable legacy of Wagnerian ideas summed up in the term "Wagnerism," and the critique of that phenomenon waged by the likes of Nietzsche, Thomas Mann, and Theodor Adorno. But retaining, for practical purposes, a focus on musical expression and "meaning" in relation to text and drama, we might just consider what becomes of these issues after the crucial encounter with the ideas of Schopenhauer in 1854.

Bryan Magee claims, with good reason, that 1854 was "the ultimately decisive year of Wagner's creative life" (2000: 225). Wagner finally began to compose the

Ring cycle, completing all of *Das Rheingold* and drafting much of *Die Walküre*. He read for the first time Schopenhauer's *The World as Will and Representation*, which continued to dominate his understanding of life and art to the end of his days; and he conceived (largely under the impress of Schopenhauer) the idea for a musical drama on the legend of Tristan and Isolde, a work which became the most radically innovative of his entire oeuvre. It was the same year, we might recall, that saw the publication of Eduard Hanslick's *Vom Musikalisch-Schönen* ("On the Beautiful in Music"), articulating a theory of "specifically musical" value in opposition to the ingrained habit of locating meaning, value, and "content" in the alleged expression of feelings or emotions (Hanslick 1986: 28). Throughout *The Artwork of the Future* and *Opera and Drama*, Wagner had applied the modifier "absolute" as a pejorative, following Ludwig Feuerbach's critique of "absolute philosophy." In this sense it described any branch of knowledge cut off from real life and pursued in isolation, turning ultimately sterile, lifeless, and irrelevant. "Absolute melody," in this sense, was mere sonic decoration or pattern-making, and "absolute music" a practice that uprooted the art from its original and necessary nourishment in words, voice, and drama. Schopenhauer's thesis that music, without any reference to words or ideas, figured the very nature of the "will" (the noumenal essence or drive he posited as preceding all forms of phenomenal "representation") gave Wagner cause to re-think his position on music as a mere means to a larger, synthetic end and his critique of music's aesthetic autonomy in modern times.

In the somewhat lopsided apologia for Liszt's symphonic poems published as an "open letter" to the *Neue Zeitschrift für Musik* in 1857, Wagner attempted momentarily to redefine the terms. "Nothing is less absolute than music (that is, as regards its phenomenal appearance), and the advocates of an absolute music clearly don't know what they are talking about; to confound their arguments it would suffice to have them point to any music without a formal basis either in corporeal motion or poetic verse" (Wagner 1888: vol. 5, 191). To this extent he is retaining earlier arguments about the origins of musical form and melody in dance, song, and the combination of these in drama. But at the same time he now declares in defense of Liszt and the honor of music: "This most splendid, incomparable, independent, and unique of all the arts . . . music can never, in any union into which it might enter, cease to be the highest, most redemptive art" (Wagner 1888: vol. 5, 191). Following Schopenhauer, but resisting Hanslick, Wagner grants to music a kind of absolute or noumenal essence while insisting that, as phenomenon or "representation," in Schopenhauer's terms, it will necessarily be conditioned by various ritual or discursive modes of human utterance. Dance, song, and drama are thus analogous to the a priori conditions of space, time, and causality that enable the representation of the "will" as perceptible phenomena.

In later writings, Wagner continues his attempted reconciliation with a Schopenhauerian notion of absolute music (music as an immediate reflection of the "will" prior to its objectification as representation of categorical Platonic ideas or forms) and his opposition to a Hanslickian formalism sidelining the role of expressive content. In the essay "On Conducting" (1869) this involves an appeal to "the sentimental genre of new music" ushered in by Beethoven, as against the older, classical "naïve" type, referring to Schiller's categories of "naïve and sentimental poetry" (Wagner 1979: 65–6). A year later, in the essay *Beethoven* commemorating the centennial of the composer's birth, he invokes the "sublime" as the category relevant to evaluating the achievement (and future potential) of post-Beethovenian music. Beethoven realized a capacity of music "thanks to which . . . it moved far beyond the realm of the aesthetically beautiful," that by which Hanslick thought to analyze it, "and into the sphere of the sublime, where it becomes freed from the constraints of any traditional or conventional forms" (Wagner 1888: vol. 9, 102). This is all consistent with a fundamental notion of dramatic music established in the "Zurich" writings, further developed in "*Music of the Future*" and revisited in the late essay "On the Application of Music to the Drama" (1879). In order to recuperate its originary potential – intuited by, but then lost with the ancient Greeks – and at the same time to sublate the formal and expressive conventions of modern tonal music of the Baroque and Classical eras, modern music should take its bearings from a new kind of drama drawing on fundamental mythic plots or archetypes and structured in such as way as to "motivate" a new level of expressive, psychological, and structural sophistication. The more fully this is achieved, the more music itself will acquire the character and even the status of drama, whose principal locus will thus cease to be identified in the text.

In the later sections (16 through 25) of *The Birth of Tragedy*, Nietzsche further developed Wagner's Schopenhauerian intuitions about the modern musical-dramatic *Gesamtkunstwerk* in relation to the original Greek tragedy. In particular, he relates Wagner's argument for replacing an aesthetics of the beautiful with one of the sublime to his own categories of the Apollonian and the Dionysian. Modern music, such as Wagner's, has the potential to reinvent the Dionysian impulses that first gave rise to the genre of tragedy. Both are reflections of noumenal essences or drives (the "will") prior to their Apollonian (or "Apolline") objectification in the form of phenomenal appearances, the figurative realm of myth.

> *The tragic myth* can only be understood as the transformation of Dionysiac wisdom into images by means of Apolline artistry; it leads the world of appearances to its limits where it negates itself and seeks to fall back into the womb of the one, true reality; at which point it seems to sing, with Isolde, its metaphysical swan-song.
>
> (Nietzsche 1999: 105)

Like the tragic myth, the role of musical dissonance and the apparent destruction of "form" in Wagner's works both figure art's ability to replicate our own relation, as living phenomena, to the all-creating and all-consuming force of the "will." Myth and music "both originate in a realm which lies beyond the Apolline; both transfigure a region where dissonance and the terrible image of the world fade away in chords of delight . . .; both justify by their play the existence of even 'the worst of all worlds'" (Nietzsche 1999: 115).

There is no doubt, of course, that Wagner channeled his understanding of Schopenhauer's philosophy into some of the central themes of his later dramas, most clearly in *Tristan und Isolde* (sexual desire as the most immediate manifestation of the "will" in human life, the urge of the lovers to transcend their individuated status as "appearance" and to return to a primal state of unitary, noumenal "essence"), but also in *Die Meistersinger* (where the simultaneous creative and destructive principle of *Wahn* already prefigures Nietzsche's idea of the Dionysian) and in *Parsifal* (sympathy with the sufferings of other living beings and the renunciation of the individual will as avenues to "redemption"). Bryan Magee goes further and proposes that Wagner's musical language was fundamentally changed by his exposure to Schopenhauer, explaining the freer, more expansive unfolding of musical designs and the intensified levels of expression in *Die Walküre* and *Tristan* (as compared to the tentative, experimental quality of *Das Rheingold*) as a response to the philosopher's views on the unique, essentially autonomous status of music as an unmediated reflection of the will (Magee 2000: chs 11 and 12). While, as suggested above, Schopenhauer did provide an account of musical autonomy more palatable to Wagner than Hanslick's version, it seems unlikely that such an abstract articulation of the matter (fairly primitive where it enters into details) could have a compositional effect, even if the chronology is roughly plausible. (Nietzsche offers a better account of a liberated modern music recuperating its archaic birthright, so to speak — but in response to Wagner, of course, not as an influence on him.) On the other hand, Magee is certainly justified in claiming that philosophical ideas "in the broadest sense, a sense that includes political and social ideas of a general nature," do "suffuse" Wagner's works (Magee 2000: 123), and that in their intended totality these works manage to integrate in viably artistic form the "mainstream traditions" ("at the point of their highest development") of Western music, theater, and philosophy (Magee 2000: 193). In other words, in assessing Wagner's contribution to the philosophy of music, we should by no means limit the discussion to the ideas he put into print, however wide-ranging those may be. The interface of those ideas with the dramatic texts of the works and their musical scores must be the ultimate proving ground of any attempt to evaluate Wagner's "philosophical" significance.

See also Adorno (Chapter 36), Aesthetic properties (Chapter 14), Composition (Chapter 47), Hanslick (Chapter 33), Music's arousal of emotions (Chapter 22), Nietzsche (Chapter 32), Opera (Chapter 41), and Schopenhauer (Chapter 31).

References

Grey, T. (2009), ed. *Wagner and his World*, Princeton: Princeton University Press.

Hanslick, E. (1986 [1891 8th edn]) *On the Musically Beautiful*, trans. G. Payzant, Indianapolis: Hackett.

Magee, B. (2000) *Wagner and Philosophy*, London: Penguin Books. (Also published 2001 as *The Tristan Chord: Wagner and Philosophy*, New York: Henry Holt and Company.)

Nietzsche, F.W. (1999 [1872/1888]) *The Birth of Tragedy and Other Writings*, ed. R. Geuss and R. Speirs, trans. R. Speirs, Cambridge: Cambridge University Press.

Schopenhauer, A. (1969 [1818, 1844]) *The World as Will and Representation*, 2 vols, trans. E.F.J. Payne, New York: Dover.

Wagner, R. (1895–99) *Richard Wagner's Prose Works*, 8 vols, trans. W.A. Ellis, London: Kegan Paul, Trench, Trübner & Co.

—— (1888) *Gesammelte Schriften und Dichtungen*, 10 vols, ed. H. von Wolzogen and R. Sternfeld, Leipzig: Breitkopf & Härtel.

—— (1973) *Wagner Writes from Paris . . . Stories, Essays, and Articles by the Young Composer*, ed. and trans. R.L. Jacobs and G. Skelton, London: Allen and Unwin.

—— (1979) *Three Wagner Essays*, trans. R.L. Jacobs, London: Eulenburg Books.

—— (1984) *Opera und Drama*, ed. K. Kropfinger, Stuttgart: Reclam.

Further reading

Adorno, T. (2005 [1952]) *In Search of Wagner*, trans. R. Livingstone, London and New York: Verso. (An influential, if often elliptical, essay in Wagnerian cultural criticism.)

Bermbach, U. (2004) *Die Wahn des Gesmtkunstwerks: Richard Wagners politisch-ästhetische Utopie*, Stuttgart and Weimar: J.B. Metzler. (Wagner's thought read from the perspectives of nineteenth-century political and social history, including themes of revolution, anti-Semitism, nationalism, and Schopenhauerian philosophy.)

Borchmeyer, D. (1991) *Richard Wagner: Theory and Theatre*, trans. S. Spencer, Oxford: Clarendon Press. (Essays on themes in Wagner's writings and stage works with reference to Enlightenment and Romantic literary history and history of ideas.)

—— (2003) *Drama and the World of Richard Wagner*, trans. D. Ellis, Princeton: Princeton University Press. (Cultural-historical essays on the operas, with chapters on Nietzsche and Mann.)

Goehr, L. (1998) *The Quest for Voice: on Music, Politics, and the Limits of Philosophy*, New York: Oxford University Press. (Issues of musical autonomy, censorship, performance, and exile, including an essay on the aesthetic, political, and philosophical "lessons" of *Die Meistersinger*.)

Grey, T. (1995) *Wagner's Musical Prose: Texts and Contexts*, Cambridge: Cambridge University Press. (Interprets leading ideas and terms concerning music, opera, and music drama in Wagner's writings in relation to contemporary music-aesthetic discourse and examples from Wagner's works.)

Kitcher, P. and Schacht, R. (2004) *Finding and Ending: Reflections on Wagner's* Ring, New York: Oxford University Press. (A study of themes and characters in the *Ring* with an emphasis on ethical values and problems.)

Kühnel, J. (1992) "The Prose Writings," in U. Müller and P. Wapnewski (eds) *Wagner Handbook*, Cambridge: Harvard University Press, pp. 565–651. (A survey of the published writings with detailed summaries.)

Liébert, G. (2004) *Nietzsche and Music*, trans. D. Pellauer and G. Parkes, Chicago and London:

University of Chicago Press. (A musical-intellectual biography, putting the relationship to Wagner in that larger context.)

Magee, B. (1997) *The Philosophy of Schopenhauer*, rev. and enlarged, Oxford: Oxford University Press. (A comprehensive primer on the philosopher's work, with extensive treatment of music and aesthetics.)

Scruton, R. (2004) *Death-Devoted Heart: Sex and the Sacred in Wagner's* Tristan und Isolde, Oxford and New York: Oxford University Press. (Introduction to the text, sources, and music of the opera, interpreting these with reference to ideas about erotic love, ritual and sacrifice, redemption, and aesthetic experience from Plato to Schopenhauer.)

Treadwell, J. (2003) *Interpreting Wagner*, New Haven: Yale University Press. (Themes in Wagner's writings read through the stage works.)

36

ADORNO

Andy Hamilton

Theodor Adorno (1903–69) is the most important writer on aesthetics of music in the twentieth century. Brought up in a rarefied artistic milieu, Immanuel Kant, G. W. F. Hegel and Karl Marx were his primary philosophical influences. He studied at Frankfurt University, and in 1925–28 was a composition student of modernist composer Alban Berg. He eulogized Berg's teacher Schoenberg as the paradigm modernist. Teaching philosophy at Frankfurt University, he became associated with the Institute for Social Research, but after the Nazi rise to power in 1933 he left for England then the United States, where he began sociological research on popular music. In 1949 Adorno returned to co-direct the re-established Institute for Social Research, becoming a leading member of the so-called Frankfurt School of contemporary Marxist philosophy. *Philosophy of Modern Music* (1949) made him famous; it represented Schoenberg and Stravinsky as opposed poles of modernism, with Stravinsky the reactionary. Adorno died in 1969. Adorno's classic work *Aesthetic Theory* was published posthumously in 1970.

Adorno's aesthetics of modernism

Adorno is the philosopher of *artistic modernism* – which must be distinguished from *modernity*, the social and cultural developments arising with the Enlightenment at the end of the eighteenth century. Modernism, in contrast, is primarily an artistic phenomenon, a sharpening and intensifying of modernity, or a response to it. It is a problematic and highly contested concept, but the consensus is that it arose in the later nineteenth century, and flourished in the first three decades of the twentieth. "The fundamental problem addressed by Adorno's aesthetics is how to philosophize about art in the absence of aesthetic norms," writes Max Paddison (1993: 2). In the era of modernism, on this view, prescriptive maxims for the production of, or critical response to, artworks, are no longer available.

Debussy's *Prélude à l'Après-midi d'un Faune* (1894) is often cited as the first fully modernist musical work. The leading theorist of musical modernism, however, was Viennese composer Arnold Schoenberg. From the first decade of the twentieth century, Schoenberg and fellow modernists fragmented tonal syntax, replacing it with various strategies, most radically what became known as *atonality*. For Schoenberg, the music of Wagner, Strauss, Debussy, and Mahler showed the breakdown of tonality. Atonality abolished the distinction between consonances and dissonances, and renounced a tonal center. Stultification of the tonal system made this "emancipation" necessary and inevitable, Schoenberg believed. However, to talk of the collapse of tonality is to subscribe to a Schoenbergian version of modernist history; one could instead refer to the evolution of tonality, since many modernists, notably Stravinsky and Bartók, continued to use key centers.

Adorno focused almost exclusively on Western art music of the eighteenth to twentieth centuries, and within that the Austro-German tradition and its avant-garde, the Second Viennese School of Schoenberg, Berg and Webern. His apparent dismissal of popular culture seems elitist. But for someone whose musical world-view was so narrow, Adorno's influence has been surprisingly broad.

Adorno and Hegel: dialectic, historicism and truth-content

As Paddison puts it, Adorno's critical sociological aesthetics of music is "interdisciplinary, densely formulated, deeply paradoxical, anti-systematic and fragmented" (2001: 165). His rich, subtle *Aesthetic Theory* unites philosophical aesthetics and criticism and history of art, hence its very apt epigraph from Friedrich Schlegel: "Philosophy of art usually lacks one of two things: either the philosophy or the art" (Adorno 1997: 366). But Adorno is steeped in the German Idealist tradition of Kant and Hegel, and develops Hegel and Marx's criticism that Kant's aesthetics ignores the historicity and socially conditioned character of autonomous art.

Adorno's theoretical works are profoundly indebted both to Hegel's dialectical method and to his historicism. He assumes Hegel's dynamic concept of contradiction, pervasive in nineteenth-century German philosophy, but in contrast to the latter's "Positive Dialectics," stresses the irreconcilable antagonism of contradictions. Titling his major work *Negative Dialectics* (1966), Adorno says that in the historical process, opposites negate each other yet refuse reconciliation or synthesis in a concept of the whole. Hence Adorno's pessimism is as widely influential as his Puritanism and apparent elitism, and of a piece with them.

His historicism is also pervasive, notably in his interpretation of the post-Romantic imperative that the artist must remain "true" to the requirements of the artistic material. For Adorno, material is not inert substance transformed by the artist, but is ineliminably historical: "material is what artists manipulate: everything from words, colors and sounds through to connections of any kind ... Forms, then, can also become material" (Adorno 1997: 148). That is, the material that the composer addresses is historically "pre-formed." Genres, forms and gestures show their historical derivation; within the structure of the autonomous artwork, this material is "re-formed" (Adorno 2006: 31–4). For Adorno, art is "concentrated social substance" that contains the contradictions of social reality. He has in mind how trumpet flourishes in a classical symphony are derived from music for military bands, and movements such as minuet and scherzo originated in dance forms.

Adorno develops these claims in a correspondence in 1929–32 with Austrian modernist composer Ernst Krenek. Krenek saw the composer as autonomous creator with absolute freedom to select material, but Adorno responded that their choice was restricted by historical possibilities: "atonality is the only possible manner of composing today . . . not because . . . it [is ahistorically] 'better' [but because] tonality has *collapsed*" (quoted Paddison 1993: 83). For Adorno, music of the past is understood from the avant-garde's position. His account explains how in the early twenty-first century it is impossible to write unironically in the style of Mahler, let alone Mozart; tonality has lost the meaning it had for them.

We have been talking of "valid" artistic procedures and authentic art. For Adorno, validity and authenticity crucially depend on *truth-content*. This concept, originating in Hegel's cognitivist conception of art, is captured in the quotation from the latter which heads the introduction to Adorno's *Philosophy of Modern Music* (1949): "In art we have to do not with any agreeable or useful child's play, but with an unfolding of the truth" (Adorno 2006: 7; Hegel 1975: vol. II, 1236). While Adorno takes the concept of truth-content from Hegel, he takes from Marx (as well as Hegel) the idea that it is a *social truth* – and from modernism that it is a fragmented, non-unitary one.

What is truth-content, especially as applied to something as apparently non-literal as music? Adorno would deny that the truth-content of a Mahler symphony is captured by metaphysical, programmatic interpretations; nor are Wagner's music-dramas decoded by literal motif-identification. For him, the first movement recapitulation in Beethoven's Ninth Symphony makes a "judicious, even judging affirmation of something that is, however, not expressly stated." On the strength of its similarity to language, Adorno believes, music constantly poses a riddle, which it never answers – but he insists that this is true of all art. Even when its medium is linguistic, what the artwork says is not what its words say, and so the cases of music and literature are not so distinct: "No art can be pinned down as to what it says, and yet it speaks" (Adorno 1992: 1). We will gain some idea of what he means by this in the section on "Autonomous music as social critique."

Adorno and Marx: music and art as commodity or social fact

To reiterate, Adorno's work arises from the Idealist tradition of Kant and Hegel, but also from Marx's historical materialist critique of that tradition. Adorno's sociological critique treats art in the context of its situation in industrialized societies. His deep affiliation to art for art's sake, and absolute music –

traditions apparently at odds with Marxist claims of social conditioning of art – is filtered through a distinctive interpretation of Marxist dialectics. (Art for art's sake frees art from a social, political or any other function; absolute music is non-functional, non-vocal, non-programmatic music for music's sake.)

Classical Marxism, commonly taken to derive from the later Marx, is a materialist theory of society and history according to which the economic circumstances under which people produce, and consume, conditions their culture. Economic determinism is a rigid form of this view, but Marx himself usually allowed an interaction between economic base and political, social and cultural superstructure, such that cultural conditions exercise some reciprocal influence on economic ones. The Frankfurt School cited the younger Marx in favoring historical rather than scientific, deterministic materialism, and stressed the importance of culture. Thus Adorno is a heterodox Marxist who questions what he regards as the "vulgar Marxist" privileging of production, and rejects the linear evolutionary scheme of classical Marxism. This position became known as Western Marxism, in contrast to the Soviet version; it questions whether proletarian revolution is now possible, since the working class has ceased to be a vehicle for social change (see Jay 1984: chs 2 and 3).

Adorno's brand of Western Marxism, in which the ideals of art for art's sake and absolute music remain salient, presents a complex and elusive treatment of the autonomy of art and music. It may seem puzzling how a Marxist could see any truth in the autonomy of art. Autonomy is normally taken to mean that art is governed by its own rules and laws, and that artistic value makes no reference to social or political value (see Geuss 2005: 161). As we saw, however, Western Marxism questioned the base/superstructure model, and Adorno's version of it offers the subtlest account of that relation.

We are now in a position to consider the central dichotomy in Adorno's aesthetic theory: between *the autonomy of art and music* (from Kant) and its *commodified nature* (from Marx). "Art's double character as both autonomous and *fait social* [social fact]" is a contradiction in the Hegelian or Marxist sense (Adorno 1997: 5). Adorno's key claim is that although autonomy and commodity status are in tension, yet each requires the other – they form a dialectical opposition. In order to explain how art and music have this "double character" as autonomous and commodified, we need first to understand exactly what Adorno means by "autonomous" in this context.

Art and music in the pre-Enlightenment era had been in the service of a direct social function arising from court, aristocracy or church. On the modernist picture that Adorno develops, music lost its direct social function with the ascendancy of bourgeois culture from the late eighteenth century; aristocratic and church patronage declined, and a non-functional "art music" developed. It was no longer the primary role of composers to write for religious services, military bands or the theater, or to produce aristocratic *Tafelmusik* – literally "table-music" – played during meals. Until the mid-nineteenth century, music lagged behind the other arts in this respect. The developing market for art music involved the appearance of public concerts, often by subscription and, after 1800, mass publication of works for the bourgeois amateur. The nineteenth-century music publisher is the equivalent of the twentieth-century record company in mediating between artist and audience. Beethoven and Chopin had suffered, or sometimes profited, from the appearance of rival editions of their work, but development of copyright helped secure precarious economic independence for composers.

I define autonomy as lack of *direct* social function, since Adorno recognizes that all art has a social function in some sense. Indeed, he develops Kant's concept of "purposiveness without a purpose" into the idea that autonomous art's social function arises precisely *from* its apparent functionlessness: "Insofar as a social function may be predicated of works of art, it is the function of having no function" (Adorno 1997: 227; here "work of art" = "autonomous work of art"). That is, autonomous art and music constitute autonomous practices that do not serve any other practice.

Adorno shows how the development of autonomous art is not of merely sociological interest. It is a process whereby art seems to be freed from narrowly didactic or merely pleasurable purposes, as moralizing, or mere entertainment. The "social" autonomy of art fosters an individualist as opposed to social taste and aesthetics, and thus the development of the "aesthetic" autonomy of art. For instance, composers of the first Viennese School – Mozart, Haydn, and Beethoven – aimed to subvert the listener's expectations in a way that their predecessors, more subservient to a social aesthetic, did not. If an artist stops working for a specific patron such as a church or a court, and offers their work for sale to those whose identities are not fully specified in advance – that is, once they begin to function within the market – it becomes easier for them to produce works that embody their own values rather than those of their patrons, thus increasing their autonomy (Berger 1997: 6).

This growing autonomy is part and parcel of the commodification of artworks, Adorno argues "The artist was born at the same time as his work went on sale" (Attali 1985: 47). Capitalism emancipates from feudalism, as Marx recognized, though it forges new chains of its own. The relation between autonomy and commodity, Adorno maintains, is dynamic; two apparently contradictory features stand in a reciprocal or symbiotic relationship. Music is not simply a reflection of society, as classical Marxism says. Adorno seems to recognize the truth in both art for art's sake and classical Marxism: he regards art and music aesthetically (as autonomous) and sociologically (as product) simultaneously.

The culture industry

The most influential concept arising from Adorno's Marxist sociological aesthetics was that of the *culture industry*: a filtering mechanism that pre-selects music and artworks and standardizes public taste according to the demands of

the capitalist market, thus diverting the revolutionary potential of the prole-
tariat. Adorno first used the term as a chapter-title in *Dialectic of Enlightenment*
(1944), co-authored with Horkheimer. The culture industry constantly promises
the new, and "perpetually cheats its consumers of what it perpetually promises"
(Adorno 1972: 139). Adorno prefers the term "culture industry" to "mass culture" because it is not a culture that arises spontaneously from the masses, but is
administered from above:

> The culture industry piously claims to be guided by its customers and to
> supply them with what they ask for. But while assiduously dismissing
> any thought of its own autonomy and proclaiming its victims its judges,
> it outdoes in its veiled autocracy, all the excesses of autonomous art . . .
> It drills them in their attitudes as if it were itself a customer.
>   (1974: 200–1; also "Culture Industry Reconsidered"
>   in Adorno 2001: 98–106).

Adorno seems to hold the elitist belief that nothing can be both popular and
artistically valuable; his critique of mass culture is unusual in being left-wing
rather than right-wing elitist. (He believed that a genuine popular culture, traditionally subversive of dominant classes, was no longer possible, because of the
culture industry.) "The composition hears for the listener" is his memorable ver-
dict on popular music – no listening effort is required – and he draws implausibly
dark, totalitarian conclusions from the mass crazes and infatuations of contemporary popular culture. "On Popular Music" (1941) diagnoses the standardization
of popular musical material (Adorno 2002: 437–69).

The culture industry is often assumed to embrace only popular music and art,
but this is a misconception. It includes art music of the past that has been transformed into "museum-art," as well as contemporary "moderate", non-modern-
ist music that compromises in order to be accessible. Mozart's Symphony No.
40 and Vivaldi's *The Four Seasons* have become popular classics and hence commodified, but unlike pop music, they were not originally a product of the culture
industry. The same work might in one era be autonomous, and in a later era
entirely commodified. Its aesthetic value, maybe its very identity, changes over
time: "Works are usually critical in the era in which they appear; later they are
neutralized, not least because of changed social relations. Neutralization is the
social price of aesthetic autonomy" (Adorno 1997: 299).

Adorno's most notorious assault on popular culture was his polemic "On Jazz"
(1936). Written under the pseudonym Hektor Rottweiler – Adorno's sense of
humor was no laughing matter – it confused commercial danceband music and
improvised jazz. (Other jazz writings are in Adorno 2002.) But the criticism in
"Farewell to Jazz" (1933) of jazz's rather predictable use of 32-bar song forms has
validity. And Adorno deserves credit for taking dance music seriously as a social
fact, rather than dismissing it as harmless entertainment.

Music of the avant-garde: Adorno's limited grounds for optimism

We have seen that through his theory of the culture industry, Adorno diagnoses a twentieth-century divide between progressive, self-reflective, and critical music which resists commodification, while alienating itself from its public – and regressive, assimilated music that uncritically accepts its commodity character as entertainment. Only authentic avant-garde music, which resists its social commodification, could be both socially conditioned and aesthetically autonomous, he believes. Ultimately it alienates itself from its audience, which is bourgeois – Schoenberg and his followers most radically.

For Adorno, Schoenberg was the exemplar of authentic art, especially in his freely atonal works of 1907–14, whose structural freedom raised expression to a new level. During the 1920s, unable to sustain the intense creative effort, Schoenberg codified atonality in the serial or 12-tone system – in effect replacing the tonal system he had destroyed. Adorno regarded this development as a neo-classical prison.

An influential post-Romantic view of artistic creation holds that artworks set up conflicts which are resolved within the frame of the work. But for Adorno, the modernist work sets up conflicts which cannot be resolved, thus rupturing its form – which becomes socially critical in reflecting the impossibility of reconciliation within society. This fracturing process can be traced back as far as Beethoven's late string quartets and piano sonatas, he believed, whose disintegration of form created bafflement in their own time. Drawing on his theory of Negative Dialectics, Adorno argues that "A successful work is not one which resolves objective contradictions in a spurious harmony, but one which expresses the idea of harmony negatively by embodying the contradiction, pure and uncompromised, in its innermost structure" ("Cultural Criticism and Society" in Adorno 1967: 32). "Success" is relative; even the authentic works will fail, but the artistic effort must be made.

Autonomous music as social critique

I have defined autonomy as lack of *direct* social function. Particular concerts will have various social functions; Adorno's claim might be said to be that they have no *intrinsic* or *direct* social function of the kind that characterizes non-autonomous music. (I am putting Adorno's claim in my own terms, trying to make sense of it without, I hope, distorting it too much.)

For Adorno, the principal social function of autonomous art in the modernist era is social critique. Only by becoming socially autonomous can art become self-conscious and socially critical. For Adorno, the key representative of art's growing autonomization was Beethoven:

> If he is the musical prototype of the revolutionary bourgeoisie, he is at the same time the prototype of a music that has escaped from its social

tutelage and is aesthetically fully autonomous . . . His work explodes the schema of a complaisant adequacy of music and society.

(Adorno 1976: 209)

This "complaisant adequacy" is the hallmark of heteronomous art, which affirms rather than challenges society.

For Adorno, autonomous art's critical role is associated with the growing concentration on form that arises with autonomy. Since it no longer fulfills a direct social function, Adorno holds, the autonomous artwork can create its own inner logic, which does not refer to anything external. In its consistency and total integration, form and content become identical; the work *is* its idea. (Heteronomous art and music, in contrast, imitates, represents, or expresses things outside of itself.) Since it arises in virtue of the artwork's form, not its content, autonomous art's social critique is not the superficial one offered by political or propaganda art that appeared with modernism – "[what is] social about art is its immanent movement against society, not its manifest opinions":

> Art . . . is social not only because of its mode of production . . . nor simply because of the social derivation of its thematic material. Much more importantly, art becomes social by its opposition to society, and it occupies this position only as autonomous art.
>
> (Adorno 1997: 227; 1976: 209)

Adorno stresses that through its dynamic, organic form – the thoroughgoing development of thematic material exemplified by the opening movement of his Fifth Symphony – Beethoven's music epitomizes socially progressive forces. This dynamic form constitutes a truth-content that is critical of *ancien régime* aristocratic society.

There are broader reasons why autonomous art and music functions as social critique. Something which by the standards of ordinary life is useless is for Adorno a salutary violation of the Enlightenment principle of universal functionality, and acquires an "irreplaceable dignity":

> By crystallizing in itself as something unique to itself, rather than complying with existing social norms and qualifying as "socially useful", it criticises society by merely existing . . . through its refusal of society, which is equivalent to sublimation through the law of form, autonomous art makes itself a vehicle of ideology.
>
> (Adorno 1997: 229, 226–7)

It is precisely though their refusal of social function that, according to Adorno, autonomous music and art acquire a critical function. By standing apart from society, they become more genuinely critical than political art. Autonomous art and music are a model of emancipation, of life lived under non-oppressive conditions. This is the only glimmer of hope from Adorno, a thoroughgoing pessimist, but not a Marxist cynic about art.

Autonomous music and the musical work

Developing these Adornian ideas, consider how liturgical music is heteronomous and has a direct social function. If a cultural outsider – an anthropologist from Mars – were to ask, during a church service, "What is the (social) function of this music?", the answer would be: religious, to uplift the spirits of the congregation and turn their thoughts to God. This music subserves the functions of the religious ceremony. There is a corresponding answer for all music with direct social function; music for dancing or military pageants is part of, or contributes to, the social occasion. These are all cases of art that is not for art's sake, but for those things distinct from art – religion, instruction, commerce, politics, entertainment, advertising. The modernist story is that prior to the separation of the value spheres in the eighteenth century, all art was for the sake of one of these other things. (This separation is discussed in Hamilton 2007: ch. 1.)

In contrast, if the cultural outsider went to a concert and asked, "What is the (social) function of this music?", no comparable answer could be given. One could acknowledge that a Bach cantata, performed in concert, was originally composed for church services; but its concert performances have no direct social function. To say that the music contributes to the social occasion of a concert is absurd; the music *is* the social occasion. This, I would argue, is the defining contrast between autonomous and heteronomous music, as Adorno conceives it.

The development of autonomous music in the later eighteenth century mirrors the appearance of the musical work (Goehr 1992). Indeed, it may be that the musical work-concept – which according to some authorities appears only in the later eighteenth century – just is the concept of autonomous art. To talk of the *artwork* is to talk of something normally without direct social function. Its appearance seems especially clear in the case of music, since it is contemporary with the separation of composition from performance. In Western music during the eighteenth and nineteenth centuries, notation became increasingly specific and prescriptive in its requirements on performers; what had once involved improvisational freedom became a matter of interpretation of essentially fixed works. The possibility of autonomous music arises only with a distinction between the enduring repeatable musical work, and music composed for a particular occasion, whether religious, courtly or military.

Functionless art and music is a deeply paradoxical or dialectical notion. Adorno has penetrating insights on how the lack of direct social function gives rise to unique secondary functions: "In a society that has been functionalized virtually through and through, totally ruled by the exchange principle, lack of function comes to be a secondary function" (Adorno 1976: 41–3). Functionless art and music acquires non-critical secondary functions in virtue of its functionlessness. Corporate hospitality events in the Tate Modern or Royal Festival Hall trade on the perceived social value of functionless art, which is vulnerable to exploitation or co-option by the capitalist marketplace. Autonomous art and music also acquire functions as cultural capital and expression of social status. Adorno's treatment of the autonomy of art and music may be Eurocentric and ignores gender issues, but it does have the social dimension at its core.

Autonomous practice: qualifying Adorno's standpoint

Adorno's treatment of autonomous music can be criticized on both factual and normative levels. Factually, it may be argued that autonomy and heteronomy are ideal artistic types present throughout history. Karol Berger, for instance, claims that most European music since ancient times falls between these ideals (2000: 116); there is no point at which the era of autonomous music began, rather there is partial autonomy in all music (see the discussion of Bach in Wolff 2000: 225–30). Berger's case is supported by the existence of traditions of "learned music" in the medieval and Baroque eras – Bach contributed to the latter through such works as *The Art of Fugue*, and *The Well-Tempered Clavier* (Ledbetter 2002: 34). During the later eighteenth century, music performed for its own sake in private began to be performed in public as so-called chamber music. As noted earlier, subscription concerts helped composers to become independent, and fostered the development of a bourgeois audience. But private performance of chamber music, which exhibited aesthetic autonomy, pre-dates the public concert, whose appearance as an institution may therefore not be quite so central as is often assumed. However, unlike Berger, I believe that earlier trends prefigure a general tendency from the late eighteenth century onward.

I have dwelt on the social dimension of artistic autonomy, which so preoccupied Adorno. This dimension illustrates a general truth about art's autonomy, however – that it stands in a reciprocal relation with its functionality or instrumentality. Adorno captures the truth that the negation of functionality is itself a kind of function. To talk of something as an artwork or musical work is to separate it from other things, and yet those other things remain connected with it. This is a paradox, an apparent but not genuine contradiction – just as the liberation of the artist through commodification of the artwork is paradoxical but, since capitalism liberates as well as constricts, not a genuine contradiction. Adorno's account is a brilliant attempt to explain this disconnection and connection, an account which overcomes the dichotomy between aestheticism and social functionalism.

See also Continental philosophy and music (Chapter 26), Hanslick (Chapter 33), Kant (Chapter 30), Music and dance (Chapter 43), Music and politics (Chapter 50), and Popular music (Chapter 37).

References

Adorno, T. (1967 [1955]) *Prisms*, trans. S. and S. Weber, Cambridge: MIT Press.

—— (1974 [1951]) *Minima Moralia: Reflections from Damaged Life*, trans. E.F.N. Jephcott, London: Verso.

—— (1976 [1962]) *Introduction to the Sociology of Music*, trans. E. Ashton, New York: Continuum.

—— (1992 [1963]) *Quasi una Fantasia: Essays on Modern Music*, trans. R. Livingstone, London: Verso.

—— (1997 [1970]) *Aesthetic Theory*, trans. R. Hullot-Kentor, London: Athlone Press.

—— (2001) "Culture Industry Reconsidered," *The Culture Industry: Selected Essays on Mass Culture*, ed. J.M. Bernstein, London: Routledge, 98–106.

—— (2002) *Essays on Music*, ed. R. Leppert, Berkeley: University of California Press.

—— (2006 [1949]) *Philosophy of New Music*, trans. R. Hullot-Kentor, Minneapolis: University of Minnesota Press.

Adorno, T. and M. Horkheimer (1972 [1944]) *Dialectic of Enlightenment*, trans. J. Cumming, New York : Seabury Press (reprint New York: Continuum, 1989).

Attali, J. (1985 [1977]) *Noise: The Political Economy of Music*, trans. B. Massumi, Minneapolis: University of Minnesota Press.

Berger, K. (1997) *A Theory of Art*, New York: Oxford University Press.

—— (2000) *A Theory of Art*, New York: Oxford University Press.

Geuss, R. (2005) "Art and Criticism in Adorno's Aesthetics," in *Outside Ethics*, Princeton: Princeton University Press, pp. 161–83.

Goehr, L. (1992) *The Imaginary Museum of Musical Works*, Oxford: Clarendon Press.

Hamilton, A. (2007) *Aesthetics and Music*, London: Continuum.

Hegel, G.W.F. (1975 [1835–8]) *Hegel's Aesthetics: Lectures on Fine Art*, 2 vols, trans. T.M. Knox, Oxford: Oxford University Press.

Jay, M. (1984) *Adorno*, London: Fontana.

Ledbetter, D. (2002) *Bach's "Well-Tempered Clavier": The 48 Preludes and Fugues*, New Haven: Yale University Press.

Paddison, M. (1993) *Adorno's Aesthetics of Music*, Cambridge: Cambridge University Press.

—— (2001) "T.W. Adorno," in S. Sadie (ed.) *The New Grove Dictionary of Music and Musicians*, 2nd edn, vol. 1, London: Macmillan, pp. 165–7.

Wolff, C. (2000) *Johann Sebastian Bach: The Learned Musician*, New York: W.W. Norton.

Further reading

Bernstein, J. (2004) "Adorno's *Aesthetic Theory*," in F. Rush (ed.) *The Cambridge Companion to Critical Theory*, Cambridge: Cambridge University Press, pp. 139–64. (An overview of Adorno's aesthetics.)

Cook, D. (1996) *The Culture Industry Revisited*, Lanham: Rowman and Littlefield. (Revisionary, denies that Adorno rejected the culture industry in its entirety.)

Haskins, C. (1989) "Kant and the Autonomy of Art," *Journal of Aesthetics and Art Criticism* 47: 43–54. (Clear discussion of a key concept for Adorno's aesthetics.)

Huhn, T. (2004) *The Cambridge Companion to Adorno*, Cambridge: Cambridge University Press. (Includes important recent articles on Adorno's aesthetics of music, especially by Paddison.)

Jarvis, S. (1998) *Adorno: A Critical Introduction*, Oxford: Polity. (Very clear general treatment.)

Paddison, M. (2002) "Music as Ideal: The Aesthetics of Autonomy," in J. Samson (ed.) *The*

Cambridge History of Nineteenth-Century Music, Cambridge: Cambridge University Press, pp. 318–42. (Excellent background on later nineteenth-century music aesthetics.)

Rosen, C. (1975) *Schoenberg*, Chicago: Chicago University Press. (Excellent treatment of Schoenberg and modernism.)

Zuidervaart, L. (1990) "The Social Significance of Autonomous Art: Adorno and Bürger," *Journal of Aesthetics and Art Criticism* 48: 61–77. (Rare case of a writer on Adorno who is concerned to develop his ideas philosophically.)

Part V
KINDS OF MUSIC

37
POPULAR MUSIC
John Andrew Fisher

Most of us have listened to popular music throughout our lives. It permeates our culture, on the radio, on TV, in the movies, and even in churches, as Contemporary Christian Rock. The musicologist Richard Taruskin describes our engagement with popular music as more than mere exposure: "Nowadays most educated persons maintain a lifelong fealty to the popular groups they embraced as adolescents" (2007: 37). The significant role that popular music plays in our lives has undoubtedly been instrumental in creating interest in popular music among music theorists. Another important factor has been a sharp decline of belief in the superior status of high culture, including classical music. As a consequence of these social and cultural changes, many music theorists have turned their attention to popular music. Where previously there were none, now there are several academic journals devoted to the study of popular music, all of which began publishing in recent decades.

Before this sea change, the philosophy of music had focused almost exclusively on purely instrumental Western classical music, and thus primarily on the notion of a musical work, on the ontology of such works, their abstract musical, aesthetic, and expressive properties, and on the resulting musical experiences of listeners. According to this model of music, the composer plays the role of an artist who creates and gives meaning to the musical work. Performers are important as interpreters of the written score who give sonic life to the abstract work, which properly remains the center of aesthetic attention. Authenticity in classical music has to do with how faithfully performers follow the composer's instructions as indicated in a score.

The attention to popular music that is now emerging offers new perspectives on the philosophy of music and more generally on the philosophy of art. Among the questions concerning music are those regarding what music merits the status of art: should popular music be considered art and its products regarded as artworks? Moreover, there is a question of the value, aesthetic or otherwise, of popular music. Skepticism has often been expressed about whether popular music has any sort of positive value – as music, as art, or even instrumentally – for society. Indeed, there are many negative critiques of popular music, from both conservative and radical directions, one of the earliest and most influential being Theodor Adorno's (1941). (See Carroll 1998 for criticism of the main philosophical critiques of mass and popular art, including those of Adorno.)

Elevating popular music to the status of art would do more than expand the purview of musicology and philosophy of music. Because popular music involves physically engaged responses (it is common for listeners to physically move, dance, and even sing along to the music), the model of appreciation at the heart of traditional aesthetic theory – that of disinterested, even disembodied, contemplation – faces a serious challenge. (For the challenge of popular art to aesthetic theory see Shusterman 1991 and Novitz 2003. For whether rock music requires different appreciative practices, see Baugh 1993, Davies 1999, and Novitz 2003.)

Consideration of popular music also forces philosophers to reconsider the ontology of music so as to account for the ways in which its forms diverge from the model of classical music sketched above. Are there aesthetically important musical artifacts of a different sort that are prominent in popular music, such as recordings (or "tracks") and improvisations? If so, do such artifacts have different aesthetic dimensions than those possessed by classical musical works? Finally, is the very picture of a work that is the result of a free and creative act of an individual composer undermined by the more complex world of mass-produced popular music, with its pervasive commercialization, collaborative authorship, and recycling of materials? (Horn 2000 questions the applicability of the work concept to popular music. For the ontology of rock music, see Gracyk 1996: 1–98, Fisher 1998, and Kania 2006.)

Even though the classical model of music with its emphasis on the abstract musical work has limited applicability to popular music, the concept of authenticity remains important. However, authenticity in popular music takes a different form, shifting from whether performers are accurately recreating a pre-existing work to a concern for their capacity to give appropriate *meaning* to the music they perform (Gracyk 1996: 219–25). Simon Frith describes the central place authenticity occupies in rock: "The rock aesthetic depends, crucially, on an argument about authenticity. Good music is the authentic expression of something – a person, an idea, a feeling, a shared experience, a *Zeitgeist*. Bad music is inauthentic – it expresses nothing" (1987: 136). Frith's own view is that quality in rock ought to be explained in some other way than by the "myth of authenticity" (1987: 137).

What is popular music?

Claims about popular music, such as the attacks on it from both ends of the political spectrum, presuppose that we can characterize what it is. However, because of the many associations of the expression "popular music," there is no *one* answer to the question "What is popular music?" (Middleton 1990: 3–7).

Further complicating the issue is the fact that the categories "popular" and "folk" both evolved as ways of referring to "the people," although from different perspectives.

In investigating the meaning of "popular music," we need to distinguish the concept or concepts expressed by *actual* usage of the term from theoretically stipulated concepts that, albeit clearer, may not explain what popular music is as we ordinarily think of it.

Popular vs. mass music

An example of a theoretical simplification is Noël Carroll's argument for replacing the notion of popular art with his conception of mass art. He argues:

> If by popular art one means the art of the common people, then there has always been what is called folk art. Moreover, if popular art just means art that is liked by lots of people, then it seems fair to say that every society has had some popular art.
>
> (1998: 185)

Carroll objects that both of these concepts of popularity apply to every type of society and hence they are *ahistorical*, whereas "the concerns that motivate contemporary theoretical discussions about the popular arts occur in a historical context where we understand that the label 'popular art' refers discursively to the arts of mechanical and electronic reproduction" (183). Accordingly, he defines his proposed replacement concept of mass art as art that is simplified for mass consumption and which is both "produced and distributed by a mass technology" (196).

Carroll's concept of mass art describes rock recordings (technologically created and distributed), but does it characterize popular music more generally? To equate the category of popular music with a category of mass music, as Carroll would define it, would imply that popular music is only possible in a modern technological society. Hence it would rule out popular music before the twentieth century and consequently many familiar applications of the concept of popular music, for example, to describe street songs from seventeenth-century England, or music in early nineteenth-century America, such as minstrel music and parlor songs. Such songs are paradigm examples of popular music rather than folk music. The problem is that applying Carroll's simplification to music would ignore categories of popular music that are neither folk music nor mass-technology music.

Another limitation of any equation of popular music with mass music is that it privileges recordings while leaving the songs that are recorded in limbo. Songs are more abstract entities than their recordings and they are not produced technologically any more than are poems; they can be recorded, arranged and performed in multiple ways and yet be the same song. A given song – for example, Dylan's "Mr. Tambourine Man" – is not to be equated with recordings of it, such as by Melanie. Nor are songs or their recorded versions to be identified with their live performances, which are also by Carroll's definition not mass art. Yet surely songs and their live performances are central to the fabric of popular music.

Popular vs. folk music

An equation of popular music with folk music would also be historically inaccurate. The historical development of the concept of popular music reflects the evolving meaning of the more basic concept of popularity. As Raymond Williams reminds us, "popular" originally referred to something *of* the people, which could mean either *open* to all the people in a society – as in "popular government" – or *able to appeal* to all the people, thus was "common," "low," or "base" (Williams 1983: 236–7). This evolved into the sense of "widely favored," which could be viewed pejoratively as the result of unseemly courting of the public. Williams suggests that we have inherited at least three related senses of "popular": (i) inferior work, (ii) work that deliberately sets out to win favor, and (iii) work that is well liked by many people.

In another early sense, a "popular tune" was one that was familiar to everyone in society and could be used effectively in a variety of types of music. Moreover, until the mid-eighteenth century, "high," "middle," and "low," as applied to music, referred not to value but to appropriateness for use in different genres of music, such as music for the church (high) or for ballad singing on the street (low).

> Public cultural material in the eighteenth century was much more fluid and contiguous than it would later become: most societies in early modern Europe possessed . . . a wide-ranging, universally shared body of knowledge. . . . The elite culture that existed at the time tended to build on and supplement this universal material rather than displace it, making the shared layer a truly communal "popular" culture in a sense of the word that disappeared later.
>
> (Gelbart 2007: 17)

From this focus on function, the Romantic age turned to categorizing music by its *origin*, by who created it (Gelbart 2007: 40–110). This led to the concept of folk music, which developed in tandem and by contrast with that of art music, each arising out of the Romantic age's valorization of, respectively, the nation (the "folk," in terminology invented by Herder) and the individual genius that created the music. Having spawned these two categories, "popular music" was left to refer to everything else; it was not pure and natural as was folk music, which arose out of a traditional community, nor was it the individual expression of a composer aspiring to new heights of organic unity and originality of musical form. Hubert Parry's 1899 address to the Folk Song Society captures the resulting contrast between folk and popular: "in true folk song there is no sham, no got-up glitter, and no vulgarity . . . Moreover, there is an enemy at the doors of folk-music which is driving it out, namely the common popular songs of the day, and this enemy is one of the most repulsive and most insidious" (quoted in Middleton 1990: 131).

The distinction between folk and popular is difficult to draw, and some would argue "ideologically dangerous" (Gelbart 2007: 5). The International Folk Music Council (IFMC) in 1954 characterized folk music in terms of evolution through oral transmission. Folk music was music that evolved through the community's creative impulse and its process of selection: "it is the re-fashioning and recreation of the music by the community that gives it its folk character" (quoted in Gelbart 2007: 2). One difficulty with this conception is to distinguish such refashioning by a traditional community from the refashioning of songs and genres of popular music by mass communities.

Another problem is to justify the notion that authenticity attaches in a special way to folk music whereas it disappears when music is made in more urban and less unified societies. Without the Romantic idealization of the "folk," what grounds the idea that traditional music (as folk music is now called) is more authentic? To be sure, it may reflect community functions, such as initiation rites, and musical traditions such as use of modal melodies and traditional instruments. But without Romantic assumptions concerning the uncorrupted life of peasants, the decadence of modern urban life, and the mythical notion of a traditional organic community, can a distinction in authenticity between traditional and popular music be maintained?

Current conceptions of popular music

With the solidification of these three contrasting categories by the early nineteenth century both classical music and folk or national music were regarded with esteem as pure and authentic, both free from the "taint of commerce" and dependent only on genius or "natural" cultural traits. Popular music, on the other hand, now differentiated from folk as well as art music, was regarded as less valuable because of its dependence on commerce and on craft rather than genius (Gelbart 2007: 257). The overlapping themes that determine the meaning and reference of the expression "popular music" as it is used today echo this complex history.

One sense of "popularity" as applied to music is quantitative popularity. In this sense, something that is popular is widely liked by relevant evaluators: "popular" as a high degree of consumption or approval. This sense presupposes reference to a class of objects and a group of evaluators. Asserting that *La bohème* is very popular means that among operas and people who listen to such music it is widely liked. Quantitative popularity does not create a *musical* category. It describes a *relation* to an audience rather than properties of the music that might define a general type of music. Quantitative popularity comes in degrees determined by the percentage of people from the relevant class who prefer or like the music. Thus, Mozart's *Marriage of Figaro* is more popular than his *La Clemenza di Tito*, but neither is popular music in the categorical sense. Still, there is little doubt that quantitative popularity shadows any discourse about popular music organized by category; accordingly, it sounds odd to describe some quantitatively unpopular alternative band's music as popular music.

To describe some music as popular in the categorizing sense is to place it in a category with descriptive content. That content is largely predicated on the two contrasts familiar from history. One common notion characterizing "popular music" is that it is meant to contrast with classical music: popular music is music that is *not* in the classical music tradition. Adorno alludes to the contrast when he says "Popular music . . . is usually characterized by its difference from serious music" (Adorno 1941: 17). His notion of serious music appears to be determined by masterpieces of Western classical music. Adorno's focus aside, however quantitatively popular a classical musical work might be, it is not popular music. This contrast can be extended cross-culturally: in South India, popular music is distinguished from Carnatic music (a classical music) although, in contrast to Western practices, Indian popular music freely mixes folk and classical elements into popular songs (Reck 2009: 274).

Popular music is also defined by the historical contrast with folk music. This distinction applies where there exists both traditional music and urban popular music, such as in Africa, where afrobeat, soukous, and other genres of African popular music are clearly different from tribal music even though they use many traditional musical materials. Although the category of popular music is a moving target, the concept of traditional or folk music is more determinate. Hence, using the IFMC notion of traditional music, we can reason that the "folk music revival" of the 1950s and 1960s produced not traditional music but a genre of popular music. The songs in that revival were either written by the musicians themselves or were from singers and traditions that were not those of the singer or their audience (e.g. Pete Seeger singing Leadbelly's "Goodnight, Irene"). In short, these were not musical performances shaped by a community out of which they grew.

Should such performances be considered inauthentic appropriations from folk sources? It cannot be appropriation in a case, such as Dylan's, where the musician writes his own songs and sings them as such, even if in the style of a folk tradition. On the other hand, singers who sing traditional songs as such but do not pretend to be of the original community can be viewed as inviting the audience to engage in an act of make-believe, imagining that they are in that community. In such a case there need be no sense of passing off a performance as something it is not, and thus it need not seem inauthentic. Yet some cases have been controversial. One much-debated example concerns white middle-class musicians performing black blues songs. This was objectionable to some, perhaps for the very reason that the white audience was indifferent to the communal origins of these songs and the white musicians received credit for what they did not create. (See Rudinow 1994 and Young 2008 for analyses of the issues.)

A prominent sub-category of popular music is "pop" music; it is Britney, not Björk. To many people, "pop" means inferior. Evidence of this is that many genres of popular music reject any association with "pop" music. Pop music in this conception is music whose function is to be consumed as an entertainment commodity by the largest possible audience and whose musical characteristics are chosen to achieve that goal. Hence, both the form and the content are necessarily dumbed down to appeal to the widest audience, which is assumed to be musically undiscerning. No wonder most genres of jazz and alternative music reject being labeled "pop."

To be sure, such genres as disco and smooth jazz are widely considered paradigms of musical superficiality. It seems doubtful, however, that all pop music is without musical merit. Much pop music is seen by both the musicians and the fans as having elements of originality as well as properties of personal expression and insight. Perhaps this is an illusion (Adorno thought so), but given that the commercial music market requires constant change, something original – for example doo-wop – is likely to result even from commercial priorities.

Frith (2004) and Richard Middleton (1990) point out that a communal identity is expressed by various genres of popular music. Fans have a picture of who they are as fans of *this* music – their values, styles, etc. If the audiences for folk music, blues, or jazz believe that the audience for "pop" music is less discriminating or virtuous than they are, this would explain why they reject that label for their music. Frith gives the example of the anger directed at Dylan in 1966 when he started playing electric rock, an episode Frith describes as "Dylan going pop." The anger was evoked by

> the betrayal of an identity, of a belief in what an artist *stood for*, and how that, in turn, reflected (and reflected back on) the identity of the listener. For Bob Dylan's folk-club followers musical taste was a key to the way they differentiated themselves from the mainstream of commercial pop consumers.
>
> (Frith 2004: 32)

Popular music as art

The fine arts have been understood since the eighteenth century to include music along with painting, dance, poetry, plays, and so forth. However, the type of music that was considered serious or fine art in the nineteenth and twentieth centuries, comparable to literature or painting, was assumed to be classical music. Is this prevailing assumption that excludes popular music from the status of art but includes almost all of classical music justified? It is surely arguable that bebop was some of the most important and original music created during the 1940s, as was the music of John Coltrane, Miles Davis, and other jazz musicians in the 1960s and also rock after 1965, for instance, in the Beatles' albums. The power and originality of that music and much popular music in many genres since then would seem to constitute a *prima facie* case that such works and performances should be considered art and the musicians artists.

Yet even friends of popular music, particularly friends of rock music, have not embraced this status; some have been indifferent to the issue, and some have rejected the status. Yet, (i) categorizing popular music as art reflects the fact that the central features of the arts in general, such as emotional expression and narrative, are also central features of most popular music, and (ii) such status supports serious attention to the expressive, formal, and representational dimensions of popular musical works, even though those dimensions take a different form in popular music than they do in classical music. Finally, *some* works of popular music are worthy of great admiration on aesthetic grounds.

Why would writers who accept the cultural importance of rock reject the label "art" for such music? Clichés about art and rock play a role. Theodore Gracyk argues that rock critic Jon Landau attacked the idea of rock as art based "on the old stereotype that art is intellectual and contrived, whereas popular culture is visceral, immediate, and 'authentic'" (Gracyk 2007: 13). The cultural theorist Dick Hebdige rejected art status for rock because it would cast the music as "timeless objects judged by the immutable criteria of traditional aesthetics" thus losing the immediacy of the music for its audience (quoted in Gracyk 2007: 14).

Gracyk too rejects the status of art for popular music. He points out that it is commonly assumed "that art status demonstrates great value" (2007: 22); accordingly, he argues that the Beach Boys' *Pet Sounds* is not art because it is flawed. However, philosophers of art have long distinguished the descriptive use of "artwork" to denominate a category of artifacts from the honorific use of the term "artwork" to praise the best of these. The master argument for the existence of the descriptive category is that there are mediocre, confused, and tepid works of art in all forms; hence, not all art is good art. Contemporary theories of art, such as Gaut's cluster account, are descriptive; they describe what makes something art, not what makes something good art. Gaut's account would clearly include much popular music because such music exhibits most of the properties that are, according to his theory, sufficient to assign an artifact to the category of art, such as the possession of aesthetic properties, emotional expression, the exhibition of an individual point of view, being an exercise of creative imagination, being the product of a high degree of skill, and so on (Gaut 2000).

Gracyk, however, objects to a similar account: "the disjunctive theory of art offers no guidance in distinguishing between better and worse Beach Boys albums. The threshold requirement for obtaining art status [on the disjunctive theory] is now so low that being a work of art confers no special merit" (2007: 24). Proponents of descriptive definitions of art, however, would claim that classifying popular music as art should not imply that all popular musical works are great artworks, any more than classifying movies, paintings, or plays as art implies that they all have great aesthetic value. Some jazz is mediocre and cliché-ridden, but some is brilliant music.

Variation in quality in popular music is actually a regular concern of fans and critics. Not only do critics produce lists of the best records, they also produce lists of the worst. Frith points out that ranking is a feature of fandom: "A self-proclaimed rock or rap or opera fan who never dismissed anything as bad would be considered as not really a *fan* at all" (2004: 19). The ability to separate good from bad, even from a subjective point of view, would seem to be impossible if Adorno had been right. He treats the audience for popular music of his day as made zombie-like by the standardization and formulaic nature of commercial mass music. "They listen atomistically and dissociate what they hear . . . [developing] certain capacities which accord less with the concepts of traditional esthetics than with those of football and motoring. . . . They are childish . . . forcibly retarded" (Adorno 1982: 286). Frith (2004) argues that really bad music is judged so by an audience because it is musically incompetent, involves genre confusions (opera singers performing pop songs), or involves expressively inappropriate emotions. This last criterion highlights that with a few exceptions modern popular music comprises songs that interrelate lyrics and musical structure, and, accordingly, are to be judged holistically, rather than as the sum of independent musical and textual components.

Beyond really bad music, listeners judge popular music by such features as derivativeness rather than originality, dependence on obvious formulas, and so on (Frith 2004). Care must be taken, though, to judge what is formulaic in popular music by its genre. As Frith points out, "the formula criticism tends to be genre-dependent; minor variations in boy band music are taken to be insignificant; minor variations in rural blues guitar tunings . . . are of great importance" (Frith 2004: 20).

The social vs. the aesthetic point of view

Given the influence of mass popular music on the public it was natural for theorists to worry about its underlying ideologies. This concern has motivated such questions as, "Does rock music reinforce capitalist domination or is it a force for social liberation?" (See, for example, Adorno 1982; Scruton 1997: 496–500; and Gracyk 1996: 218–26). However, early critiques that assumed a simple static ideology implicit in popular music in general as mass commercial product have tended to be supplanted by more nuanced views. Recent theories tend to view the social and cultural significations of a popular musical work as complex and unique to a cultural context rather than as a simple unchanging expression of a class or political ideology (Middleton 1990).

Concerns have also been raised about the values expressed by particular songs or genres of popular music. An example is the charge that heavy metal rock expresses an ideology of male dominance. The theories prevalent in popular-music studies concerning the significant impact of popular music on listeners' imaginations and sense of identity make such concerns salient. (For a critical review of these arguments, see Gracyk 2001: 174–92. For a distinction between messages "in" art and messages "through" art, see Novitz 1995.)

The emphasis of popular music studies has been sociological. Where does that leave the music as an object that individual listeners appreciate and to which they respond with enjoyment? The danger is that studying the social meanings of genres and performers necessarily views popular music from the outside rather than as an object of musical or aesthetic appreciation. To regard this perspective as revealing the underlying reality of the musical experience for a given work of music appears to assume that there is no significant aesthetic basis for the listener's individual response. When listeners feel they are responding favorably or unfavorably to the audible features of a song, are they in reality responding to social factors and significations in the music that operate independently of their conscious aesthetic perceptions?

Frith points out that the sociological approach will miss why listeners enjoy one song and not another, why some songs are hits, why distinctions are made: "The discriminations that matter in these settings occur within the general socio-logical framework. While this allows us at a certain level to 'explain' rock or disco, it is not adequate for an understanding of why one rock record or one disco track is better than another" (1987: 135). The challenge is to understand the aesthetic dimensions of popular music while acknowledging that its social functions and significations are an integral component of the music for the individual listener (Gracyk 2007).

See also Adorno (Chapter 36), Appropriation and hybridity (Chapter 17), Jazz (Chapter 39), Music and gender (Chapter 52), Music and politics (Chapter 50), Rock (Chapter 38), Sociology and cultural studies (Chapter 51), and Song (Chapter 40).

References

Adorno, T., with the assistance of G. Simpson (1941) "On Popular Music," *Studies in Philosophy and Social Science* 9: 17–48.

—— (1982 [1938]) "On the Fetish-Character in Music and the Regression of Listening" in A. Arato and E. Gebhardt (eds) *The Essential Frankfurt School Reader*, New York: Continuum, pp. 270–99.

Baugh, B. (1993) "Prolegomena to Any Aesthetics of Rock Music," *Journal of Aesthetics and Art Criticism* 51: 23–9.

Carroll, N. (1998) *A Philosophy of Mass Art*, Oxford: Oxford University Press.

Davies, S. (1999) "Rock versus Classical Music," *Journal of Aesthetics and Art Criticism* 57: 193–204.

Fisher, J.A. (1998) "Rock 'n' Recording: The Ontological Complexity of Rock Music," in P. Alperson (ed.) *Musical Worlds: New Directions in the Philosophy of Music*, University Park: The Pennsylvania University Press, pp. 109–23.

Frith, S. (1987) "Towards an Aesthetic of Popular Music," in R. Leppert and S. McClary (eds) *Music and Society: The Politics of Composition, Performance and Reception*, Cambridge: Cambridge University Press, pp. 133–50.

—— (2004) "What is Bad Music?" in *Taking Popular Music Seriously: Selected Essays*, Burlington: Ashgate, pp. 313–34.

Gaut, B. (2000) "'Art' as a Cluster Concept," in N. Carroll (ed.) *Theories of Art Today*, Madison: University of Wisconsin Press, pp. 25–44.

Gelbart, M. (2007) *The Invention of "Folk Music" and "Art Music": Emerging Categories from Ossian to Wagner*, Cambridge: Cambridge University Press.

Gracyk, T. (1996) *Rhythm and Noise: An Aesthetics of Rock*, Durham: Duke University Press.

—— (2001) *I Wanna Be Me: Rock Music and the Politics of Identity*, Philadelphia: Temple University Press.

—— (2007) *Listening to Popular Music: Or, How I Learned to Stop Worrying and Love Led Zeppelin*, Ann Arbor: University of Michigan Press.

Horn, D. (2000) "Some Thoughts on the Work in Popular Music," in Michael Talbot (ed.) *The Musical Work: Reality or Invention?* Liverpool: Liverpool University Press, pp. 14–34.

Kania, A. (2006) "Making Tracks: The Ontology of Rock Music," *Journal of Aesthetics and Art Criticism* 64: 401–14.

Middleton, R. (1990) *Studying Popular Music*, Bristol: Open University Press.

Novitz, D. (1995) "Messages 'In' and Messages 'Through' Art," *Australasian Journal of Philosophy* 73: 199–203.

—— (2003) "Aesthetics of Popular Art," in J. Levinson (ed.) *The Oxford Handbook of Aesthetics*, Oxford: Oxford University Press, pp. 733–47.

Reck, D. (2009) "India/South India," in J.T. Titon (ed.) *Worlds of Music: An Introduction to the Music of the World's Peoples*, 5th edn, Belmont: Schirmer Cengage Learning, pp. 179–212.

Rudinow, J. (1994) "Race, Ethnicity, Expressive Authenticity: Can White People Sing the Blues?" *Journal of Aesthetics and Art Criticism* 52: 127–37.

Scruton, R. (1997) *The Aesthetics of Music*, Oxford: Clarendon Press.

Shusterman, R. (1991) "Form and Funk: The Aesthetic Challenge of Popular Art," *British Journal of Aesthetics* 31: 203–13.

Taruskin, R. (2007) "The Musical Mystique: Defending Classical Music against its Devotees," *The New Republic*, 22 October, 34–45.

Williams, R. (1983) *Keywords: A Vocabulary of Culture and Society*, rev. edn, Oxford: Oxford University Press.

Young, J. (2008) *Cultural Appropriation and the Arts*, Malden: Blackwell.

38
ROCK
Allan F. Moore

Definition

Philosophies of rock are rarely explicit. It is as if contemplation of something so visceral were somehow inauthentic. And yet, philosophical assumptions about rock are endemic to its discourse, not least in respect of its identity. Both historical and geographical locations are important. "Rock" certainly does not exist prior to the 1950s, if rock'n'roll is seen as its point of origin (Peterson 1990; Everett 2009). This is frequently regarded as the case among US scholars. However, if rock is marked by the advances made particularly by Lennon, McCartney, Ray Davies and Bob Dylan, then rock gradually emerges in the mid-1960s. In this latter history, the role of the "British invasion" of US cities in 1963–64 is crucial. Whichever position one takes, there is a time before which "rock" is not part of the cultural experience. So, just what is it that does not exist prior to its originating era? At the risk of jumping ahead of myself, it seems to me important to insist that any comprehensive declarative statement ("rock is . . .") is bound to fail, for the term "rock" (like equivalent terms – "soul," "blues," "gospel," "folk," "classical") describes a set of discrete ways in which music works. First, the term describes a *style*; in other words, a means for musicians to regulate musical decisions about what sounds to make, and how to organize them temporally. Second, it describes a *genre*; in other words, a means of making the results of these decisions public, or entering into quasi-contractual relationships with agents, listeners, and other manifestations of music's institutions. Third, it describes a *practice*; in other words, a way of prescribing the (un)acceptable behavior of musicians who desire to be regarded as rock musicians. And finally, it describes a *repertory;* in other words, it categorizes individual items of music. None of these descriptions is possible without the term "rock" to organize them, while consideration of any one of these four is most effective when continuing to observe its relationship with the other three.

The four senses I have identified may often operate together. (Aretha Franklin's live recordings at a Los Angeles Baptist Church in 1972, released as *Amazing Grace*, qualify as "gospel" in all four senses.) But they are not necessarily coextensive, as can be observed in relation to The Nice's recording "America" (1968). Written by Bernstein and Sondheim for *West Side Story*, it is a "show tune" in terms of *repertory*. The Nice approach it as "rock" musicians – this defines their *practice*. It is an example of what contemporary discourse named "progressive pop," aimed at and consumed largely by a burgeoning student market; this defines its *genre*. However, its stylistic amalgam of explicit beat, improvisation and (quasi-elite) status identifies its *style* as "art rock."

This level of analysis is rarely resorted to. I deal in this section with types of comprehensive definition: the relations between "rock," "pop," and "popular," those between "recorded" and "live," and the importance of rock as "sound structure." Despite their unsuitability, comprehensive declarative statements remain popular. It seems that critics (and listeners) need to find a usable working definition, even if it is hardly "definitive," and the problems caused by a recording such as "America" are rarely given any attention. Two types of "comprehensive" definition are current, and both are explored in a recent virtual symposium where Richard Middleton argues that for definitions of popular music, "two overarching positions are visible, which we might term 'descriptivist' and 'discursivist,' respectively" (*Popular Music* International Advisory Editors 2005: 45). "Descriptivist" positions implicitly assume the possibility of listing all the features held in common by all members of the same style, genre, practice, or repertory. "Discursivist" positions define the term by declaring it the negation of everything it is not ("soul," "classical," "folk" etc.).

Neither of the positions Middleton identifies is ultimately satisfactory. An exhaustive list even of the features which define rock as a style is unachievable (Moore 2001: 1–4), while defining something against its negations takes anti-essentialism to an untenable extreme. A better approach may be by way of prototype theory (Lakoff 1987) which offers graded membership of categories, thereby according better with how we use them. Fabbri (1999) briefly explores this approach in defining musical genre. Note, though, that I am allowing that symposium's "popular music" to stand for this chapter's "rock": Between the 1960s and the rise of electronic dance music and hip-hop (variously in the 1980s and later), "rock" and "popular music" were synonymous to the music industry, in much scholarship, and to many listeners. "Rock" was therefore the mainstream, much to the dismay of those who, following a preferred position within cultural studies (e.g. Willis 1978), identified it with rebellion. This preference stems from the earliest constructions of cultural studies as a discipline, whereby an attitude of rebellion among youth was lauded and, as the most compelling expression of that attitude, rock music was identified with it. Even in more recent decades, as we shall see, a distinction between rock and popular music in general can be hard to draw.

Though "rock" is hard to distinguish conclusively from "popular music," attempts are also often made to distinguish it from "pop," usually in relation to the opposition between "authentic" rock (to which I shall return) and "commercial" pop – or to refuse such distinction (Everett 2007). Nicholas Cook ties the term "rock" to questions of authorship (an aspect of rock as *practice*), arguing that rock musicians tend to "see pop musicians as industry puppets but themselves as genuine authors" (1996: 40); as both Stan Hawkins (2002) and Fred Maus (2001) have pointed out, the Pet Shop Boys (among others) problematize this view. For Cook, at least in this article, the presence of multiple texts (i.e. different recorded versions) and multiple authorship (a consequence of the social practice of rehearsal) has the potential "for opening theory up to new perspectives, to the benefit of our understanding of all music" (Cook 1996: 40–1). Graham Vulliamy (1975) also accepted a pop–rock distinction, at a far earlier stage in rock's history, basing his decision on the views of musicians themselves, their fans, and what he then regarded (with concern) as the growing cultural legitimacy of "rock" (to which I have already drawn attention). From another sociological perspective, Gregory Booth and Terry Lee Kuhn argued that the labels we apply "relate to commonalities that are economic and transmissive in nature, and that . . . the type and nature of the music content . . . are a result of these economic and technological support systems" (1990: 414). This analysis deals with aspects of rock as *genre* and as *practice*, seeing *style* as subsidiary: As music aimed at a mass audience, "rock" here becomes an exemplar of "pop." The point is that since there are no agreed grounds for the definition of "rock" (or of "pop"), writers can supply their own and develop individual perspectives. Is "rock" subsidiary to "pop," or to "popular"? Is it distinguishable from them? Is it altogether distinct? Each position is defendable, but these definitions appear to be subjective.

However, on any understanding, we have to construct "rock" in such a way that there is something at least provisionally distinctive about it, and that distinctiveness must be analyzed for a chapter such as this to have any viability. A prominent view is that of Theodore Gracyk (1996), whose position is summarized thus by Andrew Kania: "the primary work of art in rock music is . . . [the] sound structure encoded on a recording and properly instanced through playback of a copy of the recording" (2006: 401). (This is a similar concept to Even Eisenberg's "phonography" (1988), but Eisenberg applies it to a range of musics outside anyone's conception of rock.) This ontological definition has two components: that a piece of rock music is principally a "sound structure" and that hearing the recording has primacy over hearing other things (such as live performances). However, as soon as one asks questions about that "sound structure" ("What is it?" "How does it work?" etc.), one is inevitably addressing rock as *style* (rather than as genre, practice, or repertory). This emphasis on rock as manifest *sound* is not trivial when one recognizes that, for much music, how it sounds has had little impact on how its functioning is conceived. Within academic circles, how music is structured has long taken precedence over how it sounds. Serious non-academic scholarship (at least in the popular field) has given precedence to biography, authorial intention, and lyric content. It is only among (many) everyday listeners that how the music sounds appears to have been a more important consideration.

Andrew Chester (1970) made an early attempt to formulate one difference Gracyk is concerned with: that between recorded musics and musics for live performance, although Chester distinguished between "extensional" musics dominated by pre-planning and "intensional" musics dominated by spur-of-the-moment decision-making. For Chester, rock was an instance of the latter; for Gracyk, rock seems to be an instance of the former. It is the construction of music as precisely pre-planned which has enabled the dominance of its consideration as structure, and which accords with a current of thought that has assumed rock can adequately be addressed via its notation or transcription (a normative procedure for critical attention to concert music and jazz), a misguided view which receives critiques in, for example, Moore 2001 and Zak 2001. Kevin Holm-Hudson (2001) has added to this mix a concern for intertextual reference and historical consciousness.

Indeed, it is the historical circumstances of rock's arrival which impact most on its identity. Gracyk is certainly right to insist on the essentiality of rock's historically emergent technology, although, because the distinctions between style, genre, practice, and repertory are rarely addressed, there remains space for fans of Bob Dylan, for instance, to maintain that, for some musicians, how they approach live performance is a more central concern than the issuing of recordings (e.g. Marshall 2007, esp. 189–97). But the primacy of recording over live performance inherent in Gracyk's formulation is itself historically circumscribed. Edward Macan's recent biography of Emerson, Lake, and Palmer refers to Greg Lake's view that the relationship between studio albums and live tours was that between a check and cash – "the former is merely a promise to deliver payment in the form of the latter," arguing that prior to the 1980s, live performance "served as a living, breathing *commentary* on the music, rather than a stylized . . . *presentation* of the music" (Macan 2006: 185). The rider "prior to the 1980s" is vital, since the relationship is now widely agreed to have reversed (at least until the 2008 credit crash) – a rock show, at least at the more expansive (and expensive) end of the genre, exists to re-create, as far as possible, the sound of the album.

Authenticity

Whatever rock is considered to be, discussions which reference "authenticity" dominate the discourse. As it pertains to rock, authenticity is a highly complex concept, used in different ways depending on whether it is considered an "ascribed" (contingent, interpreted) or "inscribed" (inherent) value, on whether it is class-based, and on whether it is seen as a function of performance or of composition (in any of the various ways that happens in rock). The dominant view has long been that it is inscribed, and that it identifies either a personal integrity and an ideology of self-expression, or a commitment to the maintenance of particular (originary) practices (or both). It is this identification which has allowed numerous critics to pronounce its demise. (See Born and Hesmondhalgh 2000 in particular.) And yet it has refused to vanish from music discourse. Lawrence

Grossberg (1992) broke with the monolithic view, arguing for three genre-specific authenticities: those of rock (founded in the romanticized ideology of community), of black genres (founded on the rhythmicized and sexualized body), and of self-conscious post-modernity (as in the Pet Shop Boys' honesty in the acceptance of cynical self-knowledge). Johan Fornås (1995: 275–7) generalized this analysis, producing categories of "social," "subjective," and "meta-" authenticities, validated by communities, perceivers, and producers respectively, each of which has both conservative and progressive variants.

My approach has been to view authenticity (and other values) as always ascribed rather than inscribed, not only due to a Derridean mistrust of naturalist discourses, but also through a refusal to determine who has the authority to pronounce the presence of a particular value in the face of the varied experiences of other perceivers. This produces three authenticities – of *expression*, *experience*, and *execution* – depending on whether the music is experienced as authentic with respect to some aspect of the musician producing it, the listener(s) perceiving it, or an absent other involved in its history (for instance, its original writer) (Moore 2002). Taylor (1997), writing about "world musics" has developed a different, but not altogether unrelated, tripartite system. Kivy (1995) has also argued that there is not one authenticity (but probably three); however, the restriction of his sphere of reference to that tiny minority of music we call "classical" renders his arguments out of place here.

Understanding and meaning

Here I raise questions about the way the presence of meaning is determined, the question of music's emotional content, and the idea of meaning inherent in the use of lyrics. In some respects, the question of the understanding of rock replays that of understanding other music. First, of course, is the question "What's to understand?" While many listeners listen to "classical" musics for their sensuousness alone, there is general recognition (I believe) that understanding of such musics is both possible and, on occasion, enlightening. With regard to rock, and partly resultant from its construction as a music of rebellion, there is no such recognition among most users and media commentators. In the academy, the understanding of rock was first pursued solely in terms of social function. It is only recently that questions of purely musical meaning have been broached. (For reasons of space, I take it for granted here that "purely musical meaning" is a meaningful descriptor, that music exists in and of itself aside from its perception; in some disciplinary contexts this position is denied.)

Most of the few attempts to understand musical detail in rock are either *formalist* or *semiotic*. Early work by Walter Everett exemplifies the former. In his study of the Beatles' "She's Leaving Home," he argues that as the song progresses there is a gradual divorce between the song's "surface" (i.e. every element of detail we actually hear) and its "structure" (a widely hypothesized notional pitch-entity which, through rules of transformation, generates the "surface" in a way analogous to Chomskian grammar). This divorce "symbolize[s] the girl's sought-after freedom from home, and ultimately, the distance symbolized by the 'generation gap'" (Everett 1987: 12).

The main proponent of semiotic techniques for understanding the range of popular music has been Philip Tagg, who complains (following Umberto Eco's proposal for an integrated semiotics) that most music semiotics is concerned with syntax, at the expense of semantics and pragmatics (Tagg and Clarida 2003: 51–6). Tagg's classic study (1991), by observing the semiotic references at play in the musical detail, demonstrates that the protagonist of Abba's "Fernando" deludes herself (and hence, propagandistically, us) into believing in her commitment to the revolutionary cause. Elsewhere, semiotics rarely addresses musical details (hence the general dominance of formalist analysis). Instead, valuable though they are, we are more likely to find studies such as Dave Laing's of punk, which treats "all types of sign (written, spoken, sung, played, gestured)" (1985: ix) as equivalent in their act of signifying, or Barbara Bradby's analysis of Buddy Holly's "Oh Boy!" which reads the song as an enactment of the achievement of male adolescent independence (Bradby 2002). What is absent from any of this work, with the exception of Tagg's, is adequate theorizing about method. Tagg adheres to explicit semiotic principles and invariably produces an interpretation, but he rarely addresses rock.

Disciplinary perspectives are relevant here: Tagg is a musicologist; Laing and Bradby are sociologists. But a particular disciplinary perspective does not entirely determine one's view of rock. Although writing "[f]rom a sociological perspective," Simon Frith seems to agree with Tagg, arguing that "[t]o hear combinations of sounds as music, it is necessary to know something about the conventional meanings of agreed musical elements" (1998: 109), their semiotic dimension, if you will. I am reminded here of Walter Watson's (1993) elegant, exhaustive demonstration that the answer you get depends on the question you ask, but Frith at least implies that there is a right question. What is particularly interesting is that any reference to "rock" as such, while common in his earlier work (e.g. Frith 1984) is missing from this more recent study, and yet he devotes much space to *sound structures encoded on a recording and properly instanced through playback of a copy of the recording*. Edward Kealy (1982), another sociologist, agrees with the focus on the encoding of sound, but for him this is definitional of a much broader *popular music aesthetic*: he argues that as early as the 1970s, rock musicians took control of every stage of the recording process, in contrast to those uninterested in (or incapable of) doing so, people he called simply popular musicians. So, it seems that in order to explicate an understanding of how these sounds mean, it is necessary first to categorize them (an enterprise the grounds for which, as we have seen, are not agreed).

Surely, though, rock creates meaning primarily in the emotional sphere. This seems, after all, to be a principal reason why listeners choose to spend time with music. Emotional content is readily assumed of all rock but, surprisingly, it is rarely explicitly addressed. In discussions of its emotional sphere, rock is supremely cast as a music of the body, right from Elvis Presley's earliest television appearances. Dick Bradley's comments, while among the more measured, are quite typical. He privileges the Lacanian psychoanalytic term *jouissance* to refer to "the thrills, the shivering bursts of pleasure which we sometimes experience, perhaps sexual climax is its most intense or characteristic form. . . . Rock listeners experience – and know and recognize – *jouissant* pleasure in listening" (Bradley 1992: 117–18). Although Bradley's analysis is careful, others' are less so (as Grossberg's use of a similar position above might suggest), and "the reduction of the rock body to sites of sexuality and little else" (Tagg and Clarida 2003: 71) has become a widely held assumption, due in large measure to the hold post-Lacanians maintain on contemporary cultural theory.

Both Tagg and Clarida (2003, esp. 66–73) and Frith have argued strongly against this construction. Frith problematizes the mind–body dualism as played out across a series of musics in order to undermine the simplistic equation of the rhythm of rock with the pleasures of (simulated) sex. He finds it "striking that the pleasures of rock music continue to be explained by intellectuals in terms of *jouissance*, the escape from structure, reason, form, and so forth. . . . [W]hat's involved in such assertions is not a musical (or empirical) judgment at all, but an ideological gesture, a deviant expression of respectable taste," concluding that "music is 'sexy' not because it makes us move, but because (through that movement) it makes us feel; makes us feel (like sex itself) intensely present" (Frith 1998: 144). Most prominent in Frith's analysis here is recognition and critique of the desire, or even need, of critics who wish to affirm rock's values to construct them as rebellious, or deviant in some way.

So far, I have equated the notion of "sound structure" with the "music" of rock. But what of its lyrics? After all, ask most of my students about the philosophy of music, and the question of meaning will figure highly in the answer. Ask the meaning of a song, and it is frequently reduced to the lyrics (and not even the lyrics as sung, but as they are posted on the internet). This position is countered in, for example, Moore (2005). There is little in the literature which attempts a philosophical overview of the subjects addressed in rock lyrics. Harris (1993) takes a very broad approach to *repertory*, addressing a range of themes: alienation, theology, hedonism, individuality, and idealism are particularly prominent. More specific studies address similar themes: theology, existentialism, postmodernity, identity, and the philosophy of language (Wrathall 2006, on U2); Nietzsche, existentialism, epistemology, ethics, and difference (Baur and Baur 2006, on the Beatles). Literature which demonstrates how these themes are instantiated as *music* is notable through its absence.

Evaluation

So, how do we know whether the music is any good? Most writing about rock (whether academic or not) makes implicit assumptions about value. Edward Macan, rarely among writers, is willing to be explicit about what these values might be. His procedure for evaluating the worth of the output of Emerson, Lake, and Palmer requires him to address "innovation and originality; historical significance [i.e. influence on contemporaries] . . .; compositional, arranging, and technical mastery; inter-album cohesiveness; conceptual depth . . .; production savvy" (Macan 2006: xxxiii). At one level, this is nothing more than a list, but it at least serves to organize those separate features that critics believe listeners (among whom are critics themselves, of course) can find of value. But rock, even if understood in a more limited fashion as a genre or style, is not monolithic. Wendy Fonarow, for instance, finds that the audience for "indie rock" (i.e. independent rock which first emerged from the industry shake-up initiated by punk, in the late 1970s) assesses that music through intertwined values she labels Puritan and Romantic. The Puritan encompasses a "distrust of authority, a preference for non-corporate, independently owned commercial operations, an avocation of simplicity in musical form, production, and style, a promotion of high moral standards regarding issues of sexuality and conduct, an emphasis on education, and an underlying theme of austerity and absence," but "indie's ideology expresses . . . contradictory values at every turn, demonstrating Romantic Bohemian youth still deeply embedded in a Puritan aesthetic moral system" (Fonarow 2006: 28, 183–4). Again, such detail about the values implicit in such broad categories of music is rare in the literature.

Frith argues for three forms of evaluative music discourse. The first, "the bourgeois art world [which] is the world of classical (or art) music," and the second, "the folk music world [where] ideally, there is no separation of art and life," are familiar enough; the third is "the commercial music world [whose] values are created and organized . . . around the means and possibilities of turning sounds into commodities" (Frith 1998: 36, 39, 41). This last certainly encompasses ("authentic") "rock," ("commercial") "pop," and the "popular." What is interesting about these distinctions is that although Frith follows the assumption that they are style-related, they seem not necessarily to be so. A key marker of the first category is the "autonomy" acquired by a musician no longer subject to the necessity of making his or her mark. But we could say the same of artists such as Sigur Rós, or Robert Fripp, both of whom produce forms of rock music. John Covach's exploration of the "formal types [which] apply to much of the rock repertory" (2004: 75) exemplifies the rather restrained approach to evaluation typical of this discourse. The second category is sought by many young audiences, and is found in the lack of separation between performer and audience common for many "local" performers (intimately known to their audience). This is by no means restricted to folk; where they are still to be found, pub rock acts and local club DJs exemplify this. As for the third, although rock musicians may fight against commercial pressures, most conform to them in terms of their use of management, record companies, large-scale (impersonal) tours, etc., particularly those musicians on the way to gaining a name. Recognition that these criteria of evaluation are not deeply tied to particular styles may open the way for individual listeners to recognize that their value system is under their own control, rather than being prescribed by a particular (sub-)cultural ideology. As such, this parallels the recent move from consideration of (prescriptive) musical subcultures toward less rigidly defined, even virtual, "music scenes" in the sociology of popular music. For the rock musician, I suspect that these evaluative categories may work as process: starting with Frith's second category, a successful musician will be found to have moved through the third to the first.

This may seem an unsatisfactory way to conclude. Not only do we not really know what "rock" is, but there is also no more clarity about how to understand it, what it means, or how to determine whether it is any good. Indeed, as I have intimated throughout, the most illuminating contributions to its philosophy address particular limited, circumscribed areas. More than two decades ago, Alan Durant argued that we do not understand the detailed conditions of rock fully enough to enable us to generalize effectively. He called the then-current situation "one of outstanding contradiction and diversity of practice and belief" (Durant 1986: 119). In twenty-five years, nothing much seems to have changed.

See also Music and politics (Chapter 50), Popular music (Chapter 37), Sociology and cultural studies (Chapter 51), and Song (Chapter 40).

References

Baur, M. and Baur, S. (eds) (2006) *The Beatles and Philosophy: Nothing You Can Think that Can't be Thunk*, Chicago: Open Court.

Booth, G.D. and Kuhn, T.L. (1990) "Economic and Transmission Factors as Essential Elements in the Definition of Folk, Art, and Pop Music," *Musical Quarterly* 74: 411–38.

Born, G. and Hesmondhalgh, D. (2000) "Introduction," *Western Music and its Others*, Berkeley: California University Press, pp. 1–58.

Bradby, B. (2002) "Oh, Boy! (Oh, Boy!): Mutual Desirability and Musical Structure in the Buddy Group," reprinted in Moore (2007), pp. 567–95.

Bradley, D. (1992) *Understanding Rock'n'roll: Popular Music in Britain 1955–64*, Buckingham: Open University Press.

Chester, A. (1970) "Second Thoughts on a Rock Aesthetic: The Band," reprinted in Moore (2007), pp. 111–18.

Cook, N. (1996) "Music Minus One: Rock, Theory, and Performance," *New Formations* 27: 23–41.

Covach, J. (2004) "Form in Rock Music: A Primer," in D. Stein (ed.) *Engaging Music: Essays in Music Analysis*, New York: Oxford University Press, pp. 65–76.

Durant, A. (1986) "Rock Revolution or Time-no-changes: Visions of Change and Continuity in Rock Music," *Popular Music* 5: 97–121.

Eisenberg, E. (1988) *The Recording Angel*, London: Picador.

Everett, W. (1987) "Text-painting in the Foreground and Middleground of Paul McCartney's Beatle Song, 'She's Leaving Home': A Musical Study of Psychological Conflict," *In Theory Only* 9: 5–13.

—— (ed.) (2007) *Expression in Pop-Rock Music*, New York: Routledge.

—— (2009) *The Foundations of Rock*, New York: Oxford University Press.

Fabbri, F. (1999) "Browsing Musical Spaces," reprinted in Moore (2007), pp. 49–62.

Fonarow, W. (2006) *Empire of Dirt*, Middletown: Wesleyan University Press.

Fornäs, J. (1995) *Cultural Theory and Late Modernity*, London: Sage.

Frith, S. (1984) *Sound Effects: Youth, Leisure, and the Politics of Rock'n'roll*, London: Constable.

—— (1998) *Performing Rites*, New York: Oxford University Press.

Gracyk, T. (1996) *Rhythm and Noise: An Aesthetics of Rock*, London: I. B. Tauris.

Grossberg, L. (1992) *We Gotta Get Out of This Place*, New York: Routledge.

Harris, J.F. (1993) *Philosophy at 33 1/3 rpm: Themes of Classic Rock Music*, Chicago: Open Court.

Hawkins, S. (2002) *Settling the Pop Score*, Aldershot: Ashgate.

Holm-Hudson, K. (2001) "The Future is Now . . . and Then: Sonic Historiography in Post-1960s Rock," *Genre* 34: 243–65.

Kania, A. (2006) "Making Tracks: The Ontology of Rock Music," *Journal of Aesthetics and Art Criticism* 64: 401–14.

Kealy, E.R. (1982) "Conventions and the Production of the Popular Music Aesthetic," *Journal of Popular Culture* 16: 100–15.

Kivy, P. (1995) *Authenticities*, Ithaca: Cornell University Press.

Laing, D. (1985) *One Chord Wonders*, Buckingham: Open University Press.

Lakoff, G. (1987) *Women, Fire, and Dangerous Things*, Chicago: Chicago University Press.

Macan, E. (2006) *Endless Enigma*, Chicago: Open Court.

Marshall, L. (2007) *Bob Dylan: The Never Ending Star*, Cambridge: Polity.

Maus, F.E. (2001) "Glamour and Evasion: The Fabulous Ambivalence of the Pet Shop Boys," reprinted in Moore (2007), pp. 525–39.

Moore, A.F. (2001) *Rock: The Primary Text*, 2nd edn, Aldershot: Ashgate.

—— (2002) "Authenticity as Authentication," reprinted in Moore (2007), pp. 131–46.

—— (2005) "The Persona/Environment Relation in Recorded Song," *Music Theory Online* 11, available at http://mto.societymusictheory.org/issues/mto.05.11.4/mto.05.11.4.moore.html.

—— (ed.) (2007) *Critical Essays in Popular Musicology*, Aldershot: Ashgate.

Peterson, R.A. (1990) "Why 1955? Explaining the Advent of Rock Music," *Popular Music* 9: 97–116.

Popular Music International Advisory Editors (2005) "Can We Get Rid of the 'Popular' in Popular Music?" reprinted in Moore (2007), pp. 35–48.

Tagg, P. (1991) *Fernando the Flute*, Liverpool: Liverpool University Institute for Popular Music.

Tagg, P. and Clarida, B. (2003) *Ten Little Title Tunes*, New York: Mass Media Music Scholars' Press.

Taylor, T. (1997) *Global Pop: World Musics, World Markets*, New York: Routledge.

Vulliamy, G. (1975) "A Re-assessment of the 'Mass Culture' Controversy: The Case of Rock Music," *Popular Music & Society* 4: 130–55.

Watson, W. (1993) *The Architectonics of Meaning: Foundations of the New Pluralism*, Chicago: Chicago University Press.

Willis, P. (1978) *Profane Culture*, London: Routledge & Kegan Paul.

Wrathall, M.A. (ed.) (2006) *U2 and Philosophy: How to Decipher an Atomic Band*, Chicago: Open Court.

Zak, A. III (2001) *Poetics of Rock: Cutting Tracks, Making Records*, Berkeley: California University Press.

39
JAZZ
Lee B. Brown

Does jazz have an essence?

The question, "what is jazz?" was famously ridiculed in the response attributed to Louis Armstrong: "If you have to ask what jazz is, you'll never know." The remark suggests something serious but controversial – namely, that jazz essentially *is* something or other. But what?

In 1938, one brilliant writer – Winthrop Sargeant – addressed the topic of jazz in book-length detail from a music-theoretic point of view while dodging the question of a jazz essence (Sargeant 1938). We owe the most pointed attempt to define the music to a French musicologist, composer, and jazz journalist, André Hodeir, who shocked many by his denial that jazz has any necessary connection with either improvisation or blues tonality (Hodeir 1956: 35, 85, 90, 155–6, 236). Against those who think that jazz is essentially tied to improvisation, he cites the Ellington trumpet "concerto" for Cootie Williams, in which improvisation plays virtually no role. Hodeir could have named countless other cases. Charlie Mingus's work, "Half-Mast Inhibition," for instance, lacks any musical improvisation. Against the necessity of blue tonality for jazz, Hodeir cites the famous Coleman Hawkins 1939 recording of "Body and Soul" as just one example.

Hodeir's definition of jazz is that it consists essentially of an "*inseparable but extremely variable mixture of relaxation and tension*," that is, "of swing and the hot manner of playing" (1956: 240). The idea behind the definition is a general contrast between European "classical" music and jazz with respect to the interplay between tension and relaxation. European music capitalizes upon broad alternations between these two poles – between movement and repose, for instance, or dissonance and consonance. The peculiarity of jazz, by contrast, is that tension and relaxation are deployed "at the same moment" (Hodeir 1956: 195–6). However, although Hodeir does not take pains to profile the point, it seems clear that he applies this tension–relaxation duality to jazz in two (related) ways.

First, consider the case of jazz rhythm – that is, the phenomenon of swing, which Hodeir explains in terms of a *superstructure* comprising notes strategically but eccentrically placed above a (relatively) steady typically two- or four-beat rhythmic *infrastructure* (1956: 197–9). Hodeir's characterization of note-placement in the superstructure is, to be sure, a homely one – a matter of "getting the notes and accents in the right place" (1956: 197). The words serve as a kind of placeholder for the innumerable means, liberally illustrated by Hodeir, by which soloists, given a suitable infrastructure, judiciously place notes so as to achieve the right effect. For instance, some twenty measures of the solo Louis Armstrong plays on the Hot Five recording of "Muggles" either orbit around (or play nothing but) the tone C. Heard as a European melody, one can hardly get the point of the effort. Heard as swinging music, there is no doubt about it. Stravinsky was talking about the effect when he described the giddy sensation we register when jazz tries "persistently to stress irregular accents" but "cannot succeed in turning our ear away from the regular pulsation of the meter drummed out by the percussion" (Stravinsky 1947: 30). Put otherwise, a soloist's notes will be felt as moving independently of the underlying pulse and then as being recaptured by it. Hodeir notes that, so understood, swing exemplifies one of the "Freudian paradoxes: an unpleasant tension which is associated with pleasure – that is . . . with a partial relaxation" (1956: 196 n. 2).

Second, the wording of the definition makes clear that at a higher level the tension–relaxation duality reappears, with swing as a whole now taken as a main source of relaxation and hot playing as a main source of tension. Hot playing is not defined but is, rather, illustrated by such features as exceptional or continually rising volume, distortions of sonority, and vital drive (Hodeir 1956: 224–33).

It is hard not to see Hodeir as hankering for an account that would analyze the concept jazz not simply in terms of a set of necessary but disconnected conditions, but in terms that would tell us what it is about the *interaction* of its ingredients that yields a unified effect. Thus, he looks for opportunities to show how hot playing plays a role in swing (Brown 1991: 123–5). For instance, he notes the way vibrato can serve swing by making notes dance, so to say (Hodeir 1956: 124–5). However, he has to admit that not everything about hot playing can be regarded as serving swing. Indeed, there are trade-offs between the two. Jazz that is too relaxed may lack drive, while jazz that is too hot – too driving, for instance – may leave less room for a swinging placement of notes in the superstructure (Hodeir 1956: 237–8).

An evolutionary jazz history

The range of cases just cited is one reason Hodeir refers to the relationship between tension and relaxation as "variable." Another is that in Hodeir's version of essentialism the sources of tension and relaxation in the music were only gradually brought into an effective overall relationship. Hodeir's story of jazz unfolds in three over-arching chapters – a period of growth, then of maturity (the period of classic jazz) and then, presumably, one of decline (1956: 35). From such a perspective, the essence of an art form is something toward which history moves, and from which history may eventually depart. Thus, early jazz had not fully realized the ideal balance of tension and relaxation. Indeed, it too often relied on tension alone – which could even reach "a level of [swingless] paroxysm" (Hodeir 1956: 237). (Examples would be the often frenetic performances of the Original Dixieland Jazz Band.) In fact, Hodeir grants that this kind of unbalance could be a danger even in the mature period (1956: 231–2). (Examples would include the often over-heated performances at the famous "Jazz at the Philharmonic" concerts.)

Strikingly, Hodeir notes that the overall developmental pattern exhibits one notable anomaly, namely Louis Armstrong. Given his early ability to decompose single beats into many sub-divisions, his rhythmic use of vibrato, stop-time choruses, and extensions of notes beyond their expected values, Armstrong was well ahead of the development of the music as a whole (Hodeir 1956: 34). It is as if Armstrong somehow intuitively knew the direction of the music.

Essentialism and its vicissitudes

Although Hodeir goes more deeply into the question of the essence of jazz than anyone else we might cite, the difficulties with his view are clear. First, it is open to the charge that it conflates the question, "Is this jazz?" with the question, "Is this *good* jazz?" – as judged by a set of preferred standards. The result is that remarkable "oldtime" musicians such as clarinetist Johnny Dodds are marginalized. Second, when Hodeir turns to the moderns we can see him struggling to fit them into a formula that works best for the pre-Second World War classic jazz era. However, Hodeir speaks of musicians of the so-called "cool" school – he is thinking of players such as Lee Konitz and Stan Getz – as losing touch with a sufficient degree of tension (1956: 118, 222). Even by mid-century, Hodeir noted "conflicts" breaking out that had not yet become "aggressive" as if it would be only a matter of time before they would do so (1956: 116).

Third, once we set aside Hodeir's evolutionary view of the matter, counterexamples from the full range of jazz history litter the landscape. Ornette Coleman sought a very loose "spread" rhythm that would ideally be liberated from the kind of metric consistency required for classic swing. And it is hard to see how Hodeir's views of "mature" jazz would apply to the rock-slanted rhythms of jazz-fusion or to twenty-first century free jazz. Nor does he have much to tell about the rhythmic complexities of Latin jazz. As already suggested, Hodeir is not blind to the problem. Toward the end of his main work, we find a section titled "Toward a Change of Essence?" But he might well have spoken of a loss of essence altogether.

Later writers who applied serious musical analysis to the explanation of how jazz works all owe something to Hodeir – as Gunther Schuller, a major scholar of the genre, grants (Schuller 1968: viii). Like Hodeir, they typically imagined something analogous to what F. R. Leavis termed "the great tradition" in English literature. (Indeed, a main work by the renowned Martin Williams is titled *The Jazz Tradition*.) From our perspective it is difficult to say what if anything now represents such a tradition. Against those who place their hopes on the kind of avant-gardism once represented by John Coltrane or Ornette Coleman, there are the traditionalists who see the recent neo-classicism of Wynton Marsalis at Lincoln Center as the savior of jazz. Against both stands the pop music marketplace in which jazz would seem to be either mainly lost or "saving" itself by fragmentation into pieces too small to be regarded as preserving any tradition.

Ontology

Works of jazz

If there exists an ontology of jazz, what are its *works*? One option would be to place jazz works in the same category as any number of familiar works for live performance – songs by Stephen Foster or symphonies by Beethoven, for example. The occurrence of improvisation in jazz performance ought to be no obstacle to the approach. (Consider Baroque ensemble works in which the continuo parts are only sparingly determined by antecedent instructions.) Such an ontology would fit the intuition that, in spite of their improvisational content and striking differences, a performance by Miles Davis and one by Thelonious Monk could both be of one piece – "Round Midnight," let us say.

In fact, a view of this kind has been ably articulated (Young and Matheson 2000). The basic idea is derived from the view propounded in a notable philosophical study of performance art that works for audiences might be individuated by specific sets of *instructions* used to guide performances (Thom 1992). Two jazz performances can be instances of a common work – a jazz "standard," say – when they share "a common starting point in a common but loose set of tacit instructions" (Young and Matheson 2000: 128–9). In jazz, such instructions are generally cast in what the authors term a *canonic form*, consisting of an introduction, a statement of the tune, or "head," a set of partly improvised variations on the tune, a restatement of the head, and a conclusion. The category of jazz works, according to such a view, would include songs written specifically for jazz performance, such as "Night in Tunisia" (Dizzy Gillespie) or "Django" (John Lewis) but also popular standards such as "Body and Soul" or "How High the Moon."

Some of the difficulties faced by the proposal are recognized by the authors themselves (Young and Matheson 2000: 130–2). First, much jazz music fails to conform to the canonic model. Consider "free" jazz of the sort first attempted by Lennie Tristano. We might treat such a performance as being of a work that can only have one performance, but this is an awkward implication surely. Part of the point of a free jazz performance after all is that it is *not* of a pre-existent work. Second, there exist performances – Ornette Coleman's "Lonely Woman," for instance – not based on any harmonic chord changes but rather on motifs. Perhaps the motific model and the harmonically based canonic model can be given a common characterization, but it is not obvious how.

A final technical problem with the Young–Matheson view is that jazz standards often have one or more "contrafacts," that is, tunes that share the standard's harmonic structure while going under a different title. Conversely, there exist many jazz performances that differ wildly from each other except that they are of the *same* song. This song-sorting problem, as one might term it, is how to articulate a criterion of performance-identification that avoids (1) performances of ostensibly different works turning out to be of the same work and (2) performances ostensibly of the same work turning out to be of different works. How the present view – or indeed any similar view – would handle such cases is not clear.

But the larger problem is that it may be incorrect that the field of jazz music really is a sphere of musical *works*, as was assumed by Young and Matheson, as well as by others (Hagberg 2000).

Jazz without works

Suppose the focus of critical attention with jazz performances is in fact not an *abstractum* that could be instantiated in multiple instances. Suppose, as was suggested several years ago, that the focus is instead the *specific act* of creating this music, now, as I listen, so to say (Brown 1996: 353, 366, n. 2; Kania 2008: 12–15, forthcoming). Such an option would in turn open up the possibility that the territory of jazz may simply not be inhabited by art *works*. Much depends here on an agreement about the criteria governing the concept of an art *work*, of course. Are there reasons why an ephemeral event cannot be an art work, for instance?

Much depends too on our willingness to discount the apparent fact that jazz musicians do give performances that would appear to be of works – jazz standards, for instance. The non-work view would need to maintain that, in a jazz context, playing "Body and Soul" or "Stardust" is just an occasion for improvising. But this would be a difficult position to defend. (Should we also insist that the tunes in a symphony by Beethoven or Brahms are just occasions for sonata-allegro development?) In spite of their close harmonic similarities, a jazz standard and a bebop contrafact of it have their own individuality. Bop tunes are abstract, choppy, often whimsical or playful, when compared with the songs from which they are derived. Jazz players will tend to improvise in the spirit of the tune they are playing. Furthermore, the non-work view will have to marginalize fully fledged jazz compositions by Duke Ellington and others. This would surely be implausible.

A non-ontology for jazz?

The larger problem, however, is that the field of jazz may just be too cluttered for any single unifying ontology. The Young–Matheson view may be suitable for a great many jazz performances. But it cannot deal easily with free jazz performances. The non-work view may be well suited for the latter kind of case but is implausible for the enormous multitude of cases where it *is* relevant what jazz song is played. It may be possible to work out an ontology for jazz songs or for jazz compositions. But perhaps there is no single concept – whether it be of a kind of work or of a *non*-work – that can serve as the ontological centerpiece for jazz in general (Brown, forthcoming). Further support for the negative conclusion might be gleaned from the relationship of jazz to recording technology.

Recorded jazz

The story is that after Louis Armstrong and Earl Hines performed "Weather Bird" together on a notable occasion, they listened to it again and again, amazed at what they had created. How, in spite of the event's ephemerality, did they manage to do this? Through the recording that Okeh Records had just made of the performance, of course. Is there not a sense then in which even ephemeral jazz performances may sometimes endure?

Recording technology and jazz music arrived on the scene at about the same time and their histories have been problematically intertwined ever since. Phonography's potentiality for repetition has made possible substantial features of the institutions that revolve around jazz. It is no accident that classic analyses of jazz performances – by Schuller, Williams, and others – are studies of recordings. Early in his main work on jazz, Hodeir states that the words "*work and record*" will be "used interchangeably" throughout his study (1956: 2). The painstaking analyses of specific jazz performances that he and others provide would be inconceivable without the possibility of going over the same stretches of music again and again – by means of recording technology, of course. Much the same thing is true of jazz pedagogy. In the days of shellac 78s, jazz musicians often wore out a specific set of grooves on a recording by returning the needle again and again to the solo they were studying. The study and critical appreciation of sources and models is possible thanks only to the preservation and repeated playback that phonography makes possible.

The view has been expounded that, ontologically understood, works of rock music are not compositions for live performance, but are, rather, identical with recorded *albums* or perhaps *tracks* thereon (Gracyk 1996; Kania 2006). Rock works do not have performances but have instead *playbacks* – on one's stereo or iPod. Could such a view be maintained for jazz works? It helps here to apply a distinction that has been made between two targets of attention when listening to recordings, namely, the *phenomenal* and the *active* performance (Kania 2008:

7–8, 13–14). The former refers simply to the sounds we hear when we play a CD, for instance. The latter refers to the active production of the recorded sounds by the singing or playing of musicians. Even if we would say otherwise about rock, we are surely not intended to listen to jazz recordings as sonic constructs. One's intuition is, rather, that we are intended to listen with the expectation that the phenomenal performance heard on a recording closely reflects the active production of music by musicians.

However, given modern recording strategy, the injunction to attend to the active performance in the case of recorded jazz may be facile. Even before the digital age, the editing of recorded music by cutting and splicing tape was well established. It is common knowledge that while recording for Columbia Records, Miles Davis allowed entirely different notes to be inserted into his recorded performances. Rudy van Gelder, the most distinguished jazz engineer in the past half century, explains how, after recording sessions, musicians would "line up at the door of the control room waiting to fix their mistakes." Jazz musicians nowadays, he says, want to "build their music track by track" with a result "that is more like painting . . . stroke by stroke, rather than performing in the moment" (Seidel 2006: 60).

One response to this situation is that such phonographic constructs nevertheless represent what musicians *could* have played. But as we consider further cases, this reply becomes less convincing. Consider what have been called *concept albums* such as Gil Evans and Miles Davis's *Sketches of Spain*, in which electronic fade-out is used to give the cinematic effect of a parade moving off down the street. Indeed, with much jazz recorded nowadays the final product is very distant from anything that could have been played. With typical "smooth jazz," for instance, a lead track by a melody-playing instrument, usually a saxophone or guitar, is laid over a backdrop, which consists of music samples and "pads" – that is, programmed rhythms and soft, barely perceptible timbres of choirs, strings, and so on. The music is not so much performed as laminated together according to a plan. In short, the injunction to attend to the active performance in recorded jazz is problematic.

Even in the absence of manipulation, phonography's power of exact repetition poses a specific problem for recorded jazz performances that we acknowledge to be improvised. It has been suggested that "as recorded, [such jazz] may have an entirely different phenomenology from that of the living thing" (Brown 1996: 336; see also Brown 2000: 117–18). The benefits of phonographic repeatability are obvious. But for improvised jazz, this is a strange virtue. With live improvised music one is not responding simply to the structural details of the unfolding music. One is also responding to the performer's on-the-spot choices and actions that generate those details. But our up-take of all this is surely changed with recordings. Given the repeatability of recorded performances, one soon learns to anticipate precisely how a stretch of familiar recorded improvised music is going to go at any given point. No wonder recordings have been regarded by some scholars as little more than advertisements for the living thing (DeVeaux 2006).

One response to the problem is to posit a pluralism, or at least a dualism, with further negative implications for either a unified phenomenology or ontology for jazz. With recorded improvised jazz, the focus of critical attention may be one or more kinds of things importantly different from the targets of attention in a live context. This is a somewhat paradoxical result. Precisely *because* jazz is not a thoroughgoing compositional form – because it depends so much on improvisational spontaneity – both leisurely appreciation of it and detailed discourse about it depend upon a medium that to some extent embalms the music.

Jazz and the culture wars

Social criticisms of jazz could already be heard during the first decades of the music. The lurid cover of *Etude Music Magazine* for August 1924, for instance, announced the periodical's intention to deal with "the jazz problem." Late in the twentieth century, notice was taken of a new, often shrill kind of jazz writing, which gave evidence that the post-modernist culture wars had reached jazz (Brown 1999). Perhaps the most famous philosopher who profiled jazz (indeed, all American popular music) as the *bête noire* of high musical culture was Theodor Adorno.

Jazz versus *"classical"* music

Engaging Adorno on his own terms is a Sisyphean task, since his arguments are to a great extent applications of an almost insurmountable neo-Marxist sociological metaphysics. However, bits and pieces of his thinking can be separated from this massif.

Adorno argues that the jazz musician's supposed spontaneity is a myth – indeed, that the music consists of a stereotypical recycling of basic musical patterns. He continually repeats the claim that all jazz is based on the 32-bar Broadway show tune (Adorno 1941: 17–18, 1976: 25). Adorno is apparently ignorant of the 12-bar blues form in jazz. But even if his generalization had taken that form into account, Adorno's myopic view would still not reckon with the many exceptions to it that have been detailed (Gracyk 1996: 163–4).

Adorno builds much of his criticism of jazz upon a comparison of the musical practice of jazz by the yardstick of European concert music. Only by *a priori* reasoning from dubious axioms would some of his judgments be meaningful – for example, that the "bent" notes of blue tonality can only be heard as mistakes that we try to correct in our mind's ear (Adorno 1941: 26, 1963: 126). Adorno's often bizarre charges have been diagnosed elsewhere (Brown 1992: 25).

Afrocentrism: Baraka

One might date the intramural cultural debates about jazz from 1963 when dramatist, poet, and music critic Amiri Baraka, aka LeRoi Jones, made a passionately sustained statement about the putative misappropriation of black musical sources by the white music business (Baraka 1963). The complexities of the assumptions underneath this argument have been analyzed more than once (Rudinow 1994; Gracyk 2001: 107–28; Brown 2004: 250–1; Young 2008: 34–7).

Baraka is blunt about what he regards as an inauthentic "white" jazz sound. White musicians, he says, can be "impressive" but their technical mastery is not sufficient to give them the "right" sound (Baraka and Baraka 1987: 319). There are perhaps real issues here, as one scholar's examination of the markers of "blackness" in music indicates (Tagg 1989). But the results of such studies are open to interpretation (Brown 2004: 243). Furthermore, Baraka is not interested in the issue at this level of generality. He is clear that the "Negro" of which he speaks is not an African "Negro" but an American one (Baraka 1963: ix–xii) and, consistent or not with this qualification, he clearly regards African-American music as less authentic to the extent that it defers to features derived from European musical culture. The African American, he says, has "abandoned too much of his own musical tradition in favor of a more formalized, less spontaneous concept of music" (Baraka 1963: 90). A prime example is the music of Duke Ellington, which Baraka describes as indentured to the "considerations and responsibilities of high art" (Baraka 1963: 222).

But Baraka is in danger here of a dilemma. If he hankers for an authentic African *American* music, then how could European elements be excluded? They constitute much of what American music is. Otherwise he would seem to be proposing an Afro-purist version of the music that is conceptually and historically confused. As Hodeir and others have shown, such a perspective should, if consistent, advocate the elimination of *all* the machinery of jazz borrowed from European music, including harmonic motion – even chords themselves (Hodeir 1956: 41–4; Brown 1998: 1–3). It is almost certainly true that African Americans invented jazz. However, if we analyze the elements of the music, it is hard to deny that its character, taken as a whole, is – contrary to the Afro-purist – a vectorial resultant, so to say, of African *and* European practices.

Jazz as America's "classical" music

Like Baraka, Wynton Marsalis – famous not only as a brilliant jazz and classical trumpet player, but as artistic director of jazz at Lincoln Center – has been happy on occasion to speak of the putative ineptitude of white jazz players. In response to the loaded question, "Why are the best jazz musicians black?" Marsalis replied – citing jazz pundit Stanley Crouch – that people "who invent something are always the best" at doing it. If you "celebrate less accomplished musicians . . . you cheat yourself" (Marsalis and Stewart 1994: 142, 145). (The rationale is curious, given Marsalis's *classical* trumpet expertise.) Critics have detected the effect of this opinion in Ken Burns's television series *Jazz*, which was strongly influenced by Marsalis and his mentors, Crouch and Albert Murray.

On another matter, however, Marsalis and Baraka could not agree. In the 1950s, one writer had already tried to make the case that, given that the tradition of opera and concert music was supposedly dead, jazz would take over the role of serious-but-listenable music (Pleasants 1955). The prediction has not exactly been borne out. Nevertheless, the view has made a reappearance thanks largely to the activities of Marsalis at Lincoln Center, where, since a key concert in 1987, the theme of jazz as "America's classical music" has been nurtured (Gourse 1999: 186, 199). The characterization would appear to be based upon a mainly hortatory use of "classical." However, things fall partly into place if we understand that one of Marsalis's markers of a *classical* musical form is that it is *indigenous*. He tends to see American struggles about race as definitive of Americans *as an entire people*. Hence, the negative conclusion: the music played on a typical "classical" radio station in the United States is not *American* classical music. (Even if composed and performed by Americans? – one wonders.) Jazz, however, does deserve the label. The argument is not without interest; but, as has been shown, it does put a further strain on the application of the concept of *classical* (Brown 2002).

See also Adorno (Chapter 36), Appropriation and hybridity (Chapter 17), Improvisation (Chapter 6), Ontology (Chapter 4), Performances and recordings (Chapter 8), and Rock (Chapter 38).

References

Adorno, T. (1941) "On Popular Music," *Studies in Philosophy and Social Science* 9: 17–37.
—— (1963) "Zeitlose Mode – Zum Jazz," in *Prismen: Kulturkritik und Gesellschaft*, Frankfurt: Deutscher Taschenbuch Verlag, pp. 118–32.
—— (1976 [1962]) *Introduction to the Sociology of Music*, trans. E.B. Ashton, New York: Seabury Press.
Baraka, A. (1963) *Blues People: Negro Music in White America*, New York: William Morrow (originally published under the name "LeRoi Jones").
Baraka, A. and Baraka, A. (1987) *The Music: Reflections on Jazz and Blues*, New York: William Morrow.
Brown, L.B. (1991) "The Theory of Jazz Music: 'It Don't Mean a Thing . . .'" *Journal of Aesthetics and Art Criticism* 49: 115–27.
—— (1992) "Adorno's Critique of Popular Culture: The Case of Jazz Music," *Journal of Aesthetic Education* 26: 17–31.
—— (1996) "Musical Works, Improvisation, and the Principle of Continuity," *Journal of Aesthetics and Art Criticism* 54: 353–69.
—— (1998) "Jazz" in M. Kelly (ed.) *Encyclopedia of Aesthetics*, vol. 2, New York: Oxford University Press, pp. 1–9.
—— (1999) "Postmodernist Jazz Theory: Afrocentrism Old and New," *Journal of Aesthetics and Art Criticism* 57: 235–46.

—— (2000) "Phonography, Repetition and Spontaneity," *Philosophy and Literature* 24: 111–25.

—— (2002) "Jazz: America's Classical Music?" *Philosophy and Literature* 26: 157–72.

—— (2004) "Marsalis and Baraka: An Essay in Comparative Cultural Discourse," *Popular Music* 23: 241–55.

—— (forthcoming) "Do Higher-Order Music Ontologies Rest on a Mistake?" *British Journal of Aesthetics*.

DeVeaux, S. (2006) "This is What I Do," in H. Becker, R. Faulkner, and B. Kirshenblatt-Gimblett (eds) *Art from Start to Finish: Jazz, Painting, Writing and Other Improvisations*, Chicago: University of Chicago Press, pp. 118–25.

Gourse, L. (1999) *Wynton Marsalis: Skain's Domain – A Biography*, New York: Schirmer.

Gracyk, T. (1996) *Rhythm and Noise: An Aesthetics of Rock*, Durham: Duke University Press.

—— (2001) *I Wanna be Me: Rock Music and the Politics of Identity*, Philadelphia: Temple University Press.

Hagberg, G. (2000) "Improvisation in the Arts," *Journal of Aesthetics and Art Criticism* 58: 95–7.

Hodeir, A. (1956) *Jazz: Its Evolution and Essence*, trans. David Noakes, New York: Grove Press.

Kania, A. (2006) "Making Tracks: The Ontology of Rock Music," *Journal of Aesthetics and Art Criticism* 64: 401–14.

—— (2008) "Works, Recordings, Performances: Classical, Rock, Jazz," in M. Doğantan-Dack (ed.) *Recorded Music: Philosophical and Critical Reflections*, Middlesex: Middlesex University Press, pp. 3–21.

—— (forthcoming) "All Play and No Work: The Ontology of Jazz," *Journal of Aesthetics and Art Criticism*.

Marsalis, W. and Stewart, F. (1994) *Sweet Swing Blues on the Road*, New York: Norton.

Pleasants, H. (1955) *The Agony of Modern Music*, New York: Simon and Schuster.

Rudinow, J. (1994) "Race, Ethnicity, Expressive Authenticity: Can White People Sing the Blues?" *Journal of Aesthetics and Art Criticism* 52: 128–36.

Sargeant, W. (1938) *Jazz, Hot and Hybrid*, New York: Arrow Editions.

Schuller, G. (1968) *Early Jazz: Its Roots and Musical Development*, New York: Oxford University Press.

Seidel, R. (2006) "Home Studio: Original Home Recorder," *Downbeat* 74/2: 56–8, 60.

Stravinsky, I. (1947) *Poetics of Music*, New York: Vintage Press.

Tagg, P. (1989) "Open Letter: 'Black Music,' 'Afro-American Music' and 'European Music'," *Popular Music* 8: 285–98.

Thom, P. (1992) *For an Audience*, Philadelphia: Temple University Press.

Young, J.O. (2008) *Cultural Appropriation and the Arts*, Malden: Wiley-Blackwell.

Young, J.O. and Matheson, C. (2000) "The Metaphysics of Jazz," *Journal of Aesthetics and Art Criticism* 58: 125–34.

40
SONG

Jeanette Bicknell

Song and singing are topics of immense philosophical and aesthetic interest which have received comparatively little attention from philosophers. This chapter surveys some of the main areas of philosophical interest related to song, including the definition and ontology of song, meaning in songs, and some questions surrounding vocal performance and the ubiquity of singing. For a discussion and diagnosis of the entrenched philosophical "prejudice" against songs, see Ridley (2004: ch. 3).

Defining "song"

Singing is both a performing art and a cultural practice, and it plays a part in the artistic culture and domestic life of every culture of which we know. Two related features distinguish songs from other musical forms. First, the presence of a text. Although "songs" may be composed for musical instruments (such as Felix Mendelssohn's "Songs without Words" for the piano), these are not songs in the strict sense, but works that share some characteristics with them, notably a clear melodic line and accompaniment. "Vocalise" is song without a text – a borderline case in which the voice is treated as a musical instrument and the melody is sung on a vowel sound. Second, singing is by definition a vocal activity, although the voice may be accompanied by musical instruments.

While speech and singing may be understood as contrary to one another, the distinction between them is best made not physiologically but on cultural and pragmatic grounds. Using a spectrograph, George List (1963) recorded the pitch contours of various vocal activities and found many gradations between everyday speech and singing. Speech intonation may level out and approach a monotone or be heightened and exaggerated. Examples of vocal communication falling between singing and speech, yet arguably belonging clearly to neither, include rap, children's skipping and clapping rhymes, auctioneers' chants, street sellers' calls and cries, field and street hollers, the chants used in meditation and religious practices, and calls to prayer. Whether any of these are considered examples of "song" (or indeed examples of music) depends on cultural expectations and related attitudes regarding these very categories. For example, in cultures where "music" is understood as a secular activity or has little prestige, participants may be reluctant to describe their vocal activity as singing and prefer to define it as part of a larger spiritual practice. Islamic calls to prayer may sometimes sound like songs but are not usually considered to be singing performances, and the similar role of the cantor or chazzan in Judaism is seen to be primarily moral or spiritual rather than musical.

Today we may find it natural to think of song as a hybrid form combining words and music which are likely to have been composed separately before being brought together. (See, for example, Levinson 1990.) However such an assumption is historically uninformed. In earliest times music and poetry were one; their separation – what has been called music's "emancipation" from language (Neubauer 1986) – came later. A number of theorists have argued that music originated before language or that the two have a common origin. These include Rousseau (1998) and Darwin (1981), as well as contemporary researchers (Brown 2001; Mithen 2006). The evidence we have suggests that the beginnings of poetry lay in the fitting of words to pre-existing melodies and rhythms (Winn 1981: 1). C. M. Bowra, in his study of the songs of pre-literate cultures, argues for five evolutionary stages in the development of songs: the meaningless line, the repeated intelligible line, the single stanza, the collection of stanzas into longer songs, and the collection of these songs into cycles (1962: 86). In the West, the division of poetic from musical technique can be traced to the development of writing. With another method available for preserving poetic texts, instrumental musicians could pursue melody and rhythm for their own sakes, rather than for the purpose of aiding memorization (Winn 1981: 17–18). Ancient Greek *mousiké* which had previously been a unified whole, eventually broke down into four distinct pursuits: musical composition and performance, literary composition and performance, musical theory and philosophy, and rhetorical theory (Winn 1981: 30).

Given the ubiquity of songs the world over, there are many different types of songs, sung in many different contexts and serving diverse purposes. A philosophical approach appropriate to one type of song may not be fruitful when applied to another song. I propose a three-part classification of songs. First, while any song can be performed in front of an audience, some songs are "works for performance," specifically intended to be performed, often in a formal setting (Thom 1993: ch. 1; Davies 2001: 20–5). These include art songs, songs in opera and music drama, jazz standards, and the songs recorded by professional singers for a mass media audience. Second are songs intended for "participation-performance" or communal singing. The "audience" and the performers are one in this case. Such songs include national anthems, hymns, campfire songs, and many folk songs. Even when only one person performs such a song, he or she does so less *for* an audience than *on behalf* of an audience (Zuckerkandl 1973: 27). Finally, some songs are best understood as "functional" songs because they serve specific practical or cultural purposes. Examples include lullabies, mnemonic songs, work songs, and laments. Cone (1974) proposes a different classification of songs, based partially on musical and partially on functional considerations. "Simple songs" have no accompaniment or only simple accompaniment (Cone 1974: 58). An "art song" is a poem set to a composed vocal line and united with a fully developed instrumental accompaniment. In contrast to these are "natural songs" such as ballads, in which the roles of the poet and composer are "hardly relevant" (Cone: 1974: 59). Finally, in "functional songs" the vocal persona of the song is an aspect of the actual singer, expressing himself or herself as a member of a specific community taking part in a ritual or assisting at a social event (Cone: 1974: 49–52). "Happy Birthday" is the classic example.

Meaning in songs

For the purposes of analysis we can consider a song's text separately from its other elements. What is the proper construal of the relationship between the meaning of a song's words and the melody, harmony, and rhythm to which they are set, as well as any accompanying melodies? Many different answers have been proposed. Words in songs may be "reinforced, accented, blurred, inspired to a new meaning, in a continual interplay" by accompanying music (Booth 1981: 8). It is worth noting that already by the early Christian era three distinct forms of singing were recognized, each positing a different relationship between words and music. First was the chanting of the Psalms on a single note, with rising introduction and falling cadence. The texts were essentially treated as prose. Second were the elaborated and ecstatic melismata sung to the words "alleluia" and "amen." Finally hymns, designed for congregational singing, displayed a more equal partnership between words and music, with each word set to one or at most two pitches (Winn 1981: 35–6). These different vocal practices point to different underlying attitudes toward the relationship between a song's text and its other elements.

Rhetorical models of music, which originated in ancient Greek ideas about the character-forming power of *mousiké*, dominated theorizing about musical meaning until the early modern period and continue to be significant today. Their influence remains evident in what might be called the "propositional" model of song meaning. According to this, the meaning of a song can be reduced to the meaning of its verbal text. Rousseau subscribed to a variety of this doctrine and his views are typical of his time. Language conveys ideas, but to convey feelings as well words must be set to melody (Rousseau 1998: 324). Words are thus the primary carriers of meaning and the most that music can do is to supplement them. The propositional model becomes unsatisfactory when we take a closer look at song texts (Booth 1981). Songs are a form of oral communication and as such are subject to the burdens and limitations of oral communication. Song texts tend to be highly redundant, predictable, often formulaic, convey a low density of information, and trade in familiar simplifications (Booth 1981). Folk and popular songs must be accessible to their intended audiences; this in turn requires some fidelity to familiar forms (Gracyk 2001: 18–26). So a problem arises: if the meaning of a song is nothing more than the meaning of its text, it becomes difficult to explain the endurance of songs and singing across time and space. This is because singing is not a very efficient means for conveying propositional meaning; song is music and text is not. Hence while most songs do convey a text, their meaning cannot be reduced to the propositional content of that text.

One influential account of the relationship between words and music in song is that of Jerrold Levinson (1996). He notes three dimensions that can be analyzed in this relationship: the relation of the song's text to its vocal line, the relation of a song's text to its accompaniment, and the relation of the vocal line to the accompaniment. Levinson proposes that the ideal comportment between music and text is one of "mutual suitability" or "holistic working," rather than internal matching or mirroring. He compares this relationship to that of a (happily) married couple, whose interaction with one another is mutually rewarding. In Peter Kivy's "moderate indeterminacy" view, the text of a song particularizes the emotional expressivity of the music and therefore contributes to the music's overall expressiveness (Kivy, 1989: ch. 10). Ridley (2004: ch. 3) criticizes both Kivy and Levinson for, despite outward assurances to the contrary, improperly treating songs as hybrids of music and text. Asking, as Levinson does, how closely the expressiveness of the music "matches" the emotional quality or tone of the text is to treat songs as a hybrid art form. Ridley, in opposition, argues that songs are a distinct musical form containing words. Any talk of "matching" is inappropriate because there is not one thing to match to another. Ridley notes that a text may have musical qualities before it is set to music, and that the same words read as a poem and sung in a song may have a different sonorous quality and emotional resonance. The best setting of a text to music is not one that "matches" the text in some way but rather one that shows that the composer has understood the text in question. Furthermore, music may particularize a text, just as much as text particularizes music. (For another discussion of these points, see Boykan 2000.)

Ontology

There is a story that Alice Hammerstein, daughter of lyricist Oscar Hammerstein, was once at a social gathering where someone referred to the song "Ol' Man River," saying that it was "written by Jerome Kern." She is said to have protested that no, her father wrote "Ol' Man River," and what Kern wrote was "Dum dum da dum." This anecdote, whether apocryphal or not, nicely illustrates some of the ontological complexities inherent in song. Is a song to be identified with its text, its tune, or something else? What are a song's identity conditions – do the words or the tune make a song the particular work that it is? Like many songs, the text of "Ol' Man River" is often altered in performance. To what degree can the words be changed before we have a different song? Composers have notoriously "recycled" their work, sometimes using the same melodic line to fit very different texts. Different composers have set the same texts to different melodic lines. In such cases, how are we to determine what counts as the same song? What sort of entity is a song?

The answers to such questions will depend upon one's prior ontological commitments and one's understanding of the nature of musical works and artworks more generally. Those committed to the view that musical works are types or universals will have a different take on the ontology of songs than, say, those holding the view that works are abstract particulars. What seems uncontroversial, however, is that many songs are ontologically "thin" – that is, they have few determinative properties, and many qualities of a performance will be aspects of a performer's interpretation, not of the work as such (Davies 2001: 20). This would seem to be especially true of folk songs, popular songs, and rock songs. Songs originated in non-literate societies and were originally part of oral traditions. This background influences the attitudes taken by audiences and performers alike. For example, many folk songs exist in numerous versions, and verses may be dropped or sung in a different sequence. Even songs that are works for performance may, depending on the musical tradition and audience expectations, be altered in performance and retain their identities. We are better off determining identity conditions for songs on a pragmatic, case-by-case basis.

Performance

Any act of singing – with friends at the pub, to a sleepy child, or in the course of a ritual – may be attended to as if it were a performance, but some acts of singing are intended to be listened to for their own sake. Because singers make music with their bodies, instead of or in addition to musical instruments, vocal performances have an element of subjectivity beyond that of solely instrumental performances. "The voice is the person" is both an overused metaphor for individual style and a matter of copyright law in many countries. Public performances of songs thus involve complex issues of gender, social ontology, and personal identity that are not so pronounced in instrumental performances. One consequence is that while some songs are aesthetically appropriate for any singer, in other cases incongruities may arise between what the song communicates and the singer's public persona (Bicknell 2005).

Performances of songs imply a three-way relationship between a singer, a song, and an audience. As with any human interactions, these may carry moral obligations in addition to the aesthetic obligations inherent in performance (Bicknell 2009). Different conceptions of song meaning contribute to different performance practices among singers. The degree to which a singer (and accompanying musicians) will attempt to make the words of a song comprehensible to an audience will depend on the musical genre in question and on audience expectations. In some genres, the communication of the song's melody and rhythm, and with it a dominant emotional mood, will be just as important as, or more important than, the communication of the song's lyrics. In other musical traditions, such as contemporary country music, performers must strive to make each word fully audible and comprehensible.

Vocal performances manifest similarities and differences with other kinds of musical performances, and an adequate account of musical performance must take into account the complications raised by singing. Paul Thom makes a useful distinction between a "reading" and a "rendition" of a work for performance (1993: 76–8). A reading of a work is an understanding of its content, and a rendition is the execution of a work. Renditions are based on readings of works, and may or may not be executed as planned. (For example, a singer may plan a note-perfect performance yet be unable to execute it.) Inaccuracies can occur in the reading of a work, in the plan for the execution of a reading, or in the rendition itself. Performance without interpretation cannot be an artistic ideal because of the teleology of works for performance. They are understood, both by creators and by audiences, as calling for a certain kind of "playful" attention (Thom 1993: 30–2).

Similarly, Stan Godlovitch understands musical performance as "a complex activity which co-ordinates and focuses actions, skills, traditions, and works in order to define and create musical experience for the receptive listener" (Godlovitch 1998: 50). He places more emphasis on the performer–listener axis than on the performer–composer relationship. Performers have certain categorical obligations to listeners, and performances can fail by disaffecting listeners. Performers do not have unconditional obligations to composers, although a performance might certainly fail if it misrepresents a work.

Few thinkers have focused on the intricacies and complications of singing as opposed to other kinds of musical performances. Adam Smith (1723–90) offers an insightful analysis of singing performance that deserves to be better known. In keeping with the attitudes to music then current in Britain, Smith understands music as a form of artistic representation, such that individual musical works may represent the sentiments of a particular person in a particular situation. In the case of a vocal performance, an additional layer of representation is possible. The singer can, "by his countenance, by his attitudes, by his gestures, and by his motions," convey the sentiments of the person whose situation is depicted in the song (Smith 1982: 194). The singer's acting enhances the performance and is indeed necessary for a good performance. As Smith writes, "there is no comparison between the effect of what is sung coldly from a music-book at the end of a harpsichord, and of what is not only sung, but acted with proper freedom, animation, and boldness" (Smith 1982: 194).

The composer Edward Cone raises an intriguing question about singing performance and song meaning. In listening to, say, a performance of Schubert's setting of a poem by Goethe, whose voice do we hear? He suggests four different answers. We hear the actual physical voice of the singer in question, the protagonist of the song, the poet whose words and images characterize the protagonist and the dramatic situation, and in the song's musical accompaniment we hear the voice of the composer. Yet the composer is not simply one voice among the four. Rather, the voice of the composer constitutes the "complete musical persona," and the vocal persona – the protagonist of the song – is properly understood as a character quoted by the complete persona. The complete musical persona of a song is not to be strictly identified with the composer but is "a projection of [the composer's] musical intelligence, constituting the mind, so to speak, of the composition in question" (Cone 1974: 57).

Cone's analysis of song meaning leads him to a specific account of song performance. Like Smith, he stresses the importance of dramatic impersonation. For example, when Marian Anderson sings "Swing Low, Sweet Chariot," she recreates, as a dramatic persona, the slave who originally sang the song as an authentic appeal. An ideal or "faithful" performance is one in which the physical presence and vitality of the singer turns the persona of the musical text into an immediate living being. By contrast, in an illegitimate interpretation, it is the singer (rather than the vocal persona) who is seen as embodying and "composing" the song as he or she sings. The singer fails to let us hear the persona – and hence the composer's voice behind the persona – speak for itself. Yet this is not quite the whole story for Cone. As human beings, singers must produce their own interpretations of songs and insist on their own freedom of action. But as dramatic characters, singers must be faithful to the text and to the dramatic situation. There is thus a tension between these two aspects of a singer's role, and audiences are (or should be) aware of these tensions, as they are analogues for the tension between freedom and determinism in their own lives. Cone hypothesizes that the presence of such tensions can help explain the peculiar appeal of vocal performance, and of the performing arts more generally.

Finally, it should be noted that not all singing performances are renditions of works for performance or even of songs. Singers may also improvise new lyrics for an existing song, improvise lyrics for an instrumental melodic line ("vocalese"), and singers in the jazz tradition may improvise nonsense syllables ("scat singing") in the course of a song performance.

Why sing?

The phenomenon of singing continues to be both widespread and taken for granted. The practice has not atrophied, despite instrumental music's "emancipation" from words, or the fact that ordinary non-musical verbal communication is more efficient. Composers continue to set words to music, and listeners persist in seeking out vocal music in all the genres in which it has a place. While Plato already in Book Three of his *Republic* raised the question of the power of song and argued for subjecting it to generally agreed moral imperatives, similar concerns continue to be raised about transgressive popular singing, as evidenced by the imposition of warning labels on some CDs. Why should song and singing have retained their importance? I suggest two possibilities, both related to the social nature of music and song.

First, thinkers in different traditions have described the ways in which communal singing serves to connect the subjective with the social. Victor Zuckerkandl (1973) writes that different interrelations between people are created by speaking and by singing. The spoken word presumes an "other" – the person spoken to, as opposed to the person speaking, who face each other as separate individuals. When tones are added to words and individual speech becomes communal singing, individuals who had previously faced one another are transformed into one group. Tones do not refer yet they are intended to be heard, both by the singers themselves and by others. When we sing as part of a group, we perceive the feeling of our own vocal activity within our bodies, and we hear the tones we make combining with those made by others around us. As Zuckerkandl writes, "the dividing line between myself and others loses its sharpness" (1973: 28). It seems reasonable that traces of these effects can be perceived even when we listen to others sing, and we join in with the singing imaginatively, if not audibly.

Second, singing is linked with the human desire for recognition and the obligation to recognize others. There is something ineluctably human about the voice. Hence the observation of Mladen Dolar that the impersonal or mechanically produced voice always has a touch of the uncanny (2006: 22). As Cone has argued, one cannot help but interpret a vocalist as a protagonist, rather than as the player of an instrument, even when the singer produces nonsense syllables: "For when the human voice sings, it demands to be heard, and when it is heard it demands recognition" (Cone 1974: 79).

See also Authentic performance practice (Chapter 9), Opera (Chapter 41), Popular music (Chapter 37), and Rock (Chapter 38).

References

Bicknell, J. (2005) "Just a Song? Exploring the Aesthetics of Popular Song Performance," *Journal of Aesthetics and Art Criticism* 63: 261–70.
—— (2009) "Reflections on *John Henry*: Ethical Issues in Singing Performance," *Journal of Aesthetics and Art Criticism* 67: 173–80.
Booth, M.E. (1981) *The Experience of Songs*, New Haven: Yale University Press.
Bowra, C.M. (1962) *Primitive Song*, Cleveland: World Publishing Co.
Boykan, M. (2000) "Reflections on Words and Music," *Musical Quarterly* 84: 123–36.
Brown, S. (2001) "The 'Musilanguage' Model of Music Evolution," in N.L. Wallin, B. Merker and S. Brown (eds) *The Origins of Music*, Cambridge: MIT Press, pp. 271–300.
Cone, E.T. (1974) *The Composer's Voice*, Berkeley: University of California Press.
Darwin, C. (1981 [1871]) *The Descent of Man and Selection in Relation to Sex*, Princeton: Princeton University Press.

Davies, S. (2001) *Musical Works and Performances: A Philosophical Exploration*, Oxford: Clarendon Press.

Dolar, M. (2006) *A Voice and Nothing More*, Cambridge: MIT Press.

Godlovitch, S. (1998) *Musical Performance: A Philosophical Study*, London: Routledge.

Gracyk, T. (2001) *I Wanna Be Me: Rock Music and the Politics of Identity*, Philadelphia: Temple University Press.

Kivy, P. (1989) *Sound Sentiment: An Essay on the Musical Emotions*, Philadelphia: Temple University Press.

Levinson, J. (1990) "Hybrid Art Forms," in *Music, Art, and Metaphysics: Essays in Philosophical Aesthetics*, Ithaca: Cornell University Press, pp. 26–36.

—— (1996) "Song and Music Drama," in *The Pleasures of Aesthetics: Philosophical Essays*, Ithaca: Cornell University Press, pp. 42–59.

List, G. (1963) "The Boundaries of Speech and Song," *Ethnomusicology* 7: 4–13.

Mithen, S. (2006) *The Singing Neanderthals: The Origins of Music, Language, Mind, and Body*, Cambridge: Harvard University Press.

Neubauer, J. (1986) *The Emancipation of Music from Language: Departure from Mimesis in Eighteenth-Century Aesthetics*, New Haven: Yale University Press.

Ridley, A. (2004) *The Philosophy of Music: Theme and Variations*, Edinburgh: Edinburgh University Press.

Rousseau, J.J. (1998 [1753]) "Essai sur l'origine des langues," in E. Lippman (ed.) *Musical Aesthetics: A Historical Reader*, vol. 1, New York: Pendragon Press, pp. 323–37.

Smith, A. (1982 [1795]) "Of the Nature of that Imitation which takes place in what are called the Imitative Arts" in W.P.D. Wightman and J.C. Bryce (eds) *Essays on Philosophical Subjects*, Indianapolis: Liberty Fund, pp. 176–213.

Thom, P. (1993) *For an Audience: A Philosophy of the Performing Arts*, Philadelphia: Temple University Press.

Winn, J.A. (1981) *Unsuspected Eloquence: A History of the Relations between Poetry and Music*, New Haven: Yale University Press.

Zuckerkandl, V. (1973) *Man the Musician*, Princeton: Princeton University Press.

Further reading

Clayton, M. (2008) *Music, Words and Voice: A Reader*, Manchester: Manchester University Press. (An interdisciplinary anthology about song and singing.)

41

OPERA

Paul Thom

While drawing attention to the deep aesthetic differences between the French and Italian opera in the late seventeenth century, and between the operas of Wagner, Verdi, Schoenberg, and Weill, Herbert Lindenberger judges that all these works have in common "the fact that they enact a play by means of instrumentally accompanied song" (Lindenberger 1998: 129). An opera, according to this conception, is a hybrid work that combines musical elements, in which singing predominates, with the representation of dramatic action. These are its components, which it shares with musicals and other types of music-theater. The components can be organized in a variety of ways, as when parts of the music lie outside the dramatic representation (e.g. in an independent overture or entr'acte), or when parts of the drama are unaccompanied by music (e.g. in short passages where a letter is read, or in whole stretches of spoken dialogue). Philosophical questions about opera are of two main kinds: ontological and aesthetic.

Ontology

What sort of entity is an opera? At least, you would think, it is a musical work – or, rather, it at least contains a musical work (since it also has non-musical elements). Philosophers disagree about the nature of musical works. According to some, a musical work is a really existing thing – whether it be an abstract entity such as a type of sound-occurrence (Dodd 2007), or a perduring four-dimensional concrete entity made up of performances that are related to one another by structural similarities or causal connections (Caplan and Matheson 2006). According to other philosophers, a musical work is a purely intentional object: it can only be considered as that which is authored by a composer, or that which is performed by musicians, or that which is experienced by an audience. It does not have the determinacy of a really existing thing, but exists only in the degree of determinacy with which the object of the composer's authoring, the object of the musicians' performing, or the object of the audience's experience, is presented (Ingarden 1986).

Both the realist and the intentionalist conceptions of a musical work require some fine-tuning if their use of the word "work" is to be justified (Goehr 2007).

We can adopt a minimal conception of a work for performance as a set of pre-scriptions (however "thin") enshrined in some relatively enduring form – which may exist in a material medium (e.g. as a printed score), or may exist in another medium (e.g. as an electronic encoding or a collective memory) that can be realized in a material medium.

There are several ways in which the concept of an operatic work differs specifically from the generic concept of a musical work, and they create different problems for attempts to adapt ontological theories of the musical work to the case of opera.

Since operatic works are usually the result of collaboration between a composer and a librettist, any account of operatic works will have to allow for joint authorship. The account will also have to recognize opera's hybrid nature, in the sense that its realization requires the operation of more than one art. If an opera is a type, it cannot just be a type of sound-event because operas are theatrical as well as musical works. In order to be a theatrical work an opera must specify some details about stage-action and about what (if anything) that stage-action is supposed to represent. So, if an opera is a type, then it is a type whose tokens are not just occurrences of sounds but rather human actions (singing and making music, and representational stage-movement), along with other events such as stage-effects. This creates a difficulty for Dodd's account of musical works as types of sound-occurrence. Dodd's musical ontology is combined with what he calls a "sonicist" aesthetic of music: a musical work's aesthetic interest resides solely in what it sounds like. Now, even though there are some people for whom the aesthetic interest of opera is exhausted by listening to it in recorded form, it is clear that opera is standardly designed for theatrical performance. So, considered in its wider cultural context, opera cannot be accommodated within a sonicist aesthetic. Dodd's ontology can be adapted to accommodate this feature of opera by broadening the class of types with which musical works are identified, so as to include action-types, but if this adaptation is made, sonicism will have to be abandoned.

Because an operatic work is a work for performance, its authoring can be viewed as a quasi-linguistic intentional act, in which the authors lay down pre-scriptions for what is to be done in performing the work. An opera cannot, then, simply be an action-type; neither can it simply be a fusion of performances. Not only must its performances be actions of the prescribed types but they must also be presented under the aspect that they *are to be done* in performing the work. The work somehow *regulates* its performances.

Dramatic representation

Among the actions and other events that make up an operatic performance, some are representational of a dramatically connected sequence of events. Philosophers who think of musical works as really existing things like to think of this sort of representation as a relationship between the work and the "world of the work" (e.g. Wolterstorff 1980). The world of the work is the set of propositions that the work represents as being (fictionally) true. Actually, it is misleading to speak of a "world" being represented by an opera. Operas are usually schematic works, in that what they represent falls far short of the complete determinacy that characterizes the possible worlds of modern metaphysics. The work's schematic representations are filled out in production, and further filled out by the audience's imaginations. At the end of this process, there may be something approaching a "world," but it is no longer purely "of the work" since it is just as much "of the work's production," "of the production's performance," and "of the performance's imaginative reception."

Of course, acculturated spectators manage to work out what it is that the work itself represents as being fictionally true. Are there principles underlying that skill? David Lewis thinks so. He suggests that what is true in the world of the work must at least include anything that is logically implied by what the fiction explicitly represents as being true (Lewis 1978). But this principle does not deliver all of the information that an ordinary audience member finds in a fiction. Normally our understanding of fiction outstrips the logical consequences of what is on the page or the stage.

Lewis makes a suggestion about what else might be required. He proposes that fictional worlds must remain as close as possible to the actual world, or at least to beliefs about the actual world at the time of the fiction's creation. According to this proposal, we would have to say that in the world of *Le Nozze di Figaro*, where the singers sing in Italian, the audience is entitled to assume that the characters represented by the singers speak in Spanish, because the represented action is set in Seville. This assumption would be based on the fact that in the actual world it is true that the people in Seville speak Spanish. Yet this proposal seems at odds with our experience of Mozart's opera (Kivy 1994). When we see and hear the singers singing in Italian, we assume different things about the characters they represent, depending on what happens in the production; but it would be an unusual production of *Figaro* that specifically led us to assume that the characters were speaking to one another in Spanish.

Another suggestion is that the spectators' ability to work out what is being represented is grounded not in a single way but in a plurality of ways – sometimes on conventions appropriate to various forms or styles, sometimes on the intentions of an actual or postulated author, sometimes on facts or beliefs about the actual world, and sometimes on a consideration of the rhetorical structures of the work or performance (Livingston 2005: ch. 7).

On an intentionalist approach, by contrast, we are not obliged to postulate a "world of the work" nor to ask on what principles that world is populated with propositions. Instead, we can think of the audience's activity as having an intentional object – namely, the intentional activities of authors and performers. The audience's activity is, like that of the performers, both imaginative and interpretive. And like all interpretation, it goes beyond what is given, and does so in accordance with some sense-endowing framework. The framework may be one that is appropriate to realist fiction, and if so, it will incorporate as many propositions as possible from the actual world, or from the world as it was believed to be at the time of the work's composition or performance. But there are many other possible interpretive frameworks that can be appropriate to individual operatic scenes or moments, or to whole operas. Among them there could be some in which the interpreter assumes that what is represented is a magical world – a world where personages communicate not in speech but in song, and where they are subject to the mysterious force of an unseen music. There is also an interpretive framework in which we do not need to specify what kind of communication is represented as going on between the characters. All that matters is that the singers, who represent the characters, sing to one another.

Aesthetics

To specify opera's components and its ontology is not yet to say anything about its aesthetic qualities. And yet the form is imbued with aesthetic potential, deriving partly from the potentialities of the human voice, and partly from its other components. The sonority of a voice may be infinitely various, resembling the sonority of any musical instrument, but having additionally the quality of a human utterance. The voice, as the natural organ of expression, can in the subtlest ways convey psychological states so that we not only understand what they are but also feel what it is like to have them. And the voice, as one of the instruments whereby we perform illocutionary acts, is capable of instantly conveying the sound of a command, a lament, a plea, or a cry. These aesthetic qualities, when transformed by a dramatic situation and heightened by the theatrical devices of the opera house, take on a uniquely potent form.

Music-lovers expect aesthetic unity in a musical work. But according to some thinkers aesthetic unity is bound to be elusive in opera because while musical form is built up on the basis of repetitions, dramatic form is non-repetitive and one-directional (Kivy 2002: 166). Kivy may be right in thinking that an aesthetic unity of musical and dramatic values is hard to achieve in opera; but the way he pursues his argument it applies only to a sub-class of what are ordinarily called operas – namely, to those that attempt to combine closed musical forms with dramatic representation. (He restricts the term "opera" to such cases, contrasting opera with what he calls "music-drama.")

There is, however, something in the nature of all opera (music-drama as well as opera in Kivy's restricted sense) that can make aesthetic unity hard to achieve – namely, the fact that opera is a hybrid form. It can be hard to achieve an aesthetically satisfying combination of the disparate elements in this hybrid, and oftentimes the attempt fails. The problem may be entirely internal to the work, or it may concern its performability. Within the work there may be a mismatch between music and action, as some critics find to be the case in *Così fan tutte* (Kerman 1988: 91–8). Or it may be hard to find performers in whom the requisite musical and dramatic attributes are satisfactorily combined. The difficulty of satisfactorily combining opera's disparate elements has been recognized by the creators of opera themselves, particularly at times of operatic reform, when librettists and composers have had to find new ways of formulating attainable aesthetic goals, given opera's hybrid nature and its consequent liability to fall short of its aesthetic ideals.

However, an intrinsic difficulty in a medium should not be confused with a failing in the very form. For an opera to succeed in producing an aesthetic unity of its musical and dramatic elements should be viewed as an achievement.

The *combination* of opera's elements has been thought of in various ways; for example, as juxtaposition, as synthesis, or as transformation. In his article "Hybrid Art Forms," Jerrold Levinson cites some aspects of Philip Glass's *Einstein on the Beach* as instances of juxtaposition, where

> the complexity and richness function in service of an ideal not of unity, but of complete fragmentation and rampant uncoordination. Works that achieve this sort of effect – a natural one for *juxtapositional* hybrids, in which individual artistic contributions do not formally meld with their neighbors – do so through a kind of cognitive overload.
>
> (Levinson 1990: 35–6)

Levinson states that in synthesis or fusion "the objects or products of two (or more) arts are brought together in such a way that the individual components to some extent lose their original identities and are present in the hybrid in a form significantly different from that assumed in the pure state" (Levinson 1990: 31). This description is consistent with what Peter Kivy sees as the ideal of drama-made-music – namely, to find "the completest possible coalescence of musical form with musical representation" (Kivy 1988: 254). It is well illustrated in the operatic collaborations of Mozart and Da Ponte. Transformation, according to Levinson, is "closer to the synthetic model than to the juxtapositional one, but differs from the former in that the arts combined do not contribute to the result in roughly the same degree" (1990: 32).

Operas as artworks

Many different types of aesthetic property are found in opera. Some of them are properties that may be possessed by non-vocal music; for example, a whole *scena* may be structured in a way that recalls the sonata form that is familiar from instrumental music. Some of opera's aesthetic properties, such as virtuosic vocal display, are shared with non-dramatic song. Sometimes an opera exhibits aesthetic properties of a type found also in non-musical drama: spectacle and illusion, which are found in certain types of spoken theater, have always been among the aesthetic characteristics of opera. Some of opera's aesthetic properties are, however, unique to this form. They are evident in those operas, or parts of operas, that achieve a synthesis or transformation of their components. There may be a generic description that these properties share with non-operatic properties, but what makes them *aesthetic* properties is the specific sense-modalities through which they are experienced, and in the case of an operatic synthesis these sense-modalities are multiple. Rigoletto's tragedy can be described in language that would apply equally to a spoken melodrama, but its uniquely powerful aesthetic quality is something that can be experienced only in the context of Verdi's synthesis of musical and dramatic elements.

Pleasing forms, vocal display, spectacle, and illusion alone (even when combined) do not make for art. Yet opera aspires to the status of art. Bernard Williams raises a fundamental question about opera as an art form. He points out that real opera lovers really love things such as "the end of the first act of *Tosca*, which, with its mounting excitement and the superimposition of a dark baritone declamation onto the rhythm of a tolling bell and religious ritual," and he asks, given that "the powers of opera can be exercised, not just marginally but very typically, by distinctly dubious works," how it can be that opera is a serious form. He suggests that the answer lies in opera's performative character.

> At a fine operatic performance, we are conscious of the singer's achievement and of the presence of physical style and vitality, and the sense of this reinforces the drama itself. A concrete feeling of performance and of the performers' artistry is nearer the front of the mind than in other dramatic arts.
>
> (Williams 2006: 133–4).

An alternative explanation might be that, while opera aspires to be art, its repertoire of theatrical and musical devices includes many that are effectively calculated to thrill and stir the audience, regardless of whether they are deployed for artistic ends. Charles Rosen writes wittily about the tendency of nineteenth-century opera to descend into what he calls "trash," but he acknowledges that in the hands of Meyerbeer the operatic form took "a debased but effective form with moments of great power" (Rosen 1996: 645). Certainly, he does not draw the conclusion that the operatic form is inherently unartistic.

Some of the operas of Mozart, Verdi, and Wagner are recognized as great works of art. If that is so, then it must be that these works are similar in their achievements to great works of art in some other media. Philosophers, amongst others, have tried to point to these similarities in the case of particular operas.

Bernard Williams sees Mozart's *Le Nozze di Figaro* as "one of the very greatest masterpieces of realistic art," because it "not merely displays human feelings and relations in a real social context, but shows those feelings as formed and distorted by that context, and shows also how rank can itself generate rage and loneliness, while lack of it can leave room for a greater openness" (2006: 30). Williams draws attention to the ways in which Mozart added expressive depth to the libretto; for example, in "the depths of hurt and bitterness that Mozart uncovered in the recitative 'Tutto è disposto,' and the snaking unsettled aria which follows it" (26).

Williams describes the singular aesthetic character of Verdi's operas, with particular reference to *Don Carlos*:

> Verdi's expression of his characters' typically energetic and direct reaction to the circumstances, and above all Verdi's unusual expression of that, creates in the audience a feeling of liberation, a sense of committed and energetic individual action, which is deeply invigorating. This experience is the basic, central, response to Verdi's art; almost all other responses to it grow out from, are sophistications of, that one. . . . His characters do not need to be expressing sentiments in favor of liberty and honesty: the very method of expression itself conveys the importance and value of resolute action, untrammeled response to circumstance, and integrity of character. Verdi's work sometimes directly expresses the values he believed in; in its entire conception it embodies them.
>
> (55–6)

In his remarkable philosophico-musical commentary on *Tristan und Isolde*, Roger Scruton uncovers the way the composer transforms the medieval material on which he based his libretto, deepening its humanity in the process. He celebrates Wagner's gifts as a dramatist, describing the opera's first act as "a triumph of dramatic organization" (Scruton 2004: 49). He reminds us of the music's expressive powers when he describes "the simple but poignant way" in which Wagner "captures what is meant by a 'look into' another's eyes" (41). He writes of the "sheer commanding eloquence of the orchestral mirror into which Isolde sings" (50), and of "the greatest love scene in all opera" where music gives "objective form to the inner selfhood of passion" (61).

Performance practice

Among the issues here, there are questions about the meaning, the possibility, and the desirability of "authentic" performance of opera. With regard to the aesthetic viability of combining observance of musical directives with disregard for stage-directions, it is noteworthy that the question of the "authentic" performance of an opera is actually two questions – one concerning the music, the other the staging. The two main components of an operatic work (the musical directions, and the prescriptions for stage-movement and effects) are affected in different ways by the passage of time. Generally speaking the musical directions retain their authority but the stage-directions quickly lose theirs. This being so, a latter-day producer may find that, while the music still commands respect, the stage-directions do not, and so may opt to re-interpret the staging while reproducing the music.

There are artists in the opera house as well as in composers' garrets; and some individual singers, conductors, and *régisseurs* are held in high regard for the unique artistic qualities they bring to the realization of operatic works. No one would deny this status to a Callas or a Barenboim, but some writers are reluctant to accord the status of artist to an opera director. Commenting on Peter Sellars' 1996 Glyndebourne production of Handel's dramatic oratorio *Theodora*, Jerry Fodor (2007) postulates that the art of the director is to disappear; so for him an opera director such as Sellars whose work is highly visible is no artist. This opinion is widely held among a certain type of opera-lover. Against it one can argue that there are aesthetic qualities that belong to an operatic production rather than to individual performances of that production. The production's aesthetic unity, if any, will be determined among other things by what decisions have been made regarding cuts, and what accommodations have been made in production for the singers' limitations. Here the director's contributions, and those of the musical director, will be obvious to anyone who knows the opera and its performance history. The same is true of the production's quality as spectacle. This is solely the stage director's responsibility, and given that spectacle must be constantly renewed if it is to remain spectacular, directors must regularly find new ways of creating special effects. It is also the director's role to realize an overall conception of the opera in production, and thereby to guide the imagination of the audience. If operatic productions are to achieve the status of art and not simply that of historical re-presentation, then creative directorial activity is indispensable; and there is no more reason why the director's contribution should be self-concealing than there is for claiming that the performers should be transparent.

Richard Taruskin, writing about the same production of *Theodora*, sees Sellars as trying to have it both ways: "The works are updated on the stage, embalmed in the pit." Taruskin hypothesizes that this conjunction is "a perfect paradigm of post-modernism, perhaps, and yet another unmasking of the pseudo-historicism of 'Early Music'" (1995: 263–4). Leaving aside the question whether Sellars's production was actually inspired by postmodern ideas, and the question whether Early Music can justly be accused of pseudo-historicism, two other questions should be noticed here. First, there is the question of the status of the stage-directions in pieces for theatrical performance; second, there is the question whether it is aesthetically inappropriate to pay heed to an opera's musical content while paying none to its stage-directions.

Controversy surrounds the status of stage-directions in opera, as in theater generally (Thom 1993: 86). Do they carry the same authority as the written notes; for example, when the composer explicitly approves them? On one side of this debate, Philip Gossett, in his preface to Cohen and Gigou's catalog of Parisian operatic staging manuals, describes the artistic success that can result from following the original stage-directions of certain nineteenth-century operas. He writes: "I do not think it is utopian to hope for a day when knowledge of the original staging of an opera will be considered as indispensable to a modern director as is a careful reading of the libretto" (Cohen and Gigou 1986: xii). On the other side, opera director David Pountney argues that in staging operas whose plots now lack plausibility, one may have not only to ignore the original stage directions but also to consciously undermine them (Pountney 2003).

Williams argues that there is no intrinsic conflict between "authentic" musical performance and contemporary innovation in staging, and that these two can be combined by finding "visual and dramatic equivalences, which work for us, to the expressive content both of the words, and of the music as that music, partly with the help of musicological scholarship." He cites Sellars's *Theodora* as an instance where this combination produces aesthetically satisfying results (Williams 2006: 123–4).

Opera is best thought of neither as an art form nor as a form that is inimical to art, but as a form whose hybrid nature endows it with the potential to be art and also with the potential to be rubbish. The potential to be art requires a rare concurrence of circumstances if it is to be realized in performance. Not only must the work contain an artistic conception, but also the director must have found an artistic way of liberating and enhancing that conception, or transcending it, and the performers must succeed in bringing it to life on the night. And a critical audience is not purely receptive of all this, but further interprets, actively exploring unrealized potentialities.

A satisfactory philosophy of opera should provide both an ontology and an aesthetics adequate to its topic. The ontology will have to account for the network of intentional relations that connects operatic works, productions, and performances. It will need to describe the specific ways in which representation functions in opera. A suitably nuanced aesthetics of opera will pay careful attention to the aesthetics of the operatic voice, and will explain how positive aesthetic qualities can arise from opera's hybrid elements. A comprehensive philosophy of opera as a performing art will provide a theoretical framework for evaluating the role of the director, and will cover a wide spectrum of production styles, ranging from those that attempt authenticity to those that merely take an existing work as supplying "ingredients" for a newly devised piece of music-theater (Hamilton 2007: 31).

See also Appropriation and hybridity (Chapter 17), Authentic performance practice (Chapter 9), Composition (Chapter 47), Ontology (Chapter 4), Phenomenology and music (Chapter 53), Song (Chapter 40), and Wagner (Chapter 35).

References

Caplan, B. and Matheson, C. (2006) "Defending Musical Perdurantism," *British Journal of Aesthetics* 46: 59–69.

Cohen, R. and Gigou, M.-O. (1986) *Cent ans de mise-en-scène lyrique en France (env. 1830–1930)*, New York: Pendragon Press.

Dodd, J. (2007) *Works of Music: An Essay in Ontology*, Oxford: Oxford University Press.

Fodor, J. (2007) "Life in Tune," review of Williams 2006, *Times Literary Supplement*, January 19, 3–4.

Goehr, L. (2007) *The Imaginary Museum of Musical Works: An Essay in the Philosophy of Music*, rev. edn, Oxford: Oxford University Press.

Hamilton, J. (2007) *The Art of Theater*, Malden: Blackwell.

Ingarden, R. (1986) *The Work of Music and the Problem of its Identity*, trans. A. Czerniawski, Berkeley: University of California Press.

Kerman, J. (1988) *Opera as Drama*, rev. edn, Berkeley: University of California Press.

Kivy, P. (1988) *Osmin's Rage: Philosophical Reflections on Opera, Drama, and Text*, Princeton: Princeton University Press.

—— (1994) "Speech, Song, and the Transparency of the Medium: A Note on Operatic Metaphysics," *Journal of Aesthetics and Art Criticism* 52: 63–8.

—— (2002) *Introduction to a Philosophy of Music*, Oxford: Clarendon Press.

Levinson, J. (1990) *Music, Art and Metaphysics*, Ithaca: Cornell University Press.

Lewis, D.K. (1978) "Truth in Fiction," *American Philosophical Quarterly* 15: 37–46.

Lindenberger, H. (1998) *Opera in History: From Monteverdi to Cage*, Stanford: Stanford University Press.

Livingston, P. (2005) *Art and Intention*, Oxford: Clarendon Press.

Pountney D. (2003) "Directing Grand Opera: *Rienzi* and *Guillame Tell* at the Vienna State Opera," in D. Charlton (ed.) *The Cambridge Companion to Grand Opera*, Cambridge: Cambridge University Press, pp. 131–46.

Rosen, C. (1996) *The Romantic Generation: Liszt, Bellini, Schubert, Chopin, Mendelssohn, Meyerbeer, Schumann, Berlioz*, New York: Harper Collins.

Scruton, R. (2004) *Death-devoted Heart: Sex and the Sacred in Wagner's* Tristan and Isolde, Oxford: Oxford University Press.

Taruskin, R. (1995) *Text and Act: Essays on Music and Performance*, New York: Oxford University Press.

Thom, P. (1993) *For an Audience: A Philosophy of the Performing Arts*, Philadelphia: Temple University Press.

Williams, B. (2006) *On Opera*, New Haven: Yale University Press.

Wolterstorff, N. (1980) *Works and Worlds of Art*, Oxford: Oxford University Press.

42
MUSIC AND MOTION PICTURES

Noël Carroll and Margaret Moore

Over the last two decades, interest in and research on the topic of motion-picture music – the music that is part of films, television shows, and so on – has expanded dramatically. However, there has been little attention to the philosophy of motion-picture music in the analytic tradition. Nevertheless, two problems have begun to coalesce. They are:

1. What is motion-picture music?
2. Are there implicit fictional presenters of music in the storyworld of the movie?

This chapter will review the debates surrounding these problems.

What is motion-picture music?

Jeff Smith raises the question of the "ontology" of film music in an article on film music and philosophy, stating an Aristotelian desire to establish "first principles" for the study of the philosophy of film music (Smith 2009: 189). The question "What is motion-picture music?" suggests two readings. The first is an ontological question about the nature of film music, or what kind of thing it is. The second is the classificatory question of which or what things should be counted as film music. Smith writes in terms of ontology, but his project is best construed as a classificatory project. We pursue this latter question, and do not assume that film music forms a unique ontological kind.

The main thrust of Smith's discussion is a critique of William Rosar's article "Film Music – What's in a Name?" (2002), which strikes down Rosar's essentialist definition of film music. Rosar identifies film music as original music composed in a particular style for a particular film; for example, Max Steiner's score for *Gone With the Wind*. While an essentialist definition of this sort might be useful to a musicologist studying, for example, the influence of Hollywood scores on twentieth-century musical composition, a philosopher who needs a classification identifying all and only film music in order to address further philosophical problems of film music will find such a definition too restrictive. Smith offers instead a "cluster account" of film music, which "serves to identify several possible criteria for classification" (2009: 189).

Specifically, Smith offers the following criteria as contributing toward something's counting as film music:

(1) music specially composed for use as part of a recorded audio-visual medium; (2) music used to accompany cinematic depictions of peoples, places, things, ideas, or events; (3) music used to underline aspects of a film's setting; (4) music used to communicate a film character's traits; (5) music used to signify emotion or mood in a filmed scene or sequence; (6) music used to convey a film character's point of view; (7) music used to accent depicted actions in a filmed scene or sequence; (8) music used to reinforce a film's formal features, such as its editing; and (9) music that sounds like film music.

(2009: 190)

Most of these items (2–8) identify film music in terms of the role a score or musical cue serves within the larger context of the film. It is not important whether the music is originally composed for the film, or is selected or re-orchestrated from pre-existing music. It is not important whether the music is in a Romantic or popular style. Nor is it important whether the music is diegetic, that is, occurring within the world of the filmic narrative, or non-diegetic, occurring outside the fictional world. Both are equally film music, and the differences between them are analyzed according to their function within the film. The first condition covers music composed for the purpose of inclusion in a film, even if the film director ultimately decides not to use the music for its intended purpose. This means, for instance, that Alex North's original score to *2001: A Space Odyssey* is film music, even though Kubrick decided to use pre-existing music in the final cut.

While Smith is offering a cluster account of film music, not a functional definition, many of the conditions that comprise the cluster identify artistic functions music plays in films, and as a result the definition is both redundant and incomplete. It is redundant in that music that serves any of these functions can be thought of as "modifying music" (Carroll 1988: 213–25), that is, music that comments on, or shapes the viewer's perception of, elements or events of the narrative. It is incomplete because there are likely to be possible uses of music in film that have yet to be discovered.

Another problem with Smith's cluster account is that satisfying Smith's ninth criterion does not count toward something being film music. According to Berys

Gaut's "'Art' as a Cluster Concept," which Smith invokes as his model, "a criterion is simply to be understood as a property possession of which counts as a matter of conceptual necessity toward an object's falling under a concept" (2000: 26). It is hard to see how sounding like film music would count toward a piece of music being film music as a matter of conceptual necessity. If, as Rosar suggests, portions of Hindemith's *Mathis der Maler* were called film music because they sounded like film music, then, according to Smith, this counts toward *Mathis der Maler*'s actually being film music. Similarly, by now, after so many exorcism movies, the *Dies Irae* sounds like film music, but it is no more film music now than it was before the invention of motion pictures. This condition also initiates an unwanted regress. If other works by Hindemith sound like *Mathis der Maler*, they sound like film music, and so might be counted as film music. Smith claims that none of his criteria is necessary *or* sufficient for a thing counting as film music, but without some antecedent knowledge of which things are film music, there is no principled reason that satisfying any criterion or subset of criteria is not sufficient for being film music.

Instead, we offer the following analysis:

x is motion-picture music if:

1. x is a piece of music composed for use in a movie (e.g. Steiner's scores to *King Kong* and *Casablanca*, and Bernard Herrmann's score to *Psycho*, but also North's compositions intended to be included in *2001: A Space Odyssey*),

or

2. x is an arrangement or re-orchestration of existing music made specifically for inclusion in or accompaniment to a movie (e.g. Johnny Green's arrangement of Gershwin's *American in Paris* for Vincente Minnelli's film with the same title),

or

3. x is a recording of pre-existing music appearing in a movie (e.g. numerous instances of popular songs used diegetically or non-diegetically in films such as *Pulp Fiction*).

If it is music in a movie, it is motion-picture music. This account includes everything that Rosar and Smith include in their accounts, but is sufficiently general that any future use movie-makers discover for music will automatically fall under it.

What exactly is the purpose of this analysis? Does this account identify objects metaphysically distinct from all other things? There is a reason to think that this could not be the case. On this account, every piece of non-original music that is used in a movie automatically becomes motion-picture music. Thus, Barber's *Adagio for Strings* became a particularly well-known case of motion-picture music when it was used in Oliver Stone's *Platoon*. When high-school orchestras around the country perform this piece, are they now performing motion-picture music? In a trivial sense, yes. But the vast majority of previously composed music that is used in a film retains whatever status it had prior to its inclusion. It is a notoriously difficult task to correctly state what sort of ontological thing a work of music is, but it seems that the Barber *Adagio* is still a piece of concert music, whatever *that* is, even if it also becomes motion-picture music. Are we forced to say that musical works used in films take on multiple ontological identities, or that there are now two Barber *Adagio*s, the motion-picture music and the concert piece? These questions seem motivated by the need for theoretical precision, and not by a serious problem in ontology. To avoid the unwanted consequence of large quantities of music retroactively turning into motion-picture music, the account on offer specifies that the token of the musical type *in the movie* is motion-picture music, *when it is in the movie*. Because a movie soundtrack includes a particular musical performance, it is this performed token used with the movie that becomes motion-picture music. But other tokens of a piece and the type itself – even other instances of the particular recording – remain unaffected.

This definition is meant to be deflationary: any and all music appearing in (or intended to appear in) a movie is motion-picture music. We have not learned anything interesting about motion-picture music from this definition, other than what the extension of the term is. The more interesting philosophical questions involving motion-picture music involve exactly how it functions in the film, and we will now turn to one of these.

The implicit fictional presenter

This next issue is embedded in a larger discussion about whether motion pictures have implicit fictional narrators, or as Jerrold Levinson prefers to label them, implicit fictional presenters (Levinson 1996).

What is an implicit fictional presenter? The easiest way to get a handle upon this term is to contrast the implicit fictional presenter with the explicit fictional presenter. In the newsreel segment of *Citizen Kane*, the breathless voice-over commentary that accompanies footage of the life of Charles Foster Kane is an example of explicit fictional narration. The speaker is a narrator because he tells us the story of Kane's life and he is fictional because he is a character in the fiction. Presumably, other characters, such as Bernstein, could interact with him.

However, there are also explicit fictional narrators in movies with whom the other fictional characters cannot interact. For example, the voice-over commentary by Orson Welles in *The Magnificent Ambersons* is not and could not be heard by the fictional inhabitants of the storyworld; yet Welles *qua* narrator is nevertheless a fictional being, rather than a flesh and blood person, and it is his role to narrate the fiction. These fictional beings are explicit, since we can hear them loud and clear, and we have no need to infer their presence in the film. An implicit fictional narrator, on the other hand, is one whose narrating activity we need to posit in order to explain something.

Putatively, we need to posit this fictional entity because every narrative has a narrator. Of course, the requirement that narratives possess narrators does not automatically get us implicit fictional narrators, even in cases where the story lacks an explicit fictional narrator. Why? Because there are other candidates who might fulfill the required role of narrator. The first is the actual filmmaker (or filmmakers), the person(s) who made the movie and was paid by the studio.

And if it is not the actual filmmaker, then perhaps the narrator is the implied filmmaker – that is, the filmmaker as she manifests herself in the motion picture. The implied filmmaker may, in fact, share all of her beliefs, desires, attitudes, allegiances, and so forth with the actual filmmaker, but it is also possible that she may not. The actual filmmaker may be a pessimist, yet since she is making a romantic comedy, she needs to adopt the perspective of an optimist. In other words, the implied filmmaker is how the actual filmmaker strikes us on the basis of the way in which she has shaped the motion picture in terms of its tone, its structures, its emphases, ellipses, etc. The implied filmmaker is the agency to whom we assign responsibility for the way in which the fiction is constructed. So if narratives require narrators and if the actual filmmaker is not available for the role, might not the implied filmmaker be up to the task?

The defender of implicit fictional narration denies that either the actual filmmaker or the implied filmmaker can function as the narrator of a fictional story. Why?

To begin with the actual filmmaker, she lives, so to speak, on the wrong side of the fiction operator. The filmmaker makes it true in the movie version of *Pride and Prejudice* that Darcy slights Elizabeth at the ball. She does this by mandating us to imagine that Darcy slights Elizabeth at the ball. It is true in the fiction that Darcy slights Elizabeth and yet it cannot be the actual filmmaker who is *telling us that it is true that* Darcy slights Elizabeth, since the actual filmmaker does not believe this insofar as she does not believe that Darcy or Elizabeth exist.

However, if there is no explicit fictional narrator reporting this state of affairs, who is? Remember that supposedly someone has to be telling us what is true in the storyworld, since narratives require narrators and assertions require assertors. So, there must be some narrative agency (aka the implicit fictional narrator) who is asserting thus and so inside the fiction, since only narrators inside the fiction are positioned metaphysically in such a way to *assert* thus and so from thence.

A parallel argument can be leveled at the idea that the implied filmmaker is the relevant narrator. The implied filmmaker is responsible for the way in which the fiction is *qua* movie fiction. The implied filmmaker is, we may say, the teller or presenter of the *fiction*. But it is being reported to us from within the fictional world that Darcy slighted Elizabeth. Yet if there is no explicit fictional narrator to report this truth to us from within the fiction and the implied narrator is blocked from asserting that "Darcy slights Elizabeth" for the same reason that the actual author is blocked as the possible narrating source, then we are once again left with the question of identifying the narrative agency, since narratives require narrators. So, it is urged that we must posit an implicit fictional storyteller as the pertinent narrative agency.

Of course, motion pictures narrate not only by means of words, but also by images, both visual and aural. The motion picture tells us its story by presenting us with a succession of images. In *Strangers on a Train*, first we see a man, Bruno, stretching his arm to retrieve a cigarette lighter from a sewer. Next we see a tennis match in Forest Hills, New York. The story, in large measure, is presented to us through images. But who is presenting us with these images? Who is giving access to the visage of Bruno straining to reach the lighter? Who is, in effect, inviting us to "Behold Bruno"?

It cannot be Alfred Hitchcock. Hitchcock can only present us with the image of Robert Walker, the actor who played Bruno. Yet, supposedly, Bruno is being presented to us visually so that we can see him imaginarily. Who is doing this? It must be an implicit fictional presenter – here we say *presenter* rather than *narrator* in order to acknowledge the fact that much of the "telling" in motion pictures is done through showing or presenting.

Motion pictures not only present actors who play fictional characters but they also present additional elements of the narrated episodes, such as the perspective from which they are seen and the sounds that accompany them. Of course, the sounds internal to the narrative are not the only sounds that movie audiences hear. Much of the soundtrack typically consists of non-diegetic music – that is, music which is not internal to the storyworld, but which nevertheless can comment upon its events and inflect the ways in which we perceive them. But, who, then, presents said narrated events replete with their non-diegetic accompaniments?

Specifically, what is the relation between non-diegetic movie music and the implicit fictional presenter? Just as the implicit fictional presenter asserts the existence of certain states of affairs in the fictional world by presenting them to us visually, so certain states of affairs can be revealed to obtain in the storyworld by means of the non-diegetic music that the implicit fictional presenter addresses to us. Non-diegetic music, for instance, may indicate by means of dissonant music that a character is fraught with inner turmoil. But how did we gain access to this truth within the fictional world? The implicit fictional presenter informed us by means of the non-diegetic dissonant music.

As we saw in the previous section, movie music may perform a variety of functions. A number of these functions have to do with alerting the audience to the way in which things actually stand in the fictional world. In this respect, the implicit fictional presenter may be said to tell us something about, or inform us about, or report about states of affairs in the fictional world. That is, by way of non-diegetic music, the implicit fictional presenter asserts truths that obtain within the scope of the fiction operator.

There are a number of functions by means of which the implicit fictional presenter may report, through the use of non-diegetic music, how things stand in the world of the fiction. For example, the presenter may reveal, qualify, under-line, or corroborate that a character is in such and such a psychological state. Perhaps her dreaminess is signaled by the use of strings in a high tessitura. Or the implicit fictional presenter may use non-diegetic music to foreshadow an event; often impending doom is indicated by the use of an ominous minor key. In general, the fictional presenter signifies that an event or an object is of greater importance than one might initially assume by orchestrating a scene with a pro-nounced flourish. Or the implicit fictional presenter may mobilize non-diegetic music to establish his or her attitude toward some character or event. In *Psycho*, the implicit fictional narrator presents his shock and terror at the murder of the detective by means of Bernard Herrmann's shrieking violins. And, in addition, the presenter may alert us to events in the fiction through the score, as in the case of the leitmotif of the shark in *Jaws*. Because these usages of non-diegetic music make a difference in what we take to be reports of what is true in the fictional world, we purportedly need the implicit fictional presenter as a narrative agency. Sometimes this information arrives subliminally, but often we are quite aware of it, despite the old saw that audiences do not hear movie music (Gorbman 1987).

One problem with the very idea of the implicit fictional presenter is that often things are revealed in fictions of which it is given that no one in the fictional world is aware. For example, in one episode of the television program *Six Feet Under*, we see the character Nate bury his dead wife out in the desert. It is given in the fiction that there are no other witnesses. But if the implicit fictional presenter is a denizen of the fiction, then there was at least one witness. Thus, positing the implicit fictional presenter can lead to contradictions (Currie 1995: 173–4).

One way to patch up the theory in order to avoid this problem is to deny that the implicit fictional presenter observes the events recounted. Jerrold Levinson, for example, regards the implicit fictional presenter as "a kind of perceptual pilot through the film world, rather than as an observer of it whom we opportunisti-cally inhabit" (1996: 254). Quoting George Wilson, Levinson repeats: "the nar-rator is a fictional figure who, at each moment of the film, asserts the existence of certain fictional states of affairs by showing them to the audience demonstra-tively; that is, by ostending them within and by means of the boundaries of the screen" (1996: 254). The implicit fictional presenter does not observe the things he points out, but only points to them in a way that implies "Behold."

Yet it is a bit strange to think of a person-like being, fictional or otherwise, who points to things that it cannot see. However, even if the implicit fictional presenter does not witness that which he or she shows, it still is not clear that the *Six Feet Under* counterexample can be circumvented so easily. For surely, if there is such a thing as an implicit fictional presenter acting as our perceptual pilot – showing us this and then that in the storyworld – then the implicit fictional presenter must be cognizant of that to which he is drawing our attention.

And this then allows us to reframe the *Six Feet Under* example. As the episode establishes the case, no one in the world of the story knows where Nate has buried his wife. However, if there is an implicit fictional presenter, then there is someone – a fictional narrator – in the fiction who is cognizant that Nate has buried his wife under a tree in the desert. At this point, we may be told that the implicit fictional presenter is not a cognizer. But if the implicit fictional narrator is not a cognizer, can this creature still be thought of as a narrator? A narrator is presumably person-like, especially with respect to possessing the cognitive wherewithal to do things such as telling, asserting, reporting, and so forth. So either the implicit fictional narrator is cognizant of the location of Nate's burial of his wife, thereby contradicting the story being told, or the implicit fictional narrator is bereft of cognitive powers, in which case the implicit fictional narrator does not appear to be a narrator.

At this point, an attempt might be made to balkanize the storyworld ontologically. A distinction might be drawn within the fictional domain between the world of the story and the world of the film (cf. Levinson 1993: 71–2). The world of the story is where characters such as Nate live. None of those characters, save Nate, is cognizant of what he has done with his wife's body. But there is also the fictional world of the film in which facts about the implicit fictional presenter are established. Yet this distinction not only seems ad hoc, but also violates the principle defended by friends of the implicit fictional presenter that the implicit fictional presenter and the other fictional characters are all on the same level.

The problems with the implicit fictional narrator broached so far apply to every channel of implicit fictional presentation. They pertain to the way the implicit fictional presenter might disclose something thought to be unknown by anyone in the fiction by visual or aural means – by means of a close up or some non-diegetic music. Yet there also seem to be special problems that arise when we focus on the implicit fictional presenter's use of non-diegetic music. This music does not belong to the fiction. Putatively, it is unheard by those who live inside the fiction operator. How does the implicit fictional presenter have access to it and how does said presenter wield what he cannot hear in such a way as to reveal things in the domain of the fiction?

That is, how can you assert the existence of certain states of affairs in the storyworld *by means of* music you do not or cannot hear? Maybe one way to deal with this problem is to develop the suggestion by George Wilson that we think of the implicit fictional narrator on the model of documentary filmmakers (2006: 194–7). When we digest a fiction film, we imagine that we are watching a documentary made within the world of the fiction by the implicit fictional presenter or a team of them. This then can be used to handle the question of how the implicit fictional presenter is able to wield the non-diegetic music that seemed so mysterious above. Simply put, the implicit fictional presenter has laid a soundtrack down on his documentary film.

But are we to imagine that we are seeing documentary films before the advent of cinema? Watching *Ben Hur* would require us to imagine the existence of cinema before the existence of cinema (Currie 1995: 173; Carroll 2006: 179)! Moreover, the documentary hypothesis would not really dispel problems of the sort engendered by *Six Feet Under*, since the hypothesis would require that an entire motion picture crew saw Nate, knew what he did and where he did it, despite the story's implication that no one did.

At this point, in order to block counterexamples such as *Ben Hur* but also cases such as *Six Feet Under*, it may be proposed that the implicit fictional presenters are not to be thought of as people. They are some kind of natural iconic recording devices, like mirrors, or at least the mirrors possessed by wicked witches (Wilson 2006: 195). They imprint images and presumably sounds, but without human intervention. Because these devices existed from the beginning of time, the existence of "documentaries" emerging from within fictions whose events antedate the advent of cinema are not problematic. Moreover, since these natural iconic devices are not person-like but sheer physical processes, they do not contradict the implications of films in which the events being shown are given as neither seen nor cognized by anyone.

However, this raises the question, once again, of whether they are narrators. The friends of the implicit fictional presenter are very skeptical of the notion that movies might narrate themselves – a view propounded by David Bordwell (1986: 61–6). Yet is not the notion of natural iconic recording devices that serve up the likes of an episode of *Six Feet Under* precariously close to the notion that movies narrate themselves?

One way to deflect this line of objection to the supposition of natural iconic recording devices is to claim that we need not question the inner workings of these devices – we need not worry about whether they are person-like or whether the way they operate is compatible with the minimal requirements of what counts as a narrator (Wilson 2006: 196). We need merely suppose they work.

For example, in the old *Flash Gordon* series, there is a viewing machine that allows you to see anywhere in the universe by simply turning it on. It is just given that this is how the machine operates. It is silly to bring questions about actual-world physics to bear on the world of Flash Gordon – likewise for questions about how the natural iconic recorders function.

Nevertheless, this argument rides upon a false analogy. It is true that the viewing machine in the *Flash Gordon* series is mysterious. After all, how could there be recording devices at every point in the universe? But within the fiction, it is *explicitly* given that these contraptions work as represented. So we agree with this supposition, just as we agree that vampires have the potential to be immortal. Where we are explicitly told in the fiction or genre to waive our presuppositions about how we believe the world works, we do so.

But what about when we are not explicitly told to waive our real-world presuppositions with regard to the fictional domain? What are we to think when the room that is filling up with water has entrapped the heroine? Well, obviously, that she will drown if she is submerged for too long. Why do we suppose that? Because our default heuristic when following fictions is to bring to bear on the fiction all the presumptions we make about the actual world, *unless told otherwise*, either within the fiction itself, or by its genre, or its historical context. That is, a realistic heuristic prevails, unless we are told to suspend it, as we are in the case of undying vampires (Walton 1990: 144–50).

But what does this have to do with the debate about our implicit fictional iconic recorders? Namely, that they do not enjoy the same privileges as do the video contraptions in Flash Gordon's universe. We are explicitly instructed that Flash's viewing devices work. In short, an *explicit* avowal or straightforward implication is required to withdraw the realistic heuristic (Gaut 2004: 237–46). Nevertheless, this is precisely what is not forthcoming with respect to an *implicit* fictional presenter, whether an implicit documentarian or even someone or something more exiguous. For, they are, by definition, *implicit* (Carroll 2009: 204).

But since we have not been explicitly told to waive the realistic heuristic with regard to these alleged fictional presenters, it is open to us to ask about their nature and to question, specifically, whether a story can be told about them which explains how, although putatively sheer physical processes, they can still count as narrators.

Moreover, although it may be possible to imagine that the individual shots in a documentary could be produced by some natural iconic image-maker, such as a mirror, it is much harder to imagine how an entire film, edited in a narratively intelligible fashion, could be produced by means of a sheer natural process. And undoubtedly even more daunting will be imagining that an entire non-diegetic musical track could be affixed to the visuals with such synchronized precision as a result of the interaction of blind natural forces.

At this juncture, friends of implicit fictional narration will demand to know who is narrating the story, if we rid ourselves of the implicit fictional presenter. Yet here it pays to ask ourselves whether or not we dismissed the possibility too quickly that it might be the actual or implied filmmaker, or some combination of the two. These options were rejected earlier because it was claimed that in order for things to be true in the fiction, there would have to be some narrative agency inside the fictional world that is responsible for reporting or asserting or presenting those truths. But why accept the proposition that there must be an act of asserting or reporting or telling inside the fiction in order for things to be true in the fiction?

Rather it is the actual filmmaker, or the actual filmmaker in concert with the implied filmmaker, who does this. They make this and that true in the fiction by mandating that we imagine (i.e. entertain as unasserted) certain propositional contents. For example, it is true in the fiction *The Birds* that Melanie Daniels is attacked in the attic because Alfred Hitchcock and his team of fictioneers have mandated that we imagine the propositional content: "that Melanie Daniels is attacked in the attic." Moreover, the various functions of non-diegetic movie music that friends of the implicit fictional presenter attribute to "him" can easily be attributed to the actual filmmaker or the actual filmmaker in combination with the implied filmmaker. It is Max Steiner who alerts us to the onset of *King Kong* by means of the non-diegetic music that imitates his footfalls. Steiner achieves this by mandating that we imagine that it is true in the fiction that something is coming the lovely Miss Darrow's way.

In other words, there is no pressure here to presume that there are mute acts of assertion going on within the fictional world. Thus there is no reason to posit an implicit fictional presenter as the narrator. The actual filmmaker, or the implied filmmaker, or the two in concert are sufficient to account for the narration of the movie, unless one is equivocating on the notion of a narrator by taking it to be equivalent to a teller or reporter, rather than merely being the creator of the narrative. But it is surely only on the basis of the latter sense that we concur that every narrative has a narrator.

Moreover, in the case of non-diegetic music, it seems far less strained to attribute it to the narrative agency of the actual movie-makers, perhaps in combination with the implied movie-makers, just because there are no soundtracks in the world of the fiction for the allegedly implicit fictional presenters to manipulate.

See also Definition (Chapter 1), Performances and recordings (Chapter 8), and Ontology (Chapter 4).

References

Bordwell, D. (1986) *Narration and the Fiction Film*, Madison: University of Wisconsin Press.

Carroll, N. (1988) *Mystifying Movies: Fads and Fallacies in Contemporary Film Theory*, New York: Columbia University Press.

—— (2006) "Film/Narrative: Introduction," in N. Carroll and J. Choi (eds) *The Philosophy of Film and Motion Pictures*, Oxford: Blackwell, pp. 175–84.

—— (2009) "Narration," in P. Livingston and C. Plantinga (eds) *The Routledge Companion to the Philosophy of Film*, London: Routledge, pp. 196–206.

Currie, G. (1995) *Image and Mind: Film, Philosophy, and Cognitive Science*, Cambridge: Cambridge University Press.

Gaut, B. (2000) "'Art' as a Cluster Concept," in N. Carroll (ed.) *Theories of Art Today*, Madison: University of Wisconsin Press, pp. 25–44.

—— (2004) "The Philosophy of the Movies: Cinematic Narration," in P. Kivy (ed.) *The Blackwell Guide to Aesthetics*, Oxford: Blackwell, pp. 230–53.

Gorbman, C. (1987) *Unheard Melodies*, London: British Film Institute.

Levinson, J. (1993) "Seeing, Imaginarily, at the Movies," *Philosophical Quarterly* 43: 70–8.

—— (1996) "Film Music and Narrative Agency," in D. Bordwell and N. Carroll (eds) *Post-Theory*, Madison: University of Wisconsin Press, pp. 248–82.

Rosar, W. (2002) "Film Music – What's in a Name?" *Journal of Film Music* 1: 1–18.

Smith, J. (2009) "Music," in P. Livingston and C. Plantinga (eds) *The Routledge Companion to Philosophy and Film*, New York: Routledge, pp. 184–95.

Walton, K. (1990) *Mimesis as Make-Believe: On the Foundations of the Representational Arts*, Cambridge: Harvard University Press.

Wilson, G. (2006) "*Le Grand Imagier* Steps Out," in N. Carroll and J. Choi (eds) *The Philosophy of Film and Motion Pictures*, Oxford: Blackwell, pp. 185–99.

Further reading

Kania, A. (2005) "Against the Ubiquity of Fictional Narrators," *Journal of Aesthetics and Art Criticism* 63: 47–54. (Argues against the necessity of positing fictional narrators in every narrative fiction.)

43

MUSIC AND DANCE

Robynn J. Stilwell

Thinking about music and dance has existed largely in negative space in Western culture. The *International Encyclopedia of Dance* (Cohen et al. 1998) contains no article on philosophy (tellingly, there *is* an article on aesthetics, the most "embodied" branch of philosophy); conversely, there is no mention of dance in the article on philosophy in the *New Grove Dictionary of Music and Musicians* (Sadie 2001). Large-scale works of music may contain movements that are called, well, "movements," composed of gestures arranged in patterns rooted in dance, yet musical thinking in the past couple of centuries has expunged almost all but these linguistic traces.

Western musical philosophy since the Enlightenment has often been premised upon music's ineffability and sublimity, its seeming ability to appeal directly to the mind; the "vulgar" traces of the body were almost always denied or ignored. This conception of absolute music – music without external reference – underlay the nineteenth-century symphony. This genre, which came to signify the highest musical accomplishment, is one in which "abstract" architectural edifices were built on the basic floor-plans of social dance while ballet developed as an independent theatrical art. The twentieth century produced thoughtful and musically adept choreographers such as Isadora Duncan, George Balanchine, Martha Graham, and Katherine Dunham; but while practitioners and critics were expanding both the physical and the intellectual horizons of the dance, musical thinking was still, primarily, grounded in the nineteenth-century ethos. Not until the end of the twentieth century did thoroughgoing philosophical and analytical writing about dance, and its relationship to music, start to appear.

Francis Sparshott, a rarity among philosophers in having written extensively on dance, posits that music has so much intellectual theory, and thus heft, because its materials are so artificial (constructed from insubstantial but scientifically amenable acoustic events), that theory is a way of grasping music's substance. Dance, conversely, has so little theory because its materials are the most familiar – the human body and its gestures, which seem transparent and self-evident. Music required a theoretical apparatus, based on mathematical proportion and thus, both literally and figuratively, rationality (Sparshott 1988: 90–1).

Dominant Western conceptions of music and dance derive from the Greeks. Thinkers, makers, and doers of the dance have been concerned with three fundamental – and broadly overlapping – areas of inquiry: the relationship of music and dance, their origins and connections to the other arts; the body – the medium, source, and agent of dance; and choreography – the specific, aesthetic union of music and movement.

The special relationship

> From its birth, music has registered the rhythms of the human body[,] of which it is the complete and idealised sound image.
>
> (Jacques-Dalcroze 1980: 7)

> Music . . . is the dance of the inner life, and its outward manifestation is dance.
>
> (Sparshott 1995: 222)

The nature of the connection of dance to music through the medium of the human body is at the heart of almost all philosophy regarding dance. Does dance arise from the body's response to music, or is music the audible trace of bodily movement? Even when addressed by science – listening to music lights up parts of the brain associated with both emotion and movement (Levitin 2006: ch. 6) – the origins of these intimately related arts tends to regress to a chicken-or-egg argument, a function, perhaps, of unnecessary boundaries.

For the Greeks, all arts were "of the muses," and the muse Terpsichore's art comprised both music and dance in a single, inseparable ideal of choral dance – a unitary concept common to many, if not most, cultures around the world. The differentiations for Plato were of degree rather than kind: not "music" and "dance," but "play" and "discipline," "gymnastics" (sheer activity) and "mimesis" (activity with meaning) (Plato 1900: bk. 2).

The impulse to dance and sing is natural in the young of all creatures; where humans differ is in the ability to create order and to pass on that knowledge. Ordered motion generates "rhythm," the mingling of voices creates "harmony," and the two together form "choric song" (Plato 1900: 664e–665a). Ordering requires discipline, and that discipline provides pleasure in achievement: the educated can sing and dance *well*. But is what they sing and dance *good*? For Plato, that distinction is based not on execution, but intent. His arts are mimetic – they represent, or are expressive of, emotions, states, actions; whether they represent images of virtue or vice determines their goodness (655d–656a). However, Plato opens a thin crack into which Western culture will eventually insert a wedge; choric art is ideally integrated, but he distinguishes between the arts of music, dance, and poetry, and notes that an imbalance can produce unpleasant results (669b–670b). For Aristotle, the distinction between the arts is more subtle: they differ in their medium, the objects, and the manner of imitation, though in each case imitation is produced by rhythm, language, or harmony, either singly or combined (Aristotle 1984: 1447a14–1447b29).

The mimetic principle held sway in Western music, which was ideally expressive of text, until its rapid overturn around the turn of the nineteenth century, as idealism overtook materialism (Bonds 1997). A subtext to the revolution in musical aesthetics which led to the elevation of abstract music over texted or programmatic (mimetic) music was the gradually growing distrust of or disgust with the body during the Renaissance and Reformation, enshrined in the mind/body split of the Enlightenment.

Music's lack of specific meaning, which had been seen as a liability, was suddenly its strength, providing its ability to convey the inexpressible, ineffable, and the sublime, transcending body and word. Without text or program, however, music needed structure, and this came from the human body it was "transcending": the voice or word, and the body or dance. The essential unity of poetry, music, and dance is found in the inextricable interpenetration of their principles: poetry depends on meter and repetition with variation (rhythm), rhyming and assonance (sound, not meaning), and its rhetorical flourishes rely on higher order processes, such as the "rhyming" of ideas through unexpected but satisfying juxtaposition (Ratner 1980; Adorno 2002c). Patterns of repetition and contrast create the pulse of the dance, and the musical forms that supported abstract musical expression were rooted in Renaissance dance forms: the minuet and trio retained the name and rhythms of the dance, and their rounded binary form lies at the heart of the symphonic sonata form. Sonata form itself is a dramatic principle, the interaction of characters or themes in a scheme of exposition, development, and recapitulation that one can trace directly to Aristotle's conception of tragedy.

Idealism was primarily a Germanic philosophy, in which Richard Wagner was certainly steeped, but his conception of *Gesamtkunstwerk* respects the Grecian unity. He analogizes the severing of the individual arts from each other with the Tower of Babel (Wagner 1993: 104), but his language is laden with dance imagery: "By their nature [the arts] are inseparable without disbanding the stately minuet of Art" (95). Wagner desires re-integration, but still sees music as the transcendent art. While he famously hails Beethoven's Seventh Symphony as the "apotheosis of the dance" (124), the Ninth is a greater achievement because it "anchors" itself in the "Word" and in doing so surpasses, by embodying, the other arts (126–7). Although his argument borders on logical implosion, it nevertheless fuses both philosophical strains: integration and transcendence.

Wagner's idealistic fusion was a significant influence on subsequent generations of artists, not least the American dancer Isadora Duncan, who took her inspiration from the Greeks, but explicitly filtered through "the German Masters": "Beethoven created the Dance in mighty rhythm, Wagner in sculptural form, Nietzsche in Spirit. Nietzsche created the dancing philosopher" (Duncan 1969:

48). For Duncan, the impulse to dance was not only "natural" – to be found in the human body – but also in nature itself: "Man has not invented the harmony of music. It is one of the underlying principles of life" (1969: 78). This conceptual elision of music, dance, and life is prevalent in the early twentieth century, particularly through the metaphor of rhythm, from Emile Jacques-Dalcroze's "rhythmique," a force analogous to electricity or to the chemical and physical forces of nature (Spector 1990: 116), to the driving, inspirational energy evoked by lyricist Ira Gershwin's use of the word "rhythm" (see Crawford 1993: 219). Like the later twentieth-century concept of "soul" (the African-American roots of both are probably not coincidental), this "rhythm" came from life and gave life to dance.

Duncan descends from the dominant Germanic musico-philosophical line; but, for most of the nineteenth century, theatrical dance had followed a more southerly route. Ballet arose from social dances codified in the French court of the seventeenth and eighteenth centuries, and became increasingly professional by the nineteenth. It developed as an independent art relatively late, emerging from *divertissement* within opera to a free-standing entity near mid-century. French dancer and choreographer Marius Petipa almost single-handedly created the classical ballet when he was recruited to the Imperial Theater of St. Petersburg, Russia. The two lines converge when Isadora Duncan's visit to Russia in 1904 significantly impacts many artists, including Mikhail Fokine, the first choreographer of impresario Serge Diaghilev's *Ballets Russes*. This company of Russian dancers in Paris (1909–29) worked with the most prominent composers and artists of the day, setting the foundation for the coming century of dance.

Many find in the *Ballets Russes* the closest realization of the *Gesamtkunstwerk* yet achieved – Sparshott posits that these ballets "fail" in being collaborative, rather than being the product of one artist. Diaghilev may have assembled the artists, but he would not have claimed the kind of authorship Wagner envisioned. Sparshott suggests that the company's collaborative aesthetic did not serve as the model it might have because of a philosophical clash with the individualistic mainstream of modernist art (1988: 69), though its impact was nonetheless tremendous.

One of Duncan's principal influences on Fokine, and by extension the *Ballets Russes* and its progeny, was that she did not shy away from dancing to "great music": Beethoven, Chopin, Schubert, even Wagner, implicitly restoring equality between music and dance, though this was – next to her scanty attire – the most controversial aspect of Duncan's art. Despite this redressed imbalance, the modernist ideal of individual expression (essentially an intensification rather than rejection of major Romantic principles, such as organicism and the importance of innovative "genius") emphasized division, a policing of the boundaries between and even within arts.

Sparshott has aptly compared music and dance to the hydrogen and oxygen atoms in a molecule of water (1995: 227), but this concise image has not impeded him from making some of the most nuanced examinations of the music-dance compound:

> It is often said that dance movement is characteristically movement patterned by music – or, more precisely, since one can dance without music, movement patterned as if by music. But really, dance is in some respects prior to abstract music. Time as the measure of movement depends on what is moved, and in music as pure form nothing is really moved. Should we not say that what singers and players of instruments do is already to dance, in that they perform the dance that will embody the form that the music identifies? No, better not; but one sees the point of saying it.
>
> (1988: 374–5)

The body

The human body is the medium of dance: its material, its means of communication, and the substance through which it propagates. For Wagner, this made dance the most realistic of all the arts (1993: 100). For Louis Horst, Martha Graham's musical director and mentor, the physical manifestations of dance and the basic elements of music are equivalent: rhythm is rhythm, whether manifested in sound or motion; melody is linear contour, an outline traced in space; and harmony is voice, "that inner muscular quality which is the physical essence of movement" (Horst and Russell 1967: 30) and realized in the body as "understand[ing] through contrast" (33) – what is dissonance and resolution in music becomes muscular tension and release in the body.

Horst, like Duncan, looked back beyond the received conventions of art to previous eras for his concepts. The dancing body had grown increasingly incorporeal as ballet became an art: the impetus was increasingly "up," toward lightness and ease, an aristocratic bearing unencumbered by gravity. Pointe shoes decreased the body's contact with the ground, and long tulle tutus hid the muscular work of the legs to heighten the illusion of weightlessness; dancers of Romantic ballet portrayed ethereal characters – sylphs, wilis, ghost nuns. In Petipa's classical ballet, the body regained substance and muscularity, though still through graceful characters such as swans and princesses; dance movements became more defined, and tutus were shortened for the display of athletic legs.

These bodies were disciplined, as Plato had counseled, but Isadora Duncan found them ugly, distorted by the artificiality of their training and dress. This reaction against ballet was a strong feature in modern dance; Duncan's striking recollection of seeing Eleanora Duse on stage was not about the actress's movement, but how her presence grew in stillness (Duncan 1969: 121). This outward manifestation of the inward, a return to the body and "weight," recurs frequently in modernist dance aesthetics: in the "primitive" stamping of Nijinsky's *Rite of*

Spring, in Graham's psychological dramas, in Katherine Dunham's anthropological exploration of African roots of Caribbean dance.

Ironically, it is Duncan who predicts the direction ballet (and music) will take in the twentieth century by denying ballet's ability to convey the new American. In hindsight, her words in "I See America Dancing" evoke both Aaron Copland and the Balanchine dancer: "Long-legged strong boys and girls" will dance to music that will "gush forth from the great stretches of earth, rain down from the vast sky spaces of stars, and the American will be expressed in some mighty music that will shape its chaos to Harmony" (Duncan 1969: 49).

Duncan's death comes in the same year as George Balanchine's *Apollo*: 1927. Although based in the classical Russian technique, *Apollo* presages the new, clean, athletic, disciplined, and fast American ballet. The critical inspiration for Balanchine came in the restraint of Stravinsky's music: "it seemed to tell me that I could dare not to use everything, that I, too, could eliminate" (Balanchine 1949: 81). Complementarily, American composer Elliot Carter cites Balanchine's ever-unfolding transition from one gesture to another as a key inspiration for his own composition (in Mason 1991: 166) – music is not always the leading partner.

Dance in the new American century, however, was not merely an elevated art on the theatrical stage, but also a popular pleasure, one heavily influenced by an African-American culture and aesthetic of bodily movement far removed from the one to which Duncan aspired, her "natural" beauty conditioned by her Euro-American culture. Technological advances in communications and travel after the First World War brought various dialects of body language into more vigorous contact, impossible to separate from their source cultures, whether the stain of slavery in the US or the rise of fascism in Europe, each providing a particular filter through which to view the moving body. Although himself an enthusiastic (and apparently skilled) ballroom dancer, émigré philosopher Theodor Adorno viewed the jazz dancing of his adopted American home in the 1930s with disgust; for him, the music contained no "authentic" complexity and therefore no intellectual content. The sheer appeal to the body created in the "jitterbuggers" a "spite" that they turned upon themselves in frustration:

> They cannot be altogether the spineless lot of fascinated insects they are called and like to style themselves. They need their will, if only in order to down the all too conscious premonition that something is "phony" with their pleasure.
>
> (Adorno 2002b: 468)

Adorno's own experiences could cast a pall on otherwise telling historical and sociological observations of the swing era into which he had been rather unceremoniously dumped, perhaps most dramatically in his quasi-geometric "proof" of jazz = fascism:

The effectiveness of the principle of march music in jazz is evident. The basic rhythm of the continuo and the bass drum is completely in sync with march rhythm, and, since the introduction of six-eight time, jazz could be transformed effortlessly into a march. The connection here is historically grounded; one of the horns used in jazz is called the Sousaphone, after the march composer. Not only the saxophone has been borrowed from the military orchestra; the entire arrangement of the jazz orchestra, in terms of the melody, bass, *obbligati,* and mere filler instruments, is identical to that of the military band. Thus jazz can be easily adapted for use by fascism.

(Adorno 2002a: 486)

The jazz band, he notes correctly, is rooted in the military, and each step in his historical march is essentially correct, but that last one is a doozy.

Whether as the other, the beloved object, or an accent or slang, the vernacular is inescapable in the twentieth century, always in productive tension with the cultivated. Popular music, largely African-American or otherwise "ethnic," brought the body back into music in ways in which hegemonic European culture had largely effaced. Dance historian Constance Valis Hill observes that some French-based choreographers of the 1920s adopted only the superficial "primitive" aspects of jazz, but others went deeper:

They explored the structural and dynamic aspects of jazz music such as speed, dissonance, polytonality and polyrhythms that accented, pulsed and even suspended time. They assimilated the parts of jazz dances that isolated body parts, squared the port de bras, and created new body dynamics.

(Hill 1996: 228)

Racism remains a subtext even in the enthusiastic French embrace of African and African-American dance in the 1920s; popular dance was certainly not immune. For example, in tap dance the light-footed, upward-impulsed, composed body of Bill Robinson (and his crossover audience) was seen by some black dancers as "white," whereas Eleanor Powell's low (pelvic) center of gravity and downward drive was seen as "black" (where, of course, "black" is seen as "authentic," itself a highly contested cultural construct).

A reintegration of music and dance in the body permeates the century. Critic André Levinson described Josephine Baker's dancing as if the music came from inside her (Hill 1996: 236). This embodiment of music runs through not just Elvis Presley's swiveling pelvis or the dancer-singers such as Madonna and Britney Spears, for whom the voice is adjunct to the body rather than the reverse, but more emphatically in the black gospel tradition represented in various inflections by Sam Cooke, James Brown, Jackie Wilson, Aretha Franklin, and Al Green.

Michael Jackson's riffs can seem to be generated from the impetus of his light but dynamic dancing, rather than his movements being a choreographed response to the music. At the other end of the vernacular–cultivated divide, Leslie Satin observes that in the danced "operas" of Meredith Monk, "the movement is the singing and the singing is the movement" (1996: 126). Monk herself recalls Isadora Duncan's "environmental" dancing when she says, "to find the flow I realized that in those days I could really let myself be *danced* by the air and by the space and I could let myself be *sung*" (quoted in Satin 1996: 137).

Choreography

Choreography is the constructed union of music and dance. To a great degree, it is in this practical aesthetic exploration where we find the most specific thought about the relationship between music and dance.

At choreography's peak as an independent art, the choreographer of the classical ballet in Imperial Russia is the dominant creative power, soliciting music from the specialist composer. Yet this is not *exactly* music ordered by the yard.

> Music must excite, support and guide the movement of the choreographic artists . . . In short, as the best woman is the one of whom nothing is said, the best music for ballet is that which passes almost unnoticed, for once the public's attention is directed toward the music, it means that the music is not wholly suited to the subject, although excellent in and of itself.
>
> (Valentin Skalkovsky, quoted in Wiley 1985: 8)

If this balance is appropriately struck, the music is deemed *dansante*, "which, although a quality not easily defined, is wrongly condemned as trivial" (Wiley 1985: 5–6). At its simplest, *dansante* music comprises a steady beat and melody to support (and presumably incite) the movement.

Historically, it had been possible to distinguish between music for dancing (social dance, ballet) and music such as a symphonic minuet and trio that was conceptually and rhythmically dance music, but not intended for the practical purpose of dancing. After Duncan, that distinction blurs; it becomes possible to dance to all music – or no music, although, in practice, dance without music tends to be about the absence of music or the sounds made by the dancers. Such dance is still perceived through the ordering principles we deem "musical."

Duncan, for all her embrace of "great music," counseled students, "Please don't let any one persuade you to try to dance to Debussy . . . the gesture of Debussy is all *inward* – and has no outward or upward" (1969: 107). Horst does not exactly disagree, but has a more nuanced understanding of impressionist music:

Frequently altered tempo, abrupt changes in dynamics (from a tense to a relaxed movement, from a slow to a fast or a change in space and pace) contribute to the shimmering, fragmented quality which gives the style its flavor. Although it is impossible for the human body actually to fragment itself, by these devices of interrupted line, texture, and rhythm an effect can be achieved which is similar to the one the painters attained with their broken colors.

(Horst and Russell 1967: 138)

Horst, a musician by training, conceived of (and taught) choreography according to the principles of music composition, and, like the Romantic symphonists, relied upon pre-classical dance forms for structure. One of his first rules was that composition was not an inspirational experience but based on "a conception of a theme and the manipulation of that theme" (Horst and Russell 1967: 23).

Ruth St. Denis coined "music visualization" as "a substitute for the much abused expression 'interpretive'" (Spector 1990: 209–10). "Music visualization" can be understood as merely reproducing acoustic events in the visual realm, but this superficial understanding wildly underestimates the creativity required. The same music can inspire many divergent interpretations, which can in turn influence the audience's reception of the music.

Doris Humphrey, who embraced "music visualization" both as terminology and as practice, wrote with insight and, more rare, *practicality*. Her discussion of music suitable for dance echoes Skalkovsky's: not all music is suitable for dance, particularly the "too-complex composition in general, which is so demanding of attention that it cannot make a good partner" (Humphrey 1959: 132).

But she also argues for independence, if not autonomy:

The dance should be related to, but not identical with, the music, because this is redundant – why say in dance exactly what the composer has already stated in music? . . . The ideal relationship is like a happy marriage in which two individuals go hand in hand, but are not identical twins.

(Humphrey 1959: 164)

Humphrey's conception of this "ideal relationship" is broad-ranging: dance without music "does not seem empty, or as though the bottom had dropped out, but increases concentration and attention to movement to an astonishing degree" (142). She relates that in setting a procession to Bach's Passacaglia in C minor her choreographic idea was nine bars against eight of music – but "no one noticed" (135); however, such contrasting or contrapuntal hypermeasures create a rhythmic tension, whether they are consciously noticed or not (Jordan 1996: 21).

The choreographer most associated with music–dance counterpoint is undoubtedly George Balanchine, particularly in his collaboration with Stravinsky, with whom he shared an artisan's approach to creation: "When I listen to a score by him I am moved – I don't like the word inspired – to try to make visible not only the rhythm, melody and harmony, but even the timbres of the instruments" (1949: 78). Still, rhythm is the ordering principle as well as the impetus to motion:

> Stravinsky's strict beat is his sign of authority over time; over his interpreters too. A choreographer should, first of all, place confidence without limit in this control. For Stravinsky's rhythmic invention, possible only above a stable base, will give the greatest stimulus to his own powers.
>
> A choreographer can't invent rhythms, he only reflects them in movement. . . . As an organizer of rhythms, Stravinsky has been more subtle and various than any single creator in history. And since his rhythms are so clear, so exact, to extemporize with them is improper.
>
> (Balanchine 1949: 75)

But, on a finer scale than even Humphrey, Balanchine values silence:

> A pause, an interruption, is never empty space between indicated sounds. It is not just nothing. It acts as a carrying agent from the last sound to the next one . . . An interpreter should not fear (unfortunately many do) Stravinsky's calculated, dynamic use of silence. He should give it his trust and, what's more, his undivided attention.
>
> (1949: 76)

Balanchine's choreography certainly embraces these rests and pauses: enchaînements repeat, syncopated against musical repetition so that each movement is constantly recontextualized; a rest can act as a spotlight or quotation marks, framing a movement. But the counterpoint extends far beyond the step or phrase, into the architectural: "Planning rhythm is like planning a house, it needs a structural operation" (Balanchine 1949: 75). Stravinsky echoes: "Balanchine's visualization of the *Movements* exposed relationships of which I had not been aware in the same way. Seeing it, therefore, was like touring a building for which I had drawn the plans but never completely explored the result" (1972: 34).

Twentieth-century choreography converged toward the Balanchinian counterpoint between music and dance: complex and flexible, ranging over cultivated and more vernacular styles. In theatrical and cinematic dance, the relationship between music and dance is particularly close, as a choreographer will work with a dance arranger who shapes and orchestrates the music to best support and reflect the dance, creating a unified whole. In collaboration with electronic composer Thom Willems, William Forsythe's ballets, such as . . .*In the Middle*

Somewhat Elevated . . ., often impose large-scale structures on repetitive or seemingly random musical patterns, just as individual gestures can be highlighted by – or themselves highlight – particular musical events. Even when that intimate interaction is denied, it can be found by the audience: in the intentional divergence in the collaboration of John Cage and Merce Cunningham, music and dance are composed separately, each according to its own chance operations, and what happens when they are performed together is the "work." As audiences are inextricably bound by their enculturation, however, they will unconsciously register the coincidences and contrasts of the movements and sounds as an unfolding counterpoint.

Sparshott proposes perhaps the most succinct and yet powerful means of approaching music and dance by declaring the relationship prepositional: one may dance to, with, for, against, around, across, or on top of music. This simple idea is tremendously provocative, and implicitly underlies much work in the emerging field of dance analysis. Each preposition suggests a different relationship, one that can be (and often is) grasped immediately by dancers, musicians, critics, and audiences. The challenge is to explain *how* this impression is created, though the language may remain beyond our grasp. "I am not sure I have ever seen anyone dance '*under* the music'," Sparshott concludes, "but I am by no means sure I haven't" (1995: 224).

See also Adorno (Chapter 36), Antiquity and the Middle Ages (Chapter 24), Music, philosophy, and cognitive science (Chapter 54), Plato (Chapter 28), Rhythm, melody, and harmony (Chapter 3), Visual music and synesthesia (Chapter 44), and Wagner (Chapter 35).

References

Adorno, T.W. (2002a [1936]) "On Jazz," in Adorno (2002c), pp. 470–95.

—— (2002b [1941]) "On Popular Music," in Adorno (2002c), pp. 437–69.

—— (2002c) *Essays on Music*, ed. R. Leppert, trans. S.H. Gillespie, Berkeley: University of California Press.

Aristotle (1984) *Poetics*, trans. I. Bywater, in *The Complete Works of Aristotle*, vol. 2, ed. J. Barnes, Princeton: Princeton University Press, pp. 2316–40.

Balanchine, G. (1949) "The Dance Element in Stravinsky's Music," in M. Lederman (ed.) *Stravinsky in the Theatre*, New York: Pellegrini & Cudahy, pp. 75–84.

Bonds, M.E. (1997) "Idealism and the Aesthetics of Instrumental Music at the Turn of the Nineteenth Century," *Journal of the American Musicological Society* 50: 387–420.

Cohen, S.J. et al. (1998) *International Encyclopedia of Dance: A Project of Dance Perspectives Foundation, Inc.*, New York: Oxford University Press.

Crawford, R. (1993) *The American Musical Landscape*, Berkeley: University of California Press.

Duncan, I. (1969) *The Art of the Dance*, ed. S. Cheney, New York: Theatre Arts Books.

Hill, C.V. (1996) "Jazz Modernism," in Morris (1996), pp. 227–42.

Horst, L. and Russell, C. (1967) *Modern Dance Forms in Relation to the Other Modern Arts*, New York: Dance Horizons.

Humphrey, D. (1959) *The Art of Making Dances*, New York: Rinehart.

Jaques-Dalcroze, É. (1980 [1930]) *Eurhythmics, Art and Education*, trans. F. Rothwell, ed. C. Cox, New York: Arno Press.

Jordan, S. (1996) "Musical/Choreographic Discourse: Method, Music Theory, and Meaning," in Morris (1996), pp. 15–28.

Levitin, D.J. (2006) *This is your Brain on Music: The Science of a Human Obsession*, New York: Dutton.

Mason, F. (1991) *I Remember Balanchine: Recollections of the Ballet Master by Those who Knew Him*, New York: Doubleday.

Morris, G. (ed.) (1996) *Moving Words: Re-writing Dance*, London: Routledge.

Plato (1900) *Laws*, in *The Collected Dialogues of Plato*, trans. B. Jowett, vol. 4, New York: The Jefferson Press, pp. 1–480.

Ratner, L.G. (1980) *Classic Music: Expression, Form, and Style*, New York: Schirmer Books.

Sadie, S. (ed.) (2001) *The New Grove Dictionary of Music and Musicians*, 2nd edn, London: Macmillan.

Satin, L. (1996) "Being Danced Again: Meredith Monk, Reclaiming the Girlchild," in Morris (1996), pp. 121–40.

Sparshott, F.E. (1988) *Off the Ground: First Steps to a Philosophical Consideration of the Dance*, Princeton: Princeton University Press.

—— (1995) *A Measured Pace: Toward a Philosophical Understanding of the Arts of Dance*, Toronto: University of Toronto Press.

Spector, I. (1990) *Rhythm and Life: The Work of Émile Jaques-Dalcroze*, Stuyvesant: Pendragon Press.

Stravinsky, I. (1972) *Themes and Conclusions*, London: Faber.

Wagner, R. (1993) *The Art-work of the Future, and other works*, trans. W.A. Ellis, Lincoln: University of Nebraska Press.

Wiley, R.J. (1985) *Tchaikovsky's Ballets:* Swan Lake, Sleeping Beauty, Nutcracker, Oxford: Oxford University Press.

44
VISUAL MUSIC AND SYNESTHESIA
Kathleen Marie Higgins

Visual music

The expression "visual music" is reminiscent of the proverbial square circle. It sounds like a category mistake. Music directly addresses the sense of hearing. We do not need to use our eyes to experience it.

"Visual music" might refer to visual art that tries to capture something of the character of music. Walter Pater provocatively said that all art aspires to the condition of music (1980: 106). Some visual artists overtly pursue this goal. Piet Mondrian, for example, sought to convey rhythm by means of his painting. Henri Matisse aimed to achieve impressions akin to those wrought by jazz improvisation in *Jazz*, a series of works using stenciled cut-outs.

Music has always offered visual as well as aural enjoyment, however. Until modern recording technology enabled us to separate the aural track from the activities that produce it, music was always "live," and musicians' physical movements were visually accessible to those who were relatively nearby. The enjoyment of seeing music-makers in action remains one of the attractions of live concerts today.

Vision is often directly involved in the performance of music as well. Conductors use visual signals to indicate the time and the manner in which particular musical sounds should be produced. Performers within ensembles similarly use gesture to cue each other or prompt tighter synchronization. The audience itself is sometimes involved in such gestural behavior, as when listeners make hand movements to mark rhythm in classical Indian music.

If we restrict the expression "visual music" to works within the musical medium, music can be visual in a variety of ways besides those already mentioned. First, musical notation itself is a visual means of communicating music, and often it is simply referred to as "the music." Although designed primarily for preserving musical works and facilitating coordination among performers, the score is sometimes also visually attractive. Famous historical examples of scores which are visual artworks are two constructed by Baude Cordier (*c.*1380–1440). The score for his "Belle, bonne, sage," a love chanson, is shaped like a heart, and it includes red notes which add to the score's visual appeal while also indicating rhythmic changes. For his "Tout par compass," an eternal canon, Cordier used a circular staff. To recognize their wittiness, one needs to see these scores. Even notation not obviously geared to visual pleasure is sometimes treated as visual art, as when passages of medieval notation are framed and hung on walls in the present day.

A second species of visual music includes certain avant-garde works that can only be accessed by means of sight. A performance of John Cage's *4'33"* is an example. The work consists of a pianist sitting down at the piano for precisely four minutes and thirty-three seconds, and then standing and bowing to the audience. While the non-sighted might be informed about what is going on, direct experience of this "music" depends on seeing the performance. Other avant-garde music, too, employs visually observed antics that have theatrical effect. Henry Cowell's works that instruct the performer to reach inside the piano and pluck the strings by hand, or to roll the bell of a trombone directly on the strings, would be cases in point. Although the sounds produced can be registered as non-standard by the ear, the precise character of these unconventional performance techniques would be hard to identify by means of hearing alone.

A third type of visual music is the wide array of music that is synchronized with visually perceived performance in other media. Dance and opera both fall under this category. More experimental forms, from Wagner's *Gesamtkunstwerk* to the musical performance art of the 1960s Fluxus group and beyond, employ music in explicitly multi-media productions.

Soundtracks, too, whether integrated with film, television, video, or cartoons, coordinate musical and visual processes. In most of these cases, the soundtrack is taken to be an accompaniment to a form that is more prominently visual. The music video, developed in the early 1980s, however, attempts to reverse this hierarchy, with the visual stream presented as an accompaniment to the music. (One might question whether this reversal has been completely effective. Given the dominance of the visual sense, one might argue that the music video actually relegates the music that is supposed to be the central attraction to a secondary role.)

A noteworthy species of multi-media work specifically seeks to integrate light and color into musical performance. This aspiration has led to the development of diverse, eccentric machines called color organs. One interesting instance was the ocular harpsichord constructed around 1730 by Father Louis Bertrand Castel, a Jesuit priest. He connected a frame with a series of windows to a harpsichord. When a note was sounded, one of the windows would open, revealing a color. Georg Philipp Telemann was sufficiently intrigued by this device that he wrote some pieces for it. Another famous color organ was that designed for use in Scriabin's symphony, *Prometheus: A Poem of Fire*. Scriabin had color indications written into the score for the work, and the color organ was to project colors on a screen (and ideally the audience) as the music unfolded. (For a fascinating summary of the history of color organs, see Moritz 1997.) The contemporary employment of artistic lighting in connection with rock concerts and other musical performances might be seen as a later manifestation of the same ambition to combine music with color, along with music-playing computer programs that enable individual consumers to enjoy blinking light displays accompanying musical playback.

Synesthesia

Music can also be visual as a result of synesthesia. Synesthesia occurs when the stimulation of a particular sensory mode occasions stimulation of another. I will consider musical synesthesia in both narrow and broader senses, the first being a relative rarity, the second a common phenomenon.

Idiopathic synesthesia

Musical synesthesia in the narrow sense is the spontaneous association of aurally experienced music with "phantom" percepts normally experienced through another sensory modality. This kind of synesthesia is called "idiopathic." The associations are involuntary, and they occur only "in the mind's eye" (Cytowic 1993: 76). That is, they are not intersubjectively observable, and the percepts involved tend to be incomplete objects characterized by isolated qualities that are relatively mono-dimensional (such as isolated blinking patterns or shapeless auras of color). Often non-synesthetes find a description of these percepts puzzling. Walt Disney's *Fantasia* offers some impression of this type of synesthetic experience when images of violin bows being played in an orchestra transform into moving linear flecks. Idiopathic synesthesia is relatively uncommon, and synesthetes do not share a common set of experiences. The particular phantom percepts and their specific behavior are unique to each synesthete.

The idiopathic musical synesthete's experience adds a dimension to the enjoyment of music, but it does not seem to provoke much envy (except on the part of certain artists, such as Scriabin). In fact, researchers and cultural commentators have often denigrated synesthesia. The *Oxford Companion to the Mind*, for example, characterizes synesthesia as epistemologically deficient:

> Confusion between the senses: for example, some musicians experience colours for particular notes. The effect can become dramatic in some drug states, presumably through loss of normal inhibitory mechanisms which isolate the central processing of the senses.
>
> (Gregory 1987: 765)

Certain late nineteenth- and early twentieth-century theorists of cultural decadence considered synesthesia a hallmark of degeneration. In 1895, for example,
Max Nordau asserted of synesthesia:

> It is a retrogression to the very beginning of organic development. It
> is a descent from the height of human perfection to the low level of
> the mollusc. To raise the combination, transposition and confusion of
> the perceptions of sound and sight to the rank of a principle of art, to see
> futurity in this principle, is to designate as progress the return from the
> consciousness of man to that of the oyster.
>
> (Quoted in Dann 1998: 33)

Negative views of synesthesia do not appear to be restricted to Western society.
Alan Merriam observes something similar in his interactions with the Basongye
people of Africa:

> While I do not regard my own tentative efforts as being "experimen-
> tal" in any sense, it is apropos to report that no informant among the
> Basongye either admitted to synesthesic experience or, indeed, even con-
> sidered questioning along this line to fall clearly within the bounds of
> normal sanity.
>
> (Merriam 1964: 93)

The idiosyncrasy of the perceptions involved presumably explains why many
consider idiopathic synesthesia irrelevant to musical experience at best – only
one in a hundred thousand people are idiopathic synesthetes (Gage 1998: 350–
1). It does not seem to have much to do with the musical experience for most
listeners.

Commonplace synesthesia

Musical synesthesia understood in a broader sense, however, is a common phenomenon. The appreciation of music through multiple sensory modalities is, in
fact, typical for the human species. I will defend the claim that musical experience in general has a synesthetic dimension and suggest that this helps to explain
why music is so easily associated with extra-musical phenomena, from cartoons
to ethical ideals.

That other senses besides hearing are involved in musical experience is evident
from the visual aspects of musical appreciation that we have already considered.
Musical experience also has a tactile character, which is demonstrated by the fact
that deaf people can enjoy music by means of touch.

Touch is engaged by music in virtue of the evolution of the auditory system.
The auditory system seems to have evolved from pressure-sensitive cells along

the bodies of fish. These cells enabled fish to detect movements of other entities in the water. Some of these cells eventually moved to the interior of the fish's head, becoming the vestibular system. The next stage of this evolutionary process was the development of three canals along the three dimensions of space relative to a fish's body. Each canal has a sack adjacent to it. Hairs attached to neurons at the base of each sack push their way through a layer of gelatin with calcium balls resting at the bottom. When the fish moves, the calcium balls move the hairs. This alerts the neurons and ultimately the brain as to how fast the fish is moving. At a further point in the evolutionary process, vibrations in the water were sufficient to move the calcium balls. This ability to register external vibrations amounted to a new sensory mode: hearing. (For a more detailed discussion, see Jourdain 1997: 15.)

One consequence of this origin of hearing is that the auditory system remains closely linked to the vestibular system, which enables us to maintain balance. The connection between music and dance is grounded in the direct association of these two systems (Nussbaum 2007: 99–100). Charles Nussbaum suggests another consequence of the emergence of hearing from our system for managing bodily orientation. According to Nussbaum, music exploits the very system that we use when interacting with the external world, specifically our ability to mentally model features of our environment in preparation for action. In the case of music, we mentally "represent virtual layouts and scenarios in an imaginary musical space in which the listener acts (off-line)" (Nussbaum 2007: 21). In other words, we engage in an imaginary exploration of musical space when listening to music. Music arouses our motor systems, although the overt movements they prompt are mostly inhibited. (This inhibition, however, is only relative, as can be recognized from listeners' propensity to tap their feet, to sway, to clap, and to dance.)

Nussbaum's account associates music not only with the tactile but also with the kinesthetic sense. In fact, he suggests that our ability to employ metaphors in relation to music depends more fundamentally on our tactile and kinesthetic responses than on our aural experience. He draws on George Lakoff and Mark Johnson's theory of metaphor (1980), in particular on the claim that we derive our abstract concepts from concepts related to bodily orientation and movement. Lakoff and Johnson contend that there is an asymmetry of transference between images derived from the various sensory domains: touch and kinesthetic experience dominate and provide metaphors for other sensory spheres, as opposed to the reverse. This suggests that the tactile and kinesthetic character of musical experience is more basic than its auditory character to our ability to relate to it metaphorically and to associate it with extra-musical meaning. The widespread use of height metaphors in relation to pitch provides support for this rather surprising contention.

Nussbaum's discussion suggests that our musical experience is always synesthetic. While he stresses the tactile and kinesthetic dimensions of musical synesthesia, the evidence of human discourse about music suggests that people associate music with the entire sensorium. The use of cross-modal terms in connection with music is widespread. Many such uses do relate features of music to the tactile and kinesthetic. Among these is the already noted application of the "high–low" continuum to pitch, a pattern that occurs in many languages and cultures. The German "*dür*" ("hard") and "*möll*" ("soft") in reference to major and minor modes also associates the musical with the tactile. The Kaluli of Papua New Guinea employ the spatial image of "lift-up-over-sounding" and the tactile term "hardness" to describe their musical ideal (Feld 1984: 390–2). Western tempo indications commonly designate styles of movement, which would typically be experienced visually and kinesthetically, for example, *andante*, which literally means "walking."

However, terminology from the experience of other senses is also in evidence. Another Western term indicating performance manner, *dolce*, or "sweetly," links a musical quality to flavor. "Bright" and "dark" are used so commonly in reference to music that it is easy to miss the fact that these words are most commonly linked to vision. The vocabulary of color is also pervasively applied to musical tone, as neurologist MacDonald Critchley points out:

> The metaphorical use of chromatic terms to describe auditory experiences is a literary commonplace, sometimes grossly overplayed. Oscar Wilde, for example, wrote that "her voice was exquisite . . . but it was wrong in colour." Elsewhere he referred to the vermilion lips of Salome . . . "like the scarlet blast of trumpets." Proust spoke of the "red and mysterious" appeal of the Vinteuil septet, and in another place he mentioned the "geranium scent" of the music.
>
> (Critchley 1977: 226)

Proust is not alone in associating music with smell. The Kota tribe in south India also use olfactory terms in connection with music, and the Aboriginal peoples of Australia refer to the taste or smell of a song (Wolf 2001). (See also Ellis (1985: 68), who notes that the same word is used for "taste" and "melody" in Pitjantjatjara, and Chatwin (1987: 58).)

This diversity of cross-sensory references reminds us that the senses are not as separate as we sometimes imagine. Hearing, touch, and the kinesthetic sense have a special evolutionary connection, but all the senses communicate with each other. The aberration is the case of a percept being accessed exclusively through one sense. As Merleau-Ponty observes, our senses work in tandem in ordinary perception:

> The senses intercommunicate by opening on to the structure of the thing. One sees the hardness and brittleness of glass, and when, with a tinkling sound, it breaks, this sound is conveyed by the visible glass. One sees the

springiness of steel, the ductility of red-hot steel, the hardness of a plane blade, the softness of shavings. . . . The form of a fold in linen or cotton shows us the resilience or dryness of the fibre, the coldness or warmth of the material. . . . In the jerk of the twig from which a bird has just flown, we read its flexibility or elasticity, and it is thus that a branch of an apple-tree or a birch are immediately distinguishable.

(Merleau-Ponty 1964: 229–30)

The synesthetic intermingling of sensory qualities in the phenomenology of experiencing objects is a consequence of the way our senses operate in our coming to know objects. Immanuel Kant (1998) observed that our various sensory tracks are mentally consolidated into a general representation of the external world. We take the data from vision, hearing, and touch, for example, to yield information about the same world, and this data all contributes to our mental representation of reality. In many, if not most, cases our senses apprehend objects through multiple channels simultaneously. The same table that I see is an object of touch and hearing when I rap on it.

The qualities of the table just mentioned are apprehended by distinct senses, but some qualities do not seem to be restricted to a particular sense. Long before Kant, Aristotle reflected on the fact that certain qualities of objects were simultaneously perceived by multiple senses. He termed these qualities "common sensibles":

The senses perceive each other's special objects incidentally; not because the percipient sense is this or that special sense, but because all form a unity: this incidental perception takes place whenever sense is directed at one and the same moment to two disparate qualities in one and the same object, e.g. to the bitterness and the yellowness of bile; the assertion of the identity of both cannot be the act of either of the senses.

(Aristotle 1941: 582 (425a30–425b3))

Aristotle's suggestion is that some sensory qualities are not consigned to a single sense, but are accessed by two or more simultaneously. E. M. Hornbostel (1927) similarly proposes that we experience a number of "amodal sensory qualities," such as brightness, darkness, and roughness, which are not uniquely directed toward a single sensory modality. His explanation resonates with Nussbaum's kinesthetic thesis. Hornbostel suggests that the stimulation of one sense affects another because it operates on body tonus, which is in communication with all the senses. (See also Cytowic 1989: 306.)

Gestalt psychologist W. S. Boernstein draws on Hornbostel's account to link synesthesia with human cognition. He claims that thinking developed as a means for human beings to engage in "internalized movement; i.e., a movement is first anticipated, and then carried out" (Boernstein 1970: 676). A precondition for this internalized movement is the integration of the effects of the multiple sensory modes and amodal sensory stimulation on body tonus (Cytowic 1989: 307–8). Synesthesia, in other words, is a precondition for developing the capacity to think.

Lawrence Marks spells out another connection between synesthesia and thinking. Noting that young children readily formulate associations between qualities apprehended by different sensory modes, he argues that such synesthetic "discoveries" facilitate the capacity to form metaphors. "To pass from similarity within one sense to similarity between two senses is to undergo a metamorphosis, to establish a new process, which provides an elementary basis for metaphoric resemblance" (Marks 1978: 188). Marks and colleagues propose that synesthetic association may be fundamental to cognitive development.

> Perhaps "stumbling onto" cross-modal similarities can precipitate a subsequent search for other similarities within diverse domains – in our view, the very crux of metaphor. . . . The direction of this search, we contend, is implicitly if not explicitly inward, into phenomenal experience, into the mind's eyes and ears. If so, then cross-sensory metaphors . . . may provide one key to understanding more generally the establishment in childhood of metaphoric competencies.
> (Marks, Hammeal, and Boernstein 1987: 84; see also Marks 1978: 189–91)

The connection made here between synesthesia and metaphor-formation offers insight into the cross-cultural tendency to associate musical details with non-musical content. Of course, the pitch/rhythm/timbre complex that is music (narrowly conceived) can be linked to referential language, and thus content of any sort can be grafted onto the musical stream. But not just any content will do for a given bit of music. The art of text-setting presupposes a notion of aptness in regard to how music and words are connected. Impressions of similarity between the connotations of words and the metaphors suggested by music may provide the basis for acceptable linkages.

More strikingly, metaphorical transference enables many uses of musical details to teach and reinforce patterns of importance to a society. Music is an unparalleled mnemonic, as the Australian Aboriginals recognize. They employ musical metaphors to help them navigate the environment, applying the synesthetic character of music that Nussbaum notes to very practical ends. They correlate the stream of a song with features of the physical environment. Their songs serve as literal maps, with contours and details that correspond to the shape of the land and its physical landmarks. The efficiency of this form of musical mapping is demonstrated by the fact that people from different tribes who do not share a common language can nevertheless recognize the landscape encoded in each other's songs.

Nussbaum contends that music's relationship to our internal navigational system provides the basis for our sense of music's relevance to extra-musical content. One such domain is ethical experience. Ethnomusicologists have observed that valued behavioral styles within a society are reflected in its music, if not directly instilled by it. Alan Lomax (1962) formulated the theory that a society's song style reflects the character of its ideals of social interaction, through such features as the way that male and female voices interact and how cooperative effort is organized (whether through hierarchical direction or more spontaneous emergence). Sound structure mirrors social structure as it is ideally understood (cf. Feld 1984).

The synesthetic character of musical perception also suggests an explanation for our tendency to relate visual images to music when none are directly presented. Until recent times one could only hear music in the vicinity of music-makers, so that typically listeners were able to take in the context through the whole sensorium. Modern recording technology, however, has made possible the delivery of music as a decontextualized stream of sound. In contrast to most of our experiences, the disembodied sonic stream dissociates our sensory modes, with aural/tactile apprehension being disconnected from what we perceive visually.

Nevertheless, music prompts visual reveries. Music is designed to make pattern forcefully conspicuous, and it is present to us with particular immediacy. The clarity and immediacy of music in the auditory and tactile domains makes one aware of a reality that transcends one's own body, even when one listens to a recording. Because music is so salient to us, with the same pattern manifest both aurally and tactilely, it makes listeners strongly aware of their connection with the larger world, even in the absence of visual reinforcement of the patterns the musical signal provides. Given that we relate to the larger world with our entire sensorium, the powerful impression of connection with the world that we obtain through music enlivens our senses all together, and we are motivated to respond with our entire bodies (as we do in dancing). The intensity of our aural and tactile impressions of the musical signal, by stimulating the rest of the sensorium, encourages us to seek content for the visual sense, which predominates in most of our interactions with the world. Hence, we find the combination of music with the actions of cartoon characters quite natural. The construction of programs in connection with instrumental music (a popular pastime in the nineteenth century, when absolute music had attained preeminence) also builds on our impression that a world so palpably present to touch and hearing should have a visual aspect as well. (Diana Raffman (1993) makes a case that is formally similar when she argues that the similarities between the structural features of music and language trick the mind into expecting a semantics in music, just as it finds a semantics in language.)

More theoretically, synesthesia also sheds light on the notion of the musical persona, the postulated agent that undergoes the events that instrumental music portrays. We have noted that the percept experienced by the idiopathic synesthete is something less than a fully fledged object. As Richard E. Cytowic explains, "The synesthetic percept is more like a *moment* of an incomplete object rather than the unfolding of a dream-like story with subject-object relations" (1989: 311). The musical percept, when isolated from context, is a bit like the synesthetic percept in this respect. The musical percept seems to engage in behavior, but it is difficult to characterize the nature of the agent. This difficulty has prompted some to utilize the notion of a "persona" (e.g. Levinson 2006). But the vagueness of the persona idea leads others to think we should eschew it. Peter Kivy complains, "The musical persona is such a vague, abstract, shadowy being that even 'its' sex cannot be determined" (2003: 116).

Music's synesthetic appeal, however, suggests some usefulness in the persona idea. One case in which music models extra-musical content, a possibility that the synesthetic involvement of multiple senses affords, is the common impression that the movement of music is akin to the activity of an agent. The persona notion acknowledges the indeterminate character of both behavior and agent in the auditory signal, but also reflects the fact that music suggests a world available to our whole sensorium. By speaking of a musical persona, one acknowledges the indefiniteness of any features of the "agent" who seems to behave through the music beyond the characteristics of the behavior itself. This indefiniteness makes room for the formulation of analogies between the behavior presented through the music and other content (so long as one is aware of their subjective character) as an outgrowth of our relating to music with our whole sensory apparatus engaged. The vagueness of the idea of the persona also reflects our ability to tolerate indefiniteness in our impression of an agent, much as the idiopathic synesthete has no difficulty attending to percepts of incomplete character.

Ordinary musical listening is synesthetic in that it involves the fusion of sensory streams into an integrated experience. The modeling that musical synesthesia affords is open-ended, but it is constrained by the aesthetic requirement of affective and other kinds of coherence. Charles Hartshorne draws attention to our mental tendency to form associations with music, noting that our satisfaction as listeners depends on the congruence of affect with sensory experience:

> [I]t is impossible to attend to the notes except in so far as the mind stands ready to synthesize or fuse them into a total emotional integration, involving the entire conscious being, with which they are congruent. No one can listen to complex music without thinking. . . . The art of aesthetic appreciation is to "associate" with the object solely the images and reactions whose affective content will permit the sensory content to remain in the focal center rather than such as will displace it; therefore – and this is the same thing in other words – which will find the supreme illustration of their own "spirit" in that sensory content – as all the spirit of a piece of music is concentrated in its principal theme.
>
> (Hartshorne 1934: 189)

Our senses band together when encountering music, and in tandem arouse the whole nervous system, which generates our intellectual and emotional response. Thus, synesthesia's multi-modal impact is compelling, and its forcefulness awakens the heart and the mind, along with the senses. In effect, music meets us everywhere, through all our receptive capacities. That is what we mean by "the power of music," a power that depends on synesthesia.

See also Music and dance (Chapter 43), Music and motion pictures (Chapter 42), Music's arousal of emotions (Chapter 22), and Psychology of music (Chapter 55).

References

Aristotle (1941) *De Anima*, trans. J.A. Smith, in *The Basic Works of Aristotle*, (ed.) R. McKeon, New York: Random House, pp. 535–603.

Boernstein, W.S. (1970) "Perceiving and Thinking: Their Interrelationship and Organismic Organization," *Annals of the New York Academy of Sciences* 169: 673–82.

Chatwin, B. (1987) *The Songlines*, New York: Penguin.

Critchley, M. (1977) "Ecstatic and Synaesthetic Experiences during Musical Perception," in M. Critchley and R.A. Henson (eds) *Music and the Brain: Studies in the Neurology of Music*, London: Heinemann Medical, pp. 217–32.

Cytowic, R.E. (1989) *Synaesthesia: A Union of the Senses*, New York: Springer-Verlag.

—— (1993) *The Man Who Tasted Shapes: A Bizarre Medical Mystery Offers Revolutionary Insights into Emotions, Reasoning, and Consciousness*, New York: G.P. Putnam's Sons.

Dann, K.T. (1998) *Bright Colors Falsely Seen: Synaesthesia and the Search for Transcendental Knowledge*, New Haven: Yale University Press.

Ellis, C.J. (1985) *Aboriginal Music, Education for Living: Cross-cultural Experiences from South Australia*, St. Lucia: University of Queensland Press.

Feld, S. (1984) "Sound Structure as Social Structure," *Ethnomusicology* 28: 383–409.

Gage, J. (1998) "Synaesthesia," in M. Kelly (ed.) *Encyclopedia of Aesthetics*, vol. 4, New York: Oxford University Press, pp. 348–51.

Gregory, R.L. (ed.) with the assistance of O.L. Zangwill (1987) *The Oxford Companion to the Mind*, New York: Oxford University Press.

Hartshorne, C. (1934) *The Philosophy and Psychology of Sensation*, Chicago: University of Chicago Press.

Hornbostel, E.M.v. (1927) "The Unity of the Senses," *Psyche* 7: 83–9.

Jourdain, R. (1997) *Music, the Brain, and Ecstasy: How Music Captures Our Imagination*, New York: Avon Books.

Kant, I. (1998 [1781]) *Critique of Pure Reason*, trans. P. Guyer and A.W. Wood, Cambridge: Cambridge University Press.

Kivy, P. (2003) *A Philosophy of Music*, New York: Oxford University Press.

Lakoff, G. and Johnson, M. (1980) *Metaphors We Live By*, Chicago: University of Chicago Press.

Levinson, J. (2006) "Musical Expressiveness and Hearability-as-expression," in M. Kieran (ed.) *Contemporary Debates in Aesthetics and the Philosophy of Art*, Malden: Blackwell, pp. 192–206.

Lomax, A. (1962) "Song Structure and Social Structure," *Ethnology* 1: 425–51.

Marks, L.E. (1978) *The Unity of the Senses: Interrelations among the Modalities*, New York: Academic Press.

Marks, L.E., Hammeal, R.J., and Bornstein, M.H. (1987) *Perceiving Similarity and*

Comprehending Metaphor, with commentary by L.B. Smith, Chicago: University of Chicago Press.

Merleau-Ponty, M. (1964) *Phenomenology of Perception*, trans. W. Cobb et. al., ed. J.M. Edie, Evanston: Northwestern University Press.

Merriam, A.P. (1964) *The Anthropology of Music*, Evanston: Northwestern University Press.

Moritz, W. (1997) "The Dream of Color Music, and Machines that Made it Possible," *Animation World Magazine* 2, available at www.awn.com/mag/issue2.1/articles/moritz2.1. html.

Nussbaum, C.O. (2007) *The Musical Representation: Meaning, Ontology, and Emotion*, Cambridge: MIT Press.

Pater, W.H. (1980 [1893]) "The School of Giorgione," in *The Renaissance: Studies in Art and Poetry*, (ed.) D.L. Hill, Berkeley: University of California Press.

Raffman, D. (1993) *Language, Music, and Mind*, Cambridge: MIT Press.

Wolf, R.K. (2001) "Emotional Dimensions of Ritual Music among the Kotas, a South Indian Tribe," *Ethnomusicology* 45: 379–422.

Part VI
MUSIC, PHILOSOPHY, AND RELATED DISCIPLINES

45
MUSICOLOGY
Justin London

On music and musicology

When asked "What is a musicologist?," the composer Dmitri Shostakovich purportedly said:

> I'll tell you. Our cook, Pasha, prepared the scrambled eggs for us and we are eating them. Now imagine a person who did not cook the eggs and does not eat them, but talks about them – *that* is a musicologist.
>
> (Fanning 1995: 1)

Shostakovich distinguishes musicologists from musicians and composers (who cook the eggs), as well as audiences (who eat the eggs), and, by implication, music teachers (who train the cooks). Of course, one might extend this analogy in a more sympathetic fashion, and note there may be gourmands interested in the history of cuisine (historical musicologists), or food chemistry (music theorists), or cultural traditions of cooking and eating (ethnomusicologists). But Shostakovich's parable captures a widely held point of view, namely, that true musical understanding is shown by one's ability to make or perform music, not by one's ability to talk about it.

It was not always thus. In *De Institutione Musica* (early sixth century), Boethius defines "the true musician (musicus) as the scholar who can judge poetic compositions and instrumental performances by the application of pure knowledge; this scholar is to be distinguished from the poet, who composes songs more by instinct than by knowledge, and the instrumentalist, who is little more than a skilled craftsman" (Bower 2001: 785).

Even if popular sentiment, captured by Shostakovich's complaint, lies more with the instrumentalists and poets (i.e. composers), musicology presses on. Musicology encompasses Historical Musicology, Music Theory and Analysis, and Ethnomusicology. The evolution of these sub-disciplines is sketched out in the next section of this chapter. It is then followed by a discussion of the practices of historical musicology and music theory, and the philosophical entanglements those practices involve. (Ethnomusicology is given its own treatment in Chapter 49 in this volume.)

Two general observations, however, are useful at the outset. First, musicology is tied to a canon; for the most part, this has been Western art music from the Middle Ages through the present. While the musicological canon has broadened considerably in the last quarter-century, music outside the Western art tradition has long been the province of other scholars. Non-Western music has been (until recently) the domain of ethnomusicology while jazz and popular musics were investigated by scholars in fields ranging from English Literature to Sociology. With Western art music as its paradigmatic practice, certain presumptions – a written tradition which fixes a work in tangible form, a strong distinction between composers and performers, an emphasis on the primary parameters of pitch and rhythm – become normative for the discipline. Second, musicology is grounded in and on the study of artifacts, since these form the evidentiary basis for the discipline as musicologists scrutinize manuscripts and printed scores, letters, diaries, concert reviews, and so forth. The focus on these materials (and the lives and activities that generate them) necessarily colors the ontological and epistemic commitments of the discipline. It is telling that historical musicologists and music theorists often refer to these artifacts as the musical "work," even though most, if asked what a musical work is, are likely to espouse to something like the "simple view" of musical ontology proposed by Julian Dodd (2009), a combination of type/token theory and sonicism.

A very brief history of modern musciology

Musicology in its modern sense began in the late eighteenth and early nineteenth centuries. While there were important music dictionaries and encyclopedias published earlier in the eighteenth century, the turn of the nineteenth century saw another advance in music scholarship with works such as Heinrich Koch's *Musikalisches Lexikon* (1802), Johann Forkel's biography of Bach (1802), and F.-J. Fétis's *Biographie Universelle des Musiciens* (1835). There was a parallel advance in musical performance, as exemplified by Mendelssohn's revival of Bach's *Saint Matthew Passion* in 1829. Events such as these were the impetus for both the birth of the art music canon and a broader sense of the musical past as concert repertoires extended well beyond the current generation of composers and their immediate forebears.

With the interest in both the compositions of earlier figures, and regional and national musical traditions (part and parcel of rising nationalism), the mid-nineteenth century saw the birth of modern critical editions of complete works of individual composers (e.g. the Bach-Gesellschaft edition began in 1851; Beethoven in 1862; Mozart in 1877). At the end of the century, government-sponsored anthologies of Austrian, German, and Bavarian music were begun. All of these projects took decades to complete; many are still in use today.

Guido Adler's seminal text on "the origin, method, and aims of *Musikwissenschaft*" (1885) encapsulated the disciplinary distinctions for the next century. His "scientific musicology" was divided into two broad areas: historical and systematic. The historical area included paleography (notation), the taxonomy of forms, the laws or rules of particular practices and style, and the history of musical instruments. Adler's systematic area was far broader, as it encompassed music theory, aesthetics and psychology, music education and musicianship training, and ethnomusicology (which he termed "comparative musicology").

In the first half of the twentieth century, with the preparation of complete editions and other archival projects in full swing, musicology concerned itself primarily with completing its map of the past. This was an era of positivism, and musicological practice reflected the intellectual tenor of the times. The principal tasks were (a) preparing authoritative editions of scores, including transcriptions of medieval and renaissance music in modern notation, (b) establishing accurate composer biographies and work chronologies, and (c) unearthing the works of secondary composers and thus "connecting the dots" between the recognized masters. The wider access to historical sources also informed the first phases of the authentic performance practice movement, with its emphasis on the use of "original" instruments, smaller ensembles, proper ornamentation, and other aspects of performance practice.

Musicology in the second half of the twentieth century can be regarded as a reaction to the first. To be sure, archival and codicological work continued, especially as new techniques in print and sketch studies refined the chronology and authentication of works. But now the dots were un-connected, as the works of lesser known composers came to be understood in their own right, rather than as precursors to (or derivations from) those of their better known contemporaries. The authenticity movement matured, with strong reactions to the pedantry of the first generation of its practitioners, while at the same time expanding its remit from Renaissance and Baroque music into eighteenth- and nineteenth-century repertoire. (For a fuller discussion of early music and issues of authenticity see Chapter 9, "Authentic performance practice," in this volume.) Perhaps the most significant development in post-Second World War musicology was its hermeneutic turn. Musicology today most often aims to provide a thicker discursive context for musical works and genres by applying the methods and frameworks of reception history, feminist theory and gender studies, Marxist theory, post-colonial theory, and other forms of textual criticism.

The latter half of the twentieth century also saw a number of disciplinary fissures, due to a combination of the growing number of musicologists and their growing sub-specializations, as well as tensions between structuralist and post-structuralist approaches. The Society for Music Theory split from the American Musicological Society in 1977; other notable foundings were those of the Sonneck Society/Society for American Music (1975), the International Association for the Study of Popular Music (1981), and the Center for Black Music Research (1983), and in the UK, the Society for Music Analysis (1992).

Current practice in historical musicology

As Glenn Stanley notes in his essay in the *New Grove Dictionary*, historical musicology currently falls into two basic categories: (1) an empirical-positivistic practice, "with an emphasis on locating and studying documents and establishing objective (or would-be objective) facts about and from them," and (2) a theoretical-philosophical practice that (a) "addresses general historiographical problems such as change and causality, periodization, and biography, or (b) that addresses art-historical/musically-specific issues such as forms, styles, and the historical context of works and repertoires" (2001: 492). In both practices the objects of study/evidence employed may be autograph manuscripts, first printings, as well as subsequent editions of scores (documenting how a work was received and transmitted, including historical accretions); composers' personal documents such as letters, diaries, and (especially) work sketches; contemporaneous reviews and essays; musical instruments and descriptions; and pictures, photographs, and other iconographic materials. In addition the "theoretical-philosophical practice" may include secondary sources such as contemporaneous writings on philosophy, language, and culture, as well as more recent critical and meta-critical discourse.

The Summer 2009 issue of the *Journal of the American Musicological Society* is a telling sample. "The Allure of Dissolution: Bodies, Forces, and Cyclicity in Schubert's Final Mayrhofer Songs" by Blake Howe is an interpretive analysis of those songs in light of theories of embodiment and disability; "Lessons with Stravinsky: The Notebook of Earnest Andersson (1878–1943)" by H. Colin Slim examines both Stravinsky as pedagogue and the work of Andersson, a little known American composer; and "Alfred Schnittke's *Nagasaki*: Soviet Nuclear Culture, Radio Moscow, and the Global Cold War" by Peter J. Schmelz is an examination of Schnittke's piece as propaganda and as a window into Soviet culture. As is evident here, the bulk of current historical musicology is engaged not in empirical-positivistic practice, but in the critical interpretation of musical works: what they mean (or meant); why they were composed; and how they may inform a larger historical, intellectual, or aesthetic discourse.

As they pursue such projects, historical musicologists are necessarily entangled in a number of philosophical thickets. Four will be considered here. The first may be termed "the problem of the elusive object," related to the ontology of the musical work. Are works, in fact, determinable? For example, if we define musical works in Levinsonian terms as historically indexed sound structures together with their performance means (Levinson 1980), can we actually determine what that structure is and what its performance means are? Much of the empirical-positivistic tradition has concerned itself with nailing down these particulars –

getting the notes and instruments right, in other words. Hence the efforts to produce definitive editions, which use source comparisons and other means of codicological sleuthing to provide the modern performer with an "urtext."

At the same time, musicologists have always been aware of the "openness" of works they seek to capture in a critical edition. These range from the compositional accretions in the Middle Ages and Renaissance – in the motet tradition alone one finds a veritable menagerie of musical transmogrifications – to the practice of ornamentation in Baroque instrumental music to substitute arias in Mozart operas to differing arrangements of Duke Ellington. The early music movement has especially had to confront the under-determined nature of musical scores in considering questions such as instrumentation (often unspecified), size of performance forces (also unspecified), text placement (often vague), and chromatic alterations ("musica ficta"). What musicological research has shown is that in many traditions, neither the sound structure nor the performance means can be fixed by the tangible form of music notation, both because (a) in some cases there was no determinate sound structure or performance means to be fixed, and/or (b) all notational systems under-specify the sonic and performance particulars of the music.

In worrying about getting the notes right, musicologists also have had to confront problems of authorial intention – call this the "Bassoons in Beethoven" problem. In Beethoven's Fifth Symphony, the French horn famously intones the second theme of the first movement; in the recapitulation, since the key has changed the horn call is written for bassoon, presumably because the natural horns in E-flat could not play the theme in C (or at least not as resoundingly, even if they re-crooked). In the later nineteenth-century performance tradition, when valved horns became commonplace, the bassoon call was taken back by the horns. The presumption here is that had such French horns been available, Beethoven would have used them. Note that this takes the conception of the musical work to a level beyond what is given by the score. For even if the problems of notational specificity and accuracy could be solved, it may not really indicate what sound-structure and performance means are constitutive of the work; to determine *that*, one must imagine what the composer would have intended to write down in musical notation if ideal performance resources had been available to him or her.

From composer intentions relative to the musical utterance – what sounds should be made, and how – we move to problems related to the meaning of those sounds. Musicologists work hard to provide an accurate contextualization of older music, allowing us to understand the conditions under which a work was written and first heard. This includes topical references (both musical and nonmusical), the background of its initial audience, its subsequent reception, and so forth. All which, hopefully, allows us to have a full and proper understanding of works from times and places different from our own. But consider Mozart's Serenade in D (K. 320), which uses a theme based on a Viennese posthorn call, hence the work's nickname. Musicologists can tell us what posthorns were, what they sounded like, and so on, so modern audiences can understand this non-musical reference. But this understanding falls short of providing the *experience* of an eighteenth-century listener, who had first-hand knowledge of the posthorn's call in everyday life. No matter how detailed the program notes, they cannot restore the familiar and perhaps humorous effect Mozart intended in using this sonic quotation. This is akin to the difference between getting a joke (which the musicologist's work allows me to do) and finding it funny (which it cannot – see Cohen 1999).

Perhaps even more musicological effort is spent trying to uncover (or at least propose) what a composer intended his or her composition to mean. This can be thought of as the Shostakovich version of the Humpty-Dumpty problem. As is known to philosophers of language, just because a speaker S intends utterance U to mean M it does not entail that listeners will grasp M. And likewise, just because listeners grasp some meaning M^*, even if warranted, it does not follow that M^* is what the speaker intended. In other words, meaning is multiply defeasible. Moreover, one can also ask whether U has the grammatical resources, both syntactically and semantically, to convey M. Thus even if S intends M, and listeners grasp M, this grasp may not be in virtue of U, but simply the fact that S says anything at all in a given context. Consider, then, the considerable debates over the meaning of much of Shostakovich's music – is it wry satire and criticism of the Stalinist regime which denounced him, or is just derivative bombast? Much hinges here on what Shostakovich intended to mean, what listeners (both then and now) believed Shostakovich to mean, and the extent to which those intentions might be encoded in the music. Musicological investigations have focused mostly the first point, presumed the second, and tended to ignore the last. Cases such as Shostakovich show, however, how a thick discursive/cultural context can allow instrumental music to do some fairly heavy semantic lifting, especially when one acknowledges a communicative intent on the part of the composer above and beyond conveying a particular musical structure to the listener (see, for example, Davies 2007 on intentions, or at least our "uptake" of those intentions, as constitutive properties of works).

Music theory and analysis

As Robert Gjerdingen has pointed out, "a cynic might conclude that [music theory] has often provided little more than a technical apparatus in support of the current aesthetic doctrine" (Gjerdingen 1999: 166). While music theories and analyses may make claims to broad generality, especially if they are cast in naturalistic terms (Cook 2002), they are not value neutral, and always reflect the context of a time, place, and musical practice. In addition, it is often difficult to tell whether a given music-theoretic assertion is the tail or the dog, relative to the aesthetic doctrine, let alone who is doing the wagging. This depends on the interest of the theorist (and perhaps her reader): whether the aim is to use a composition (or compositions) to promote a particular aesthetic doctrine, or vice-versa.

Just as there is a distinction between "doing music" (performance, composition), and "talking about music" (musicology), as noted at the beginning of this chapter, within music theory there are similar fissures. This is reflected in the distinction between "theory," a consideration of the nature of musical sounds and their general principles of organization, and "analysis," the explication of the structure and "meaning" of particular musical works. Somewhat ironically, just as Shostakovich valorized doing over talking, in music theory analysis is often valorized over more abstract theories, as evidenced by the weight and authority given to musical examples and the broadly held tenet that speculative theories are only as good as the analytical insights they may generate.

Another way of mapping the music theory terrain has been proposed by Carl Dalhaus: a three-fold division of *speculative*, *regulative*, and *analytic* traditions (Dalhaus 1984). As Thomas Christensen notes, these three are often intertwined (Christensen 2001, 2002). The speculative tradition is perhaps the oldest, going back to Pythagoras. It is concerned with the nature and being of music. The regulative addresses practical problems of notation, grammar, and pedagogy; here we find prescriptions regarding chord progressions, the construction of counterpoint, and so on. The analytic tradition is the youngest of the three, exemplified by E. T. A. Hoffman's landmark review of Beethoven's Fifth Symphony in 1810. In analyses we find most clearly Gjerdingen's "technical apparatus in support of the current aesthetic doctrine" (1999: 166). Analyses may also document or dissect compositional method; this was especially typical of composer-theorists in the second half of the twentieth century such as Stockhausen and Babbitt. Analysis may extend beyond single works to consider entire repertories; William Caplin's taxonomy of thematic types and their functions in Haydn, Mozart, and Beethoven is a good example of this (Caplin 1998). Such taxonomic analysis is an important element in the historical documentation of a compositional style, genre, or oeuvre, and hence there is an important relationship between historical musicology and music theory in the analytic tradition.

In the analytic branch, the objects of study and evidence employed are musical scores, composer sketches, other analyses, and hearing ascriptions, that is, claims about the relative importance of musical events and the connections between them, based on the analyst's experience of the music. The analyses of Heinrich Schenker and his many students exemplify this approach. In the regulative branch, the objects of studies and evidence are one and the same: one is presented with exemplars, or sets of exemplars, that are thought to be typical of a style or practice. These exemplars serve as models for well formedness within that style, and are to be emulated in subsequent compositions. Lastly, in the speculative branch of music theory the objects of study can be basic formal types (e.g. lists of all possible five-note scales or chords; all possible rhythmic permutations

within an eight-beat measure, etc.) as well as examples from a particular literature. Speculative theories proceed by making arguments regarding the kinds and
nature of the relationships between them. Examples of recent speculative theory
include the group-theoretic approach of David Lewin (1987) or recent models
of harmony cast in terms of geometric spaces (Callender, Quinn, and Tymoczko
2008).

Just as with historical musicology, music theorists often stumble into philosophical thickets of their own. The first thicket is the music theorist's version
of the "problem with musical notation," for musical notation is the music
theorist's stock-in-trade. Most musical analyses are analyses of musical scores,
and score elements, rather than sounds or sound-structures. This is analogous
to basing one's theories and analyses of architecture on the study of blueprints
and site plans, rather than actual buildings. Given the difficulties involved in
capturing the details of musical performances, at least until very recently, this
reliance on musical scores was inevitable. Yet music notation evolved to capture what Leonard B. Meyer termed the "primary parameters" of pitch (melody
and harmony) and time (rhythm and meter) (1989: 14); the familiar five-line
musical staff is a stylized plot of pitch and time on the vertical and horizontal
dimensions of a continuing coordinate system. Notational traditions from the
Middle Ages to the present day do not capture the "secondary parameters"
of timbre, texture, and loudness. There are, of course, valid practical reasons
for this, as musical notation serves to tell performers what to do in order to
produce the sounds needed to instantiate a particular piece. Moreover, we usually regard the primary parameters as work-determinative: a certain pattern
of note intervals and rhythmic durations is precisely what makes something
an instance of "Happy Birthday." Change those intervals and/or rhythms and
one no longer has that tune. But play "Happy Birthday" loud or soft, or on
a trumpet or on a flute, and one still has "Happy Birthday." So far, so good.
However, as psycho-acousticians have shown, musical parameters are not per-
ceptually/epistemically discrete. For example, timbre and harmony are not distinct aspects of auditory perception: tones fuse into complex spectral blends,
and most instruments produce fairly rich, chord-like spectra. Thus manipulations of "harmony" (i.e. chord voicing) may be experienced as variations in
timbre, and vice-versa, and this is indicative of the gap between the structures
that musical scores represent versus the structures that we hear.

Music analysis tends to be composer-centric, and this centricity is manifest in
a number of ways. First, analyses of musical structure(s) are often couched in
terms of how the composer (presumably) thought about the musical materials
used and the relations she thought obtained amongst them. The presumption is
that an understanding of compositional method is necessary for an understanding of the work so composed. Yet this does not follow. Just as one need not
know the details of impasto technique to understand and appreciate a Van Gogh
painting – as their effect is clear to the viewer – one need not know the details

of a clever chromatic modulation to experience the effect of hearing a melody transformed from one harmonic landscape to another, as if by magic. In a similar fashion, analyses will often focus on a piece as a solution to some compositional puzzle or problem – a "composing out" of a particular contrapuntal framework, or tracing the way in which the composer may have/must have conceived of the relations between various harmonic pillars in a piece, for example. This is not surprising, given the close ties between music theory and composition noted above. Yet this parallels the musicological problem of determining the meaning of a piece through an examination of the composer's intentions: how a composer composed may remain opaque (absent first-hand testimonials), and, just as in the Shostakovich example, such accounts may miss the mark as to how the piece actually works for most listeners. This reveals a confusion between understanding and appreciating of the process by which a work is created versus understanding and appreciating the end product of that process.

The goal of much music analysis, if not most, is to highlight the features of a work whose aesthetic value is never in doubt; music analysis almost never examines a bad work to dissect its flaws (Littlefield and Neumeyer 1992 is an exception), though at times it may be marshaled to make the case for a relatively unknown piece or composer. Mostly, however, one sees discussions of the usual suspects, the most prominent works by the canonical composers of the Western Art Music tradition. While some analyses purport to demonstrate the "unity and coherence" of masterworks (something that would seem to require no demonstration), others, more promisingly, aim to get the reader to hear or notice certain features or relationships that she had not done on previous listenings. In so doing, they make their case for the value of the music, and may deepen our experience of it. Yet there is a problem lurking here, the "I just don't hear it that way" problem.

Suppose an analysis claims that a certain piece starts with a melody, and ends with the same melody in inversion, such that it is now "upside down" (i.e. with all its intervals reversed, going down where it initially went up and vice versa). If I have already noticed this fact, the analysis does not add to change my experience or understanding of the piece; rather, my experience confirms the analysis – in which case the analysis is of little value. If I had not noticed this before, I may have an "aha" moment, but does this change my experience of the piece? Knowing that a given relationship is present may not make it aesthetically salient (see Levinson 1997 regarding large-scale form). Moreover, Mark DeBellis (1995) has pointed out that the efficacy of such analyses depends on whether our listening experience is, in his terms, "weakly" or "strongly non-conceptual." If our hearing is weakly non-conceptual, then both analytically informed and analytically "naive" listeners recognize the melodic inversion, but the naive listeners cannot articulate their recognition in terms of an analytic ascription; they "know but cannot say." If our hearing is strongly non-conceptual, however, the inability of naive listeners to articulate something like "the ending is the beginning upside down" means that they do not grasp the relationship at all. Thus if listening is strongly non-conceptual, then the analysis can change both how and what I hear, and though the analysis may be true, it also may generate the very evidence claimed to support its thesis. Moreover, what happens when the analysis fails to convince in the strongly non-conceptual case – if I "just don't hear it that way." We have no way of adjudicating the truth-claims of the analysis, as the analyst and the reader simply are not hearing the same music. For the analyst hearing "the ending *as* an upside-down beginning" entails the belief that "the ending *is* an upside-down beginning." For the analytically informed listener, hearing is believing, and believing is hearing (London 1996).

See also Analysis (Chapter 48), Authentic performance practice (Chapter 9), Ethnomusicology (Chapter 49), Music theory and philosophy (Chapter 46), Notations (Chapter 7), Ontology (Chapter 4), and Understanding music (Chapter 12).

References

Adler, G. (1885) "Umfang, Methode und Ziel der Musikwissenschaft," *Viertelharsschrift für Musikwissenschaft* 1: 5–8, 15–20.

Bower, C. (2001) "Boethius," in Sadie, vol. 3, pp. 784–86.

Callender, C., Quinn, I., and Tymoczko, D. (2008). "Generalized Voice-Leading Spaces," *Science* 320: 346–48.

Caplin, W. (1998) *Classical Form: A Theory of Formal Functions for the Instrumental Music of Haydn, Mozart, and Beethoven*, New York: Oxford University Press.

Christensen, T. (2001) "Musicology, §II: Disciplines of Musicology, 2. Theoretical and Analytical Method," in Sadie, vol. 17, pp. 494–8.

—— (2002) "Introduction," in T. Christensen (ed.) *The Cambridge History of Western Music Theory*, Cambridge, Cambridge University Press, pp. 1–23.

Cohen, T. (1999) *Jokes,* Chicago: University of Chicago Press.

Cook, N. (2002) "Epistemologies of Music Theory," in T. Christensen (ed.) *The Cambridge History of Western Music Theory,* Cambridge, Cambridge University Press, pp. 78–105.

Dalhaus, C. (1984) *Die Musiktheorie im 18. und 19. Jahrhundert, Erster Teil: Grundzüge einer Systematik*, Geschichte der Musiktheorie vol. 10, F. Zaminer (ed.) Darmstadt, Wissenschaftliche Buchgessllschaft.

Davies, S. (2007) "Versions of Musical Works and Literary Translations," in K. Stock (ed.) *Philosophers on Music*, Oxford: Oxford University Press, pp. 79–92.

DeBellis, M. (1995) *Music and Conceptualization*, New York: Cambridge University Press.

Dodd, J. (2009) *Works of Music: An Essay in Ontology*, Oxford: Oxford University Press.

Fanning, D. (ed.) (1995) *Shostakovich Studies*, Cambridge: Cambridge University Press.

Gjerdingen, R.O. (1999) "An Experimental Music Theory?" in N. Cook and M. Everist (eds) *Rethinking Music*, Oxford: Oxford University Press, pp. 161–70.

Levinson, J. (1980) "What a Musical Work Is," *Journal of Philosophy* 77: 5–28.

—— (1997) *Music in the Moment*, Ithaca: Cornell University Press.

Lewin, D. (1987) *Generalized Musical Intervals and Transformations*, New Haven: Yale University Press.

Littlefield, R. and Neumeyer, D. (1992) "Rewriting Schenker: Narrative–History–Ideology," *Music Theory Spectrum* 14: 38–65.

London, J. (1996) "Hearing is Believing: A Review-Essay of Mark DeBellis' *Music and Conceptualization*," *Current Musicology* 60/61: 111–31.

Meyer, L.B. (1989) *Style and Music: Theory, History, and Ideology*, Chicago: University of Chicago Press.

Sadie, S. (ed.) (2001) *The New Grove Dictionary of Music and Musicians*, 2nd edn, London: Macmillan.

Stanley, G. (2001) "Musicology, §II: Disciplines of Musicology, 1. Historical Method," in Sadie, vol. 17, pp. 492–94.

46

MUSIC THEORY AND PHILOSOPHY

Judy Lochhead

Introduction

Music theory is one of the oldest traditions of writing about music, even if now it is one of the least understood outside of professional musical studies. From one perspective, music theory defines the basic materials and concepts by means of which music is composed, performed, heard, and discussed: intervals, scales, rhythms, meters, register, and so forth. From another perspective, music theory addresses emergent properties of musical organization, speculating on higher levels of musical organization that reflect on the nature of musical understanding: principles of scale generation, chord roots, hyper-metrical design, formal continuity, and so forth. In both its practical and its speculative modes, music theory is a type of thought about music that permeates all aspects of musical activity: composing/creating, performing, listening as well as the attendant discourse about music. And as a type of contemplation on the nature of musical experience, music theory has strong points of similarity to philosophy: both conceptualize the nature of the human experience of and with the world.

While both music theory and philosophy are sometimes characterized as contemplation of the world rather than as an active living of it, the distinction of thinking and doing does not fully hold. In both instances, contemplation which takes the form of conceptual understanding has a productive affect on behavior. In the particular case of music theoretical contemplation both the practical and the speculative modes of music thinking play a central role in how music is created, performed, and heard. As types of inquiry, both philosophy and music theory share this reflexive relation to the world. Music theory then might be understood as a sub-genre of philosophical thought.

The productive role that philosophy and music theory play with respect to the nature of human behaviors in and understandings of the world is not unique. Scientific modes of understanding also have a similarly reflexive relation to the world, and music theory often allies itself with such modes. Indeed a broader history of music theory might profitably distinguish how particular theoretical models variously associate with either a more scientific or philosophical type of inquiry. In some of the earliest writings of the Ancient world in the Western tradition, it is worth noting that philosophical and scientific modes of thought were linked through writings on music and mathematics, and hence this toggling between different modes of inquiry in the history of music theory is a feature of the earliest layers of thought more generally.

Here I focus on some of the particular ways that music theory has intersected with philosophical thought from the earliest instances in Ancient philosophy until the present. That intersection ranges from being a focal feature of the theoretical model to a background contextual frame. On one hand, for some Ancient authors music theory was an integral part of their philosophical thought, or for some music theorists since the mid-nineteenth century, particular philosophical concepts explicitly shaped a model or approach. On the other hand, a particular music theoretical approach may be understood to embody the broader philosophical concept of its historical era. This chapter, focusing on the most explicit intersections of music theory and philosophy, presents in a chronological ordering of several select cases in which a particular philosophical tradition intersects explicitly with the work of a particular theorist. This historical survey of such intersections is necessarily non-comprehensive and thus often entails large historical gaps. The chapter concludes with a few observations on why music theory is related in fundamental ways to the broader goals of philosophical thought generally.

Intersections in the Ancient and Medieval historical eras – music theory as philosophy

In its earliest manifestations in Ancient and Medieval eras, music theory was coupled with arithmetic, geometry, and astronomy as fields that correlated the occurrence of natural phenomena to number and numerical relationships. As allied fields of study, these disciplines became known in the Middle Ages as the Quadrivium and mastery of these fields was considered preparatory to philosophical endeavors. Several Ancient and Medieval authors have a notable standing in both philosophy and music theory; some important examples include Pythagoras (fl. second half of the sixth century BCE), Aristoxenus (fourth century), and Boethius (c.480–524/5) (see Chapter 24, "Antiquity and the Middle Ages," in this volume).

While there is controversy over the status of Pythagoras as an actual historical figure and the record of his ideas comes through later authors, Philolaus (fl. second half of the fifth century BCE) and Archytas (fl. first half of the fourth century BCE), Pythagorean ideas have played a prominent role in both philosophy and music theory. Most notably is the Pythagorean principle of the numerical basis of the truth of the world. This principle was carried forward and developed by

Philolaus and Archytas, and then later by the mathematician Euclid (fl. 300) through various observations about the proportional relation between string length and interval (octave = 2:1; perfect fifth = 3:2; perfect fourth = 4:3; whole-tone = 9:8) and the generation of the octave scale through sub-divisions of the perfect fourth. Further, Pythagorean principles hold that the numerical relationships that are manifest in the acoustical properties of intervals also hold in the relations between the orbiting speeds of celestial bodies. This correlation, known as the Harmony of the Spheres, became a central tenet in Ancient philosophy. Resting on the observation of mathematical relationships that inhabit the acoustical phenomena of music, the correlation is the basis of the central philosophical thesis for music theoretical writing. This ancient sense of cosmic harmony – the music of the spheres – is adapted in Plato's *Timaeus* when he claims that the unity heard in harmonious musical intervals is an imitation of divine harmony (see Chapter 28, "Plato," in this volume).

Aristoxenus (fl. fourth century BCE) wrote the treatise *On Harmonics*, which is the oldest work of music theory for which substantial fragments exist. As a disciple of Aristotle, he was critical of a simple application of the Pythagorean emphasis on number. Instead, Aristoxenus argued that music theory should be a self-standing mode of inquiry (not a sub-area of mathematics). It should focus on sound, not simply on numerical proportions, and it should be subject to scientific principles of understanding as put forward by Aristotle. And from what remains of his *On Harmonics*, we may surmise that Aristoxenus attempted to develop a comprehensive and coherent system of musical phenomena, starting with simple things (sounds) and proceeding through more complex phenomena and relations. Aristoxenus developed the idea of genus, according to the disposition of intervals within a tetrachord, and defined three genera (enharmonic, chromatic, and diatonic) based on the ordering of intervals. He also developed a concept of *tonoi* as "positions of the voice . . . [used] in singing a melody" (Bélis: 2009). While that part of the treatise describing the *tonoi* has been lost, the term apparently refers to what we would today call transpositions of a scale. (See Barker 2004 for translation and discussion of writings by several Ancient Greek theorist-philosophers.)

Aristoxenus's treatise did not, however, address musical practice directly and hence was not intended for those who would create or perform music. He maintained a strong distinction between the scientific study of music and practical issues of music-making, claiming that practical matters were a matter of skill (*technē*) and not of science (*epistēmē*). In the context of the fourth century BCE, study of the structures of musical phenomena was philosophy. (See Mathiesen 1999 for a comprehensive discussion of Ancient Greek music and musical thought.)

Several centuries later, in the early Middle Ages, a renewed interest in the philosophical treatises of Antiquity resulted in works that transmitted early writings on philosophy and hence music through a kind of glossed paraphrase. Boethius was the first to explicitly define the Quadrivium as the systematic study of arithmetic, geometry, music, and astronomy. Boethius's *De institutione musica* (Boethius 1989, written *c*.500) is believed to be one of a series of treatises that he planned on the topics of the Quadrivium. Boethius's treatise largely recounts the ideas of earlier philosopher-music theorists, but at the same time it clarifies and extends some of the ideas of these earlier Greek authors. Of particular note is Boethius's articulation of the earlier distinction between cosmic and psychic harmony as *musica mundana* and *musica humana* and his addition of a third category of *musica instrumentalis*, which is performed and heard music. (See Bower 1981 for an account of the role that Boethius's musical theory played in philosophical thought generally.)

From Antiquity through the early Middle Ages music theory was understood as an integral part of philosophy, and indeed concepts of interval and scale in connection with the abstract principle of harmony were central philosophical concepts. While such philosophical concerns with music were not focused on the actual practice of sounding music, they did lead to music theoretical work that made that connection explicitly. Later writers in the Middle Ages, notably Aurelian of Réôme (fl. 840–50 CE) and Hucbald (*c*.840–930), explicitly addressed musical practice, initiating the split of music theory from philosophy. However, it must be noted that these authors relied on the theoretical principles concerning interval and scale defined by the earlier philosophers and hence the relation between music theory and philosophy remained.

Intersections of philosophy and music theory in the eighteenth and nineteenth centuries

With the advent of Enlightenment ideas and methods in the seventeenth century, new approaches to music theory emerged, and once again a significant intersection with philosophical thought occurred. The French philosopher René Descartes (1596–1650) played a central role in defining the emerging scientific thought and empirical methods of the Enlightenment. He and another French philosopher Marin Mersenne (1588–1648) both wrote music theoretical treatises. Descartes's treatise on music, *Compendium musicae* of 1618 (Descartes 1961), and Mersenne's various writings on music were directly influential on the thinking of the French composer and theorist Jean-Philippe Rameau (1683–1763). Known equally for his musical composition and theoretical work, Rameau embodied the ideals of Enlightenment thought in several ways. Interested in the pursuit of musical knowledge, Rameau did not eschew musical practice but instead embraced it fully in his compositional work. And further, Rameau viewed current musical practices, especially that of harmony in its modern sense, as phenomena requiring a Cartesian method of systematic explanation using rational principles. Rameau's most significant contribution appeared in the 1722 *Traité de l'harmonie reduite à ses principes naturels* (Rameau 1971). Here he argues that in early eighteenth-century musical practice there are a limited number of chord types – the triad and the seventh chord. The observation follows from an assertion that a tone and its octave are identical and hence that disparate chords may in fact be related through inversion of the pitch constituents of each. Further, Rameau claimed that a single note serves as the source not only of a chord but also of the notes of a key. He calls this source a "root" note which functions as the founding or fundamental note of a chord. Rameau then asserts that if one tracks the sequence of chord roots in music of the early eighteenth century, it is possible to determine a limited number of sequence types (sequences of chord roots are governed by intervals of a perfect fifth or fourth). Rameau's theory of chord structure and of chord relations has had a significant role in shaping music practice and thought about it, and while his ideas may not have such notoriety as those of Descartes, the effects of his musical theory is audibly present in the music that has been composed since the eighteenth century. And it is good to remember that as an active composer and music theorist, Rameau was centrally involved at the highest levels of European intellectual life with notable, often contentious, exchanges with such authors as Jean-Jacques Rousseau (1712–78), Denis Diderot (1713–84), and Jean le Rond d'Alembert (1717–83). (See Christensen 1993 for a detailed account of Rameau's theories in its cultural and intellectual context.)

Music theory in the late eighteenth through the nineteenth centuries continued the Enlightenment concern with systematic and rational explanation of musical phenomena, with particular emphasis on the generation of the fundamental harmonic units of musical practice: the major and minor triads. While explanation based in the "natural" phenomena of the overtone series could account for the major triad (the first six pitches of the overtone series form a major triad), no comparable basis for the minor triad can be derived from the overtone series in any rationally consistent way. Moritz Hauptmann (1792–1868), a German theorist and composer, turned toward a dialectical understanding in his 1853 treatise, *Die Natur der Harmonie und Metrik* (Hauptmann 1991). Hauptmann argued that the major and minor triads may be understood in dialectical terms as below, where I = unity; II = duality, and III = synthesis:

C	E	G		F	A-flat	C
I	III	II		II	III	I

In the case of the minor triad, the note of unity is not the root of the triad but rather its fifth, but in both cases the third is the synthetic component that reunites the other two into a larger unity. The logical generation of the minor triad may be understood to mirror that of the major triad, linking the two in a larger system of musical logic. In rejecting an empirical basis for systematic musical knowledge, Hauptmann embraced the tradition of German idealist philosophy and affirmed the music theoretical goals of systematic explanation of musical practice that was initiated in the eighteenth century.

Intersections in the twentieth and twenty-first centuries

The revolutionary changes in compositional aesthetic and specifically in the nature of pitch organization in the early years of the twentieth century necessitated new theories of compositional technique. One notable theory of pitch organization (the twelve-tone technique) was advanced by Austrian composer-theorist Arnold Schoenberg (1874–1951), and while it has no explicit reliance on a specific philosophy, Schoenberg's theory may be linked through concept and method with the philosophy of the Logical Positivists (see Wright 2007). Schoenberg's insistence on a logical and systematic process of pitch choice in the twelve-tone technique – repeated statements of an ordered sequence of the twelve chromatic notes in linear or simultaneous combination – echoes the scientific rationalism of such philosophers as the early Ludwig Wittgenstein, Moritz Schlick, Rudolf Carnap, and Hans Reichenbach. At about the same time, another Austrian composer-theorist, Heinrich Schenker (1868–35), advanced a reactionary theory of musical structure focused on common practice music that built upon principles of German Idealist philosophy and specifically on a Goethian organicism (for more on Schenker's philosophical foundations see Korsyn 1988; Solie 1980; Blasius 1996). Premised on the notion of a background triad (the *Ursatz*) that unfolds over the time of a movement or work, Schenker proposes a theory of ideal structure that is manifest in the surface details of a work. Nonetheless, the methodology of Schenker's theory, which defines precise concepts for the analytical determination of the ideal structure from the musical surface, resonates with the concern for empirically determinable meanings that was a central principle of Logical Positivist philosophy in the early years of the twentieth century.

In the years immediately following the end of the Second World War, science and scientific methods became a standard for knowledge and permeated music theoretical work explicitly, both in Europe and the United States. In Europe, the post-war reconstruction efforts included an emphasis on cultural production, and the project of rebuilding extended to musical composition. Composers, responding to the intellectual climate of the time, explicitly articulated the need for a systematic and logical approach to compositional technique. And they often borrowed the general principles and methods of contemporary philosophers, especially those from Logical Positivism and its extensions in the United States as analytic philosophy. In Europe, composers such as Pierre Boulez, Karlheinz Stockhausen, and György Ligeti wrote music theoretical or analytical articles premised on the value of a systematic basis for music composition; they developed various extensions of Schoenberg's twelve-tone technique into the domains of rhythm, timbre, texture, and dynamics in the effort to create and reveal systems of musical structure that are based on a logical foundation. Writing in the German journal *Die Reihe* that provided an intellectual platform for the post-war composers, Henri Pousseur, a French composer-theorist, made explicit the belief that the link between composition and theory rested on an "unerring trust in the structural solidarity that exists between the world and our intellectual tools," a belief he explicitly links to the French philosopher Gaston Bachelard (1884–1962) (Pousseur 1959: 44). Much of Bachelard's work was focused on the philosophy of science and on the nature of the "scientific state of mind" that for Pousseur dictated an integrated creative and research program that through speculative thought projects new musical forms.

In the United States, a similar emphasis on an integrated theoretical and compositional endeavor was linked explicitly to analytical philosophy through the composer-theorist Milton Babbitt. With training in both music and mathematics, Babbitt turned toward the principles of post-war analytical philosophy as the intellectual platform for a compositional technique founded on a systematic music theoretical basis. In a now infamous 1958 article with the provocative title "Who Cares if You Listen?" (the title assigned by an editor), Babbitt likened the activities of the contemporary composer-theorist to those of the research scientist in a university setting (Babbitt 2003). Like research in theoretical physics, music theoretical research is the site of speculative thought about the possible structures of the world. In the case of music theory, speculative research about musical structure and musical hearing is deemed a necessary part of the composer's creative process. Babbitt used the concepts and methods of Logical Positivism and its later manifestation as analytical philosophy, building explicitly upon ideas of such philosophers as Rudolf Carnap and W. V. O. Quine, to establish a ground for music theoretical discourse. For Babbitt, the creation of a precise and rigorous musical theoretical discourse assures that statements about music are objectively verifiable and hence have meaning (Babbitt 1965: 11). Using the principles of mathematical set-theory, Babbitt expanded Schoenberg's twelve-tone system not only by serializing rhythm, timbre, dynamics, and texture (as did the Europeans) but also by further developing a concept of "combinatoriality" which allows for more complex ways to compositionally present the twelve-note set.

In both the United States and Europe, composers in the years following the Second World War embraced a model of the composer-theorist with the same sort of vigor as did Rameau in the eighteenth century. At each of these historical junctures, the advent of new philosophical world-views provided a creative and intellectual stimulus for discourse in and about music. Composer-theorists, such as Boulez, Stockhausen, and Babbitt, were centrally engaged in the philosophical and intellectual discourse of their time and produced historically important work in both the compositional and the theoretical domains, and philosophical thought provided the link between the aesthetic and discursive modes of thought. While developments in Europe and the United States were roughly parallel in the post-war years with respect to newly composed works and their relation to speculative music theory, another strand of music theory developed in the United States.

Because of political and social conditions in Europe in the years before and during the Second World War, proponents of Schenkerian theory emigrated to the United States and established a strong base of operations in the Northeast. Despite its retrospective philosophical roots and its focus on canonic music of the past, contemporary composers in the United States embraced the Schenkerian analytical method because it promised a precise and systematic description of musical phenomena and asserted a precise musical meaning premised on the triad as ideal structure. While critical of Schenker's regressive political and social views, the same composer-theorists who developed a new technical discourse for the composition and analysis of recent music also praised Schenker's theory for its systematic and logical approach to tonal music. Babbitt, for example, understood Schenker's theory not simply as empirical study of musical practice but rather as a speculative extension of structural possibility that "enable[s] music to progress in a profound sense" (Babbitt 1952: 262).

The dominant music theoretical traditions in the United States and Europe in the years following the Second World War were founded on the general principles of Logical Positivism and its various extensions and revisions in analytical philosophy in the United States. These theories include those focused on twelve-tone techniques, set theory, and transformational theory. Indirectly this included Schenkerian approaches to musical structure as well as the generative theory of tonal structures developed by composer Fred Lerdahl and Ray Jackendoff, the latter based on principles of Chomskyan linguistics (Lerdahl and Jackendoff 1983). But in the United States, another strand of music theoretical inquiry arose in the late 1970s and was informed by Continental philosophy, including phenomenology and various sorts of post-structuralist thought.

A number of authors writing in the 1960s and 1970s had produced more general aesthetic approaches to music using concepts from phenomenological philosophy, including those by F. Joseph Smith (Smith 1979), Alfred Pike (Pike 1970), and Victor Zuckerkandl (Zuckerkandl 1956). In the late 1970s, Thomas Clifton developed a more specifically music theoretical approach that built primarily upon both the general philosophical principles and the investigative procedures of Edmund Husserl (1859–1938) and to a lesser extent on Maurice Merleau-Ponty's (1908–61) philosophy of embodiment (Clifton 1983). Husserl's concept of intentionality, in which the "things" of experience arise as a relation between the objects of the material world and our apprehension of them, stood at the core of his philosophical approach and necessitated a radical investigation of the nature of the things of experience. This investigative turn had a strong resonance with music analysis as a sub-branch of music theoretical work, and the strong analytical and hence empirical nature of Clifton's work reflects this Husserlian strand of phenomenological thought. And following out the Husserlian questioning of the "natural standpoint," that is, the sense that the world is "given" to us through perception, Clifton proposes new theoretical models of music's temporality and spatiality that extend traditional notions of musical structure in the domains of pitch, rhythm, texture, and timbre.

Another analytical model premised on a Husserlian concept of temporal experience was developed by theorist David Lewin, who moved the model in the direction of music cognition (Lewin 1986). Other music theoretical work has turned toward later developments of phenomenological philosophy. My own from the early 1980s can serve as an example. While steeped in Husserlian investigative methodology, it depends more on ideas from Martin Heideggers's (1889–1976) extensions of Husserl's philosophy. In particular, I employ an analytical methodology that engages Heidegger's distinction between the manifest and latent features of the things of experience. This distinction asserts that the manifest features of experience, that is, the features that have perceptual presence, take their full meaning from the latent features which have no such perceptual presence. The distinction requires that a full understanding of experience must go beyond simple experiential presence. Applied to music, this distinction plays a role in defining an analytical framework that takes account of the multiplicity of meanings of musical phenomena (Lochhead 1982). And in a more recent article, the embodiment philosophy of Merleau-Ponty provides a foundation for an analytical method demonstrating how bodily intentionality plays a role in understanding the gestural features of musical phenomena (Fisher and Lochhead 2002).

In the 1990s another strand of music theoretical work based in corporeal intentionality emerged from a more recent and American embodiment philosophy. Using concepts of embodied cognition from linguist George Lakoff and philosopher Mark Johnson, several authors have sought to explain both musical concepts and the music to which they refer in terms of conceptual metaphors which bear the trace of the body (Lakoff and Johnson 1980; Johnson 1987; Saslaw 1996). Branching off from Merleau-Pontian notions of corporal intentionality, the embodiment philosophy of Lakoff and Johnson has moved recently into the domain of cognitive science, a turn that has been matched in music studies in the work of Lawrence Zbikowski (Zbikowski 2002) and Arnie Cox (Cox 2001).

The impact of Continental philosophy on music theory is ongoing and developing in several new directions. For instance, recent interest in the philosophical work of Gilles Deleuze and Félix Guattari amongst music theorists promises new approaches to music theory (e.g. Hulse and Nesbitt 2010). But it is worth noting at this juncture that the music theoretical focus on musical experience and cognition through the lens of Continental philosophy has had a significant impact on who writes theory. While the authors influenced by Logical Positivism and analytic philosophy tended to be composer-theorists in the early and middle years of the twentieth century, the authors influenced by Continental philosophy tend to be theorists, assuming a critical stance toward musical understanding.

Conclusion

This brief and select historical survey of the intersections between music theory and philosophy suggests the depth and variety of the connections between these two fields of thought. While philosophical thought contained music theory in the Ancient world, it is typical in the modern world for music theorists to frame their work around existing philosophical thought. Nonetheless, it is possible to observe some commonalities in the larger goals of philosophical and music theoretical endeavors. Both reflect on the nature of the world (including music) and our experience of it and both establish concepts and methods of address that shape the world – in other words both stand in a reflexive relation to the world. Thus, while it is no longer recognized as such, it is useful to think of music theory as a kind of philosophy of the musical world.

See also Analysis (Chapter 48), Analytic philosophy and music (Chapter 27), Antiquity and the Middle Ages (Chapter 24), Continental philosophy and music (Chapter 26), The early modern period (Chapter 25), Phenomenology of music (Chapter 53), Plato (Chapter 28), Rhythm, melody, and harmony (Chapter 3), and Understanding music (Chapter 12).

References

Babbitt, M. (1952) "Review of Structural Hearing by Felix Salzer," *Journal of the American Musicological Society* 5: 260–5.
—— (1965) "The Structure and Function of Music Theory," *College Music Symposium* 5: 49–60.
—— (2003 [1958]) "Who Cares If You Listen?" [aka "The Composer as Specialist"], *The Collected Essays of Milton Babbitt*, ed. S. Peles with S. Dembski, A. Mead, and J. Straus, Princeton: Princeton University Press, pp. 48–54.
Barker, A. (2004) *Greek Musical Writings II: Harmonic and Acoustic Theory*, Cambridge: Cambridge University Press.
Bélis, A. (2009) "Aristoxenus," *Grove Music Online* in *Oxford Music Online*. 6 December 2009, available at www.oxfordmusiconline.com/subscriber/article/grove/music/01248.
Blasius, L. (1996) *Schenker's Argument and the Claims of Music Theory*, Cambridge: Cambridge University Press.
Boethius, A. M. S. (1989 [c.500]) *Fundamentals of Music*, trans. with introduction and notes by C. Bower, New Haven: Yale University Press.
Bower, C. (1981) "The Role of the *De Institutione Musica* in the Speculative Tradition of Western Musical Thought," in M. Masi (ed.) *Boethius and the Liberal Arts: A Collection of Essays*, Bern/Frankfurt/Las Vegas: Peter Lang, pp. 157–74.
Christensen, T. (1993) *Rameau and Musical thought in the Enlightenment*, Cambridge: Cambridge University Press.
Clifton. T. (1983) *Music as Heard: A Study in Applied Phenomenology*, New Haven: Yale University Press.
Cox, A. (2001) "The Mimetic Hypothesis and Embodied Musical Meaning," *Musicae Scientiae* 5: 195–209.
Descartes, R. (1961 [1650]) *Compendium of Music*, trans. W. Robert, Rome: American Institute of Musicology.
Fisher, G. and Lochhead, J. (2002) "Analyzing from the Body," *Theory and Practice, Journal of the Music Theory Society of New York State* 27: 37–68.
Hauptmann, M. (1991 [1853]) *The Nature of Harmony and Meter*, trans. W.E. Heathcote, New York: Dover [reprint of the 1893 translation].
Hulse, B. and Nesbitt, N. (2010) *Sounding the Virtual: Gilles Deleuze and the Theory and Philosophy of Music*, Aldershot: Ashgate.

Johnson, M. (1987) *The Mind in the Body: The Bodily Basis of Meaning, Imagination and Reason*, Chicago: University of Chicago Press.

Korsyn, K. (1988) "Schenker and Kantian Epistemology," *Theoria: Historical Aspects of Music Theory* 3: 1–58.

Lakoff, G. and Johnson. M. (1980) *Metaphors We Live By*, Chicago: University of Chicago Press.

Lerdahl, F. and Jackendoff, R. (1983) *A Generative Theory of Tonal Music*, Cambridge: MIT Press.

Lewin, D. (1986) "Music Theory, Phenomenology, and Modes of Perception," *Music Perception: An Interdisciplinary Journal* 3: 327–92.

Lochhead, J. (1982) *The Temporal Structure of Recent Music: A Phenomenological Investigation*, Ph.D. diss., State University of New York at Stony Brook.

Mathiesen, T.J. (1999) *Apollo's Lyre: Greek Music and Music Theory in Antiquity and the Middle Ages*, Lincoln: University of Nebraska Press.

Pike, A. (1970) *A Phenomenological Analysis of Musical Experience and Other Related Essays*, New York: St. John's Press.

Pousseur, H. (1959 [1957]) "Outline of a Method," in H. Eimert and K. Stockhausen (eds) *Die Reihe* vol. 3: *Musical Craftsmanship*, trans. L. Black, Bryn Mawr: Theodore Presser, pp. 44–88.

Rameau, J.-P. (1971 [1722]) *Treatise on Harmony*, trans. with notes and an introduction by P. Gossett, New York: Dover.

Saslaw, J. (1996) "Forces, Containers, and Paths: The Role of Body-Derived Image Schemas in the Conceptualization of Music," *Journal of Music Theory* 40: 217–43.

Smith, F.J. (1979) *The Experiencing of Musical Sound: Prelude to a Phenomenology of Music*, New York: Gordon and Breach.

Solie, R. (1980) "The Living Work: Organicism and Music Analysis," *19th-Century Music* 4: 147–56.

Wright, J. (2007) *Schoenberg, Wittgenstein, and the Vienna Circle*, Bern: Verlag Peter Lang.

Zbikowski, L. (2002) *Conceptualizing Music: Cognitive Structure, Theory, and Analysis*, New York: Oxford University Press.

Zuckerkandl, V. (1956) *Sound and Symbol: Music and the External World*, trans. W. Trask, New York: Pantheon Books.

Further reading

Boretz, B., Morris, R., and Rahn, J. (eds) (2008) *Perspectives of New Music* 46/2. (Includes a forum on G. Deleuze and F. Guattari, *A Thousand Plateaus*, featuring articles by B. Boretz, J. Rahn, M. Gallope, and M. Scherzinger.)

Christensen, T. (ed.) (2002) *The Cambridge History of Western Music Theory*, New York: Cambridge University Press. (Articles by prominent authors on music theoretical issues in broad historical perspective.)

Palisca, C. and Bent, I. (2009) "Theory, theorists," in *Grove Music Online. Oxford Music Online*, available at www.oxfordmusiconline.com/subscriber/article/grove/music/44944. (Provides an excellent overview of the broad sweep of the history of music theory.)

47

COMPOSITION

Roger Scruton

Notation

The composer is sometimes thought of as a person who *writes* music. But in the historical scheme of things, writing music is the last in a series of activities, which begin with *making*, pass to *remembering* and therefore *repeating* music, and thence to *writing* music *down*, and only then, when notation has developed, to the art of composing straight onto the page. At all stages in that process music is *composed* – that is to say, created through the ordering of sound along melodic, rhythmic or harmonic dimensions. The development of notation enables composers to dispense with the feats of memory that once were needed, just as the writing down of Greek verse put the Homeric rhapsodes out of business. And musical notation makes it possible to build structures – such as the permutational structures of Schoenberg and Stockhausen – which could not be achieved if the only way of moving around the piece was by remembering and anticipating.

Some philosophers have argued that music is not composed but *discovered*. After all, a work of music is identical neither with the notes written down, nor the sounds made in reading them. It is more like a rule for producing those sounds, or a "sound structure," or a "sound type": an abstract entity that is not located in a place or a time, any more than a number is. In this connection, Julian Dodd has defended a kind of musical Platonism, arguing that works of music do not begin to exist at any particular time, and therefore are not brought into existence by the composer. Works of music are discovered, in something like the way in which mathematical proofs are discovered (Dodd 2007). Other philosophers, notably Jerrold Levinson and Stephen Davies, have argued that there are kinds of abstract entity, musical works among them, which come into existence at a certain time, and are appreciated for qualities, such as their originality, which are essentially connected to their temporal nature (Levinson 1980; Davies 2001).

Whatever we think of this dispute, it should be clear that it is not specifically about music. A work of poetry is identical neither with the words on the page nor with a particular act of reading, writing or thinking them. But most of us believe that poets *create* their poems; in other words, that there is a *first* time that the relevant word tokens were spoken, written or imagined. Likewise with composition: the Platonist position reminds us that creating a work of music means doing something *for the first time*. So what exactly is it that the composer does?

In approaching this question we must recognize that music has many uses and arises in many ways. There is improvised music, as well as music written down and ring-fenced against change. There is music for dancing and marching, music for listening, music for worshipping, and "music while you work." There are traditions such as our Western one in which the repeatable work has emerged as all-important, and in which a developed system of notation enables people to compose without performing, and to leave permanent records of what they have invented. And there are traditions such as the Indian one, in which melodies and their elaborations are memorized, but in which notation is schematic and incomplete.

This does not mean that there are no "works" of Indian classical music. There are plenty of them, but they are not identified through scores. The Indian raga comprises four elements: a mode, a rhythmic cycle or *tala* which allots time values to successive notes, a melody occupying an entire cycle, and a sequence of diminutions or *raginas*, born from the basic phrases of the work. Traditional notation was never sufficient to encompass the result, which might last for an hour or more, and astonishing feats of memory were required of traditional musicians – feats made possible only by the absorption of the raga into religious worship, and by the religious discipline of the musicians. (The case resembles that of Gregorian chant which, like the classical raga, was only sketchily notated and has had to be revived after a period of forgetting.) Nevertheless, even though imperfectly notated, the ragas have existed, some of them for centuries, as individual works, realized, to be sure, in contrasting performances but, like musical works in our Western tradition, the record of original creative acts which are represented in performance. And although many of these works are anonymous, not a few are attributed to specific composers such as Tyâgarâja (1767–1847), whose works, memorized by his pupils and disciples, have been passed on and revered not merely as interesting musical objects, but as the creations of an interesting soul (Jackson 2000: 268–70).

Almost all musical traditions have named melodies – named usually from the song that is sung to them. Many have notated classics. The notation may be (like that of the Indian ragas and much classical Chinese music) more ambiguous than the Western classical tradition would countenance. But in all traditions, ours included, notation underdetermines performance and identifies works of music only when read in the context of a performance tradition. Many "Baroque" classics – and most of the Bach cantatas – are notated with a figured bass, leaving the instrumentalists to work out the accompanying voices for themselves. Nevertheless we love and admire these works as *works*, make the same distinction between work and performance as we would in the case of a Strauss tone-poem or a Schubert song, study the sources in order to know how best to compose out the middle parts, and in doing so believe that we are in relation to a *composition*, the act of an individual who intended us to hear the result. Whenever we identify a *work* of music, we suppose a composer at the back of it, whose intention we follow as we listen or play.

Performances and playbacks

Of course, when improvisation by the performer is a fundamental component in what the audience enjoys, the work takes on another character – less the music itself than a template for producing it. And since the invention of recording, and the mass reproduction of specific musical events, individual performances can acquire a kind of eternal and transcendent character comparable to that of the classical masterpieces. There then arises a new kind of work – the work composed *as* a template for improvisation, of which perhaps only a few recordings achieve the status of classics. An example is Thelonious Monk's "'Round Midnight," rightly esteemed for its authoritative harmonic sequence and soulful melody, but existing in countless performances, some by Monk at the piano, some by the Monk Quartet, some by other musicians using other forces, all differing in every respect that the tradition of jazz improvisation allows and encourages. Only some of the extant versions of "'Round Midnight" achieve the heights, or depths, of melancholy soulfulness that Monk coaxed from the piano, and all listeners will have their favorites. Nevertheless there really is a musical work which is "'Round Midnight," and the work concept is as usefully applied in such a situation as for a Mozart symphony. In the case of "'Round Midnight," much more is left to the performer's discretion than is left by the score of a Mozart Symphony, and a talent *of the same kind* as the composer's is needed, if the performance is to be truly successful. (Peter Kivy (2007) has gone further, arguing that, in every tradition, the performance is a work of art, independent of the work of art that is performed.) Nevertheless, it would surely be as correct to identify Thelonious Monk as the composer of "'Round Midnight" as it would be to identify Mozart as the composer of the "Jupiter" Symphony.

Just as recording techniques have permitted the immortalization of performances, so have they also permitted a new kind of composition, in which performance is by-passed altogether. There has emerged a class of "works for playback," as Stephen Davies has called them: works programmed by the composer into the device that transmits them in audible form (Davies 2001: 25). Early examples of such work, composed onto magnetic audio-tape, were called *musique concrète* by their pioneer, Pierre Schaeffer, whose *Cinq études de bruit* appeared in 1948. Since the emergence of digital methods of creating and storing sound patterns, electronic music has become like photography: something that everyone can produce, regardless of talent, with electronic dance music (EDM) taking over night-clubs around the globe. Whether we can still speak of EDM as composed is a moot point: there is certainly no way of recuperating from it the elaborate communicative intentions that can be heard either in a classical sonata or in a jazz improvisation. With EDM we reach the boundary of the interpersonal world, beyond which lies the desert where the machines are dancing.

Composer and audience

Composition, in the tradition of Western music, has generally been distinguished from performance, even when composer and performer are one and the same. The composer is creating a work of art, whose performances may vary, but which is the single vehicle of an original creative intention. As a rule, composers intend their works to be heard *as* individual products, and therefore as acts of communication with an audience. And this intention is tacitly understood by the audience, and incorporated into the listening culture. Hence a composed work is heard differently from a folk song. True, not all music which we hear as folk music arose spontaneously, "by an invisible hand," from a tradition of communal music-making. Some folk music must surely have been the result of individual inspiration – there can be no other explanation of artful melodies such as the English folk song "Lovely Joan" or the Tudor Court song "Greensleeves," or the Negro spiritual "Swing Low Sweet Chariot," or the songs collected by Canteloube in the Auvergne. Nevertheless a folk song is heard as the voice of a community. It is not one person who is expressing his or her feelings through this music, but a collective soul. The folk song is heard as the residue of countless experiences, as the record of shared emotions and a shared form of life. And when composers use folk melodies it is often in order to present consciously, in the centre of the audience's attention, a voice which is not that of the individual, but that of the community, extended in time. Such is the effect of folk melody in the last act of Stravinsky's *Petrouschka*, for example, in Vaughan Williams's first Norfolk Rhapsody or in Copland's *Appalachian Spring*.

From the philosophical point of view, the act of composition should be understood as the intentional creation of music for the attention of an audience. Schoenberg famously dismissed the need for an audience as a weakness that composers should strive to overcome (Schoenberg 1984: 54). But he was not aiming his compositions into the void: he had *another audience* in mind, one made of people like himself, who listen in silent concentration, without doing irrelevant and unmusical things such as clapping. Even if composers write only for an *imaginary* audience, it is the experience of the audience that is the true target of their intention. The reason for this is clear: it is only *in the ear of the beholder* that music exists. Music is not sound, nor is it the symbols in which the sound is encoded. Music is the object of a certain kind of perception – a process that we hear *in* sounds, in something like the way in which we hear language in the sounds of the human voice. It is, as Gurney put it, "ideal movement" heard in a sequence of sounds (Gurney 1880). A person writing marks on a piece of paper, and intending thereby to give instructions for the production of sounds, is not yet writing music. Only if the intention is to produce sounds *in which music can be heard* does notating sounds count as composing.

To put it another way: composing music occurs within a cultural context, and this context is one of making, listening to, and moving with music. Take the context away and the act of writing down sounds will no longer be an act of composing music. Of course music can be heard in all kinds of sounds which were not intended as music – in the bubbling of a brook, in the clatter of a train on the tracks, in the songs of songbirds. But the compositional intention always reaches beyond the sound, to the musical perception. When a composer places in his music something intended to be heard *as uncomposed sound*, as did Respighi with recorded birdsong in *The Pines of Rome*, this is heard as a sound which enters the music from outside, rather than as an organic part of it. Messiaen, in *Le catalogue des oiseaux*, makes birdsong out of music, not music out of bird-song, and the musical intention flows continuously from beginning to end of each piece.

The cultural context ensures that musical elements have a significance beyond that imposed on them by the composer. It is not possible to divest the diatonic scale and the tonal triads of their resonance, which has been acquired over centuries of usage. It is indeed largely because of this resonance that music is an effective vehicle of communication – one that equals language in the range and complexity of the experiences that it conveys, as any musical person can discover by listening to the 600 or so Schubert songs. Any departure from the traditional and accepted set of expectations must involve an attempt to create a new audience, one that can hear music in sounds that hitherto have been outside the musical fold. This has been the task of composers in our time, and it is not an easy one. As Schoenberg saw, the emancipation of the dissonance requires the creation of audiences who feel no longing for resolution and cadence, who can hear simultaneities instead of chords, and who can navigate through music in which there are no privileged pitch classes to create the equivalent of a tonal center (see Chapter 3, "Rhythm, melody, and harmony," in this volume). Eventually Schoenberg hit on serial organization as a way of creating new expectations in the audience. The permutational order of a serial composition prevents any single pitch class from emerging as a tonic, and so encourages audiences to hear a sequence of simultaneous pitches, rather than a harmonic progression. But permutation also puts a serious obstacle in the way of musical comprehension, with many pitches heard as simply "put into" the music, rather than growing out of its intrinsic movement.

The ear of the beholder can hear sounds as music only if it can recognize the movement of one phrase to the next, the development of a musical argument, and the repetition of important phrases, rhythms and harmonies. This is as true of large-scale symphonic movements as it is true of the simplest pop song. The great structures built by Bruckner, for example, depend at every point on the memorable phrases and harmonies which he implants in the ear of the listener, and which he allows to develop through a syntactical process that deploys all the resources of short-term memory in order to build long-term effects. It is surely significant that there are few convincing lengthy structures in serial music outside the operas of Berg, in which the dramatic action serves to bring cohesion and sequence to what is happening in the orchestra. Even so, Berg's music is episodic, and dependent at every point on sudden transitions of mood.

Pure music and musical drama

This raises an interesting philosophical question. When does music develop from its own inner resources, and when does it depend upon something outside itself? Wagner's ambition in his music dramas was to create drama *from* the musical movement, rather than to pin the music to a drama that moved independently. And it is arguable that in the second act of *Tristan und Isolde*, up to the entry of King Marke and his entourage, Wagner succeeded in doing this. But it was a rare achievement, seldom to be emulated thereafter and anticipated before only by Mozart in the Da Ponte operas and *The Magic Flute*. Much composition today, by contrast, involves composing to an action, a text, or a drama, which pre-exists the composition and lays strict limits to its form. Thus film music has emerged as a new *use* of music, in which musical development is subordinate to an action that obeys no musical laws. This makes composition in one sense easy: you do not need musical material that will sustain the piece unaided. But it also seems to downgrade the result. It is significant that there is little great music for the film that has entered the concert repertoire. Maybe the greatest example, indeed, is the piece of film music that Schoenberg composed – for a film that was purely imaginary! And when film music *does* survive beyond the context of its original use, it usually ceases to be heard as "filmic" – witness, for example, Prokoviev's *Alexander Nevsky* cantata, or Vaughan Williams's *Sinfonia Antartica*.

There is an interesting contrast here with ballet music. There is great music for the ballet by Tchaikovsky, Stravinsky, Bartók, Ravel, and others. This music has survived in the concert hall often long after its choreographic application has been forgotten, but is still heard as dance music. What explains this? One suggestion is that in ballet the dance follows the movement of the music, and does not constrain it; whereas in film scores the music follows the movement of the drama, and loses track when the action changes. When rescued for the concert hall, as in the Vaughan Williams symphony just mentioned, the idea of a narrated *action* is left behind.

The contrast here sheds light, I believe, on the central mystery of composition, which is the art of using melodic, rhythmic, and harmonic material to form continuous sequences that make sense in themselves, and move of their own impulse toward closure. In choosing that material, the composer is in some way foreseeing all that will unfold from it, and foreseeing the final stasis in which the life of the music has run its course. For Hanslick this was the paradigm of musical composition, in which the primary inspiration is not a text or an image but a purely musical idea, conceived in the imagination of the composer, and subjected to a purely musical development (Hanslick 1986: 33–5). It seems easier to understand how this is done, with the old building blocks of the arpeggiated tonic and dominant chords – as in the classical style – and the old sequential forms of sonata, theme and variations, and so on. But how it is done with material such as the motto theme of Berlioz's *Symphonie fantastique*, or with uncharted forms such as those of Debussy's *La mer* remains mysterious.

This returns us to the controversy, pivotal to the development of Western classical music in the nineteenth century, between the followers of Wagner and the followers of Brahms, the former arguing that the fixed structures of the classical symphony and sonata had exhausted themselves, and that music must henceforth develop along *dramatic* lines, either following a text, or taking its inspiration from the movement of extra-musical ideas, as in the tone poems of Liszt, Wagner's father-in-law – the Brahmsians arguing the opposite. It is in fact rather difficult to locate the controversy here, given that Wagner's own music is so majestically symphonic in form, and can in many cases stand alone in the concert hall without a text – the "Prelude and Liebestod" from *Tristan und Isolde* being a celebrated example, and a triumph of "absolute" music that has never since been equaled. Brahms uses one of his own songs – the second "Regenlied" – to wonderful effect in the last movement of the G major Violin Sonata, and the great symphonies of Mahler go from song to sonata and back again without the faintest suggestion of conflict. Nevertheless, there is undoubtedly something correct in Hanslick's observation, that musical order comes from the development of *musical* ideas, and that text and drama are in some away outside the music, even if acting as an inspiration to the composer and a completion of the expressive atmosphere.

See also Analysis (Chapter 48), Classical aesthetic traditions of India, China, and the Middle East (Chapter 23), Gurney (Chapter 34), Hanslick (Chapter 33), Improvisation (Chapter 6), Notations (Chapter 7), Ontology (Chapter 4), Performances and recordings (Chapter 8), Rhythm, melody, and harmony (Chapter 3), and Wagner (Chapter 35).

References

Davies, S. (2001) *Musical Works and Performances*, New York: Oxford University Press.

Dodd, J. (2007) *Works of Music: An Essay in Ontology*, New York: Oxford University Press.

Gurney, E. (1880) *The Power of Sound*, London: Smith, Elder, and Co.

Hanslick, E. (1986 [1891 8th edn]) *On the Musically Beautiful*, trans. G. Payzant, Indianapolis: Hackett.

Jackson, W. (2000) "Religious and Devotional Music: Southern Area," in A. Arnold (ed.) *The Garland Encyclopedia of World Music, Vol. 5 South Asia: The Indian Subcontinent*, New York: Taylor and Francis, pp. 259–71.

Kivy, P. (2007) "*Ars Perfecta*: Towards Perfection in Musical Performance?" in *Music, Language and Cognition: And Other Essays in the Aesthetics of Music*, New York: Oxford University Press, pp. 111–34.

Levinson, J. (1980) "What a Musical Work Is," *Journal of Philosophy* 77: 5–28.

Schoenberg, A. (1984) *Style and Idea: Selected Writings of Arnold Schoenberg*, ed. L. Stein, Berkeley: University of California Press.

48

ANALYSIS

Joseph Dubiel

Defining analysis

It seems safe to assume that the effect of music depends not only on its individual sounds, but also on how the sounds are put together. This assumption gives us a subject of study. Often the subject is called musical *structure*, and the study of it *analysis* (if the focus is on individual cases) or *theory* (if the focus is on generalization). The terms' vaguely scientific aura reflects the idea that patterns and relationships in musical compositions play a role in *causing* the experiences of music that fascinate us, which is reasonable enough. But obviously the causal power is not all within the sound. We get musical experiences only if we go along with the music, by paying attention in certain ways, believing and wanting certain things, and participating in the appropriate contexts. For this reason, the work that we call analysis of music might also be understood as interpretation of music, focusing on attributes of compositions likely to matter to listeners with certain interests. Rather than liken music analysis to a chemical assay, we might liken it to close reading of literature. This is not a perfect analogy, either: compared to close reading, the analysis of music is usually more overtly technical, often engaging issues of perception that have no close parallel in literary study. And music analysis tends not to address questions of biography or historical context to the degree that is routine in literature. There is no deep or compelling reason why it could not, but, in the world of music scholarship as we find it, analysis is recognized, at least informally, as primarily the study of patterned sounds and their perceptual interpretation.

When we try to characterize music analysis further than that – especially in a philosophical context – we find that it is neither a precisely defined practice nor a unified one. Perhaps relatedly, we also find that it is not a practice in which goals and methods are extensively discussed. The theoretical discourse around analysis concentrates on narrower issues: particular musical techniques and relations.

The most positive way to describe this state of affairs might be to say that music analysts typically work close to the notes, giving intellectual expression to a kind of involvement that is also enacted in composing, performing, and listening; and that music analysis is undertaken to assuage many different kinds of curiosity. One analyst might be concerned chiefly with showing how each successive event of a beloved composition is somehow the right thing for the composition to have done. Another might be interested in imagining how the composer's choices could have been made; another, in deriving ideas that might be put to work in new compositions. Still another might be most interested in developing a closer relationship to a musical work, by finding more to hear in it and by becoming more aware of how it does what it does. Another might be trying to test some music-theoretical generalizations, using an individual composition as a case study. Many other possibilities can be imagined.

It is easy to sense how all of these ambitions are related, though they are not exactly parallel. They all depend on the expectation of a significant connection between the structure of music and the qualities that we are able to ascribe to the sounds in combination. This connection is the foundation of all the other inquiries.

The ineliminable music-analytic activity, then, is the drawing of a connection between the structure found by an analysis and someone's experience – actual or potential – of the music. If we find that we cannot relate a pattern in the composition to a way of hearing the music, then it is not clear that we should consider the pattern to be part of musical structure. This is not meant to be a point about the essence of structure, or of music. It is meant to situate analysis among the various kinds of music study, by pointing out the kind of information that analysis most characteristically addresses.

Here is a simple example. It is a fact about Josquin's *Missae Hercules Dux Ferrariae* that its subject, the succession D-C-D-C-D-F-E-D in equal note values, begins with, and devotes most of its length to, an alternation of two pitches. It is also a fact that the notes of this subject are derived from the Latin phrase "Hercules Dux Ferarriae," naming the nobleman Josquin intended to honor, by the extraction of the phrase's sequence of vowels, e-u-e-u-e-a-i-e, and the reinterpretation of these vowels as the vowels of the note names that were used in the Renaissance, re-ut-re-ut-re-fa-mi-re. The first of these facts obviously is something we could hear; indeed, a particularly interesting feature of this generally rather austere composition is its varying exhibition of and concealment of the repetition, especially as it interacts with the repetitions and near-repetitions of text that are scripted in the Roman Catholic mass. The second of these facts is something we can *know*, and our knowledge of it might even help us to appreciate the first fact, by directing our attention to an otherwise unprepossessing theme, among many more demonstrative ones – adjusting our priorities as listeners, we might say – or by inflecting the music, in our minds, as an ingenious musical working-out of an artificial premise. But this second fact does not seem to be of the right sort to figure in our *auditory* experience in any more direct way. The second kind of fact is not unimportant, by any means, but it is less characteristic of the work we call analysis than the first kind.

The identity of music analysis, then, may lie in the disciplined narrowness of the kind of information with which it is most concerned – while the kinds of knowledge it develops, and the kinds of arguments it makes, are diverse. The rest of this chapter surveys some possibilities.

Conceptualizing what we hear

The first benefit we might derive from a discipline of talking about what we hear is a better awareness of what we hear. (This is the side of analysis that is most like criticism.) Philosophically minded readers will be familiar with the paradoxical aspect of this apparently straightforward point: if our formulations are checked for correspondence to what we hear, and we can tell more or less directly whether they are right, then what do we learn by making these formulations? Musicians have a tradition of accepting a bad answer to this question, namely, that we are bringing to consciousness experiences of which we were formerly unconscious. But (as Mark DeBellis puts it) "listening to music is a full-blooded conscious experience if there ever was one" (DeBellis 1995: 45). The gain in awareness that comes from articulating an experience should not be understood as moving it from unconscious to conscious, but from one kind of consciousness to another: as the addition of *conceptual* awareness to perceptual awareness.

Here is an example. In an article about the methodology of analysis, Edward T. Cone says that the recapitulation of the second movement of Beethoven's E Major Piano Sonata Op. 109 "bursts in upon the development" (at measure 105; the music is shown in Figure 48.1) (1989: 42). Simple and obvious as it is, this description does some work for us. It recognizes that the event in question sounds hasty and disconnected – which is all the more remarkable for an event that, by most accounts, represents a crucial moment in the movement's form. The description might help sensitize us to this peculiarity. If we remember how the beginning of this movement burst in on the tranquil, mellow ending of the preceding movement, we might also recognize that an unusual approach to the

Figure 48.1 Beethoven, Piano Sonata in E, Op. 109, second movement, measures 93–115

recapitulation helps to recapture that feeling, even though the second movement has been brusquely energetic all the way along.

Or we might not. It is important to acknowledge that the work accomplished by the description depends on the state of awareness of the listener who reads it, who may or may not have given attention to this aspect of the recapitulation, may or may not have been startled in relation to a contrary expectation, may or may not have the knack of putting something like this into words. The differences are pragmatic ones, not logical ones. We talk partly to *find out* whether other people hear what we hear. In most cases (exchanges between sane participants in a shared musical culture), we find out that, to some degree they do, to some degree they do not, and – most important – to some degree we do not know because we cannot be sure how much our perceptual awareness changes when it takes on a new conceptual aspect. Music theorists do not always remember to focus on the value of interpersonal exchange in itself when trying to explain the discipline; but one of the most rewarding challenges in analytical work can be the effort to make one's hearing accountable to others.

This said, one of the times when we know our awareness has changed is when we acquire a concept that we did not have before. Had you ever thought about the possibility of a composition's recapitulating, not only the melody, harmony, and texture of its beginning, but also the startling suddenness of it? Once you do, you get a lot of other possibilities to think about, including, of course, recapitulations *different* in suddenness from what they recapitulate, whether the material itself changes or not, and you realize that all the other recapitulations you know can be assessed from this point of view. Your awareness takes on another dimension.

In the best of cases, then, even a bit of description as innocuous as "bursts in" can prove to be a considerable conceptual resource – provided it can be connected to a musical experience that specifies its meaning and opens it to further implications. (We are talking about meaning as the attribution of qualities, in this case backed up by concepts, that is, not meaning as reference. Musical meaning begins in hearing-as.) Thinking through these implications may produce an expanded sense of musical possibility, one that affects subsequent experience as well.

Accounting for what we hear

Now, if a composition can do something – elicit an experience in us – it must have a *way* of doing it. In the second movement of Beethoven's Op. 109, the means to make the recapitulation "burst in" include an irregularity in the harmonic succession. Instead of approaching the tonic harmony from the dominant harmony – a progression so deeply entrenched in tradition that many theorists have tried seriously to represent it as inherently logical – this movement jumps to the tonic from the dominant *of* the dominant, simply leaving out the intervening (and conventionally pivotal) dominant harmony. We can understand the irregularity at two levels: first is the simple fact that the move to the tonic is *unusual*; second is the more specific fact that the unusual feature is an elision, and so the arrival of the tonic is *premature*.

When we learn this, what exactly do we learn? By now, one aspect of the answer may be predictable: we might learn any number of things, depending on the point of view from which we come to the information. As we came to it in this discussion, we already had an impression of the effect of the music, of the recapitulation blasting in with unusual haste or pressure. To this impression, we have now added a degree of understanding of how the music elicits it, through the deployment of an exceptional harmonic succession. If we are at all technically minded as musicians, the use of this peculiar succession may be a point of interest in itself, and the way the music does what it does may be a point of further appreciation. (See Walton 1993 and Guck 1993 for a good discussion of this redoubled appreciation.)

Finding what we might hear

But we might have come to be interested in this musical moment by a different route. We might have noticed the unusual succession first, as a technical fact of music theory, without any particular thought about the experienced quality of "bursting in." This, too, is a common direction for analytical thinking to follow. Assuming that we are right in believing the succession to *be* unconventional (or, more fastidiously, assuming we are right in believing in the coherence and the relevance to this piece of the conventions from which the progression departs), we might wonder what is going on. Often this wonder finds expression in a "why" question, such as "why does the music do that?" or, more naturalistically, "why did Beethoven do that?" Music theorists ask such questions all the time. Under scrutiny, such questions usually make better sense as indirect ways of inquiring about something else.

One important unclarity in these "why" questions is whether they are asking for a *cause* or a *reason*. (We need not engage the question of whether and how a reason should be considered to *be* a cause, as long as we agree that some reasons are not causes.) Do we have some hope of discovering a force that guided Beethoven's hand? His supernatural genius? His subconscious? Such a question, and such answers, are not unknown in the history of music theory, but they are not central today. Do we hope to discover some other sense in which the music was compelled to do what it did? Logical necessity? An inherent structure of tonality? (The latter one would be particularly hard when the event that interests us is a *departure* from normal progression.) Such a question, and such answers, may be central in music theory today; if so, this not altogether good.

The article from which we have drawn the example of Beethoven's Op. 109 is a case in point. In it, Cone asserts a standard of analysis, as opposed to mere description, which his own productive phrase "bursts in" does not yet meet. He says that true analysis should try to *explain*, of each musical event, "why it occurs: what preceding events have made it necessary or appropriate, toward what later events its function is to lead" (1989: 41). In pursuit of such an explanation, Cone offers more information. The first phrase of the recapitulation ends on the dominant (measure 108), the second on the tonic (measure 112). Thus the harmony preceding the recapitulation (the dominant of the dominant), though not immediately resolved (to the dominant) by the beginning of the recapitulation, might be heard to resolve later, at the first point of articulation within the recapitulation. And then this resolving harmony (the dominant) in turn might be heard to resolve (to the tonic) at the next such point. Thus "the whole passage is bound together in a cadential II-V-I" (Cone 1989: 42; Cone's expression "II-V-I" represents a different way of conceptualizing the normal harmonic progression to which this whole discussion refers, namely, dominant of dominant, to dominant, to tonic).

This information is interesting from many points of view – but how is it relevant to Cone's ostensible question of why the elision occurs? How would the occurrence of the dominant harmony at the end of a phrase do anything to cause or motivate the omission of a dominant just before the phrase begins, much less to make it "necessary?" (It should be noted that there is nothing in the least unusual about the occurrence of a dominant at the end of the phrase; this may even be the *most* normal harmony to find in that position.) Cone actually seems to be pursuing a different question, something along the lines of: what makes such an event *acceptable*? That is, if a piece is going to omit a significant harmony from a standard progression, especially at a major point of articulation, are there any implications? Any constraints? Or can a composer just *do* that? (Could composing really be that easy?)

Cone does not ask these questions. We are considering them because they may reflect the impulse behind his work better than his explicit precepts do. In any event, questions such as these might be more answerable than his demand for a show of cause. They at least orient the discussion toward the unusual succession consequences – the effects for the sake of which it might have been written.

A particularly interesting feature of Cone's discussion is where it locates the consequences: in listeners, not simply in the score. He argues that our sense of missing the dominant harmony will send us into the recapitulation with a preoccupation, an unusually strong perceptual sensitivity to this harmony when it eventually does occur – and this will rebalance our impression of the recapitulated phrase. To our sense of this phrase as abrupt in its onset, we add the further sense that the phrase's intrusion does not simply cancel the preceding harmonic progression, and that the phrase manages somehow to be embedded within a completion of that progression. Remarkably, this happens without any change in the notes of the phrase, which is repeated exactly as it was played at the beginning. (Eventually there is a compositional change as well, when the end of the theme in the recapitulation is overlapped by the beginning of a rearranged restatement in measure 112.)

What Cone achieves by this analysis is a sense of the unusual event as meaningful rather than arbitrary, as having implications rather than as momentary and whimsical. It apparently is easy to mistake this desired sense of significance for the sense of logical necessity called for in Cone's statement of analytical purpose, because analysts make the mistake all the time – perhaps even cultivate the mistake, unconsciously, in order to make the discipline seem more decisive and powerful than it could realistically be.

This mistake is particularly likely to find its way into the important analytical practice of searching a piece for recurring patterns, especially patterns that are somewhat idiosyncratic. The harmonic succession that has engaged our interest in the second movement of Op. 109 is a perfect example of this. Unusual though it may be, we can find other instances of it, at reasonably prominent moments in the piece. To do this, we may have to generalize our description of the succession slightly; there may not be any other instances of exactly the move we found at the moment of recapitulation, from the dominant of the dominant directly to the tonic, omitting the dominant, in E minor. But if we identify the chords independently of these specific functions, simply as an F-sharp major triad moving to an E minor triad, then we can recognize the same succession occurring several times shortly before the recapitulation, from measure 96 to measure 97 and from measure 100 to measure 101. Admittedly each of these occurs across a phrase boundary, between the end of a clearly defined unit and the beginning of another (the second unit usually a modified repetition of the first), so that the sense of "progression" is somewhat attenuated. But the same is true of the approach to the recapitulation, so this is actually a plus: the phraseological discontinuity is something that all these passages have in common, in addition to the chords they include.

Meanwhile, we could generalize our description of the harmonic succession in another way, characterizing it as one from (major) dominant triad to (minor) subdominant triad, in whatever key. A succession of this kind is embedded within the main theme of the movement, every time it occurs. Like the instances leading to the recapitulation, this succession crosses a local boundary, from the end of the first phrase (measure 108, corresponding to measure 4 of the original statement) to the beginning of the second (measure 109, corresponding to measure 5). This is a very interesting configuration: the first phrase ends in a state of comprehensible incompletion (a half cadence, for those who have the technical language), and the start of the second phrase does not immediately respond to that incompletion, as though some other course of action was more pressing. Eventually there are responses, both at the end of the second phrase (as Cone points out), and, sooner but less directly, in the *second* harmony of the second phrase. The first thing we get, though, is a jolt of energy, one whose direction does not exactly fit the circumstances, but does not totally disrupt them, either, so that things can be worked out as the phrase goes along.

With this sense of the first theme in mind, we can attribute another layer of meaning to the way the recapitulation bursts in. Not only is this music set up to recapture the unspecific startle of its first occurrence, which was produced by contrasts with the first movement that are not recovered here in the middle of the second movement (loud against quiet, minor against major, forceful against gentle), but it also creates its new startle specifically from a characteristic of harmonic discontinuity that was already inherent within it, at its own phrase boundary. It does this by opportunistically seizing on a harmonic succession that had occurred, as if inadvertently, during the repetitions of a short unit near the end of the development. Those repetitions seem like a momentary loss of direction; then it is as though the recapitulation eagerly recognizes its cue in them, and jumps in without waiting for conventional preparation. (It does not hurt a bit that the repeated unit has developed from, and still resembles, the bass line of the beginning of the theme.)

In this little analysis, we have treated the recurrence of the harmonic succession as we have treated the other technical facts we have encountered, including the unusual harmonic succession itself: we have tried to work out what its effect might be on our experience of the music. In our original observation of the unusual succession, it was unmistakable that this interpretive step was needed – because that fact was just a single fact, leaving it obvious that we needed to ask, "what *about* that?" But connecting several instances of a harmonic pattern may feel enough like a substantive accomplishment in itself that the need for further work is not felt so acutely. At least this is what seems to happen fairly often in music analysis. Analysts often present information about similarities between moments in a piece as though it is self-evidently interesting, or self-evidently relevant to the character of the music. That enterprise is facilitated when the character attributed to the music is somewhat abstract or schematic, something like "logic," or "coherence," or "unity" (as though this could be determined without reference to what, in particular, the piece is doing). By lowering its attributive sights in this way, analysis can get an explanandum that seems to be within the reach of explanation by uninterpreted technical information. As a bonus, the analyst is spared the demands of working out a nuanced description of a musical experience (something for which musical training does not necessarily provide much preparation), *and* the discourse is allowed to seem relatively impersonal, logical, and determinate, rather than subjective and mushy. (Maus 1993 considers further significance for these issues of discursive style.)

There is one context for analysis that might enable us to look at this recurrent mishap more favorably, namely, that of modernist composition. There an important intellectual project has been to study the music of the classical canon as a source of ideas for new music that would not rely on all of the conventions of that canon (such as tonality and sonata form). In pursuit of this project, it makes perfect sense to be preoccupied with patterns and regularities in a piece that are not necessarily conventional, that are instead specific to that piece. It might be possible to give such regularities a larger role in the creation of new pieces. And for this purpose, the identification of idiosyncratic regularities might be a higher priority than the characterization of their exact effect.

This is a good time to acknowledge that we have not devoted much attention to the kind of conventional, well-entrenched theories of music that we have occasionally relied on in our identification of chords, and phrases, and recapitulations. Instead, we have concentrated on conceptions of lesser scope, more specific to the music at hand. One reason is that a resumé of those theories could easily have consumed the entire length of this chapter; given the availability of several good surveys of analysis (such as Bent 1987 and Cook 1987), it seemed more important to deal with conceptual issues here. And the fact is that these broader theories raise no issues that we have not already dealt with. In the little bit of analysis we have done, it has been possible to see what happens to the ideas that flow from these theories when they are put to work in specific instances. Each report made in the terms of a harmonic or formal theory still has to be interpreted in relation to its context in a particular piece, to see how it interacts with other facts to produce an effect in that context.

Prospects

No matter what the mixture of technical and ordinary language in an analysis, the evaluation of the analysis ultimately depends on its implications for hearing the music. Not describing musical experience can only make an analysis elliptical; it cannot change the basic logic. Neither, then, can the effort to frame analysis as primarily the explanation of why the composition is the way it is, because the only workable explanations will be functional ones, claiming that the score is arranged so that the music will elicit some experience in a listener. The causal connections in the argument, if any, will be from the structure to some hearing of the music by someone – actual, possible, or imagined.

For the best of reasons, music analysis cannot be expected ever to be a very powerful discipline, if power means the production of determinate, verifiable results. The phenomena to which it is directed, namely, our experiences of music, are various. We can expect not only their details but also their ontologies to be different, from piece to piece and listener to listener. Even trusty concepts such as "recapitulation" are apt to take on idiosyncratic inflections in relation to specific pieces (and to gain in interest by doing so). And every piece will somewhere involve entities and relationships peculiar to it – like our elliptical harmonic succession that remains peculiar even as it becomes a habit, and the character of impulsive yet not destructive rashness that it helps to create in the second movement of Op. 109.

If there are ways to make music analysis empirically stronger, they probably will depend on its discourse becoming more candidly subjective and relative – because it is in musical experience that the data lie. In particular, it will be an urgent matter for analysis to think more about the specific attributes of listeners, who now tend to be represented abstractly and generally, with little reference to the variety of their interests and dispositions. To say this is more to point toward a frontier than to report on the present state of the literature.

See also Aesthetic properties (Chapter 14), Composition (Chapter 47), Musicology (Chapter 45), Music theory and philosophy (Chapter 46), Notations (Chapter 7), Ontology (Chapter 4), Phenomenology of music (Chapter 53), Style (Chapter 13), and Understanding music (Chapter 12).

References

Bent, I. (1987) *Analysis*, New York, Norton.

Cone, E.T. (1989 [1960]) "Analysis Today," in *Music: A View from Delft: Selected Essays of Edward T. Cone*, (ed.) R.P. Morgan, Chicago: University of Chicago Press, pp. 39–54.

Cook, N. (1987) *A Guide to Musical Analysis*, London: Dent.

DeBellis, M. (1995) *Music and Conceptualization*, Cambridge: Cambridge University Press.

Guck, M.A. (1993) "Taking Notice: A Response to Kendall Walton," *Journal of Musicology* 11: 45–51.

Maus, F.E. (1993) "Masculine Discourse in Music Theory," *Perspectives of New Music* 31.2: 264–93.

Walton, K.L. (1993) "Understanding Humor and Understanding Music," *Journal of Musicology* 11: 32–44.

Further reading

Babbitt, M. (1987) *Words about Music: The Madison Lectures*, eds S. Dembski and J.N. Straus, Madison: University of Wisconsin Press. (Informal demonstration of analysis at work, oriented to composition.)

Dubiel, J. (2000) "Analysis, Description, and What Really Happens," *Music Theory Online* 6/3, available at http://mto.societymusictheory.org/issues/mto.00.6.3/mto.00.6.3.dubiel. html. (Inquiry into this supposed distinction, with a reply by Allen Forte and rejoinder by the author.)

—— (2004) "Uncertainty, Disorientation, and Loss as Responses to Musical Structure," in A. Dell'Antonio (ed.) *Beyond Structural Listening?: Post-Modern Modes of Hearing*, Berkeley and Los Angeles: University of California Press, pp. 173–200. (About differences between structural attributions and their correlated experiences.)

Guck, M.A. (2006) "Analysis as Interpretation: Interaction, Intentionality, Invention," *Music Theory Spectrum* 28: 191–209. (Close to the frontier.)

Hanninen, D.A. (2004) "Feldman, Analysis, Experience," *Twentieth-Century Music* 1: 225–51. (Discusses music often called unanalyzable, making many important points of method; related to, but strikingly different from, Hirata.)

Hirata, C.C. (2003) *Analyzing the Music of Morton Feldman*, Ph.D. diss., Columbia University. (Discusses music often called unanalyzable, making many important points of method; related to, but strikingly different from Hanninen.)

49

ETHNOMUSICOLOGY

Peter Manuel

While it is not surprising that Western music aesthetics has overwhelmingly focused on post-Renaissance Euro-American art music, recent decades have seen a growing interest in aesthetic aspects of non-Western music traditions. Ethnomusicological studies of these have enhanced our understanding and appreciation of diverse world musics and their cultural contexts, as well as highlighting ways in which Western music aesthetics is unique and distinctive or, alternately, comprises themes and approaches of broad cross-cultural applicability.

It should be pointed out that much music outside the geographical West – be it modern commercial popular music or neo-traditional art music, not to mention imported Western genres themselves – may be produced and apprehended in ways not markedly different from that of familiar genres in the West. Accordingly, many Western analytical approaches – whether Leonard Meyer's theories of the dynamics of tension and resolution (Meyer 1956), or the ongoing academic debates on the nature of the psycho-acoustic process – might be fruitfully applied to a variety of global genres, from Indian classical music to a pop song played in an African nightclub. However, in many traditional cultures worldwide, one can find a rich and dramatic variety not only of musical styles but also of conceptions of musical meaning, much of which could be understood as constituting distinctive forms of music aesthetics.

Issues of scope, definition, and analytical approach

The cross-cultural study of music aesthetics involves a set of initial problems and challenges pertaining to the definition, delimitation, or identification of concepts of "aesthetics" and even "music." In many ways these questions parallel and recapitulate discussions by anthropologists and some historians of art regarding the proper approach to non-Western visual arts, especially in non-literate traditional societies (see, e.g. Maquet 1986; d'Azevedo 1973). Restrictive modern conceptions of "art" or "music" as denoting entities produced solely for disinterested aesthetic pleasure, free from any overt social function, would tend to eliminate from consideration a vast realm of expressive activities or products that we might otherwise well consider to be "artistic" or "musical." Just as many cultures do not have words for "art" per se, some do not have terms for "music" as a general category (though they might have terms for specific entities such as "drumming" or "song"). Likewise, in some cultures, genres (such as chanting of the Quran) which we might regard as overtly "musical" might not be included in the category of "music." Although defining "music" may remain as elusive and impossible as defining "art," a working conception might involve the oft-quoted notion of "humanly organized sound" supplemented by the consideration that the sonic entity involve creative manipulation of form for its own sake in order to incarnate feeling or cultural meaning, in a public medium, with sensuous effect (Anderson 2004: 7; Armstrong 1975: 11).

If "music aesthetics" is understood in the narrow sense of scholarly attempts to rationally explain musical enjoyment and evaluation, then we might well conclude that there is relatively little in the way of music aesthetics per se to be found outside the Western or cosmopolitan academy (not to mention before the eighteenth-century writings of Alexander Baumgarten and other philosophers). Alan Merriam, in his *The Anthropology of Music* (1964) offered a somewhat more elaborate definition of the Western conception of "the aesthetic," with special reference to music, in an effort to assess its cross-cultural applicability. Merriam defined it as involving (1) psychic distance [that is, a kind or degree of disinterested, detached appreciation], (2) manipulation of form for its own sake, (3) attribution of emotion-producing qualities to music conceived strictly as sound, (4) attribution of beauty to the art product or process, (5) purposeful intent to create something aesthetic, and (6) a presence of a philosophy of the aesthetic (1964: 261–9). He concluded that the Flathead Indians and the Basongye (a Congolese ethnic group), whom he had researched, did not have a music aesthetic in this sense, and that the Western concept of the aesthetic, as he defined it, would prove to be of limited universal applicability.

Subsequent scholars of world music have been less interested in demonstrating the absence of such a narrow Western notion of the aesthetic in the cultures they study, than in exploring, in a more positive sense, what sorts of ideas (explicit or implicit) about music they do in fact have. Such scholars have sought to construct and employ a conception of "aesthetics" that is specific enough to retain some coherence and substance but broad and flexible enough to accommodate the extant rich and vast body of cross-cultural thought about music. As explored in several studies, such a conception of cross-cultural music aesthetics could include: the presence and nature of evaluative criteria for music; the relation of these criteria to judgments about other arts, natural phenomena, social interactions, moral behavior, or the like; the coherence of ideas about music with an indigenous worldview; and the ways that musical form or "sound structure" can be seen to reflect such a broader value system, cosmology, or epistemology, constituting a "philosophy of music" that mirrors a more general philosophy of life. Robert Kauffman's study of Shona Rhodesian music (1969), for example, argued that a native "aesthetic" could be articulated as reflecting morphology (classification of art types), psychology (human reactions and related behavior patterns), and value theory (relating art and music to other aspects of culture). Some such concerns cohere with broader conceptions of music aesthetics used even in reference to Western (including pre-Renaissance) culture, as specified, for example, by Francis Sparshott, that is:

> attempts to explain what music means; the difference between what is and what is not music, the place of music in human life and its relevance to an understanding of human nature and history, the fundamental principles of the interpretation and appreciation of music, the nature and ground of excellence and greatness in music, the relation of music to the rest of the fine arts and to other related practices, and the place or places of music in the system of reality.
>
> (1980: 120).

The fact that such a "philosophy of music" may not be explicitly articulated in many traditional cultures poses a fundamental challenge to the ethnographer, whose uncovering of such an aesthetic may thus depend on extensive fieldwork, involving, among other things, asking the right questions of the right informants. However, the scholarly attempt to discover cases of such "ethnoaesthetics" is laden with inherent dangers. Some ethnographers (e.g. Merriam 1964: 271) have argued that the notion of an "unvoiced aesthetic" or "functional aesthetic," as posited, for example, by David McAllester among the Navajo (1954), is a contradiction in terms (akin to the notion of an "implicit [music] theory," where "theory," in order to be a meaningful concept, should be defined precisely as the conscious use of abstract concepts such as meter and mode to describe music). Similarly, while a few scholars (e.g. Chernoff 1979: 153) have contended that non-verbal actions (such as might illustrate approval or disapproval of a performance) should be recognized as a kind of aesthetic discourse, one could also argue that such suppositions expand the notion of "music aesthetics" to the point where it ceases to have any meaning. Certainly Merriam is correct in suggesting the importance of distinguishing aesthetic notions that are actually articulated by culture bearers, as opposed to those merely hypothesized by ethnographers.

Accordingly, scholars have generally attempted to ground their theses about "ethnoaesthetics" in statements by informants, although this ethnographic quest is far from unproblematic. It is all too easy for the fieldworker, eager to "discover" some unique and distinctive "unvoiced aesthetic," to inadvertently put words in his or her informants' mouths, to rely excessively on a single voluble but idiosyncratic informant, to misinterpret general evaluative statements as implying a body of aesthetic criteria, or to impute coherent philosophical notions to statements or actions unable to bear such interpretive weight. (For admonitions against such errors, see, e.g. Merriam 1964: 273; Ladd 1973; Seiber 1973; Maquet 1986). As noted in reference to the study of visual arts, tendentious scholars run the risk of inappropriately imposing Western concepts, or, alternately, of exoticizing and "essentializing" people whose aesthetic notions and worldviews might not in fact be as unique as the ethnographer argues them to be (see, e.g. Agawu 2003). Such imputations of an all-encompassing worldview in a given culture may also negate the degree of autonomy that art and music might have in that society, and the degree of agency that musicians might enjoy (see, e.g. Chernoff 1979: 155, 194). A final consideration is the need to avoid unsustainable generalizations about a culture based solely or even primarily on art or music.

Other questions and problems of scope, definition, and focus arise in the cross-cultural study of music aesthetics. In representational visual arts, the occasionally useful distinction between form and content (i.e. that entity which is being represented) finds a certain counterpart in vocal idioms with varying degrees of relative importance of (musical) form and lyric content. There are many forms of "text-driven" vocal performance – such as religious chant or a narrative epic ballad – in which a lyric of primary aesthetic or ritual focus is rendered melodically, whether in the form of an ornamented reciting tone or a simple, repeated stock melody. Such genres may lie on a continuum between heightened speech and music (or song), depending on the extent to which the purely "musical" or formal aspects are subjects of aesthetic interest, or are able to demonstrably enhance the impact of the text. Susanne Langer (1953: ch. 10) has written insightfully on the process by which, in song, the lyric text is fully "assimilated" into music, losing its status as poetry. However, genres such as *tarannum* recitations of Urdu *ghazals,* or Cuban *punto guajiro* (whose vocalists call themselves *poetas*/poets rather than "singers") may be regarded as "song" or music only with fundamental qualifications.

Another kind of analytical conundrum is presented by the variety of laments and other vocal events found worldwide that constitute or incorporate overt weeping. Modern Western scholars of music aesthetics continue to debate whether music actually "expresses" emotion (rather than "being expressive of" it); however, there is general agreement with the point made by Langer (1953: 141–2) and others, that music performance (like any artistic endeavor) does not constitute a form of direct emotional expression (or that any such expression as might occur is extraneous and probably even detrimental to the aesthetic process). However, the existence of several kinds of lachrymose lament traditions in world music problematizes this otherwise persuasive argument. (See, e.g. Feld 1982: ch. 3 regarding the New Guinean Kaluli; Merriam 1964: 266 regarding the Musongye; and Tiwary 1978 regarding the "tuneful weeping" of North Indian villagers.) One might be inclined to categorize such events as ritualized and stylized forms of weeping rather than as any kind of song or music per se. However, some evidence – such as Steven Feld's accounts of his informants' interest in his recordings of their weeping songs – suggest that they may represent distinctive (and not uncommon) confluences of aesthetic creativity and direct emotional expression.

Related to the contrast or complex relation between form and content is the equally problematic distinction between functional art and autonomous art created purely for disinterested aesthetic enjoyment. Hence, for example, the designation of "craft" rather than "art" for a knife, where the ornamentation on the handle constitutes an "add-on" to an essentially utilitarian object. Correspondingly, just as European art music was not really "emancipated" from court and ritual functions until the eighteenth century, so does most music-making in traditional societies fall into some category of being "functional" rather than autonomous. While purely recreational forms of music may exist, more typical in such cultures is music's use to worship a deity, praise a patron, accompany repetitive manual labor, stylize the rendition of a narrative ballad, or dignify and celebrate a wedding or childbirth. As with visual arts, however, the functional aspects of such performances are often inseparable from aesthetic dimensions, such that a study of musical aesthetics need not restrict itself to purely recreational or concert musics constituting "art for art's sake." Most kinds of Balinese dance-drama, for example, are functional in the sense that they are conceived partly as a performance for the Hindu gods. However, as Edward Herbst notes, the gods are connoisseurs, such that the artistic merit of the performances is essential to their ritual efficacy (1997: 122). Similarly, in Afro-Latin religious ceremonies such as those of Brazilian *macumba* and Cuban *santería*, the artistry and flair of the drumming and singing are essential to inducing the gods to manifest themselves in the form of spirit possession (in Chernoff 1979: 124). Maquet has observed that some overtly functional objects, such as the African chief's stool or scepter, are typical loci of aesthetic interest, insofar as they are intended to display his power and even connoisseurship (Maquet 1986: 62); similarly, Kwabena Nketia points out that the Akan chief's drum ensemble serves a similar "function," whose efficacy is dependent on its beauty or aesthetic excellence (Nketia 1973). Likewise, it is extremely common worldwide for religious music with an explicit religious function to be performed by professional musicians who do not necessarily share the faith of their patrons (such as the Muslim professionals who perform for North Indian Hindu events). In such cases, it may be natural for many such musicians to conceive their music in more explicitly aesthetic rather than utilitarian terms. Such considerations need not imply that the functional aspects of a music genre are irrelevant, but an attempt to understand the music aesthetics of a given society should by no means exclude from consideration genres which have utilitarian dimensions. Merriam's argument about the absence of a modern Western "aesthetic" in some technologically primitive traditional societies should thus constitute a starting point rather than a disincentive for further inquiry.

Case studies

With such considerations in mind, several ethnomusicologists and anthropologists have explored notions of music aesthetics, broadly conceived, in a variety of cultures outside the Euro-American mainstream, using diverse analytical approaches and generating a correspondingly varied range of findings. Taken collectively, these studies do not begin to constitute a comprehensive global mapping of music aesthetics, especially since scholars have been particularly interested in isolated, traditional, and often demographically small groups whose worldviews are especially likely to differ from those of the modern world. Nevertheless, the studies undertaken do provide a sense of the richness and variety of vernacular music aesthetics cross-culturally.

In many non-Western societies, evaluative criteria and allied notions of music aesthetics are explicit, especially in the case of the highly evolved and elaborate philosophies of art in the traditional high cultures of East and South Asia. If R. F. Thompson (1973) had to go to some effort to elicit evaluative statements from Yoruba informants about statues, researchers such as John Chernoff (1979) have been able to find West African musicians happy to expound at length on their notions of musical aesthetics. In larger societies with well-established literary traditions, evaluative criteria about music and the arts are also explicit; hence A. J. Racy has been able to document evaluative terms and conceptions in urban Egyptian music culture, while several scholars have described Javanese and Balinese concepts about music (Racy 1998).

Rather than illustrating an exotic worldview, a primarily "functional" conception of music, or a markedly distinct sort of aesthetic approach, the evaluative statements voiced by West Africans and others can often be seen to reflect a fundamentally aesthetic attitude toward music that is not dramatically different from that of the West. Chernoff (1979) quotes at length from his Ghanaian drum teacher, a particularly articulate and reflective artist who dilates on the proper approach to playing the lead *dondon* drum – when and how often to switch from one pattern to another, how to relate it to the accompanying parts, or to a dancer, and so on. Some of the teacher's commentary explicitly relates performance to social ethics, stressing, for example, how impulsive, showy, and self-indulgent playing can reflect a lack of emotional sensitivity and respect for tradition. While such comments might be interpreted as reflecting a certain "African" sensibility, they could easily be applied to a variety of music idioms, from salsa piano playing to Irish fiddling. At the same time, even in societies with an unproblematically aesthetic attitude toward music, evaluative and descriptive terminology and statements are sometimes surprising and distinctive, and may be of particular use to outsiders attempting to understand the music. For example, Indo-Trinidadian tassa drum music, with its flashy pyrotechnics and thunderous volume, might be typically characterized by a foreign listener as wild and raucous; yet when performers and other insiders praise a given player or ensemble, they invariably describe it as "sweet."

Ethnographers of non-Western music cultures have taken special interest in aesthetic statements by informants that are especially reflective of their particular cultural contexts and broader social or philosophical notions, or that suggest aesthetic preferences that obtain in other expressive media and sensory domains. Thompson, for example, notes the sometimes explicit appreciation of composure, poise, and relaxed self-control – as opposed to frenzied abandon or catharsis – in some Congolese and West African drumming and dancing; such an attitude, he argues, can be seen to reflect a broader "aesthetic of the cool" which is valued in social behavior and other aspects of life (Thompson 1966). Barbara Tedlock finds a different sort of extra-musical resonance in the evaluative statements made by her Zuni acquaintances, especially those who praise certain songs as *tso'ya* – a term imperfectly glossed as "clear, new, beautiful" used to characterize a variety of phenomena (Tedlock 1986: 189). In reference to song, *tso'ya* could refer to its large melodic contour, clear articulation of lyrics, chromatic passages, and incorporation of two contrasting melodies. A line of identically clad dancers would be distinguished as *tso'ya* by its inclusion of a single member in a brightly contrasting outfit. In the natural world, *tso'ya* could characterize the vividly contrasting colors on a swallowtail butterfly or a collared lizard. Tedlock argues that the recognition and valuing of *tso'ya* reflect a "Zuni aesthetic" which is distinctive and internally consistent.

Of particular interest to ethnomusicologists have been the ways in which cosmologies or worldviews in a given society can be reflected or rearticulated in formal aspects of music, in such a way that sound structure seems to mirror social structure. Particularly influential in this regard have been Feld's writings on the Kaluli, a relatively isolated ethnic group of some 1500 people living in the New Guinea highlands. In his book *Sound and Sentiment* (1982), Feld explored, among other things, the intriguing coherences between song, myth, and folk ornithology, including the belief that the voices of the forest birds represent deceased ancestors. Feld focuses in particular on ceremonial songs in which sung melodies patterned on bird calls and accompanied by drums consecrated with bird blood reach a stage at which they "harden," in local parlance, provoking weeping; at the same time, such songs are valued by Kaluli informants not merely (or even) as seances or funerary laments, but for their aesthetic values and skillfully rendered formal features. In a subsequent article, Feld expanded on the intriguing ways that singing and drumming – typically with multiple, contrasting, out-of-sync patterns – recapitulate forest sounds (again, especially, the raucous sound of multiple, contrasting bird calls) and even the forms of Kaluli conversation, with its constant seeming cacophony of group interjections and interruptions (Feld 1988). Of special interest, as Feld notes, are the ways the Kaluli use the term *dulugu ganalan* – roughly, "lift-up-over-sounding" – as a descriptive term not only for such sounds but also for the effective aesthetic deployment of such a texture in music.

Turning to the geographically proximate but socially distant high cultures of Bali and Java, ethnomusicologists have posited similar iconicities between music structure and epistemologies in the sophisticated musics performed on gamelans – large ensembles dominated by metal gongs and xylophones. Judith and Alton Becker have noted how Javanese conceptions of time are dominated to a distinctive extent by various sorts of cycles – not merely Gregorian, solar, and lunar, but also a set of vernacular calendrical periodicities (Becker 1979; Becker and Becker 1981). It is not coincidental, they argue, that Javanese gamelan music is governed – in a more overt and elaborate form than most metered musics – by time-cycles (*gongan*), whose expressive power derives from their "iconicity" or coherence with local cosmology.

Susan Walton posits yet another sort of iconicity in Javanese gamelan music. She notes that recurrent in Javanese philosophy is the belief in an ineffable, perhaps esoteric, "inner" (*batin*) level of meaning and reality that underlies most worldly, external (*lahir*) appearances (Walton 2007: 35). Although traceable to local interpretations of Sanskritic *rasa* aesthetic theory and Sufi mysticism, such conceptions inform colloquial worldviews as well as learned, literary discourse. Just as Sanskrit philosophy (especially that of the eleventh-century Abhinavagupta) linked aesthetic relish of *rasa* to a blissful state of heightened consciousness, so gamelan music seems to reflect the state of collective meditative transcendence sought by local Sufi mystics. Moreover, the notion of an elusive "inner melody" implicit in the layered polyphony of the gamelan can be seen as a quintessential *batin* entity (Walton 2007: 35).

Other scholars have undertaken similar attempts to relate vernacular aesthetic criteria (whether explicit or "unvoiced") to broader beliefs and values. Margaret Kartomi (1993) has sought a correspondence between Sumatran Mandailing ensemble music and a local tolerance of socially contrasting "freedom and cooperative mores." Charles Keil has posited a relation between Nigerian Tiv music structure and an affinity toward "circles and angles" in visual aesthetics (Keil 1979). Naturally, ethnomusicologists, like other scholars, need not limit their scholarly output to reporting the "emic" statements of cultural insiders, but may contribute much by advancing interpretations, however speculative. Nevertheless, as suggested above, such endeavors run risks of being more fanciful than empirical, and of creating rather than documenting iconicities.

Some writers have opined that such correlations between worldview and musical form are precisely the sort of thing that distinguishes "primitive" societies from the post-Renaissance West, where the fine arts have enjoyed an autonomy and an explicitly "disinterested" mode of appreciation that allegedly liberate them from any extra-musical influences or conditioning. Others, however, have challenged the notion of such autonomy, from various viewpoints. For instance, the Western preference for closed, symmetrical musical forms – such as sonata form, or familiar song formats like the 32-bar AABA form, in contrast to open-ended, additive forms like a strophic narrative ballad – reflects a broader post-Renaissance aesthetic preference for unified, formally complete art works, such as the novel, or a painting deploying perspective and a realistic foreground–

background dialectic. It has been persuasively argued that this aesthetic, voiced in the fifteenth century by Leon Alberti, in which all parts must cohere with the unified whole, should not be seen as a purely formal, autonomous development, but as part of a semiotic revolution conditioned by the advent of capitalism and industrial technology, which generated an unprecedented degree of concern with rationalization of all aspects of life, and a new emphasis on the bourgeois self as opposed to the feudal collective (see, e.g. Marothy 1974; Hauser 1957: 15; Manuel 2002).

Modernity and traditional aesthetic systems

The advent of modernity has had dramatic effects on traditional music cultures worldwide, bringing mass media, the sounds of global pop styles, and new modes of musical production, reception, and patronage even to the New Guinean highlands. Conversely, some traditional musics – from Tibetan chant to pygmy singing – have come to be recycled as "world beat" exotica in the West, posing some of the same questions of audience reinterpretation as raised by the familiar "African mask problem" decades earlier. One of the most overt, widespread, and dramatic changes wrought by such developments on non-Western music cultures is what could be called an aestheticization process. The spread of commercial pop styles, whether local or imported, places a new emphasis on musics that are purely recreational, and thus largely free of the "functional" considerations that might condition the form and meaning of work songs, religious music, life-cycle commemorations, praise songs, and the like. Thus, commercial pop musics bring with them not only dramatically new sounds and styles but also a quintessentially and primarily aesthetic mode of appreciation, oriented toward a "distinterested" form of reception (that might include energetic social dance).

In many countries, from Uganda to Trinidad, songs and dances are disembedded from their traditional contexts and performed by folkloric groups on stage, often in the format of competitions. Judges use scorecards whose criteria ("stage presentation," "attire," "group coordination," etc.) are explicitly aesthetic, regardless of how central such considerations were in traditional settings. In such situations, the exclusive emphasis on aesthetic aspects may be new, but the criteria themselves may derive from (and constitute intriguing articulations of) traditional evaluative norms.

A form of aestheticization can also result when traditional genres are rearticulated as modern popular musics, whether presented for local or foreign audiences. For example, the music of the griots of West Africa's Senegambia region traditionally foregrounded the genealogical praise lyrics sung for its patrons, with the instrumental accompaniment (on *cora* lute or wooden xylophone) being of secondary importance. Several griots, however, have successfully marketed their music to Western "world beat" audiences, in the process de-emphasizing the lyrics (which are in any case unintelligible to foreigners), foregrounding the melodious instrumental playing, and effectively "liberating" the art from its traditional social function (Racanelli 2009). Such changes need not be nostalgically lamented as alienating or commercializing, as they can stimulate new sorts of musical creativity and dynamism.

See also Analysis (Chapter 48), Classical aesthetic traditions of Asia and the Middle East (Chapter 23), Music and dance (Chapter 43), Musicology (Chapter 45), Notations (Chapter 7), and Understanding music (Chapter 12).

References

Agawu, K. (2003) *Representing African Music: Postcolonial Notes, Queries, Positions*, New York and London: Routledge.

Anderson, R. (2004) *Calliope's Sisters: A Comparative Study of Philosophies of Art*, 2nd edn, Upper Saddle River: Pearson Prentice-Hall.

Armstrong, R.P. (1975) *Wellspring: On the Myth and Source of Culture*, Berkeley: University of California Press.

Becker, J. (1979) "Time and Tune in Java," in A.L. Becker and A. Yengoyan (eds) *The Imagination of Reality: Essays in Southeast Asian Coherence Systems*, Norwood: Ablex, pp. 197–210.

Becker, J. and Becker, A. (1981) "A Musical Icon: Power and Meaning in Javanese Gamelan Music," in W. Steiner (ed.) *The Sign in Music and Literature*, Austin: University of Texas Press, pp. 203–15.

Chernoff, J. (1979) *African Rhythm and African Sensibility*, Chicago: University of Chicago Press.

d'Azevedo, W. (ed.) (1973) *The Traditional Artist in African Societies*, Bloomington: Indiana University Press.

Feld, S. (1982) *Sound and Sentiment*, Philadelphia: University of Pennylvania Press.

—— (1988) "Aesthetics as Iconicity of Style, or 'Lift-up-over-Sounding': Getting into the Kaluli Groove," in *Yearbook for Traditional Music* 20: 74–113.

Hauser, A. (1957) *The Social History of Art*, vol. II, New York: Vintage.

Herbst, E. (1997) *Voices in Bali: Energies and Perceptions in Vocal Music and Dance Theater*, Hanover: Wesleyan University Press.

Kartomi, M. (1993) "Comparative Musicology and Music Aesthetics," in *Systematische Musikwissenschaft* 1: 257–82.

Kauffman, R. (1969) "Some Aspects of Aesthetics in the Shona Music of Rhodesia," *Ethnomusicology* 13: 507–11.

Keil, C. (1979) *Tiv Song: The Sociology of Art in a Classless Society*, Chicago: University of Chicago Press.

Ladd, J. (1973) "Conceptual Problems Relating to the Comparative Study of Art," in d'Azevedo, pp. 417–24.

Langer, S.K. (1953) *Feeling and Form: A Theory of Art*, New York: Scribner.

Manuel, P. (2002) "Modernity and Musical Structure: Neo-Marxist Perspectives on Song Form and its Successors," in R. Qureshi (ed.) *Music and Marx: Ideas, Practice, Politics*, New York: Routledge, pp. 45–62.

Maquet, J. (1986) *The Aesthetic Experience: An Anthropologist Looks at the Visual Arts*, New Haven: Yale University Press.

Marothy, J. (1974) *Music and the Bourgeois, Music and the Proletarian*, Budapest: Akademiai Kiado.

McAllester, D. (1954) *Enemy Way Music: A Study of Social and Esthetic Values as Seen in Navaho Music*, Cambridge: Peabody Museum.

Merriam, A. (1964) *The Anthropology of Music*, Chicago: Northwestern University Press.

Meyer, L. (1956) *Emotion and Meaning in Music*, Chicago: University of Chicago Press.

Nketia, J.H.K. (1973) "The Musician in Akan Society," in d'Azevedo, pp. 79–100.

Racanelli, D. (2009) *Diasporic* Jeliya *in New York: A Study of Mande Griot Repertoire and Performance Practice*, Ph.D. diss., Graduate Center of the City University of New York.

Racy, A.J. (1998) "Improvisation, Ecstasy, and Performance Dynamics in Arabic Music," in B. Nettl (ed.) *In the Course of Performance: Studies in the World of Musical Improvisation*, Chicago: University of Chicago Press, pp. 95–112.

Seiber, R. (1973) "Approaches to Non-Western Art," in d'Azevedo, pp. 425–34.

Sparshott, F.E. (1980) "Aesthetics of Music," in S. Sadie (ed.) *The New Grove Dictionary of Music and Musicians*, vol. 1, London: Macmillan, pp. 120–34.

Tedlock, B. (1986) "Crossing the Sensory Domains in Native American Aesthetics," in C. Frisbie (ed.) *Explorations in Ethnomusicology: Essays in Honor of David P. McAllester*, Detroit: Information Coordinators, pp. 187–98.

Thompson, R.F. (1966) "An Aesthetic of the Cool: West African Dance," *African Forum* 7: 85–103.

—— (1973) "Yoruba Artistic Criticism," in d'Azevedo, pp. 19–59.

Tiwary, K. (1978) "Tuneful Weeping: A Mode of Communication," *Frontiers: A Journal of Women Studies* 3: 24–27.

Walton, S. (2007) "Aesthetic and Spiritual Correlations in Javanese Gamelan Music," *Journal of Aesthetics and Art Criticism* 65: 31–41.

50
MUSIC AND POLITICS

James Currie

In 1970, the composer Gavin Bryars founded the Portsmouth Sinfonia so that works from the Western classics could be performed by musicians who had not been formally trained within that music's normal traditions and were often quite unskilled on their instruments. The frequently carnivalesque egalitarianism of the concerts – Bryars has amusing anecdotes in this regard (Griffiths 1985: 151–2) – suggests that during this period the Portsmouth Sinfonia and Bryars were swept up in the sometimes rampant politicized iconoclasm that character- ized the immediate cultural aftermath of the upheavals of 1968; it would encour- age us to think of Bryars as an example of a far-from uncommon phenomenon – a post-1945 composer attempting to bring political transformation into coor- dination with musical practice. Indeed, it was at this time that Bryars became good friends with the pianist John Tilbury, who then subsequently became part of Cornelius Cardew's Scratch Orchestra, the famous experimental group that quickly politicized itself along the lines of the Maoist Marxism then prevalent in radical left-wing circles in Western Europe. Bryars, however, never joined the Scratch Orchestra, and when in the mid-1980s Paul Griffiths asked him whether he had not been tempted, he answered "Not really. I could sympathize politi- cally, but I thought that the combination of politics and artistic activity was what in philosophy one would call a 'category mistake.' The criteria for evaluating excellence in each were different, and therefore to apply criteria from one to the other seemed to me inappropriate" (1985: 155).

Bryars had read philosophy at Sheffield University (1961–64), so we can take seriously that "category mistake" invokes Gilbert Ryle's vision of a phi- losophy that is concerned with "the replacement of category-habits by category- disciplines" (1949: 8). From this perspective, if the common phrase "music is political" is a category mistake, then the job of philosophy should be to get rid of it and reassert that the "logical type or category to which a concept belongs is the set of ways in which it is logically legitimate to operate with it" (Ryle 1949: 8). One might argue that this project has little bearing outside of concerns regarding the logical cleanliness of philosophy itself, and to a degree Ryle concurs. After all, if a category mistake can be a myth, nevertheless a "myth is, of course, not a fairy story," and people can often function perfectly well under misconceptions. However, there is a subtly Enlightenment ethos of emancipation underlying Ryle's project. For example: "Many people can talk sense with concepts but cannot talk sense about them; they know by practice how to operate with concepts, anyhow inside familiar fields, but they cannot state the logical regulations governing their use" (Ryle 1949: 7). The key phrase here is "inside familiar fields," with its mildly deprecatory implications of habit and convention. If from a pragmatic position it might be argued that we only know something by means of the conventions that dictate its use, from an Enlightenment perspective the home offered by these conventions can keep us in the dark regarding other possibilities. As this chapter will show, there are indeed benefits to be claimed for the sense of belonging that, from Johann Herder's counter-Enlightenment writings in the eighteenth century (Berlin 2000: 168–242) through to bell hooks's African American feminist critique today (2009), has been propounded as a predominant life-enhancing value. But Ryle's continuation opens up a possible correlation between belonging and vulnerability, since for him people who conceptually operate solely within a zone of familiarity "are like people who know their way around their own parish, but cannot construct or read a map of it, much less a map of the region or continent in which their parish lies" (1949: 8).

What if the parish starts to malfunction, necessitating a new understanding of how it should be traversed, or a means of getting out of it? A category mistake, it would seem, is fine only as long as the context in which it functions continues to work. When that ceases to be the case, it needs to be scrutinized. I argue likewise and so will *not* be motivated here by the more frequently stated aim of arriving at one thing, a kind of music/politics symbiosis in which music is always looking with interest beyond itself to where politics lies. Rather, I wish to contemplate the advantages of a fork in the road that denotes two (music and/or politics). Influenced by a common theme in post-war French philosophy, particularly that of Gilles Deleuze and Félix Guattari, I will be more concerned with the singularity of different practices, and so will seek to emphasize the places were music is, in a neutral sense, self-involved and, thus, indifferent to the political (Deleuze and Guattari, 1994).

Collaborative politics

When music and politics are under discussion today in broadly conceived postmodern discourses, indifference rarely gets presented attractively. In general, this is because it is viewed less as a mere sign of a lack of shared concerns than as an overdetermined attempt to create space and avoid the feelings of vulnerability that occur when the Other is perceived to be too close. Thus, an indifferent space between music and politics gets interpreted symptomatically, as a denial either of the proximity of the relationship between the two, or even as a mask for the absence of any proper relationship of difference at all. What I will call collaborative politics argues against such indifference, claiming that if what we want, in the broad and fully emancipatory sense, is space, then we need to proceed by means of paradox, and bring music and politics closer rather than further away. Categories are the mistake; category mistakes, merely the attempt to rectify them.

Collaborative politics argues that music is embedded within what I will call human belongings: the specific realms of human activity and meaning-making that enable us to belong to a certain social locality and which, in turn, therefore belong to us. To ignore such embeddedness would be to attempt to ignore that human world. Lawrence Kramer writes that "classical music can become a source of pleasure, discovery, and reflection tuned not only to the world of the music, rich though that is, but also to the even richer world beyond the music" (2007: 6). Music is here a privileged site for a broadly conceived politics of relationship formation; in collaborating with the world, music encourages us do likewise: "classical music enlarges the capacity of all music to attach itself, and us, more closely to whatever we care about" (Kramer 2007: 33). This is essentially a therapeutic politics whose basic message is that *we are not* until we collaborate with, and heal the wound that divides us from, *that which is*. And since "that which is" here denotes socially produced human belongings, we are not, therefore, until we collaborate with collaboration itself. As a result, the implied political subject here looks rather like the music valorized by collaborative politics. Kramer writes that he wants to "reject the idea that there's a deep musical truth that loose talk about meaning and expression obscures and dumbs down. The meaning and expression are what matters" (2007: 8). Likewise, the subject of collaborative politics redresses the balance of the normative aesthetic categories around which it could be understood to be organized, by rejecting form (the "deep structural truth" that supports the autonomy of the subject from within) in favor of content (human belongings). In order for music to be political, subjects must be social. Without such category mistakes, both music and subjects would be meaningless not only in the literal sense, but also ethically, lacking in the value that makes human life meaningful.

But if human belongings are our earth, why do they need music acting as a gravitational force so that we might remain grounded upon them? Rather than being an esoteric abstraction alienating us from human belongings, music qua music seems to be a privileged means of allowing for that relationship; in order for the one (human belongings), there must be two (human belongings *and* music). Collaborative politics attempts to suture such problematic splitting through assertions such as Kramer's that "Music is our premier embodiment of the drive for attachment" (2007: 33). Since music here is merely a manifestation of a constitutive feature (the drive for attachment) of human belongings themselves, we cannot properly talk about two. In fact, in this instance, the displacement of the drive for attachment onto music makes music itself into a virtual human, a kind of cyborg. Music is now somewhat uncannily endowed with a kind of human agency, like Frankenstein's electrically vivified monster. As Kramer's continuation attests, "[Music] works, it grips and grasps us," and so resurrects us from our condition of alienated non-engagement, since this contact is "almost with the electricity of touch" (2007: 33).

However, ravished into this state of arousal by the musical cyborg that we have created, to what do we then attach ourselves? Unless we are either frigid or too-cool-for school, we respond reciprocally, and attempt to embrace the music itself – through dance, movement, attentive listening, singing along, or the canceling out of distractions, by closing the eyes or turning down the lights. Admittedly, one might argue that what allows us to get entrapped in music is attraction to the traces in the music of the very human belongings that had initially motivated the music's production. However, it would be debatable to conclude that what keeps us lodged there is merely this content (our identity, name, beliefs, and so on). Surely something else, however mediated, also comes into play! Otherwise there would be no need for the embarrassing disorientation occurring when you hit the ground after the music is over, no sobering sense of return after a moment of forgetting, such as we experience when we step out of the concert hall and quotidian concerns resume their whisperings in our ears, like profanities insinuated from the lips of some minor malevolent sprite. Maybe the reason we seek expression for human belongings through such saucy fooling around with music – which, *pace* Kramer, seems noticeably less efficient than just confronting the meanings directly – is precisely so as to fool around with music. Perhaps the human belongings are just a ruse.

Continuing in this aestheticist vein, we could note the seemingly sublime experiences that we can have of music of whose culture and time we have next-to-no understanding. I, for example, listen to North Indian Rāgas, and yet, without any particular pride, I can confess to having never made the effort to find out anything about their "cultural contexts." Of course, one might argue here that I merely prove the opposite point by means of an unfortunate case study, and that what keeps me attached to North Indian Rāgas is precisely not their music, per se, but rather that the music presents itself as a screen onto which I can project the shoddy Orientalist fantasies of my own culture and so reaffirm my sense of belonging to it. As Carolyn Abbate has rightly pointed out, music is decidedly sticky: "Words stick to it, as anyone who has tried to get the 'lyrics' for Schubert's Unfinished Symphony out of his head knows all too well. Images and corporeal gestures stick as well" (2004: 523). And so of course do racist political fantasies. But if, as reception history and film music attest, almost anything can attach itself to the same piece of music, then music is also potentially indifferent to human belongings, like a dog that stares out blankly from the series of anthropomorphic costumes in which its lonely owner has it dressed.

If the world of human belongings requires the world of music in order to keep us bonded to it, then that would imply that human belongings are in some sense insufficient in-and-of-themselves for the humans for whom, collaborative politics asserts, they are fundamental; likewise if human belongings are being employed merely to allow for a musical romp in the hay. In both cases, the presence of an autonomous musical trace reveals a lack within human belongings and so is potentially performing the function of critique – a function which the following shows to be appropriate.

Collaborative politics seeks to keep us bonded to human belongings either in order to preserve them against the damaging large-scale political forces of the present or as an assertion of human belongings' ability to be housed in accordance with presently existing political frameworks. Collaborative politics therefore tends to claim that it is possible to separate and shield certain kinds of human belongings from mediation by large-scale political forces; it asserts the power of locality and particularity to resist being fully consumed by universality. But why can human belongings remain meaningfully and productively autonomous in the face of such politics when collaborative politics asserts that music itself cannot be autonomous of human belongings? Admittedly, the two situations may not be comparable, so to ask such a question could constitute a category mistake. But the discrepancy might also be evidence of a perspectival trick whereby the political and the musical are made to appear as smaller (less powerful) than they actually are so that we can be successfully convinced of the primary value of human belongings.

Considering the political, the rhetorical justification for collaborative politics' potentially covert move would be necessitated by the fact that today's large-scale political forces frequently *do* decimate local-level human belongings. And so to center a politics today solely on human belongings would be tantamount to an escapist denial of the political per se. For in the present global problematic, the political is, as Alain Badiou has written, "something that – in the categories, the slogans, the statements it puts forward – is less the demand of a social fraction or community [i.e. the subjects of human belongings] to be integrated into the existing order than something which touches on a transformation of that order as a whole" (2002: 109). For example, take the numerous examples of indigenous peoples defending their lands (and so their social faction, community, human belongings) against violent incursion by pan-global forms of capitalism. Since the logic of capital is structurally constituted so that it cannot retreat and respect a zone of difference, indigenous groups have to strive for some kind of transformation of the existing order as a whole in order to secure their human belongings; this accounts in part for the development of socialist and Marxist revolutionary politics in areas such as the Mexican states of Oaxaca and Chiapas, or in Evo Morales's Bolivia. In order to be effective sources of resistance, their human belongings must undergo dialectical mediation with regard to the universalized forms of capitalism by which they are threatened. As a result, they can no longer be human belongings in and of themselves. If this does not happen, indigenous peoples would end up like the parishioners using category mistakes in Ryle's metaphor, and so they would be more vulnerable to being annihilated.

The stark conclusion here, therefore, is that if human belongings cannot produce the means for understanding how their own existence is threatened, then they are not life-enhancing. The potential autonomy of music merely exacerbates such a conclusion, for if, in part, we can sustain elevated degrees of attraction to music precisely because something in it exceeds the trace of the human belongings out of which it and we ourselves emerge, then that suggests that there is a need that human belongings per se can not fulfill.

The politics of critique

Collaborative politics, then, is ideological to the degree that it works to exclude from circulation the understanding that human belongings are in fact *not* enough. By comparison, what I call the politics of critique makes this assertion into its founding credo. Within the politics of critique, the function of the music is no longer to attach us to that which already exists and can be known (in the sense of being articulated through language with regard to its meanings). More dialectical in orientation than collaborative politics, it points, on the one hand, toward a different condition of social life yet to come; and on the other, engages in the paradox of giving voice to that which, at present, cannot be known in the normative sense. The former, for example, is an *idée fixe* in the work of Jacques Attali. Music "heralds, for it is *prophetic*. It has always been in its essence a herald of times to come" (1985: 4). It "makes audible the new world that will gradually become visible . . . it is not only the image of things, but the transcending of the everyday, the herald of the future" (1985: 11). "Music was, and still is, a tremendously privileged site for the analysis and revelation of new forms in our society" (1985: 133). Regarding the latter, Lydia Goehr, talking of the German Romanticism that informs her own position, writes that the purely musical" came to serve,

> as a repository for all that which could not be captured by a philosophical theory constrained solely by the authority of reason . . . "The purely musical," more specifically, served as a general metaphor symbolizing a repository for all that was unknowable by ordinary cognitive or logical means.
>
> (Goehr 1998: 18)

Rather than seeking the collaborative political end of keeping present that which potentially threatens to recede into the past, the politics of critique thus attempts to draw that which seemingly is not yet into that which already is. Predominately dialectical, what it values in human belongings is their potential for becoming as opposed to their ability to constitute themselves as what G. W. F. Hegel might have referred to as immediacies – the kinds of self-enclosed systems into which collaborative politics can sometimes strive to transform human belongings. Because it is the underlying formal lack (in Hegel's terms, negativity) in that which has been conceptually determined that allows for such becoming, the politics of critique aims to encourage as a constitutive feature of human practices, the keeping open of the gaps, silences, and fissures that this lack creates; to invoke the famous passage in Hegel's preface to the *Phenomenology* (1977: §32), it seeks to keep us tarrying with the negative, for through a paradoxical exchange, by being exposed to the fact that our concepts are less, we get the magnificence of more, the full presence produced by an absence. Thus, as we move from the politics of collaboration to the politics of critique, and from belongings to becomings, the active subjects implied by these politics shift their orientation from content (what they are) to form (the constitutively open structure that allows for what else they might be). In doing so they attain what Goehr refers to as their authentic voice, the source of their autonomy.

Goehr writes that "a practice is always *more than* any theory which either describes and or prescribes it" (1998: 38); it contains an excess that is produced by the inability of the theory to fully determine it. However, when we seek to eradicate that excess – by forcing what we can articulately understand things to be (which is another way of saying their theories) to appear indistinguishable from their potentiality (their practices) – then situations lose their "openness" and so we get less. "To leave a theory limited [in other words, constitutively open] and its corresponding practice undetermined allows competing political ideals and conflicting expressions of those ideals to exist within a single practice" (Goehr 1998: 38); it is productive of what she calls "large mindedness" (Goehr 1998: 41), which is the precondition in her argument for a highly pluralized yet intensely dialectically mediated social life. Without the potential for becoming that is engendered by such "large mindedness," "individuals lose their expressive potential or autonomy, and the community within which they live becomes . . . 'defunct'" (Goehr 1998: 38). Attali takes the point to a higher rhetorical pitch, asserting that the large mindedness of becoming is, in fact, the defining value of human life itself. Thus, the politically repressive nature of the world in which we live is indicated by the fact that "Our society mimics itself, represents and repeats itself." It is as if "our society" were suffering from some fatally narcissistic disorder, constantly striving to see, and so preserve, the reflection of what it already is. But as the myth of Narcissus attests, if we cannot see something other than ourselves, then we die. And so this mirroring of the existent social structures only occurs as a result of an economy: in short, "instead of letting us live" (Attali 1985: 134). Our revolt against this economy occurs when we strive for "the emergence of the free act, self-transcendence, pleasure in being instead of having" (Attali 1985: 134). Instead of belongings.

For my argument, the advantage of the politics of critique lies in the fact that it does not have to hedge around the issue of musical autonomy. Rather than being a hindrance to the attainment of its political vision, the music qua music is one of the privileged markers not only of the feasibility of that political vision, but also of its presently existing reality. This does not imply that music is unmediated. "Undoubtedly," Attali writes, "music is a play of mirrors in which every activity is reflected, defined, recorded, and distorted"; there is no question, "Art bears the mark of its time" (1985: 5). Critical politics is here in thorough agreement with collaborative politics; we cannot compose, perform, or listen to music outside of our historical moment. But the politics of critique acknowledges that musical material is mediated in a way that is different to the essentially more linguistic orientation of human belongings, and, moreover, that this difference makes a difference with regard to our positioning in relationship to our historical moment when music is present.

The historical roots in modernity for this veneration of music's difference to language lie in the late eighteenth century. Previously, music had tended to be thought of as inferior because it could not point to the world with the same purportedly efficient lack of ambiguity as language. From the turn of the nineteenth-century onwards, however, it was precisely this ambiguity that started to seem attractive, and it has held a certain line of attention ever since (for example, from the Schlegels, Schopenhauer, and Nietzsche, through to Adorno and Goehr). The reason for this interest can be reduced to consideration of this truism: that music can seem incredibly meaningful even though we are often at a loss to say, beyond the application of a somewhat Neanderthal expressive labeling system, what it actually means. Frequently one hears the report: that music has given articulation for a listener to something that had been too profound to be touched by words; that it is as if, to give one of Adorno's variations on this theme, "We do not understand music – it understands us" (1998: xi); that exposure to music when it does this makes life more meaningful.

Thus, if music is insufficient as a normative form of meaning, conversely, music frequently reveals that meaning itself is lacking with regard to what makes life meaningful. And if music shows meaning to be insufficiently meaningful, and meaning also, in this instance, attaches us to what is, then music shows us that meaningfulness arises not solely from increasing our proximity to the existent, but from the possibility that even from our position inside a historical condition we can expand the relational space between ourselves and what is and so create distance. Thus, Goehr writes that in the nineteenth century, "The idea that a philosopher should become a musician was dependent upon seeing in music, or, rather, in the musician, the capacity to view the world at a distance" (1998: 32). This, for example, would explain the strange sense of expansiveness and release that is frequently attendant on musical expression, even when, as for example with melancholic music, the condition to which it refers is one that when experienced for real produces a physiological sensation of weighty incarceration (see Goehr 1998: 22). For Goehr, this space that music qua music produces within the existent is political because it allows for what she refers to as a "freedom within": "The key to this notion of *freedom within* is the idea that music is immanent and social, but it is not merely or instrumentally social. Rather, it aspires to be resistantly social through its purely musical form" (Goehr 1998: 13). Music thus opens up the possibility of life being otherwise and in doing so embodies not so much "our drive for attachment" as perhaps our drive for dignity.

Within the politics of critique, humans subjects act as if they are just engaging with music for music's sake, "Doing for the sake of doing," "Playing for one's own pleasure," as Attali puts it. And yet by doing so it transpires they are doing something else, "Inventing new codes, inventing the message at the same time as the language," creating the "conditions for new communication" (Attali 1985: 134). Thus, the "purely musical" is never pure, which accounts for why Goehr, through recourse to Wagner, makes it interchangeable with "the purely human" (Goehr 1998: 46). Admittedly, for Goehr, the "purely human is deliberately empty of specific or 'prejudicial' content." And thus "In being empty, this regulative ideal perhaps remains essential, but it is not regressively essentialist" (Goehr 1998: 130). Nevertheless, by preserving the word "human," she draws attention to a constitutive limit of both collaborative politics *and* the politics of critique: that they function only by thinking of musical activity as an expression of either self or group, of the human's desire for relationship either to their own subjectivity, or to the subjectivities of others. Thus, "Music is political already in virtue of the fact that music is a practice of human expression or performance working itself out in the world, in particular communities" (Goehr 1998: 128). In short, in most of today's talk about music and politics, we are dealing with a profound imbalance, since there is almost no consideration of the possibility of an outside to politics, however broadly conceived. Of course, for the purposes of an effective politics, this may indeed be a necessary rhetorical move; for philosophy, however, it is sophistry.

Music and the limits of politics

So what if some human activity is motivated by the pleasure that is taken precisely by engaging with something that it not completely inside the practices of human subjectivity and its social manifestations? Such engagement may indeed be beneficial to the human project; swimming in the sea may do wonders for my mood and may make me into a "better human." But I do not go swimming in order to be a better human. Moreover, the fact that my swimming may be incorporated beneficially into the economies of my human subjective/social life does not mean that it is merely such; since most things can do more than one thing, what something is cannot be reduced to what it does. After all, I may love swimming so much that I am prepared to trash my human belongings (by breaking appointments, ignoring responsibilities) just so I can get more sea time. Undoubtedly, there is often a miasma of humanly produced meanings flying around me whilst I am swimming. But I am not simply swimming in them – unless I can somehow float without water. And anyway, if I dive under the water, I can momentarily be free of them. The fact that my freedom soon reaches its limit when I must come up for air, does not eradicate the pleasure created when, through underwater swimming, I am briefly in excess of my normal human inscription. In fact, one might argue that the focused physical and mental effort necessary to be in excess and the pleasure that is the prize are mutually emboldening.

To make the leap now from swimming in the sea to engaging with music would involve an unacceptable analogy between water and musical material, as if music were nature. However, although the making of music is (leaving aside birds and computers) done by humans, the resulting musical sounds are no more human in themselves than a chair. Music exhibits not only a degree of ineradicable indifference to its origins – a feature that is merely exacerbated by the nomadic proclivities of musical recordings – but, like nature, a certain indifference to human subjectivity altogether. As a result, music is the darkest form of democracy, for the most depraved of humans can still be magnificent listeners, composers, or performers. Likewise, a man does not drown because he is a racist, but because his swimming fails him. To assert, as a Goehr might, that a serial killer's "subjective freedom . . . to be musical" opens up the possibility of the serial killer being otherwise is only tautologically true: self-evidently he is capable also of being a musician. But to conclude that in becoming a musician the serial killer opens up a gap within his serial killing activities through which a more human human could materialize is to make a dubious association of talent/proclivity with the Good. In part, this association emerges from the use of an inappropriate metaphor: openness. Like swimming under water, composing, performing, and listening well to music emerge less from an initial opening up of ourselves to how we might be otherwise, than from an initial skill for focusing on abilities we already have, or have developed, onto certain materials (water, musical sound) in the hope of then being able to momentarily experience the pleasure of exceeding our normal inscriptions. We cut things out, not let things in. The pleasure gained from such exceeding is self-justifying, and so not compromised when it fails to open up productive transformations in subjective/social life. This is not to say that it cannot. However, it is to acknowledge that when it does, it is not as a result of music being political, but more often from a kind of moral luck produced by the mad chance of where music happens to land when it finds itself thrown onto the roulette wheel of the human project.

But if music and politics are two separate singularities, why has so much discourse of the past twenty-five years sought to show otherwise? I offer the following conclusion as a provocation for further debate. The wide-spread circulation of "music as politics" is a symptom, the overdetermined affect produced by the attempt to repress the awful truth: that in the period beginning in the late 1970s – including Thatcher, Reagan, New Labour, aggressive Neo-Liberalism, and the exponential increase of the power of corporations over all aspects of everyday life – the political has increasingly been lacking, castrated. Music, amongst other things, has had to appear as political in order to mask this lack. For Bryars in the early 1970s, by comparison, this was not necessary. With 1968 and other events still reverberating as a productive catalyst in the political imagination, there was still the possibility of politics, and so of that something else too: music. However, today, in the presiding discourses, we have to ask: do we have either at all?

See also Adorno (Chapter 36), Continental philosophy and music (Chapter 26), Plato (Chapter 28), and Value (Chapter 15).

References

Abbate, C. (2004) "Music – Drastic or Gnostic?" *Critical Inquiry* 30: 505–36.

Adorno, T. W. (1998) *Beethoven: The Philosophy of Music*, trans. E. Jephcott, ed. R. Tiedemann, Palo Alto: Stanford University Press.

Attali, J. (1985) *Noise: The Political Economy of Music*, trans. B. Massumi, Minneapolis: University of Minnesota Press.

Badiou, A. (2002) *Ethics: An Essay on the Understanding of Evil*, trans. P. Hallward, New York and London: Verso.

Berlin, I. (2000) *Three Critics of the Enlightenment: Vico, Hamann, Herder*, ed. H. Hardy, London: Pimlico.

Deleuze, G. and Guattari, F. (1994 [1991]) *What Is Philosophy?*, trans. H. Tomlinson and G. Burchell, New York: Columbia University Press.

Goehr, L. (1998) *The Quest for Voice: Music, Politics, and the Limits of Philosophy*, Berkeley: University of California Press.

Griffiths, P. (1985) *New Sounds, New Personalities: British Composers of the 1980s in Conversation with Paul Griffiths*, London: Faber and Faber.

Hegel, G.W.F. (1977 [1807]) *Phenomenology of Spirit*, trans. A.V. Miller, Oxford: Oxford University Press.

hooks, b. (2009) *Belonging: A Culture of Place*, New York and London: Routledge.

Kramer, L. (2007) *Why Classical Music Still Matters*, Berkeley: University of California Press.

Ryle, G. (1949) *The Concept of Mind*, London: Hutchinson.

51

SOCIOLOGY AND CULTURAL STUDIES

Anthony Kwame Harrison

Preliminaries

Sociology has a long history of inquiry into music and the social activities surrounding it. Starting with Georg Simmel's (1968) early reflections on music's functions in structuring social relationships, some concern for music and the norms and values governing its production, meaning, and reception have been part of the sociological project since its disciplinary outset. While this interest in music as an aspect of social life has remained constant, during the final decades of the twentieth century, and now continuing into the twenty-first, the sociology of music has blossomed to include a variety of theoretical orientations and methodological approaches, as well as a range of topics of study. Much of this expansion has been connected to the development of cultural studies as a left-of-center sociological offshoot that has taken up an ambitious theoretical analysis of popular music as one of its central pillars. Consequently, any review of the sociological study of music would be remiss to ignore the exchanges of ideas, orientations, and methodologies that have existed between the discipline of sociology (properly defined) and this most established of its successor discourses. Acknowledging the considerable overlap and cross pollination that has occurred between the two disciplines, I present a single treatment of the state of the field – hereinafter referred to as the "sociology of music." My purpose is less to provide a comprehensive overview than to lay out some of the major themes and concerns that have dominated the field since the mid-1970s, and to make the case that the sociological study of music makes an important contribution to our ongoing efforts to understand the human condition.

Before proceeding, a few points of clarification and qualification are in order. The United Kingdom, a nation with no notable history of rigorous sociological orthodoxy (Anderson 1968), was a logical birthplace for cultural studies. Amidst the social and political turmoil of the 1960s, and pushed by a generation of academics who came of age during the post-war changes in economies, technologies, and the music industry itself, cultural studies was born out of liberal sociologists' and literary critics' recognition of the undeniable social relevance of music. Its emergence within a nation that once boasted of having an empire upon which the sun never set served to nourish its engaged postcolonial stance and implicit rejection of empiricism. Cultural studies developed as a product of and logical participant in the rise of post-structural and postmodern intellectual thought, both of which brought forth a wider appreciation for interpretive frameworks of analysis. Although it has matured into a field that straddles multiple disciplines, its roots are most firmly within the tradition of sociological inquiry.

A second point of clarification regards the scope of this chapter. Given cultural studies's British beginnings and the extent and influence of contemporary work being done by English-speaking scholars, my discussion of recent scholarship is largely centered on the Anglophone world, particularly the work of scholars situated within the United States and United Kingdom. Such a focus puts me in the somewhat delicate position of having to reconcile a British sociological tradition of heterodox approaches and orientations with an American tradition that has often aspired to emulate the technical expertise of the alleged "harder" social sciences. Of course neither this nor the dichotomy between proper sociology and cultural studies are as neat or absolute as I have presented them here. Nevertheless, it is important to recognize that there are epistemic tensions surrounding the legitimation of knowledge and the relationship between researchers and research subjects found within certain corridors of the field.

The third point has to do with terminology, specifically my usage of the idiom "popular music." There is an elaborate history within music-related scholarship of differentiating between "serious" and "popular" music forms. Serious or "art" music – that falling within the Western "classical" canon – has generally been regarded as having a musical autonomy that allows for its analytical treatment as great work existing above and outside the social contexts from which it emerges and passes through. Such a view has been especially prominent within more aesthetically oriented fields such as musicology and music theory. Popular music, on the other hand, has largely been thought of as a contaminated and/or corrupting form caught up in the intricacies of modern social life. Some recent scholarship within the sociology of music has worked to dismantle this dichotomy (see DeNora 1995). None of this withstanding, for my purposes here, it seems wise to maintain some sense of distinction and to clarify that I use the term "popular music" in reference to any of the commercially produced twentieth-century (and now twenty-first-century) music forms including but not limited to those fitting broadly within the genres blues, jazz, country, rhythm and blues, rock, reggae, rap, and electronic.

Sociological inquiries into music are chiefly concerned with the social contexts in which it is produced, circulated, consumed, and/or evaluated. As such, over the last half-century sociologists and cultural studies scholars have been pioneers in the study of popular music forms. The same perceived qualities that have encouraged music scholars within other fields to avoid popular music have made it particularly appealing to those within the sociological tradition. Popular music's omnipresence as a feature of everyday life and its economic presence as a billion-dollar industry with important connections to several other industries make it too conspicuous for sociologists to ignore. For the most part, the sociology of music has stayed away from evaluations of "good" versus "bad" or "greater" versus "lesser" musics. In this respect, an adherence to sociology's traditional edict of value-neutral scholarship (Weber 1949) has endured. Rather than making such evaluations, sociology of music scholars seek to understand the conditions and processes that inspire their development and contribute to their maintenance.

Sociological foundations

Contemporary sociology organizes itself around three principal theoretical perspectives, each of which can be linked to the ideas of foundational sociological thinkers. Although the various approaches and methodologies that comprise much of the recent work within the sociology of music often extend, straddle, and more generally complicate these paradigmatic boundaries, a basic familiarity with each of the three perspectives allows for a better understanding of where and how contemporary scholarship corresponds with and breaks from established sociological traditions.

The first and arguably most fundamental of these paradigms is *structural functionalism*. Strongly influenced by Émile Durkheim's theories of social integration and collective conscience, structural functionalism is based on the idea that society "works" because of the stability, organization, and interdependence of its various components (see Durkheim 1947). Rather than chaos, social life is characterized by patterned behaviors and interactions – what sociologists refer to as social structures – that have evolved and continue to endure because of the particular social purposes they serve. Thus, on a grand scale, institutions such as marriage, religion, and education can each be understood and explained as having one or more social functions. John Ryan and Michael Hughes's article "Breaking the Decision Chain" (2006) is a good example of recent sociology of music scholarship that fits within this framework. The article begins from the functionalist premise that, with the demise of genuine folk (music) communities, the music industry has come to serve the important role of mediating between music artists and audiences. Ryan and Hughes go on to structure their arguments regarding the drawbacks of contemporary do-it-yourself music production around the idea that the music producer – who occupies a prominent position in the music industry chain of production (Ryan and Peterson 1982) – plays a key function in steering the complex collaborative processes designed to ensure that music commodities are crafted to appeal to the people responsible for promoting and distributing them, and ultimately to the mass public. Consequently, in the absence of professional music production consultation, self-producing musicians struggle to reach their artistic and audience potentials.

The second perspective, which is most prominently associated with the ideas of Karl Marx, is referred to as *conflict theory*. In contrast to functionalists' attention to social structures and stability, conflict theorists emphasize competition, inequality, and change as intrinsic qualities of social organization. Certainly most would agree with the functionalist view that societies exists through series of patterned activities, beliefs, and institutions, yet in doing so conflict theorists stress how social order is arrived at via social control – the distribution of power being the key variable in this dynamic. Marxism has historically had a strong presence within the sociology of music. The two most important centers of twentieth-century sociological music thought – the Frankfurt School (highlighted by the work of Theodor Adorno) and the Birmingham School – both embraced Marxist principles, albeit in vastly different ways. Adorno saw popular music as a product of commercial cultural industries designed to shape, distract, and pacify the mass public (see Horkheimer and Adorno 1993). This view is generally referred to as the massification perspective. The scholars of the Birmingham School's Centre for Contemporary Cultural Studies (CCCS) situated music at the center of collective youth associations – or subcultures – and theorized style as improvised resistance (Hebdige 1979).

The third and final sociological perspective is *symbolic interactionism*. Whereas structural functionalism and conflict theory both examine how broad (macro) patterns of social organization shape society, symbolic interactionism focuses on individual behaviors, shared meanings, and the ways in which people's everyday actions shape the social construction of reality. In doing so, interactionists pay considerable attention to matters of agency as well as the dialogic relationship between self and society. Notable "forefathers" of this tradition include Max Weber, W. E. B. DuBois, and George Herbert Mead. Andy Bennett's (1999a) study of white hip-hoppers in northeast England uses an interactionist approach to explore the various ways in which white youth, in the absence of a sizable black community, articulate their claims to hip-hop legitimacy. Interactionism's interpretive framework has developed in opposition to functionalism's positivist and empiricist leanings. Not surprisingly, cultural studies – with its emphases on the politics of style and meaning – has aligned most strongly with conflict and symbolic interactionist orientations.

Popular music and sociology

Sociology emerged in response to conditions of modernity. Simply put, the field could not exist without some conception of society and the complexities inherent within it. As such, the analytic focus of the discipline has followed changes in social organization, activity, and administration – particularly in the "West" but now spreading to include more of the globalized world. The contemporary state of the sociological study of music reflects this parallel evolution of society and scholarship.

A number of important occurrences preceded the discipline's current diversity of approaches and subject matters. Within North America and Europe – the traditional homes of sociological analysis – the late nineteenth and early twentieth centuries brought forth a proliferation of musical styles. Factors contributing to this include: (a) improvements in instrument making and manufacturing; (b) the myriad non-Western influences introduced through the colonial encounter; (c) the use of music in the service of nationalism; (d) the invention and development of recording technologies; and (e) the beginnings of the modern music industry (Martin 1995). Although most sociologists of the early twentieth century concentrated on Western "art" music (see Sorokin 1937; Weber 1958), their appreciation for the social factors impacting it helped to cultivate the discipline's burgeoning interest in the ways in which music mirrored the increasing complexity and heterogeneity of modern social life.

Popular music's ascendance as a subject of sociological study issued from a second proliferation of musical styles linked to important changes in the music industry (Peterson 1990) and the development of the post-Second World War youth market (Bennett 2001). Advances in music playback technologies, most notably the increased portability, miniaturization, and personalization of listening devices, have had an accelerating effect on the everyday nature of music experience. This expanding ubiquity of popular music has made it an important feature in research on contemporary identity construction (see Gilroy 1993; Pisares 2006).

The cultural studies-led impetus to focus on popular music was prompted by the recognition of new forms of collective identification and differentiation among British post-war youth. Both the use of popular music in the political protests of the 1960s and the recognition of subcultural style as creative resistance (see above) encouraged sociologists to abandon earlier massification models. This resulted in innovative attempts to identify music's dynamic and varied uses.

Within the academy particularly, the establishment of offshoot fields such as black studies, ethnic studies, and women's studies introduced new discourses which worked to further de-center the sociology of music's traditional Western classical bias. Shifts in the size and demographic make-up of national university systems – through the GI Bill in the United States and the Robbins Report in the United Kingdom – also fueled this change. Indeed, many participants in the early wave of popular music scholarship came from relatively humble backgrounds and were themselves products of these post-war shifts. By the close of the twentieth century, the rise of a consumer-driven academic model was encouraging more topics of everyday interest into university curriculums. Beyond music's general appeal to college-aged people, courses which examine its social implications and dynamics also satisfy the increased interest in social/market research found within the business world.

Approaches

Over the last thirty years the sociological study of music has grown to feature several notable approaches which span the range of the macro–micro, empirical–interpretive, and functional–critical dualities outlined above. In terms of focus, although certainly not in terms of theory or predisposition, we can categorize these in accordance with the two major twentieth-century schools of sociology of music thought.

Cultural industries focus

One major thrust of recent sociological scholarship has continued the cultural industry focus of the Frankfurt School; yet it has broken from its unidirectional slope of massification theorizing. The most prominent approach to emerge out of this branch of research is the *production of culture* perspective best associated with the work of Richard Peterson (see Peterson and Anand 2004). Starting from an organizational systems framework that emphasizes design, structure, and decision-making processes, and influenced by Howard Becker's work on cooperative creativity and "art worlds" (Becker 1982), the production of culture approach only tangentially addresses the question of whether cultural commodities are products of industries of mass manipulation. Rather, this perspective recognizes cultural production as a coordinated field of activity, and maintains that the sociology of culture (or music) should be most concerned with understanding the nature of such coordination in mediating between industries and audiences (see the above discussion of Ryan and Hughes 2006). The production of culture model proposes that symbolic production takes place at the nexus of six individually analyzable constraints: technologies, laws and regulations, industry structure, organizational structure, occupational careers, and markets. This approach is by no means limited to the sociological study of music. It has been used to examine industries as distinct as book publishing houses (Powell 1985) and French wineries (Ulin 1996). Furthermore, only a handful of the music-specific scholarships go through the rigors of detailing all six aspects of the production of culture model (see Peterson 1990). Still, an analysis of any of the six (or any combination) with some attention to the importance of the others marks a project as fitting within the general production of culture approach. It is therefore regarded as one of the leading "schools" of contemporary sociology of music research.

A notable derivative of the production of culture perspective is the *circuit of culture* model developed by Paul du Gay. Rather than using the organizational field of production as its central focus, the circuit of culture looks to examine the representations, social identities, production activities, consumptive uses, and regulations surrounding specific cultural objects. Du Gay's pioneering application of this model was used to construct a sociological biography of the Sony

Walkman (1997). Similar music-based applications have been conducted on 12-inch singles (Straw 2002), hip-hop cassette tapes (Harrison 2006), and compact discs (Straw 2009).

One of the chief criticisms leveled against the production of culture perspective is that its attention to organization and process has come at the expense of issues of power (Hesmondhalgh 2002). This criticism is tempered by the realization that analyses of the production arena often furnish some understanding of who benefits. But at its core, the production of culture perspective adheres more to Durkheimian notions of functional operation than Marxian views on competition and inequality. This, if nothing else, marks a significant departure from the Frankfurt tradition. There have been cultural industry analyses that more systematically take up questions of power and resistance. A key tension in much of this work has been the relationship between independent and majors record labels (see Roberts 2002) – particularly in an era when lines separating the two are often difficult to discern (Negus 1999). Other studies have explored the creative autonomy of local musicians and the role of music-making activities in structuring social life (Finnegan 1989).

Music and identification

Although the market forms one of Peterson's six production of culture factors, it is rarely treated as a powerful determinant. To the contrary, the production of culture perspective tends to disempower audiences by emphasizing the creation of demand. The focus on consumers becomes the domain of a broad network of approaches that I collectively lump under the heading "music and identification." There is a lengthy history within the sociology of music generally and the study of popular music specifically of investigating the appeal of particular music genres to defined taste publics – usually delineated along the axes of generation, class, race, ethnicity, and sometimes gender. Such approaches commonly involve survey research. These models often show parallels between a demographic group's history of participation and representation in a given music genre and their appreciation of it. More elaborate theorizing has been prompted by the need to explain seeming disjunctures – for instance, the appeal of reggae music among white British youth (Jones 1988).

The early work by the CCCS sought to apply a logic of parallels to the music preferences of specific youth subcultures. This came to be known as *homology* theory (Willis 1978). The concept of homology is based on a synchronism between the values and aesthetic codes that members of a subculture aspired toward and the music they listened to. Thus, to cite a classic study done by Dick Hebdige, the "soulless, frantically driven music" of punks, was consistent with their ripped fashions, spiked hair, drug preferences, and "insurrectionary poses" (1979: 114). Research of this sort has been critiqued for being overly abstract, subjective, and problematically deterministic (Clarke 1990).

Nevertheless, a general adherence to the homology principle, whether applied to style, social structure, or local culture, continues to inform a good deal of sociology of music research. For example, homological considerations typically underlie content analyses of cultural materials. The interpretive frameworks employed in much of this work have made it more accepted within cultural studies than within the discipline of sociology properly defined.

In the early 1990s, research conducted on music taste groupings began to reveal new patterns of eclectic high-status consumption. This came to be known as the *omnivore* thesis (Peterson and Simkus 1992). It proposes that whereas elite consumers once distinguished themselves through the consumption of high-brow cultural products, by the end of the twentieth century such statuses were increasingly conveyed through diverse tastes. Thus, rather than through just classical music, high cultural standing may be communicated through music collections that include jazz, blues, rock, reggae, Brazilian samba, and Moroccan Gnawa trance. There are good indications that such omnivorous tendencies are also increasingly found among middle-class consumers. In an era of rising omnivorousness, I believe sociologists have been right to pay particular attention to the popular music varieties that are often left off omnivores' music playlists (Bryson 1996) – for any assertion of taste is also an assertion of distaste and research suggests that even omnivores are selective in their taste patterns (Peterson and Simkus 1992).

Another significant music and identification approach looks specifically at how music is employed in the service of identity construction. From this perspective, musical experiences (whether performing or listening) are seen as instances of self-in-process (Frith 1996). Such scholarship is founded on earlier research examining the social–psychological functions of music in society – which include helping to manage and express emotions, and organizing memories (Frith 1987). The notion of subcultural capital (Thornton 1995), which – building off the theories of Pierre Bourdieu (1984) – is defined as an alternative taste hierarchy within the terrain of youth culture, has become an important concept through which identity construction via music activity is theorized. Mapping subcultural capital becomes a means of understanding dynamics of boundary maintenance, belonging, and power within youth social collectivities.

Music scenes

Critiquing the rigidity of subculture as a serviceable analytic construct, starting in the 1990s popular music scholars began using alternative, multifocal models such as post-subculture (Muggleton 2000), neotribe (Bennett 1999b), and music scene (Straw 1991). Of these, the *music scene* perspective has gained the most currency. Music scenes are theorized as social spaces in which producers, musicians, and fans come together to create and sustain structures and sentiments of social cohesion (Peterson and Bennett 2004). Such a framework succeeds in consolidating the two dominant foci of sociological music scholarship – namely, production and consumption – through an emphasis on locality. The wide-scale acceptance of this perspective was preceded by research examining music's role in the construction of space and place (see Stokes 1994). It was also fueled by a tradition of research on local music-making practices (see Cohen 1991). Recent music scene scholarship has expanded to include translocal and virtual scenes (Peterson and Bennett 2004). This perspective has been additionally effective in promoting the use of qualitative and particularly ethnographic research methods (Cohen 1993) – once primarily the domain of ethnomusicology. And there is an emerging body of sociological music research that uses ethnography to explore music's role in ordering aspects of everyday life (see DeNora 2000).

One area where the sociology of music has been sparse is in its examination of music within non-Western societies – again, most of this work has been left to ethnomusicologists. This is unfortunate since comparative cross-cultural analyses would likely lead to better understandings of particulars and universals with regards to music. Certainly enough has transpired to illustrate how ethnocentric notions about Western classical music's inherent superiority once limited the field. The favorable reception of the music scene model could very well encourage more sociological studies of localities outside the traditional sociological geography.

Authenticity

During the last twenty years, the concept of *authenticity* has become central to the sociology of music theorizing. Authenticity gets fabricated through the music industry (Peterson 1997). It is also a prized feature of subcultural capital (Harrison 2009). Similarly most music enthusiasts seek out authentic musical experiences (Grazian 2003). Authenticity's appeal as a conceptual unit lies in the fact that it provides music sociology scholars with a means to negotiate the treacherous terrain of music evaluation. Rather than judging music as better or worse, authenticity, which is never naturally occurring but rather "a discursive trope of great persuasive power" (Stokes 1994: 7), functions as the essential quality that for most listeners makes music good.

Further research in the sociology of music would do well to explore the zones in which inauthentic music is most widely appreciated. Even with some awareness of the music industry's hit-making practices – think "American Idol" – millions of people still enjoy the most popular of inauthentic "pop music" forms (see Frith 2001). In some respects, the music and identification field's focus on subcultures and distinct music scenes has limited its attention to the dynamics impacting pop music identification. There is still much consolidating to be done.

Conclusion

The last thirty years have brought tremendous advances to sociological music scholarship, including the development of sophisticated theoretical models, the adoption of various methods of inquiry, and the introduction of new epistemological paradigms. Sociological studies of music proceed from the recognition that music is both a product of and an instrumental force in shaping social processes. Music's creation, reception, and evaluation are influenced by the nature of the circumstances in which they occur; at the same time, music is regularly pressed into action within a variety of social settings (DeNora 2000). The sociology of music therefore seeks to understand and explain music as a dynamic societal phenomenon embedded in a wide range of social contexts.

Early sociological studies of music tended to use it as a case study through which to illustrate a particular theoretical claim (Martin 1995). In the post-war period, music forms themselves became subjects of sociological investigation. Recent sociology of music scholarship has matured to the point of recognizing music as a highly synergetic process which organizes social activity and structures social relations.

Thus, music sociology has taken up the difficult challenge of uncovering the situational bases upon which everyday evaluations of music are made, as well as the commercial operations that often underlie them. In this respect, the music sociologist must also be a social critic. It is his or her task to examine and make sense out of the distinct connections between aesthetic conventions, social structures, and social relations that comprise musical life.

See also Adorno (Chapter 36), Continental philosophy and music (Chapter 26), Ethnomusicology (Chapter 49), Music and politics (Chapter 50), Popular music (Chapter 37), and Rock (Chapter 38).

References

Anderson, P. (1968) "Components of the National Culture," *New Left Review* 50: 1–57.

Becker, H. (1982) *Art Worlds*, Berkeley: University of California Press.

Bennett, A. (1999a) "Rappin' on the Tyne: White Hip Hop Culture in Northeast England – an Ethnographic Study," *Sociological Review* 47: 1–24.

—— (1999b) "Subculture or Neo-tribes? Rethinking the Relationship Between Youth, Style and Musical Taste," *Sociology* 33: 599–617.

—— (2001) *Cultures of Popular Music*, Philadelphia: Open University Press.

Bourdieu, P. (1984) *Distinctions: A Social Critique of the Judgment of Taste*, trans. R. Nice, Cambridge: Harvard University Press.

Bryson, B. (1996) "'Anything But Heavy Metal': Symbolic Exclusion and Musical Dislikes," *American Sociological Review* 61: 884–99.

Clarke, G. (1990 [1981]) "Defending Ski Jumpers: A Critique of Theories of Youth Subcultures," in S. Frith and A. Goodwin (eds) *On Record: Rock, Pop and the Written Word*, London: Routledge, pp. 81–96.

Cohen, S. (1991) *Rock Culture in Liverpool: Popular Music in the Making*, Oxford: Clarendon.

—— (1993) "Ethnography and Popular Music Studies," *Popular Music* 12: 123–38.

DeNora, T. (1995) *Beethoven and the Construction of Genius: Musical Politics in Vienna 1792–1803*, Berkeley: University of California Press.

—— (2000) *Music in Everyday Life*, Cambridge: Cambridge University Press.

du Gay, P. (1997) "Introduction," in P. du Gay, S. Hall, L. Janes, H. Mackay, and K. Negus (eds) *Doing Cultural Studies: The Story of the Sony Walkman*, London: Sage, pp. 1–5.

Durkheim, É. (1947 [1893]) *The Division of Labor in Society*, trans. G. Simpson, New York: Free Press.

Finnegan, R. (1989) *The Hidden Musicians: Music-Making in an English Town*, Cambridge: Cambridge University Press.

Frith, S. (1987) "Towards an Aesthetic of Popular Music," in R. Leppert and S. McClary (eds) *Music and Society: The Politics of Composition, Performance and Reception*, Cambridge: Cambridge University Press, pp. 133–49.

—— (1996) "Music and Identity," in S. Hall and P. du Gay (eds) *Questions of Cultural Identity*, London: Sage, pp. 108–27.

—— (2001) "Pop Music," in S. Frith, W. Straw, and J. Street (eds) *The Cambridge Companion to Pop and Rock*, Cambridge: Cambridge University Press, pp. 26–52.

Gilroy, P. (1993) *The Black Atlantic: Modernity and Double Consciousness*, London: Verso.

Grazian, D. (2003) *Blue Chicago: The Search for Authenticity in Urban Blues Clubs*, Chicago: University of Chicago Press.

Harrison, A.K. (2006) "'Cheaper Than a CD, Plus We Really Mean It': Bay Area Underground Hip Hop Tapes as Subcultural Artefacts," *Popular Music* 25: 283–301.

—— (2009) *Hip Hop Underground: The Integrity and Ethics of Racial Identification*, Philadelphia: Temple University Press.

Hebdige, D. (1979) *Subculture, The Meaning of Style*, London: Methuen.

Hesmondhalgh, D. (2002) *The Cultural Industries*, London: Sage.

Horkheimer, M. and Adorno, T.W. (1993 [1944]) *Dialectic of Enlightenment*, trans. J. Cumming, New York: Continuum.

Jones, S. (1988) *Black Culture, White Youth: The Reggae Tradition from JA to UK*, London: Macmillan.

Martin, P.J. (1995) *Sound and Society: Themes in the Sociology of Music*, Manchester and New York: Manchester University Press.

Muggleton, D. (2000) *Inside Subculture: The Postmodern Meaning of Style*, Oxford: Berg.

Negus, K. (1999) *Music Genres and Corporate Cultures*, London: Routledge.

Peterson, R.A. (1990) "Why 1955? Explaining the Advent of Rock Music," *Popular Music* 9: 97–116.

—— (1997) *Creating Country Music: Fabricating Authenticity*, Chicago: University of Chicago Press.

Peterson, R.A. and Anand, N. (2004) "The Production of Culture Perspective," *Annual Review of Sociology* 30: 311–34.

Peterson, R.A. and Bennett, A. (2004) "Introducing Music Scenes," in A. Bennett and R.A. Peterson (eds) *Music Scenes: Local, Translocal, and Virtual*, Nashville: Vanderbilt University Press, pp. 1–15.

Peterson, R.A. and Simkus, A. (1992) "How Musical Tastes Mark Occupational Status Groups," in M. Lamont and M. Fournier (eds) *Cultivating Differences: Symbolic Boundaries and the Making of Inequality*, Chicago: University of Chicago Press, pp. 152–86.

Pisares, E.H. (2006) "Do You Mis(recognize) Me: Filipina Americans in Popular Music and the Problem of Invisibility," in A.T. Tiongson, E.V. Gutierrez, and R.V. Gutierrez (eds) *Positively No Filipinos Allowed: Building Communities and Discourse*, Philadelphia: Temple University Press, pp. 172–98.

Powell, W.W. (1985) *Getting into Print: The Decision Making Process in Scholarly Publishing*. Chicago: University of Chicago Press.

Roberts, M. (2002) "Papa's Got a Brand-New Bag: Big Music's Post-Fordist Regime and the Role of Independent Music Labels," in N. Kelley (ed.) *Rhythm and Business: The Political Economy of Black Music*, New York: Akashic Books, pp. 24–43.

Ryan, J. and Hughes, M. (2006) "Breaking the Decision Chain: The Fate of Creativity in an Age of Self-Production," in M. Ayers (ed.) *Cybersounds: Essays on Virtual Music Culture*, New York: Peter Lang, pp. 239–53.

Ryan, J. and Peterson, R.A. (1982) "The Product Image: The Fate of Creativity in Country Music Songwriting," in J.S. Ettema and C.D. Whitney (eds) *Individuals in Mass Media Organizations: Creativity and Constraint (Sage Annual Reviews of Communication Research* 10), Beverly Hills: Sage, pp. 11–32.

Simmel, G. (1968 [1882]) "Psychological and Ethnological Studies on Music," in *The Conflict in Modern Culture and Other Essays*, trans. K.P. Etzkorn, New York: Teacher's College Press, pp. 98–140.

Sorokin, P.A. (1937) *Social and Cultural Dynamics*, vol. 1, New York: Bedminster.

Stokes, M. (1994) "Introduction," in M. Stokes (ed.) *Ethnicity, Identity and Music: the Musical Construction of Place*, Oxford: Berg, pp. 1–28.

Straw, W. (1991) "Systems of Articulation, Logics of Change: Communities and Scenes in Popular Music," *Cultural Studies* 5: 368–88.

—— (2002) "Value and Velocity: The 12-inch Single as Medium and Artefact," in K. Negus and D. Hesmondhalgh (eds) *Popular Music Studies*, London: Edward Arnold, pp. 164–77.

—— (2009) "The Music CD and Its Ends," *Design & Culture* 1: 79–92.

Thornton, S. (1995) *Club Cultures: Music, Media and Subcultural Capital*, Cambridge: Polity.

Ulin, R.C. (1996) *Vintages and Traditions: An Ethnohistory of Southwest French Wine Cooperatives*, Washington: Smithsonian Institution Press.

Weber, M. (1949 [1904]) "'Objectivity' in Social Science and Social Policy," in E.A. Shils and H.A. Finch (eds and trans) *Max Weber on the Methodology of the Social Sciences*, New York: Free Press, pp. 50–112.

—— (1958 [1921]) *The Rational and Social Foundations of Music*, trans. D. Martindale, J. Riedel, and G. Neuwerth, Carbondale: Southern Illinois University Press.

Willis, P. (1978) *Profane Culture*, London: Routledge and Kegan Paul.

52

MUSIC AND GENDER

Fred Everett Maus

Overview

Scholarly studies of gender and sexuality became highly visible during the late 1980s and 1990s, constituting an unusual conjunction of music research and political involvement. When female scholars wrote from feminist perspectives, or self-identified gay, lesbian, and bisexual scholars wrote from anti-homophobic perspectives, the research was also personal, highlighting aspects of individual identity.

Studies of gender became especially important in historical musicology and ethnomusicology. Various fora emerged, including the series of biannual conferences, "Feminist Theory and Music," that began in 1991. Monographs and edited collections appeared (Bowers and Tick 1986; Koskoff 1987; Citron 1993; Solie 1993; Cook and Tsou 1994). A journal, *Women & Music: A Journal of Gender and Culture*, appeared from 1997. Lesbian, gay, bisexual, transgender and queer/questioning (LGBTQ) studies became visible and well-organized in historical musicology (Brett, Wood, and Thomas 1994). From 1997, the American Musicological Society offered an annual award, the Philip Brett Prize, for LGBTQ studies of music. The second edition of the *New Grove Dictionary of Music and Musicians* (Sadie 2001), the leading English-language encyclopedia of musicology, added articles such as "Feminism," "Gay and Lesbian Music," "Gender," and "Women in Music."

Work on gender and sexuality in popular music studies mostly developed independently of academic musicology and ethnomusicology, partly through connections between popular music studies and sociology, partly through journalism (Frith and McRobbie 1990; Gill 1995; Whiteley 1997). Meanwhile, some scholars in historical musicology extended their analysis of gender and sexuality from classical music to popular music (McClary 1991).

Any socially oriented study of music-making deals with social life that is structured by differences of gender and sexuality. The history of European art music includes the frequent exclusion of women from careers in composition, the acceptance and power of female performers in certain restricted contexts, and the prominence in twentieth-century Europe and America of gay male composers. Popular music industries offer distinct roles for men and women (Leonard 2007), and have made complex use of the imperfectly hidden presence of gay men and lesbians as pop performers. Popular music audiences and fandoms typically involve aspects of gender and sexuality. The groups described by ethnomusicologists often have different musical practices for men and women; until recently, ethnomusicology gave less attention to women's musics. Musical practices reflect and contribute to the gender and sexuality arrangements of their social settings.

Relations of gender and sexuality to musical meaning may be less obvious. Still, at least when music has representational aspects, there are relations to gender and sexuality. Male/female difference and heterosexuality are central in almost all operatic plots. In song or program music, gender and sexuality are often pertinent. Schumann's *Dichterliebe* and Berlioz's *Symphony Fantastique* articulate masculine perspectives on heterosexual love. The male protagonist in each work expresses resentment toward the woman in the story because she fails to return his desire; this displays his assumption of masculine entitlement. When audiences or critics treat such works reverently, rather than questioning the protagonist's understanding of his situation, they show unselfconscious misogyny, which feminist criticism can appropriately disparage.

Representational aspects may seem to belong to libretti, song texts, and programs rather than to "music itself." But criticism treats music as expressive in these contexts, and music helps to create gendered personalities for operatic characters and other characters depicted in musical works. An account of gender in such representational works should extend to consider the contribution of music to the representation of gender.

Instrumental, non-programmatic music may seem to raise special challenges for the interpretation of meaning in relation to gender and sexuality. Such music has been relatively recalcitrant to interpretation of meaning generally. If gender and sexuality cannot be shown pertinent to meaning in absolute music, then the project of gender and sexuality studies seems to encounter an important limitation, precisely in its encounter with some of the most prestigious music.

McClary on musical meaning

The rest of this chapter will focus on a particular account of musical meaning. The selection of Susan McClary's ideas for close examination is not arbitrary. *Feminine Endings* (McClary 1991), the most famous feminist musicological book in English, is central in the development of the field, and offers a lucid account of musical meaning. It could have been equally appropriately to focus instead on the work of another major figure such as Suzanne Cusick or Philip Brett; in its brief but intense history, study of gender, sexuality, and music has opened too many promising avenues to introduce them all in a brief chapter.

As Cusick argues, McClary's work contributes to music criticism, understood as a discourse of interpretation and evaluation of musical works (Cusick 1999). Criticism offers accounts of particular musical examples; McClary supports her readings with provocative generalizations about musical meaning. A discourse called music criticism emerged, in the musicology of the 1970s and 1980s, as an area of controversy (Maus 2001a). Several established musicologists championed criticism as a type of scholarly writing on music, distinct from factual historical research and technical musical analysis, different partly in its concern for musical meaning. McClary began publishing during the time that Joseph Kerman (1985) and Leo Treitler (1989) consolidated their critiques of musicology; at that time, music criticism seemed, to many scholars, central to the future of music scholarship. McClary brought feminism directly into a recently established area of progressive scholarship. Her work ascribes meaning to music in several distinct ways.

Sexual interpretation of pitch syntax

A defining attribute of music criticism, as understood through the 1970s and 1980s, was its contrast with technical music analysis. Analysis dealt with structures of sound, typically not addressing issues of meaning, evaluation, or experience. Advocates of music criticism often suggested that analysis was inadequate for understanding music. But critics typically affirmed that analysis provided crucial descriptive resources for music criticism.

Edward Cone, recommending a turn to "hermeneutics," wrote that "if verbalization of true content – the specific expression uniquely embodied in a work – is possible at all, it must depend on a close structural analysis" (1982: 235). Many critics followed him in wishing to connect content closely to the sonic detail that analysis describes.

McClary (1991) agrees that analysis can lead to an understanding of certain aspects of meaning. Unlike many music critics, she also shows a particular interest in technical music theory, the abstract discipline that offers technical generalizations about groups of compositions.

McClary devotes special attention to tonality, the type of pitch organization that prevails in eighteenth- and nineteenth-century concert music and much subsequent music. *Feminine Endings* does not usually challenge the technical accounts of music theorists, though it challenges ideological assumptions that surround music theory, offering to place technical description within new ideological contexts such as feminism and gay studies.

For instance, McClary (1991: 12–13, 136) seems to accept Heinrich Schenker's technical theories as a broadly accurate account of tonality. In this, McClary differs from other proponents of music criticism who argue that Schenkerian analysis misrepresents pitch relations (e.g. Treitler, Kerman).

Following the mainstream of music theory, McClary understands tonal syntax in terms of long-range goal-directedness: tonality makes it possible for music to "arouse and channel desire" (1991: 12). Goal-directedness appears throughout a tonal composition: locally in the movement of each phrase toward a cadential harmony, more broadly in long-range, hierarchized motion toward structural goals, as articulated in Schenker's theory.

In linking goal-directedness to meaning and experience, McClary suggests that "music is very often concerned with the arousing and channeling of desire, with mapping patterns through the medium of sound that resemble those of sexuality" (1991: 8). More strongly, "music itself often relies heavily upon the metaphorical simulation of sexual activity for its effects" (1991: 12). The goal-directedness of tonal music, as described in technical terms by Schenker and other theorists, creates "simulations of sexual desire and release" (1991: 13). While accepting as discoveries the technical claims of Schenker and other theorists, McClary goes beyond music theory, connecting technical information directly to iconic representation by virtue of "simulation" or resemblance.

This simulation links music to sexual politics. McClary argues that evaluations of music may intervene, inexplicitly, in the politics of gender and sexuality, because the grounds for valuing certain kinds of music may derive from the kinds of sexual experience that the music treats as normative. According to McClary, some of the most admired classical music evokes types of sexual experience – not only goal-directed, but climax-oriented and impatient with tenderness – that count as masculine in the settings within which classical music has been created and performed. McClary describes other kinds of musical pleasure, associated with feminine sexuality, that favor non-goal-oriented enjoyment – "relatively noncoercive modal techniques that delight in the present moment, rhythms that are grounded in the physicality and repetitiveness of dance," "a quality of timeless, sustained hovering," or "a prolonged moment of musical jouissance" (1991: 119, 125, 145). McClary suggests that classical composers and audiences neglect these pleasures in favor of purposeful motion toward cadential goals. But she finds the less goal-directed pleasures in some music by women, and considers exemplification of these pleasures to be politically valuable. McClary finds similar positive qualities in the second movement of Schubert's "Unfinished" Symphony. The opening "drifts through time by means of casual, always pleasurable pivots," and "Schubert tends to disdain goal-oriented desire per se for the sake of a sustained image of pleasure and an open, flexible sense of self" (McClary 1994: 215, 223). With Schubert, McClary suggests that these qualities articulate an alternative masculinity and, tentatively, she suggests links to same-sex eroticism. McClary specifies that the sexualities and gender identities that she describes are culturally constructed, rather than natural.

Musemes of gender and sexuality

McClary draws on musical semiotics, correlating particular musical features with meanings. Though she does not use the terms, these meaningful features could be called "topics" (Ratner 1980) or "musemes" (Tagg 2000a, 2000b). McClary concentrates on musemes with a clear relation to gender and sexuality. She refers to these as "the common semiotic codes of European classical music: the gestures that stereotypically signify 'masculine' or 'feminine,' placidity or violence, the military or the domestic realm" (1991: 68).

McClary suggests that development of these "codes" began in seventeenth-century opera, which required musico-dramatic depiction of different types of men and women. Generally, she does not develop a list of musemes or provide a detailed historical account of their development. She may seem unsystematic about her identification of musemes; for instance, in comparison with Leonard Ratner, whose work grounds the identification of eighteenth-century topics in historical treatises, providing a list of topics as well as labeling them in compositions. McClary counts on widespread familiarity with musemes, continuing to the present day, and sometimes seems to dismiss issues of justification: "any five-year-old has sufficient experience from watching Saturday morning cartoons to verify most of the signs I will need" (1991: 68).

McClary's ad hoc approach allows flexibility in taking account of many different aspects of specific musical passages. In describing a theme by Tchaikovsky, which she summarizes as "sultry, seductive, and slinky," she not only mentions chromaticism – a museme signifying alluring but untrustworthy qualities – but rapid, fragmentary iterations in different registers and "stagnant" but "irrational" qualities of motion (1991: 71). A strength of McClary's musematic analyses is her unwillingness to rest at the stage of labeling: McClary identifies musemes in order to integrate them into an interpretation of an extended passage.

The narrative of sonata form

As with goal-directedness, McClary's account of sonata form makes bold use of familiar theoretical material. Standard accounts of sonata form bring together harmonic and thematic issues. Accordingly, McClary's interpretation of sonata form draws on both harmonic structure and the semiotic aspects of themes. In treating sonata form as a kind of narrative, that is, as a form that communicates a story, McClary's work relates, once more, to the music criticism of the 1970s and 1980s, in which comparisons of music and narrative became a prominent interpretive approach (Maus 2001b).

In sonata form, according to McClary, music moves toward a second key area, at once strongly desired and destabilizing. Subsequently, a sonata-form composition achieves stability by returning persuasively to the opening key, establishing the "consolidated identity" of the protagonist (1991: 14). For McClary, this is a gendered narrative, depicting a masculine protagonist who goes out to conquer and returns triumphant. The second key area, combining allure and danger, has qualities attributed, in misogynist thought, to women. The return to the original key for a long concluding section restores the stable identity of an implied protagonist, thereby overcoming the feminine harmonic threat.

As McClary indicates, critics from A. B. Marx on have noted the stereotypical "masculine" and "feminine" qualities of first and second themes in sonata form (MacClary 1991: 13; Marx 1997: 133). For McClary, the use of such musemes (which she finds in mid-eighteenth-century symphonies, as well as the nineteenth-century symphonies of Marx's day) intensifies the gendered, masculinist narrative of sonata-form compositions. The opening of a sonata-form composition establishes a protagonist, through stability of tonality and through musemes signifying masculinity. Succeeding events depict the attraction of a destabilizing second key area, associated with musemes signifying femininity. The eventual transposition of feminine musemes to the initial key represents a triumph of masculine subject-construction at the expense of feminine independence.

McClary on musical experience and social function

Along with these interpretations of aspects of music, McClary's descriptions indicate a consistent relation between musical content and the experiences of listeners. She finds no clear distinction, in musical experience, between feelings and experiences depicted in the music and feelings and experiences that one imagines oneself having: to hear music is, among other things, to imagine having certain experiences. Since, in *Feminine Endings*, McClary regards tonality as a means of simulating sexual experience, listening to tonal music becomes, in her treatment, an activity of imagining oneself having sexual experiences. Listeners experience sexual desire and release, simulated through tonality, as though it is their own. Someone who listens to an exciting approach to a musical climax, the music finally "bursting through the barrier with a spasm of ejaculatory release," does not merely witness the depicted experiences of an external protagonist. Rather, the "cathartic fulfillment" in the music "mysteriously becomes our own experience of libidinal gratification" (1991: 112–13). This contagious quality makes music, as McClary describes it, a powerful way of communicating experience.

McClary's interpretations of music, and her consequent evaluations, derive in part from ideas about functions of music, which go along with generalizations about the settings within which music functions.

The broad background of McClary's account is a succession of historical social arrangements in which relations of men and women are asymmetrical, men having various forms of power over women. One form of subordination of women consists in men's power to determine public representations of gender and sexuality in ways that serve their interests, representing men's prejudices about women as objective fact, and failing to acknowledge unwelcome aspects of women's subjectivities. The content and consequences of public representations of gender and sexuality are central to McClary's feminist position.

McClary depicts European and American classical music, along with recent US popular music, as expressing the preferences and subjectivities of men. Men have usually composed this music, in settings where men have economic power to determine the creation and performance of music; men have also produced much of the critical discourse for interpreting and evaluating music. If, as McClary affirms, music has representational capabilities, its depictions are likely to reflect the beliefs and desires of certain men. If women's beliefs and desires differ from those of the men who shape public musical life, these different attitudes are not likely to appear in music. When male-authored musical works depict women, as they do in opera and many other texted works, it is more certain that the women reflect the male authors' conceptions of women than that they match women's conceptions. Because of male domination of discourse about music, exposure of this masculinist bias has been unlikely.

One function of music, then, is to circulate certain men's ideas about the world. Another, more specific function, in McClary's account, is to lead people – men and women – to feel these ideas as their own. This results from the contagious quality of music, which "is often received (and not only by the musically untutored) as a mysterious medium within which we seem to encounter our 'own' most private feelings" (1991: 53).

As a vivid medium for communicating experiences, music can teach people ways of feeling and thinking. "It is in accordance with the terms provided by language, film, advertising, ritual, or music that individuals are socialized" (1991: 21). "Music teaches us how to experience our own emotions, our own desires, and even (especially in dance) our own bodies. For better or worse, it socializes us" (1991: 53). The content, and exclusions, of music create a shared sense of what is possible and valuable. In McClary's view, musical practices have helped to create consensus attitudes about gender and sexuality, held viscerally and unreflectively, that favor the interests of men rather than women. The socializing role of music shows the importance of feminist critique of male hegemony in music, and creates the context for female-authored resistant musical practices.

At times, McClary emphasizes an opposite side of music: musical activities have sometimes seemed feminine or feminizing. This may seem at odds with her claim that music typically advances men's interests, but the possible conflicts between musicality and masculinity can also explain a defensive over-emphasis, in musical contexts, either on masculinity or on a kind of neutrality that distances music from any associations with gender and sexuality.

Evaluation of McClary's ideas, and alternatives

From within the framework of music criticism, how might one evaluate McClary's account of musical meaning? And are there aspects of McClary's account, deriving from a commitment to the norms of music criticism as it developed during the 1980s, to which one might seek alternatives?

Feminine Endings is intentionally polemical, and its assertions often receive less evidential or argumentative support than they might. This leaves McClary's claims open to dismissal, but does not mean that her positions are wrong. One range of questions about the book is how one might attempt to give fuller support to its positions (Fink 2004). As noted, McClary regards listening as a process of identification with the experiences evoked in the music. Kendall Walton's ideas (1997) could contribute to a fuller account: he suggests that listeners typically imagine of their own musical experience that it is their own experience of feelings.

In associating goal-oriented pitch syntax with iconic representation of sexual experience, McClary is correct about some music, most obviously Wagner's *Tristan* and some other late Romantic compositions. It is uncertain how generally the association with sexuality extends into cadential patterns or goal-directedness in other styles of music. In not addressing this question, McClary leaves for others the exploration of a range of meanings that directed motion may have. No doubt, critical interpretation needs other models besides sexuality: movement toward orgasm is not the only goal-directed experience with which listeners are familiar, and the sound of some music (for instance, in Haydn's characteristic major-mode *allegro* style) might not direct listeners toward sexual associations. One model, different from McClary's but perhaps appropriate to some music, is to think of cadences as articulations, rather than as hotly desired goals. Cadences are often formulaic and non-individualized in comparison to preceding parts of a phrase; perhaps, sometimes, they serve mainly to mark a boundary, like a picture frame. To pursue McClary's identification of musical and sexual goals convincingly, in the cases where it is apt, one would need to explore alternative accounts for other cases, rather than simply accepting her identification universally. This issue is not simple; evaluation of the role of sexuality in musical experience cannot be determined simply by introspection, as sexual meanings in music and elsewhere are subject to disavowal and unawareness.

Similar considerations apply to McClary's account of sonata form, which she states generally but which seems more apposite to some compositions than to others. Strauss's *Don Juan*, for instance – not in sonata form, but making related use of thematic and harmonic patterning – plainly identifies its masculine hero with the opening key and thematic material, and depicts his attractions to women through modulations to new keys with contrasting thematic material. But in many other compositions, for instance, the first movement of Beethoven's "Spring" Sonata, McClary's generalization seems less pertinent. Charges of overgeneralization appear often in discussions of *Feminine Endings*.

In readings of particular musemes, McClary usually seems to operate intuitively, on the basis of an insider's competence with codes, rather than explicitly giving evidence for her interpretations. More explicitly documented accounts could take various forms; for instance, turning to historical treatises or reception history, as documented in reviews and other historical texts. One could survey texted musical literature for consistent associations of verbal features with musical features. Assuming with McClary that meanings of musemes have been stable to the present, one could conduct empirical research using present-day listeners. The first two approaches are familiar in musicology; over the last decades, Philip Tagg has pursued the latter two. *Ten Little Title Tunes* expands Tagg's earlier account of musemes through extensive collection and analysis of written description of music by hundreds of respondents (Tagg and Clarida 2003). In gathering data, Tagg played music excerpts, identifying each as music for a film scene and asking what the scene would be.

As indicated, McClary's use of analysis in 1991 was continuous with the work of other critics, and she showed more interest in music theory than most critics. However, a skeptical attitude toward theory and analysis may be appropriate, partly on feminist grounds. Theory and analysis emphasize the urgency of goal-directed motion, and McClary interprets this as reflecting a masculine valorization of goal-driven sexuality. But what if the masculine ideology that McClary detects belongs to the discourse created by male theorists and analysts, rather than the music they describe? Perhaps some descriptions of music overestimate the importance of goals, thereby constituting performances of masculinity on the part of the authors.

Consider William Caplin's description of the first cadence in Mozart's Sonata in G, K. 283: "The composer allows the melody to hold itself insistently on the fifth scale-degree . . . the cadential function is delayed by means of further tonic prolongation . . . The pent-up energy created by frustrating expectations of melodic and harmonic closure is finally released in a flurry of sixteenth-notes" (1998: 47–8). Music possessing such qualities would, as McClary suggests, invite associations with male sexual climax. But Caplin's description seems over-wrought and simplistic in relation to Mozart's gentle, elusive music, with its intricate rhythmic ambiguities. Arguably, Caplin's passage exemplifies a common analytical defect, the inapposite use of a simplistic model of tension and climactic release. In understanding why such models are widespread, it may be appropriate to evoke masculinity, but as a quality of theoretical and analytical discourse, rather than of the music it attempts to describe. Perhaps feminism should be suspicious of descriptive tools that originate in a male-dominated culture of music scholarship. Perhaps the theoretical and analytical preoccupation with goals is problematic, something to get past in articulating other qualities of musical sound and motion.

Similar concerns arise in relation to gendered models of sonata form in A. B. Marx and other writers (Marx 1997: 133). In the presence of formal interpretations that repeat gender stereotypes, one might question the gender politics of the authors who create these texts and the cultures that circulate them, rather than of the compositions they purport to describe. The focus on large-scale form may, itself, distort musical experience in the interest of a simple, drastic conceptual mastery. Jerrold Levinson argues that musical listening consists, above all, in the experience of a succession of moments of varying qualities, an experience poorly represented by discursive identification of large-scale formal patterns (Levinson 1997). While Levinson does not relate his account to gender and sexuality, he finds in much musical experience the sustained, moment-by-moment pleasure that McClary associates with historical constructions of femininity. Arguably, much in music theory, analysis, and aesthetics is a defensive masculine discourse, an effort to deny aspects of musical experience that may be felt as feminizing (Maus 1992, 1993, 2004; Guck 1994).

Most broadly, *Feminine Endings* follows conceptions of music criticism in offering definite interpretations of compositions. This goal is open to challenge. A focus on critical interpretation of compositions seems to disregard the role of performers. Cusick (1994a) argues that this privileges mental over physical engagement, relying on a hierarchized opposition linked to gender difference. And it disregards the effects that performance decisions may have on the possible interpretations of a composition; different performances may render various critical interpretations more or less believable. Outside the context of gender and sexuality, a new interest in the contributions of performers has been a significant strand of recent Anglophone musicology (see especially Taruskin 1995).

Further, by stating definite interpretations of compositions, McClary seems to marginalize the activity of listeners in forming individualized, idiosyncratic relations with music. While McClary's interpretations urgently sound feminist themes, their univocality may, in itself, suppress difference. If progressive politics of gender and sexuality aspires to recognize individual difference within identity categories, including difference of cognitive and sensuous experience, such suppression is problematic. Contrary to McClary's critical practice, many scholars of gender and sexuality have turned to autobiographical description of their interpretive relations to music, offering descriptions of compositions that claim no general authority, representing only personal understandings that are richly interwoven with personal experiences of gender and sexuality (Koestenbarum 1993; Cusick 1994b; Pegley and Caputo 1994; Maus 1996; Brett 1997).

It is important to develop approaches to gender, sexuality, and musical meaning that go beyond the norms of music criticism, questioning music criticism's reliance on syntactic and formal analysis, and challenging its neglect of performance and the varied subjectivities of musicians and listeners. One should also acknowledge the elegance and resourcefulness of McClary's feminist account of musical meaning. This range of issues and approaches will remain a lively area of inquiry for some time.

See also Analysis (Chapter 48), Music and politics (Chapter 50), Musicology (Chapter 45), Music theory and philosophy (Chapter 46), Sociology and cultural studies (Chapter 51), and Understanding music (Chapter 12).

References

Brett, P. (1997) "Piano Four-Hands: Schubert and the Performance of Gay Male Desire," *19th-Century Music* 21: 149–76.

Brett, P., Wood, E., and Thomas, G.C. (eds) (1994) *Queering the Pitch: The New Gay and Lesbian Musicology*, New York: Routledge.

Bowers, J. and Tick, J. (eds) (1986) *Women Making Music: The Western Art Tradition, 1150–1950*, Urbana: University of Illinois Press.

Caplin, W.E. (1998) *Classical Form: A Theory of Formal Functions for the Instrumental Music of Haydn, Mozart, and Beethoven*, Oxford: Oxford University Press.

Citron, M. (1993) *Gender and the Musical Canon*, Cambridge: Cambridge University Press.

Cone, E.T. (1982) "Schubert's Promissory Note: An Exercise in Musical Hermeneutics," *19th-Century Music* 5: 233–41.

Cook, S.C. and Tsou, J.S. (eds) (1994) *Cecilia Reclaimed: Feminist Perspectives on Gender and Music*, Urbana: University of Illinois Press.

Cusick, S. (1994a) "Feminist Theory, Music Theory, and the Mind/Body Problem," *Perspectives of New Music* 32: 8–27.

—— (1994b) "On a Lesbian Relation with Music: A Serious Effort Not to Think Straight," in Brett, Wood, and Thomas, pp. 67–83.

—— (1999) "Gender, Musicology, and Feminism," in N. Cook and M. Everist (eds) *Rethinking Music*, Oxford: Oxford University Press, pp. 471–98.

Fink, R. (2004) "Beethoven Antihero: Sex, Violence, and the Aesthetics of Failure, or Listening to the Ninth Symphony as Postmodern Sublime," in A. Dell'Antonio (ed.) *Beyond Structural Listening? Postmodern Modes of Hearing*, Berkeley: University of California Press, pp. 109–53.

Frith, S. and McRobbie, A. (1990 [1978]) "Rock and Sexuality," in S. Frith and A. Goodwin (eds) *On Record: Rock, Pop, and the Written Word*, London: Routledge, pp. 371–89.

Gill, J. (1995) *Queer Noises: Male and Female Homosexuality in Twentieth Century Music*, Minneapolis: University of Minnesota Press.

Guck, M.A. (1994) "A Woman's (Theoretical) Work," *Perspectives of New Music* 32: 28–43.

Kerman, J. (1985) *Contemplating Music: Challenges to Musicology*, Cambridge: Harvard University Press.

Koestenbaum, W. (1993) *The Queen's Throat: Opera, Homosexuality, and the Mystery of Desire*, New York: Poseidon Press.

Koskoff, E. (ed.) (1987) *Women and Music in Cross-Cultural Perspective*, New York: Greenwood Press.

Levinson, J. (1997) *Music in the Moment*, Ithaca: Cornell University Press.

Leonard, M. (2007) *Gender in the Music Industry: Rock, Discourse, and Girl Power*, Aldershot: Ashgate.

Marx, A.B. (1997) *Musical Form in the Age of Beethoven: Selected Writings on Theory and Method*, ed. and trans. S. Burnham, Cambridge: Cambridge University Press.

Maus, F.E. (1992) "Hanslick's Animism," *Journal of Musicology* 10: 273–92.

—— (1993) "Masculine Discourse in Music Theory," *Perspectives of New Music* 31: 264–93.

—— (1996) "Love Stories," *Repercussions* 4: 86–96.

—— (2001a) "Criticism: General Issues," in Sadie, vol. 6, pp. 670–73.

—— (2001b) "Narratology, narrativity," in Sadie, vol. 17, pp. 641–43.

—— (2004) "The Disciplined Subject of Musical Analysis," in A. Dell'Antonio (ed.) *Beyond Structural Listening? Postmodern Modes of Hearing*, Berkeley: University of California Press, pp. 13–43.

McClary, S. (1991) *Feminine Endings: Music, Gender, and Sexuality*, Minneapolis: University of Minnesota Press.

—— (1994) "Constructions of Subjectivity in Schubert's Music," in Brett, Wood, and Thomas, pp. 205–33.

Pegley, K. and Caputo, V. (1994) "Growing up Female(s): Retrospective Thoughts on Musical Preferences and Meanings," in Brett, Wood, and Thomas, pp. 297–313.

Ratner, L.G. (1980) *Classic Music: Expression, Form, and Style*, New York: Schirmer Books.

Sadie, S. (ed.) (2001) *The New Grove Dictionary of Music and Musicians*, 2nd edn, London: Macmillan.

Solie, R.A. (ed.) (1993) *Musicology and Difference: Gender and Sexuality in Music Scholarship*, Berkeley: University of California Press.

Tagg, P. (2000a [1979]) *Kojak: 50 Seconds of Television Music. Towards the Analysis of Affect in Popular Music*, 2nd edn, New York: Mass Media Music Scholars' Press.

—— (2000b [1991]) *Fernando the Flute*, 2nd edn, New York: Mass Media Music Scholars' Press.

Tagg, P. and Clarida, B. (2003) *Ten Little Title Tunes: Towards a Musicology of the Mass Media*, New York: Mass Media Music Scholars' Press.

Taruskin, R. (1995) *Text and Act: Essays on Music and Performance*, Oxford: Oxford University Press.

Treitler, L. (1989) *Music and the Historical Imagination*, Cambridge: Harvard University Press.

Walton, K. (1997) "Listening with Imagination: Is Music Representational?" in J. Robinson (ed.) *Music and Meaning*, Ithaca: Cornell University Press, pp. 57–82.

Whiteley, S. (ed.) (1997) *Sexing the Groove: Popular Music and Gender*, London: Routledge.

53
PHENOMENOLOGY OF MUSIC

Bruce Ellis Benson

Phenomenology and music are linked both historically and theoretically. On the one hand, already in phenomenology's infancy music was a topic of consideration by "proto-phenomenologist" Carl Stumpf, who used the concept of tonal "fusion" to explain musical consonance or harmony (Stumpf 1890). Early phenomenologists, such as Waldemar Conrad, Hans Mersmann, and Gustav Güldenstein, attempted phenomenologies of music with varying degrees of fidelity to strict phenomenological method (Conrad 1908; Mersmann 1922–23, 1925; Güldenstein 1928). On the other hand, the way in which we hear a melody becomes a crucial part of Edmund Husserl's explanation of internal time consciousness (Husserl 1991: 5–53). Phenomenology has been widely used as a way to explore music, particularly the ontology of musical works and our experience of musical sound.

To see how phenomenology can and has been utilized to study music, we need to begin with some basic aspects of phenomenology.

Introduction to phenomenology

Widely recognized as the founder of the phenomenological movement, Husserl laid out the basic contours of phenomenology. With the slogan "to the things themselves," Husserl insisted that all theorizing begin with an analysis of the basic phenomena as they appear (1983: 35). What he calls the "transcendental reduction" is the suspending of preconceptions, ontological beliefs, and theories in order to provide a direct and pure investigation. Once one has effectively "bracketed" such assumptions, one can apprehend the phenomena precisely as they appear to consciousness and unencumbered by any preconceptions. Then, the next goal is an "eidetic reduction," in which the specific phenomenon is reduced to its essential features. Husserl employs what he terms "free imaginative variation" to determine what properties of an object are essential and those that are merely accidental. The result is a "descriptive" phenomenology that leads to an "eidetic" phenomenology and then on to a "constitutive" phenomenology, in which the one considers how an object develops before us. That is, constitutive phenomenology considers the levels of experience and temporal phases that found the fully constituted essence of an object.

Various objects, including pieces of music, appear to us and develop over time. Husserl's account of internal time consciousness explains how we are able to experience a phenomenon over time. We "intend" (that is, perceive or apprehend) an object in the moment. Yet that object has continuity for us both because of "protention" (in which we anticipate the continuance of the object) and "retention" (in which the object is retained by short-term and then long-term memory). Using these basic concepts, Husserl explains how we hear a melody. The notes which have just been played are "retained" in our memory and those which we currently hear "protend" (with varying degrees of determinacy) in the direction of the future. Even though past notes fade away, we are able to intend them and hear them as constituting a whole that exists over time. Thus, we are able to hear these tones as a melody, rather than simply a random sequence of tones.

Of course, Husserl's phenomenology undergoes a number of changes as it develops. There are aspects of his thought – such as his emphasis on the centrality of the individual transcendental consciousness – that have led others to characterize his philosophy as "solipsistic." Yet, particularly as Husserl's thought matures, he comes to insist that the "I" always exists in a community and that community is part of the "life-world" – the environment in which we find ourselves that is composed of both nature and culture. An important development in Husserl's later philosophy (though anticipated by aspects in his early philosophy) is the strong emphasis on history. Thus, in Husserl's later philosophy, there is the recognition of the historical, cultural, and communal condition in which we live.

Although Martin Heidegger's phenomenology is in many ways indebted to Husserl, Heidegger's description of the subject is far more significantly "grounded" in practical experience. His term for human existence is "Dasein," which he describes as "being-in-the-world" (1962). That is, we are so fundamentally connected to the world that our existence cannot be thought apart from it. Further, Heidegger points out that we are "interpretive" beings whose understanding is always from within a cultural and intellectual horizon. As beings who are fundamentally "hermeneutical" in nature, our entire interaction with the world is one in which the things that we encounter take on meaning precisely by way of their relation to us. Not surprisingly, Heidegger's account of time makes it constitutive to Dasein's very existence. We are fundamentally pointed toward the future and thus we understand the future in terms of our own potential and possibilities. An important aspect of this future-oriented account is the use of interpretation in understanding. This is a point Heidegger's student, Hans-Georg Gadamer, develops in great detail. The most fundamental way of knowing, Heidegger argues, is interpretive; that is, Dasein takes concepts and meanings already available, and uses them to understand the world. This is called the hermeneutical circle because Dasein cannot get behind these concepts and justify them. Instead, they must be assumed for any understanding to be possible. When our expectations fail to line up with the phenomena adequately, if (as Gadamer memorably puts it) we are "pulled up short," then our interpretations must be revised (Gadamer 1989: 268). Thus, there is a fundamental difference between Husserl and Heidegger that will become particularly evident in phenomenologies of music that follow one or the other thinker. Although Husserl does recognize the importance of the life-world in his later thought, a Husserlian orientation takes our experience of music to be relatively pure and direct. Accordingly, from a Husserlian perspective, musical works have a kind of ideal and thus unchanging character that is not affected by performance practice or development of a musical tradition. However, if one considers both music experience and the ontological nature of musical works from Heidegger's hermeneutical standpoint, then one takes them to be thoroughly grounded in lived, practical experience and also only understandable from a actual, given perspective. Phenomenologists of music influenced by the work of Maurice Merleau-Ponty (who follows Husserl and Heidegger) emphasize this sense of being "culturally situated" even more, since Merleau-Ponty goes further than Heidegger in making the self truly "intersubjective" (Merleau-Ponty 2002: 402–25). A further aspect of Merleau-Ponty's thought is that we are embodied beings and so we do not relate to music as disembodied minds but as beings whose bodily existence means that we have both a mental and a "bodily" intelligence.

With these basic features of phenomenology in mind, we turn now to some specific examples of how phenomenology has been applied to music. Although quite a number of specific phenomenologies of music could be cited, our attention will be to some of the more influential and most developed ones.

Roman Ingarden: the ontology of the musical work

Simply glancing at the title of Roman Ingarden's phenomenology of music – *The Work of Music and the Problem of Its Identity* (1986) – tells the reader what is at stake for Ingarden. Although Ingarden intends his investigation into music to count as a true phenomenology (that is, driven by "the things themselves"), he is quite sure that pieces of music count as "works" and that they have discrete boundaries. Moreover, his phenomenology is restricted to musical works of the "classical music" tradition, with the result that much of what he says is simply not applicable to other sorts of music (though Ingarden seems to be completely unaware of this point). Ingarden's goal is to spell out what a musical work *is*; in other words, it is a project of "ontology," an attempt to explain the "being" of a musical work. Ingarden maintains that the work of music is above and beyond both the score and the performances of the work, so that its identity is unaffected by either. Effectively, it exists as an ideal object that can be instantiated at any time or in any place. Yet the problem is whether such a clear line of separation between this "work itself" and the score and performances can be drawn. Ingarden goes to great lengths to preserve these distinctions.

On the one hand, Ingarden recognizes that the score plays a highly important role, one that goes beyond merely "recording" the piece. In fact, while he wishes to give the "work itself" priority over scores or performances, in his account the score ends up taking on a centrality which almost seems to eclipse that of the composition, since the written notes serve to "determine mediately how the musical work should be structured and what qualities it should have" (Ingarden 1989: 25). Yet the problem with scores in general is that any given piece of music is always much more than a score, since it has attributes that the score cannot account for alone. "Because of the imperfection of musical notation, the score is an incomplete, schematic prescription for performance" (Ingarden 1986: 116). Thus, scores are *in principle* never complete: they are always "riddled with places of indeterminacy [*Unbestimmtheitsstellen*]" (Ingarden 1989: 90). Thus, rather than isomorphically reflecting a composition, scores do so only imperfectly. Moreover, it seems safe to say that, even with a far superior notational system, these indeterminate aspects would likely not disappear.

On the other hand, since performances by their very nature cannot avoid filling in the contours of a composition (i.e. its places of indeterminacy), variations among performances appear to come dangerously close to threatening the identity of the "work itself." Ingarden's solution to the obvious problem of the differences between the work and its performances is an *Irrelevanzsphäre* – a sphere of irrelevance. What Ingarden means is that the limits of a musical work are somewhat flexible and small variations in performance, such as different tempi or dynamics or even a false note, do not affect the "work itself." A certain degree of room for variation is allowed, but this variation is *irrelevant*. Ingarden maintains that not only is a work not *dependent* upon its performances but it is also not even *affected* by them – in *any* way. "Only the performances of the work are susceptible to influence by the subjective and Objective differences . . . the work itself stands outside their domain" (Ingarden 1989: 12). Here, Ingarden reflects the influence of Husserl rather than Heidegger.

Ingarden is aware that these distinctions are somewhat problematic precisely because of his attentiveness to the phenomena. Performances have the function of *presenting* a composition and making a musical experience possible: without a performance, there is literally nothing to be heard. Further, in presenting a musical composition, a performance thereby lends it a concrete existence and, in so doing, removes its indeterminacies. At least in terms of our experience, the "work itself" and its performances remain fundamentally inextricable. Ingarden's solution of the *Irrelevanzsphäre* remains problematic in that it is likewise "indeterminate." That is, where does the "work itself" end and the "irrelevant" bits begin? Ingarden denies that musical works undergo change over time. Instead, he contends that, though a piece of music remains the same, it is composed of a variety of possibilities for interpretation. Ingarden's account leaves us with significant problems. To what extent is the composition distinguishable from the score that preserves it in written form? Do performances serve only to *present* works to us, or do they somehow help to define and shape the work? Ultimately, Ingarden admits that "strictly speaking, we never become acquainted with a given musical work as the ideal aesthetic object in its entire fullness" (Ingarden 1989: 108), which is to say that we never really come to know the "work itself."

While Ingarden is hardly the only phenomenologist who has attended to the ontological nature of musical works, his is the best known and most developed. Yet other phenomenologists have applied the phenomenological method to questions of musical performance and listening.

Listening and sound: the description of hearing music

In more recent phenomenological treatments, there has been a move away from questions of ontology to a concern for what is involved in making and listening to music. Since phenomenology – like philosophy in general – has been so dominated by visual metaphors, F. Joseph Smith has proposed an "akumenology" that shifts the emphasis from sight to sound – an important move in the development of phenomenology of music. Borrowing heavily from Husserl, Smith provides an account of temporality that focuses on temporal phrases and how music is perceived by the listener. When we listen to music, we hear tone sequences in the present that are strongly related to both the past (by way of short-term memory) and the future (by way of anticipation). "In musical sound original impression, retention, and protention acquire a synthetic unity of their own" (Smith 1979: 108). We first synthesize musical phenomena in a passive way, and only later turn to active explanation and categorization. Given that our experience of music is "pre-intellectual," Smith advocates moving away from thinking of ourselves as metaphysical subjects and instead as embodied listeners who hear music prior to intellectual categorization. Such a move effectively leads to critiques of two competing accounts. The first is that traditional music theorists usually think of music in terms of numbers and so disconnect musical theory from musical practice. In such analysis, the actual sensory reception of music is lost to theoretical explanation. Second, Smith calls for moving away from Husserl's eidetic analysis to what Smith calls an "echotic reduction," "since we would not be interested in the *eidos* of musical sound but rather in its phenomenological *echos*, as sonorous essence" (1979: 30).

For Smith, music is ultimately a communal, intersubjective experience that brings together the pre-predicative, sensitive experience of the listener with the community of composers, performers, and listeners. When we make music together, we enter into a communal experience that requires a dialogical exchange and receptivity to the other. "The discordant voice of the other calls me to a sharing of the world . . . to a going outside and *beyond myself* by offering my hand, my heart, even my whole bodily being to the other" (Smith 1979: 36). Using the example of a chamber ensemble, Smith points out that each member – who is fully capable of being a soloist – must give up that freedom and submit to the aspirations of the group in order to work together. Of course, music is also "made" by the listener being an active participant in the whole process, for it is only at the moment of *hearing* that music truly exists. Thus, "the receptivity of the listening subject is a necessary correlate to the activity of the speaker or the musician" (Smith 1979: 111). Extending Heidegger's hermeneutical standpoint, Smith's phenomenology significantly widens and deepens our thinking regarding the musical experience.

Much like Smith, Don Ihde criticizes the tradition of Western philosophy as problematically "visualist" in nature. While we have gained much from this perspective, we have also had a "relative inattentiveness to the global fullness of experience and, in this case, to the equal richness of listening" (Ihde 2007: 8). Ihde makes a distinction between what he calls "first" and "second" phenomenology, with the first given attention to the richness of the experience and the second to the essential historicality of that experience. Thus, drawing on Heidegger, Ihde points out that sound and music only have their significance within a given world and thus are mediated by way of culture and history. Being highly influenced by Merleau-Ponty, Ihde emphasizes the embodied aspect of our engagement with music. He terms our experience of music "dance," for the entire body is affected by music. One is reminded of Friedrich Nietzsche's comments on dancing and life, for Ihde speaks of music "enticing" us to dance and "bodily listening" as the mode of proper engaging with music: "The call to dance is such that *involvement* and *participation* become the mode of being-in the musical situation" (Ihde 2007: 156).

In the second edition of his book *Listening and Voice* (2007), Ihde considers how recording has affected musical taste, the role that instrumentation plays in the production of music, and the ways in which these relationships have changed as technology has developed. As to taste, rock and popular music have come to dominate the musical scene, with classical music becoming less important. Much popular music relies on electronic amplification in its live production and that amplification becomes as much a part of the created piece of music as any other aspect. Because of its mode of production, popular music is particularly well suited for recording. Conversely, in classical music, the limits of electronic reproduction are immediate and likewise often detrimental. Even with the best technology, the live experience of classical music can only very imperfectly be captured by recording. Of course, recording presents limits for other types of music too. Idhe also notes a significant difference in the way rock and popular music are both made and experienced from that of classical music. With developments in technology, the trajectory of musical instrumentation in rock and pop music is away from music that is performed first-person without instruments or else instruments very closely connected to the body (such as instruments that are dependent upon the human breath or touch) to instruments that are much less connected to the body (an electronic synthesizer being a particularly good example).

Ihde reminds us that our experience of music is very strongly culturally mediated. A taste for rock or pop music provides a clear example of that. Likewise, with its heavy dependence upon improvisation that arises out of a long and complex tradition, jazz is likewise highly situated culturally and historically. Both result from developments in technology and the popular appropriation of forms of folk music, such that the production of music and the musical experience have changed quite significantly, and the descriptive categories first employed by Ingarden have little purchase on these new forms of music. What is needed is a closer attention to the historical worlds in which such new forms are developed and used by musical participants. That recognition leads us to the vital role of the *context* (musical and otherwise) in the entire experience of making and listening to music.

Aural context: the hermeneutics of music

The recognition that music is always situated within a cultural setting means that hermeneutics – the interpretive element in composing, performing, and listening to music – must be given its due. Musical concepts and possibilities do not arise from nowhere but rather from within a particular social and artistic context. Lawrence Ferrara strives to provide what he would consider to be a "holistic" approach to music that brings together phenomenology and more traditional approaches to music. Specifically, he uses what he would call the "descriptive-phenomenological" method to describe our actual experience of the music as heard in time, the "hermeneutical-phenomenological" method to explain the particular worldly context in which music arises and is heard, and the "conventional-formal" method to analyze musical form. Ferrara insists that only within such a broad consideration of music can we come to understand it in all of its dimensions. If we take the descriptive approach, we can understand music as an object that occurs in the time–space continuum. The goal of such a description is to accomplish what Husserl sought in his "bracketing" of assumptions in order to achieve an immediacy or direct apprehension of the music. By way of the hermeneutical approach, we can come to understand the world of the composer (as well as that of the performer and listener). This approach allows us to understand the particularities of these various worlds. It is the adding of the traditional or formal musical analysis to these two other methodologies that marks Ferrara's work as unlike that of Smith. Ferrara claims that these methodologies do not compete with one another; rather, they provide a holistic, even if "eclectic" approach, in that each of them informs and supports the others. Thus, the description of sound-in-time and the analysis of the musical form and syntax work together to ground the referential insights that emerge from hermeneutical description. Ferrara speaks of the "interplay of a work's multi-levels of significance" and insists that only a methodology that takes them all into account can do them justice (Ferrara 1991: 33). All of these ways of considering music are dedicated to allowing a piece of music to show itself as it truly is. While it may be that there is some aspect of the musical work that is ideal, this account of the musical work is clearly set against abstracting the work from the influence of its time, history, and culture.

There are ten steps to Ferrara's eclectic method. The first is that of considering the historical framework of the piece in the context of both music history and the composer's other compositions. Next, one attempts to get an idea of the basic structure of the piece by repeated listenings. Step three requires careful attention to a piece's syntax, or how a piece of music is constructed. The fourth step is an explicitly phenomenological description of the music as heard in time. A search for musical representation (i.e. in what sense a piece of music might "represent" something) marks the fifth step. A consideration of the way in which a piece of music expresses or represents human feelings or emotion is the sixth step. In step seven, one pays attention to the composer's "onto-historical world," the world out of which the piece arises. Step eight is about listening to the music and hearing how the previous steps interact with one another. Creating a guide to performance, commenting on such things as tempi, dynamics, and the basic "message" of the piece, is step nine. Finally, step ten is a kind of "meta-critique" of the entire process in which one considers the pros and cons of the method through which one has just gone and how these stages interact with one another. Thus, to whatever extent Ferrara's method is appropriate only to Western or even only Western classical music, such a mitigated appreciation of this method is anticipated by the self-critical aspect of step ten, in that the method itself is weighed for its veracity and appropriateness to the musical phenomenon it is analyzing.

Ferrara's method brings together the various strands of phenomenology and traditional music analysis that results in a robust description of a piece of music, in terms of its origin, its ontology, and its effect upon the listener. Such a method is hermeneutical in nature, since it takes for granted both that pieces of music cannot be considered apart from their cultural and historical context and that our descriptions and experiences of them are inevitably interpretations that are colored by our own cultural and historical context(s). Whereas Ingarden's phenomenology of music does recognize that pieces of music have a historical context, that context is largely downplayed. Further, Ingarden denies the possibility that later contexts in which music is performed or heard might somehow have an effect upon the ideal object known as the "work itself."

Yet it is precisely this attention to context, particularly the varying contexts over the lives of pieces of music, to which Bruce Ellis Benson pays particular attention. His phenomenology – very much a kind of hermeneutics of music – is particularly concerned with what musicians *do*. Although much of his account is concerned with classical music, it also focuses on the kind of improvisation one finds in jazz. Indeed, Benson advances a potentially controversial thesis – that music of all types is thoroughly improvisational in nature. To be sure, such a proposition seems counterintuitive in regard to classical music, in which we usually assume a kind of "repetition" model. According to such a model, the composer is the "true" creator and the performer merely an "intermediate transformer station" (Paul Hindemith) or "a kind of middleman" who "exists to serve the composer" (Aaron Copland) (Benson 2003: 12). Benson argues that this conception of composer, performer, and musical work is problematic on various counts.

First, Benson deconstructs the idea of a musical work as composed by a musical "genius" who "magically" gets ideas from nowhere. Although this Romantic idea still dominates much of our thinking about composers and compositions, Benson shows that it is a relatively *new* idea that certainly was not prevalent in Renaissance or Baroque music. Despite it being a kind of "regulative ideal" for classical compositions, when one examines what composers actually do it becomes clear that this ideal is not borne out in practice, even in classical music (Benson 2003: 42–52). The reality is that composers often borrow ideas from other composers (or themselves), go through a complicated and sometimes quite tortured process of composition, have quite differing levels of determinacy of how they intend their compositions to sound, and in some cases (Beethoven being a particularly good example) are not content with the end result.

Second, even when performers *think* they are "merely" repeating what the composer has written, Benson argues that they are always filling in those places of indeterminacy that Ingarden rightly realized are part of any piece of music. By examining what performers think they are doing by using period instruments and performance techniques, it becomes clear that they are adhering to an ideal that simply would not have been part of what most composers would have or *could have* intended, precisely because it is a thoroughly modern ideal that most composers would not have had in mind. The reality is that, for pieces of music that have been in existence for more than a century, there have been varying ways of interpreting them that have been deemed "acceptable." Ingarden speaks of pieces as having a "sphere of irrelevance," but exactly what aspects of a piece would be considered "irrelevant" are themselves changing.

What, then, becomes of the musical work? On Benson's view, what the composer creates is only the beginning, not the end. True, composers play an enormous role in creating musical works, at least in classical music as performed today. Yet performers are also part of the creative process and so are more than simply mouthpieces for the composer. Indeed, listeners also play a role in the final form that a musical work takes. But, if these observations are correct, then a musical work is a somewhat problematic object. Rather than being an ideal object that is fully formed from its beginning, it is instead something that takes shape over time. Contrary to Ingarden, pieces of music are continually changing, given different performing and listening practices and conditions. This is why Benson concludes that *improvisation* is fundamental to the musical experience. Pieces of music both arise by way of improvisation in the composition process and improvisation continues to form their shape in terms of performances and listeners.

Conclusion

Although these are only representative samples of work in musical phenomenology, it should be clear that the phenomenological method is designed to attend to the musical experience itself, rather than the analysis of scores. Music is experienced in time by fully embodied beings whose experience of music is just as bodily as it is mental. Further, music-making is something that is fundamentally intersubjective, and even a performance by a musician in a practice room is still very much connected to a social and historical context. Finally, by attending to the musical phenomena, it becomes clear just how much music is dependent upon particular traditions and their preconceptions that allow for composition, performance, and listening to music of different sorts. Only when music is set in its proper context can it be fully experienced and appreciated.

See also Analysis (Chapter 48), Continental philosophy and music (Chapter 26), Music theory and philosophy (Chapter 46), Ontology (Chapter 4), Performances and recordings (Chapter 8), Psychology of music (Chapter 55), and Understanding music (Chapter 12).

References

Benson, B.E. (2003) *The Improvisation of Musical Dialogue: A Phenomenology of Music*, Cambridge: Cambridge University Press.

Conrad, W. (1908) "Der asthetische Gegenstand," *Zeitschrift für Ästhetik und allgemeine Kunstwissenschaft* 3: 71–118.

Ferrara, L. (1991) *Philosophy and the Analysis of Music: Bridges to Musical Sound, Form, and Reference*, Westport: Greenwood.

Gadamer, H.-G. (1989 [1960]) *Truth and Method*, trans. J. Weinsheimer and D.G. Marshall, New York: Continuum.

Güldenstein, G. (1928) *Theorie der Tonart*, Stuttgart: Klett.

Heidegger, M. (1962 [1927]) *Being and Time*, trans. J. Macquarrie and E. Robinson, New York: Harper and Row.

Husserl, E. (1983 [1913]) *Ideas Pertaining to a Pure Phenomenology and to a Phenomenological Philosophy, First Book: General Introduction to Pure Phenomenology*, trans. F. Kersten, Dordrecht: Kluwer

—— (1991) *On the Phenomenology of the Consciousness of Internal Time (1893–1917)*, trans. J.B. Brough, Dordrecht: Kluwer.

Ihde, D. (2007) *Listening and Voice*, 2nd edn, Albany: State University of New York Press.

Ingarden, R. (1986) *The Work of Music and the Problem of Its Identity*, trans. A. Czerniawski, ed. J.G. Harrell, Berkeley: University of California Press. (This text is virtually identical with the section on music in Ingarden 1989; however, it is a translation of Ingarden's Polish version of the text [rather than the German version] and differs at some crucial junctures.)

—— (1989) *Ontology of the Work of Art: The Musical Work, The Picture, The Architectural Work, The Film*, trans. R. Meyer with J.T. Goldthwait, Athens: Ohio University Press.

Merleau-Ponty, M. (2002 [1945]) *The Phenomenology of Perception*, trans. C. Smith, New York, Routledge.

Mersmann, H. (1922–23) "Versuch einer Phänomenologie der Musik," *Zeitschrift für Musikwissenschaft* 5: 255–62.

—— (1925) "Zur Phänomenologie der Musik," *Zeitschrift für Ästhetik und allgemeine Kunstwissenschaft* 19: 372–88.

Smith, F.J. (1979) *The Experiencing of Musical Sound: Prelude to a Phenomenology of Music*, New York: Gordon and Breach.

Stumpf, C. (1890) *Tonpsychologie*, vol. 2, Leipzig: Hirzel.

Further reading

Lochhead, J. (1982) *The Temporal Structure of Recent Music: A Phenomenological Investigation*, Ph.D. diss., State University of New York at Stony Brook. (An important example of musicology that applies phenomenology to music theory.)

Sadai, Y. (1980) *Harmony in Its Systematic and Phenomenological Aspects*, trans. J. Davis and M. Schlesinger, Jerusalem: Yanetz. (A composer who writes on music theory and phenomenological method.)

Wiskus, J. (2008) "The Universality of the Sensible: On Plato and the Musical Idea according to Merleau-Ponty," *Epoché: A Journal for the History of Philosophy* 13: 121–32. (A music theorist who incorporates contemporary phenomenology, including Merleau-Ponty.)

54
MUSIC, PHILOSOPHY, AND COGNITIVE SCIENCE
Diana Raffman

Philosophers of music (and also music theorists) have recognized for a long time that research in the sciences, especially psychology, might have import for their own work. (Langer 1941 and Meyer 1956 are good examples.) However, while scientists had been interested in music as a subject of research (e.g. Helmholtz 1875; Seashore 1938), the discipline known as *psychology of music*, or more broadly *cognitive science of music*, came into its own only around 1980 with the publication of several landmark works. Among the most important of these were *The Psychology of Music* (1982), a collection of papers edited by the psychologist Diana Deutsch, and *A Generative Theory of Tonal Music* (1983) by music theorist and composer Fred Lerdahl and linguist Ray Jackendoff. These works and others made possible the first attempts to apply scientific research to philosophical issues concerning music (e.g. Raffman 1993; DeBellis 1995).

Since the 1980s, of course, a great deal of research has been done in cognitive science, philosophy, and music. For philosophers, there are perhaps three topics with respect to which findings in the cognitive sciences are most likely to be germane – the nature of musical understanding, the role of emotions or feelings in music, and the evaluation of musical works. This brief overview will describe some of the scientific research that has been done on these topics, and then indicate how it might be philosophically significant.

Scientific research

In his 1976 Norton Lectures at Harvard, Leonard Bernstein had floated, but not developed, the idea that tonal music might have a grammar analogous to the generative grammar that Noam Chomsky (1965) had proposed for natural language. Lerdahl and Jackendoff (1983) developed Bernstein's proposal into a detailed set of analytical rules, that is, a grammar, designed to capture an experienced listener's unconscious mental representation of a musical stimulus. (An experienced listener is familiar with a given idiom, here "classical" tonal music, but has no formal training.) The musical grammar contained metrical and grouping rules governing rhythmic structure, and higher-level time-span and prologonational rules governing certain interactions between rhythm and pitch. Lerdahl and Jackendoff hypothesized that conscious musical experience, characterized by feelings of tension, resolution, stability, and the like, was the result of unconsciously analyzing a musical stimulus – recovering its structure – according to these grammatical rules, much as a speaker–hearer's conscious understanding of a sentence was supposed to be the result of unconsciously analyzing a linguistic stimulus according to the rules of the linguistic grammar. In fact, Lerdahl and Jackendoff conceive of conscious musical experience as the listener's *understanding* of a piece of music. In a subsequent book, *Tonal Pitch Space Theory* (2001), Lerdahl has expanded upon the pitch component of the musical grammar. Here he proposes that the events of a tonal work are heard (understood) as traversing a path through a multidimensional space defined by the relative distances among pitches, chords, and keys.

In designing their musical grammar, Lerdahl and Jackendoff naturally employed the investigative methods of music theory and linguistics; in particular, they took musical and linguistic *intuitions* as their evidence. But the idea of a significant link between music and language has also received support from research in psychology and neuroscience. For example, it appears that melodic contexts can influence the perception of speech (e.g. Koelsch et al. 2005; Dilley and McCauley 2008), and harmonic contexts can influence phoneme monitoring (Bigand et al. 2001). Shared structures have been observed in speech prosody and musical melody and rhythm (Patel 2008); and ERP (evoked response potential) measures of neural activity reveal that in tasks involving both musical and linguistic syntactic integration, interference occurs between the two processes (Patel et al. 1998). (The same kind of interference shows up in behavior as well; see, for example, Fedorenko et al. 2009.) Musical training appears to facilitate second language learning (Slevc and Miyake 2006); and fMRI (functional magnetic resonance imaging) studies indicate that some musical and linguistic processes activate the same areas of the brain (Tillman et al. 2006). In an overview of the biology and evolution of music, Tecumseh Fitch (2006) concludes that various "design features" of music and language suggest an overlap of the two domains. (See Levitan 2006 and Patel 2008 for sustained defense of this idea.)

Another driving innovation in the cognitive science of music was the introduction, by psychologists Carol Krumhansl and Roger Shepard (1979), of the *probe tone* test of experienced listeners' mental representations of tonal pitch structure. In contrast to Lerdahl and Jackendoff, Krumhansl and Shepard were interested in the experienced listener's standing knowledge (mental representation) of tonal pitch structure, rather than in the understanding of particular pieces. (Presumably some standing or "static" knowledge of tonal pitch structure is mobilized in the understanding of any particular piece.) They wanted to find out whether the pitch relationships postulated by music theory – the circle of fifths, the system of major and minor triads, scales, and keys, etc. – are psychologically real. In each trial in a probe-tone task, the listener hears a brief musical passage, then a short silence, and then one of the twelve chromatic pitches (the probe tone). The listener's task is to rate how well the probe tone "fits" with the context of the preceding musical passage. This process is typically repeated for each of the twelve chromatic pitches, the idea being that the probe tones allow the researcher to probe the musical representations in the listener's mind at a given moment. The ratings that emerged from Krumhansl and Shepard's tests indicated that experienced listeners possess complex hierarchical representations of tonal pitch structure – indeed, a good deal of the fundamental pitch structures recognized by music theorists. This knowledge is what enables listeners to recognize wrong notes in a performance and to produce (sing) the final pitch in an unfamiliar melody when the preceding notes are provided, among other things.

A further significant line of scientific research grew out of the work of music theorist Leonard Meyer (1956), often credited as the first theorist to take account of psychological research. (Meyer was himself influenced by the philosopher Susanne Langer (1941).) Meyer argued that understanding a piece of music involves having certain "undifferentiated feelings" of tension and release in response to it (1956: 18). General features of human perceptual psychology (e.g. gestalt principles of grouping and continuation), together with our knowledge of tonal structure and musical style, engender certain (musical) expectations in us when we listen to music. When our expectations are either violated or fulfilled, we experience a feeling of tension or release, respectively.

Meyer's views were later formalized by Eugene Narmour (1990) and also developed into psychological theories of musical *expectancy*. For example, Jamshed Bharucha and Keiko Stoeckig (1986) had subjects perform a series of priming tasks that revealed their harmonic expectancies. On each trial the subject heard a musical passage in a given key. The passage was followed by a single target chord, and the subject's task was to say whether the target chord was in-tune or out-of-tune. It emerged that subjects were faster in their responses when the target chord was harmonically related to the key of the initial passage, and so was expected, than when it was unrelated. The same result was obtained when the task was to classify the target as major or minor, or to identify its timbre.(Bharucha (e.g. 1987) is one of few researchers who have reformulated their theories of tonal pitch cognition within the framework of parallel distributed processing or connectionism.) More recently David Huron (2006) has proposed an elaborate five-stage theory of expectation which he applies to music perception. Echoing Meyer, Huron argues that the fulfillment and violation of musical expectations evoke emotional responses in the listener.

Much of the research described above is grounded in the idea that as we are exposed to performances of tonal music, we abstract or "infer" from those stimuli the basic structures postulated by music theorists. However, in recent years there has emerged a competing, radically empiricist conception of the learning of tonal pitch structure. According to some *statistical learning* models (e.g. Krumhansl 1990; Huron 2006), our acquisition of knowledge (representations) of tonal pitch structure depends upon merely statistical, rather than structural, properties of the pitch-time events in a musical stimulus. In a review of Krumhansl, Huron writes:

> [T]he tonal hierarchy correlates well with the distribution of [pitches]for musical passages; play a pitch often enough, and the tonic will tend to drift towards that pitch. The correlation between the tonal hierarchy and probabilities of various pitches within tonal music are consistently high (average r = 0.88). Krumhansl exploits this fact to develop a remarkably successful yet simple key-finding algorithm. Third, by cross-correlating the distributions for different keys it is possible to generate a spatial representation of interkey distances . . . [When] Krumhansl applies multi-dimensional scaling to her response data[,] the "circle of fifths" pops right out – showing that this theoretical construct is not simply a fanciful abstraction, but bears real cognitive import.
>
> (1992: 180)

Unsurprisingly, the idea that learning pitch structure is statistically based is controversial. Of course the tonic is the pitch occurring most often in a tonal work, critics object, because the work is composed by a mind that represents the tonic as the most important pitch. This does not explain how listeners recover the pitch structure of the work: listeners would "find" the tonic even if the tonic was not the most frequent pitch; indeed, even if the tonic did not occur at all. (One could certainly write such a piece.) Jones points out that "adults rely heavily on rhythmic properties to differentiate melodies; they have difficulty identifying a learned melodic sequence if its original rhythm changes, even when temporal segmentations and statistical pitch properties are unchanged" (2010). Indeed, if recovery of pitch structure is statistical, then we ought to be able to recover the structure of any arbitrary pitch system, simply in virtue of the fact that different pitches occur in it with different frequencies; but there is considerable evidence that we cannot recover twelve-tone pitch structure (Gibson 1995; Krumhansl 1990), just for example.

However acquisition works, the idea that tonal pitch structure is psychologically real stands on firm ground. Recent fMRI experiments provide additional confirmation. In their 2002 paper in *Nature*, Petr Janata and his colleagues report the discovery of activation patterns in the cortex corresponding to the relationships among tonal keys. They write:

Western tonal music relies on a formal geometric structure that determines distance relationships within a harmonic or tonal space. In functional magnetic resonance imaging experiments, we identified an area in rostromedial prefrontal cortex that tracks activation in tonal space. Different voxels [i.e. three-dimensional pixels] in this area exhibited selectivity for different keys. Within the same set of consistently activated voxels, the topography of tonal selectivity rearranged itself across scanning sessions. The tonality structure was thus maintained as a dynamic topography in a cortical area known to be at a nexus of cognitive, affective, and mnemonic processing (2167). . . . [W]hat changed between sessions was not the tonality-tracking behavior of these brain areas but rather the region of tonal space (keys) to which they were sensitive. This type of relative representation provides a mechanism by which pieces of music can be transposed from key to key, yet retain their internal pitch relationships and tonal coherence (2169).

What Janata and colleagues found is that each key (C major, C minor, D major, etc.) activates a unique assembly of neurons in the frontal cortex in a given hearing. On another occasion (hearing the same music or different music), that assembly may be activated by a different key, but the relationships among the keys are preserved. (See also Brattico et al. 2006 for relevant findings.)

Of particular interest to philosophers of music will be the scientific studies of music and emotion. (See Juslin and Sloboda 2001 for a good overview.) I have already mentioned Meyer's and Langer's important work on musical feelings; psychologists have taken their views as a point of departure. Like philosophers of music, psychologists of music disagree as to whether musical emotions are (1) ordinary emotions such as sadness, happiness, and fear, or (2) some sort of thin versions of ordinary emotions, or (3) feelings special to music or to aesthetic experience generally, or (4) more like moods. Obviously there are *some* non-trivial differences between musical and ordinary emotions, for example with respect to their antecedent causes and behavioral consequences; and musical feelings do not seem to involve any cognitive appraisal, which is required by some theories of (non-musical) emotion. An experiment by Marcel Zentner, Stéphanie Meylan, and Klaus Scherer (2000) suggests that the frequency of some emotions differs as between musical and "ordinary" contexts. For example, their subjects' (experimental) diaries reflected that nostalgia, awe, and enchantment occurred more often in musical than in ordinary contexts, while the situation was reversed for anger and fear. Also, physiological concomitants of musical emotions coincide only partially with those of ordinary non-musical emotions (Krumhansl 1997).

Until fairly recently most psychological research on musical emotion investigated the "perception" of emotion in, or the expression of emotion by, a musical work, as opposed to the "induction" or evocation of emotion in the listener (e.g. Wedin 1972). (For a helpful overview, see Gabrielsson and Juslin 2002.) In general, happiness and sadness, which are strongly associated with tempo and mode (major vs. minor), are the emotions most consistently said to be expressed by music. Relatively louder music is heard as being relatively more animated, triumphant, and activated, but can also be heard as tense or angry, while relatively softer music sounds more tranquil or melancholy. This bias toward the study of perceived emotion may be explained in part by the fact, noted by philosophers (e.g. Kivy 2001: 147), that perceived emotions often occur in the absence of felt emotions, that is, listeners often attribute an emotion to a piece of music without themselves feeling that emotion; but not, in general, vice versa (Hunter and Schellenberg 2010). Whatever the explanation, psychologists are now devoting more attention to induced musical emotions. Zentner et al. (2000) found that instructing subjects to rate emotions induced by musical stimuli, rather than emotions expressed by those stimuli, produced very different results. Other studies indicate that induced and perceived emotions are correlated (i.e. same music, same emotion whether induced or perceived), but perceived emotions were rated as being stronger than induced or felt emotions (e.g. Evans and Schubert 2008).

Perhaps the most interesting question about music and emotion concerns the relationship between musical feelings (perceived or induced) and specific musical structures. For example, John Sloboda (1991) found that tears accompanied harmonic descent through the cycle of fifths to the tonic; shivers or chills accompanied enharmonic changes, new harmonies, and sudden changes in loudness; and racing pulse went along with repeated syncopation and earlier-than-expected occurrences of important pitch-time events. In a study focusing on listener's physiological responses, Krumhansl (1997) had subjects listen to three kinds of musical excerpts: sad (i.e. sadness-expressing) ones, characterized by inter alia slow tempos, minor keys, and relatively constant dynamics; scary ones, characterized by faster and more irregular tempos and dynamic levels; and happy ones, characterized by relatively fast tempos, major keys, and fairly constant dynamics. (Classification of the excerpts as sad, scary, or happy was confirmed by uniform and consistent judgments of the subjects.) It turned out that listening to the sad excerpts was associated with felt sadness and also with (inter alia) decreased pulse rates and increased blood pressure; listening to scary excerpts was associated with felt fear and also with increased breathing rates and decreased finger temperature; and listening to the happy excerpts was associated with felt happiness and also with decreased respiration depth ("shallower" breathing). Krumhansl writes:

> These results suggest that musical emotions are reflected in psychophysiological measures . . . These psychophysiological changes are behavioural indicators that listeners experience emotions when listening to music. Not only do listeners verbally report emotional responses to music with considerable consistency, music also produces physiological changes that correspond with the type of musical emotion.
>
> (1990: 350–1)

In related research, listeners have been shown generally to prefer musical consonance to dissonance and happy-sounding music to sad-sounding; however, the appeal of sad-sounding music increases when listeners feel tired or sad (Hunter and Schellenberg 2010). This last finding may help to explain why listeners often enjoy listening to sad music – otherwise a puzzle for the view that music induces emotions.

The experiments described above are only a tiny sample. Virtually nothing has been said here about the scientific research on musical performance, composition, or improvisation, on the role of rhythm, meter, and timbre in music perception, or on musical deficits such as amusia, to name a few; and aspects of all of these may be relevant to philosophy. (Popper et al. 2010, Hallam et al. 2009, and Peretz and Zatorre 2003 provide excellent surveys of the scientific literature.) That said, let us now look briefly at some philosophical implications.

Some philosophical implications

Musical understanding

Philosophers have advanced a variety of views about the nature of musical understanding; for example, that it consists of feeling certain emotions (Davies 1994), or in imagining that we are feeling certain emotions (Walton 1990), or in recognizing the musical expression of certain emotions (Kivy 2001). And while any of these accounts may be partly correct, the apparent psychological reality of detailed tonal structure and its importance in determining the character of music perception suggest that grasp of tonal structure must play a central role. (As we saw, Lerdahl and Jackendoff define musical understanding in terms of the recovery of musical structure.)

In particular, research in music cognition lends support to the idea that understanding a piece of music involves the representation of movement through a tonal space (e.g. Lerdahl 2001). Philosophers have argued over whether talk of movement in a space is metaphorical when applied to music, and if so, whether the metaphor can be replaced by purely musical terminology (e.g. Budd 1985; Scruton 1983; Kania 2007). Malcolm Budd is surely right that the spatial terminology can be replaced, but this does not mean that musical movement is wholly non-spatial. The scientists' thought is that the tonal pitch relationships in a musical work are isomorphic to, and hence can be theoretically modeled and psychologically represented as, certain spatial relationships. There is no obvious reason why such a representation must be metaphorical. At the very least, there is no obvious reason why talk of musical *movement* must be metaphorical. For one thing, surely there is a perfectly literal sense of the word "move" in which it means something like "develop" or "proceed" or "progress" or "grow." It is hardly coincidental that music theorists use the term "progressions" to refer to transitions among harmonies, or that they characterize fast (slow) changes of harmony as fast (slow) harmonic *motion*. For another thing, musical motion may be a kind of apparent motion, rather like the apparent motion we experience when looking at a row of lights that flash serially in quick succession. Nothing moves; rather, it appears as if something (a light?) moves.

The observed commonalities between musical and linguistic structure, processes, and neural mechanisms suggest that the understanding of music is also importantly analogous to the understanding of language. One possible view is that, in music as in language, understanding is the result of grammar-driven operations defined over acoustic stimuli; in other words, understanding consists in the grasp of musical or linguistic structure. In the musical case, that grasp of structure is consciously experienced as certain specifically musical feelings of tension, stability, resolution, and so forth. The idea that having an ordinary emotion or mood, even weak versions of them, could constitute musical understanding suffers from the fact that however closely such emotions are *correlated* with musical events, or even caused by musical events, they do not possess the requisite normativity. In most cases it is hard to see what could justify claiming that a listener (*a fortiori* a performer or composer) has made a mistake, has misunderstood the music in virtue of feeling or failing to feel a certain mood or emotion in response to it, or in virtue of hearing or failing to hear a certain musical passage as expressing a certain emotion. In contrast, musical feelings of tension and stability and the rest, which result from the recovery of tonal structure, do possess the requisite normativity. If a listener hears an authentic cadence or a 4–3 suspension as increasing in tension or instability, *a fortiori* if she identifies an authentic cadence as (e.g.) a deceptive one, she is mistaken. An authentic cadence just is, in part, a progression from instability to stability (see Raffman 1993: 37–56, for elaboration).

Music and emotion

According to the so-called cognitivist view of musical emotion, endorsed notably by Peter Kivy (1990), listeners recognize the expression of emotions by musical works but do not typically feel those emotions themselves; in the scientific terminology used above, musical emotions are perceived but not induced or felt. In support of this view, Kivy claims that "there are no behavioral symptoms of listeners actually experiencing [emotions] when attending to music" (1990: 151). The psychological, physiological, and neuroscientific research described above suggests otherwise. Listeners are able to make uniform and consistent reports (verbal behaviors) of the emotions they experience in listening to music; they undergo uniform and consistent physiological changes while listening to music; and fMRI studies suggest that the mental representation of tonal pitch structure is underwritten by parts of the cortex that are implicated in affective experience.

Evaluation of music

No doubt the psychological findings concerning our preferences for consonance over dissonance and for happy music over sad, etc., may have implications for the evaluation of musical works. Also, generally speaking, the artistic merit of a work must depend at least in part upon its comprehensibility: it is difficult to see how a (humanly) incomprehensible work could be a great work. The latter point raises a question about the evaluation of atonal, specifically twelve-tone or serial, pieces of music. As indicated above, research on pitch perception has revealed that even expert listeners are probably not able to recover serial pitch structures to any significant extent. Lerdahl (1988) has suggested that serial pitch structure, which is not hierarchical, does not provide a good "ecological fit" with human perceptual and cognitive systems, and so is difficult or even impossible for us to recover (understand) aurally. Consequently, if musical understanding essentially involves grasp of the structure of a work, a question may arise about the artistic merit of twelve-tone pieces (Cavell 1976; Taruskin 1996; Tymoczko 2000; Raffman 2003; Levitan 2006).

See also Analysis (Chapter 48), Arousal theories (Chapter 20), Evaluating music (Chapter 16), Music and language (Chapter 10), Music's arousal of emotions (Chapter 22), Psychology of music (Chapter 55), Resemblance theories (Chapter 21), and Understanding music (Chapter 12).

References

Bernstein, L. (1976) *The Unanswered Question: Six Talks at Harvard by Leonard Bernstein*, Cambridge: Harvard University Press.

Bharucha, J. (1987) "Music Cognition and Perceptual Facilitation: A Connectionist Framework," *Music Perception* 5: 1–30.

Bharucha, J., and Stoeckig, K. (1986) "Reaction Time and Musical Expectancy: Priming of Chords," *Journal of Experimental Psychology: Human Perception and Performance* 12: 403–10.

Bigand, E., Tillman, B., Poulin, B., and D'Adamo, D.A. (2001) "The Effect of Harmonic Context on Phoneme Monitoring in Vocal Music," *Cognition* 81: B11–B20.

Brattico, E., Tervaniemi, M., Näätänen, R., and Peretz, I. (2006) "Musical Scale Properties are Automatically Processed in the Human Auditory Cortex," *Brain Research* 11: 162–74.

Budd, M. (1985) "Understanding Music," *Proceedings of the Aristotelian Society*, supp. vol. 59: 233–48.

Cavell, S. (1976) "Music Discomposed," in *Must We Mean What We Say? A Book of Essays*, Cambridge: Cambridge University Press, pp. 180–212.

Chomsky, N. (1965) *Aspects of the Theory of Syntax*, Cambridge: MIT Press.

Davies, S. (1994) *Musical Meaning and Expression*, Ithaca: Cornell University Press.

DeBellis, M. (1995) *Music and Conceptualization*, Cambridge: Cambridge University Press.

Deutsch, D. (1982) *The Psychology of Music*, San Diego: Academic Press.

Dilley, L.C., and McAuley, J.D. (2008) "Distal Prosodic Context Affects Word Segmentation and Lexical Processing," *Journal of Memory and Language* 59: 294–311.

Evans, P., and Schubert, E. (2008) "Relationships between Expressed and Felt Emotions in Music," *Musicae Scientiae* 12: 75–99.

Fitch, W.T. (2006) "The Biology and Evolution of Music: A Comparative Perspective," *Cognition* 100: 173–215.

Fedorenko, E., Patel, A.D., Casasanto, D., Winawer, J., and Gibson, E. (2009) "Structural Integration in Language and Music: Evidence for a Shared System," *Memory & Cognition* 37: 1–9.

Gabrielsson, A., and Juslin, P. (2002) "Emotional Expression in Music," in R.J. Davidson, K.R. Scherer, and H.H. Goldsmith (eds) *Handbook of Affective Sciences*, Oxford: Oxford University Press, pp. 503–34.

Gibson, D. (1995) "Theoretical Assumptions and Aural Experiences in the Pitch-Class Set Domain," *Music Theory Explorations and Applications* 4: 17–25.

Hallam, S., Cross, I., and Thaut, M. (2009) *The Oxford Handbook of Music Psychology*, Oxford: Oxford University Press.

Helmholtz, H. von (1875) *On the Sensations of Tone as a Physiological Basis for the Theory of Music*, trans. A. Ellis, London: Longmans (reprint 1954, New York: Dover).

Hunter, P.G., and Schellenberg, E.G. (2010) "Music and Emotion," in Popper, Jones, and Fay, pp. 129–64.

Huron, D. (1992) Review of Carol L. Krumhansl, *Cognitive Foundations of Musical Pitch*, *Psychology of Music* 20: 180–185.

—— (2006) *Sweet Anticipation: Music and the Psychology of Expectation*, Cambridge: MIT Press.

Janata, P., Birk, J., Van Horn, J.D., Leman, M., Tillman, B., and Bharucha, J. (2002) "The Cortical Topography of Tonal Structures Underlying Western Music," *Science* 28: 2167–70.

Jones, M.R. (2010) "Music Perception: Current Research and Future Directions" in Popper, Jones, and Fay, pp. 1–12.

Juslin, P., and Sloboda, J. (2001) *Music and Emotion: Theory and Research*, New York: Oxford University Press.

Kania, A. (2007) "The Philosophy of Music," in E.N. Zalta (ed.) *The Stanford Encyclopedia of Philosophy*, available at http://plato.stanford.edu/entries/music/.

Kivy, P. (1990) *Music Alone: Philosophical Reflections on the Purely Musical Experience*, Ithaca: Cornell University Press.

—— (2001) *New Essays on Musical Understanding*, Oxford: Clarendon Press.

Koelsch, S., Gunter, T.C., and Sammler, D. (2005) "Interaction between Processing in Language and in Music: An ERP Study," *Journal of Cognitive Neuroscience* 17: 1565–79.

Krumhansl, C. (1990) *Cognitive Foundations of Musical Pitch*, Oxford: Oxford University Press.

—— (1997) "An Exploratory Study of Musical Emotions and Psychophysiology," *Canadian Journal of Experimental Psychology* 51: 336–52.

Krumhansl, C., and Shepard, R.N. (1979) "Quantification of the Hierarchy of Tonal Functions within a Diatonic Context," *Journal of Experimental Psychology: Human Perception and Performance* 5: 579–94.

Langer, S. (1941) *Philosophy in a New Key: A Study in the Symbolism of Reason, Rite and Art*, Cambridge: Harvard University Press.

Lerdahl, F. (1988) "Cognitive Constraints on Compositional Systems," in J. Sloboda (ed.) *Generative Processes in Music*, Oxford: Oxford University Press, pp. 231–59.

—— (2001) *Tonal Pitch Space Theory*, Oxford: Oxford University Press.

Lerdahl, F., and Jackendoff, R. (1983) *A Generative Theory of Tonal Music*, Cambridge: MIT Press.

Levitan, D. (2006) *This is Your Brain on Music: The Science of a Human Obsession*, New York: Dutton.

Meyer, L.B. (1956) *Emotion and Meaning in Music*, Chicago: University of Chicago Press.

Narmour, E. (1990) *The Analysis and Cognition of Basic Melodic Structures: The Implication-Realization Model*, Chicago: University of Chicago Press.

Patel, A. (2008) *Music, Language, and the Brain*, Oxford: Oxford University Press.

Patel, A.D., Gibson, E., Ratner, J., Besson, M., and Holcomb, P. (1998) "Processing Syntactic Relations in Language and Music: An Event-Related Potential Study," *Journal of Cognitive Neuroscience* 10: 717–33.

Peretz, I., and Zatorre, R. (eds) (2003) *The Cognitive Neuroscience of Music*, New York: Oxford University Press.

Popper, A., Jones, M.R., and Fay, R. (eds) (2010) *Springer Handbook of Auditory Research (Vol. 36): Music Perception*, New York: Springer.

Raffman, D. (1993) *Language, Music, and Mind*. Cambridge: MIT-Bradford Books.

—— (2003) "Is Twelve-Tone Music Artistically Defective?" *Midwest Studies in Philosophy*, 27: 69–87.

Scruton, R. (1983) "Understanding Music" in *The Aesthetic Understanding: Essays in the Philosophy of Art and Culture*, London: Methuen, pp. 77–100.

Seashore, C. (1938) *Psychology of Music*, New York: McGraw-Hill.

Slevc, L.R., and Miyake, A. (2006) "Individual Differences in Second Language Proficiency: Does Musical Ability Matter?" *Psychological Science* 17: 675–81.

Sloboda, J. (1991) "Musical Structure and Emotional Response: Some Empirical Findings," *Psychology of Music* 19: 110–20.

Taruskin, R. (1996) "How Talented Composers Become Useless," *The New York Times*, March 10, H31.

Tillman, B., Koelsch, S., Escoffier, N., Bigand, E., Lalitte, P., Friederici, A.D., von Cramon, D.Y. (2006) "Cognitive Priming in Sung and Instrumental Music: Activation of Inferior Frontal Cortex," *NeuroImage* 31: 1771–82.

Tymoczko, D. (2000) "The Sound of Philosophy: The Musical Ideas of Milton Babbitt and John Cage," *The Boston Review*, October/November, available at http://bostonreview.net/BR25.5/tymoczko.html.

Walton, K. (1990) *Mimesis as Make-Believe: On the Foundations of the Representational Arts*, Cambridge: Harvard University Press.

Wedin, L. (1972) "A Multidimensional Study of Perceptual-Emotional Qualities in Music," *Scandinavian Journal of Psychology* 13: 241–57.

Zentner, M.R., Meylan, S., and Scherer, K.R. (2000) "Exploring Musical Emotions across Five Genres of Music," presentation at 6th International Conference of the Society for Music Perception and Cognition, August 5–10, Keele, UK.

55
PSYCHOLOGY OF MUSIC
Eric Clarke

Early history

Writing on the relationship between music and human behavior goes back to classical antiquity – and in a broad sense the psychology of music therefore has a very long history. The Greek philosophers Aristoxenus, Plato, and Aristotle all made important contributions to an understanding of the nature of musical materials and their effects on people, and were very aware of the power of music to cause both psychological and social unrest, as well as its capacity to calm, soothe, divert or give pleasure. Important though these writings are from a historical perspective, and in their continuing influence on contemporary psychology of music, what would now be recognized as the psychology of music dates from the rise of psychology itself in the second half of the nineteenth century. The two most influential figures in early music psychology were Hermann von Helmholtz and Carl Stumpf, representing very different theoretical positions, but both focusing principally on what might be called "the elements of music": the sensations of pitch, rhythm, intensity, and timbre. This can be seen both as reasonable – since there is a certain logic in looking at what might be thought of as the building blocks of music (pitches and rhythms) as a first step; and as ideologically loaded – positioning music as an object, separated from human activity and divorced from its context. Helmholtz's and Stumpf's approaches were the forerunners of contemporary psychoacoustics, the study of relationships between acoustical events (frequencies, durations, and intensities) and their psychological counterparts (pitches, timbres, rhythms, and loudness).

Helmholtz was an experimental psychologist, committed to the idea that an understanding of the physics of sound could be combined with an understanding of the physiology of the auditory system to provide an explanation of music and musical experience (Helmholtz 1954 [1885]). His explanation of consonance and dissonance, for example, depended on the idea that the patterns of vibration in the inner ear, created by dissonant combinations of sounds, produced interference patterns which were perceived as a quality of beating or roughness. A physical attribute (the frequencies of the components of two or more notes) is directly related to a physiological attribute (a pattern of vibration on the basilar membrane of the inner ear) that results in a perceptual experience (consonance or dissonance). From these physical and physiological principles, Helmholtz ultimately hoped to develop an empirically based scientific account of musical aesthetics.

Stumpf was also interested in using experimental findings, but committed to the primacy of human experience, and in this sense anti-reductionist in outlook. He too developed a theory of consonance and dissonance, which took account of acoustical theory, but also prioritized the intuitions and reported experiences of expert musicians. An accomplished musician himself, he was acutely aware of the highly differentiated perceptual sensitivities that musicians develop, and of the significant effects of local and wider context on people's musical judgments – an attitude that is difficult to reconcile with Helmholtz's more physicalist outlook. Stumpf's sensitivity to the impact of context led him to a much broader interest in the music of other cultures than was typical for many of his contemporaries, making him an important figure in the early development of ethnomusicology. In many ways, Helmholtz and Stumpf represent two different approaches to music psychology that are still apparent more than a century later: Helmholtz stands for an empirical scientific approach, whose aim is to explain the complexity of human musical experience in terms of a linked chain of physical, physiological, and psychological mechanisms; Stumpf represents a tradition that argues for the irreducibility of human experience, open to systematic investigation, but thoroughly embedded in its social and cultural context.

After the work of Helmholtz and Stumpf, research in music psychology did not cease altogether, but the trickle of publications from 1900 to the late 1960s remained disparate in both subject matter and approach, with the consequence that a coherent field or discipline never really took shape. An exception is the program of research carried out by Carl Seashore at the University of Iowa in the 1920s and 1930s. Seashore's achievement was to develop new ways to study musical performance with a detail and precision that had never been possible before (summarized in Seashore 1967), using musically realistic materials played by expert musicians.

Mainstream Anglophone psychology was dominated by behaviorism from the 1920s to the early 1960s, during which period there was an intense concentration on the observable behavior of humans and other animals, and a resistance to theorizing about mental states and processes. With the work of the linguist Noam Chomsky (1957), and a growing number of psychologists on whom Chomsky's work had a dramatic influence (e.g. Miller, Gallanter and Pribram 1960), came the cognitive revolution – a radical change in psychology in which the emphasis turned emphatically away from behavior toward the mental processes and internal representations that might be inferred from the manifest capacities of human subjects. The connection with language (through Chomsky's work) is significant: language is a distinctively human capacity that is endlessly creative, and yet rule-governed – as shown by native speakers' sensitivities to "unacceptable" utterances. You do not have to be a trained linguist to know that there is something wrong with the utterance "Green furiously ideas sleep colourless," while "Colourless green ideas sleep furiously," though semantically anomalous, is perfectly acceptable grammatically.

In simple terms, Chomsky's approach to language was to assert that linguistic competence must be understood as the expression of a small number of powerful grammatical rules that both constrain the otherwise infinite possibilities of a language and, at the same time, permit an indefinite number of new utterances to be created. Chomsky's theory quickly became immensely influential in linguistics, and was also adopted by many psychologists who saw the possibility to extend this principle beyond language into many other aspects of human behavior. A rule-based approach seemed to offer a powerful way to understand vision, motor skills, memory, creativity – and music.

Like language, music seems to be infinitely creative and yet highly structured, and just as Chomsky proposed that people's language use could be explained by what he called a generative grammar (a finite set of rules that could generate, or analyse, an infinite number of utterances), so others saw this as a way in which to understand how competent listeners make sense of completely new pieces of music – as long as they are in a familiar style. Musical style is the equivalent of a language, and a piece is like an utterance – a sequence of sounds that may never have been encountered before, but uses principles that are familiar from many other instances. This seemed to be a very powerful way in which to understand all kinds of phenomena in music psychology: melodies that are easy to remember conform to a readily identifiable pattern or "grammar" (Deutsch and Feroe 1981); music that is interesting and emotionally engaging is rule-governed, but does not simply adhere slavishly to those rules – arousing but not always confirming a listener's expectations (Dowling and Harwood 1986); and expressive playing can be understood as a performer's systematic, but not entirely predictable, use of rules that relate musical structure to expressive gestures and transformations (Clarke 1988).

Recent history

Around 1980 there began a dramatic increase in the productivity, profile, and wider acceptance of the psychology of music, with the founding of a number of important journals, and a stream of significant book publications (e.g. Davies 1978; Deutsch 1982; Lerdahl and Jackendoff 1983; Sloboda 1985; Dowling and Harwood 1986). The strong emphasis in the great majority of the work published at this time (and which remains a dominating theme) was on the relationship between musical structure and psychological processes, most obviously expressed in the title (and contents) of Howell, Cross and West's (1985) *Musical Structure and Cognition*. The fundamental question addressed by this approach was how listeners perceive, remember, evaluate, and distinguish between different musical sequences, and the primary theoretical framework took mental representations of musical structures as its central principle.

Consider the following example: do listeners find it easier to remember tonal melodies than atonal melodies; and if so, why? A standard way to research this kind of question is to construct a series of melodies which differ in tonality while keeping other properties the same (rhythm, register, average interval size, tempo, etc.). The melodies might then be played to a group of listeners who are subsequently tested for the accuracy of their memory either by singing back each melody as soon as they have heard it, or by judging whether a "comparison melody" is the same or different from the original. In this research paradigm, the key to understanding what listeners remember, and the kinds of mistakes that they make, is presented as a function of the kind of internal representation that they form; and the research question is a search for the most appropriate, powerful, or plausible model of listeners' internal representations, based on evidence for the tunes that they find easy or difficult to remember, and the patterns of errors that they make in laboratory studies.

Research from the 1980s is dominated by proposals for the kinds of models that might explain listeners' behavior, using geometrical, mathematical, computational and rule-system approaches. In 1992, John Sloboda wrote a review of what he regarded as the most influential published research in the psychology of music in the period 1980–1990, focusing on the leading journal *Music Perception* (Sloboda 1992). Overwhelmingly, the most influential publications were concerned with hierarchical representations of musical structure, presented in more or less formalized terms; and foremost amongst these models was Fred Lerdahl and Ray Jackendoff's *A Generative Theory of Tonal Music* (1983) – a book-length study of the ways in which the perceptions and intuitions of experienced listeners to tonal music might be understood by means of an explicit cognitive rule system. After a period in the 1960s and 1970s when the relatively small volume of research in music psychology was largely focused on highly abstracted and rather un-music-like materials (isolated pitches and durations), Lerdahl and Jackendoff's theory coincided with, and stimulated, an engagement with more musically realistic materials.

With the spread of music psychology from psychology departments into music departments, a further transformation of the field began to take place, the consequences of which are still evident. The structuralist-cognitive phase of music psychology – typified by Lerdahl and Jackendoff's theory and Carol Krumhansl's influential empirical work – had been consistent with prevailing trends in both music theory and musicology (a preoccupation with formalist analysis, and structuralism more generally); and with cognitive science – the institutionally powerful combination of psychology with artificial intelligence and computer science. A reaction against what was perceived as the quantitative and formalist character of these traditions began to develop in the early 1990s, and music psychology – without abandoning the cognitive tradition that it had embraced so effectively – started to branch out in more qualitative, social, and developmental directions. An example is Jeanne Bamberger's book *The Mind Behind the Musical Ear* (1991), which used a detailed study of a small number of children to explore the specific character of children's musical minds. The approach was directly influenced by the work of the developmental psychologist Jean Piaget, and made use of far more qualitative methods and individually tailored materials and procedures than is typical of cognitive methods with adults. A practical reason for this is that many standard empirical research methods are simply inappropriate for infants and young children: you cannot ask a six month old (nor, probably, a six year old) to rate a melody on a numerical scale, or to indicate whether two melodies are the same or different. Ingenious methods *have* been devised to assess whether very young infants can discriminate between musical materials (see below), but the developmental psychological research of the 1980s and 1990s (for instance, looking at children's songs or invented notations) often started out with a qualitative and descriptive approach, recording (in the broad sense of that term) what it was that children did musically in relatively naturalistic situations.

Research on performance (which saw dramatically increased activity in the later 1980s) also began to branch out from the generative, and structuralist approach into more social domains concerned with communication both between performers, and between performers and their audiences. This connected with research in musical emotion and meaning – and various kinds of qualitative or more mixed (qualitative and quantitative) methods began to develop. Rather than looking only at the digital data of performance, researchers also began to pay proper attention to what performers said about their own performances (e.g. Chaffin, Imreh and Crawford 2002). Ethnomusicologists had been arguing for decades for the importance of paying close attention to the behaviors and discourses of musicians in their own cultures, and the ethnomusicological technique of participant observation (observing and describing a musical culture from the "inside") showed how revealing it can be to try to understand "musicking" (Small 1998) through close interaction with indigenous musicians. The sociologist Tia DeNora has also been influential in this regard, her book *Music in Everyday Life* (2000) documenting some of the many ways in which people encounter and use music in their daily lives, through interviews, diaries, and covert or participant observation.

Current trends

As the programs of international conferences indicate, a broadly cognitive approach still dominates the psychology of music. Because the frequency processing characteristics of the ear are an obvious and fascinating aspect of its anatomy and physiology, and because of the enormous emphasis on pitch in music theory, music psychology was for a long time also dominated by studies of pitch. More recently, however, rhythm and timing have attracted increasing research attention, partly as a reaction against the dominance of pitch, and partly because of the way that rhythm in its broadest sense is crucially involved in musical performance and communication. From the earliest developmental interactions to the most skilled expert performances, the control of time has been shown to be a crucial and fascinating aspect of human musicality (Malloch and Trevarthen 2008).

Educational and "everyday life" perspectives have gained considerable momentum (e.g. Clarke, Dibben and Pitts 2010), together with research into emotion, meaning, and the social functions of music (e.g. Juslin and Sloboda 2001; North and Hargreaves 2008). This trend reflects a recognition of the limitations of laboratory-style research on what has often been presented as the "fundamentals" of music (the perception and cognition of "primary" musical materials – pitches, rhythms, melody). The "primary materials" outlook is based on a specific view of music (as an object, abstracted from its contexts, uses and circumstances) that was increasingly challenged within musicology in the last decade of the twentieth century, and the prospect of an all-conquering cognitive science of music, powered by the methods and principles of the physical and computational sciences, has started to look very much less plausible than it once did to some people.

Alongside developing interests in a more social and applied approaches, there are also perspectives offered by biological and cultural evolution (Cross 2003; Wallin, Merker and Brown 2000); and an awareness of the importance of the body in music – ranging from the "macro" level of bodily gesture and movement in the production and perception of music, to the "micro" level of neuroscientific studies of music and the brain (e.g. Peretz and Zatorre 2003; Patel 2008).

Excesses and deficits

As music psychology has changed and developed, it has inevitably been preoccupied with, or conversely blind to, different questions at different times. If we confine ourselves to the period since 1980, then the overriding preoccupation of the cognitive psychology of music (up to the mid-1990s) was the question of musical structure: how listeners formed mental representations of musical structures as they heard or remembered music, and how performers made use of, or responded to, musical structures as they played music expressively or tried to read and memorise it. Tonal and rhythmic structures have dominated, and other aspects of musical structure and sound (such as timbre, dynamics, texture, and spatialization) have received less attention. The cultural positioning of music psychology (its domination by Anglo-American researchers) has meant that classical Western tonal music has been the overwhelming focus of attention, and investigations of the musics of other cultures have usually been somewhat superficial – and virtually always motivated by the kind of cross-cultural comparison of which ethnomusicologists are often understandably suspicious. It is all to easy for a comparison of Western listener behavior with, for example, Javanese listeners to start off with deeply rooted ethnocentric assumptions (about the nature and function of listening, for instance) which then ensure that a similarly ethnocentric "result" will be found. The same broad problem often applies to investigations of the music of sub-cultures that are geographically much closer to home (pop and jazz), but which may also involve radically different basic assumptions and kinds of behavior.

The concentration on cognition meant that for a long time emotion and meaning in music remained virtually an untouched subject. The argument for this was that people's emotional responses to music, and what music might mean to them, were so unpredictable and idiosyncratic, and so dependent on personality, or biographical and contextual factors, that it was simply impossible to make progress in that direction in any systematic or empirically defensible fashion. Only more recently has the research community become impatient with this attitude – not only because the "holy grail" of understanding how people pick up and represent structure never seemed to get any nearer, but also because the foundational commitment to a structuralist approach has been seriously questioned on more fundamental grounds. Research on emotion in music, in relation to both listening and performing, has now become a much more active area, as have the related themes of embodiment, gesture, meaning, and the functions of music in everyday life.

These developments have brought about a convergence between music psychology, ethnomusicology, and the sociology of music (Cook 2008), but with significantly different agendas and conceptual frameworks, allowing substantially different questions to be addressed. Take, for example, the case of jazz musicians playing together. From a broadly sociological/ethnomusicological perspective, the primary focus of interest here might be the ways in which those musicians talk about their experiences, how they construct their own sense of identity and musical value within that context, descriptions of the kinds of interactions that can be observed between them in performance, and perhaps an analysis of the power and authority structures that control those interactions. By contrast, music psychologists have been more concerned with trying to understand how it is that performing musicians in this kind of improvising context can control the time-course and specific content of their interactions from the point of view of sensorimotor control and communicative interaction, and what they are specifically doing to produce, for instance, a sense of "groove," or a "laid back" feel, and how that might be affected by context and intention. There is a complementarity between these kinds of approach, and connecting threads between these different views of common ground are starting to emerge in relationships between music psychology, ethnomusicology, the sociology of music, anthropology, archaeology, and ecology (e.g. Clarke 2005; Miell, MacDonald and Hargreaves 2005; Mithen 2005).

One of the blindspots of earlier psychology of music was a rather stark de-socialization of its subject matter – a tendency to treat musical behavior as the cognitive skills of an individual listener, performer or composer. In part, this reflects a dominating view within older musicology and music theory in which music is seen in a distinctly abstracted and autonomous light: organized sound in time. This view of music fitted rather too neatly with the ways in which music might be investigated in a laboratory context, which for most of the twentieth century was how psychological research was generally carried out. In part this can be attributed to the grip that a positivist empiricism, based on laboratory methods and hypothesis testing, has had on music psychology and psychology more generally – and perhaps the discipline's desire to associate itself with the prestige of the natural sciences. Since this dominant paradigm had such a powerful impact on what was regarded as the appropriate subject matter, it is important to have some sense of what the typical methods used in music psychology have been.

Methods

Not surprisingly in the light of its history, music psychology has inherited many of its methods from psychology generally, and experimental cognitive psychology more specifically. The cognitive revolution of the late 1950s and early 1960s was as much a revolution in methods as anything else, and many of these were imported directly into music research. Typical laboratory studies involve the presentation of controlled musical materials to individual participants ("subjects") who are required to judge items on numerical scales of various kinds, to indicate whether pairs of items are the same or different, to judge whether a specific chord in a sequence is in tune or not (the speed at which the judgment is made acting as an indicator of various kinds of cognitive processing); or in a method developed by Carol Krumhansl and known as the "probe-tone technique" (Krumhansl 1990), to judge how well a single note fits with various kinds of prior context. Studies of musical performance have usually tried to capture specific aspects of what performers do in controlled but reasonably realistic ways. Detailed studies of the timing, dynamics, articulation, and physical movements of skilled musical performances, using numerical data extracted from recordings of one kind or another, and analyzed using standard statistical methods can investigate a whole range of research questions about expression, emotion, communication, and style change.

There are some significant advantages to carrying out this kind of quantitative research: the data are clearly defined, the methods are well established, the principles are widely known and accepted in the general scientific community, and the analytical techniques are readily available in standard computer software. Nonetheless, there are limitations: many kinds of musical behavior are complex and continuous and cannot easily be reduced to the discrete judgments that quantitative research typically requires. If the aim is to investigate listeners' fluctuating emotional responses to music, for example, then it can be hard to design a realistic study that produces neat, quantitative data. There have been attempts to capture more continuous quantitative data – for instance, by asking listeners to move a computer mouse around so as to convey their changing emotional response to music – but it is equally likely that a researcher will ask participants to talk freely about what they heard, or keep a written or spoken diary of their listening and responses to music over a significant period of time. These are qualitative data – potentially rich and complex statements that cannot be reduced to points on a scale – and they present different challenges and opportunities to the researchers that use them.

Until the 1990s, qualitative research was regarded as the poor relation of its more hard-nosed quantitative counterpart, but qualitative research is now more widely accepted and correspondingly more methodologically developed. There are accepted ways to analyze qualitative data that provide frameworks within which to analyze complex and often messy qualitative data (spoken language, diaries, open-ended interviews, video images) with a degree of system and rigor. Social and developmental psychology have always been much more ready to use a qualitative approach, often combined with quantitative methods of the kind that are typically found in questionnaires. If you are interested in finding out about teenagers' musical preferences, for example, it is likely that you will both want to talk to some teenagers in an informal and open-ended way and, perhaps, send out a questionnaire to a much larger sample to get some kind of overview. The interviews will yield qualitative data (recorded conversations), and the questionnaires might produce quantitative data, if the questions ask for ratings, or multiple-choice answers.

Certain kinds of research necessarily require the use of rather specialized methods, and working with young, preverbal infants is one such example. Even very young infants have been found to turn to look at objects or events they find interesting, and to suck faster on a dummy. With equipment that can monitor direction of gaze or sucking rate, researchers have been able to investigate the music perceptual capacities and preferences of infants that are days or even just hours old.

Finally, research into music and neuroscience requires particularly specialized methods and equipment. The various kinds of brain-imaging techniques, such as Functional Magnetic Resonance Imaging (fMRI), Magneto-encephalography (MEG), and Electro-encephalography (EEG), are different ways of monitoring how much activity is going on in different areas of the brain in more or less direct ways. All of these techniques have their own particular strengths and weaknesses, determining the kinds of study in which they can be used. Some are extremely invasive for the participant, who may have to lie with his or her head completely engulfed by what looks like a very large and noisy tumble dryer. The information that can be gathered about different regions of brain activity is potentially fascinating, and rapid advances have been made since the 1990s in what is known about general (as well as musically specific) brain functioning; but it is obviously very hard under these physical circumstances to involve people in anything like realistic musical activities.

This highlights a pervasive problem in music psychology research: the balance between realism and control, sometimes expressed as the question of ecological validity. Musical experiences are often complex, time varying, context-dependent, individually variable, and easily disrupted by extraneous interventions; and are embedded in historical processes, cultural circumstances, value systems, and the complex mediations of technology and material culture. Some, such as Theodor Adorno (1948: 32–3), have concluded that an effective psychology of music is simply not possible. A more optimistic and constructive conclusion might recognize that a full account of the human engagement with music cannot possibly be framed within one disciplinary context, however hybrid that discipline, but that an account that *excludes* any consideration of human psychology must be fatally inadequate.

See also Ethnomusicology (Chapter 49), Music and language (Chapter 10), Music education (Chapter 56), Music, philosophy, and cognitive science (Chapter 54), Phenomenology and music (Chapter 53), Sociology and cultural studies (Chapter 51), and Understanding music (Chapter 12).

References

Adorno, T.W. (1948) *Philosophy of Modern Music*, trans. A.G. Mitchell and W.V. Blomster, London: Sheed and Ward.

Bamberger, J. (1991) *The Mind Behind the Musical Ear*, Cambridge: Harvard University Press.

Chaffin, R., Imreh, G., and Crawford, M. (2002) *Practicing Perfection: Memory and Piano Performance*, Mahwah: Lawrence Erlbaum.

Chomsky, N. (1957) *Syntactic Structures*, The Hague: Mouton.

Clarke, E.F. (1988) "Generative Principles in Music Performance," in J. Sloboda (ed.) *Generative Processes in Music*, Oxford: Clarendon Press, pp. 1–26.

—— (2005) *Ways of Listening: An Ecological Approach to the Perception of Musical Meaning*, New York: Oxford University Press.

Clarke, E.F., Dibben, N., and Pitts, S.E. (2010) *Music and Mind in Everyday Life*, Oxford: Oxford University Press.

Cook, N. (2008) "We Are All (Ethno)Musicologists Now," in H. Stobart (ed.) *The New (Ethno)musicologies*, Lanham: Scarecrow Press, pp. 48–70.

Cross, I. (2003) "Music and Biocultural Evolution," in M. Clayton, T. Herbert, and R. Middleton (eds) *The Cultural Study of Music: A Critical Introduction*, London: Routledge, 19–30.

Davies, J.B. (1978) *The Psychology of Music*, London: Hutchinson.

DeNora, T. (2000) *Music in Everyday Life*, Cambridge: Cambridge University Press.

Deutsch, D. (ed.) (1982) *The Psychology of Music*, New York: Academic Press.

Deutsch, D. and Feroe, J. (1981) "The Internal Representation of Pitch Sequences in Tonal Music," *Psychological Review* 88: 503–22.

Dowling, W.J. and Harwood, D.L. (1986) *Music Cognition*, New York: Academic Press.

Helmholtz, H. (1954 [1885]) *On the Sensations of Tone*, New York: Dover.

Howell, P., Cross, I., and West, R. (eds) (1985) *Musical Structure and Cognition*, New York: Academic Press.

Juslin, P. and Sloboda, J.A. (eds) (2001) *Music and Emotion: Theory and Research*. Oxford: Oxford University Press.

Krumhansl, C.L. (1990) *Cognitive Foundations of Musical Pitch*, New York: Oxford University Press.

Lerdahl, F. and Jackendoff, R. (1983) *A Generative Theory of Tonal Music*, Cambridge: MIT Press.

Malloch, S. and Trevarthen, C. (eds) (2008) *Communicative Musicality Exploring the Basis of Human Companionship*, Oxford: Oxford University Press.

Miell, D., MacDonald, R., and Hargreaves, D.J. (eds) (2005) *Musical Communication*, Oxford: Oxford University Press.

Miller, G., Gallanter, E., and Pribram, K. (1960) *Plans and the Structure of Behavior*, New York: Holt, Rinehart and Winston.

Mithen, S. (2005) *The Singing Neanderthals. The Origin of Music, Language, Mind and Body*, London: Weidenfeld and Nicolson.

North, A.C. and Hargreaves, D.J. (2008) *The Social and Applied Psychology of Music*, New York: Oxford University Press.

Patel, A.D. (2008) *Music, Language and the Brain*, Oxford: Oxford University Press.

Peretz, I. and Zatorre, R.J. (eds) (2003) *The Cognitive Neuroscience of Music*, Oxford: Oxford University Press.

Seashore, C.E. (1967 [1938]). *Psychology of Music*. New York: Dover.

Sloboda, J.A. (1985) *The Musical Mind. The Cognitive Psychology of Music*, Oxford: Oxford University Press.

—— (1992) "Psychological Structures in Music: Core Research 1980–1990," in J. Paynter, T. Howell, R. Orton and P. Seymour (eds) *Companion to Contemporary Musical Thought*, London: Routledge, pp. 803–39.

Small, C. (1998) *Musicking: The Meanings of Performing and Listening*, Hanover: University Press of New England.

Wallin, N.L., Merker, B. and Brown, S. (eds) (2000) *The Origins of Music*, Cambridge: MIT Press.

56

MUSIC EDUCATION

Philip Alperson

Philosophical interest in music education

Though philosophical thinking about music education is as old as Plato's *Republic* and the subject has in recent years attracted the attention of some philosophically minded music educators, the philosophy of music education has not received much attention by contemporary philosophers, certainly as compared with the attention given by philosophers to other questions about music such as the ontology of musical works and the nature and role of musical form and musical expressiveness.

The relative lack of attention to music education among contemporary philosophers is itself a philosophically interesting question. Music-making is, after all, one of the oldest of human activities: a bone flute found in the Hohle Fels Cave in Germany dates back at least 35,000 years. Music is nowadays widely considered to be one of the "fine" or major arts, a prime example of artistic activity in which sensuous objects possessing salient qualities of form, expression, and symbolism are created by artists expressly for the directed attention of others, for whom these works are thought to repay repeated scrutiny. Musical practice is also frequently regarded as an exemplary case of craft, an activity in which particular sets of skills and knowledge are deployed in order to bring about certain kinds of ends. Music often bears an intimate, if complicated, relationship to the public sphere by dint of its potential for personal, public, and social expression. In these ways, music is nearly universally acknowledged to hold an important place in the realm of human affairs. If we grant the premise that education is one of the central means by which human thought, beliefs, ideals, and practices are articulated, preserved, and transmitted from one generation to another, questions about the nature and goals of music education ought to be of great interest to philosophers.

There are of course many important philosophical questions about education in general, such as the role of education in human development, whether the goal of education ought to center on the transmission of knowledge, the education of the citizenry, emancipation and freedom from oppression, social justice, the inculcation of correct habits or virtue, indoctrination into the faith, the training of skills, principles for the establishment of curricula and teacher training programs, and so on. In the context of a philosophical inquiry into music education in particular, one might expect philosophers to address themselves to more specialized questions: What is there to learn about music? What is it about musical practice that ought to be subject of education? To what extent should music education be concerned with the training of musical skills and musicianship, or with listening skills and familiarity with a repertory, with factual information about historical musical practices, or with digital and electronic techniques for composing and performing music? Should music education include discussions of philosophical or music-theoretical issues? To what extent should music education focus on the formal aspects of music, its expressive or symbolic meanings, or the instrumental purposes that music might serve such as entertainment, the facilitation of religious or other states of mind, the transmission of culture, virtue, or the education of the soul? What is – or should be – the connection between music education and the education of taste or sensibility? To whom should education be addressed? Should the primary audience of music education be potential practitioners, whether amateur or professional, or musical audiences? Should music education address itself to the general public or the musical elite? What is the relationship between formal institutions such as conservatories and schools of music and informal learning environments such as bars, clubs, garages, and internet chat rooms, and what implications, if any, do these various kinds of settings have for music education? Are the goals of "music appreciation" classes different from the goals of conservatory training? What institutions and methodologies (such as Suzuki, Kodály, Orff, Dalcroze, and solfège) are most appropriate to the attainment of those goals we identify for music education? To what extent and in what ways are the goals of music education affected by the particularities of individual historical, cultural, social, and national contexts?

Musical practices

Ultimately, answers to questions such as these will depend on how one understands the nature of musical practice itself and how one construes the core values of that practice. But this observation raises a further complication. There is no single non-contentious understanding of what constitutes musical practice. Consider for example the base definition of music one finds in the *Concise Oxford English Dictionary*: "the art or science of combining vocal or instrumental sounds (or both) to produce beauty of form, harmony, and expression of emotion" (Soanes and Stevenson 2004: 942). Even to the extent that one thinks of music as "art," we must remember that the history of the meanings and applications of the term "art" is complex (see Shiner 2003). And, in any case, there are surely instances of music – work songs, anthems, dirges, religious chants, and so on – whose main function is not necessarily tied to a concept of art, much less to the requirement that musical sounds produce beauty of form, harmony, or the expression of emotion. The truth of the matter seems rather to be that music, like all multifaceted and culturally embedded practices and social experiences, comprises a network of multiple overlapping and at times even conflicting sub-practices, any number or combination of which might be apt candidates for preservation and transmission and, hence, for education. In this sense, the philosophy of music education recapitulates the historical and conceptual context surrounding most of the central questions of the philosophy of music. Given these complexities, perhaps the wisest plan of attack then is not to attempt a totalizing account of the philosophy of music education at the outset but rather to look into some of the domains of musical meaning and value that music educators have thought worthy of focused attention.

Musical analysis

Let us take as a starting point that music is an activity dealing with sounds. One of the chief fascinations of music is that its very materials have intrinsic interest of at least two sorts. First, sounds are sensuous objects and the ways in which they are heard in combination interest us as audibly sensitive creatures. Second, it is a striking fact that sounds and their combinations are tied to mathematical ratios and that musical sounds may become a subject of mathematical analysis. The mathematical side of music manifests itself not only with respect to tonally based features of music such as scales, modes, melodies, and harmonies but also with respect to rhythm, timbre, and texture.

It is possible, then, to think of musical education chiefly in terms of the identification, analysis, and appreciation of musical materials and sound structures presented in time, whether that study is conducted along mathematical lines, phenomenological lines, or a combination of both. The phenomenological approach traces its lineage to Aristoxenus, the mathematical approach to Pythagoras (see Chapter 24, "Antiquity and the Middle Ages," in this volume). In either case musical analysis seeks to identify the materials of music and to examine how music, considered as sequential structures of sound, works – that is, the way in which musical sounds function.

To the extent that music education focuses on the analysis of the nature of musical materials and structures, it directs our attention to a central domain of musical meaning. The presumption of musical analysis is that analysis enhances one's understanding of specific musical works and performances, that it adds to our understanding of the creation, performance, and appreciation of musical styles and technical matters with respect to harmony, counterpoint, and composition, and that it helps to develop and refine those skills relevant to these aspects of music.

Musical analysis may at first glance seem to be a more or less purely descriptive affair. It is, however, inescapably normative. The questions of what is to count as musical material and where one is to look for musical function are necessarily drawn from and favor particular musical styles, periods, and preferences. Heinrich Schenker's emphasis on melodic and harmonic structural development (Schenker 1979), for example, seems well suited to much European music from the seventeenth through the mid-nineteenth century in which tonal development is the pre-eminent organizational feature. It is arguably less congenial to motivically driven development (i.e. development where melodic or rhythmical figures are employed as the primary unifying elements), not to mention music written during and after the so-called breakup of tonality where loyalty to tonal centers is attenuated or rejected entirely. Conversely, mathematical models designed to cope with relationships of elements in atonal music – for example, models based on set theory (Forte 1973) – are not well suited to capture the felt dynamic effects of tension and resolution central to tonal music. More fundamentally than these questions of applicability, musical analysis implicitly assumes that the meaning and value of music are to be found primarily in musical form, a position for which philosophical defense is required.

Strict aesthetic formalism

It is possible to anchor the music educational interest in sound structures under the philosophical purview of aesthetic formalism. The basic presupposition of this line of thought rests on a view of music as one of the "fine arts," having as its goal the production of objects (works of art) whose main value derives from their very contemplation. The view, classically formulated in a discourse stretching from Shaftesbury, Hutcheson, and Baumgarten to Kant (Shaftesbury 1991 [1711]; Hutcheson 1973 [1725]; Baumgarten 1954 [1735]; Kant 1914 [1790]), was coincident with the rise of performance venues such as court salons and the concert hall in which composers, performers, and listeners were seen to be engaged in the collective activity of the presentation and appreciation of repeatable works, autonomous objects created for the express purpose of satisfying "disinterested" apprehension. According to aesthetic formalism, the qualities appropriate to such an attitude are qualities of form: qualities of design or structure, without reference to concepts or the practical significance of what might be thought to be represented or expressed in the work. We derive pleasure from such experience, Kant had argued, from the harmonious free play of the cognitive powers of the imagination and the understanding in the contemplation of "purposiveness without purpose" (1914: 79). On this line of thought music education is a species of aesthetic education: the goal of music education should consist in the training of the ability to produce and to respond properly to such objects.

We can distinguish two basic versions of aesthetic formalism based on differing understandings of the qualities deemed relevant to disinterested aesthetic experience. On what we can call the "strict" version of aesthetic formalism, the relevant properties are construed relatively narrowly as perceptual properties of a certain sort: the sensual, syntactic, and structural properties of musical works – the sorts of properties congenial to certain forms of musical analysis and which Eduard Hanslick famously designated "tonally moving forms" (1986: 29). The relevant qualities of musical form include aesthetic properties pertaining to melody, harmony, rhythm, texture, the dynamic qualities of music, the flow of musical events, the effect of repetition and other structural features on expectation, and so on.

Musical educational programs based on strict aesthetic formalism identify these undeniable attractions of musical forms in motion, inculcate modes of attention appropriate to such displays, provide technical vocabularies, devise instructional methods, and articulate the standards enshrined in the canon of works thought to best instantiate aesthetic achievements in the history of music. In this context an important task of musical education is the development of connoisseurship, what in an earlier era would have been called "the education of taste." It is tempting at this point to characterize the view as elitist but it must also be remembered that in focusing on perceptual properties, the view connects with the familiar idea that the appreciation of music is at some level at least something akin to a human universal.

On the other hand, strict aesthetic formalism does not accord well with the intuitions of a great many listeners. However alluring the attraction of the formal side of music, and even if we set to one side the question of the myriad roles of music in practical matters and social experience, people generally think that, if musical art is anything, it is an expressive art, an art intimately tied to the emotions. The expressivity of music does not sit easily with strict aesthetic formalism. One can of course, as Hanslick himself did, bring the idea of musical dynamism under the rubric of musical form (1986: 11). We certainly hear musical forms as musically tensive, creating musical conflict, leading toward musical resolutions, and so on. But listeners also typically hear what are often called "garden variety" emotions in the music they listen to. It may not do justice to our experience to enlist such broad terms as "sadness" or "happiness" or "pathos" to describe these experiences but we feel that something like this is going on in the music. If we cannot find exactly the right words to describe our expressive experiences of music, we yearn to do so.

Enhanced aesthetic formalism

Considerations such as these may not close the door on aesthetic formalism, however. It is possible to save the idea of aesthetic experience and the attitude appropriate to its contemplation by widening the range of what might be thought to be a candidate for appreciation from an aesthetic point of view. On the strict version of aesthetic formalism, the relevant properties were said to be perceptual and structural qualities and their relations as presented in time. It is possible, however, to argue that expressive and even representational properties can be appreciated from an aesthetic point of view. We distinguish for example the "murder" of Desdemona by Othello on stage from an actual homicide. Analogously, we might say of music education that its goal is to enhance our understanding of the aesthetic side of music including what expressive and representational potential the music might have. Let us call this the "enhanced" version of aesthetic formalism. We may regard this view as a formalist view in at least two senses: (1) one can still say that what one is focusing on are properties and their structural relations, the way in which, say, expressive properties are worked out, and (2) one can argue that it is *through* an apprehension of the formal properties that the expressive properties are made manifest. On the enhanced view, the musical working out of expressive properties is what captures our aesthetic attention. This move directly addresses the criticism of strict aesthetic formalism that it concentrates on an overly narrow range of musical properties while still holding onto the idea that an apprehension of music is at root an aesthetic affair.

One might even take a further step and claim that the working out of expressiveness in music can provide the basis for an understanding of the expressive side of life. That is, one might advance a *cognitivist* version of the enhanced aesthetic formalist position, arguing that in some sense understanding the expressive side of musical works from an aesthetic point of view provides knowledge about our inner lives, enriching our imaginative understanding of feeling, perhaps even deepening our empathetic relationship with other human beings, in each case providing a means to the education of feeling.

The cognitivist version of enhanced aesthetic formalism has in fact been quite influential in contemporary music education circles. It has been championed most notably by the music educator Bennett Riemer (2003) who draws from the expressivist views of the philosopher Susanne Langer (1953) and the writings of the psychologist Howard Gardner on "musical intelligence" (1983). The view has been defended in recent years by the philosopher Roger Scruton. Scruton argues that music shares an important feature with human life – organized movement – and that our sympathetic response to music is "a way of shaping our inner life to fit the perceived life of another" (2007: 61). Music education, then, should aim to train people to hear the movement that lies in the music, especially by attending to the structural relationships and developments enabled by tonality. In this way music has a deep cultural, and specifically moral, significance: it helps to develop our emotional knowledge, concerning what to do and what to feel (Scruton 1997, 2007). The view harkens back to Friedrich Schiller's famous claim that beauty can confer on a person social character, that "through Beauty we arrive at freedom" (1954: 27).

The cognitivist version of enhanced formalism has considerable attraction for educators. Not only does the view expand the range of proper music interest beyond what was sanctioned by the strict view but it also explicitly claims a measure of depth and importance in human affairs for music and, by extension, for music education. By focusing on expressive and other sorts of meaning that would have been regarded as "extra-musical" on the strict view, the cognitivist version of enhanced musical formalism underwrites methods for identifying, creating, and evaluating expressive musical meaning, goals relevant to practitioners and non-specialists alike.

On the other hand, the view depends strictly on the possibility of developing an adequate philosophical theory of what, on the strict version of aesthetic formalism, would have been regarded as extra-musical. The strict version strove to maintain the autonomous nature of musical meaning. On the enhanced version we are in need of a theory to explain how exactly expressive, representational, or symbolic meaning is related to formal qualities and the sense in which such meanings are to be understood aesthetically. In the specifically cognitivist variant of the view we also expect an account of the sense of knowledge put in play by the theory. Questions such as these about musical expression, representation, symbolization, and knowledge, have been the subject of extensive philosophical discussion and go beyond the scope of the present chapter. But in the context of the kinds of claims being made for music education, it is important to highlight two other questions of central concern. With respect to the cognitivist version in particular one is prompted to ask: what is the warrant for claiming that people who develop their imaginative understanding of musical expressiveness in fact increase their understanding of human emotion, much less deepen their empathetic understanding of other people? It is well known that some of the cruelest people in history have apparently had sophisticated appreciations of music. Scruton, in considering the general problem of the "evil aesthete" acknowledges that there is no a priori reason why an acquaintance with culture should enliven real sympathies, arguing that no institution and no art yet devised has been able to prevent atrocities (Scruton 2007: 41–3). That allowance, however, simply provides more fodder for the skeptic. And with respect to all versions of aesthetic formalism we may ask, what exactly is the place of specifically aesthetic understandings of music in the context of the myriad practices of music more generally?

Praxialism

Philosophical approaches to music education that rest on strict and enhanced versions of aesthetic formalism have as their subject a particular range of musical practice: music as an art. Such broader cultural functions as music is thought to have are accommodated under the general rubric of aesthetic experience. As we noted at the outset, however, music is produced and enjoyed in a wide range of contexts and circumstances in which music can be understood as having many different kinds of functions. Many of the functions that music might serve come quickly to mind: supporting religious rituals and states of mind, sustaining ethical and political institutions and principles, providing instructional and didactic support, enhancing interpersonal and communal socialization, stimulating military and athletic passions, and so on. The list is indefinitely large. The aesthetic properties of music may – and often do – play a part in these contexts but they are not necessarily central to them.

Praxialism is an approach to the philosophy of music and music education that seeks to address such concerns by proceeding from the diversity of musical practices in particular cultures. The basic outlines of the view were articulated by Philip Alperson (Alperson 1991, 2008) and have been developed by music educators (Elliott 1995; Regelski 1996). Alperson argues that music is itself best understood as an amalgam of forms of human activities defined in terms of the specific skills, knowledge, and standards of evaluation appropriate to such practices. The view calls into question the hard distinction between the intrinsic and the instrumental values of music, arguing that the philosophy of music should take as its subject not only the specifically aesthetic values of music deriving from the sensuous, structural, and referential aspects of music, but also the artistic values of music pertaining to the larger cultural and social significance that have been a part of musical practice since antiquity. The view has affinities with Christopher Small's discussions of the social experience of music-making (Small 1998), with some contemporary currents in what is called the "new musicology" that bring to musicological study issues concerning feminism and gender studies, race studies, and national, political, and social formations (Kerman 1985; Kramer 1990; McClary 1991, 2000; Subotnik 1991), and with contemporary approaches in ethnomusicology (Nettl 1983).

Some theorists (e.g. Elliott 1995: 125–8) have supposed that the praxial view is inconsistent with or antithetical to an aesthetic-based approach. There is no principled reason, however, why, on a praxialist view, the creation, performance, or appreciation of music undertaken with respect to aesthetic properties should be excluded or devalued. Such a position would be inconsistent with a principle tenet of praxialism, that philosophical theorizing should be driven by actual human practice. Nor would praxialism seek to change the emphasis in music education classrooms from "high art" or "serious" music to "low art" or "pop" or "folk" music. Rather, more radically, it aims to cut through such value-laden categories. The praxial approach may include an examination of the connection between aesthetic and non-aesthetic functions, where relevant, in matters pertaining to both the production and the reception of music. The view encourages a position of value pluralism with respect to musical styles and musical activities. Moreover, it is important to keep in mind that arguments can be made for the extra-aesthetic significance of aesthetic experience, as Scruton has done from a Schillerian and Kantian point of view, as Heidi Westerlund has done from a Deweyan perspective (Westerlund 2003), and as Theodore Gracyk has done by looking at the connections between aesthetic experience and the articulation of gender and racial identity in rock music (Gracyk 2001).

621

Praxialism poses its own problems. It is a contextualist view. That in itself does not distinguish it from aesthetically based views since it is possible to argue that the understanding of aesthetic properties, terms, and appropriate habits of mind must be understood in the context of the history of development of aesthetic theory and practice. What does distinguish the view is its embrace of anthropological, sociological, and social and political concerns that take the philosophy of music and the philosophy of music education beyond the confines of aesthetic considerations. The question here is not simply how accounts of aesthetic and extra-aesthetic experiences can be reconciled in cases where such a relation is postulated. The concern is broader, asking what the object of philosophical inquiry into music ought to be. This is an issue that goes to the heart of the question of the nature, methodology, and aims – not only of the philosophy of music and music education but also of philosophical inquiry itself.

See also Analysis (Chapter 48), Antiquity and the Middle Ages (Chapter 24), Ethnomusicology (Chapter 49), Evaluating music (Chapter 16), Expression theories (Chapter 19), Kant (Chapter 30), Hanslick (Chapter 33), and Sociology and cultural studies (Chapter 51).

References

Alperson, P. (1991) "What Should One Expect from a Philosophy of Music Education?" *Journal of Aesthetic Education* 25: 215–42.
—— (2008) "The Instrumentality of Music," *The Journal of Aesthetics and Art Criticism* 66: 37–51.
Baumgarten, A. (1954 [1735]) *Reflections on Poetry*, trans. K. Aschenbrenner and W.B. Holter, Berkeley and Los Angeles: University of California Press.
Elliott, D. (1995) *Music Matters: A New Philosophy of Music*, New York: Oxford University Press.
Forte, A. (1973) *The Structure of Atonal Music*, New Haven: Yale University Press.
Gardner, H. (1983) *Frames of Mind: The Theory of Multiple Intelligences*, New York: Basic Books.
Gracyk, T. (2001) *I Wanna Be Me: Rock Music and the Politics of Identity*, Philadelphia: Temple University Press.
Hanslick, E. (1986 [1891 8th edn]) *On the Musically Beautiful*, trans. G. Payzant, Indianapolis: Hackett.
Hutcheson, F. (1973 [1725]) *An Inquiry into the Original of our Ideas of Beauty and Virtue: In Two Treatises*, The Hague: Martinus Nijhoff.
Kant, I. (1914 [1790]) *Kant's Critique of Judgement*, trans. J.H. Bernard, 2nd edn, London: Macmillan.
Kerman, J. (1985) *Contemplating Music: Challenges to Musicology*, Cambridge: Harvard University Press.
Kramer, L. (1990) *Music as Cultural Practice, 1800–1900*, Berkeley: University of California Press.
Langer, S. (1953) *Feeling and Form: A Theory of Art*, New York: Scribner's Sons.
McClary, S. (1991) *Feminine Endings: Music, Gender, and Sexuality*, Minneapolis: University of Minnesota Press.
—— (2000) *Conventional Wisdom: The Content of Musical Form*, Berkeley: University of California Press.

Nettl, B. (1983) *The Study of Ethnomusicology*, Urbana: University of Illinois Press.

Regelski, T. (1996) "Prolegomenon to a Praxial Philosophy of Music and Music Education," *The Finnish Journal of Music Education* 1: 23–39.

Riemer, B. (2003) *A Philosophy of Music Education: Advancing the Vision*, Upper Saddle River: Prentice-Hall.

Schenker, H. (1979 [1935]) *Free Composition*, trans. and ed. E. Ostler, New York: Longman.

Schiller, F. (1954 [1795]) *On the Aesthetic Education of Man*, trans. R. Snell, New Haven: Yale University Press.

Scruton, R. (1997) *The Aesthetics of Music*, Oxford: Oxford University Press.

—— (2007) *Culture Counts: Faith and Feeling in a World Besieged*, New York: Encounter Books.

Shaftesbury, A. (1991 [1711]) *Characteristics of Men, Manners, Opinions, Times*, Cambridge: Cambridge University Press.

Shiner, L. (2003) *The Invention of Art: A Cultural History*, Chicago: The University of Chicago Press.

Small, C. (1998) *Musicking: The Meanings of Performing and Listening*, Hanover: Wesleyan University Press.

Soanes, C. and Stevenson, A. (2004) "Music," in C. Soanes and A. Stevenson (eds) *The Concise Oxford English Dictionary*, 11th edn, Oxford: Oxford University Press.

Subotnik, R. (1991) *Developing Variations: Style and Ideology in Western Music*, Minneapolis: University of Minnesota Press.

Westerlund, H. (2003) "Reconsidering Aesthetic Experience in Praxial Music Education," *Philosophy of Music Education Review* 11: 45–62.

INDEX

2001: A Space Odyssey (film) 457, 458
Abba (pop group) 421
Abbate, Carolyn 549
Abhinâvabharati 246, 248
Abhinavagupta 542
absolute music: in Adorno's aesthetics 393–4;
  in aesthetic formalism 146, 147–8; arousal
  of listeners' emotions 233–4, 236–7; and
  expression of emotion 204, 208, 223,
  239–40; Hanslick's theory 361, 363–4,
  366–7, 523; neglect of body in concept
  of 468, 470; and profundity 151, 152–3;
  as theme in Wagner's writings 366, 382–4,
  386–7, 523; value of 155, 161, 162, 163,
  see also pure music
"absolute opera", Wagner 383
abstract forms: in descriptions of music 517,
  537; genre of absolute music 468;
  in Gurney's ideas on music and
  emotions 372, 375–6, 377, 378
Academy of Sciences, Paris 318
acoustics 15, 19, 21; analytic
  approaches 295, 298; and "music
  visualization" 476, *see also*
  psychoacoustics
Adler, Guido 497
Adorno, Theodor 84, 123, 311, 385;
  aesthetics of modernism 391–2, 553; on
  autonomous art and music 392–3, 394–5,
  397–400; biographical sketch 391; critique
  of popular music 36–7, 396, 406, 410,
  413, 560; on culture industry 395–6;
  on different kinds of listening 36–7; on
  jazz 433, 473–4; Marxist thought 393–4,
  395, 560; on technology 195; view of
  psychology of music 612
aesthetic formalism 145–8; enhanced
  version 618–20; strict version 617–18,
  618–19, 620
aesthetics: in analytic philosophy 297;
  approaches in ethnomusicology 535–9;
  and appropriation in music 178–80;
  arousal of emotions in music 233–4,

238, 241; artistic medium 53–5;
  authentic performance practice 99;
  Bourdieu's ideas 288–90; and challenge
  of popular music 406, 412, 414, 421;
  in Chinese philosophy of music 251–2;
  choreography and dance 475–8; elements
  of style 138, 141; in evaluation of
  music 165, 167, 168–9, 170–3, 174;
  explorations in ethnomusicology 540–3;
  expressive qualities of music 201;
  Hanslick's study 362–6, 366–7; and
  human attachment to music 549;
  ideas in early modern period 273,
  275, 277, 281, 296; importance of
  Gurney 371; Indian music 245–50; Kant's
  ideas 328–37; in Levinson's definition
  of music 9–10, 11, 55; and McClary's
  music criticism 578; modernity and
  traditional cultures 543–4; ontology of
  Beethoven's *Hammerklavier* 43, 43–4,
  45–6; opera 449–54; and praxial approach
  to music education 621–2; properties of
  music 144–53; sonic manifestations of
  musical works 85, 155; and technology
  in performance 196; in understanding
  music 123, 127, 128; value of music 157,
  157–8, 161, 162; value of musical
  instruments 189
affect: doctrine of *Affektenlehre* 275, 296;
  and emotional reaction to music 213,
  235–6; in function of music 104, 106;
  in musical appreciation 160, 163; and
  sensory experience of music 489; use of
  language for 105
African American culture: harmful
  misrepresentation of 183–4; influences on
  dance 471, 473, 474
African American music: appropriation by
  non-African Americans 176–7, 177, 179,
  179–80, 181–2, 183, 434, *see also* black
  music; blues; jazz
African dance 473
African music 129, 137, 177, 410, *see also*

structuralism: and Bourdieu's ideas 287;
connection between music and
language 488; as dominating work
in psychology of music 605–6, 609;
in music theories 512, 606; trends in
musicology 497, 606
structure: addressed in formalist
music education 619; in Ferrara's
phenomenology of music 588; and
memorable qualities in musical
works 521–2; in music analysis 525,
526–7, 618; music and relationship with
emotions 597; as prolongational in music
and language 109–10, *110*; in psychology
of music 593, 595–6, 598, 605–6, 608–9;
superstructure and infrastructure of
jazz 426–7
"studio performance", rock music 51
Stumpf, Carl 581, 603, 604
style: in authentic performance practice 97–8;
elements in Western music 138–41; in
evaluation of rock 423; in everyday
contexts 134; and genre 136, 140; issues
of appropriation and hybridity 178, 179–
80; and ownership 182; in performer's
persona 96; and praxial approach to
music education 621; proliferation and
diversity in West 561; in regulative music
theory 501; in rock 416, 417, 418, 419;
subcultures 560, 561; and understanding
of music 130–1, 134–6, 141–2, 159, 605;
in Western music tradition 135, 136–8
subcultures: in psychological studies of
music 609; in sociological studies of
music 560, 561, 563–4, 564
subjectivism 6, 7, 287
the sublime: as aesthetic property of
music 150; in Kant's aesthetics 332–3;
in Wagner's aesthetics 387; in Western
musical philosophy 468, *see also*
transcendence
Sufism 249, 254, 542
Sullivan, Arthur *see* Gilbert and Sullivan
Sumatra, Mandailing ensemble music 542
Sumeria 70
suspension 32–3, *33*, 34
"Swing Low Sweet Chariot" (song) 520
swing music 141, 426, 426–7
symbolic interactionism 560
symbolism: in Chinese music 251; in Langer's
account of music 299
symphony: as genre 140; in Wagner's musical
aesthetics 381, 382, 383–4, 523
syncopation 25, *25*, 597
synesthesia: commonplace 483–90;
ideopathic 482–3; representations of
ragas 247, 249

syntax: in Ferrara's hermeneutical approach
to phenomenology 587–8, *588*; in
language and music 108–9; and surface
and structure of rock 420–1, *see also* pitch
syntax
synthesis *see* fusion/synthesis
synthesized music 85, 195
Syrian Christians 253

tablatures 71, 72
Tafelmusik ("table-music") 394
Taffanel, Claude-Paul 189
Tagg, Philip 421, 422, 577
tap dance 474
Tartini, Giuseppe 78
Taruskin, Richard 97, 405, 453
taste: and appeal of genres 563–4; in
Bourdieu's ideas on aesthetics 288,
289, 564; and deviance of rock 422;
and evaluation of music 166–7, 167–8;
Gurney's view 379; impact of recorded
music on 586–7; in Kant's aesthetics of
beauty 331; and music education 615,
618, *see also* olfactory terms
Taurelle, Geneviève 177
Taylor, Yuval 95–6
Tchaikovsky, Peter Ilich 522, 573
Te Kanawa, Kiri 179
techne 188, 191, 196, 197, 508
technical thinking 190–1, 196
technology 187–8, 586–7; recordings 87,
431, *see also* digital technology;
instrumental technology; internet
Tedlock, Barbara 541
Telemann, Georg Philipp 481
tempo 71, 78
tension 219, 226, 617, 618; in Meyer's
theory 535, 594
Terpsichore 469
text: in forms of vocal performance 538;
as outside of music in compositions 523;
in songs 437, 438, 439–40; in Western
conception of music 438, 470, *see also*
language; words
texture: in music theory and analysis 502,
618; in musical style 138, 139, 140–1
theatre: combined media 50; in concept of
opera 447; music–dance relationship
477–8; Rousseau's views 324, 326
themes: appropriation of 176; in classical
instrumental music 28; listener's
understanding of 158, 159; in musical
expressiveness 205, 207; Sibelius's Second
Symphony 52
Theon of Smyrna 262, 267
theory: approaches in historical
musicology 498; in ethnoaesthetics 537;